GUIDE TO PASSING

W9-AZL-005

PSI REAL ESTATE Exam

5TH EDITION

Lawrence Sager

Tim Meline
Consulting Editor

This publication is designed to provide accurate and authoritative information in regard to the subject matter covered. It is sold with the understanding that the publisher is not engaged in rendering legal, accounting, or other professional service. If legal advice or other expert assistance is required, the services of a competent professional person should be sought.

President: Roy Lipner
Publisher: Evan Butterfield
Managing Editor, Print Products: Louise Benzer
Development Editor: Anne Huston
Managing Editor, Production: Daniel Frey
Quality Assurance Editor: David Shaw
Creative Director: Lucy Jenkins

Copyright 1992, 1994, 1997, 2000, 2004 by Dearborn™ Real Estate Education,
a division of Dearborn Financial Publishing, Inc.®

Published by Dearborn™ Real Estate Education,
a division of Dearborn Financial Publishing, Inc.®
30 South Wacker Drive
Chicago, IL 60606-7481
(312) 836-4400
http://www.dearbornRE.com

All rights reserved. The text of this publication, or any part thereof, may not be reproduced in any manner whatsoever without permission in writing from the publisher.

Printed in the United States of America.

05 06 10 9 8 7 6 5 4 3

Library of Congress Cataloging—in—Publication Data

Sager, Lawrence.
Guide to passing the PSI real estate exam / Lawrence Sager. — 5th ed.
p. cm.
ISBN 0-7931-8834-2
1. Real estate business—United States—States—Examinations, questions, etc.
I. Title
HD1381.5.U5 S24 2005
333.33'0973—dc22

2004-009566

CONTENTS

Preface vii

Acknowledgments vii

About the Author ix

About the Consulting Editor ix

1. Use of the Manual 1

Examination Information 2
Salesperson Examination 3
Broker Examination 5

2. Examination and Study Strategies 6

Preparing for the Exam 6
Developing Test Questions 8
Sample Questions 9
How to Analyze a Question 11
Exam Strategy 14
Study Strategy 16

3. Property Ownership 18

Outline of Concepts 18
Diagnostic Test 26
Matching Quiz 30
Answer Key: Diagnostic Test 31
Answer Key: Matching Quiz 33

4. Land-Use Control and Regulations 34

Outline of Concepts 34
Diagnostic Test 42
Matching Quiz 44
Answer Key: Diagnostic Test 45
Answer Key: Matching Quiz 46

5. Valuation and Market Analysis 47

Outline of Concepts 47
Diagnostic Test 52
Matching Quiz 55
Answer Key: Diagnostic Test 56
Answer Key: Matching Quiz 58

6. Financing 59

Outline of Concepts 59
Diagnostic Test 67
Matching Quiz 70
Answer Key: Diagnostic Test 71
Answer Key: Matching Quiz 72

7. Laws of Agency 73

Outline of Concepts 73
Diagnostic Test 77
Matching Quiz 81
Answer Key: Diagnostic Test 82
Answer Key: Matching Quiz 83

8. Mandated Disclosures 84

Outline of Concepts 84
Diagnostic Test 87
Matching Quiz 89
Answer Key: Diagnostic Test 90
Answer Key: Matching Quiz 90

9. Contracts 91

Outline of Concepts 91
Diagnostic Test 96
Matching Quiz 99
Answer Key: Diagnostic Test 100
Answer Key: Matching Quiz 102

10. Transfer of Property 103

Outline of Concepts 103
Diagnostic Test 109
Matching Quiz 111
Answer Key: Diagnostic Test 112
Answer Key: Matching Quiz 113

11. Practice of Real Estate 114

Outline of Concepts 114
Diagnostic Test 120
Matching Quiz 123
Answer Key: Diagnostic Test 124
Answer Key: Matching Quiz 125

12. Real Estate Mathematics Review 126

Percentages 126
Rates 128
Area and Volume 129
Depreciation 132
Capitalization 132
Prorations 133
Amortization 135
Calculator Financing 137
Math Review Test 138
Mathematics—Matching Quiz 143
Answer Key with Explanations 144
Answer Key: Matching Quiz 147

13. Specialty Areas 148

Outline of Concepts 148
Diagnostic Test 154
Matching Quiz 156
Answer Key: Diagnostic Test 157
Answer Key: Matching Quiz 158

14. Brokerage Management 159

Outline of Concepts 159
Diagnostic Test 167
Matching Quiz 169
Answer Key: Diagnostic Test 170
Answer Key: Matching Quiz 171

15. Salesperson Examinations 172

Salesperson Examination I 173
Salesperson Examination I: Answer Key with Explanations 182
Salesperson Examination II 188
Salesperson Examination II: Answer Key with Explanations 195
Salesperson Examination III 200
Salesperson Examination III: Answer Key with Explanations 208

16. Broker Examinations 212

Broker Examination I 213
Broker Examination I: Answer Key with Explanations 224
Broker Examination II 229
Broker Examination II: Answer Key with Explanations 237

Appendix A

Mathematical Formulas at a Glance 241

Appendix B

Mathematics Practice and Review 243
Answer Key with Explanations 251

Appendix C

Web Site and Palm Directory 255

Glossary 256

PREFACE

The growing complexity of the real estate business has been accompanied by an increased emphasis on real estate education. Evidence for this emphasis is the trend toward state requirements for both prelicense and continuing education. Accordingly, many states currently employ professional testing organizations to aid them in the development and administration of licensing examinations. One of these organizations is PSI Examination Services, Glendale, California, which has developed widely used licensing exams for real estate professionals.

The focus of this study guide is preparation for PSI's real estate salesperson and broker licensing examinations. Of the existing books devoted to preparing for real estate licensing exams, this was the first study guide geared specifically to the current format of the PSI examination. The PSI exam is distinctive and challenging. As such, it warrants the specialized focus of *Guide to Passing the PSI Real Estate Exam.*

This book is intended to guide prospective licensees in their preparation for the exam. It is intended to *direct* their effort. The study aids presented will help the student make the best use of his or her preparation time. It is hoped that this study guide will enable the prospective salesperson or broker to achieve success not only on the licensing exam but ultimately in the dynamic field of real estate.

ACKNOWLEDGMENTS

My thanks to all those who participated in the preparation of this text. I am especially grateful for the comments and advice of: Consulting Editor Tim Meline, GRI, DREI, e-pro, Iowa Real Estate School; Daniel Conte, Appraisal and Real Estate School of Connecticut; Keith Donaldson, Donaldson Educational Services; Darlene Mallick, J.D., LL. M., Anne Arundel Community College, REALTOR® and broker, Mallick & Associates, Maryland and Pennsylvania; Farhad Rozi, Training Director and Instructor, Long & Foster Institute of Real Estate; Teresa Sirico, Teresa Sirico REALTOR® LLC, Greater New Haven Association of Realtors; and Donald White, DREI, Gambrills, MD.

This book is dedicated to my wonderful wife, Adrienne, for all of her support and encouragement.

ABOUT THE AUTHOR

Lawrence Sager is a licensed real estate broker, certified residential appraiser, AQB certified USPAP Instructor, and REALTOR®. He holds a master's degree in urban land economics from the University of Illinois and is Real Estate Coordinator at the Madison Area Technical College. His writings have appeared in numerous publications on real estate and related fields.

Sager has acted as research consultant for Madison Area Technical College, the University of Wisconsin, and other public and private organizations. He is a Certified Fair-Housing trainer and has served as president of the Community Reinvestment Alliance, Madison, Wisconsin. He has worked with the Wisconsin Real Estate Examining Board as a course writer and as the assistant executive secretary in the certification of educational programs for real estate licensure. He is a member of the Professional Standards Committee of the REALTORS® Association of South Central Wisconsin as well as the Appraiser Application Advisory Committee of the Wisconsin Department of Regulation and Licensing and the Advisory Committee on Continuing Assessor Education of the Wisconsin Department of Revenue. He is also a member of the Governor's Council on Real Estate Curriculum and Examinations. He is the author of *Guide to Passing the Real Estate Exam (ACT), Wisconsin Real Estate: Practice and Law,* and the 1980 and 1983 editions of the *Wisconsin Real Estate Manual*. He is also the author of *Guide to Passing the PSI Real Estate Exam Software* and a CD-ROM, *Real Estate Law and Practice in Wisconsin.* Sager also serves as an expert witness in the areas of real estate practice and law as well as competency of real estate licensees.

ABOUT THE CONSULTING EDITOR

Tim Meline, GRI, DREI, e-pro, graduated with a degree in education from the University of Northern Iowa and has been a licensed REALTOR® since 1976. He has been Iowa Realty's Director of Education and Training as well as Director of the Iowa Real Estate School since 1978. He is an active instructor for the Iowa Association of REALTORS® and serves as a peer reviewer on the Complaint Committee of the Iowa Real Estate Commission.

In 2002 Tim assisted in the creation of *Iowa Real Estate Basics* and *Iowa Real Estate Exam Prep,* also published by Dearborn™ Real Estate Education. Both products are used across the state of Iowa to help candidates pass the real estate licensing exam.

He has served as President of the Des Moines Area Association of REALTORS® and has chaired three Habitat for Humanity builds. Tim was recognized by his board as REALTOR® of the year in 2000 and received Honorable Mention in 2003 for the Iowa Association of REALTORS® Good Neighbor Award. In 2004 he was awarded Humanitarian of the Year by the Des Moines Area Association of REALTORS®.

Use of the Manual

The aim of this manual is to prepare you on as many levels as possible to pass the real estate licensing examination compiled by the PSI Examination Services, Glendale, California. The *Guide* addresses two primary aspects of test taking:

1. the structure and format of the exam, and

2. the content of the exam.

The organization of the *Guide* follows these two basic concerns. In addition to suggesting the most efficient use of this manual, Chapter 1 provides specific information about the PSI organization, testing procedures, and the test itself. Chapter 2, "Examination and Study Strategies," is intended to familiarize you with the *format* of the questions in the PSI exam and suggests a strategy for optimizing test scores. Several studies have shown that given two examinees of equal ability and subject knowledge, the one who is more familiar with the form and style of the test will consistently score better than the other. Accordingly, Chapter 2 discusses the mechanics and the strategies of a test. It explains, for example, the parts of a question and how a typical question is developed. It illustrates how to analyze a question for clues to the right answer and how to determine what skills the question is intended to measure. Particular attention is given to the types of questions used by PSI in its real estate licensing examinations.

Chapter 2 also presents a strategy for optimizing test results by using the diagnostic exams following the content outlines presented in Chapters 3 to 11, 13, and 14. Chapter 12 is a test of real estate mathematics.

Chapter 15, "Salesperson Examinations," and Chapter 16, "Broker Examinations," afford an opportunity to take sample exams to measure your knowledge and the test-taking skills you have gained. New to the 5th edition are three appendices containing additional math practice and pertinent reference material for new salespersons:

- Appendix A: Mathematical Formulas at a Glance
- Appendix B: Mathematics Practice and Review (50 typical math-related problems that real estate practitioners encounter, with solutions)

- Appendix C: Web Site and Palm Directory

The Glossary is a handy reference list of real estate terms and definitions.

EXAMINATION INFORMATION

The PSI salesperson exam contains from 110 to 120 multiple-choice questions. Ample time is allowed to complete the test.

The exam has two parts. The first part is an 80-question test that measures your understanding of real estate practices and principles common to all the participating jurisdictions. Discussions provide a breakdown of the divisions of the national test and their relative importance in the exam.

The second part of each exam (30 to 40 questions) is the state test. The questions focus on real estate regulations and practices and state statutes that are unique to each jurisdiction. More information on the content of this part of the exam can be obtained from your real estate commission.

All questions on the salesperson examinations are multiple choice, with four alternatives. (Formats are discussed in detail in Chapter 2, "Examination and Study Strategies.") Objective or multiple-choice questions are advantageous because they can accurately test several different levels of an applicant's knowledge in a limited amount of time and can be scored quickly.

Each answer has the same value—no penalty is imposed for wrong answers. This means that it will benefit you to answer all the questions on the exam as best you can. The answer sheet should be free of all marks except filled-in ovals and identifying information; marking more than one answer to a question counts as a wrong answer.

Examinees must pass both the national section and the state section of the test. The required percentage of correct answers varies from one licensing commission to another; this information is available from your local jurisdiction. PSI policy is to send score reports only to those examinees who have failed. Each of these reports indicates the examinee's scores on each of the two major sections of the exam (national and state), as well as on the various content areas in each major section. The scores represent the examinee's performance on a scale of 0 to 100. At present, PSI does not allow an applicant to review her or his examination.

On the day of your real estate exam, take your test center admission ticket, personal identification, several number-two pencils, an eraser, and a watch to the testing center. Many jurisdictions allow examinees to use silent, battery-powered calculators, although these calculators cannot have alphabetic keypads or paper tape. Slide rules also are allowed, but you should be able to work the math problems without such aids. No other paper or aids should be taken to the test site.

Standard instructions and procedures are part of the written exam booklet and probably will be read to you by a test supervisor before you begin the exam. When you get your test booklet, read the directions completely. When you receive your answer sheet from the test supervisor, be sure to enter your identifying information on it properly.

A majority of the states using PSI currently are having their examinees take the exam by computer. Taking the PSI examination by computer is simple; neither computer experience nor typing skills are required for taking the test, which requires you to use fewer than 12 keys. Upon being seated at the computer terminal, you will be prompted to confirm your name, identification number, and the examination for which you are registered.

An introduction to the computer and keyboard will appear on the screen prior to your starting the exam. The time allowed for this introduction will not count as part of your exam time.

The introduction includes a sample screen display telling you to press "1", "2", "3", or "4" to select your answer or to press "?" to mark for a later review. You then press "enter" to record your answer before moving on to the next question. You may change your answer as often as you like before pressing "enter." Note that during the examination, the time remaining for your examination will be displayed at the top of the screen and updated as you record your answers. If you have time remaining after you have answered every question in the examination, you will be given the opportunity to review all of the questions in the examination. You also will have the choice of reviewing only those questions that you marked for review or ending your examination and seeing your results. You may change your answers during the review options. You may repeat the review options as time allows.

For further examination information you may visit the PSI Web site at *www.psiexams.com.*

SALESPERSON EXAMINATION

The content order in Chapters 3 through 13 of this text follows the organization of the basic areas of PSI's national salesperson test.

Chapters 3 to 11 and 13 end with a brief examination of the topics covered in each section. These pretests, called "diagnostic tests," will help you determine your particular strengths and weaknesses and thus indicate which section of the examination needs additional review. They will identify the specific real estate concept, terminology, or application that you do not fully comprehend. The answers for each pretest are keyed to the page with the information you need to know for that subsection. The recommended procedure for using these sections is to take the diagnostic tests, then check your answers against the answer key provided at the end of the pretest. If your evaluation of your wrong answers indicates that you misunderstand the topic, study the chapter again. If your evaluation on the pretest indicates that you understand the concept but missed the question because of its structure, then reread Chapter 2, "Examination and Study Strategies." If math is a problem area, check Chapter 12 for a basic real estate mathematics review.

When you feel sufficiently prepared, turn to the 80- or 100-question sample exams in Chapter 15 (for salesperson) or Chapter 16 (for broker). These exams closely approximate an actual PSI exam in content and format. They offer an opportunity to thoroughly test your knowledge and test-taking skills. The answer key and its explanations will help you identify your problem topics, based on the results of your diagnostic tests and the sample exam. Consider consulting real estate principles and practice texts if you missed a significant number of questions that relate to a specific topic.

PSI test specifications for salespeople

In the national portion of the real estate licensing examination for salespersons, PSI has defined its testing priorities and outline as follows:

- **Property Ownership** (7 questions) Covers general topics such as classes of property, land characteristics, encumbrances, types of ownership, and descriptions of property.
- **Land-Use Controls and Regulations** (7 questions) Covers the kinds of restrictions that can limit property use, including public restrictions, such as zoning ordinances and building and housing codes, and private restrictions, such as those identified in deed restrictions.
- **Valuation and Market Analysis** (7 questions) Covers the methods used to estimate value, competitive market analysis, and transactions requiring formal approval.
- **Financing** (8 questions) Covers a knowledge of financing alternatives and practices of financial institutions.
- **Laws of Agency** (10 questions) Covers agency relationships, common types of agency, disclosure of agency, and compensation.
- **Mandated Disclosures** (6 questions) Covers property disclosure forms, inspection, and material facts.
- **Contracts** (10 questions) Covers topics such as offer/purchase agreements, counteroffers, leases as contracts, and rescission and cancellation agreements.
- **Transfer of Property** (7 questions) Covers topics such as title insurance, deeds, escrow or closing, and tax aspects.
- **Practice of Real Estate** (10 questions) Covers fair housing laws, advertising, ethical issues, and broker/salesperson agreements.
- **Mathematics** (5 questions) Covers general math concepts, property tax calculations, and mortgage and lending calculations.
- **Specialty Areas** (3 questions) Covers topics such as property management and commercial/business property.

BROKER EXAMINATION

The broker exam is composed of 100 to 150 questions (80 to 100 in the national test and, usually, 25 to 50 in the state test) and lasts up to five hours. Chapter 16 of the *Guide*, "Broker Examinations," contains a discussion of the broker exam, one 80-question and one 100-question sample exam. The answer key that follows includes discussions of the answers and references to the page numbers that cover the topics. Broker management is covered in Chapter 14.

The concepts-to-understand outlines and diagnostic tests in Chapters 3 to 11, as well as Chapters 13 and 14, the math review in Chapter 12, and the sample exams in Chapters 15 and 16 should be of considerable study value to the prospective broker in preparing for the exam.

PSI test specifications for brokers

In the national portion of the real estate licensing examination for brokers, PSI includes the same categories covered in the salesperson exam, with the exception of Wisconsin. The difference between the two national tests is the proportion of questions in each category. The distribution in the broker exam is as follows:

- **Property Ownership** (7 questions)
- **Land-Use Controls and Regulations** (7 questions)
- **Valuation and Market Analysis** (6 questions)
- **Financing** (7 questions)
- **Laws of Agency** (10 questions)
- **Mandated Disclosures** (7 questions)
- **Contracts** (10 questions)
- **Transfer of Property** (6 questions)
- **Practice of Real Estate** (10 questions)
- **Mathematics** (6 questions)
- **Specialty Areas** (4 questions)

The state supplement exam for brokers contains approximately 25 to 50 questions and is based on a state's statutes, rules, and contractual forms. Some of the states, such as Wisconsin, develop their own broker exams, in cooperation with PSI.

Examination and Study Strategies

The PSI real estate examinations are achievement tests that candidates must pass before they can work as salespeople or brokers in their states. An achievement test measures an individual's proficiency in a given field. The ultimate objective of the license exam is to maintain the standards of the industry and to protect the public from persons not qualified to practice real estate sales and brokerage. The exam, therefore, tests

- the knowledge applicants have gathered through license-preparation courses and individual study and
- the ability of the applicants to use that knowledge in real estate applications.

PREPARING FOR THE EXAM

Mental and physical preparation

Multiple-choice tests demand a special type of mental preparation. While memorizing definitions, terms, and formulas, keep in mind that some questions also will require you to apply your knowledge to novel situations. Concentrate on real estate principles as you study, and try to *apply the principles and facts to real-life situations.*

An excellent method of preparing for an exam is to take similar tests prior to the actual exam. You can gain important percentage points simply by being an experienced test taker. The more similar to the actual exam the practice test is in content and format, the more you will benefit. This is the strategy behind the presentation of the diagnostic tests and the salesperson and broker exams in this manual. You will earn a better score if you are in top physical and mental shape the day of the test. It is a good idea to review your notes within the 48 hours before the exam. Get your normal amount of rest the night before the exam; it is *not* wise to stay up all night in a panic-stricken effort to cram. Eat normally, but do not have a heavy meal before going to the test.

Your *attitude* is at least as important as your metabolic state. You should be prepared, determined, and positive. A small amount of anxiety is natural—it can even help you do your best—but too much anxiety is a handicap.

Taking the exam

Upon checking in for the examination, you will be required to show the necessary identification as well as verify and sign the candidate roster. You will also be required to sign the PSI Cheating Policy Statement and Candidate Consent Form. The proctor will then bring up the candidate information screen. You must review the information and ensure its accuracy. You must report any errors immediately. You will then be assigned a seat and the proctor will generate the exam. You will then be directed to enter the testing room and go to an assigned seat and begin the exam. When you actually begin the exam, read directions and questions carefully, not quickly. Be sure you understand each question completely before answering. Read each question twice to make sure of the question being asked.

A major cause of test errors is simply failure to think. Many tests measure judgment and reasoning, as well as factual knowledge. Always try to choose the *best* answer to a question; more than one alternative may be partially correct. Do not look for trick questions; choose the most logical answer to the premise of each question. Statistically, your first answer is likely to be the correct answer so do not change it unless you are absolutely sure you have made an incorrect answer.

Words used in the questions will have their standard meanings unless they are special real estate terms. It sometimes helps to rephrase a question if you are not sure of the answer. For example, you may suspect that **4** is true in the following item:

- In holding a deposit delivered with an offer, which of the following would be the best place to put the money, provided you had no instructions to the contrary?
  1. In your office safe
  2. In a neutral depository in the buyer's name
  3. In your checking account
  4. In a neutral depository

By rephrasing mentally, "The best place to put a deposit delivered with an offer would be in a neutral depository," you can clarify your thoughts about **4** being the correct answer. Be careful, though, not to change the meaning of the question when you rephrase it.

Pacing

Work through the exam at a comfortable rate. You are allowed ample time to finish the exam; however, you should work as rapidly as you can without sacrificing accuracy. Budget your time before you begin the exam. If you are not taking the test on a computer, keep a watch handy. Plan on having more than half the questions answered before half the exam time has elapsed. NOTE: With the computer you do not have to waste time shading in your answers—and your results are immediate.

You may want to take a short break halfway through the exam. If you are ahead of schedule, you can afford to look up from your paper; take several deep, slow breaths; stretch your legs; relax in your seat; and rest for a minute or two. This breaks physical and mental tension and helps prevent mistakes.

As you work through the exam, answer the easy questions first—they are worth the same number of points as the hard ones, and they will build your confidence. Mark difficult items and time-consuming calculation problems and return to them later. You may find clues in later questions; or, if time runs out, you will have all the sure points. Do not give hurried answers just because you are intimidated by the number of questions. Most objective items are not very time consuming. Do not become discouraged if the exam seems difficult. No one is expected to get a perfect score.

DEVELOPING TEST QUESTIONS

The PSI exams are the result of collaboration by real estate experts and educators. How the tests for salespeople and brokers are organized and how many questions are associated with each topic of the exam were covered in Chapter 1, "Use of the Manual." This section discusses the mechanics of test building.

Both the broker and the salesperson exams are completely multiple choice. Each test usually includes two types of questions. The first type tests your knowledge of general real estate, and the second tests your ability to apply this knowledge to specific real estate situations. The parts of a typical multiple-choice question are shown in the examples below:

- When a claim is settled by a title insurance company, the company acquires all rights and claims of the insured against any person who is responsible for the loss. This is called
  1. escrow.
  2. abstract of title.
  3. certificate of title.
  4. subrogation.

The stem

The first step in developing a question is to write the *stem*, or *lead.* The stem provides all the information necessary to determine the correct response. It usually does not include irrelevant or extraneous information; the exceptions generally are items dealing with mathematics.

The stem can be an incomplete statement, as in the preceding example, or a question.

- A lease provides a minimum rent of $250 per month plus 5 percent of annual gross income over $100,000. If the tenant did $145,000 in business last year, what total rent was paid?
  1. $3,000
  2. $5,250
  3. $4,500
  4. $7,250

The answer is **2.** Although the direct question lead tends to be somewhat less ambiguous than the incomplete statement, it usually is slightly longer and contains fewer clues to the correct response.

The alternatives

The distractors then are written, with the correct keyed response embedded among the choices. In the PSI exam, the alternatives are presented in a multiple-choice format. The multiple-choice format, as illustrated in the preceding example, supplies four separate alternative answers. In this format, you are asked to consider four possible answers, alone and in combination. Study the following example:

- Listing agreements include which of the following?
  1. An open listing only
  2. An exclusive-right-to-sell listing only
  3. An open listing and an exclusive-right-to-sell listing
  4. A contract for deed

The answer is **3.** The purpose of distractors is to differentiate between well-prepared examinees and those who do not know the subject. Test developers often use popular misconceptions or even true statements that do not apply to the stem as distractors. Questions that do use true statements as distractors test not only your knowledge but also your judgment concerning the relevance of that knowledge. The difficulty of a question depends on the quality, or plausibility, of the distractors. In the worst case, where you have no idea which answer may be correct, the chance of answering it correctly is 25 percent because, theoretically, one out of four questions could be answered correctly just by guessing. Answering the question becomes much easier, and the odds of guessing correctly much higher, if one or two responses can be immediately eliminated.

SAMPLE QUESTIONS

The questions on the exam are not set up to trick you. You will, however, encounter several exam questions on the broker's exam that are more complex than the majority of the questions. Such questions are usually in a situational (story) format. You will need to read each question carefully to know exactly what is being asked before you begin to formulate your answer.

Several examples of questions that seem to be the most difficult for examinees are illustrated in this section. These include questions involving superfluous facts, reading comprehension, multistep math, value judgments, and best answer.

Superfluous facts

Exam questions frequently contain superfluous facts that are not needed to answer the questions.

For example:

- A family paid $50,000 for their home five years ago, making a $10,000 down payment. Their monthly payment, including interest at 7¾ percent, is $286. The interest portion of their last payment was $225.27. What was the approximate loan balance before their last payment?
  1. $29,480.64
  2. $34,880.52
  3. $44,283.87
  4. None of the above

The answer is **2.** The only facts needed to answer this question are the amount of the last interest payment and the rate of interest. To solve, simply multiply the amount of the monthly interest, $225.27, by 12. Then divide the result by the interest rate, 0.0775, to get the approximate loan balance.

Reading comprehension

Another type of question you may find on the test requires that you read each word extremely carefully for comprehension.

For example:

- Closing of a transaction for a residential property is set for April 19, 2005. The seller has a three-year insurance policy that expires June 25, 2006. The seller has prepaid a three-year premium of $555. The buyer is to take over the policy as of the date of closing. The amount credited to the buyer at closing is
  1. $185.00.
  2. $202.99.
  3. $231.25.
  4. None of the above

The answer is **4** because the prorated amount of the prepaid insurance would be *debited* to the buyer.

Multistep math

A type of question that frequently appears on PSI exams involves mathematics problems that require several steps.

For example:

- A woman bought a house at exactly the appraised value. She negotiated a loan through a savings-and-loan association at 75 percent of the appraised value. The interest rate was 9 percent. The first month's interest was $405. What was the approximate selling price of the property?
  1. $54,000
  2. $60,000
  3. $72,000
  4. None of the above

The answer is **3.** To answer this question, first multiply $405 by 12 to get the approximate annual interest ($4,860). Then divide $4,860 by the interest rate, 0.09, to get the amount of the loan ($54,000). Finally, divide $54,000 by 0.75 to find the appraised value ($72,000), which is the same as the purchase price. Sometimes a candidate who understands the mathematical process can use the answer key and work backward.

$$\$72,000 \times 75\% \ (0.75) = \$54,000 \times 9\% \ (0.09) = \$4,860 \div 12 \text{ months} = \$405$$

Value judgments

A few questions on the exam may require you to make value judgments.

For example:

- A broker listed a small house for $86,000, obtaining an executed sales contract on it within six weeks at $85,000. The broker learned there was an existing $75,000 first mortgage and a $5,000 second mortgage on the property. The broker knew the real estate could be refinanced on a new $70,000 first-mortgage loan. The holder of the second mortgage told the broker he was willing to discount his $5,000 note, selling it for $4,500. The buyer has $20,000 cash and qualifies for a new $70,000 first-mortgage loan. The broker should
  1. say nothing to be seller about refinancing and allow the transaction to close.
  2. tell the seller the second mortgage can be paid off at a $500 discount.
  3. tell the holder of the second mortgage the property is sold and, therefore, he or she should demand the full amount of $5,000.
  4. buy the second mortgage himself at the $500 discount.

The answer, of course, is **2.** As an agent of the seller, the broker must act in the seller's best interest.

Best answer

You will frequently be asked to choose the best answer from alternatives when the ideal answer is not present.

For example:

- A broker listed a beachfront home at $263,000. Three weeks later, the broker was fortunate to obtain a full-price offer on the beach house. Stopping by the house after the sales contract was executed and in force, the broker was appalled to see a large foundation crack. Two days later the broker noticed the crack had been carefully repaired. The broker knew the seller was unaware of the crack because she had extremely poor eyesight. The broker suspected that the crack had been fixed by the seller's son-in-law, a building contractor. The broker should
  1. disclose the fact of the crack to the buyer.
  2. immediately cancel the sales contract.
  3. keep quiet about the crack because it has been repaired.
  4. confront the son-in-law with his suspicions and threaten to sue.

The best alternative available here is **1.** It would be ideal to inform the seller of the crack, requesting permission to inform the buyer, but that alternative does not appear here. Note that this question also asks you to make a value judgment.

HOW TO ANALYZE A QUESTION

Apparent content

In general, the PSI exams are designed to measure your real estate knowledge and skills. Multiple-choice questions can test much more than your recall of specific facts. The PSI exam will, in fact, test how well you understand a given concept; whether you can apply rules to real-life situations; and how well you can analyze, synthesize, and evaluate information, then arrive at a correct conclusion. If you can determine what ability the question is trying to measure, it will help you become a more effective test taker. The levels of skill the PSI exam seeks to measure are illustrated by the following examples:

Example 1

■ How many acres are there in a section?

1. 16
2. 36
3. 200
4. 640

The answer is **4.** This is an example of *recall*, or recognition. The point of the question is to find out if you know this fact about sections—logic does not help much in determining the answer. The *factual question* is the easiest type to recognize.

Example 2

■ Brokers owe their primary fiduciary duty to which of the following?

1. The principal
2. The lender
3. The public
4. The real estate commission

The answer is **1.** This type of question seeks to measure your understanding of the concept of fiduciary duty—and who it involves. *Comprehension questions* such as this often require you to identify real estate principles, laws, or practices.

Example 3

■ An investor leases a 20-unit apartment building for a net monthly rental of $5,000. If this figure represents a 7.5 percent return on investment, what is the original cost of the property?

1. $80,000
2. $200,000
3. $800,000
4. None of the above

The answer is **3.** Multiply the monthly rental by 12 to get the rental income ($60,000). Then divide $60,000 by 7.5 percent (0.075) to get the investment cost ($800,000). *Application questions* such as this are one level higher than comprehension questions. They ask you to use recall or understanding to solve a new real estate–related problem. Knowledge of real estate laws, regulations, principles, and practices must be applied to concrete situations encountered on the job. Math problems are usually of this type.

Example 4

■ Which of the following types of financing would be the most appropriate for a young veteran who has just used most of his savings to complete his degree in engineering and now would like to buy a house for his family?

1. A conventional mortgage
2. An installment contract
3. A VA mortgage
4. An FHA mortgage

The correct answer is **3.** At this point you are being tested not only on the concept of financing but also on your ability to weigh each of the options and come up with the best answer. *Analysis items* gauge your ability to identify parts of a whole, understand the relationships among the parts, or identify the way that these elements are organized. You may have to differentiate between reasons and conclusions or indicate the relative importance of causes or factors. This question involves more than recall, for all the options are true. You must take your thinking one step further.

Example 5

■ Which of the following types of listing agreements affords the broker the most protection?
1. An open listing
2. An exclusive-agency listing
3. A net listing
4. An exclusive-right-to-selling listing

The correct answer is **4.** *Evaluation questions* such as this one test your ability to determine the best solution or to judge value in some manner. Often you must use recall, comprehension, analysis, *and* synthesis to arrive at the answer.

Studies show that items testing the lower levels of cognition (recall or recognition) are easier than application, comprehension, and higher-level questions. However, items testing the higher cognitive functions often can be solved by using general intelligence rather than specific real estate knowledge. Your score can be improved simply by exercising logic. You can turn this to your advantage by reasoning through difficult problems using the following seven steps:

1. Read the items carefully to determine the general subject that the item is testing and exactly what is asked.
2. Reread the question for essential facts and qualifiers.
3. Eliminate answers that you know are incorrect.
4. Rephrase the problem (often helpful).
5. Determine what principles or formulas are necessary and how to solve the problem.
6. Apply relevant information to arrive at a solution.
7. Reread the question and check the answer.

Try this item for practice:

■ If an offer to purchase is received under certain terms and the seller makes a counteroffer, what is the prospective purchasers' legal position?
1. They are bound by the original offer.
2. They must accept the counteroffer.
3. They are relieved of the original offer.
4. They must split the difference with the seller.

The answer is **3.** How do you use the seven steps to arrive at that answer? In step 1, you determine that the subject is whether an offer is binding under certain circumstances. In step 2, you reread the question to determine that the prospective purchasers make an offer and the seller makes a counteroffer. In step 3, you eliminate any obviously incorrect answers—in this case, response **4.** Step 4 suggests rephrasing the problem: "If the buyers make an offer under certain terms and the seller makes a counteroffer, the buyers. . . ." Step 5 is performed so automatically for this type of question that you may not be conscious that you are doing it. You need to know that an offer is not binding on the prospective purchasers once a counteroffer has been made. In step 6 you determine that alternative **3** is correct. Step 7 ensures that you have understood the question and have marked the right answer.

Although this logical process may seem long or complicated, your mind will accomplish it automatically within a few seconds once you train yourself to think or reason through questions.

EXAM STRATEGY

Many people study diligently and simply show up at the examination site without having given any thought to a strategy for taking the test. To maintain your confidence, poise, and positive mental attitude, you should start the examination with a game plan for taking the test.

We suggest that you develop your own strategy for completing the test. Following is an example of an exam strategy:

Unless testing is computer-generated, start with the state examination. It is the shorter test, comprising 40 to 50 questions. Read each question once to determine the particular subject matter of the question. Read the question a second time, and concentrate on determining the correct response. If you are uncertain of the correct answer, eliminate obviously incorrect responses. If you still are uncertain of the single best answer, ask the computer to record the number for future review of the choice selected and move on to the next question. Then continue to the national exam, again answering the questions you know and skipping the questions you are uncertain about. By doing this, you divide the test into two parts:

1. the part you know, which you answer quickly and efficiently and remove from further consideration, and
2. the part you do not know but have managed to isolate, to which you can devote the remainder of your test time.

If math is your strength, you should next complete the math. There will be approximately ten math questions on the exam. After completing the math (on a mental high), your strategy is to go back to the state portion, then the national portion, and make a second pass through the exam. Do this until both tests have been completed.

Multiple-choice items often test not only your knowledge of specific points but also your ability to relate other information to the point. Many important topics have more than one question allotted to them. The correct answer to one question often can be found in some portion of another, so jot down the numbers of the questions that you think contain clues. This will help you in rechecking answers or answering questions you skipped.

If math is not your strength, do not let yourself be intimidated by the calculation problems. A good approach to math questions is to estimate the answer before actually working the problem. Figure neatly and carefully—this reduces error; then compare your answer with your original estimate. If they are different, you may have misplaced a decimal or used the wrong equation. If you cannot tell from the problem what equation to use, make up a simple, similar problem and determine the equation from that. If you cannot solve a problem, or if you obtain an answer that is not one of the options, check to see if you used all the figures given in your calculations. If you cannot solve a math problem in the usual way, you sometimes can find the correct solution by working backward from the given answers.

Math problems often use varying units that must be converted. You may have to change income per month to income per year before applying a formula, or you may have to convert square feet to acres before proceeding with a calculation.

If you really have no idea how to solve a math problem and must guess blindly, eliminate the two most extreme numerical answers and mark one of the remaining choices. This tactic is not always correct, but the odds favor it.

After completing every question on the exam, proofread your answer sheet if you are taking the exam with an answer key. Make sure that your answers are next to the correct numbers, that you did not misread any of the questions, and that you marked the answer you intended for each item. By using extra time to correct any careless mistakes, you may boost your score significantly. *Do not change an answer unless you are sure the new one is correct. Studies show that an examinee's first response usually is correct and that changes will decrease the score.*

By developing an exam strategy similar to this, you will be in command—not the exam.

Exam strategy

- Remember that questions are industry-related; know the vocabulary.
- Read all questions and answers thoroughly before choosing the best answer.
- Eliminate answers that are incorrect.
- Do not go back and change answers; do not second-guess yourself.
- First, complete the questions you know the answers to, then return to the questions you are unsure of.
- Psychologically prepare yourself.

STUDY STRATEGY

The following gives you a strategy for studying and incorporating the diagnostic tests and outlines of concepts to understand in Chapters 3 through 13.

Chapters 3 through 13 correspond to testing areas on the PSI exam for salesperson: "Property Ownership," "Land Use Controls and Regulations," "Valuation and Market Analysis," "Financing," "Laws of Agency," "Mandated Disclosures," "Contracts," "Transfer of Property," "Practice of Real Estate," "Mathematics," and "Specialty Areas." Chapter 14 covers "Brokerage Management." Each chapter begins with an "Outline of Concepts to Understand" for the subject area. This is followed by the "Diagnostic Test," its "Answer Key," and a test score box. Take the Diagnostic Test and analyze your results before reviewing the content outline. If your progress score suggests that you need improvement, use the test results to establish your priority areas for study.

Keep in mind that the outline format of the concepts is designed primarily to organize your real estate knowledge concisely. If you are having difficulty with a particular topic, consult real estate practice and theory texts for a comprehensive explanation of the topic. *Modern Real Estate Practice* (published by Dearborn Real Estate Education) provides a solid core of information.

How to use the progress score

After completing and correcting the diagnostic test, count the number of questions missed and enter that number in the box under "Your Score" after "Total Wrong." Then subtract the number of incorrectly answered questions from the total points. Finally, analyze your results by finding where your score of correct answers falls in the "Range" column; the rate corresponding to your score describes your progress. Your score will fall under "Good," "Fair," or "Needs Improvement."

For example:

PROPERTY OWNERSHIP

Rating	Range	Your Score	
Good = 80% to 100%	30–37	Total Number	37
Fair = 70% to 79%	26–29	Total Wrong	– 6
Needs improvement = Lower than 70%	25 or less	Total Right	31

Passing Requirement: 26 or Better

If your score on a diagnostic test is rated Good, this area is one of your strengths. However, we suggest that a student should strive for a 90-percent-correct score before taking the actual exam. A rating of Fair or Needs Improvement in a subject suggests this is an area you need to concentrate on.

Developing a strategy for studying

After you have pinpointed the areas that need particular study, you can begin studying the material in the concepts-to-understand outline. To increase the effectiveness of your study time, we suggest that you follow these rules.

Organize your study time. Educators suggest that the regular short study periods are better than lengthy cram sessions. You should study when you are at your best mentally and physically; this may be early in the morning. The following chart will help you organize your study time in relation to the specific areas on the examination.

Scheduled Hours for Study

NATIONAL EXAM	M	T	W	Th	F	Sa	Su	TOTAL
Property Ownership								
Land Use Controls and Regulations								
Valuation and Market Analysis								
Financing								
Laws of Agency								
Mandated Disclosures								
Contracts								
Transfer of Property								
Practice of Real Estate								
Mathematics								
Specialty Areas								

STATE EXAM	M	T	W	Th	F	Sa	Su	TOTAL
Real Estate Law								
Rules and Regulations								
Special State Considerations								

Study in depth. It is important to realize that you cannot simply read the text in preparing to complete the exam successfully. You must arrive at a thorough understanding of the subject matter. This can be easily achieved by writing a sample test question to yourself about the paragraph you have just read. It is a good practice to outline the thoughts of the paragraph in your own words or develop relationships between items. In other words, create mental images that will help you recall difficult concepts. Acronyms are useful when memorizing a series of items. For example, the five duties that an agent owes to a principal are COALD: care, obedience, accounting, loyalty, and disclosure. During this stage, you should work alone.

Regularly review material studied. In many cases this can be accomplished by having a study partner assist you in reviewing your knowledge of vocabulary words, concepts, and relationships. This also can be achieved by taking regular exams on the subject matter. Following are some other tips:

- Make flash cards with terms on the front and definitions on the back.
- Tape-record terms: say the term, pause, then give the definition.
- Encourage group or one-on-one discussion.

Property Ownership

OUTLINE OF CONCEPTS

I. Property Ownership

A. Classes of property

1. Real property—the land and anything permanently affixed to it; includes the interests, benefits, and rights inherent in the ownership of real estate.
2. Personal property—movable objects (chattels) that do not fit into the definition of real property; conveyed by bill of sale.
3. Fixture—an item of personal property that has been converted to real property by being permanently affixed to the land or building.
4. A fixture that is permitted to be and is detached from the land or the building would revert to personal property (severance).
5. Trade fixture—an item installed by a commercial tenant according to the terms of a lease and removable by the tenant before the expiration of the lease—personal property.
   a. If not removed, the trade fixture becomes real property of the building owner by accession.

II. Land Characteristics

A. Physical

1. Immobile—the geographic location of a parcel of land is fixed—can never be changed.
2. Indestructible—the long-term nature of improvements plus permanence of land tends to create stability in land development.
3. Unique or nonhomogeneous—all parcels differ geographically and each parcel has its own location.

B. Economic

1. Scarcity—although there is a substantial amount of unused land, supply in a given location or of a specific quality can be limited.
2. Improvements—placement of an improvement on a parcel of land affects value and use of neighboring parcels of land.
3. Permanence of investment—improvements represent a large fixed investment; some, such as drainage and sewerage, cannot be dismantled or removed economically.
4. Area preference, or situs—this refers to people's choices and desires for a given area.

C. Legal descriptions
  1. Metes and bounds
     a. Begins at a specific point and proceeds around boundaries of parcel by reference to linear measurements and directions.
     b. Boundaries established on basis of actual distance between monuments (fixed objects).
     c. A boundary must return to the point of beginning so that the land described is fully enclosed.
  2. Rectangular (government) survey
     a. Based on measurements from base lines and principal meridians.
     b. Base lines run east and west; principal meridians run north and south.
     c. Designed to set up checkerboard pattern of identical squares over specific area.
        (1) Parallel vertical lines six miles apart divide land into strips east and west of the principal meridian that are referred to as *ranges*.
        (2) Parallel horizontal lines six miles apart divide land into strips north and south of the baseline that are referred to as *tiers*.
        (3) The grid that divides the land into townships is formed by superimposing these two sets of lines.
           (a) A township is six miles square (36 square miles).
           (b) A township contains 36 sections; each section is a square mile and contains 640 acres (one acre = 43,560 square feet).
           (c) Sections are numbered from the northeast corner; the first row of six sections runs east to west, the second row west to east, and so on, with section 36 located in the southeast corner of the township.
           (d) The land description is based on references to either a section or some portion of a section, such as one quarter-section (160 acres) or one half-section (320 acres).
           (e) A typical description: the NE¼ of the SW¼ of Section 4, Township 3 North, Range 2 east of the Principal Meridian.
           (f) To determine the number of acres in a rectangular survey legal description, multiply all the denominators and divide the result of this multiplication into 640 acres. NW¼ of the SW¼ $= 4 \times 4 = 16$ divided into 640 $= 40$ acres.
  3. Subdivision plats
     a. Location of an individual parcel is indicated on a map of the subdivision, which is divided into numbered blocks and lots.
     b. Each parcel is referred to a lot, block, subdivision name, city, and state.
  4. Street address: an informal reference; too unreliable for a legal description because you cannot walk the boundaries.

III. Encumbrances

A. A charge, claim, or liability that attaches to and is binding on real estate.

B. General classifications of encumbrances

1. Liens—affect the title
    a. A lien is a charge against property that provides security for a debt or obligation of the property owner.
    b. If the debt is not repaid, the lienholder has the right to have it paid out of the debtor's property, generally from the proceeds of a court or foreclosure sale.
    c. A specific lien relates to specific property; a general lien, such as a judgment or court decree, applies to all the debtor's property.
    d. Possible specific liens against an owner's real estate include real estate taxes, mortgages, and mechanics' liens.
    e. Real estate taxes and special assessments usually take priority over all other liens, regardless of date.
    f. In some states, mechanics' liens may be given priority over previously recorded liens because mechanics' liens revert to the date the work was started, not to when the lien was recorded.
2. Encumbrances that affect the physical condition and /or use of the property include encroachment, easements, and restrictions.
    a. Deed restriction—a deed restriction or restrictive covenant is a private limitation on the use of property. Developers use it to make their new neighborhoods appealing to certain buyers. These restrictions can be enforced by a court injuction.
    b. Easement—an easement is a right acquired by one party to use the land of another party for a specific purpose.
        (1) Easement appurtenant
            (a) An easement annexed to ownership for the benefit of such parcel of land.
            (b) Requires that there be two tracts of land, either contiguous or noncontiguous, owned by different parties.
            (c) The tract over which the easement runs is known as the *servient tenement*; the tract that benefits from the easement is known as the *dominant tenement.*
            (d) Appurtenant easements "run with the land" and are not terminated by the sale of either the servient or dominant tenement.
        (2) Easement in gross—a mere personal interest in or right to use the land of another, such as the right of way for a pipeline; there is no dominant tenement, just a servient tenement.
        (3) Easement by necessity—arises when there is no other access to a property by a street or public way and the easement is required by necessity rather than for convenience.
        (4) Easement by prescription
            (a) Acquired when the claimant has made use of another's land for the prescriptive period, generally from 5 to 20 years.

(b) Claimant's use must have been continuous, without the owner's approval, visible, open, and notorious. Successive periods of use by different parties may establish a claim for an easement by prescription.

(5) License

(a) Permission to enter the land of another for a specific purpose, such as permission to park in a neighbor's driveway or to go hunting on another's property.

(b) Differs from easement in that it can be canceled or terminated by licensor at any time.

(6) Encroachments—illegal extension of a building or some other improvement, such as a wall or fence, beyond the boundaries of the land of its owner and onto the land of an adjoining owner.

IV. Interests in Land

A. Interests in real estate—feudal versus allodial rights

1. Feudal—system of land ownership in which the king or government held title to the land; the individual was merely a tenant who held rights of use and occupancy at the sufferance of the overlord.
2. Allodial—system in which an individual can hold land free and clear of any rent or service due the government; system under which land is held in the United States.

B. Limitations on ownerships—individuals' ownership rights are subject to certain rights of government:

1. Police power—power of the state to establish legislation to protect public health and safety and promote general welfare.
2. Eminent domain—right of government to acquire private property for public use while paying just compensation to the owner through a process known as condemnation.
3. Escheat—reversion of real estate ownership to the state after a statutory time period has elapsed, as provided by state law, when an owner dies and leaves no heirs or no will disposing of the real estate or when the property is abandoned.
4. Taxation—charge on real estate to raise funds to meet the public needs of the government.

C. Estates in land

1. Refers to degree, quantity, and nature of interest that a person has in real property for a lifetime (life estate) or forever (inheritable freehold).
2. Freehold estates—estates of indeterminable length, such as those existing for a lifetime or forever.
3. Fee simple
   a. Highest type of interest in real estate recognized by law.
   b. Holder entitled to all rights incident to property.
   c. Continues for indefinite period and is inheritable by heirs of owner.
4. Defeasible fee (qualified, conditional, determinable, or base fee)
   a. Continues for an indefinite period; may be inherited.
   b. Estate extinguished on the occurrence of a designated event, the time of such occurrence being uncertain.

c. May be based on either certain or uncertain event.

D. Life estate
1. Limited in duration to life of life tenant or life or lives of some other designated person or persons.
2. Not an estate of inheritance, because estate terminates at the death of the life tenant or the designated person.
3. May be created for the life of another person (estate pur autre vie).
4. Future interests in the property after the death of the life estate owner.
   a. Remainder interest—if the deed or the will names a third party to whom title will pass on the death of the life estate owner, then such party is said to own remainder interest.
   b. Reversionary interest—if the deed does not convey remainder interest to a third party, then on the death of the life estate owner, full ownership reverts to the original fee simple owner or, if he or she is deceased, to heirs.
5. Usually limited to the lifetime of the owner of the life estate (life tenant). An exception would be an estate pur autre vie.

E. Life tenant
1. Interest in real property is time-ownership interest.
2. Generally not answerable to the holder of future interest (remainderman).
3. Has limited rights, that is, can enjoy the rights of the land but cannot encroach upon the rights of the remainderman.
4. May not commit waste (permanently injure the land or property).
5. Entitled to possession of the property and to all income and profits arising from property during the term of ownership.
6. Life interest may be sold, leased, mortgaged, or gifted but may be of little value because all interest must be forfeited at the death of the life tenant; remainder interest cannot be encumbered by the life tenant.

F. Legal life estates
1. Curtesy—husband's life estate in all inheritable real estate of the deceased wife.
2. Dower—wife's life estate in all inheritable real estate of the deceased husband.
3. Many states have abolished curtesy and dower in favor of the laws of descent and distribution, by which the surviving spouse is frequently allowed to take a specific portion of the estate in fee rather than life estate.
4. Inchoate—a right not yet perfected.

G. Homestead
1. Tract of land owned and occupied as the family home.
2. In states with homestead-exemption laws, a portion of the area or value of land is exempted, or protected, from judgment for unsecured debts.

V. Freehold Estates

A. Ownership by natural persons
1. In severalty—one owner
2. In co-ownership—two or more owners

a. Tenancy in common
   (1) Each owner holds an individual interest in severalty.
   (2) Each owner can sell, convey, mortgage, or transfer his or her interest without the consent of the other co-owners.
   (3) Upon the death of a co-owner, the individual interest of the deceased passes to heirs or devisees according to the will; there is no right of survivorship.
   (4) Tenants in common may partition the land.
b. Joint tenancy
   (1) Owners have the right of survivorship, which states that all title, right, and interest of a deceased joint tenant in certain property passing to the surviving joint tenants by operation of law is free from claims of heirs and creditors of the deceased.
   (2) Four unities—title, time, interest, and possession—are required to create a valid joint tenancy.
   (3) Termination results from the destruction of any of the four unities.
   (4) Joint tenants may partition the land.
c. Tenancy by the entirety
   (1) Owners must be husband and wife.
   (2) Owners have the right of survivorship.
   (3) Title may be conveyed or encumbered only by the deed signed by both parties (one party cannot convey a one-half interest).
   (4) Usually no right of partition.
d. Community property (marital property)
   (1) Husband and wife may have sole ownership of the separate or individual property if it was owned solely by either spouse before the marriage or was acquired by gift or inheritance after marriage.
   (2) Husband and wife are equal partners in the community or marital property (property acquired during the marriage).
   (3) Upon the death of one spouse, the survivor automatically owns one-half of the community property, the other half being distributed according to the deceased's will.
   (4) Antenuptial agreements are contracts (prior to marriage) that preserve separate property ownership.

3. In trust—by a third person for the benefit of another
4. Ownership by a business organization
5. Partnerships
   a. Association of two or more persons to carry on business as co-owners and share in the profits and losses of that business
   b. Types of partnerships
      (1) General—all partners participate in the operation of the business and may be held personally liable for business losses and obligations.
      (2) Limited
         (a) Includes general as well as limited, or silent, partners.
         (b) General partner runs the business.
         (c) Although limited partners do not participate, they may

be held liable for business losses, but only to the extent of their investment unless they take an active role in management.

6. Corporations
   a. Ownership in severalty—corporations are considered by law to be a single entity.
   b. Each stockholder's liability for losses generally is limited to the amount of investment.
7. Syndicates—joining together of two or more parties to create and operate a real estate investment.

VI. Leasehold Estates

A. Types of Leasehold Estates
   1. Tenanacy on estate for years—lease for a definite period of time terminating automatically without notice by either party.
   2. Tenancy from year-to-year or periodic estate—lease for an indefinite period of time without a specific expiration date; notice must be given to terminate.
   3. Tenancy at will—lease that gives the tenant the right to possess with the consent of the landlord for an indefinite period of time; terminated by either party giving notice or by the death of either the landlord or the tenant.
   4. Tenancy at sufferance (holdover tenancy)—tenant continues to hold possession without the consent of the landlord.

B. Types of Leases
   1. Gross lease—tenant pays a fixed rent, while landlord pays all taxes, insurance, etc.
   2. Net lease—tenant pays rent plus all or part of property charges.
   3. Percentage lease—usually provides for minimum fixed rent plus a percentage of the portion of tenant's business income that exceeds a stated minimum
   4. Graduated lease—provides for specified rent increase at set future dates
   5. Index lease—allows rent to be increased or decreased periodically based on agreed index such as the change in the government cost-of-living index

VII. Other Important Terms

A. Accession—acquiring the title to additions or improvements to real property as a result of accretion of alluvium or annexation of fixtures (including accession of trade fixture not removed by the tenant prior to lease termination).
   1. Accretion—increase in land resulting from soil deposited by the natural force of water.
   2. Alluvion—actual soil-increase deposit resulting from accretion.

B. Appurtenances—rights belonging to land.

C. Assignment—transfer of rights and/or duties under a contract.

D. Attachment—procedure by which property of debtor is placed in the custody of the law and is held as security, pending the disposition of a creditor's suit.
   1. Rights can be assigned, unless the contract expressly forbids assigning them.

   2. Obligations often can be assigned, but the original party is secondarily liable for them.

E. Benchmark—permanent metal marker embedded in cement, used as a reference to indicate the elevation above sea level and actual physical location.

F. Cloud on title—any claim that may impair the title to a property

G. Cul-de-sac—street open at only one end and generally with a circular turnaround at the other end.

H. Datum—horizontal plane from which elevations are measured.

I. Erosion— gradual washing away of soil caused by flowing water or air.

J. Estovers—legally allowed necessities, such as the right of a tenant to use timber on leased property to support a minimum need for fuel or repairs.

K. Fixtures—personal property that has been affixed to and becomes part of the real property.

L. Good consideration—love and affection with no monetary measure of value.

M. Inchoate right—a right not yet perfected, such as a wife's interest in her husband's property while he is still alive. After his death the inchoate right ripens into a consummate right of dower.

N. Laches—court doctrine that bars a legal claim because of undue delay to assert the claim.

O. Lis pendens (Latin term for action pending)—recorded document that creates constructive notice that an action relating to a specific property has been filed in court.

P. Novation—also a transfer of rights and/or duties under a contract
   1. Original contract canceled.
   2. New contract negotiated and drawn, with the same parties or a new second party.
   3. Original party, if replaced, not liable.

Q. Parol-evidence rule—law that states that no prior or contemporary oral or extraneously written agreement can change the terms of the contract.

R. Quiet-title action—court action to establish the title to a specific property, for example, where there is a cloud on the title.

S. Statute of frauds—law that requires that certain contracts be in writing before they can be enforced; contracts for the sale of land and leases of more than one year are generally required to be in writing and signed by all parties.

T. Statute of limitations—law that refers to the length of time within which a party may sue.

U. Valuable consideration—consideration with a monetary measure of value.

V. Waste—abuse by one holding less than a fee estate that results in permanent injury to the land or property.

W. Writ of attachment—writ filed during a lawsuit that prevents the debtor from transferring title to the property involved in the suit.

DIAGNOSTIC TEST

1. The term *situs,* or place where something is situated, refers to
   1. uniqueness.
   2. area preference.
   3. immobility.
   4. scarcity.
2. Which of the following is a physical characteristic of land?
   1. Indestructibility
   2. Scarcity
   3. Permanence of investment
   4. Situs
3. The owner of a life estate in property
   1. does not pay real estate taxes.
   2. is entitled to possession of the property.
   3. may not receive income from the property.
   4. is not responsible for all repairs to the property.
4. Three individuals own a motel as tenants in common. One of the individuals decides to sell all of her assets. She may legally
   1. sell, because a tenant in common may sell her portion of assets if a majority of the co-owners also agree to sell.
   2. not sell, because a tenant in common's interests always remain encumbered.
   3. sell, because a tenant in common has an undivided interest in real property that is transferable.
   4. not sell, because there is a right of survivorship.
5. Which of the following statements is FALSE?
   1. Fixtures that are purchased, paid for, and installed after the execution of a mortgage are subject to liens of the mortgage.
   2. When a landowner tears down a fence, with the intention that it be permanently removed, and piles the material on the land, such material is real property.
   3. Generally, trade fixtures that were installed by the tenant are personal property.
   4. A hot-water heater installed on the property becomes a fixture.
6. Specific liens would NOT include which of the following?
   1. Mortgage liens
   2. Judgments
   3. Real estate taxes
   4. Mechanic's liens
7. A farmer purchased land with no access to a street or public way. After an unsuccessful attempt to gain access through negotiation he was able to gain access through an
   1. easement appurtenant.
   2. easement in gross.
   3. easement by necessity.
   4. easement by prescription.
8. A woman built a fence that extended beyond the boundary of her property onto her neighbor's property. This is an example of
   1. laches.
   2. an easement by necessity.
   3. an encroachment.
   4. an appurtenant easement.
9. A grandmother owned a life estate measured by her own life in residence. She leased the property for five years using a standard lease contract. Shortly thereafter, she died. The lease was
   1. valid only as long as she was alive.
   2. valid for five years.
   3. invalid because she, as an owner of a life estate, cannot lease property.
   4. valid for up to one year after her death.
10. An electrician did some rewiring in a home for which he has not yet been paid. One month after the work was completed, the electrician drove by the home to discover a For Sale sign on the property. The electrician should
    1. file a mechanic's lien.
    2. offer to purchase the house.
    3. obtain injunctive relief.
    4. sue the listing broker.

11. A tenant failed to remove her trade fixtures prior to the expiration of her lease, which resulted in the landlord acquiring title to the trade fixtures. Acquiring property in this way is known as
    1. accession.
    2. novation.
    3. laches.
    4. partition.

12. Included among the legal requirements of taking title to real property as tenants in common is that
    1. ownership interest must be equal.
    2. each co-owner's interest may be conveyed separately.
    3. a co-owner cannot will his interest in a property.
    4. the last survivor owns the property in severalty.

13. A homeowner employed a contractor to build a swimming pool on his property. Upon completion of the swimming pool, the contractor filed a lien to receive payment of the contract fee. Such filing could be considered any of the following **EXCEPT**
    1. a specific lien.
    2. an encumbrance.
    3. a general lien.
    4. a mechanic's lien.

14. A family buys a 40-year-old house, and the broker tells them the garage was built 30 years ago. Because the buildings are located on a "postage-stamp–sized" lot, the family hires a surveyor who tells them the garage extends six inches onto the neighbor's lot. Because the husband has taken a real estate course, he realizes that this might be a prescriptive easement and through court proceedings could become
    1. a dominant easement.
    2. a license.
    3. a servient easement.
    4. adverse possession.

15. A man has an unrecorded claim affecting the title to another man's property. The owner has been trying to sell the property, and the man with the claim is concerned about the possibility of it selling before a judgment of some kind is obtained. To protect himself, the man with the claim should
    1. file a lis pendens, which means litigation pending.
    2. publish a notice in the newspaper.
    3. bring a quick summary proceeding.
    4. notify the owner that any attempt to sell the property will be considered fraud.

16. *X* and *Y* own adjoining parcels of real estate. *X* has granted *Y* an easement over his property for ingress and egress. If *Y* decided to sell his land to *Z*, which of the following would be true?
    1. The status of the dominant and servient tenements will not change.
    2. The easement will be terminated, for *Y* no longer is the owner of the property.
    3. *X* may sell the easement to the new owner.
    4. To be valid, the deed of conveyance of *Y* to *Z* must specifically mention the easement.

17. Legal seizure of property to be held for payment of money pending the outcome of a suit to enforce collection is
    1. a lis pendens.
    2. an attachment.
    3. a writ of execution.
    4. an abstract of judgment.

18. Two individuals bought a building and took title as joint tenants. One of the owners died testate. The remaining owner now owns the building
    1. as a joint tenant with rights of survivorship.
    2. in severalty.
    3. in absolute ownership under the law of descent.
    4. subject to the terms of the deceased owner's will.

19. A husband and wife own property as tenants by the entireties. The husband dies and his will names their son as inheritor of the property. Which of the following statements is correct?
    1. The son and his mother own the property as tenants in common.
    2. The son owns the property in severalty.
    3. The son and his mother own the property as joint tenants.
    4. The son has no interest in the property.

20. Two brothers may take title to income property in unequal shares under which of the following?
    1. Severalty
    2. Tenants by the entirety
    3. Joint tenants
    4. Tenants in common

21. A contractor builds an addition to a house for a contract price of $52,000 and records his mechanic's lien notice. Before making any payment, the owner has the house jacked up and put on a platform prior to moving it to another location. The contractor should
    1. have his attorney prepare and record a covenant.
    2. file an encroachment notice.
    3. record an attachment.
    4. have his attorney prepare and record a notice of lis pendens.

22. Legal descriptions may NOT be based on
    1. the government survey.
    2. metes and bounds.
    3. a street address.
    4. a survey.

23. A land description that begins at a specific point and proceeds around the boundaries of a parcel by reference to linear measurements and directions is based on
    1. metes and bounds.
    2. the rectangular survey.
    3. a subdivision plat.
    4. a survey.

24. In the government survey system
    1. base lines run east and west.
    2. principal meridians run east and west.
    3. base lines run north and south.
    4. a township contains 26 sections.

25. A section contains
    1. 43,560 square feet.
    2. 640 acres (more or less).
    3. 160 square rods.
    4. 320 square rods.

26. You and your sister own a house. Your sister would like to sell her interest in the house to her cousin. You and your sister own the house under which of the following?
    1. Tenancy by the entirety
    2. Tenancy at will
    3. Tenancy in common
    4. Estate for years

27. A plumber sells his home, in which he has installed washerless faucets. After the contract has been executed, he decides to replace the faucets with standard faucets. Which of the following is true?
    1. The plumber may remove the faucets at any time.
    2. Standard faucets are a good replacement.
    3. The plumber can be held liable for removing the faucets because they are fixtures that were in place before the contract was signed.
    4. This question should be decided by the broker who took the listing.

28. Which of the following forms of ownership may only be held by a wife and husband?
    1. Tenancy in common
    2. Tenancy by the entirety
    3. Tenancy at will
    4. Joint tenancy

29. *R* sold his house; it included a water softener, which he had bought the previous year. *R*'s water softener would be classified as
    1. chattel.
    2. personalty.
    3. a trade fixture.
    4. a fixture.

30. You bought a property that measured ½ mile by ½ mile. How many acres did you purchase?
    1. 17.78 acres
    2. 36 acres
    3. 92.83 acres
    4. 160 acres

31. You are traveling directly from Section 6 to Section 36 of the same township. You are traveling
    1. northeast.
    2. southwest.
    3. northwest.
    4. southeast.

32. *B* holds a life estate in a house measured against his life. *B*'s life estate is
    1. an estate of inheritance.
    2. an example of a future interest.
    3. limited in duration to the life estate owner's life.
    4. a non-freehold estate.

33. A man and woman own their house as tenants by the entirety. Which of the following statements would NOT correctly describe the status of their ownership?
    1. Each owner has the right of survivorship.
    2. The owners must be husband and wife.
    3. Either owner may convey a one-half interest in the house to a third party.
    4. Title may be conveyed only by a deed signed by both parties.

34. The county zoo holds title to its land with the condition that if it charges admission fees, the title will revert to the original grantor of the estate. This is an example of a
    1. fee-simple estate.
    2. defeasible fee estate.
    3. legal life estate.
    4. conventional life estate.

35. An owner purchased a lot two blocks away from other homes that were built around a lake. The owner's deed cited an easement across another lakeside lot to gain entry onto the lake. What type of easement describes this situation?
    1. Easement by necessity
    2. Easement in gross
    3. Contiguous easement appurtenance
    4. Noncontiguous easement appurtenance

36. A farmer purchased a parcel of agricultural land described as the N ½ of the SW ¼ and the S ½ of the NW ¼. How many acres are in this legal description?
    1. 10 acres
    2. 80 acres
    3. 160 acres
    4. 320 acres

37. Before getting married, a husband bought an apartment building. After he became married, he decided to sell the building. The buyer's attorney required the husband's wife to sign a quitclaim deed. What interest of the wife did the attorney want released?
    1. Inchoate dower
    2. Common law
    3. Antenuptial
    4. Community property

MATCHING QUIZ

The column on the right contains brief memory links to important terms in Chapter 3. *Write the letter of the matching term on the appropriate line.*

A. Trade fixtures	1. ______Incomplete or a right not yet perfected
B. Situs	2. ______Revocable permission to use another's land
C. Township	3. ______A commercial tenant's removable fixtures
D. Specific Lien	4. ______No right of survivorship where the heirs inherit the deceased person's percentage of ownership
E. Servient Tenement	5. ______Contractual substitution of obligations from one party to another
F. Appurtenance	6. ______Latin for "litigation type action" is pending
G. Dominant Tenement	7. ______Joint tenancy with the right of survivorship
H. Prescriptive Easement	8. ______Something "in addition to," such as a right of way across someone else's property
I. License	9. ______Money or commodity used in a contract
J. Escheat	10. ______An easement created by open, notorious, hostile, and continuous usage
K. Remainderman	11. ______Easement is placed on this tenement
L. Inchoate	12. ______No heirs, therefore the government becomes owner
M. Tenancy in Common	13. ______Favorable site or preferred location
N. JTWROS	14. ______36 sections with each section having 640 acres
O. Datum	15. ______Tenement easement user
P. Valuable Consideration	16. ______The person to whom a life estate goes upon the death of the life tenant
Q. Novation	17. ______Doctrine that says if you fail to exercise a right within a reasonable time you could lose your right to act at a later time; the basis for statute of limitations laws
R. Laches	18. ______A special assessment
S. Lis pendens	19. ______Elevation benchmark
T. Meridians	20. ______Parallel vertical lines (N and S) six miles apart

ANSWER KEY WITH EXPLANATIONS: DIAGNOSTIC TEST

1. **(2)** Situs is used interchangeably with area preference. (18)

2. **(1)** Scarcity, permanence of investment, and situs are economic characteristics of land. (18)

3. **(2)** The life estate owner is responsible for paying real estate taxes and is entitled to all income and profits as well as being responsible for all repairs on the property. (22)

4. **(3)** Tenants in common have the right to sell their interest in a property without the consent of the other co-owners. (23)

5. **(2)** The fence material has been severed from the real estate and returned to personal property status. This is called severance. (18)

6. **(2)** Judgments are general liens; mortgage liens, real estate taxes, and mechanic's liens are specific liens. (20)

7. **(3)** An easement by necessity is acquired when the property is landlocked. An easement appurtenant requires two parcels, a dominant and a servient tenement. An easement in gross involves one parcel. Buried utility lines are examples of easements in gross found on a single parcel. (20)

8. **(3)** *Laches* refers to the inability to enforce a right because of undue delay in asserting it. Easements are rights to use the land of others. An encroachment is the unauthorized use or intrusion onto the property of another. (21)

9. **(1)** A life estate may be leased, but that interest is forfeited upon the death of the life tenant or the person whose life is the measurement. (22)

10. **(1)** The electrician cannot prevent the property from being sold; however, he can file a mechanic's lien to protect himself from not being paid. (20)

11. **(1)** Novation involves a transfer of liability from one debtor to another. Partition is a court procedure to divide co-tenants' interests in real property when parties do not agree to terminate. (18)

12. **(2)** The other answers are legal requirements of joint tenancy. (23)

13. **(3)** A mechanic's lien is a specific lien and an encumbrance. A general lien would apply to all of the homeowner's property. (20)

14. **(4)** A prescriptive easement is similar to adverse possession in that if one uses another's property for a statutory period of time, one may acquire a real property interest. The difference is that a prescriptive easement gives one the right to use, while through adverse possession the courts can grant ownership of the land that has been adversely occupied. (20–21)

15. **(1)** The claimant cannot prevent the property owner from selling his property. A lis pendens will provide public notice that a lawsuit affecting title to the property has been filed in court. (20)

16. **(1)** An appurtenant easement has been created and is considered a real property interest. Once created, the status of the dominant and the servient tenement remain the same. The easement runs with the land and therefore is not considered separate from the property. As a result **Z** acquires the easement. (20)

17. **(2)** Lis pendens was described above. A writ of execution is a court order directing the county sheriff to seize and sell the property of a debtor. An abstract of judgment is a summary of judgments that have become public record. (24)

18. **(2)** The remaining owner automatically takes title to the property under the right of survivorship. The joint tenancy is effective only until one owner remains; the surviving owner then holds title in severalty. (22)

19. **(4)** Tenancy by the entirety is characterized by the right of survivorship. The husband has no right to transfer his interest by will. The wife will hold an interest in severalty. (23)

20. **(4)** Severalty refers to one owner while tenancy by the entirety requires the owners to be hus-

band and wife. Joint tenancy requires equal shares of ownership. (24)

21. **(3)** An attachment places an encumbrance (lien) upon debtor's property held as security for a possible judgment obtained by an attaching creditor. (24)

22. **(3)** A street address does not tell a surveyor how large the property is or where it begins and ends and, therefore, is not acceptable as a legal description. (19)

23. **(1)** Metes and bounds is an accepted method of legal description. (19)

24. **(1)** Principal meridians run north and south, while a township contains 36 sections. (19)

25. **(2)** A section is one mile square and contains 640 acres (more or less). The reason for the "more or less" is that every 24 miles from the original base line and 24 miles from the principal meridian are correction lines and guide meridians. On either side of these lines the acres are either more or less. An acre contains 43,560 square feet. (19)

26. **(3)** Tenants by the entirety must be husband and wife. Tenancy at will and estate for years are types of leases. (23)

27. **(3)** Unless otherwise agreed, the faucets are considered fixtures that would be included in the selling price. (18)

28. **(2)** Tenants in common and joint tenants do not have to be related. A tenancy at will is not a form of ownership. (23)

29. **(4)** The water softener is a fixture or real property. The other answers are personal property. (18)

30. **(4)** $2 \times 2 = 4$
640 acres $\div$ 4 = 160 acres (19)

31. **(4)** Section 6 is in the upper left hand corner and section 36 is in the lower right hand corner. (19)

32. **(3)** A life estate is a freehold estate that terminates upon the death of the owner of the life estate. (22)

33. **(3)** Tenants by the entirety may not convey their property unless they both agree and sign the deed. (23)

34. **(2)** A defeasible fee estate may be terminated upon the violation of a condition found in the deed. (21)

35. **(4)** The two lots don't touch; therefore, they are noncontiguous, and because the easement involves two parcels, it is an easement appurtenant. An easement in gross involves only one parcel of land. (20)

36. **(3)** The solution requires an understanding of the word *and. And* means "addition." In this problem we have two legal descriptions that need to be added together: N ½ of the SW ¼ **AND** S ½ of the NW ¼. To find the solution, multiply the denominators and divide the results into 640 (total number of acres in a section). $2 \times 4 = 8$; 640 divided by 8 = 80; **AND** $2 \times 4 = 8$; 640 divided by 8 = 80. The answer is 80 + 80 = 160. (19)

37. **(1)** When the husband sold the property, the wife had an inchoate dower interest. By signing the quitclaim deed, she relinquished her future dower interest. If the husband precedes his wife in death, then her inchoate interest would be removed and replaced with her actual dower rights. The attorney didn't want the wife to be able to come back in the future and claim any dower rights. (22)

TEST SCORE

PROPERTY OWNERSHIP			
Rating	**Range**	**Your Score**	
Good = 80% to 100%	30–37	Total Number	37
Fair = 70% to 79%	26–29	Total Wrong	–
Needs improvement = Lower than 70%	25 or less	Total Right	

Passing Requirement: 26 or Better

ANSWER KEY: MATCHING QUIZ

1. L
2. I
3. A
4. M
5. Q
6. S
7. N
8. F
9. P
10. H
11. E
12. J
13. B
14. C
15. G
16. K
17. R
18. D
19. O
20. T

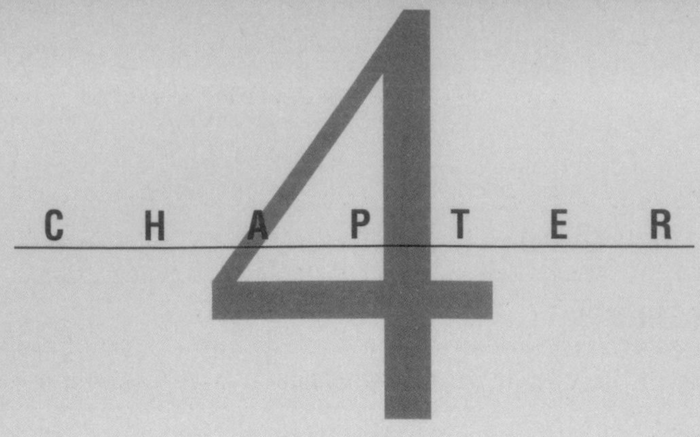

Land-Use Control and Regulations

OUTLINE OF CONCEPTS

I. Local, State, and Federal Government Land Rights

A. Police power—power of the state to promulgate laws aimed at promoting the general welfare and protecting public health and safety; examples of the use of police power include zoning, building codes, environmental protection; enabling acts are created by states to grant zoning power to municipal governments.

B. Taxation—power to tax real estate to meet the public needs of the government.

C. Eminent domain—power of the government to acquire private property for public use while providing just compensation (comdemnation) for the property owner.

D. Escheat—state laws that provide for ownership of real estate to revert to the state when the owner dies intestate and leaves no heirs or when the property is abandoned.

E. Water rights—ownership of water and land adjacent to it as determined by state law, which is based on either the doctrines of riparian and littoral rights or on the doctrine of prior appropriation; owners generally have the right to use water so long as they do not pollute or interrupt the flow.

1. Riparian rights—rights granted to owners along a nonnavigable river or stream.
2. Littoral rights—rights granted to owners along an ocean or large lake.
3. Prior appropriation—the right to use water is controlled by the state rather than by the adjacent landowner. A person must show a beneficial use for the water, such as crop irrigation, in order to secure water rights.

II. Control of Land Use

A. Public land-use controls—under police power, each state has the authority to adjust regulations required for protecting public health, safety, and the general welfare.

1. Zoning—zoning laws are local laws that regulate and control the use of land in the community, generally pertaining to the height, bulk, and use of the buildings. Powers to zone are conferred on municipal governments by state enabling acts.
   a. Nonconforming use—use in existence prior to the passage of a zoning ordinance and allowed to continue even though it does not conform
      (1) If property that exists as nonconforming is destroyed, it cannot be rebuilt without the approval of the zoning authority.
   b. Variance—approval by a zoning authority that allows an individual to deviate from the zoning requirement.
   c. Conditional use permit—allows for a use that does not conform with existing zoning but is necessary for the common good, such as locating a medical clinic in a primarily residential neighborhood.
   d. Downzoning—land zoned for residential or commercial use is rezoned for conservation only; it also applies to changes from dense to less-dense usage. The state generally is not responsible for compensating property owners for any loss of value unless the court finds that a "taking" of value has occurred, such as land being rezoned from residential to conservancy.
   e. Buffer zone—a land area that separates one land use from another; a park that separates a residential neighborhood from a shopping center.
   f. Spot zoning—reclassification of a small area of land for use that does not conform to the zoning of the rest of the area.
   g. Planned unit development (PUD)—planned mix of diverse land uses such as housing and recreation in one comprehensive plan.
2. Building codes—ordinances that specify standards for construction, maintenance, and demolition.
3. City plan specifications—a master plan to guide physical development of a community.
4. Subdivision regulations—apply to the location of streets, minimum lot size, etc.
5. Environmental protection laws
   a. Federal—examples include National Environmental Policy Act, Clean Air Act.
   b. State—many states, counties, and cities have passed their own environmental legislation.

B. Private land-use controls—restrictions specified by the owner in the deed when conveying the property.
C. If conflict exists between a zoning ordinance and a deed restriction, the more restrictive of the two takes precedence.
D. Taxation on real estate
   1. Real estate taxes generally take priority over other liens; may be enforced by the court sale of real estate that is free of other liens.
   2. Ad valorem tax (Latin for "according to the value")—includes taxes levied on real estate by various governmental units and municipalities.

3. Assessment—appraisal of value for tax purposes by an assessor representing the municipality in which the property is located.
4. Equalization factor—used in some states to correct general inequalities in statewide tax assessment.
5. Computation of tax rate
   a. The taxing district adopts a budget that identifies the amount of income to be raised from real estate taxes.
   b. To arrive at the tax rate, divide the amount of money required for the budget by the total assessed value of all properties within the taxing district. For example, if the taxing district must raise $600,000 from real estate taxes and the total assessed value is $10,000,000, the tax rate would be $600,000 ÷ $10,000,000 = 0.06, or 6 percent.
   c. The tax rate may be expressed in mills. For example, 40 mills = 4% of the taxable value; 45 mills = 4.5% of the taxable value.
   d. The tax bill for a property is calculated by applying the tax rate to the taxable value of the property; for example, a home assessed for tax purposes at $200,000 and using a tax district rate of 45 mills, or 4.5% of the taxable value, would be required (annually) to pay $9,000. Divided by 12, the monthly tax obligation would be $750.
6. Special assessments—special taxes levied on real estate; require property owners to pay for improvements that specifically benefit their real estate (installation of a curb and gutter, streets, water system, sewers, etc.).

III. Floodplain, Wetlands, and Shoreline Regulations

A. Floodplain—portions of land located near running bodies of water, such as rivers or lakes, that are subject to flooding; government controls generally restrict building in a floodplain.
B. Wetlands—areas of land where groundwater is close to or at the surface of the ground for a period of time each year that may produce swamps, floodplains, or marshes; because these areas of land are prone to flooding, they are covered by various federal, state, and local controls, such as zoning for conservation.
C. Shoreline regulation—zoning laws that reflect environmental as well as health and safety concerns; usually require zoning of all lands within a given distance of all navigable waters in each state; generally include tree-cutting rules, setback requirements for structures, filling and grading controls, dredging regulations, minimum standards for water supply and waste disposal, minimum lot sizes and widths, and subdivision regulations.

IV. Health and Safety Codes

A. Building codes
   1. Specify construction standards that must be met when erecting, maintaining, or demolishing buildings.
   2. Generally identify requirements for electrical wiring, sanitary equipment, and fire-prevention standards.
   3. Enforced by issuing building permits that verify compliance with building codes and zoning ordinances.

4. The building inspector issues a certificate of occupancy when the completed structure has been inspected and found satisfactory.
5. Issuing a building permit does not take precedence over the violation of a deed restriction.

V. Environmental Concerns

A. Pollution and environmental risks in real estate transactions
   1. Increasing public awareness of and concern about pollution problems and their health and economic effects have had significant consequences on real estate sales and values.
   2. The actual dollar value of real property can be affected significantly by both real and perceived pollution.
   3. The cost of cleaning up and removing pollution may be much greater than the dollar value of the property before pollution occurred.
   4. In some areas of the United States, mortgage and title insurance approval may depend on the inspection of the property for hazardous substances and proof of their absence.

B. Role of real estate licensees regarding environmental risks in real estate transactions
   1. Be alert to the possibility of pollution and hazardous substances on the property being sold.
   2. Ask clients about the possibility of hazardous substances associated with the property.
   3. Expect increasing numbers of questions from customers concerned about pollution.
   4. Consider the consequences of the potential liability in real estate transactions where hazardous substances may be involved.
   5. Contact government agencies and private consulting firms for information, guidance, and detailed study; real estate licensees often, however, do not have the technical expertise required to determine whether hazardous material is present on or near the property.
   6. Be scrupulous in considering environmental issues and exercise a high degree of care in all real estate transactions.

C. Hazardous substances of concern to real estate professionals
   1. Radon gas—an odorless radioactive gas produced by the decay of radioactive materials in rocks under the earth's surface.
      a. Radon is released from the rocks and finds its way to the surface; usually it is released into the atmosphere. Radon comes into a house through holes in the foundation or basement or crawl space.
      b. Long-term exposure is believed to cause lung cancer.
      c. The U.S. Environmental Protection Agency (EPA) has established radon levels that are thought to be unsafe.
      d. Testing techniques have been developed that allow homeowners to determine the exact quantity of radon in their homes.
      e. If a home is determined to have radon gas, the seller may, if the contract requires, be obligated to remediate the hazard, whether the danger is actual or only perceived.
      f. Most homes with elevated levels of radon can be fixed for between $500 and $2,500, with an average cost of about $1,200.

2. Asbestos—material used for many years as insulation on plumbing pipes and heat ducts and as general insulation because it is a poor heat conductor; also was used in floor tile and roofing material.
   a. Relatively harmless if not disturbed; can become life-threatening during its removal because of accompanying dust.
   b. Exposure to asbestos dust may exist if
      (1) the asbestos ages and starts to disintegrate. This disintegration is referred to as being friable.
      (2) remodeling projects include the removal of asbestos shingles, roof tile, or insulation that can cause the dust to form in the air and expose people in the area to the health hazard.
3. Urea-formaldehyde foam insulation (UFFI)—a synthetic material generally used to insulate buildings prior to 1978. It was banned because of its toxic out-gassing. The toxicity known as volatile organic compounds (VOC) escaped into a dwelling for several years after its application. Today insulators use a nontoxic spray to insulate buildings.
   a. Typically pumped between walls as a foam that later hardens and acts as an insulating material.
   b. Becomes dangerous because of gases released from the material after it hardens.
4. Lead poisoning—lead is a mineral that has been used extensively because of its pliability, its ability to impede water flow, and its rust resistance.
   a. Becomes a health hazard when ingested.
   b. Sources of lead poisoning
      (1) Peeling or flaking paint
      (2) Water supply systems
   c. Federal regulations on lead-based paint disclosure
      (1) Owners of residential properties built before 1978, when the use of lead-based paint was banned, will have to disclose to buyers or renters the presence of known lead-based paint hazards, if known to owner (seller) or landlord.
      (2) A lead-based paint disclosure statement must be attached as a separate item to all real estate sales and lease contracts on pre-1978 residential properties.
      (3) Real estate practitioners must distribute to buyers and renters a federal lead hazard pamphlet but are not responsible for ensuring that people read and understand the brochure.
      (4) Buyers will have up to 10 days to have a lead-risk assessment performed on the property if they want one.
      (5) Exemptions from the regulations are provided for housing for the elderly and disabled, provided children are not regularly present; for vacation homes and short-term rentals; for foreclosure sales; and for single-room rentals within dwellings.
5. PCBs (polychlorinated biphenyls)—used in the manufacture of electrical products such as voltage regulators as well as in paints and caulking materials

   a. PCBs haven't been used since 1977; however, they still are dangerous because many of the products containing them are still in operation.
   b. An environmental consultant can assess the property and recommend procedures for cleanup.
6. Waste-disposal sites—landfill operations
   a. Landfill—a specific site that has been excavated and should be lined with either a clay or a synthetic liner to prevent leakage of waste material into the local water system.
   b. Construction and maintenance of a landfill operation is heavily regulated by state and federal authorities.
   c. Landfills at improper locations and improperly managed sites have been sources of major problems; for example, landfills constructed in the wrong type of soil will leak waste into nearby wells, causing major damage.
   d. Real estate licensees must be aware of such facilities within their areas and take appropriate steps when dealing with potential clients.
7. Underground storage tanks—used in residential and commercial settings for many years.
   a. In the United States there are an estimated 3 million to 5 million underground storage tanks that hold hazardous substances such as gasoline.
   b. Risk occurs when containers become old, rust, and start to leak.
   c. Toxic material may enter the groundwater, contaminate wells, and pollute the soil.
   d. Sources of pollution
      (1) Older gas stations with steel tanks that develop leaks through oxidation (rusting).
      (2) Underground containers used to hold fuel oil for older homes
   e. Recent federal legislation calls for removal of such tanks and all the polluted soil around them.
8. Groundwater contamination
   a. Groundwater includes runoff at ground level as well as underground water systems that are sources of wells for both private and public facilities.
   b. Sources of contamination
      (1) Waste-disposal sites
      (2) Underground storage tanks
      (3) Pesticides and herbicides typically used in farming communities
   c. The only protection for the general public against water contamination is heavy government regulation.
   d. Once contamination is identified, its source can be eliminated; the process often is time-consuming and may be very expensive.
9. Electromagnetic fields (EMFs)—generated by movement of electrical currents.

a. High-tension power lines reflect a major concern with regard to EMFs.
b. The potential for EMFs being a health hazard is a source of controversy; however, they are suspected of causing cancer and related health problems.
c. Real estate licensees should be aware of continuing research on EMFs.

10. Mold—an organism that may cause allergic reactions and, therefore, is an environmental issue. Annual maintenance checks (around toilets, showers, and sinks) help to detect mold in its early stages. Dehumidifiers, proper ventilation, perimeter drainage, and sump pumps help avoid mold by removing water from the property. Most homeowners' insurance companies set dollar limits for mold claims or make mold problems an exclusion to the homeowner's policy.

D. Agencies administering federal environmental laws
1. Environmental Protection Agency (EPA)
   a. Toxic Substance Control Act
   b. Resources Conservation and Recovery Act
   c. Federal Clean Water Act
2. U.S. Department of Transportation—administers the Hazardous Materials Transportation Act
3. The Occupational Safety and Health Administration (OSHA) and the U.S. Department of Labor—administer standards for all employees working in the manufacturing sector
4. Federal government encourages state and local governments to prepare legislation in their areas

E. Statutory law
1. Resource Conservation and Recovery Act (RCRA) of 1976—created to regulate the generation, transportation, storage, use, treatment, disposal, and cleanup of hazardous waste
2. The Comprehensive Environmental Response Compensation and Liability Act (CERCLA) was created in 1980.
   a. Established fund of $9 billion called Superfund to clean up uncontrolled hazardous waste dumps and respond to spills.
   b. Created a process for identifying liable parties and ordering them to take responsibility for cleanup.
   c. Liability under Superfund consideration to be strict, joint and several, and retroactive.
      (1) Strict liability—owner is responsible to the injured party without excuse.
      (2) Joint and several liability—each individual owner personally responsible for the damages in whole; if only one owner is financially able to handle the total damage, that owner will have to pay all of it and attempt to collect the proportionate share of the rest from the owners.
3. Leaking Underground Storage Tanks (LUST) regulations—established in 1984
   a. Governs the installation, maintenance, monitoring, and failure of underground storage tanks
   b. Aimed at protecting groundwater in the United States through release prevention, detection, and correction

4. Superfund Amendments and Reauthorization Act (SARA)—created in 1986
    a. Established stronger cleanup standards for contaminated sites
    b. Substantially increased the funding of the Superfund
    c. Attempted to clarify the obligation of the lenders
    d. Created the concept called innocent landowner immunity

F. Agents' Responsibilities
    1. Most state laws DO NOT hold listing agents or buyers' agents to a standard of discovery. This is why most states have passed a seller's property disclosure act. With this new legislation the burden to disclose both known and latent property defects (to the buyer) is shifted to the seller. However, if listing agents know or have been made aware of the material defect, they must obviously disclose what they know. A buyer's agent is held to the same standard. Discovery, no. Disclosure, yes.

VI. Deed Restrictions or Covenants

A. Private restrictions written into deeds or leases that limit the use of property—for example, restrictions on the type or size of the building.
B. May be terminated by the affected necessary parties by a quitclaim deed or mutual release properly recorded.
C. Generally enforced by means of a court injunction.
D. Adjoining lot owners in a subdivision can lose the right to the court's injunction by inaction, under the doctrine of laches (the loss of a right through undue delay or failure to assert the right).
E. Deed restrictions or covenants differ from deed conditions in that violation of a condition can give the grantor the right to take back ownership; this right does not apply where a violation of a private restriction occurs.

VII. Water Rights

A. Riparian rights—rights of owners of land adjacent to a river or stream
B. Littoral rights—rights of owners adjacent to commercially navigable lakes, seas, and oceans.
C. Amount of land owned adjacent to water may be affected by the following:
    1. Accretion—land increase caused by water's action leaving soil deposits; if water recedes, new land would be acquired by reliction.
    2. Erosion—the slow loss of soil caused by wearing away of land by wind or rain.
    3. Avulsion—sudden loss of land caused by act of nature such as an earthquake.
    4. Doctrine to prior appropriation—with exception of limited domestic use, right to use water is controlled by the state instead of the owner of land adjacent to the water.
    5. Alluvion—an increase in land ownership created by the gradual addition of deposited matter from running water. Alluvion is the clay, silt, sand, or gravel deposited by accretion.

DIAGNOSTIC TEST

1. When the county board adversely acquires land for a freeway, it is exercising the power of
   1. zoning.
   2. environmental protection laws.
   3. escheat.
   4. eminent domain.
2. One example of the use of police power by a city is
   1. taxation.
   2. eminent domain.
   3. laches.
   4. environmental protection laws.
3. A building housing an insurance agency existed before the property was rezoned residential. The insurance agency building has now grandfathered in. This is an example of
   1. a variance.
   2. a nonconforming use.
   3. spot zoning.
   4. a planned unit development.
4. An investor purchased a large parcel of land zoned for commercial development, but right after the purchase he learned that the land was rezoned by the city for recreational use. This is an example of
   1. eminent domain.
   2. downzoning.
   3. nonconforming use.
   4. a planned unit development.
5. Zoning laws that include tree-cutting rules, dredging regulations, and waste disposal exemplify
   1. subdivision regulations.
   2. city plan specifications.
   3. shoreline regulations.
   4. deed restrictions.
6. Radon generally enters a house through the
   1. roof.
   2. basement floor.
   3. chimney.
   4. windows.
7. A mineral used for many years as insulation on heat ducts is
   1. asbestos.
   2. lead.
   3. urea-formaldehyde foam.
   4. radon.
8. Which of the following was an insulating material pumped between the walls of a house and banned from use in the 1970s?
   1. Asbestos
   2. Radon
   3. Urea-formaldehyde foam
   4. Lead
9. A material once used extensively because of its ability to impede water flow is
   1. lead.
   2. asbestos.
   3. urea-formaldehyde foam.
   4. radon.
10. Which of the following statements most correctly describes a waste-disposal site?
    1. Construction is relatively unregulated by state authorities.
    2. Landfills at appropriate locations have been sources of major problems.
    3. Real estate licensees need not be concerned about such facilities within their areas.
    4. Landfills constructed on the wrong type of soil may leak water into nearby wells, causing major damage.
11. All of the following may be sources of groundwater contamination **EXCEPT**
    1. underground storage tanks.
    2. waste-disposal sites.
    3. pesticides used on farms.
    4. cement.
12. All of the following requirements generally are covered by building codes **EXCEPT**
    1. fire-prevention standards.
    2. electrical wiring.
    3. sanitary equipment.
    4. minimum number of square feet of land area per apartment unit.

13. Strict liability means that
    1. an owner is responsible to an injured party without excuse.
    2. each owner is personally responsible for damages as a whole.
    3. liability extends to people who have owned the site in the past.
    4. an owner is not responsible to an injured party.

14. Which of the following terms refers to a dangerous health hazard that can occur when asbestos ages and starts to disintegrate and become airborne?
    1. Radon
    2. Friable
    3. Bacteria
    4. Oxidation

15. Which of the following statements concerning deed restrictions is NOT true?
    1. Violation of a deed condition may result in the forfeiture of title to real property.
    2. Encumbrances in the form of deed conditions generally run with restricted land into the indefinite future.
    3. The penalty for violation or breach of a restrictive covenant is more severe than that for breach of a restrictive condition.
    4. The general goal of deed restrictions is to protect the value of all properties in a development.

16. Which of the following best describes a buffer zone?
    1. An industrial park located between a shopping center and a residential neighborhood
    2. A highrise apartment complex located between a commercial development and a townhouse subdivision
    3. A recreational area located between a residential area and an office park
    4. A sound barrier located alongside a major highway

17. Police-power controls include all of the following **EXCEPT**
    1. city plan specifications.
    2. building codes.
    3. zoning.
    4. deed restrictions.

18. A tire company has a manufacturing plant located in an area that recently has been zoned residential. The company is allowed to operate under the new zoning ordinance. However, if the plant is completely destroyed by fire, the company may
    1. appeal for an exculpatory provision.
    2. not construct another tire plant in the neighborhood without being granted a zoning variance.
    3. not construct another tire plant in the neighborhood under any conditions.
    4. reconstruct the tire company in the same neighborhood.

19. Which of the following provides for monetary compensation to an owner in the event that the owner's property is taken to build a new freeway?
    1. Taxation
    2. Condemnation
    3. Escheat
    4. Police power

20. A recorded restriction is best described as
    1. a limitation on use.
    2. a condition.
    3. a lien.
    4. a lien and an encumbrance.

21. A property is assessed at $300,000, the taxing body uses a 52% assessment ratio (rollback percentage), and 40 mills is the tax rate. What is the monthly property tax?
    1. $520
    2. $1,200
    3. $1,560
    4. $6,240

22. A buyer made an offer on a building subject to an inspection. During the due diligence period disintegrating airborne asbestos fibers were discovered. This condition is called
    1. encapsulating.
    2. friable.
    3. disintegrating.
    4. radon.

23. A potential homeowner should have a certified inspector check around toilets, showers, sinks, and basement walls to detect what kind of problem?
    1. radon
    2. carpenter ants
    3. methane gas
    4. mold

MATCHING QUIZ

The column on the right contains brief memory links to important terms in Chapter 4. *Write the letter of the matching term on the appropriate line.*

A. Eminent domain	1. ______Ownership of land resulting from an actual soil increase as a result of accretion
B. Condemnation	2. ______Legislation creating an innocent landowner defense
C. Nonconforming use	3. ______Land areas used for conservation
D. Variance	4. ______Law that determines the height and length requirements for stairs
E. Downzoning	5. ______The only commercial building in a residential neighborhood said to have “grandfathered in”
F. Ad valorem	6. ______“According to value”
G. Building code	7. ______Changing land use that diminishes land value
H. Radon	8. ______Method by which government takes and pays for private property
I. Friable	9. ______Restrictions requiring all neighborhood homes be painted earth tones
J. Lead	10. ______Oversees federal environmental issues
K. LUST	11. ______Odorless radioactive gas
L. EPA	12. ______Permission from the city government to build closer to a lot line than normally allowed by zoning
M. CERCLA	13. ______An increase in land due to the gradual addition of clay, silt, sand, or gravel
N. SARA	14. ______Sudden washing away of land
O. Wetlands	15. ______Right of the government to take private property for public use or benefit
P. Restrictive covenants	16. ______The characteristic name for disintegrating asbestos
Q. Avulsion	17. ______Known as the “Superfund”
R. Accretion	18. ______Leaking underground storage tanks
S. Alluvion	19. ______In the bloodstream this can cause mental retardation

ANSWER KEY: DIAGNOSTIC TEST

1. **(4)** Eminent domain is the right of the government to take private land for public use or public benefit. The property owner has a right of appeal and must be paid just compensation. Zoning and environmental protection laws do not provide monetary compensation in the event that a property owner suffers a loss in value. Escheat is a law that provides for title to real estate to pass to the state when an owner dies intestate and leaves no heirs or abandons the property. (34)

2. **(4)** Taxation and eminent domain are not exercised under the police power. Laches refers to the equitable doctrine that bars a legal claim because of undue delay in asserting the claim. (34)

3. **(2)** A nonconforming use property is one that existed before the zoning classification changed. It was there first, hence the name *grandfather clause*. A variance allows one to deviate from the zoning ordinance. Spot zoning allows for reclassification of land for nonconforming use. A planned unit development (PUD) creates a special zoning district for a developer. (35)

4. **(2)** Downzoning involves an economic taking, whereas eminent domain results in a complete taking. A planned unit development is an example of contract zoning in that a developer has his or her plan approved by the municipality, thereby establishing a special planning district based on the developer's own plans. A nonconforming use is allowed to continue after a zoning ordinance prohibiting it has been established for the area. (35)

5. **(3)** Shoreline regulations are zoning laws that reflect environmental and safety concerns within a given distance of all navigable waters. Subdivision regulations deal with location of streets, etc., while city plan specifications or master plans guide the growth development of a community. Deed restrictions are private land-use controls. (36)

6. **(2)** Radon may also enter the house through the basement walls, crawlspace, or uncovered sump pit areas. (37)

7. **(1)** Lead was used in paint and plumbing systems. UFFI was used to insulate buildings. Radon was discussed above. (38)

8. **(3)** Asbestos was used as insulation on heating pipes and ducts as well as in floor tile and roofing material. Radon is an odorless radioactive gas that generally enters through the basement of a house. Lead was used in water pipes and paint. (38)

9. **(1)** Lead impedes water flow. Asbestos is still used today but is often encapsulated with latex paint to prevent it from becoming airborne (friable). UFFI has been banned and replaced today with a nontoxic material that is sprayed into a wall cavity and then expands. Radon is an odorless gas that can migrate into a house through the basement floor as it works its way up through the ground under the house. (38)

10. **(4)** Agents should be aware of landfills and make appropriate disclosures. (39)

11. **(4)** Leaking underground storage tanks are a major source of groundwater contamination. Pesticide use and waste disposal also may contaminate groundwater. (39)

12. **(4)** The minimum number of square feet of land area per apartment unit would be regulated by the local zoning ordinance. (35)

13. **(1)** For example, an individual who knowingly buys contaminated land can also be liable for damages even though she had no involvement in the events leading up to the contamination. (40)

14. **(2)** Friable is the term that describes the dangerous condition that exists when asbestos begins to deteriorate and becomes airborne. Radon is a radioactive by-product of radium. Various forms of bacteria are found in water. Oxidation is another name for rust. (38)

15. **(3)** Restrictive covenants are statements in a deed that limit the use of ownership of real estate. The breach of a covenant would result in damages. The breach of a condition may result in the loss of title. (41)

16. **(3)** A buffer zone is a land area that separates one land use from another such as residential from commercial, as when a recreational area is located between a residential area and an office park. (35)

17. **(4)** Police-power controls are public land-use controls. Only deed restrictions are private land-use controls, and therefore incorrect. (34)

18. **(2)** If a nonconforming use is destroyed, as in the case of the tire manufacturing plant, it cannot be rebuilt without the approval of the zoning authority. (35)

19. **(2)** Eminent domain is the right or the authority of the government to acquire private property for public use or public benefit. Condemnation is the process for actually acquiring the property. Escheat is a state law that provides that if a decedent dies intestate and has no heirs, the decedent's property will revert to the state. Taxation is a process by which the government raises funds necessary for it to operate. The police power is the right of the government to protect the public welfare through such measures as zoning and building codes. (34)

20. **(1)** A restriction would be classified as an encumbrance. The violation of a restriction would not generally result in loss of title as it would in the case of a violation of a condition. (35)

21. **(1)** $300,000 × 52% = 156,000 × 4% = $6,240
$6,240 divided by 12 = $520 monthly tax (36)

22. **(2)** Friable describes deteriorating asbestos. Encapsulation remedies the problem by painting over the asbestos with a heavy latex paint. (38)

23. **(4)** Mold is the end result of a moisture problem. Once mold dries it can become airborne, and then it poses a health threat to those allergic to the mold spores. (40

TEST SCORES

LAND-USE CONTROLS AND REGULATIONS			
Rating	**Range**	**Your Score**	
Good = 80% to 100%	18–23	Total Number	23
Fair = 70% to 79%	16–17	Total Wrong	–
Needs improvement = Lower than 70%	15 or less	Total Right	

Passing Requirement: 16 or Better

ANSWER KEY: MATCHING QUIZ

1. S	**6.** F	**11.** H	**16.** I
2. N	**7.** E	**12.** D	**17.** M
3. O	**8.** B	**13.** R	**18.** K
4. G	**9.** P	**14.** Q	**19.** J
5. C	**10.** L	**15.** A	

Valuation and Market Analysis

OUTLINE OF CONCEPTS

I. Financial Institutions Reform, Recovery, and Enforcement Act (FIRREA) and the Appraisal Industry

A. The collapse of many savings and loan associations as a result of the surge into unsound investments was at least partly the consequence of questionable property appraisals.

B. Congress introduced appraisal regulation by passing FIRREA in 1989.

C. Appraisals performed as part of a federally related transaction must comply with state standards and must be performed by a state-certified or state-licensed appraiser.

D. State appraiser licensing requirements and appraisal standards must meet minimum levels set by the Appraisal Standards Board and Appraisal Qualifications Board of the Appraisal Foundation, a national group of representatives of major appraisal and related organizations.

II. Appraisal and Value

A. Appraisal—an opinion of value; a detailed estimate of a property's value by a professional appraiser.

B. Competitive market analysis (CMA)—used by the broker or the salesperson to help the seller determine a listing price for the property; basically, a comparison of prices of recently sold and currently for sale properties that are similar in location, style, and amenities to the property of the listing seller. CMA will generally estimate market value as likely to fall within a range of figures. CMAs can also guide a purchaser in formulating an offer.

C. Value

1. Definition—the present worth of future benefits arising from the ownership of real property.
2. Characteristics necessary for a property to have value in the real estate market include "DUST":
    a. Demand—need supported by purchasing power.
    b. Utility—capacity to satisfy human wants and needs.

c. Scarcity— finite supply.
d. Transferability—transfer of ownership rights with relative ease.

D. Market value
1. Most probable price a property will bring in a competitive market, allowing for reasonable time to find a knowledgeable purchaser.
   a. The buyer and seller are not under pressure to act.
   b. Payment is made in cash or equivalent.
2. Typical goal of an appraiser, although a property may have different values at the same time.
3. Estimated price (compare to market price, which is the actual selling price).

III. Principles of Valuation

A. Highest and best use—most profitable use to which a property may be adapted, given legal constraints.
B. Substitution—the value of a property tends to be set by the cost of purchasing an equally desirable and similar property.
C. Supply and demand—the price of a property will increase if the supply decreases and will decrease if the supply increases.
D. Conformity—maximum value is realized if the land use conforms to existing neighborhood standards.
E. Increasing and decreasing return—improvements to land and structures produce a proportionate increase in value until some point beyond which the impact of improvements begins to decrease, until improvements cause virtually no change in the property value.
F. Competition—high levels of profits attract competitors into an industry; increase in competition results in decreased profits throughout the industry.
G. Change—no economic or physical condition remains constant.
H. Contribution—the value of any component of property consists of what its addition contributes to the value of the whole property.
I. Anticipation—value can increase or decrease in anticipation of some future benefit or detriment that will affect the property.
J. Plottage—the principle of combining contiguous property, and, by doing so, increasing the value of the new property. The greater efficiency of land use allows the new value to exceed the combined values of the individual parcels. For example, a strip mall was created from three parcels of vacant land each worth $50,000. After these contiguous properties were combined, the land value became $200,000. The actual process of combining these properties into one is called assemblage.
K. Balance is achieved when adding improvements to land and structures will increase the property value.
L. Regression—the principle between dissimilar properties: the worth of the better property is affected adversely by the presence of the lesser-quality property.
M. Progression—the worth of a lesser property tends to increase if it is located among better properties.

IV. Approaches to Value

A. Cost approach
1. Based on the principle of substitution

2. Steps of cost approach
    a. Estimate the land value.
    b. Estimate the replacement cost of the improvements.
    c. Estimate the depreciation.
    d. Deduct the depreciation from the replacement cost.
    e. Add the land value to the depreciated cost of improvements—do not depreciate land.
3. Depreciation—generally applies to a wasting asset, such as a building
    a. Physical deterioration (wear, tear, poor maintenance)—may be curable or incurable.
    b. Functional obsolescence—may be curable or incurable (outdated items, poor design).

    c. External obsolescence (economic, environmental, or locational)—loss of value due to factors outside the property: is always incurable.
    d. Most reliable approach for special-purpose buildings such as churches and schools.

B. Market/data approach (sales comparison or direct sales)

Contributory Value			
Square Footage	$25 per square foot	**Full and ¾ Baths**	$3,500
Brick	4% more than frame construction	**½ Bath**	$1,500

	Subject Better: Add	**Comparable Better: Subtract**	**SBA and CBS**
Subject Property	**Comparable # 1 $200,000 (SOLD)**	**Comparable #2 $212,000 (SOLD)**	**Comparable #3 $205,000 (SOLD)**
1,500 Sq. Ft. Ranch	1,300 Sq. Ft.	1600 Sq. Ft.	1600 Sq. Ft.
Frame Construction	Frame Construction	Brick	Frame
1¾ Bathrooms	1 Bath	1¾ plus ½ Baths	1 ½ Baths
Adjust for Sq. Footage	200 × 25 = $5,000 **add**	100 × 25 = $2,500 **subtract**	100 × 25 = $2,500 **subtract**
Adjust for Brick	No Adjustment	$210,000 × 4% = 8400 **subtract**	No Adjustment
Adjust for Bathrooms	$3,500 **add**	½ bath = $1,500 **subtract**	½ Bath = $1,500 **add**
Adjusted Value	$208,500	$199,600	$204,000

1. A value estimate is obtained by comparing the subject property with recent sales of comparable properties through adjustment of sales prices of comparables. Comparable properties used in an analysis should be "arm's length" or a normal market transaction involving willing buyers and willing sellers, as opposed to a foreclosure sale, an auction, or a sale to a relative.
2. Four areas of adjustment
   a. Date of sale
   b. Location
   c. Physical characteristics
   d. Terms of the sale
3. The adjustment process involves three basic steps:
   a. Adjust the price of the comparable for any difference between the comparable and the subject property (the property being appraised). With your dollar adjustments remember to always mirror your subject property.
   b. C.B.S.—*Comparable better subtract* from the comparable the difference between the comparable and the subject property.
   c. S.B.A.—*Subject better add* to the comparable the difference between the comparable and the subject property.
4. Considered the most reliable of the three approaches in appraising residential property.

C. Income capitalization approach
1. Based on the present value of the rights to future income
2. Steps in the income approach
   a. Estimate the annual potential gross income.
   b. Deduct the vacancy and rent loss to arrive at the effective gross income.
   c. Deduct the annual operating expenses to arrive at the annual net operating income.
   d. Estimate the capitalization rate.
   e. Apply the capitalization rate to the annual net income.
3. Formula for capitalization rate: net income ÷ capitalization rate = value.
4. As risk increases, the rate of return increases and the value decreases, and as the risk decreases, the rate of return decreases, the value increases and vice versa.
5. Gross rent multiplier (GRM)
   a. Used as a substitute for the income approach in appraising a single-family home.
   b. Formula for GRM: sales price ÷ monthly rental income = GRM.
   c. Monthly rental income × GRM = estimated market value.
6. Gross income multiplier (GIM)
   a. Used as a quick way to appraise commercial and industrial properties.
   b. Formula for GIM: sales price ÷ annual rental income = GIM.
7. Most reliable approach for income-producing property.

V. Steps in the Appraisal Process

A. State the problem.
B. List the types of data needed and the sources.

C. Gather, record, and verify the general data.
D. Gather, record, and verify the specific data.
E. Gather, record, and verify the data for the valuation approach needed.
F. Analyze and interpret the data.
G. Reconcile the data for the final value estimate.
H. Prepare the appraisal report.

VI. Neighborhood Analysis

A. Neighborhood—homogeneous grouping of individuals or businesses within, or as part of, a larger community.
B. Residential neighborhoods generally pass through four stages: growth, stability, decline, and revitalization.
C. Factors to consider in analysis
   1. Physical—street pattern, relation to the rest of the community.
   2. Economic—rent levels, new construction.
   3. Social—population density, frequency of crime.
   4. Governmental—zoning, special assessments.

VII. Ethics of Appraising

A. The appraiser should have no present or planned interest in the property being appraised.
B. The appraiser should have no personal interest in the property being appraised or the parties involved.
C. The appraiser should not improperly disclose the confidential parts of an appraisal report.

VIII. Other Important Terms

A. Amenities—the tangible and intangible neighborhood benefits beyond the property's boundaries description. Examples include proximity to schools, transportation, other homes of equal to or greater value, parks, etc.
B. Capitalization—a mathematical process for estimating a property's value using a proper rate of return on investment and anticipated annual net income.
C. Capitalization rate—the rate of return a property will produce on the owner's investment.
D. Comparables—sold properties listed in the appraisal report generally equivalent to the subject property.
E. Reconciliation—final step in the appraisal process, in which the appraiser reconciles the estimates of value received from the different approaches to arrive at a final estimate of the market value for the property being appraised. The most relevant approach receives the greatest weight in determining the opinion of value.
F. Replacement cost—construction cost at current prices of property that would not necessarily be an exact duplicate of the subject property but would serve the same purpose or function as the original.
G. Reproduction cost—construction cost at current prices of an exact duplicate of the subject property.
H. Subject property—property being appraised
I. URAR—Uniform Residential Appraisal Report

DIAGNOSTIC TEST

1. The characteristics required for a property to have value include all of the following **EXCEPT**
   1. effective demand.
   2. scarcity.
   3. depreciation.
   4. transferability.
2. Which of the following laws require that appraisals performed as part of a federally related transaction must comply with federal standards and be performed by a state-certified or state-licensed appraiser?
   1. Financial Institutions Reform, Recovery, and Enforcement Act (FIRREA)
   2. Regulation Z
   3. RESPA
   4. Statute of Frauds
3. You own land worth $40,000 and your building has a replacement cost of $160,000. What would be the value if the appraiser used a depreciation rate of 30 percent?
   1. $148,000
   2. $152,000
   3. $188,000
   4. None of the above
4. Which of the following does NOT apply to the definition of market value?
   1. Both buyer and seller must be well informed.
   2. Market value is the average price that a property will bring.
   3. Both buyer and seller must act without undue pressure.
   4. Payment must be made in cash or its equivalent.
5. The annual net income for an office building is $20,000. If an owner realized a 9 percent return on her investment, the value of the building would be
   1. $1,800.
   2. $22,222.
   3. $222,222.
   4. $285,714.
6. You look at four similar houses for sale in the same area and choose the house with the lowest asking price. You probably are basing your decision on the principle of
   1. highest and best use.
   2. substitution.
   3. contribution.
   4. conformity.
7. A builder developed a subdivision in which the demand for homes was great. He sold the last lot in his subdivision for a much higher price than that for which he had sold the first lot in the area. This example illustrates the principle of
   1. highest and best use.
   2. substitution.
   3. conformity.
   4. supply and demand.
8. In appraising a special-purpose building such as a post office, the most reliable approach to an indication of its value would generally be the
   1. cost approach.
   2. market/data approach.
   3. income approach.
   4. sales comparison approach.
9. Which of the following is an example of locational obsolescence?
   1. Termite damage
   2. Negligent care of property
   3. A zoning ordinance allowing a decrease in the minimum lot size
   4. Poor architectural design
10. Economic obsolescence does NOT result from
    1. adverse zoning changes.
    2. a city's leading industries moving out.
    3. an inharmonious land use in a neighborhood.
    4. outdated kitchens.
11. Depreciation generally applies to
    1. the building only.
    2. the land only.
    3. both the land and the building.
    4. the net income of the building.

12. A principal factor for which adjustments must be made in using the market/data approach is
    1. depreciation.
    2. the date of sale.
    3. the amount of real estate taxes.
    4. the cost of replacement.

13. An appraiser is estimating the value of a building that has a net income of $5,000 per quarter and a capitalization rate of 8 percent. What is the value of this property?
    1. $25,000
    2. $62,500
    3. $250,000
    4. $312,500

14. An appraiser is using the gross-rent-multiplier (GRM) method to estimate the market value of a single-family home. The home has an annual gross income of $7,200, with quarterly expenses of $900. The recognized GRM for the neighborhood is 110. The appraiser's estimate of value is likely to be
    1. $22,000.
    2. $33,000.
    3. $66,000.
    4. None of the above

15. The GRM is used in the
    1. market/data approach.
    2. income approach for office buildings.
    3. cost approach.
    4. income approach for single-family homes.

16. An office building recently sold for $600,000, with a monthly rental income of $5,000. The GIM for the property was
    1. 120.
    2. 100.
    3. 10.
    4. None of the above

17. In determining the value of a 20-unit apartment building, the appraiser has established the gross income from rents. After deducting the loss for vacancies and collection losses from this gross income, the appraiser would have established the
    1. net income.
    2. spendable income.
    3. gross income.
    4. effective gross income.

18. What is the first step an appraiser would take to arrive at an estimated value using the income approach?
    1. Determine annual potential gross income.
    2. Determine operating expenses.
    3. Determine effective gross income.
    4. Determine the vacancy rate.

19. An airport routing was changed, with the result that airplanes flew over a residential area. The subsequent loss in value caused by the airplane noise would be best described as
    1. physical depreciation.
    2. functional obsolescence.
    3. external or economic obsolescence.
    4. eminent domain.

20. Which of the following factors would be considered in the market/data or sales comparison approach to value?
    1. Conditions under which property was sold
    2. Annual gross income
    3. Replacement cost
    4. Original cost

21. Outmoded plumbing fixtures are an example of
    1. curable physical deterioration.
    2. curable functional obsolescence.
    3. incurable physical deterioration.
    4. curable external obsolescence.

22. In the income approach to appraisal, if the net income was $42,000 and the capitalization rate was 12 percent, to find the value of the property the appraiser would
    1. multiply the income by the capitalization rate.
    2. multiply the capitalization rate by the net income.
    3. divide the net income by the capitalization rate.
    4. divide the capitalization rate by the net income.

23. *D* lived in a house with a well. The groundwater entering the homeowner's well became contaminated and lessened the value of *D*'s home. The loss in value is an example of
    1. physical deterioration.
    2. external obsolescence.
    3. functional obsolescence.
    4. regression.

24. The appraiser profession is regulated at the national level by
    1. Congress.
    2. the FDIC.
    3. the national real estate commission.
    4. the Appraisal Foundation.

25. Which of the following reflects the stages through which a neighborhood passes?
    1. Growth, decline, stability, and revitalization
    2. Growth, stability, decline, and revitalization
    3. Decline, growth, stability, and revitalization
    4. Decline, growth, revitalization, and stability

26. Gross rent multipliers are generally used in appraising
    1. forms.
    2. shopping centers.
    3. single-family homes.
    4. hotels.

27. You purchased an apartment building for $600,000 nearly 6 years ago. The building accounted for 80 percent of the purchase price. If the building's economic life is estimated to be 60 years, what is the current total depreciation of the property?
    1. $36,000
    2. $48,000
    3. $60,000
    4. $72,000

28. *R* purchased an office building with an annual effective gross income of $208,000 and expenses of $74,000. What capitalization rate was used by *R* to arrive at a value of $1,576,470?
    1. 7.5 percent
    2. 8.5 percent
    3. 9.5 percent
    4. 10.5 percent

29. *M* was appraising a three-bedroom house. *M* had a comparable with four bedrooms that sold for $160,000. *M* makes an adjustment of $5,000 to the comparable for the difference in the number of bedrooms. The adjusted sales price of the comparable will be
    1. $155,000.
    2. $165,000.
    3. $170,000.
    4. None of the above

30. If the house you are appraising has central air conditioning valued at $2,500 and your comparable does not, you will adjust the sales price of the comparable by
    1. – $2,500.
    2. + $2,500.
    3. – $1,250.
    4. None of the above

31. A home's value is increased because of its proximity to schools, parks, and transportation lines. These neighborhood sites are referred to as
    1. features.
    2. benefits.
    3. amenities.
    4. attachments.

32. A bike trail that enhances the value of a neighboring home is called
    1. a feature.
    2. a benefit.
    3. an amenity.
    4. None of the above

33. What phrase describes a neighboring property that was sold to a relative for 75% of its market value?
    1. arm's length
    2. less than arm's length
    3. comparable property
    4. reconciliation property

34. A comparable property sold for $250,000, and it has 200 more square feet than a subject property. If square footage contributes $30 per square foot, what is the adjusted value of the comparable?
    1. $250,000
    2. $260,000
    3. $244,000
    4. $256,000

MATCHING QUIZ

The column on the right contains brief memory links to important terms in Chapter 5. *Write the letter of the matching term on the appropriate line.*

A. CMA	1. ______ Combining all three appraisal approaches to determine an indicated value
B. Scarcity	2. ______ Results from building in excess of the value of the neighborhood
C. Substitution	3. ______ What principle appraiser uses to determine maximum value by comparing equally desirable substitutes
D. Diminishing returns	4. ______ Essential to creating value
E. Assemblage	5. ______ The process when net income is divided by an investor's desired percent of return
F. Plottage	6. ______ The act of combining contiguous property to increase the value of the combined property
G. Progression	7. ______ A cracked foundation wall
H. Land	8. ______ Value is enhanced by a home's proximity to a beautifully shaded park
I. Physical deterioration	9. ______ Diminished value due to airplane landing routes over a neighborhood
J. Functional obsolescence	10. ______ A three-bedroom two-story home with only one bath
K. External obsolescence	11. ______ Reporting tool to help agents determine a price range for a property
L. Capitalization	12. ______ The universal appraisal report
M. GRM	13. ______ Phenomenon that happens when buying the least expensive home in the most expensive neighborhood
N. GIM	14. ______ Sales not influenced by unusual circumstances used to determine the market value of a property
O. Amenities	15. ______ In the cost approach this is added back after subtracting depreciation from replacement cost new
P. Comparables	16. ______ A name for sold homes used in a CMA
Q. URAR	17. ______ The theory that greater utilization or efficiency of contiguous property increases value
R. Reconciliation	18. ______ Sold price divided by annual income
S. Arm's length or most	19. ______ Dollar value of any housing component measured probable sales price by its worth using "paired sales" in an open market
T. Contribution	20. ______ Sold Price divided by monthly rents

ANSWER KEY WITH EXPLANATIONS

1. **(3)** Depreciation is used in the cost approach to value. (48–49)

2. **(1)** FIRREA became effective in 1989. (47)

3. **(2)** Replacement cost of building

Replacement cost of building		$160,000
Depreciation of 30%		×.30
Depreciation		48,000
$160,000 Replacement Cost – Depreciation of $48,000	=	$112,000
Added land value	=	$ 40,000
Value	=	$152,000

(49–51)

4. **(2)** Appraisers do not average to determine market value. Appraisers work from comparable transactions to arrive at an estimate of market value for the subject property. (48)

5. **(3)** Income ÷ Rate = Value
$20,000 ÷ .09 = $222,222 (50–51)

6. **(2)** The principle of highest and best use deals with the most profitable use. Contribution refers to cost and benefits of a particular improvement. Conformity is a factor in the stability of property values; zoning is an example of conformity. (48)

7. **(4)** A limited supply combined with a great demand will result in a higher price for lots. (49)

8. **(1)** The cost approach is most applicable to the appraisal of a special-purpose building. (48–49)

9. **(3)** Decreasing lot size is locational obsolescence. Termite damage and negligent care are physical deterioration. Poor architectural design represents functional obsolescence. (49)

10. **(4)** Economic obsolescence is a loss in value due to factors outside the property. Functional obsolescence is a loss in value due to a deficiency in the floor plan or design of a building. (49)

11. **(1)** Land is not depreciated; it is assumed that the land value will be recovered at the end of the economic life of the building. (49)

12. **(2)** Time, location, physical characteristics, and terms of sale are factors considered in the market or sales comparison approach. (50)

13. **(3)** $5,000 per quarter × 4 = $20,000 annual net income
$20,000 ÷ .08 capitalization rate = $250,000 value (50)

14. **(3)** $7,200 gross ÷ 12 = $600 × 110 = $66,000 value (50)

15. **(4)** The GRM is used as a substitute for the income approach in appraising a single-family home. (50)

16. **(3)** $5,000 monthly rental income × 12 months = $60,000 annual gross income
Selling price of $600,000 ÷ Gross annual rental income = $600,000 ÷ $60,000 = 10 (50)

17. **(4)** The gross income would be reflected in the first step of the operating statement. Annual net income is the bottom line in the operating statement and serves as the basis for capitalization of the income stream. (50)

18. **(1)** Annual potential gross income is based on 100% of economic or market rent plus other income such as income from vending machines. Effective gross income is annual potential gross income minus vacancy and rent loss. Operating expenses include fixed expenses such as real estate taxes and variable expenses such as management expenses. The vacancy rate is used to calculate effective gross income. (50)

19. **(3)** External or economic obsolescence is a loss in value from factors external to the property. (49)

20. **(1)** Conditions under which the property was sold would be used in the market/data approach. Cost would be used in the cost approach; annual gross income would be used in the income approach. (49–50)

21. **(2)** Functional obsolescence is a loss in the value due to deficiency in the floor plan or design of a building. The obsolescence would be

curable if it were economically feasible to update the plumbing fixtures. Economic or external obsolescence is assumed to be incurable only because it is caused by factors outside the property. (49)

22. **(3)** The capitalization approach was discussed above. (50)

23. **(2)** This is an example of external obsolescence, which would generally be incurable, depending on the cost to cure. (49)

24. **(4)** Congress delegated the regulatory responsibility to the Appraisal Foundation. (47)

25. **(2)** There are numerous examples in cities like Chicago and New York where neighborhoods have gone through the entire process, resulting in higher than ever property values. (51)

26. **(3)** The gross rent multiplier is used as a substitute for the income approach in the appraisal of a single-family home. (50)

27. **(2)** \$600,000 × .80 = \$480,000 value of building
\$480,000 ÷ 60 years = \$8,000 annual depreciation charge
\$8,000 × 6 years = \$48,000 current total depreciation. (50)

28. **(2)** \$208,000 annual effective gross income – \$74,000 expenses = \$134,000; \$134,000 ÷ \$1,576,470 = .085 = 8.5 (50)

29. **(1)** C.B.S.—Comparable Better Subtract
\$160,000 price of comparable – \$5,000 adjustment for one bedroom = \$155,000 adjusted sales price of comparable (50)

30. **(2)** S.B.A.—Subject Better Add. The subject property is better than the comparable; thus you add the value of the air conditioning to the sale price of the comparable. (50)

31. **(3)** Amenities are neighborhood facilities and services that enhance a home's value but are always outside of the property. Swimming pools, 3-car garages, decks, etc. that are on the property are called features. (51)

32. **(3)** An amenity is always outside the confines of the property, but it adds value because of its proximity. (51)

33. **(2)** Arm's length transactions describe those that mirror the definition of market value. Less than arm's length transactions do not reflect market value and, therefore, are not included in the appraiser's analysis. (49–50)

34. **(3)** 200 sq. ft. × \$30 sq. ft. in contributory value = \$6,000. Then take the sold price of \$250,000 and subtract the square footage amount of \$6,000 to arrive at the adjusted value of \$244,000. In other words, if everything else was the same between the two properties, the subject property would most likely sell for \$244,000. (50)

TEST SCORE

VALUATION AND MARKET ANALYSIS			
Rating	**Range**	**Your Score**	
Good = 80% to 100%	27–34	Total Number	34
Fair = 70% to 79%	24–26	Total Wrong	–
Needs Improvement = Lower than 70%	23 or less	Total Right	

Passing Requirement: 24 or better

ANSWER KEY: MATCHING QUIZ

1. R
2. D
3. C
4. B
5. L
6. E
7. I
8. O
9. K
10. J
11. A
12. Q
13. G
14. S
15. H
16. P
17. F
18. N
19. T
20. M

Financing

OUTLINE OF CONCEPTS

I. Theories of Mortgage Law

A. Lien theory—the mortgage is viewed as a lien on real property in many states.

B. Title theory—the lender is viewed as the conditional owner of mortgaged land in some states.

C. Intermediate theory—a number of states allow the lender to take possession of the mortgaged real estate on default.

II. Mortgage Loan

A. Mortgage origination—the lending institution that originally qualifies the borrower, orders the appraisal, initiates the Uniform Residential Loan Application (FNMA 1003), and charges a loan origination fee.

B. Mortgage—a document by which the mortgagor (borrower) places a lien on the property in favor of the mortgagee (lender) as security for debt.

C. Note—promise to repay debt; a negotiable instrument.

III. Trust Deed—Three-Party Instrument Used in Place of a Mortgage in Some Areas of the Country

A. Conveys real estate as security for loan to a third party, the trustee

B. Trustee holds the title on behalf of the lender, known as the beneficiary; the trustee is the legal owner, and the beneficiary is the holder of the note; the borrower retains the equitable title to the property, and the deed of the trust becomes the lien against it

C. The trustee may commence a foreclosure action if the borrower (trustor) defaults; a reconveyance deed returns title to trustor when trust deed has been paid in full.

IV. Types of Loans

A. Amortized loan, or fixed payment—equal monthly payments credited first to interest due, then applied to the loan balance.

B. Graduated payment mortgage—allows for smaller payments in the early years and increased payments in the later years. Causes negative amortization by adding the early years of deferred interest to principle.

C. Straight or interest-only loan—allows for payments of interest only with a lump-sum payment of principal at maturity.

D. Balloon payment—payments of principal and interest are paid to the lender over a relatively short period; the outstanding principal balance is due in a lump sum at a predetermined future date (partially amortized loan payment plan).

V. Mortgage Provisions

A. Acceleration clause—if the borrower defaults, the lender has the right to declare the entire debt due and payable.
B. Assignment—the mortgagee becomes the assignor and executes assignment to the assignee, who becomes the new owner of the mortgage and debt.
C. Defeasance clause—the mortgagee is required to execute the release or satisfaction of the mortgage when the note is fully paid.
D. Alienation (due-on-sale) clause—if the borrower sells the property, the lender has the choice of either declaring the entire debt due and payable or allowing the buyer to assume the loan.
E. Buying "subject to" versus assuming—if the property is sold "subject to" the mortgage, the buyer is not personally liable to pay the entire debt (the seller remains liable); if the buyer assumes the mortgage, he or she becomes personally liable for payment of the entire debt. The seller is secondarily liable.
F. Subordination agreements—a subordination clause is one that grants or permits a subsequent mortgager to take priority in lien structure.

VI. Mortgage Foreclosure and Redemption

A. Judicial foreclosure
   1. Lender sues the borrower in court; obtains judgment and court order to sell.
   2. Property sold at public sale to the highest bidder.
B. Nonjudicial foreclosure
   1. The mortgage generally must include a power-of-sale clause.
   2. A notice of default must be recorded and a public sale advertised in the newspaper.
   3. The property is sold at a public sale to highest bidder.
C. Strict foreclosure—the court may award title to the lender.
D. Deed in lieu of foreclosure—mortgagor gives deed to mortgagee when mortgagor is in default under terms of mortgage; this allows mortgagor to avoid foreclosure.
E. Redemption—process by which the borrower regains interest in the property.
   1. Equitable redemption
      a. Occurs prior to public sale.
      b. If the borrower pays the amount due plus the costs prior to the public sale, the mortgage is reinstated.
      c. If not redeemed, the property is sold at a public sale to the highest bidder.
   2. Statutory redemption
      a. Occurs after public sales in some states and continues for a period of time specified by law.
      b. The borrower may pay to the foreclosure purchaser the sale price in full plus costs.

F. Deficiency judgment—if the property is sold and the proceeds are insufficient to pay the mortgage and foreclosure costs, the difference is a deficiency; the lender usually can sue the original borrower for the difference (process of deficiency judgment).

VII. Types of Mortgages

A. Conventional

1. Payment of the debt based solely on the borrower's ability to pay, with security provided by the mortgage; neither insured nor guaranteed by government agency.
2. Lender sets the terms subject to many of the rules established by the secondary mortgage market. Loans originated by some institutions are sold to investors in the secondary market. Other institutions keep the loans they make; these are called portfolio loans.
3. Loan-to-value ratio (LTVR) depends on the borrower's credit risk and/or size of the down payment. For example, if a borrower put down 10 percent of a $200,000 home, then the LTV ratio would be 180,000 (200,000–20,000) divided by 200,000, or 90 percent.
4. If the loan-to-value ratio exceeds a given level, 80 percent for example, the lender may require private mortgage insurance (PMI).
5. Internet lenders provide borrowers with another viable origination option. However, online lending can be tricky, and some counseling should be sought before borrowing mortgage money online.

B. Federal Housing Administration (FHA) insured

1. FHA insures approved lenders against loss on loans made on real property.
2. Interest rates float with the open market.
3. The borrower finances an up-front FHA insurance premium of 1.50 percent (which may be partially refundable); borrower then pays a monthly (nonfinanceable) insurance premium (MIP) based on ½ percent of the mortgage amount.
4. Mortgaged property must be appraised by an FHA-approved appraiser.
5. FHA does not allow a prepayment penalty.
6. FHA mortgages are assumable with qualification.
7. Discount points are generally used to reduce the interest rate (1 point = 1 percent of the loan balance); these are generally negotiated between the seller and the buyer.

C. Department of Veterans Affairs guaranteed (DVA loans)

1. DVA does not allow a prepayment penalty.
2. A DVA loan may be assumed by a qualified nonveteran.
3. DVA guarantees home loans for eligible veterans or eligible dependents with little or no down payment.
4. The interest rate is set by the market.
5. DVA does not charge the borrower for the guarantee; however, the borrower must pay up to a 3 percent funding fee to the DVA, on any no–down-payment loan, in addition to any other fees.
6. Mortgaged property must be appraised by a DVA-approved appraiser.

7. DVA sets a limitation on the loan amount of four times the amount of the veteran's entitlement guarantee.
8. DVA guarantees the lender up to $60,000 of the loan balance. Most investors are comfortable purchasing a loan four times that amount (4 × 60,000 = $240,000) made to a qualified veteran.
9. Discount points generally are negotiated between the seller and the buyer.
10. In some cases, the DVA will make direct loans to eligible veterans or their dependents.
11. DVA requires appraisers to complete a Certificate of Reasonable Value (CRV); the DVA guarantee is based on either the amount of the CRV or the selling price, whichever is less.
12. National Guard members and reservists with at least six years of service now are eligible for DVA-guaranteed loans.

D. Rural Development and Farm Agency (formerly Farmers Home Administration)
   1. Rural Development makes and guarantees housing loans to people with low incomes in rural areas in communities of 10,000 population or less.
   2. Farm Service Agency makes and guarantees loans to farmers and ranchers.

E. Rural Economic and Community Development services, makes, and guarantees loans to homeowners in rural areas.

F. Privately insured
   1. Depending on the buyer's credit score, the buyer may obtain a conventional loan for up to 103 percent of the property's appraised value.
   2. The buyer is charged the market rate of interest plus reasonable insurance premium costs.
   3. The borrower's insurance protects the lender against loss on the upper 20 to 25 percent portion of the loan.
   4. PMI insurance premiums are made a part of the borrower's monthly payments.
   5. As property values rise and the loan-to-value ratio becomes 80 percent or less, the PMI insurance may be dropped.
      a. Requires either the lender's or investor's approval and generally a new appraisal
      b. Insurance must generally be held for two years, and the mortgagor must have a 20 percent equity to request that the insurance be dropped; when the mortgagor's equity position reaches 22 percent, the lender is required to drop the insurance.

G. Purchase-money mortgage—given by the buyer to the seller as part of the purchase price (owner financing); legal title passes to the buyer.

H. Blanket mortgage—covers more than one property or lot; generally includes a partial-release clause.

I. Package mortgage—includes real estate and (expressly) all fixtures and appliances located on the property.

J. Open-end mortgage
   1. Secures the note executed by the borrower to the lender and any future advances of funds by the lender to the borrower.

2. Terms usually restrict an increase in debt to a limit of either the original debt or a specified amount in the mortgage.
3. Additional loan amounts are figured at prevailing interest rates.

K. Construction loans
1. Generally short-term or interim loan to finance construction of an improvement.
2. Periodic payments or draws made by the lender to the owner for work completed since the previous payment.

L. Wraparound mortgage (all-inclusive second deed of trust)
1. Allows the borrower who is paying an existing mortgage to obtain additional financing from a second lender.
2. New lender agrees to keep up payments on the existing loan; gives the borrower a new, increased loan at a higher interest rate.
3. The new lender makes payments on the original loan; the borrower makes payments to the new lender on the larger loan in an increased amount.

M. Graduated-payment mortgage—only used during times of high interest rates.
1. Initial payments are low but increase over the life of the loan.
2. Allows the buyer to purchase a home with monthly payments lower than those on a level payment.
3. Aimed at helping first-time buyers who have increasing income potential.

N. Adjustable-rate mortgage
1. Contains interest-rate provision related to a selected index.
2. The interest rate may be adjusted periodically (either up or down). A margin is added to the index to determine the interest rate.
3. ARMs can be converted to fixed-rate mortgages (FRMs). They are fixed for either 5 or 7 years and then are annually adjusted.

O. Reverse annuity mortgage
1. Allows the borrower to receive periodic payments from the lender on the equity in the home.
2. The note becomes due on a specific date, at the sale of the property, or at the death of the borrower.

P. Participation mortgage—lender receives interest and an equity position in a project, known as equity kicker, or a percentage of the income of the property.

Q. Buydowns
1. Temporary—To help the borrower qualify for a loan, the seller agrees to subsidize the buyer's PI payment. For example, if the interest rate is 7% and the seller agreed to help finance a 2 – 1 buydown loan, then the borrower would make an initial payment based on a 5% interest rate the first year and 6% the second year. The seller would subsidize the buyers's PI payment 2% the first year (7% – 2% = 5%) and 1% the second year (7% – 1% = 6%). In the third year the temporary subsidy goes away and the buyer's payment is based on a 7% interest rate.
2. Permanent—In order for the borrower to qualify for a larger than usual loan, discount points can be paid at closing to permanently buy down the existing interest rate. For example, if a borrower qualified to make an $1,100 PI payment, amortized over 30 years

at 5.50% ($5.68 per $1,000), then the amount mortgaged would be ($1,100 divided by 5.68) $193,662. However, if the sellers paid enough discount points to permanently buy down the interest rate to 5.00% (instead of 5.50%), then the amount mortgaged would be increased to ($1,100 divided by 5.37) $204,842.

VIII. The Money Market

A. General characteristics
   1. Money may be viewed as a means of payment, storehouse of purchasing power, standard of value.
   2. Money market is regulated by the federal government through the Federal Reserve System and the U.S. Treasury.

B. Federal Reserve System (Fed)
   1. Regulates the flow of money through member banks by controlling reserve requirements and discount rates.
   2. Tempers the economy through open-market operations.

C. U.S. Treasury
   1. In effect, our nation's fiscal manager.
   2. Responsible for supervising the daily fiscal borrowing and spending operations of the federal government.

IX. Sources of Real Estate Financing

A. Savings and loan associations
   1. Principal function: to promote thrift and home ownership.
   2. Regulated on the national level by the Office of Thrift Supervision.
   3. Deposits are insured by the Savings Association Insurance Fund (SAIF) for up to $100,000 per depositor; SAIF is part of the FDIC.
   4. Local in nature

B. Commercial banks
   1. Prefer short-term loans but have been significant participants in residential mortgage lending.
   2. Deposits are insured by the Bank Insurance Fund (BIF) for up to $100,000 per depositor; BIF is part of the FDIC.

C. Mutual savings banks
   1. Primarily savings institutions in the northeastern United States.
   2. Active in mortgage market.
   3. Prefer FHA and DVA loans.

D. Life insurance companies
   1. Prefer long-term commercial, industrial loans.
   2. Seek equity position in projects financed.
   3. Regulated by state law.

E. Mortgage banking companies
   1. Originate loans with their own money and money belonging to other institutions and from other sources (pension funds, private individuals).
   2. Service loans they originate.

F. Mortgage brokers—originate loans for other lenders but do not service loans.

G. Sale of state mortgage bonds
   1. Authorized by federal government.
   2. Lower interest rates are usually charged to low-income and moderate-income buyers.

3. Usually for first-time buyers only.

H. Owner assisted

1. Contract for deed, land contract.
2. Take back second mortgage.

X. Secondary Mortgage Market

A. Market in which loans are bought and sold after they have been originated and funded.

B. Warehousing agencies play a major role in the secondary market by purchasing a number of mortgage loans and assembling them into packages for resale to investors.

C. Major warehousing agencies

1. Federal National Mortgage Association (FNMA)—Fannie Mae
   a. Publicly traded corporation authorized to purchase conventional as well as FHA and DVA loans.
   b. Raises funds to purchase loans by selling government-guaranteed FNMA bonds at market interest rates.
2. Government National Mortgage Association (GNMA)—Ginnie Mae
   a. Federal agency designed to administer a special assistance program and to work with the FNMA in secondary market activities.
   b. Can join forces with the FNMA in times of tight money and high interest rates; through a tandem plan, the FNMA can purchase high-risk, low-yield loans at full market rates, while the GNMA guarantees payment and absorbs the difference between low-yield and current market prices.
   c. Government agency authorized to purchase government insured FHA mortgages; government-guaranteed VA mortgages; and government-subsidized Rural Development Mortgages from intermediaries in the secondary mortgage market.
3. Federal Home Loan Mortgage Corporation (FHLMC)—Freddie Mac
   a. Government-chartered corporation created to provide secondary mortgage market for conventional loans.
   b. Has the authority to purchase conventional, FHA, and DVA mortgages; pool them; and sell bonds in the open market with mortgages as security.

XI. Property Insurance

A. Required to obtain mortgage; figured annually and often budgeted monthly.

B. Various types of polices like renters insurance (HO-4), homeowners insurance (HO-2 or HO-3), and condominium insurance (HO-6) for interior surfaces.

C. CLUE (claim activity and property damage) reports are ordered by most insurance companies on property being purchased. (CLUE is an acronym for Comprehensive Loss Underwriting Exchange). Insurers use the report to ascertain patterns of possible future claims and adjust their insurance premiums according to risk.

XII. Closing Statements (settlement statement or adjustment sheet)

A. Related to the completion of the real estate transaction, when the seller delivers title to the buyer in exchange for payment of the purchase price by the buyer.
B. Detailed accounting of real estate transaction; shows all funds received, all charges and credits made, all funds paid out.
C. Prepared by the broker, escrow office, attorney, or any other person designated to process the details of the sale.
D. Indicates how all closing costs plus prepaid and unpaid property expenses are allocated between the buyer and the seller.
E. Closing statement procedures generally reflect local custom as well as state and federal laws (for example, RESPA).

XIII. Other Important Terms

A. Amortized mortgage (direct-reduction loans)—regular monthly payments, applied first to the interest, with the balance to the principal, over the term of the loan.
B. Balloon payment—final payment of the loan; larger than previous payments and repays the debt in full.
C. Equity—value of the owner's interest in the property; the difference between the value of the property and all the liens on the property.
D. Subordination agreement—changes the order or priority of the liens between two creditors.
E. Usury—charging a rate of interest in excess of the maximum rate allowed by state law.
F. Seller financing—the seller of the real estate provides financing for the sale by taking back a secured note in the form of a purchase-money mortgage, land contract, or deed of trust.
G. Disintermediation—lenders experience a rapid withdrawal of funds into alternative investments which weakens the lender's position in the money market.
H. Arbitrage—profitable difference between interest rates in financing arrangements such as wraparound mortgages.
I. Hypothecation—pledging property as security for the loan without losing possession of it.
J. Impound account—trust account created to set aside funds for the future needs of a property, for example, to provide funds for the payment of real estate taxes and renewal premiums for insurance.
K. Discount points—money expressed in the form of a percentage. A point equals one percent of the loan amount. For example, if two discount points were paid on a $200,000 loan, the amount would be $200,000 × 2% or $4,000. Often the seller is asked to pay a discount point or two in order to help the buyer obtain financing.

DIAGNOSTIC TEST

1. All of the following statements concerning real estate financing are correct **EXCEPT**
   1. the mortgage generally is considered a lien.
   2. the mortgagee is the lender.
   3. an owner of property by whom the mortgage is executed is called a mortgagor.
   4. a promissory note is security for a mortgage.
2. A promissory note is NOT
   1. a negotiable instrument.
   2. evidence of debt.
   3. a document in which the debtor agrees to repay the stated loan.
   4. evidence of title.
3. Which of the following payment plans allows for periodic payments of interest only, with the principal due as a lump sum payment at maturity?
   1. Amortized
   2. Flexible
   3. Straight
   4. Balloon
4. All of the following are participants in the secondary mortgage market **EXCEPT**
   1. FHLMC.
   2. FNMA.
   3. FDIC.
   4. GNMA.
5. Which of the following is NOT characteristic of a conventional loan?
   1. It is neither insured nor guaranteed by public agency.
   2. Security rests on the borrower's ability to pay and the collateral pledged.
   3. It is never insured by a private agency.
   4. The ratio of the loan to the value of the property usually does not exceed 80 percent without private mortgage insurance.
6. Department of Veterans Affairs (DVA) guarantees a lender from 25 to 50 percent of the loan balance on a Veterans Administration (VA) loan, up to
   1. $25,000.
   2. $36,000.
   3. $46,000.
   4. $60,000.
7. Which of the following is NOT characteristic of a Federal Housing Administration (FHA) loan?
   1. A mortgage insurance premium is charged.
   2. The lender is insured against loss.
   3. The maximum mortgage debt is determined by a formula.
   4. The FHA provides the money for the loan.
8. Which of the following is NOT characteristic of a DVA loan?
   1. The loan is guaranteed.
   2. Only an eligible veteran or eligible dependents of veterans, as well as reservists and National Guard members who have served for six years, may qualify for the loan.
   3. The loan is insured.
   4. Little or no down payment is required.
9. A mortgage that covers more than one parcel of real property is
   1. a junior mortgage.
   2. a blanket mortgage.
   3. a package mortgage.
   4. an open-end mortgage.
10. Granting a conventional loan requires that the borrower provide the lender with which of the following?
    1. Sales contract and hypothecation instrument
    2. Mortgage and promissory note
    3. Deed of trust and sales contract
    4. Mortgage and letter of intent
11. A graduated-payment mortgage
    1. contains an interest-rate provision related to a selected index.
    2. is granted for a term of 3 to 5 years and is secured by a long-term mortgage of up to 30 years.
    3. allows a buyer to purchase a home with initial monthly payments lower than the level-payment, amortized mortgage.
    4. allows the mortgagor to borrow additional money during the term of the loan, up to the original amount of the mortgage.

12. Under judicial foreclosure, the
    1. mortgage generally must include a power-of-sale clause.
    2. court may award title to the lender.
    3. lender sues the borrower in court and obtains a judgment and court order to sell.
    4. lender may sell the property without obtaining a judgment.
13. The process by which a mortgagor regains his or her interest in a property is called
    1. foreclosure.
    2. redemption.
    3. a deficiency judgment.
    4. laches.
14. You financed the purchase of a home by means of a deed of trust. Until you pay off the debt, title will be held by the
    1. trustee.
    2. trustor.
    3. seller.
    4. beneficiary.
15. The tandem plan involves
    1. the VA and FHA.
    2. Fannie Mae and Freddie Mac.
    3. Fannie Mae and Ginnie Mae.
    4. Ginnie Mae and Freddie Mac.
16. Which of the following statements about FHA mortgages is FALSE?
    1. FHA mortgages require a larger down payment than VA mortgages.
    2. There is no prepayment penalty.
    3. FHA mortgages are assumable provided the new borrower qualifies.
    4. FHA mortgages are not assumable.
17. The difference between interest rates in financing arrangements such as wraparound mortgages is called
    1. equity.
    2. usury.
    3. disintermediation.
    4. arbitrage.
18. On the FHA loan, the buyer would NOT be required to
    1. provide mortgage insurance to protect the lender.
    2. meet FHA credit standards.
    3. find an approved lender willing to make the loan.
    4. make a 20 percent down payment on the loan.
19. A mortgage on four lots with a partial release clause would be
    1. a wraparound mortgage.
    2. a blanket mortgage.
    3. a package mortgage.
    4. an open-end mortgage.
20. Funds for Department of Veterans Affairs (DVA) loans usually are provided by
    1. HUD.
    2. the secondary mortgage market.
    3. Freddie Mac.
    4. approved lenders.
21. Charging a rate of interest in excess of the maximum rate allowed by law is
    1. laches.
    2. hypothecation.
    3. subordination.
    4. usury.
22. Pledging property as security for a loan without losing possession of it is
    1. a subordination agreement.
    2. hypothecation.
    3. an impound account.
    4. seller financing.
23. A veteran buys a home with a DVA-guaranteed loan. Two years later, the veteran sells the home to a buyer who, with the lender's approval, assumes the veteran's loan. In this situation, the veteran is
    1. responsible for paying an insurance fee charged by the DVA.
    2. responsible for paying the loan origination fee.
    3. no longer financially responsible if the buyer defaults six months later.
    4. financially responsible if the buyer defaults six months later.
24. If a lender charges a borrower two points on a $60,000 loan, what will be the service charge for points?
    1. $120
    2. $1,200
    3. $2,400
    4. None of the above

25. Reserve requirements for banks are controlled by which of the following federal agencies?
    1. FNMA
    2. GNMA
    3. Federal Deposit Insurance Corporation (FDIC)
    4. The Federal Reserve

26. The insurance report that tells about previous insurance claims is
    1. CLUB
    2. CLUE
    3. CASE
    4. COST

27. In order to help a buyer qualify for financing, a homeowner paid money to the lender to subsidize the buyer's PI payment for three years. This type of loan is called a(n)
    1. ARM.
    2. permanent buydown.
    3. temporary buydown.
    4. contract for deed.

28. A buyer asked a seller to pay two points to permanently lower the buyer's interest rate. This type of loan is called
    1. graduated payment mortgage.
    2. wraparound.
    3. purchase-money mortgage.
    4. buydown.

29. A buyer purchased a home and asked the seller to pay 2½ discount points equaling $4,000. How much money did the buyer want to borrow?
    1. $100,000
    2. $160,000
    3. $170,000
    4. None of the above

30. If a buyer can afford a PI payment of $1,200 and the amortization rate for a 5½ percent 30-year mortgage is $5.68 per thousand, how much money can the buyer afford to borrow? (Round to the closest dollar.)
    1. $115,680
    2. $116,816
    3. $211,268
    4. $211,286

MATCHING QUIZ

The column on the right contains brief memory links to important terms in Chapter 6.
Write the letter of the matching term on the appropriate line.

A. Mortgagor
B. Mortgagee
C. Straight loan
D. Balloon payment
E. Amortized
F. Acceleration clause
G. Defeasance clause
H. Alienation clause
I. Judicial foreclosure
J. Redemption
K. Deficiency judgment
L. Arbitrage
M. FHA
N. DVA or VA
O. Discount point
P. Blanket mortgage
Q. Package mortgagee
R. Hypothecation
S. GNMA
T. Usury

1. ______Fixed P & I payment where the principal portion increases with each payment
2. ______Government-insured loan
3. ______Recovery after default
4. ______Due-on-sale clause
5. ______A higher yield is realized from the difference in interest rates charged for the use of the same money a second time.
6. ______Government-guaranteed loan
7. ______Final and larger payment pays the entire balance
8. ______The borrower in a mortgage loan transaction
9. ______This loan covers more than one parcel of property
10. ______Interest-only loan
11. ______Pledging something as collateral without giving up possession of it
12. ______Result of a lawsuit for the collection of the rest of a debt owed
13. ______The holder of the mortgage
14. ______Interest rate exceeds legal limit
15. ______Applies when a debt is defeated (paid) and a release is filed to return the collateral pledged
16. ______Clause that calls the balance owed because of the borrower's default
17. ______Purchases government-insured and guaranteed loans on the secondary market
18. ______Court-ordered sale following a borrower's default
19. ______Computed as a percent of the loan
20. ______This type of loan includes both real and personal property

ANSWER KEY: DIAGNOSTIC TEST

1. **(4)** In some states, the mortgage creates a lien on the property; the note is the promise to repay the debt. (59)
2. **(4)** The promissory note is evidence of the debt but not evidence of title. Deeds are the instruments that convey title and provide evidence of ownership interest. (59)
3. **(3)** The amortized, flexible, and balloon all provide for payment of principal. (59)
4. **(3)** The FDIC insures checking and savings accounts up to $100,000 per account. (62)
5. **(3)** Conventional loans may be insured by a private agency. (61)
6. **(4)** The veteran is entitled to a loan up to four times the amount of the entitlement. (61–62)
7. **(4)** The FHA will not provide money for a loan. However, the VA will provide the money for a loan where the supply of money is scarce. (61)
8. **(3)** An FHA loan provides public mortgage insurance for which the buyer pays an insurance premium. The VA does not charge the veteran for the guarantee of the loan. (61–62)
9. **(2)** A blanket mortgage would be used to finance the development of a subdivision and is applied to more than one parcel of land. A partial-release clause is used in order for the developer to sell individual lots out from under the blanket. (62)
10. **(2)** A deed of trust is used in place of a mortgage in states such as California. A mortgage or deed of trust and a note are required for a conventional loan. The mortgagee creates a lien on the property as security for the debt. The note is a promise to repay the debt. (59)
11. **(3)** An adjustable-rate mortgage uses an index note. An open-end mortgage allows for borrowing additional money up to the original loan amount. (59)
12. **(3)** Judicial foreclosure is one of the three alternative procedures available to the lender for mortgage foreclosure. Nonjudicial foreclosure does not require the lender to sue the borrower in court. Under strict foreclosure, the court may award title to the lender. Strict foreclosure happens after a delinquent borrower has been served adequate notice giving him or her a deadline to pay off the debt. If the deadline is missed, the property is awarded to the lender and no sale takes place. (60)
13. **(2)** Foreclosure is related to the redemption period, which may end with the foreclosure sale (equitable redemption) or after the foreclosure sale (statutory redemption). If the lender does not recover what is owed by the borrower, it may sue for a deficiency judgment. Laches was discussed above. (60)
14. **(1)** The trustor is the borrower and the beneficiary is the lender. (59)
15. **(3)** Freddie Mac is a warehousing agency in the secondary mortgage market. VA and FHA are not involved in the secondary mortgage market purchase of mortgages. (65)
16. **(4)** FHA and VA mortgages are assumable with qualification. (61)
17. **(4)** Equity is the difference between what an asset is worth and what is owed on it. Usury laws limit the interest rate that can be charged to borrowers by lenders. Disintermediation refers to an outflow of funds from a lender which limits the lender's lending capacity. (66)
18. **(4)** The cash investment on an FHA-insured loan is 3 percent of the sales price or appraised value plus closing costs. Gift letters may be used for the required down payment. The maximum mortgage formula for houses over $50,000 is 97.75 percent. (61)
19. **(2)** A wraparound mortgage is a second mortgage wrapped around a first mortgage. A package mortgage is used to purchase both real and personal property like a motel. An open-end mortgage allows for future advances of funds by the lender to the borrower. (62)
20. **(4)** Freddie Mac functions in the secondary mortgage market; HUD is a regulatory agency. (61–62)

21. **(4)** Subordination allows a lender to agree to consent to a subsequent mortgage having legal priority thus placing the original lender in a lesser position. Laches refers to the inability to assert a legal right because of undue delay in asserting it. Hypothecation is pledging property as security for a loan without giving up possession of the property. Usury is charging an interest rate higher than that allowed by state law. (66)

22. **(2)** An impound account is a trust account established for funds to meet the customary requirements of a property, e.g., taxes and insurance. Subordination and hypothecation were discussed above in answer 21. A land contract would be an example of seller financing. (66)

23. **(3)** Both the DVA and FHA require buyers who assume existing mortgages to be qualified to do so. Therefore, the original buyer's liability is assigned to the new buyer in a process called novation. (61–62)

24. **(2)** One point is one percent of the loan amount. $60,000 × 0.02 = $1,200. (61)

25. **(4)** FNMA and GNMA function in the secondary mortgage market. The FDIC insures lenders' checking and savings accounts. (64)

26. **(2)** CLUE is an acronym for Comprehensive Loss Underwriting Exchange report. (66)

27. **(3)** A temporary buydown allows the seller to prepay some of the buyer's interest in order to subsidize his or her payment. This effectively buys the interest rate down on a temporary basis. For example, in a 7 percent market, using a 2 – 1 buydown, the interest rate is artificially reduced by 2 percent the first year and 1 percent the second year. In other words, the buyer makes a payment based on 5 percent the first year and 6 percent the second. At the beginning of the third year the subsidy goes away and the buyer pays the full freight. (63–64)

28. **(4)** Often a buydown loan enables the purchaser to qualify for a larger mortgage because of the lower interest rate. The lower rate is created by the seller's willingness to pay the discount points, which is often considered *prepaid interest.* (63–64)

29. **(2)** $4,000 is 2.5% of the borrowed amount. $4,000 ÷ 2.5% = $160,000. (66)

30. **(3)** Divide the PI payment of $1,200 by $5.68 to find the number of thousands to borrow. $1,200 ÷ $5.68 = 211.27 × 1,000 = $211,268 (59).

TEST SCORE

FINANCING			
Rating	**Range**	**Your Score**	
Good = 80% to 100%	24–30	Total Number	30
Fair = 70% to 79%	21–23	Total Wrong	–
Needs Improvement = Lower than 70%	20 or less	Total Right	

Passing Requirement: 21 or Better

ANSWER KEY: MATCHING QUIZ

1. E	**6.** N	**11.** R	**16.** F
2. M	**7.** D	**12.** K	**17.** S
3. J	**8.** A	**13.** B	**18.** I
4. H	**9.** P	**14.** T	**19.** O
5. L	**10.** C	**15.** G	**20.** Q

CHAPTER 7

Laws of Agency

OUTLINE OF CONCEPTS

I. **Laws of Agency**
   A. The brokerage business is one of agency; the broker is hired by the principal to become her or his agent.
      1. The broker is considered an agent who consents to represent the interest of another party who delegates authority to him or her.
      2. The principal is the party who delegates to the agent the authority to represent the principal's interest in a transaction.
      3. *Agency* refers to the fiduciary relationship between the agent and the principal.
      4. *Fiduciary* describes the relationship of trust and confidence between principal and agent. Sometimes the broker (agent) is referred to as a *fiduciary.*
      5. The client is the principal to whom the agent gives counsel and advice.
      6. The customer is the third party for whom a service is provided.
      7. The principal is obligated by contract to compensate the agent and to cooperate with and not hinder the agent's ability to fulfill the fiduciary obligations.
      8. Single agency involves a broker representing either the seller or buyer in a transaction; limitation avoids conflicts and results in loyalty and client-based service to just one client.
      9. If allowed, subagency is brought about where one broker, generally the seller's agent, appoints other brokers (with authorization of the seller) to assist in carrying out client-based functions on behalf of the principal; cooperating brokers have the same fiduciary responsibilities to the seller as the listing broker.
   B. The broker owes a fiduciary duty to the principal, who may be the seller, buyer, lessor, or lessee of property; the broker must perform duties of "COALD": care, obedience, accounting, loyalty, and disclosure for the principal.
   C. The broker owes a fiduciary duty to the principal (client) but is obligated to disclose to the customer all known material facts about a property. Most state laws require the seller to disclose deferred maintenance and latent defects to the buyer.
   D. General agent versus special agent

1. A general agent is one authorized by another to negotiate contracts for that person in a given range of matters.
2. A general agent (for example, a property manager) is authorized to represent the principal in all matters concerning one area of the principal's interest.
3. A special agent is authorized to represent the principal in one specific transaction; a real estate broker is a special agent.
4. A broker is a special agent employed by a seller to find a buyer for the seller's property or employed by a buyer to assist in the buying process.
5. As a special agent, the real estate broker is not authorized to sell property or bind the principal to any contract.

E. To be entitled to a brokerage commission, a broker must
   1. be a licensed broker.
   2. be the procuring cause of the sale/purchase.
   3. be employed by the principal.
   4. act according to the laws of agency.

F. When a broker is employed by a seller and finds a buyer who is ready, willing, and able to purchase on the terms and conditions of the listing or on any terms acceptable to the seller, the broker is entitled to the commission even if
   1. the sale is not completed because of the principal's default.
   2. the buyer cancels because of the seller's fraud, of which the broker had no knowledge.

G. Real estate brokers may share a commission only with their own salespeople or with other licensed brokers.

H. Real estate brokers may not offer legal advice; only a licensed attorney may do so.

I. Dual agency—without both parties' prior written, mutual knowledge and consent, the broker is prohibited from representing both a seller and a buyer in the same transaction.

J. The broker must exercise reasonable care when representing the principal.

K. The broker is obligated to act in good faith and conform to the principal's legal instructions and authority.

L. The broker may not act as both agent and the party to a transaction without prior knowledge and consent of all.

M. All offers must be presented by the broker to the principal promptly when received.

N. A fixed place of business must be maintained by the broker.

O. The broker may be required to deposit all funds entrusted to her or him in a trust account or do what all parties agree should be done with the funds and may not commingle such funds with operating funds.

P. The broker generally is prohibited from placing blind ads—those that do not identify the broker as the advertiser.

Q. The broker's commission is negotiable between the client and the broker, is specified in the agency agreement, and is computed as a percentage of the total amount of money involved, but may be expressed as a flat fee; net listings generally are not allowed in most states.

R. Buyer agency—the broker may be hired by a potential buyer; the broker and the buyer usually draw up a buyer agency agreement. The buyer/broker must

1. be fair and honest to the seller, but owes greater responsibility to the buyer, including duties of skill and care to promote and safeguard the buyer's best interest.
2. disclose to the buyer pertinent facts (which he or she might not be able to disclose if a subagent of the seller) such as the seller is near bankruptcy or the property is overpriced.
3. use negotiating strategy and bargaining talents in the buyer's best interest.

S. The transactional broker (nonagent or facilitator) is not an agent of either party. The transactional broker
   1. assists the buyer and seller with formalities and necessary paperwork required for transferring ownership of real property.
   2. is expected to treat all parties honestly and competently and is equally responsible to both.
   3. may not disclose confidential information to either party and may not negotiate for either the seller or buyer.

T. Designated Brokerage—this agency model allows the designated broker to appoint agents within the office to singularly represent either a seller or buyer to the *exclusion* of every other agent in the office.

U. Broker protection clause—states that the property owner will pay the listing broker a commission if, within a specified number of days after the listing expires, the owner transfers the property to someone the broker originally introduced to the owner.

V. Cooperative brokers—generally selling brokers, who work with the listing broker to bring the seller and buyer together.

II. Salespersons

A. Salespersons are responsible only to the brokers under whom they are licensed and can carry out only those responsibilities assigned by their brokers.

B. Salespersons have no authority to make contracts or receive compensation directly from principals.

C. All salespersons' activities must be carried out in the name of their supervising brokers.

D. Salespersons may work under brokers either as independent contractors or as employees.

E. Salespersons are compensated on the basis of agreements between themselves and their brokers.

F. Salespersons may not place ads without identifying their associated brokers unless allowed under state law.

G. Salespersons are agents of their brokers and either subagents or appointed agents of the party represented.

H. All listings are taken in the name of the brokerage.

III. Broker's Ethics

A. Fraud
   1. Fraud versus puffing
      a. Fraud is a misrepresentation of facts known to be false, made with the intent to deceive and relied on by the injured party to his or her detriment; it also includes intentional or negligent nondisclosure of pertinent facts by silence.

b. Puffing is an opinion or exaggeration that no one relies on for decision making, for example, "This is the most beautiful view in the county."

2. Fraudulent acts not only are unethical but can result in the revocation and suspension of a broker's license.

B. Code of Ethics—standards of ethical conduct subscribed to by members of the National Association of REALTORS® or other real estate trade organizations. Sections of the REALTORS® code have been made a part of the rules and regulations governing the conduct of real estate licensees in many states.

IV. Antitrust Law

A. Antitrust law prohibitions

1. Allocation of customers or markets—agreement among brokers to divide their markets and refrain from competing for each other's business; division may take place on a geographic basis or on a certain price range of homes
2. Price fixing—conspiracy among brokers to set prices for their services, rather than negotiate such fees
3. Boycotting—two or more businesses conspire against other businesses to reduce competition
4. Tie-in agreements—agreements to sell one product only if the buyer purchases another product as well
5. People violating the Sherman Antitrust Act may be found guilty of a felony punishable by a maximum $100,000 fine for an individual and three years in prison.
6. In a civil suit a broker found guilty of a violation of the Sherman Antitrust Act is liable for triple damages plus attorney's fees and court costs.

DIAGNOSTIC TEST

1. *A* agrees to buy *B*'s real estate for $123,000. *A* signs a sales contract and deposits $12,300 earnest money with *B*'s broker, *C*. *B* is unable to show good title, and *A* demands the return of his earnest money from *C*, as provided in the contract. What should *C* do?
   1. Deduct the commission and return the balance to *A*
   2. Deduct the commission and pay the balance to *B*
   3. Return the entire amount of earnest money to *A*
   4. Pay the entire amount to *B* to dispose of as *B* sees fit

2. A broker employs several salespeople at her office. Early one day one member of the sales staff submits a written offer with an earnest money deposit on a house listed with the broker. Later the same day another salesperson submits a higher written offer on the same property, also including an earnest money deposit. The broker, in accordance with the policy of her office, does not submit a second offer unless the first has been presented and *rejected* by the seller. In this case the seller accepts the first offer, so the seller is not informed of the second offer. In this situation, the broker's actions are
   1. permissible, provided the commission is split between the two salespeople.
   2. permissible, if such arrangement is written into the salespeople's employment contracts.
   3. not permissible, because the broker must submit all offers to the seller.
   4. not permissible, because the broker must notify the second buyer of the existence of the first offer.

3. An owner listed her home for $98,000, and the listing broker told the prospective buyer to submit a low offer because the seller was desperate. The buyer offered $96,000 and the seller accepted. In this situation
   1. the broker was unethical, but because no one was hurt, the broker's conduct is not improper.
   2. the broker violated the agency relationship.
   3. the broker's action was proper in obtaining a quick offer.
   4. any broker is authorized to encourage bidders.

4. A salesperson desires to advertise a property without including the brokerage name. This situation is allowed when
   1. the salesperson is the listing agent.
   2. the salesperson includes his or her name in the ad.
   3. the salesperson is the actual owner and advertising as a for sale by owner.
   4. the salesperson is willing to pay for the ad.

5. A doctor listed his home with a broker under an exclusive-right-to-sell agreement. The listing salesperson and her broker signed the listing contract. Which of the following statements does NOT correctly describe the relationship among the parties?
   1. The broker has a fiduciary relationship with the seller.
   2. The salesperson has a fiduciary relationship with the broker.
   3. If the salesperson dies, the listing contract will be terminated.
   4. If the broker dies, the listing contract will be terminated.

6. A real estate broker is usually
   1. a special agent.
   2. a universal agent.
   3. a general agent.
   4. an ostensible agent.

7. Which of the following is FALSE concerning a real estate broker?
   1. All offers must be presented by the broker to the principal.
   2. Brokers may place blind ads.
   3. A fixed place of business must be maintained by the broker.
   4. The broker's commission usually is specified in the listing agreement.

8. Which of the following is FALSE concerning a real estate salesperson?
   1. The salesperson is responsible to the broker under whom she or he is licensed.
   2. All of a salesperson's activities must be carried out in the name of his or her principal broker.
   3. The salesperson must work under the broker as an independent contractor.
   4. A salesperson is compensated on the basis of an agreement between herself or himself and the broker.

9. You are a broker who has listed a home for a neighbor. Which of the following terms describes your relationship with the seller?
   1. You are a subagent of the seller.
   2. The seller is your client.
   3. The seller is your customer.
   4. The seller is your agent.

10. A man who owned a single-family house had his unlicensed son-in-law do the electrical work in preparing his home for sale. The man did not disclose this to the broker at the time of executing the listing. After completion of the sale, the new owner suffered a financial loss because of the faulty electrical wiring done by the owner's son-in-law. The broker
    1. could be reprimanded for not forewarning the purchaser.
    2. is innocent of any wrongful act.
    3. will be held liable for monetary damages suffered by the purchaser.
    4. should have arranged for a proper electrical inspection prior to the sale.

11. A home is listed for $100,000 and sells for $90,000. The broker's commission is 7 percent of the selling price. The commission is
    1. $630.
    2. $700.
    3. $6,300.
    4. $7,000.

12. You are a broker acting as a facilitator in the sale of a house without being an agent of either party. You are a(n)
    1. buyer's broker.
    2. cooperative broker.
    3. listing broker.
    4. transactional broker.

13. The responsibilities of a broker in an agency relationship include
    1. managing the property.
    2. providing financing.
    3. accountability for funds received.
    4. accepting an offer for the seller.

14. The listing broker owes fiduciary duty to the
    1. buyer.
    2. lender.
    3. seller.
    4. buyer's attorney.

15. When a broker lists a property, the broker may
    1. reject an offer for the seller's property.
    2. bind the seller to a contract.
    3. advertise the seller's property.
    4. offer legal advice to the seller.

16. A broker has received several offers for a property he has listed. The broker must present each offer to the seller
    1. promptly on receipt.
    2. individually.
    3. as soon as the seller has decided on any previous offer.
    4. prior to the seller deciding on any previous offer.

17. A salesperson sells a property listed by her broker. The salesperson may accept her share of the commission from
    1. the seller.
    2. her broker.
    3. the buyer.
    4. the buyer's attorney.

18. Which of the following is a violation of the broker's fiduciary relationship with a seller?
    1. The broker charges no commission.
    2. The broker charges a 40 percent commission.
    3. The broker tells a prospective buyer the lowest price the seller will accept.
    4. The broker tells a prospective buyer the highest price the seller will accept.

19. Which of the following statements does NOT correctly describe a fiduciary?
    1. A fiduciary owes loyalty to the principal.
    2. A fiduciary must conform to the principal's legal instructions.
    3. A fiduciary is an agent.
    4. A fiduciary is a neutral third party.

20. A salesperson is working under a broker. The salesperson may
    1. work under the broker as an independent contractor.
    2. place an ad without identifying the broker.
    3. receive a commission directly from a seller.
    4. receive a commission directly from another broker.

21. A special agent is best described as someone who
    1. has power of attorney.
    2. has authority to sell a property.
    3. has authority to represent a principal in a specific transaction.
    4. has authority to represent a principal in all matters concerning an area of the principal's interest.

22. A broker presents a seller with a written offer to purchase. The broker is responsible for
    1. explaining the advantages or disadvantages of the offer to the seller.
    2. explaining the legal implications of accepting the offer.
    3. binding the seller to the offer.
    4. preparing the title search once the offer is accepted.

23. A broker is listing her neighbor's home. The commission should be determined by
    1. the size of the broker's firm.
    2. rates approved by the Real Estate Commission.
    3. rates approved by the local Board of REALTORS®.
    4. negotiation with her neighbor.

24. A broker recently has listed a home under an exclusive-right-to-sell listing contract. The broker generally will earn his commission when
    1. he submits an offer to purchase to the seller.
    2. the seller signs an offer to purchase.
    3. he finds a buyer ready, willing, and able to buy on the terms of the listing.
    4. the closing has taken place.

25. A broker has earned a commission on the sale of her listing by another broker. The listing broker may pay part of her commission to
    1. the selling broker.
    2. the selling salesperson.
    3. the out-of-state salesperson who referred the seller to her.
    4. the buyer's attorney.

26. A broker has just received an earnest money payment on an offer to purchase. The broker must place the earnest money in his
    1. trust account.
    2. business account.
    3. personal checking account.
    4. savings account.

27. A salesperson working for a broker has just written an offer to purchase on her broker's listing in which the buyer has written a check for earnest money and stated that the broker hold the funds. Which of the following statements describes how the earnest money payment should be handled?
    1. The salesperson should place the earnest money in her checking account and await the closing of the transaction.
    2. The salesperson should give the earnest money check to the seller's attorney.
    3. The salesperson should place the earnest money check in a safe deposit box until the transaction is concluded.
    4. The salesperson should give the earnest money check to her broker for deposit in the broker's trust account.

28. A licensed real estate broker who engages the services of a licensed salesperson on the basis that the broker can direct what the salesperson can do but not how it is done has
    1. engaged an independent contractor.
    2. discriminated illegally.
    3. practiced steering.
    4. established an employer-employee relationship.

29. A broker's license can be revoked if he or she
    1. advertises property for sale without including the salesperson's name in the ad.
    2. negotiates a commission based on what the broker says is the rate set by the local board of REALTORS®.
    3. pays a commission that exceeds the customary rate.
    4. advertises free market analysis as a means of obtaining listings.

30. What is the listing broker's legal responsibility to a prospective purchaser?
    1. The broker must not use fraud or deceit.
    2. The broker must help the buyer get the lowest price possible.
    3. The broker is only a middleperson. Neither the buyer nor the seller can charge her or him with avoiding a legal duty.
    4. There is none at all.

31. To create agency requires two things: delegated authority and
    1. a compensation agreement.
    2. a written agency agreement.
    3. reasonable care.
    4. consent to act.

32. A designated broker authorized an agent to singularly represent a seller, to the exclusion of everyone else in the office. This agent is called
    1. a subagent.
    2. a dual agent.
    3. an appointed agent.
    4. an affiliated licensee.

MATCHING QUIZ

The column on the right contains brief memory links to important terms in Chapter 7.
Write the letter of the matching term on the appropriate line.

A. Principal
B. Delegated authority
C. Consent to act
D. Fiduciary
E. Loyalty
F. Dual agency
G. Commingling
H. Protection clause
I. Single agency
J. Subagent
K. Puffing
L. Fraud
M. REALTOR'S Code of Ethics
N. Boycotting
O. Tying arrangement (tie-in)
P. Client
Q. Customer
R. Obedience
S. Care
T. General agent

1.______ Standard of ethical behavior for REALTORS®
2. ______Unlawful mixing of the broker's money and his or her client's funds
3.______ The person or entity that delegates authority in order to create an agency relationship
4.______ A property manger who has several duties to perform for his or her principal
5.______ A duty to a principal that includes confidentiality
6.______ Giving a seller an Estimate of Proceeds to determine their net before listing their home is an example of this agency duty.
7.______ A relationship where an agent represents only one party
8.______ With permission, representing both sides of the same transaction
9.______ An illegal action where two brokers agree not to cooperate with a third broker
10.______ Agent's exaggerated opinion
11.______ Intentional misrepresentation
12.______ An agent's agent
13.______ Extends the period of time that a seller agrees to pay a commission
14.______ The principal's act that creates agency
15.______ Type of duty required of an agent when asked by an owner not to place a For Sale sign in the yard
16.______ To create agency the principal delegates authority, and the broker must do this
17.______ A type of relationship based on trust and confidence
18.______ Requiring a buyer to list his or her current home with the same agent in order to purchase a new home
19.______ Someone you work with
20.______ Someone you work for

ANSWER KEY WITH EXPLANATIONS: DIAGNOSTIC TEST

1. **(3)** *B* is not entitled to any compensation, as she was responsible for breaching the contract. *C* cannot deduct commission because the sale did not close. (73)

2. **(3)** Brokers are responsible for submitting all offers to clients. (73–74)

3. **(2)** The broker owes loyalty to the client as part of the fiduciary responsibilities. The broker should encourage the buyer to make his or her highest and best offer. (73)

4. **(3)** A broker is prohibited by most state laws from advertising listed property without using the name of the brokerage in the ad. Agents likewise are prohibited from running blind ads whether they are the listing agent or willing to pay for the ad. The only exception is if the agent desires to advertise the sale of his or her own property. Normally these sales don't involve the brokerage; they resemble for-sale-by-owner transactions. (74)

5. **(3)** The salesperson works on behalf of the broker but is not necessarily a party to the contracts prepared by him. While the listing contract is taken by the salesperson, the contract is between the doctor and the broker. Unless there is an agreement to the contrary, listings are considered the property of the broker.(73)

6. **(1)** A special agent has a specific responsibility as compared to a general agent who has greater responsibilities such as a property manager. A universal agent has newly unlimited authority. (73–74)

7. **(2)** The blind ad was discussed in Question 4. (74)

8. **(3)** A salesperson may work under a broker as either an employee or an independent contractor. (75)

9. **(2)** The listing broker is the agent of the seller. (75)

10. **(2)** The broker would not be responsible for disclosing something which he would have no way of knowing. (73)

11. **(3)** Commission is based on the selling. $90,000 × 7% (0.07) = $6,300. (74)

12. **(4)** A transactional broker is also referred to as a nonagent whose job is to help the parties with the paperwork and procedure required to complete the transaction. (75)

13. **(3)** Accountability is part of the fiduciary relationship. (73)

14. **(3)** The listing contract creates an agency relationship and thus a fiduciary duty to the seller. (73)

15. **(3)** The listing broker is responsible for marketing the property. The broker would not have the authority to respond to an offer for the client or to offer legal advice. (73–74)

16. **(1)** The broker must present all offers simultaneously. The broker does not have the right to withhold offers from the seller. (74)

17. **(2)** A salesperson is an agent of the broker and may not accept real-estate–related compensation from anyone except his or her broker. (74)

18. **(3)** The commission is negotiable. A buyer's broker could suggest that the client offer the lowest price a seller might accept. (74)

19. **(4)** The broker has a fiduciary duty to work in the best interest of his or her client. (73)

20. **(1)** Blind ads are prohibited. A salesperson may receive a commission only from the broker for whom she is working. (75)

21. **(3)** The incorrect answers reflect the authority of a universal agent. (74)

22. **(1)** A broker may not give legal advice nor bind a seller to an offer. A title company licensed by the state insurance commission or an attorney or a title insurance abstractor would do the title search. (73–74)

23. **(4)** Commissions are negotiable. A rate approved by more than one broker would be a violation of antitrust law. (74)

24. **(3)** The commission is earned when a full-price cash offer consistent with the terms in the listing is presented to the seller. The commission is received at the closing. (74)

25. **(1)** Commissions must be shared on a broker-to-broker basis. (74)

26. **(1)** Brokers are required to set up a trust account for earnest money payments unless otherwise agreed to by the buyer and seller. (74)

27. **(4)** The salesperson is required to give all earnest money to her broker. The listing broker is responsible for holding the earnest money in his trust account. (75)

28. **(1)** A broker cannot control salespeople's working conditions as in an employer-employee relationship. An agent is not required to follow illegal instructions such as discrimination. (75)

29. **(2)** Negotiating commissions on the basis of the board rate would be an example of violating antitrust laws dealing with price-fixing. The broker's name must be included in an ad but it is not necessary to include the name of the salesperson. It is perfectly legal for the broker to advertise a free market analysis as a means of soliciting listings. (76)

30. **(1)** The listing broker must treat the customer fairly, but is required to get the seller the highest price possible. (75–76)

31. **(4)** Neither compensation nor a written agreement is necessary to create agency. Delegated authority and consent to act are the only two things necessary to create agency. (73)

32. **(3)** In states that allow appointed agency, a designated broker appoints agents to singularly represent either buyers or sellers. An appointed agent is authorized to represent either the seller or a buyer to the exclusion of everyone else in the office. Consensual dual agency takes place when the appointed agent simultaneously represents both the buyer and seller in the same transaction. (75)

TEST SCORE

LAWS OF AGENCY			
Rating	**Range**	**Your Score**	
Good = 80% to 100%	26–32	Total Number	32
Fair = 70% to 79%	23–25	Total Wrong	–
Needs improvement = Lower than 70%	22 or less	Total Right	

Passing Requirement: 23 or Better

ANSWER KEY: MATCHING QUIZ

1. M	**6.** S	**11.** L	**16.** C
2. G	**7.** I	**12.** J	**17.** D
3. A	**8.** F	**13.** H	**18.** O
4. T	**9.** N	**14.** B	**19.** Q
5. E	**10.** K	**15.** R	**20.** P

Mandated Disclosures

OUTLINE OF CONCEPTS

I. **Agency Disclosure**
   A. Disclosure of the agency relationship is required in every state; it is generally required at the first meaningful contact with a buyer or seller.
   B. Dual agency is not allowed unless all parties agree to it; however, dual agency is illegal in some states. The disclosure should be made before the individual discloses any confidential information to the broker.

II. **Property Disclosure**
   A. Latent defects—a hidden structural defect that would not be discovered by ordinary inspection, such as a part of the property being built partly on an adjoining property or a zoning violation.
      1. Seller has duty to discover and disclose any known latent defects that threaten personal safety or structural soundness.
      2. Buyers have been able to receive damages or terminate the offer to purchase in a case where a seller did not reveal known latent defects.
      3. Some states require a seller of residential property to provide a property condition report for all prospective buyers.
      4. Some states also require the licensee to discover and disclose to prospective buyers any material facts that may affect the property's desirability or value in spite of the seller's lack of knowledge or failure to disclose.
   B. Environmental disclosures
      1. A real estate broker should be able to notice potential environmental hazards in a property that would be readily apparent to a real estate broker and urge that the buyer or seller have the potential hazard evaluated by a qualified third party.
      2. Broker should be aware of the Comprehensive Environmental Response Compensation and Liability Act (CERCLA) of 1980 which was amended as the Superfund Amendment and Reauthorization Act (SARA) of 1986.
         a. Established fund of $9 billion called Superfund to clean up uncontrolled hazardous waste dumps and respond to spills.

   b. Created a process of identifying liable parties and ordering them to take responsibility for the cleanup.
   c. Liability under Superfund is considered to be strict, joint and several, and retroactive.
      (1) Strict liability—owner is responsible to the injured party without excuse.
      (2) Joint and several liability—each individual owner is personally responsible for the damages in whole; if only one owner is financially able to handle the total damage, then that owner will have to pay all and attempt to collect the proportionate share of the rest of the owners from them.
      (3) Retroactive liability—liability for actions before CERCLA was passed. For example, in the Love Canal case all the waste was dumped long before CERCLA was passed in 1980, but the release of that waste was current and causing injury after the statute was enacted. Retroactive liability means that parties found responsible for causing a release are liable even if their actions occurred prior to CERCLA's enactment.
   d. In 2001–2002 the Brownfields Revitalization and Environmental Restoration Act and subsequent Small Business Liability Relief and Brownfields Revitalization Act were enacted to further reduce the risk of innocent landowners who purchased once environmentally contaminated real estate. This legislation helped to rejuvenate many deserted, defunct, and derelict toxic industrial sites by diminishing the innocent landowner's liability exposure and providing them with the opportunity to expense cleanup costs rather than capitalize them.

C. Brokers should be familiar with environmental hazards known to be common to their market area.
D. The listing broker and selling broker, if a subagent, must inform the seller or lessor of their obligations for environmental disclosures under the Residential Lead-Based Paint Hazard Reduction Act of 1992 for dwellings built prior to 1978:
   1. Homebuyers must be alerted to any lead-based paint or related hazards.
   2. Homebuyers must be given an agreed-upon time period for the opportunity to conduct a lead-based paint inspection or risk assessment at their expense.
   3. A Certification and Acknowledgment of Disclosures must be attached to the offer to purchase.
   4. A copy of the Certification and Acknowledgment must be kept by the seller and both agents for three years after closing or the beginning of the lease.
E. Material facts for seller's agent include
   1. disclosure of all offers,
   2. buyer's ability to offer a higher price (in most states),
   3. disclosing names of prospective buyers as well as any relationship, such as buyer being related to licensee, and
   4. disclosure of known material defects in property.

F. Material facts for buyer's agent include
   1. disclosing property deficiencies,
   2. disclosing provisions of offer to purchase that are not favorable to the buyer,
   3. recommending the lowest price the buyer should offer regardless of the list price, and
   4. disclosing how long the property has been listed.

DIAGNOSTIC TEST

1. Broker *M* is going to contact customer *P* who would like to see one of *M*'s listings. *M* should make his agency disclosure
   1. prior to meeting with *P*.
   2. prior to discussing *P*'s financial qualification and type of house desired.
   3. prior to actually showing the listed property.
   4. prior to writing an offer to purchase.
2. Which of the following would not be classified as a latent defect?
   1. An unknown underground oil tank
   2. Hidden structural damage
   3. A large crack in the living room ceiling
   4. A cracked heat exchanger in the furnace
3. Which of the following statements does NOT correctly describe the status of dual agency?
   1. Dual agency is legal in all states.
   2. Dual agency is not allowed unless all parties agree to it.
   3. Disclosure of dual agency should be made when preparing an offer to purchase.
   4. Disclosure of dual agency should be made prior to the closing of a real estate transaction.
4. The Comprehensive Environmental Response, Compensation, and Liability Act was amended in 1986 to protect innocent landowners from cleanup liability through which legislative action?
   1. SARA
   2. FIREEA
   3. Title VIII
   4. Title X
5. The Residential Lead-Based Paint Hazard Reduction Act of 1992 does not require that
   1. the seller disclose any lead-based paint or related hazards.
   2. homebuyers be given an agreed-upon time period for the opportunity to conduct a lead-based paint inspection or risk assessment at their own expense.
   3. a Certification and Acknowledgment of Disclosure be attached to the offer to purchase.
   4. a copy of the Certification and Acknowledgment be kept by only the listing broker.
6. The Residential Lead-Based Paint Hazard Reduction Act of 1992 requires that copies of the Certification and Acknowledgment be kept for
   1. one year after closing.
   2. two years after closing.
   3. three years after closing.
   4. five years after closing.
7. Which of the following statements would NOT be a material fact to be disclosed by a seller's agent?
   1. The buyer's ability to make a higher offer
   2. Disclosure of a roof that leaks
   3. Discussion of the advantages of an offer to purchase
   4. Knowledge of active infestation of termites
8. Which of the following statements would NOT be a material fact to be disclosed by a buyer's agent?
   1. Disclosure of how long the property has been listed
   2. Buyer's ability to make a higher offer
   3. Recommend the lowest price the buyer should offer regardless of the list price
   4. Disclosure of provisions of offer to purchase that are not favorable to buyer
9. Which of the following does NOT correctly describe the status of agency disclosure?
   1. Disclosure is required in some states.
   2. Disclosure is required at the first meaningful contact with a buyer.
   3. Disclosure is required at the first meaningful contact with the seller.
   4. Disclosure is required in every state.
10. CERCLA is a law that deals with
    1. fair housing legislation.
    2. environmental legislation.
    3. appraisal legislation.
    4. banking legislation.

11. Legislation that has helped resurrect deserted, defunct, and derelict toxic industrial sites is known as
    1. DNR.
    2. Waste field.
    3. Due diligences.
    4. Brownfields legislation.

12. An owner had a grease fire and it spread to the ceiling. The kitchen was remodeled and the charred ceiling joists were sealed with paint. When the seller sells the property, the hidden charred ceiling joists should be disclosed as
    1. nothing because they were repaired.
    2. discoverable defects.
    3. caveat emptor.
    4. latent defects.

13. What federal legislation would a community call upon to clean up a toxic waste site?
    1. HUD
    2. Regulation Z
    3. CERCLA
    4. Title VIII

14. If a buyer's agent knows that the house her buyer desires to purchase has been stigmatized by a recent murder-suicide, what ethically should the buyer's agent do?
    1. Remain silent to protect the seller
    2. Remain silent because the incident didn't harm the structure
    3. Disclose it to the buyer after the purchase agreement is signed
    4. Disclose it to the buyer before the buyer writes an offer

MATCHING QUIZ

The column on the right contains brief memory links to important terms in Chapter 8.
Write the letter of the matching term on the appropriate line.

A. Agency disclosure	1. ______	Illegal form of representation
B. Latent defect	2. ______	Legislation that helps revitalize defunct areas of contamination
C. Seller's Property	3. ______	Legislation requiring the seller to reveal the Disclosure Act property's condition
D. CERCLA	4. ______	Innocent landowner defense legislation
E. SARA	5. ______	Known as the Superfund
F. Brownfields	6. ______	Federal law gives the buyer 10 days after offer acceptance to do this
G. Strict liability	7. ______	Potential cause of mental retardation in children
H. Joint and several liability	8. ______	Informing sellers and buyers of your working relationship
I. Retroactive liability	9. ______	Persons are individually held liable for damages along with the group
J. Lead poisoning	10. ______	Not discoverable by an ordinary inspection
K. Disclosed dual agency	11. ______	Liability extending back to previous owners
L. Undisclosed dual agency	12. ______	Owner is responsible without excuse
M. Lead-based paint	13. ______	Legally representing both the seller and buyer in the assessment same transaction
N. Lead-based paint	14. ______	Informing a potential buyer about the proximity of a landfill
O. Agent mandatory disclosure of a material fact	15. ______	Mandatory federal disclosure for this hazardous substance found in housing built prior to 1978

ANSWER KEY: DIAGNOSTIC TEST

1. **(2)** While this is generally correct, you should check with your state licensing board on the disclosure timing. (85–86)
2. **(3)** A latent defect would not be discovered by an ordinary inspection. (84)
3. **(1)** Dual agency is not legal in some states. Moreover, dual agency is not allowed in any state unless all parties agree to it. (84)
4. **(1)** SARA (Superfund Amendments and Reauthorization Act) was enacted to create an innocent landowner defense against the strict liability interpretation of CERCLA. (84)
5. **(4)** A copy of the Certification and Acknowledgment must be kept by the seller and both agents. (85)
6. **(3)** Copies must also be kept for three years after the beginning of a lease. (85)
7. **(2)** Property defects caused by deferred maintenance. (85–86)
8. **(2)** A seller's agent would be required to disclose the buyer's ability to make a higher offer unless prohibited by state law. (85–86)
9. **(1)** Agency disclosure is required in every state; therefore, the first response is incorrect. Agency disclosure is generally required at the first meaningful contact with either a buyer or seller. (84)
10. **(2)** Environmental legislation that funds federal money for the cleaning up of toxic waste sites; also called the Superfund. (84–85)
11. **(4)** Brownfields legislation guidelines give individual states the authority to determine how to clean up defunct and derelict toxic industrial sites. (85)
12. **(4)** Latent defects are hidden structural defects that can't be discovered by ordinary inspection. These defects can potentially threaten the soundness or safety of the property. *Caveat emptor* means "buyer beware," but with seller property disclosure laws that kind of thinking is unfair and unacceptable. (84)
13. **(3)** CERCLA is also known as the Superfund. HUD enforces fair housing laws; Regulation Z is legislation that requires lender disclosure of the cost of credit; and Title VIII is fair housing legislation. (84–85)
14. **(4)** The buyer's agent has an ethical duty to tell the buyer everything he or she knows that relates to the decision-making process unless the disclosure violates the law, such as the racial composition of a neighborhood. (84)

TEST SCORE

MANDATED DISCLOSURES			
Rating	**Range**	**Your Score**	
Good = 80% to 100%	11–14	Total Number	14
Fair = 70% to 79%	10	Total Wrong	–
Needs Improvement = Lower than 70%	9	Total Right	

Passing Requirement: 10 or Better

ANSWER KEY: MATCHING QUIZ

1. L	**5.** D	**9.** H	**13.** K
2. F	**6.** M	**10.** B	**14.** O
3. C	**7.** J	**11.** I	**15.** N
4. E	**8.** A	**12.** G	

Contracts

OUTLINE OF CONCEPTS

I. **Voluntary Agreement between Legally Competent Parties to Do or Refrain from Doing Some Legal Act, Supported by Legal Consideration**

II. **Essential Elements of a Valid Contract**
   - A. Competent parties—must be of legal age and mentally competent.
   - B. Offer and acceptance (mutual assent)—must be a "meeting of the minds."
     1. Any offer or counteroffer may be withdrawn at any time prior to acceptance by the offeree.
     2. A counteroffer invalidates the original offer.
   - C. Legality of object—purpose must be legal
   - D. Consideration—an act of forbearance, or the promise thereof, given by one party in exchange for something from the other. Forbearance is a promise not to do something that a party is legally entitled to do.
   - E. Description of real estate—must be accurate.
   - F. Written and signed—generally required by the statute of frauds for most real estate contracts.

III. **Contract Classifications**
   - A. Expressed—parties state terms and show intentions in words; may be either oral or written.
   - B. Implied—agreement demonstrated by acts and conduct.
   - C. Bilateral—both parties promise to do something; one promise is given in exchange for another.
   - D. Unilateral—only one party makes a promise; if the second party complies, the first party is obligated to keep the promise, such as an option or open listing.
   - E. Executed—both parties have fulfilled their promises and thus performed the contract.
   - F. Executory—something remains to be done by one or both parties.

IV. **Legal Effect of a Contract**
   - A. Valid—complies with all essentials of a contract; binding and enforceable on both parties.
   - B. Void—lacks an essential element of a valid contract; has no legal effect.

C. Voidable—appears to be valid on its surface but may be disaffirmed because one of the parties signed when a minor, when under duress, or as a result of fraud or misrepresentation.
D. Unenforceable—appears to be valid, but neither party may sue the other to force performance; for example, an oral agreement to pay a commission.

V. Discharge of Contract

A. Performance—all terms carried out.
B. Substantial performance—party remains liable because the contract was not completed exactly as required.
C. Mutual agreement—parties agree to cancel.
D. Operation of law—voided by minor or because of fraud or the expiration of the statute of limitations.

VI. Default/Breach of Contract

A. Buyer recourse if seller defaults:
   1. Rescind, or terminate, the contract and recover the earnest money.
   2. Sue for specific performance.
   3. Sue the seller for damages.
B. Seller recourse if buyer defaults:
   1. Declare the contract forfeited.
   2. Rescind the contract and keep all or part of the deposit as liquidated damages.
   3. Sue for specific performance.
   4. Sue for damages.

VII. Types of Listing Agreements

A. Open listing
   1. The seller may employ any number of brokers.
   2. The seller is obligated to pay a commission only to the broker who produces a buyer (procuring cause).
   3. If the seller personally sells the property without the aid of any broker, the seller is not obligated to pay the commission.
B. Exclusive-agency listing
   1. Only one broker is authorized to act as the exclusive agent of the principal.
   2. The seller retains the right to sell the property without obligation to the broker.
C. Exclusive-right-to-sell listing
   1. One broker is given the exclusive right to sell the property.
   2. The seller gives up the right to sell the property without paying the broker's commission.
   3. The broker receives the commission regardless of who sells the property.
D. Net listing
   1. The list price is based on the amount of money the seller will receive if the property is sold, plus the commission.
   2. If the property is sold, the seller receives only the net amount for which the property was listed, and the broker retains the remainder.

3. Because of the uncertainty of the selling price, sellers could sacrifice thousands of dollars to dishonest real estate agents; therefore, net listings are prohibited in many states.

E. All listings are agreements between the broker and the seller, not the salesperson. Accordingly, if a salesperson leaves his or her broker, all of the listings taken by the salesperson remain the property of the listing broker.

F. Types of buyer agency agreements
   1. Exclusive right agreements—the buyer must compensate his or her agent whenever purchasing a property of the type described within the period described.
   2. Exclusive agreement—the buyer's agent is assured of buyer loyalty relative to any other agents. The buyer may, however, purchase property on his or her own without the assistance of an agent and thus without any compensation being due to the buyer's agent.
   3. Open agreement—the buyer can work with more than one buyer's agent at the same time but owes compensation only if the buyer uses the services of a buyer's broker.
   4. Situations where it is appropriate for a buyer to enter into a relationship with buyer broker
      a. A family business relationship or friendship exists, which makes it difficult for broker to be completely loyal to the seller.
      b. Working with former seller clients as buyer customers.
      c. A buyer prefers to have the agent as her advocate.
      d. A broker is buying for himself; he must disclose that he is a licensed agent and representing himself and not a seller.

G. Ways in which buyer's broker can be compensated
   1. Retainer fee.
   2. Gives buyer incentive to perform contract.
   3. Fee may be refundable or nonrefundable.

H. Flat or fixed fee
   1. Can calculate a straight fixed fee.
   2. The fee can be paid by the buyer or as a co-op fee by the seller.
   3. The hourly fee should reflect the market as well as what other professionals are receiving.
   4. Percentage fee
      a. Can be a percentage of the sales price or MLS (multiple-listing service) co-op fee.
      b. Creates a disincentive for buyer's broker to get a lower price for buyer.

VIII. Termination of Listings or Buyer Agency Agreements

A. Operation of law
   1. Contracting with an individual while she or he is in a state of diminished capacity.
   2. Death or incapacity of either party.
   3. Destruction of the property or change in the property use because of an outside force.
   4. Bankruptcy of either party, at option of trustee.

B. Acts of the parties
   1. Mutual consent

2. Completion of the objective
3. Expiration
4. Revocation by the principal
5. Renunciation by the agent
   a. Subject to liability for damages caused by revoking or renouncing the agreement

IX. Contract for the Sale of Real Estate

A. Required by the statute of frauds to be in writing to be enforceable.
B. Sets forth all details of the agreement between the buyer and the seller for the purchase and sale of real estate.
C. When the contract has been prepared and signed by the purchaser, it is an offer to purchase the subject real estate.
D. An offer becomes accepted when the sellers sign and the signed offer is delivered back to the buyer (offeror).
E. More detailed than the deed itself because the contract in effect dictates the contents of the deed and all other terms and conditions of the transaction.
F. After both the buyer and the seller have executed the sales contract, the buyer acquires the interest in the land, known as an *equitable title,* or sometimes called an insurable interest.
G. A "time is of the essence" contract must be performed in the time specified; any party who does not perform on time is guilty of breach of contract.

X. Earnest Money Deposits—Not Required for a Legal Contract

A. Generally give evidence of intention to carry out the terms of contract.
   1. Usually must be held by the broker in a special trust, or escrow, account.
   2. Cannot be commingled, mixed with a broker's operating funds, or converted to a broker's own use.
   3. The amount is generally determined by negotiation between the buyer and seller.
   4. A deposit is not legally required to create a valid contract.

XI. Options

A. Contract by which the optionor (owner) gives the optionee (prospective buyer) the right to buy at a fixed price within a stated period of time.
B. The optionee pays the fee for the option right and assumes no obligation to make any other payment until the optionee decides, within a specified time, to either exercise the option right or allow the option to expire.

XII. Installment Contract/Contract for Deed/Land Contract

A. Means of financing a purchase: the buyer gives the seller a nominal down payment and regular periodic payments over a number of years, including interest.
B. Legal title to real estate remains in the vendor's (seller's) name during the term of contract.
C. The vendee (purchaser) takes possession when the contract is executed.
D. The vendee will not receive the deed to the property until the entire purchase price has been paid.

E. The vendee has the equitable title during the life of the contract.

XIII. Other Real Estate Contractual Concepts

A. Counteroffer—new offer made in response to an offer received; the original offer is, in effect, rejected and cannot be accepted thereafter unless it is revived by the offeror.
B. Amendments—licensees in many states are required to fill out amendment forms to change the language in either the listing contract or the offer to purchase.
C. Cancellation agreements—forms used to terminate a transaction; used in some states by a broker to get a written release from both the buyer and the seller to authorize the refund of earnest money.
D. Leasing agreements—written or oral contracts between the tenant (lessee) and the landlord (lessor); transfers the right to exclusive possession and the use of the landlord's real property to the lessee for a stated consideration (rent) and for a specified period of time; the statute of frauds requires that a lease for more than one year be in writing to be enforceable.
E. Addendum—adds further terms and conditions to the approved forms, thus incorporating them into the legal document; may or may not require preparation by an attorney.
F. Contingency—a condition in a contract that requires a certain event or events to happen before the contract is complete. Sometimes referred to as "subject to" clauses. Contingency clauses have three distinguishing features:
   1. Actions needed to satisfy the contingency.
   2. Time frame within which actions must be performed.
   3. Statement identifying (if necessary) who will be responsible for paying any related costs.
G. Broker's protection clause—states that the property owner will pay the listing broker a commission if, within a specified number of days after the listing expires, the owner transfers the property to someone the broker originally introduced to the owner.

DIAGNOSTIC TEST

1. A contract in which the intentions of the parties are shown by their actions is
   1. an expressed contract.
   2. an implied contract.
   3. an executory contract.
   4. a bilateral contract.

2. Which of the following is NOT an essential element of a contract?
   1. An earnest money deposit
   2. Legality of object
   3. Offer and acceptance (mutual assent)
   4. Competent parties

3. The lessee in a leasing agreement is the
   1. tenant.
   2. property manager.
   3. landlord.
   4. rental agent.

4. A lease that is signed by a person who is 17 years of age (still a minor) is
   1. unilateral.
   2. void.
   3. illegal.
   4. voidable.

5. Contracts for sale of real estate must be in writing to be enforceable, according to the
   1. statute of limitations.
   2. parol evidence rule.
   3. statute of frauds.
   4. real estate commission.

6. A broker lists a home for $80,000. The broker brings an offer to the seller for $78,000, which is rejected by the seller. The broker obtains another offer, for $80,000, for the seller. Before she can deliver the offer, however, the offeror withdraws it by calling the broker at the seller's home. There is
   1. an implied contract.
   2. a unilateral contract.
   3. an executory contract.
   4. no contract.

7. You have entered into an option contract with an optionee who has 30 days to exercise his option. The option is what kind of contract?
   1. Voidable contract
   2. Unilateral contract
   3. Unenforceable contract
   4. Bilateral contract

8. Which of the following contracts are prohibited or discouraged in most states?
   1. Option
   2. Land contract
   3. Open listing
   4. Net listing

9. Without discussing price, you order dinner in a restaurant. You are required to pay for the dinner through what kind of contract?
   1. Bilateral
   2. Express
   3. Voidable
   4. Implied

10. A broker and a seller have signed an open listing contract. This agreement is an example of
    1. a unilateral contract.
    2. an executed contract.
    3. a bilateral contract.
    4. an unenforceable contract.

11. Which of the following correctly describes an open listing?
    1. The seller may employ any number of brokers.
    2. Only one broker is authorized to act as agent for the seller.
    3. The broker is entitled to a commission regardless of who sells the property.
    4. The broker's commission is based on the excess over the sales price stated in the listing.

12. A salesperson obtains a written offer to purchase a home that she has listed for sale. The seller accepts the offer, and the salesperson promptly telephones the purchaser to notify him of the acceptance. Because the purchaser lives in a nearby town, the salesperson informs him that she will deliver a copy of the contract in three days. The salesperson has an enforceable contract when
    1. the seller signs the acceptance.
    2. the offer to purchase is presented to the seller.
    3. the acceptance is telephoned to the salesperson representing the purchaser.
    4. a copy of the contract is delivered to the purchaser in three days.

13. A contract that lacks legal object is considered to be
    1. voidable.
    2. unenforceable.
    3. void.
    4. canceled.
14. Which of the following might NOT legally terminate a listing with a broker?
    1. Bankruptcy of the client
    2. Insanity of the broker
    3. Inability of the broker to find a buyer within a reasonable amount of time
    4. An economic depression
15. *A* gave an option on her property for 90 days to *B* and received a cash consideration of $100. *B* later assigned the option to *C* for a valuable consideration. Before expiration of the option, *A* stated that she no longer wanted to sell the property. Which of the following is correct?
    1. The option is void, because an option cannot be assigned.
    2. The option is not binding on *A*, for $100 is not sufficient consideration.
    3. *C* would have a good chance in court to compel *A* to sell to him, if he exercises the option before its expiration date.
    4. *A* can refuse to sell, because the consideration paid by *C* was not in cash.
16. Both the buyer and the seller agree to wait until the broker's exclusive-right-to-sell listing has expired. They then have a third party buy the home. After a short while, the third party conveys ownership to the interested buyer, who was introduced to the owner by the listing broker. In this case,
    1. the broker is not entitled to a commission because the listing expired.
    2. if the listing broker can prove collusion, he or she may collect a full commission.
    3. the broker may sue both the buyer and the seller for the commission.
    4. the broker is entitled to his commission because he performed the task for which he was hired.
17. Procuring cause would not be required for a broker to receive a commission in a(n)
    1. open listing.
    2. exclusive-right-to-sell listing.
    3. net listing.
    4. exclusive agency listing.
18. When a broker sold a property, the sales contract contained the following statement: "Buyer to accept property in 'as is' condition." However, both the seller and the broker knew the plumbing was in a major state of disrepair but did not tell the buyer. Would an action for damages against the broker, based on fraud, be successful?
    1. No. The "as is" provision in the contract is evidence of a meeting of the minds.
    2. No. The contract specifically stated that the property was being sold "as is."
    3. Yes. The duty to disclose a material fact cannot be avoided by an "as is" provision.
    4. Yes. "As is" refers only to exterior defects.
19. A broker brings a seller an offer-to-purchase contract for the listed price of $114,500, with the stipulation that the seller must furnish a title insurance policy to prove marketable title. The seller refuses the offer. The broker
    1. can collect full commission because sellers must always provide title insurance.
    2. can collect one-half of the commission.
    3. can collect nothing.
    4. can collect one-half of the first month's mortgage payment.
20. A seller listed her home with a broker. Shortly thereafter, the seller telephoned the broker and withdrew the exclusive-right-to-sell listing. A week later, she sold the home to her neighbor for a higher price than the price on the listing. In this situation, which of the following is true?
    1. The owner has the right to terminate the listing at any time without being liable for monetary damages incurred by the original listing broker.
    2. Under an exclusive right-to-sell listing, the broker is not entitled to a commission if the property doesn't sell.
    3. The broker is not entitled to a commission because the seller obtained a better price than she would have received through the broker's efforts.
    4. If the owner withdrew the listing, after the broker spent money on it, the owner is liable to the broker for damages.

21. A salesperson for a broker listed an owner's home under an exclusive-right-to-sell listing contract. Which of the following statements correctly describes this situation?
    1. The listing belongs to the salesperson.
    2. If the principal sells his own house, he will not have to pay a commission.
    3. The listing belongs to the broker.
    4. The listing belongs to both the salesperson and the broker.

22. An owner gives an exclusive-right-to-sell listing to a broker for a six-month period. During the exclusive period, the owner also gives an open listing to another broker who produces a buyer. What is the owner's liability for payment of a commission?
    1. Only one commission must be paid, which both brokers share on a 50/50 basis.
    2. The owner is liable only to the first broker for the payment of a commission.
    3. The owner is liable for payment of a commission to both brokers.
    4. The owner is liable only to the second broker for the payment of a commission.

23. A buyer has contracted with a seller to purchase property. The contract was ratified on January 10. The closing was on March 31. What is the status of the contract on April 1?
    1. Void
    2. Anticipatory
    3. Executed
    4. Executory

24. An exclusive-right-to-sell contract is a unilateral contract and may be considered
    1. a conveyance.
    2. an employment contract.
    3. an option.
    4. a contingency agreement.

25. A salesperson
    1. may receive a commission directly from a principal.
    2. can carry out activities in his or her own name.
    3. is responsible primarily to the broker under whom she or he is licensed.
    4. may place a blind ad.

26. A buyer's offer requires that the seller pay for a licensed termite inspector to inspect a house. If active infestation exists, the buyer can either agree to have the property treated or walk. This part of an offer is best known as
    1. a condition.
    2. a contingency.
    3. a chattel.
    4. a cloud.

27. An offer is made and presented to a seller for acceptance. After the offer is signed by the seller, it must be delivered to the buyer(s). Which response best describes proper delivery of an offer?
    1. The seller's signature on the offer to purchase
    2. The buyer's agent's cell phone call to the buyer to say, "Congratulations"
    3. The buyer's agent's actual delivery of a copy of the signed agreement to the buyer
    4. The buyer's verbal acceptance of the offer over the phone

28. If a buyer offers to purchase a home for $350,000 subject to the sale of the buyer's home, what is the subject to sale called?
    1. Contingency
    2. Condition
    3. Cloud
    4. Cancellation

29. A tenant decided to purchase a farm on an installment land contract for deed with a ten-year balloon. During the ten years, what kind of title does the vendee have in the farm?
    1. Legal
    2. Conditional
    3. Equitable
    4. Substantial

MATCHING QUIZ

The column on the right contains brief memory links to important terms in Chapter 9.
Write the letter of the matching term on the appropriate line.

A. Consideration
B. Earnest money
C. Expressed contract
D. Implied contract
E. Unilateral contract
F. Voidable contract
G. Specific performance
H. Open listing
I. Exclusive right to sell
J. Net listings
K. Listing contracts
L. Statute of frauds
M. Equitable title
N. Legal title
O. A purchase agreement
P. Acceptance
Q. Optionor
R. Vendee
S. Counteroffer
T. Contingency

1. ______ In a real estate office these contracts are the property of the broker
2. ______ Prior to acceptance these are considered offers
3. ______ A type of title also known as an insurable interest
4. ______ Pumping gas prior to paying is an example of this type of contract
5. ______ A type of title that one receives as the deed is delivered
6. ______ Notification and delivery to buyers of their signed offer by the seller
7. ______ Requires contracts of sale such as purchase agreements to be in writing
8. ______ Type of listing stating, regardless of who procures the buyer, the listing broker gets paid
9. ______ Only the real estate firm who procures the buyer gets paid by the seller
10. ______ A contract with a minor
11. ______ An option is an example of this type of contract
12. ______ A court order requiring a promise made to be carried out
13. ______ Because of the uncertainty of the selling price, this type of listing is prohibited in most states
14. ______ If specified in the contract, this can be used as liquidated damages
15. ______ A legal requirement to create a valid contract that can be good and signed by an offeror or valuable
16. ______ A contract in which the parties state the exact terms
17. ______ This act by the offeree invalidates an original offer
18. ______ A termite inspection is an example of this prerequisite to settlement
19. ______ The person who owns the property and has a signed an option contract with a potential buyer
20. ______ The buyer in a land contract for deed

ANSWER KEY WITH EXPLANATIONS: DIAGNOSTIC TEST

1. **(2)** An expressed contract would be oral or written. An executory contract is one in which parties to the contract have not fulfilled their contractual obligations. An accepted offer to purchase would be an example of a bilateral contract. (91)

2. **(1)** Earnest money can be used as consideration to create a contract, but it is not essential. A contract to purchase a home may be written with the agreement that a check is to be written at closing for the full amount. To create a contract requires consideration, but the consideration may be a promise to pay the full amount at closing in return for the owner's property. (91)

3. **(1)** The landlord is the lessor. A property manager is considered a general agent because of the broad responsibilities assumed on the property owner's behalf. (95)

4. **(4)** A minor may enter into a contract; however, upon reaching majority age the minor may either ratify (accept) or disaffirm (reject) the contract. (92)

5. **(3)** The statute of limitations is the period of time within which one may judicially challenge a contract. The real estate commission is a regulatory body that is responsible for enforcing rather than making the laws of a state. The parol evidence rule provides that prior or contemporaneous oral agreements modifying a written contract will not be admitted in a court of law to modify or contradict a written contract. (94)

6. **(4)** An offer can be withdrawn at any time prior to notification of acceptance. (91)

7. **(2)** An option is a unilateral contract until the optionee chooses to exercise the option right to buy, at which time it becomes a bilateral contract. The optionor may not void the contract, which is enforceable by the optionee. (94)

8. **(4)** Options and installment land contracts are commonly used; the open listing is generally allowed but used rather infrequently. (92)

9. **(4)** The ordering of the dinner is considered an implied contract. An express contract is one where words have been exchanged, whereas in an implied contract the parties' conduct often demonstrates their willingness to enter into a contract. (91)

10. **(1)** A bilateral contract would require two promises. An open listing would be enforceable but clearly is not an executed contract as the parties must perform. (92)

11. **(1)** Answer number 4 would be a net listing while number 2 would be an exclusive agency or exclusive-right-to-sell listing. The seller in an open listing has the right to sell the property herself without paying the listing broker a commission. (92)

12. **(4)** The contract is not enforceable until binding acceptance occurs, which generally involves the delivery of the signed and accepted contract to the seller or buyer. (94)

13. **(3)** A contract that does not have legal object is void. A voidable contract is valid but may be disaffirmed depending on the parties involved. An enforceable contract is one that meets the test of a valid contract. (91)

14. **(4)** A listing contract may be terminated by acts of the parties or by operation of law. (93–94)

15. **(3)** The optionor promises to sell and has no right to cancel; the optionee has the choice of exercising the option right. (94)

16. **(2)** The broker's rights would be based on the broker protection clause. (92)

17. **(2)** The open and exclusive agency listings allow the sellers to sell the property personally on their own without owing the broker a commission. (92)

18. **(3)** The broker is required to disclose any known material fact that might affect the decision of the buyer. In an "as is" contract it is always best to define what is "as is." Is the plumbing in the bathroom "as is"? Or is the wiring in the entire house "as is"? Or is the entire property "as is"? (91)

19. **(3)** The contingency is not consistent with the terms of the listing, thus relieving the seller of the obligation to pay a commission to the broker. (95)

20. **(4)** The sellers have the power to terminate but not necessarily the right, which could result in the seller being liable for damages. The listing is a unilateral contract between the seller and the broker. As such, the broker could hold the seller to the agreed contract and simply withdraw the listing until the agreed time ran out. However, in most cases brokers who agree to termination hold the seller liable for possible marketing expenses. If the broker had a protection clause in the listing contract, the courts would probably award the broker a commission. (92)

21. **(3)** The salesperson is not a party to the contract. The exclusive right-to-sell provision prevents the seller from being able to avoid paying a commission. (92)

22. **(3)** The first broker is protected under the exclusive-right-to-sell provision; the second broker is entitled under procuring cause. (92)

23. **(3)** The closing means that the contract is no longer anticipatory or executory. (91)

24. **(2)** The listing contract is both a unilateral contract and an employment agreement. It is considered a unilateral contract because the seller obligates himself or herself to pay a commission only if a buyer is procured by the broker. However, the broker doesn't promise the seller that emphatically he or she will find a buyer. The broker only promises to try. Therefore, what legally exists is a promise for an act, which is the definition of a unilateral contract. (92)

25. **(3)** The salesperson works for the broker and may not receive commission from anyone other than the broker for whom he or she works. Blind ads are prohibited. (93)

26. **(2)** A contingency best describes this situation. Although the offer is conditioned upon the inspection, all of the elements of a contingency exist to make it the best answer. (95)

27. **(3)** Delivery means actual acceptance of the offer; therefore, until the buyer has received either a hand-delivered or faxed copy of the agreement, acceptance hasn't taken place. (91)

28. **(1)** The subject to sale is called a contingency. (95)

29. **(3)** Equitable title is sometimes referred to as an insurable interest. Legal title is passed ten years later when the deed is transferred to the vendee by the vendor. (94–95)

TEST SCORE

CONTRACTS			
Rating	**Range**	**Your Score**	
Good = 80% to 100%	23–29	Total Number	29
Fair = 70% to 79%	20–22	Total Wrong	–
Needs improvement = Lower than 70%	19 or less	Total Right	

Passing Requirement: 20 or Better

ANSWER KEY: MATCHING QUIZ

1. K
2. O
3. M
4. D
5. N
6. P
7. L
8. I
9. H
10. F
11. E
12. G
13. J
14. B
15. A
16. C
17. S
18. T
19. Q
20. R

Transfer of Property

OUTLINE OF CONCEPTS

I. **Deeds—Transfers of Title**
   A. By descent
      1. Every state has a law known as the statute of descent and distribution.
      2. When a person dies intestate, the decedent's real estate and personal property pass to her or his heirs according to statute.
   B. By will
      1. A will takes effect only after the death of the testator; until that time any property can be conveyed by the owner.
      2. State laws usually require that on the death of a testator, his or her will must be filed with the court and probated to pass title to the devisees, although title, upon death, automatically vests in such devisees (will) or distributees (intestate). Title to property may not be in abeyance.
   C. By involuntary alienation—transferred without owner's consent
      1. Escheat—when a person dies intestate and leaves no heirs or abandons the property, title to her or his real estate passes to the state.
      2. Eminent domain—the federal, state, or local government may take the private property for public use through a suit for condemnation; the owner must be given just compensation.
      3. To satisfy debts—debt is foreclosed, the property sold, and the proceeds of the sale applied to pay off the debt.
      4. Natural forces
         a. Accretion—slow accumulation of soil, rock, and so on deposited by the movement of water on the owner's property.
         b. Erosion—gradual tearing away of the land by the action of natural forces.
         c. Avulsion—sudden tearing away of the land by the action of water or earthquake.
         d. Reliction—new land is acquired as water recedes.
      5. Adverse possession—actual, visible, hostile, notorious, exclusive, and continuous possession of another's land under a claim of title; periods of time may be tacked on by successive owner/tenants.

D. Voluntary alienation—either gift or sale; to transfer title during his or her lifetime, an owner must use some form of deed or conveyance.
   1. Deeds—written instruments of conveyance from owners (grantors) to the recipients (grantees).
      a. General warranty deed—contains promises and covenants
         (1) Provides the greatest protection of any deed.
         (2) Covenant of seisin—the grantor has the title and possession and has the right to convey.
         (3) Covenant against encumbrances—the grantor warrants that the property is free from any liens or encumbrances except those specifically stated in the deed.
         (4) Covenant of quiet enjoyment—the grantor guarantees that the title is good against a third party.
         (5) Covenant of further assurance—the grantor promises to obtain and deliver any instrument required to make the title good against third parties.
         (6) Covenant of warranty forever—the grantor guarantees that if the title fails, the grantee will be compensated for the loss sustained.
      b. Special warranty deeds—the grantor warrants only that the property was not encumbered during the time that the title was held, except as noted in the deed.
      c. Bargain and sale deed—contains only an implied warranty that the grantor holds an interest in the property. The grantor may choose to add warranties to the deed making it similar to a special warranty deed.
      d. Quitclaim deed—contains no warranties and conveys only such interest, if any, that the grantor may have when the deed is delivered but conveys that interest completely; often used to cure a defect in title.

E. Types of proof of title
   1. Abstract of title and lawyer's opinion
      a. Abstract of title—condensed history of all instruments on record affecting the title to the property.
      b. Attorney's opinion of title to the property—the buyer's attorney examines the abstract for flaws and prepares a written opinion of the condition of ownership.
   2. Torrens system
      a. A certificate of title accompanied by the owner's signature is filed with the registrar's office and used to verify future transfers.
      b. Title to Torrens—registered property never can be acquired through adverse possession.
   3. Certificate of title—prepared by an attorney without preparation of an abstract; attorney provides an opinion on the ownership of title; is not a title insurance policy.

F. Title insurance
   1. Protects insured against loss resulting from certain defects in the title, such as a forgery or defect in the public record, other than those exceptions listed in the policy.

2. Most standard coverage policies will not cover situations arising from questions of survey, defects of which the policyholder has knowledge, or unrecorded documents.
3. Extended coverage policies will cover additional risks that may be discovered only by inspection of the property, including unrecorded rights of persons in possession, or by examination of an accurate survey.
4. It is an indemnity contract.

II. Escrow Process

A. In some states this is the means by which the parties to a contract carry out the terms of their agreement.
B. Parties appoint a third party to act as an escrowee, or escrow agent.
C. In the sale of real estate, the seller's deed and the buyer's money are deposited with an escrow agent under an escrow agreement that sets forth conditions to be met before the sale will be consummated.
D. The escrow agent holds the deed and, when the title conditions and other requirements of the escrow agreement have been met, records the deed. Then the title passes and the sale is complete.

III. Deed Requirements

A. Requirements for a valid conveyance
   1. Grantor—must have legal existence, be of legal age, and be legally competent to convey the title.
   2. Grantee—must be named in the deed in such a way that he or she can be identified.
   3. Consideration—must be acknowledged by the grantor; in most states, consideration must be stated in dollars.
   4. Granting clause—must contain words that state the grantor's intention to convey the property.
   5. Habendum clause—follows granting clause when necessary to define the terms of ownership to be enjoyed by grantee.
   6. Description of real estate—must use a legal description that is understood by all parties.
   7. Signature of grantor—must be signed by all the grantors named in the deed; sometimes a seal is required.
   8. Acknowledgment—provides evidence that the signature is voluntary and genuine; not essential to the validity of the deed unless required by state statutes.
   9. Delivery and acceptance—actual delivery of the deed by the grantor and either actual or implied acceptance by the grantee.
   10. Exceptions and reservations ("subject-to" clauses)—should specifically note encumbrances, reservations, or limitations that affect the title being conveyed, such as liens, easements, and restrictions.

B. Recording of deeds and conveyance of title
   1. The title generally passes to the grantee when the executed deed is delivered and accepted.
   2. Exceptions:
      a. Torrens property—the title transfer when deed has been examined and accepted for registration.

   b. Closing in escrow—the date of delivery is generally the date that it was deposited with the escrow agent; if the escrow does not close, no title passes.
3. Recording a deed or taking possession of a property gives constructive notice to the world that one has rights in the property.
4. An unrecorded deed is valid between the parties to a transaction.

IV. Legal Versus Equitable Title (broker only)

A. Equitable conversion
   1. A doctrine of law that gives title to property to a buyer under an executory contract in certain situations before legal title has been transferred to the buyer.
   2. Upon creation of binding offer to purchase, the seller holds legal title for the buyer, who has equitable title.
   3. The seller holds legal title as security for the purchase price.
   4. Risk of loss also becomes buyer's responsibility; this applies in some states.
   5. Many states have adopted the Uniform Vendor and Purchaser Risk Act, which states that the risk of loss shifts to the buyer only if possession or legal title has been transferred to the buyer. The contract may and usually does specify who assumes the risk of loss.

B. Equitable title (insurable interest)
   1. Buyer's ownership interest in real property, which occurs when an offer to purchase becomes binding upon the parties.
   2. Interest may be conveyed by deed, will, etc.
   3. Interest converts to legal title upon delivery and acceptance of deed.

V. Real Estate Settlement Procedures Act (RESPA)

A. Created to ensure that the buyer and seller have knowledge of all the settlement costs before closing.

B. Requirements
   1. Lenders must give a copy of the special information booklet, *Settlement Costs and You,* to each loan applicant.
   2. The borrowers must be provided with a good-faith estimate of the settlement costs by the lenders no later than three business days after the receipt of the loan application.
   3. The loan closing expenses must be prepared on a Uniform Settlement Statement (HUD Form 1).
   4. RESPA explicitly prohibits the payment of kickbacks and prohibits referral fees when no services are actually rendered.

C. RESPA regulations apply only to transactions involving new first-mortgage referral loans for one-family to four-family dwellings generally financed by the federally related mortgage loan.

VI. Tax Benefits

A. Capital gains
   1. As of 1997, a married couple may exclude as much as $500,000 from capital gains tax for profits on the sale of a principal residence if they file jointly.
   2. Homeowners who file as individuals are entitled to a $250,000 exclusion each.

3. There is no limit on the number of times homeowners may take advantage of this benefit, as long as the homeowners have occupied the property as their residence for at least 24 months of the past five years.
4. A 1998 law lowers the required holding period for a noncorporate taxpayer from 18 to 12 months for long-term capital gain.

B. Penalty-free withdrawals from IRAs
   1. People buying homes for the first time may make withdrawals from their tax-deferred individual retirement funds (IRAs) for down payments on their homes without paying a penalty.
   2. The withdrawals are limited to $10,000.

C. Home-related expenses that are tax deductible for the owners
   1. Some loan origination fees
   2. Interest paid on mortgages on first and second homes
   3. Real estate taxes but not penalties for late payment
   4. Discount points on loans
   5. Prepayment penalties on loans

VII. IRS Regulations

A. Independent contractors and employees—under the "qualified real estate agent" category in the Internal Revenue Code, meeting three requirements can establish independent contractor status. This allows agents to report their brokerage income on IRS 1040 Schedule C as "self-employed."
   1. The individual must have a current real estate license.
   2. The individual must have a written contract with the broker that contains the following clause: "The salesperson will not be treated as an employee with respect to the services performed by such salesperson as a real estate agent for federal tax purposes."
   3. Ninety percent or more of the individual's income as a licensee must be based on sales production, not on the number of hours worked.

   Note: The broker should have a standardized agreement for this purpose drafted or reviewed by an attorney.

B. 1099 Forms
   1. IRS rules require closing agents to report details of closing to the IRS using IRS Form 1099 S.
   2. Reports must be submitted for sales or exchanges of residences with four or fewer units.
   3. Commissions paid to salespeople by brokers also must be reported on IRS Form 1099 MISC.

C. Declarations of value
   1. Documents of statements of value that accompany every deed or contract to be recorded in the registrar of deeds office.
   2. Statements of value are used by local and state tax officials for assessment purposes and for determining conveyance tax owed to state or municipality.

D. Imputed interest
   1. The IRS will impute, or assign, interest at a prescribed rate, computed monthly, on an installment contract that fails to include an interest rate or states an unreasonably low rate.
   2. Although no interest is paid, buyers may deduct for tax purposes imputed interest per annum on unpaid balances.
   3. Rate for determining whether interest should be imputed and the amount of interest that should be imputed is based on the applicable federal rate (AFR).
   4. AFR is one of three rates, depending on whether the debt instrument is:
      a. Short term—not more that three years
      b. Midterm—more than three years but not more than nine years
      c. Long term—more than nine years
   5. IRS issues alternative AFRs on a monthly basis.
   6. Installment sales of less than $3,000 are not covered by the imputed interest law.

E. 1031 tax-deferred exchange
   1. Under Section 1031 of the IRS Code, real estate investors can defer taxation of capital gains by making a property exchange.
   2. A property owner may exchange his or her property for another property and have tax liability on the sale only if additional capital or property is received.
   3. Tax on an exchange is deferred rather than eliminated.
   4. Properties involved in exchange must be of like kind.
      a. Like kind refers to any real property to be held for income purposes or investment; excludes dealer property or residences.
   5. Additional capital or personal property included in a transaction to even out the exchange is considered boot; the party receiving boot is taxed at the time of the exchange.
   6. You must use a qualified intermediary to hold the money in the tax-deferred exchange.

DIAGNOSTIC TEST

1. The deed that provides the buyer the greatest protection is the
   1. bargain and sale deed.
   2. general warranty deed.
   3. quitclaim deed.
   4. specialty warranty deed.
2. A warranty deed generally will transfer title to the grantee when it is
   1. acknowledged.
   2. signed by the grantee.
   3. signed by the grantor.
   4. delivered and accepted.
3. Which of the following would be an example of voluntary alienation?
   1. Sale
   2. Eminent domain
   3. Escheat
   4. Adverse possession
4. A grantee has received an executed, notarized deed. The grantee takes possession of the property but does not record the deed. The conveyance is
   1. invalid between the parties and valid as to third parties with constructive notice.
   2. valid as between the parties and valid as to the subsequent recorded interests.
   3. valid as between the parties and invalid as to subsequent recorded interests without notice.
   4. invalid as between the parties.
5. Which of the following statements does NOT correctly describe a properly executed will?
   1. It takes effect only after the death of the devisee.
   2. It specifies who will inherit the owner's property.
   3. It must conform to the state statute.
   4. It cannot supersede state laws of dower and curtesy.
6. Generally, title insurance coverage extends to
   1. defects known to the buyer.
   2. liens listed in the policy.
   3. defects listed in the policy.
   4. defects not found in the public record.
7. A deed must be signed by the
   1. grantor.
   2. vendee.
   3. grantee.
   4. vendor.
8. What do the following situations have in common?
   - I. A man's property is taken by the city and used for a new highway.
   - II. A woman's land gradually is wearing away because of wind.
   - III. A developer's property is sold at a foreclosure sale.

   1. They will require the use of a warranty deed to transfer title.
   2. They are all examples of voluntary alienation of title.
   3. They are all examples of eminent domain.
   4. They are all examples of involuntary alienation.
9. *A* and *B* have entered into a binding offer to purchase. *B* will buy *A*'s house. Which of the following statements correctly describes the status of the transaction?
   1. *A* will have equitable title until closing.
   2. *B* will have legal title when the offer to purchase becomes binding on both parties.
   3. *A* will have legal title until the offer becomes binding, at which time *A* will hold equitable title.
   4. *A* will hold legal title until closing, and *B* will hold equitable title until closing.
10. Which of the following statements does NOT correctly describe equitable title?
    1. Upon creation of a binding offer to purchase, buyer holds equitable title.
    2. Equitable title converts to legal title upon delivery and acceptance of the deed.
    3. If so specified, it may be conveyed by deed.
    4. It may not be conveyed by will.

11. The need for a loan closing to be prepared on a Uniform Settlement Statement is a requirement of
    1. Regulation Z.
    2. the federal fair housing laws.
    3. Government National Mortgage Association (GNMA, or Ginnie Mae).
    4. RESPA.

12. The requirement that a lender give each loan applicant a copy of *Settlement Costs and You* is created under
    1. Federal Home Loan Mortgage Corporation (FHLMC, or Freddie Mac).
    2. Federal Housing Administration (FHA).
    3. RESPA.
    4. Regulation Z.

13. Which of the following is NOT a requirement for establishing independent contractor status for a salesperson?
    1. The individual must have a current real estate license.
    2. Ninety percent or more of the individual's income as a licensee must be based on sales production.
    3. The individual's income must be based on the number of hours worked.
    4. The individual must not be included in the company hospitalization and retirement program.

14. The person conducting the closing must report details on closing to the IRS on
    1. IRS Form 1099.
    2. IRS Form 1099 S.
    3. IRS Form 1099 MISC.
    4. IRS Form 1099 R.

15. Section 1031 of the Internal Revenue Code allows real estate investors to do which of the following when making a property exchange?
    1. Avoid the capital-gains tax only if the exchange is of like kind.
    2. Phase out the capital-gains tax.
    3. Defer the capital-gains tax.
    4. Avoid the capital-gains tax even if the exchange is not of like kind.

16. A single person listed a house and accepted an offer from a buyer. Then, before closing, the person married. At closing the other spouse signed a deed to relinquish an inchoate interest in the property being sold. What kind of deed would be used to convey their inchoate interest without imposing any legal obligations to defend its title?
    1. Quitclaim
    2. Bargain and sale
    3. Special warranty
    4. General warranty

17. When a grantor appears before a notary, the notary attests that the grantor is who he or she says they are and that their signing is
    1. legal.
    2. deliberate.
    3. voluntary.
    4. insured.

18. RESPA requires that borrowers be provided with a good faith estimate of settlement costs by lenders no later than how many business days after the loan application?
    1. One
    2. Two
    3. Three
    4. Four

MATCHING QUIZ

The column on the right contains brief memory links to important terms in Chapter 10. *Write the letter of the matching term on the appropriate line.*

A. Acknowledgment	1. ______ Means of conveyance by the trustor
B. Reconveyance clause	2. ______ Follows granting clause and starts with "To have and to hold"
C. Covenant of seisin	3. ______ The person who conveys title to someone else by deed
D. Constructive notice	4. ______ Insurance that protects against loss from title defects
E. Grantee	5. ______ The grantor's expression that he or she has possession and the right to convey the property
F. Grantor	6. ______ Grantor guarantees that title is good against third parties who might bring court actions to establish superior title
G. Abstract of title	7. ______ In the presence of a notary, "I am who I say I am and my act is voluntary"
H. Title insurance	8. ______ Clause requiring the return of the trust deed to the trustor
I. Trust deed	9. ______ A summary made from the recorded legal history of a property
J. Habendum clause	10. ______ The person who receives title by deed
K. Covenant of quiet enjoyment	11. ______ Dying without a will
L. Devise	12. ______ Settlement costs legislation
M. Testate	13. ______ Uniform Settlement Statement
N. Intestate	14. ______ The transfer of real property by will
O. IRS Code 1031	15. ______ Type of notice given by recording a deed
P. 1099 MISC	16. ______ A very high percentage of this person's income is based on sales production
Q. RESPA	17. ______ A type of deed that conveys title without imposing any future title liability on the grantor
R. Quitclaim deed	18. ______ IRS reporting form for commissions paid
S. HUD Form 1	19. ______ Dying with a valid will
T. Independent contractor	20. ______ IRS code that governs tax-deferred exchanges

ANSWER KEY WITH EXPLANATIONS: DIAGNOSTIC TEST

1. **(2)** The general warranty deed provides the buyer with the greatest protection. The quitclaim deed provides the buyer with the least amount of protection. A special warranty deed protects the buyer against title defects but only during the ownership period of the grantor. (104)

2. **(4)** The title transfers once the deed is delivered and accepted by the grantee. It is signed by the grantor; the grantee's name must appear on the deed, but the deed is not signed by the grantee. The deed is often notarized, and the notary attests the grantor's acknowledgement that the grantor signature is a voluntary act and that they are in fact who they say they are. The notarized signature is an attempt to keep forged documents from being recorded. (105)

3. **(1)** Obviously a sale is a voluntary alienation; all the other responses are examples of involuntary alienation. Eminent domain is the right of the government to take private property for public use or public benefit if just compensation is paid to the landowner. Escheat applies when a person dies without a will and without heirs capable of inheriting and the government then takes ownership of the abandoned property. Adverse possession is the open and notorious use of another's land under a claim of right or color of title. (104)

4. **(3)** The grantee must give constructive notice that he has an interest in the property. Constructive notice is given by recording the deed in the registrar of deeds office or by occupying the property. (105–106)

5. **(1)** A devise is a gift of real property by will. The deviser is the donor of the gifted real property, and the devisee is the recipient of the real property. (103)

6. **(4)** Title insurance does not cover liens or defects listed in the policy. (104–105)

7. **(1)** The vendor is the seller in a land contract; the vendee is the buyer. The grantee must be identified in the deed but does not have to sign it. (105)

8. **(4)** Selling and gifting property are examples of voluntary alienation. (103)

9. **(4)** *B* will have equitable title until closing, after which *B* will have legal title. (106)

10. **(4)** The seller maintains legal title and the buyer has equitable title until the closing takes place and the deed transfers to the buyer. (106)

11. **(4)** Regulation Z requires disclosure of cost in credit transactions. The Federal Fair Housing laws prohibit discrimination against groups of people identified as protected classes. GNMA functions in the secondary mortgage market. (106)

12. **(3)** Freddie Mac buys and sells mortgages in the secondary mortgage market. The FHA provides public mortgage insurance for home loans. Regulation Z requires credit cost disclosure and provides for right of rescission in certain types of credit transactions under certain conditions. (106)

13. **(3)** One of the three IRS requirements for independent contractor status is that 90 percent or more of the individual's income as a licensee must be based on sales production, not on the number of hours worked. (107)

14. **(2)** IRS rules also require brokers to report commissions paid to salespeople on IRS Form 1099 MISC. (107)

15. **(3)** Section 1031 of the IRC does not allow real estate investors to either avoid or phase out the capital gains tax; it only allows for the deferring of the tax. (108)

16. **(1)** A quitclaim deed is used to convey title without imposing any liability on the grantor to defend its quality. (104)

17. **(3)** The act must be voluntary. By the deed being signed in the presence of a notary, the recorder's office is confident that the grantor's signature has not been forged. (105)

18. **(3)** RESPA allows three (3) business days or 72 hours to receive a good faith estimate from the lender. The purpose of this legislation is to empower the consumer with accurate and timely information about the actual settlement costs they are expected to pay at closing. (106)

TEST SCORE

TRANSFER OF PROPERTY			
Rating	**Range**	**Your Score**	
Good = 80% to 100%	14–18	Total Number	18
Fair = 70% to 79%	12–13	Total Wrong	–
Needs improvement = Lower than 70%	11 or less	Total Right	

Passing Requirement: 12 or Better

ANSWER KEY: MATCHING QUIZ

1. I
2. J
3. F
4. H
5. C
6. K
7. A
8. B
9. G
10. E
11. N
12. Q
13. S
14. L
15. D
16. T
17. R
18. P
19. M
20. O

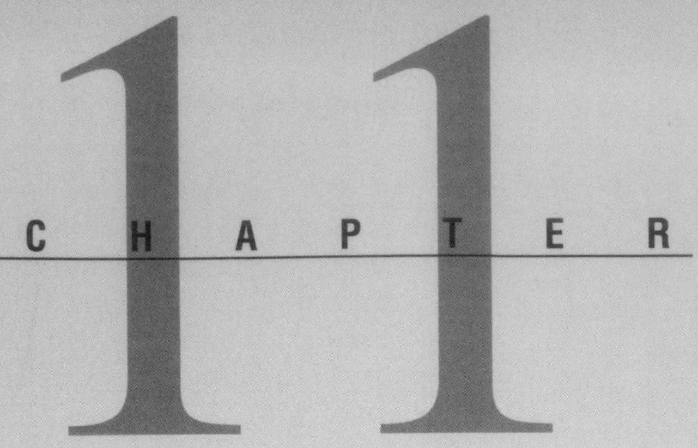

Practice of Real Estate

OUTLINE OF CONCEPTS

I. **Federal Fair Housing Laws**
   A. Civil Rights Act of 1866—prohibits racial discrimination in the buying, renting, selling, holding, or conveying of real and personal property.
   B. Federal Fair Housing Act of 1968—provides that it is unlawful to discriminate on the basis of race, color, religion, or national origin when selling or leasing residential property.
      1. In 1974, the Housing and Community Development Act added gender to the list of protected classes.
   C. An amendment to the federal fair housing laws went into effect in March 1989 adding handicap and familial status to the list of protected classes and giving the U.S. Department of Housing and Urban Development (HUD) more enforcement authority.
      1. The new amendment defines familial status as one or more individuals who have not reached the age of 18 being domiciled with a parent or another person who has or is seeking legal custody.
         a. A person who is pregnant also is included in the definition of *familial status.*
         b. All properties must be made available under the same terms and conditions as available to all other persons unless a property meets the standards for exemption as "housing for older persons."
      2. The new amendment defines disability as a physical or mental impairment that substantially limits one or more of a person's major life activities.
         a. A definition of *disability* does not include the current illegal use of or addiction to a controlled substance.
         b. Persons who have AIDS are protected under the handicapped classification as are persons in an addiction recovery program.
         c. Persons renting a dwelling are required to permit handicapped persons to make modifications of existing premises at their

own expense, if these modifications are necessary to afford full enjoyment of the premises.

d. In a rental property situation, a landlord may condition the agreement to allow modifications upon an agreement to restore the interior of the premises to the premodification condition. (It is a legitimate landlord action to limit occupancy based on honest square footage limits.)
e. There are a number of accessibility and usability requirements covering certain types of newly constructed residential buildings that must be met under federal law; access is required for common-use and public areas of the building as well as adaptive and accessible design for the interior of the dwelling units.
f. A licensee may not disclose to a seller or landlord that a prospective buyer or tenant is a member of a protected class.
g. Alcoholics and drug addicts who have been diagnosed, treated, and are not currently addicted are protected under federal fair housing laws; they are considered to have a disability. However, convicted drug dealers are not covered under any condition.
h. People diagnosed as mentally ill are also protected under the federal laws.
    (1) Mentally ill people do not have to be currently receiving treatment to be protected under the law.
    (2) If a mentally ill tenant is behaving inappropriately and reasonable action such as counseling has not solved the problem, the tenant may be evicted. In other words, a landlord does not have to tolerate such behavior by a mentally ill tenant.

3. Types of illegal activity under familial status include
    a. Charging higher security deposits.
    b. Segregating families within buildings.
    c. Segregating families in certain buildings.
    d. Maintaining "adults-only" complexes that do not constitute housing for older adults, which will be hereinafter defined shortly.
4. Types of illegal activity under provisions for the handicapped include
    a. Refusal to permit reasonable modifications that are necessary for the full enjoyment at the renter's expense.
    b. Refusal to make reasonable accommodations in rules, policies, practices, or services.
    c. Failure to design and construct for first occupancy, as of March 1991, an accessible route into and through a dwelling.
5. The 1988 amendments also provide that certain properties may be restricted for occupancy by the elderly.
    a. The amendments provide an exemption from the familial status protection for housing intended for or occupied solely by persons 62 years of age or older or housing intended for or

occupied by at least one person 55 years of age or older per unit.

   b. Properties complying with the "55-or-older" exemption must have at least 80 percent of the units occupied by at least one individual who is 55 years of age or older.
   c. Exemption properties also must publish policies and procedures that demonstrate the intent to provide housing for these individuals.

6. The 1988 amendments do not require that housing be made available to
   a. Individuals whose tenancy would constitute a direct threat to the health or safety of other individuals or that would result in substantial physical damage to the property of others.
   b. Individuals who have been convicted of the illegal manufacture or distribution of controlled substances.
7. The 1988 amendments also made significant changes to the enforcement mechanisms under the Federal Fair Housing Act of 1968, including
   a. Authorizing administrative law judges to award both economic and noneconomic damages, injunctive relief, and reasonable attorney fees and to impose civil penalties against violators of the act.
   b. Expanding the statute of limitations for initiating administrative proceedings from 180 days to one year after the alleged discriminatory housing practice.
   c. Authorizing administrative law judges within HUD to hold contested case hearings.
   d. Requiring HUD to proceed with cases on behalf of any person alleging that she or he has been the victim of housing discrimination, regardless of whether the alleged victim provides his or her own legal counsel.
8. Remedies under the new amendments include
   a. A civil penalty against the respondent, not exceeding $10,000 for the first offense.
   b. A penalty not exceeding $25,000, if another offense was committed within the past five years.
   c. A penalty not exceeding $50,000, if two or more discriminatory practices have been found in the past seven years.
   d. An order for "appropriate" relief that may include actual damages, injunctive relief, and "other equitable relief."
   e. A recommendation for disciplinary action against a named respondent whose licensure by a governmental agency is related to the complaint (including license suspension or revocation).
9. Other prohibited discriminatory acts include
   a. Refusing to sell, rent, or negotiate with any person as a means of discrimination.
   b. Changing terms for different individuals as a means of discrimination.
   c. Making discriminatory advertising statements.
   d. Representing that a property is unavailable as a means of discrimination.

e. Blockbusting—making a profit by inducing owners to sell because of the prospective entry of minorities into the neighborhood.
f. Redlining—discriminatory denial of loans or insurance to people in selected areas, regardless of their qualifications.
g. Steering—leading prospective homebuyers to specific areas or avoiding specific areas either to maintain or to change the character of an area.
h. Denying membership in a multiple-listing service (MLS) or related groups as a means of discrimination.

10. Exemptions from the law
    a. Sale or rental of a single-family home if the home is owned by a person who does not own more than three such homes at one time and if certain conditions exist:
        (1) A broker is not used.
        (2) Discriminatory advertising is not used.
        (3) If the owner is not currently living in the home or was not the most recent occupant, only one such exempt sale has been made within any two-year period.
    b. Rental rooms or units in an owner-occupied one-family to four-family dwelling.
    c. Dwelling units owned by religious organizations may be restricted to persons of the same religion if membership is not restricted on the basis of race, color, sex (or gender), national origin, disability, or familial status.
    d. Lodgings of a private club may be restricted to members as long as the lodgings are not operated commercially.

D. Equal Housing Poster—the 1974 amendment to the 1968 Federal Fair Housing Act requires that the Equal Housing Opportunity logo (poster) be posted with the agent's license.

E. Federal Equal Credit Opportunity Act—prohibits discrimination against credit applicants on the basis of race, color, religion, national origin, sex, marital status, age (if the applicant is of legal age), or dependency on public assistance; it requires that all rejected credit applicants be informed, in writing, of the reasons for credit denial within 30 days.

II. Americans with Disabilities Act (ADA)

A. This 1990 law affects real estate licensees because it addresses the rights of individuals with disabilities in employment and public accommodations.

B. The ADA provides for the employment of qualified job applicants regardless of their disabilities.

C. Any employer with 15 or more employees as of July 26, 1994 must adopt nondiscriminatory employment procedures and make reasonable accommodations to enable an individual with a disability to perform in her or his employment.

D. The ADA (Title III) states that individuals with disabilities have the right to full and equal access to businesses and public services; thus, building owners and managers must be sure that obstacles restricting those rights are eliminated.

E. The ADA also provides comprehensive guidance for making public facilities accessible.
F. The law seeks to protect property owners from incurring burdensome expense to extensively retrofit an existing building by recommending reasonable achievable accommodations that will accomplish the purpose of providing access to the facility and services.
G. Because it costs less to incorporate accessible features in the design than to retrofit, new construction, including remodeling, must meet higher standards, being readily accessible and usable.
H. Types of alterations that might be made to public facilities and services include
   1. Attaching grab bars to a restroom stall.
   2. Providing automatic-entry doors.
   3. Adjusting the height of a pay telephone to make it accessible to a person in a wheelchair.
   4. Converting information on real estate listings to large-print or audio format.
I. The ADA provides for enforcement by allowing several remedies for a person who is discriminated against, including
   1. A temporary or permanent injunction.
   2. The court may grant any equitable relief that the court considers appropriate.
   3. A civil penalty of up to $50,000 may be assessed for a first violation of the law, and a penalty of up to $100,000 may be assessed for any subsequent violation.

III. Truth-in-Lending Law

A. Regulation Z
   1. Disclosure requirements
      a. Require disclosure of cost in credit transactions.
      b. Customer has the right to rescind in some types of credit transactions under certain conditions, for example, a second mortgage.
   2. Coverage of Regulation Z
      a. Loans to individuals are covered for all real estate credit transactions for personal, family, and household purposes, regardless of the amount involved.
      b. Loans to individuals are covered for non–real-estate credit transactions for personal, family, and household purposes up to $25,000.
   3. Agreements not covered
      a. Personal property credit transactions for amounts over $25,000
      b. Real estate purchase agreements
      c. Business or commercial loans
      d. Loans with four or fewer installments
      e. Loans made without interest charges
      f. Loans to government agencies
      g. Assumptions with no change in terms
      h. Agricultural loans for amounts over $25,000
   4. Requirements of Regulation Z regarding finance charges
      a. All finance charges as well as the true annual interest rate must be disclosed to the customer before the transaction is completed.

   b. Finance charges must include interest, loan fees, points, service charges, finder's fees, credit fees, and property and credit insurance.
   c. The finance charge must be stated as the Annual Percentage Rate (APR).
5. Requirements of Regulation Z regarding liens on residences
   a. A "cooling off" period is required when liens will be placed on a principal residence; the borrower has the right to rescind the transaction up to midnight of the third business day following the transaction or until delivery of the disclosure statement, whichever is later.
   b. The right to rescind does not apply to loans to finance the purchase or initial construction of a house.
6. Advertising
   a. Regulation Z does not require brokers to advertise credit terms; if lenders advertise some credit details; however, they must fully disclose the terms.
   b. Specific credit terms (trigger terms) may not be advertised unless the ad includes all of the information below in c.
   c. Full disclosure of terms
      (1) Amount of down payment
      (2) Amount of loan or cash price
      (3) Finance charges as annual percentage rate
      (4) Number, amount, and due dates of payments
      (5) Total of all payments except where advertisement relates to first mortgage
7. Regulation Z is administered by the Federal Trade Commission (FTC) and promulgated by the Federal Reserve System (FRS).
8. Penalties for noncompliance
   a. Violation of an administration order enforcing Regulation Z is $10,000 for each day the violation continues.
   b. Engaging in an unfair or deceptive practice may result in the imposition of a fine of up to $10,000.
   c. A creditor may be liable to a consumer for twice the amount of the finance charge, from a minimum of $100 to a maximum of $1,000, plus court costs, attorney's fees, and any actual damages.
   d. Willful violation constitutes a misdemeanor and is punishable by a fine of up to $5,000 or one year's imprisonment or both.

B. Agent Supervision (See Chapter 14 on Brokerage Management)

DIAGNOSTIC TEST

1. You are receiving a mortgage from your local bank. Regulation Z requires your bank to disclose
   1. your right to rescind within three business days.
   2. the amount of your closing costs.
   3. the annual percentage rate.
   4. penalties to the bank if they do not comply with the laws.
2. The federal fair housing laws prohibit discrimination on the basis of
   1. sexual orientation.
   2. political beliefs.
   3. marital status.
   4. sex.
3. Persuading someone to sell by telling her or him that minorities are moving into the neighborhood is illegal and is called
   1. redlining.
   2. blockbusting.
   3. testing.
   4. teering.
4. Which of the following is exempted from the federal fair housing laws?
   1. Rental of rooms in an owner-occupied five-family dwelling
   2. Rental of an owner-occupied five-family dwelling
   3. Rental of a single-family home when a broker is used
   4. Lodgings of a private club when the lodgings are not operated commercially
5. The practice of channeling potential buyers of one race into one area and potential buyers of another race into another area is known as
   1. canvassing.
   2. blockbusting.
   3. redlining.
   4. steering.
6. A real estate broker may
   1. refuse to rent to a qualified minority person.
   2. solicit listings in a minority neighborhood.
   3. refuse to negotiate with a minority person.
   4. change the terms of sale for a minority person.
7. The federal fair housing laws prohibit which of the following types of private housing?
   1. A Lutheran organization giving preference to its members in renting
   2. A Norwegian advertising his house for "Norwegians only"
   3. The Elks Club operating a rooming house on a nonprofit basis
   4. A Masonic Lodge operating a rooming house when the lodgings are not operated commercially
8. Which of the following categories is NOT protected against discrimination under the federal fair housing laws?
   1. Religion
   2. Familial status
   3. Disabled status
   4. Lawful source of income
9. The denial of a loan by a lender would NOT be a violation of federal fair housing laws if it were based on
   1. lack of income.
   2. sex.
   3. age.
   4. marital status.
10. Which of the following laws provides comprehensive guidance for making public facilities accessible?
    1. RESPA
    2. Regulation Z
    3. Federal fair housing laws
    4. Americans with Disabilities Act (ADA)
11. Which of the following activities would be legal under the familial status category of the federal fair housing laws?
    1. Charging higher rents for people with pets
    2. Charging higher security deposits for families with children
    3. Segregating families within buildings
    4. Segregating families in certain buildings

12. Which of the following agreements would be covered by Regulation Z?
    1. A personal property credit transaction for $30,000
    2. A commercial loan
    3. An agricultural loan for $15,000
    4. A loan to an individual for a personal property credit transaction for $20,000

13. Which of the following finance charges would NOT be used by a bank to calculate the annual percentage rate for disclosure to the borrower?
    1. Loan fees
    2. Credit fees
    3. Home inspection fees
    4. Service charges

14. "Trigger terms" relates to
    1. the ADA.
    2. federal fair housing laws.
    3. RESPA.
    4. Regulation Z.

15. The right of rescission provided by Regulation Z is for a time period of
    1. two business days following the transaction or until delivery of the disclosure statement, whichever is later.
    2. three business days following the transaction or until delivery of the disclosure statement, whichever is later.
    3. four business days following the transaction or until delivery of the disclosure statement, whichever is later.
    4. five business days following the transaction or until delivery of the disclosure statement, whichever is later.

16. The Americans with Disabilities Act became law in
    1. 1968.
    2. 1989.
    3. 1990.
    4. 1994.

17. Converting information on a real estate listing to large-print or audio format would be a response to
    1. federal fair housing laws.
    2. the Americans with Disabilities Act.
    3. Regulation Z.
    4. RESPA.

18. The Americans with Disabilities Act (ADA) would NOT require which of the following alterations to be made to public facilities and services?
    1. Attaching grab bars to a restroom stall
    2. Providing automatic entry doors
    3. Providing an automatic sprinkler system
    4. Converting real estate listing information to large print or audio format

19. Which of the following rental practices would be legal under federal fair housing laws?
    1. A property manager discloses to the landlord that a prospective tenant is a minority
    2. A property manager charges a mother and her six-year-old son a higher security deposit than another woman with no children
    3. A rental agent refuses to rent an apartment to a person who is a convicted drug dealer
    4. A property manager refuses to rent to a blind man because he has a seeing-eye dog and the property does not allow dogs.

20. The Civil Rights Act of 1866 prohibits discrimination in housing on the basis of
    1. religion.
    2. race.
    3. sex.
    4. handicap

21. Which of the following is not a protected class under the Federal Equal Credit Opportunity Act?
    1. Marital status
    2. Age
    3. Sexual orientation
    4. Dependency on public assistance

22. Disclosure of cost in a credit transaction is required by
    1. RESPA.
    2. Regulation Z.
    3. the Federal Equal Credit Opportunity Act.
    4. the 1968 Federal Fair Housing Act.

23. According to the Federal Equal Credit Opportunity Act, a rejected credit applicant must be informed, in writing, of the reason for credit denial within
    1. 3 days.
    2. 10 days.
    3. 30 days.
    4. 90 days.

24. A second violation of the Americans with Disabilities Act can result in a civil penalty of up to
    1. $10,000.
    2. $25,000.
    3. $50,000.
    4. $100,000.

25. Regulation Z is administered by the
    1. Federal Trade Commission.
    2. Department of Housing and Urban Development.
    3. Federal Reserve System.
    4. Federal Housing Administration.

26. A landlord allowed a tenant confined to a wheelchair to make several minor physical changes to an apartment. These changes are called
    1. disability accomodations.
    2. familial accomodations.
    3. trade fixture modifications.
    4. reasonable accommodations or modifications.

27. Which of the following is a legitimate landlord action under fair housing's familial status?
    1. Charging a higher security deposit for families with children
    2. Segregating families within a building
    3. Segregating families into certain buildings
    4. Limiting occupancy based on honest square footage limits

28. Most states require real estate licenses to be conspicuously displayed by their broker. What else is the broker of a real estate office required to conspicuously display?
    1. EHO poster
    2. Listings
    3. Civil Rights Act of 1866
    4. ECOA legislation

MATCHING QUIZ

The column on the right contains brief memory links to important terms in Chapter 11.
Write the letter of the matching term on the appropriate line.

A. Civil Rights Act of 1866	1. ______ The Federal Fair Housing Act of 1968
B. HUD	2. ______ Prohibits property discrimination based on race
C. AIDS	3. ______ Inducing owners to sell because of entry of minorities into neighborhoods
D. Reasonable	4. ______ American legislation that gives disabled people accommodations equal employment rights
E. Familial status	5. ______ Protected under HUD's disability definition of the Fair Housing Act
F. Title VIII	6. ______ Protected class that includes persons who are pregnant
G. EHO poster	7. ______ Segregating families with children to certain buildings or floors within a building
H. 62 years and older	8. ______ Fair housing enforcement agency
I. Blockbusting	9. ______ An authorized discrimination age for senior housing exempt from familial status
J. Redlining	10. ______ Intentionally not loaning money in transition neighborhoods
K. Steering	11. ______ Lenders must use this to clearly state for comparative purposes the cost of their loans
L. Federal Trade Commission	12. ______ Legislation that requires disclosure for the cost of credit
M. ECOA	13. ______ Showing minorities only targeted neighborhoods rather than the entire market
N. ADA	14. ______ Tenant granted permission to put in bathroom grab bars and raise electrical outlets
O. Regulation Z	15. ______ Legislation protecting against discrimination in lending
P. Discrimination	16. ______ Required to be conspicuously displayed in real estate, appraising, and lender offices
Q. Annual Percentage Rate	17. ______ Under certain conditions these organizations may be allowed to discriminate
R. Religious organizations	18. ______ Agency that enforces Regulation Z

ANSWER KEY WITH EXPLANATIONS: DIAGNOSTIC TEST

1. **(3)** Regulation Z requires lenders to inform borrowers of the true cost of credit, which includes the Annual Percentage Rate (APR). Kickbacks or referral fees are prohibited. (118–119)
2. **(4)** Some states and local governments prohibit discrimination on the basis of sexual orientation, political beliefs, and marital status. (114)
3. **(2)** Redlining is denying loans or insurance to people in selected neighborhoods regardless of their qualifications. Testing is done to enforce the law, and steering restricts freedom of choice. (116)
4. **(4)** The exemption applies to up to four units of owner-occupied rental housing. (117)
5. **(4)** Canvassing involves personal solicitation of opinions or sentiments which is generally legal. Blockbusting and redlining were discussed above and are illegal.(116)
6. **(2)** Discrimination is treating people differently when they are members of a protected class. (116–117)
7. **(2)** Religious organizations and private clubs may discriminate under certain circumstances. An individual homeowner must comply with certain conditions to be exempt from federal fair housing laws. (117)
8. **(4)** Nevertheless, lawful source of income is a protected class in some states. The Federal Equal Credit Opportunity Act also protects borrowers in a similar manner. (114)
9. **(1)** Lack of income is an acceptable reason for denying a loan, provided all lawful sources of income are considered as discussed above. (117)
10. **(4)** Regulation Z is the Truth-in-Lending Law. Ginnie Mae functions in the secondary mortgage market. Federal fair housing law does not deal with accessibility to public facilities. (117–118)
11. **(1)** Since pets are not a protected class, landlords may charge higher rents for renters with pets. (115)
12. **(4)** A loan to an individual for a personal property credit transaction for no more than $25,000 would be covered by Regulation Z. (118–119)
13. **(3)** Home inspection fees are not related to the finance charges. (119)
14. **(4)** Brokers advertising credit terms must fully disclose terms of credit if they use "trigger terms." (119)
15. **(2)** It is important to emphasize that the right of rescission does not apply to loans to finance the purchase or initial construction of a house. (119)
16. **(3)** Moreover, an amendment to the 1968 Federal Fair Housing Act to add handicapped and familial status as protected classes became effective in 1988. (117)
17. **(2)** The 1968 Federal Fair Housing Act includes handicapped as a protected class, but the specific measures are identified in the ADA. Regulation Z requires disclosure of cost in a credit transaction. RESPA is aimed at protecting consumers from abusive lending practices. (117–118)
18. **(3)** The fire codes would require the providing of an automatic sprinkler system. (117–118)
19. **(3)** Convicted drug dealers are never protected under federal fair housing laws. (115)
20. **(2)** The Civil Rights Act of 1866 makes clear that there is no situation in which racial discrimination may be practiced. (114)
21. **(3)** Sexual orientation is a protected class in nine states; however, it is not protected under federal housing or lending laws. (117)

22. **(2)** RESPA provides consumer protection with regard to closing procedures and costs. The Federal Equal Credit Opportunity Act prohibits credit providers from discriminating against members of certain protected classes. The 1968 Federal Fair Housing Act prohibits discrimination in the sale or rental of housing. (118–119)

23. **(3)** The Federal Equal Credit Opportunity Act also states that a borrower is entitled to a copy of the appraisal report, paid for by the borrowers. (117)

24. **(4)** A penalty of up to $100,000 may be assessed for any subsequent violation of the Americans with Disabilities Act. (118)

25. **(1)** Regulation Z is promulgated by the Federal Reserve System. (118–119)

26. **(4)** Under federal law the tenant is allowed (at the tenant's expense) to make reasonable modifications. (117–118)

27. **(4)** The landlord is allowed to limited the number of people in a unit based on square footage. (115)

28. **(1)** The Equal Housing Opportunity poster with the logo of an equals sign inside the outline of a house. (117)

TEST SCORE

PRACTICE OF REAL ESTATE			
Rating	**Range**	**Your Score**	
Good = 80% to 100%	22–28	Total Number	28
Fair = 70% to 79%	20–21	Total Wrong	–
Needs improvement = Lower than 70%	19 or less	Total Right	

Passing Requirement: 20 or Better

ANSWER KEY: MATCHING QUIZ

1. F
2. A
3. I
4. N
5. C
6. E
7. P
8. B
9. H
10. J
11. Q
12. O
13. K
14. D
15. M
16. G
17. R
18. L

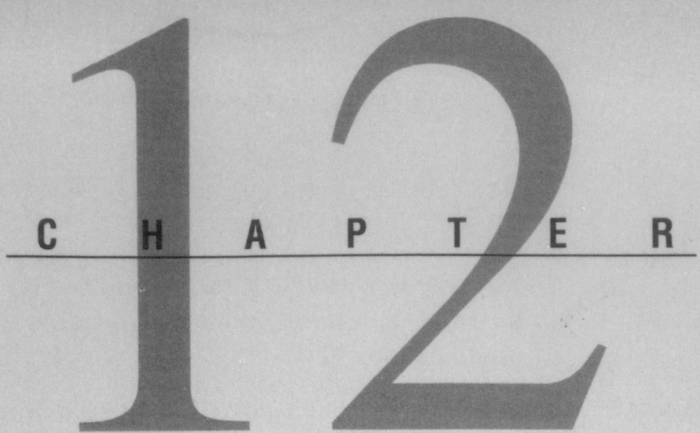

Real Estate Mathematics Review

This review is designed to familiarize you with some basic mathematical formulas that are used most frequently in the computations required on state licensing examinations. These same computations also are important in day-to-day real estate transactions. If you think you need additional help in working these problems, you may want to order a copy of *Mastering Real Estate Mathematics,* 7th edition, by Ralph Tamper (Chicago: Dearborn™ Real Estate Education, 2002).

PERCENTAGES

Most calculators have a key with a % sign on it called the percent key. This key converts percentages into decimals for calculation purposes. For example, if you need to compute a 6% commission on a $200,000 sale, enter $200,000 and then multiply (×) it by 6 and touch the % key to compute the commission. $200,000 × 6% = $12,000.

Many real estate computations are based on the calculations of percentages. A percentage expresses a portion of a whole (or total) that is expressed as 100. For example, 50 percent means 50 parts of the 100 parts constituting the whole. Percentages greater than 100 percent contain more than one whole unit. Thus, 163 percent is one whole plus 63 parts of another whole. Remember that a whole is always thought of as equaling 100 percent.

60% = 0.60   7% = 0.07   175% = 1.75

To express a percentage as a fraction, place the percentage over 100. For example:

$$50\% = \frac{50}{100}$$

These fractions then may be reduced to make working the problem easier. To reduce a fraction, determine the highest number that will divide both the numerator and denominator evenly—that is, with no remainder—then divide each of them by that number. For example:

25/100 = 1/4 (both numbers are divided by 25)

49/63 = 7/9 (both numbers are divided by 7)

- A broker is to receive a 7 percent commission on the sale of a $50,000 house. What will the broker's commission be?

$$0.07 \times \$50{,}000 = \$3{,}500 \text{ broker's commission}$$

Percentage problems contain three elements: *percentage, total,* and *part.* To *determine a specific percentage of a total,* multiply the percentage by the whole. This is illustrated by the following formula:

$$\text{percent} \times \text{total} = \text{part}$$
$$5\% \times 200 = 10$$

This formula is used in calculating mortgage loan interest, brokers' commissions, loan origination fees, discount points, the amount of earnest money deposits, and income on capital investment.

A variation or inversion on the percentage formula is used to find the total amount when the part and percentage are known. Therefore:

$$\text{total} = \frac{\text{part}}{\text{percentage}}$$

- A broker received a $3,600 commission for the sale of a house. The broker's commission was 6 percent of the total sales price. What was the total sales price of this house?

$$\text{total sales price} = \frac{\$3{,}600}{0.06} = \$60{,}000$$

Simplified, the equation looks like this: $3,600 = 6% of x. To solve this equation both sides are divided by 6% to cancel the 6% out of the right side of the equation. The result looks like this: $3,600 divided by 6% OR .06 = (6% ÷ 6%) x. So *$3,600 divided by 6% or .06 = $60,000.*

Another way of looking at this same problem is to translate the algebraic formula into a simple sentence. **Divide any part by its % of the total and you'll find the total number.**

We know that $3,600 is 6% of the total. Therefore, if that number ($3,600) is divided by *6% or .06* then the resulting number must be the total. The solution is figured like this: $3,600 ÷ *6% or .06* = $60,000.

Lets try another example. Statistically, a move-up buyer's next home is (on the average) 52% higher than his or her current home. If a seller is asking $200,000, what is the estimated value of a potential buyer's current home?

What do we know? We know that $200,000 represents both the value of the buyer's current home and 52% more. Therefore, the $200,000 listed property is 152% of the unknown total. Accordingly, the part ($200,000) divided by its percentage of total *(152% or 1.52)* will result in the total. *$200,000 ÷ 152% = $131,579.* Thus, for target marketing purposes the listing agent should target market in a $138,000 neighborhood in order to find prospective move-up buyers.

FIGURE 12.1

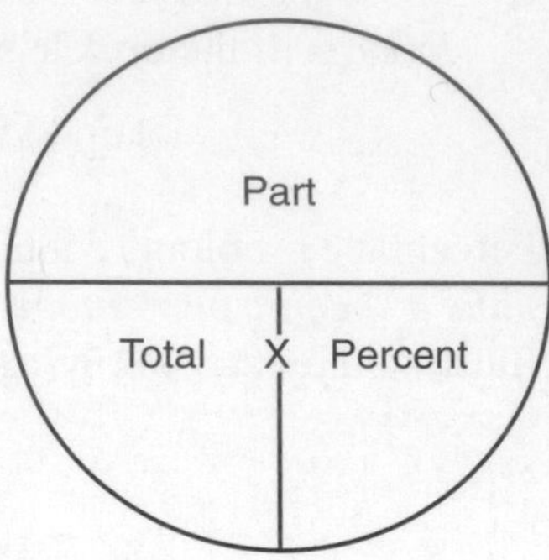

This formula is used in computing the total mortgage loan principal still due if the monthly payment and interest rate are known. It also is used to calculate (1) the total sales price when the amount and percentage of commission or earnest money deposit is known, (2) the interest due if the monthly payment and interest rate are known, and (3) the market value of property if the assessed value and the ratio (percentage) of assessed value to market value are known.

To determine the percent when the amounts of the part and the total are known:

$$\text{percent} = \frac{\text{part}}{\text{total}}$$

This formula may be used to determine the tax rate when the taxes and assessed value are known or the commission rate if the sales price and commission amount are known.

An easy way to remember the *formula* (or part, percent, and total) is with the diagram in Figure 12.1. First draw the circle and divide it in half; then divide the bottom half in half. Put the term *part* in the top half of the circle and the other two terms in the two bottom portions.

Next, substitute the known amounts for the words that represent those amounts. The word that remains represents the element you are solving for. If the terms for which you have figures are below the line that divides the entire circle in half, multiply them to find the third element; if one figure is above the other, divide the top term by the bottom one.

RATES

Property taxes, transfer taxes, and insurance premiums usually are expressed as rates. A rate is expressed as cost per unit; for example, in a certain county tax is computed at the rate of $50 per $1,000 of assessed value. The formula *for computing rates* follows:

$$\frac{\text{value}}{\text{unit}} \times \text{rate per unit} = \text{total}$$

- A house assessed at \$50,000 is taxed at an annual rate of \$25 per \$1,000 assessed valuation. What is the yearly tax?

  Step 1 \$50,000 ÷ 1,000 = 50
  Step 2 \$50 × \$25 = \$1,250 total annual tax

AREA AND VOLUME

Area

People in the real estate profession must know how to compute the area of a parcel of land or to figure the amount of living area in a house. *To compute the area of a square or rectangular parcel,* use this formula:

$$\text{area} = \text{length} \times \text{width } (A = l \times w)$$

- What is the area of a rectangular lot 200 feet long by 100 feet wide?

$$200' \times 100' = 20{,}000 \text{ square feet}$$

Area is always expressed in square units.

To compute the width of a rectangular parcel, use this formula:

$$\text{width} = \frac{\text{area}}{\text{length}}$$

- What is the length of a rectangular lot that measures 40 feet wide and has an area of 3,600 square feet?

$$\frac{3{,}600 \text{ sq. ft.}}{40 \text{ ft.}} = 90 \text{ feet}$$

To compute the amount of surface in a triangular-shaped area, use one of these formulas:

$$\text{area} = 1/2 \text{ (base} \times \text{ height) } [A = 1/2 \text{ (b} \times \text{h)}]$$

or

$$\text{area} = \text{(1/2 base)} \times \text{height } [A = (1/2 \text{ b}) \times \text{h}]$$

The part of an equation enclosed in parentheses is always computed before any other part of the equation. The base of a triangle is the bottom, the side on which the triangle rests. The height is an imaginary line extending from the point (or vertex) of the uppermost angle straight down (perpendicular) to the base (see Figure 12.2).

FIGURE 12.2

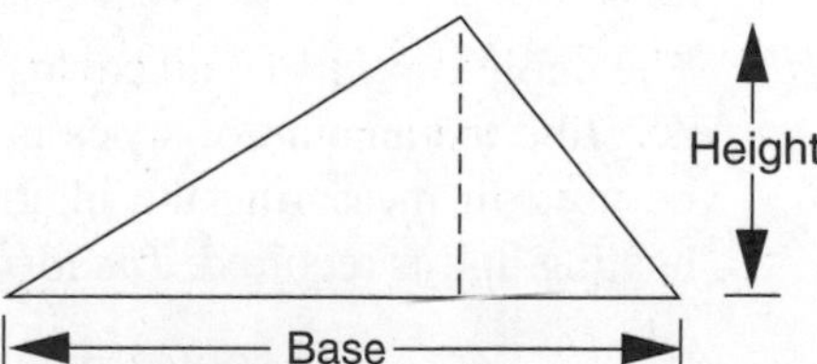

- A triangle has a base of 50 feet and a height of 30 feet. What is the area?

$$1/2\ (50' \times 30') = \text{area in square feet}$$
$$1/2\ (1{,}500) = 750 \text{ square feet}$$
or
$$50 \div 2 = 25 \times 30 = 750 \text{ square feet}$$

To compute the area of an irregular room or parcel of land, divide the shape into regular rectangles, squares, or triangles. Next, compute the area of each regular figure and add the areas together to obtain the total area.

- Compute the area in the hallway in Figure 12.3:

FIGURE 12.3

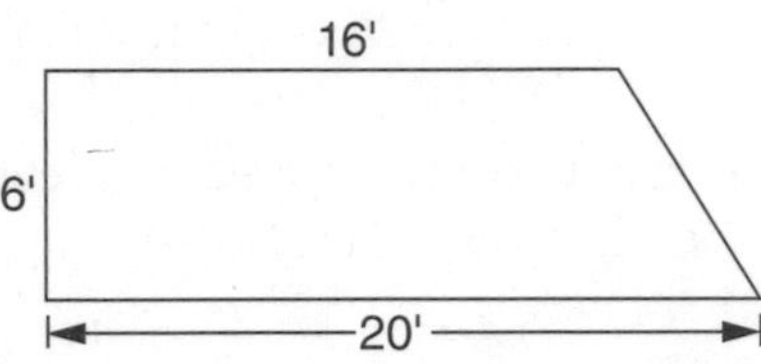

First, make a rectangle and a triangle by drawing a single line through the figure as shown in Figure 12.4.

FIGURE 12.4

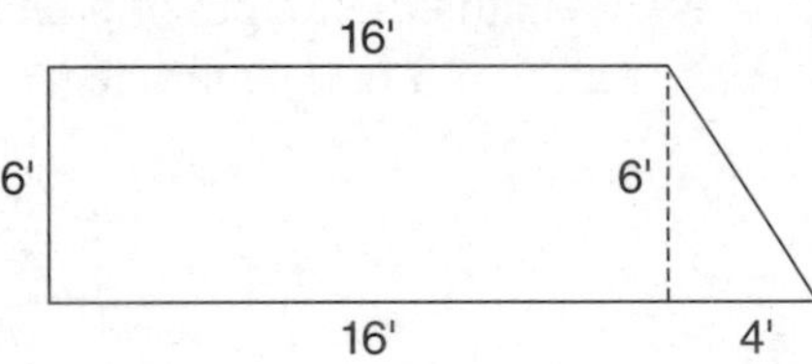

Compute the area of the rectangle:

area = length × width   16' × 6' = 96 square feet

Compute the area of the triangle:

area = 1/2 (base × height) = 1/2 (4' × 6') – 1/2 (24) = 12 square feet

Add the two areas:

96 + 12 = 108 square feet total area

Volume

The cubic capacity of an enclosed space is expressed as volume. Volume is used to describe the amount of space in any three-dimensional area. For example, it would be used in measuring the interior airspace of a room to determine what capacity heating unit is required. *The formula for computing cubic or rectangular volume* is

volume = length × width × height *(V = lwh)*

FIGURE 12.5

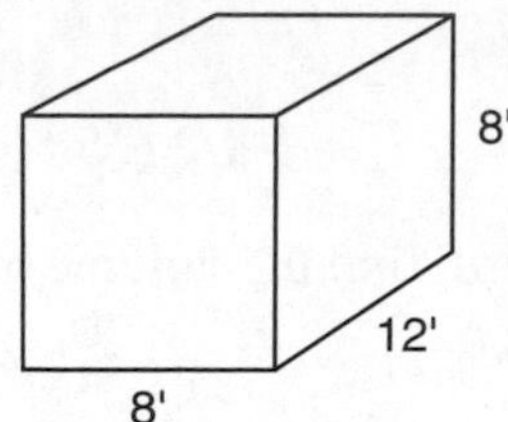

■ The bedroom of a house is 12 feet long and 8 feet wide and has a ceiling height of 8 feet (Figure 12.5). How many cubic feet does the room contain?

$$8' \times 12' \times 8' = 768 \text{ cubic feet}$$

Volume is always expressed in cubic units.

This next section may not be test material for salespersons but qualifies as required knowledge for brokers.

To compute the volume of a triangular space, such as the airspace in a house with a peaked roof, use the following two formulas:

$$V = lwh$$

and

volume = 1/2 (base × height × width) [V = 1/2 (bhw)]

What is the volume of airspace in the house shown in Figure 12.6?

FIGURE 12.6

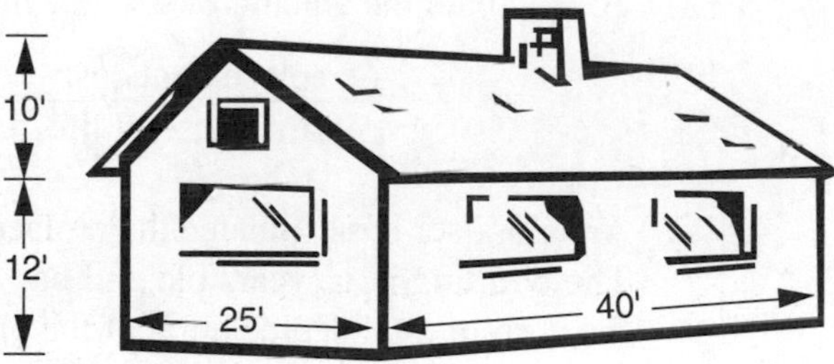

First, divide the house into two shapes, rectangular and triangular, as shown in Figure 12.7:

FIGURE 12.7

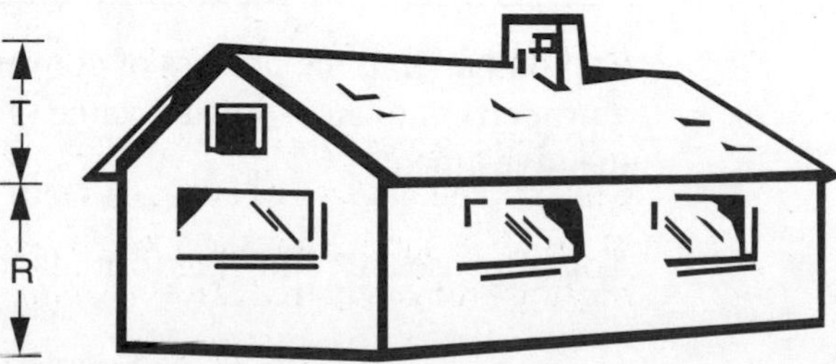

Second, find the volume of T.

volume = 1/2 (base × height × width)

1/2 (25' × 10' × 40') = 1/2 (10,000) = 5,000 cubic feet

Third, find the volume of R.

25' × 10' × 40' = 10,000 cubic feet

Finally, add volumes *T* and *R*.

5,000 + 10,000 = 15,000 cubic feet of airspace in the house

Cubic measurements of volume are used to compute the construction costs per cubic foot of a building, the amount of airspace being sold in a condominium unit, and the heating and cooling requirements for a building.

Be sure that when you compute either area or volume, all dimensions are in the same units of measure. For example, you cannot multiply two feet by six inches; you have to multiply two feet by 1/2 foot, or 24 inches by 6 inches.

DEPRECIATION

Depreciation is used in appraisal to calculate the loss of value in a building due to all causes. It is the difference in value between a new building and the existing building being appraised. It is not related to the IRS method of depreciation.

You should be familiar with the straight-line method of depreciation, which allocates the total depreciation over the useful life of a building in equal annual amounts.

To calculate the amount of straight-line depreciation use this formula:

$$\frac{\text{replacement cost}}{\text{years of useful life}} = \text{annual charge for depreciation}$$

An appraiser has estimated the replacement cost of an office building at $200,000. The building is 16 years old and has an estimated useful life of 50 years. What is the current total depreciation of the property?

$$\frac{\$200{,}000}{50} = \$4{,}000 \text{ annual depreciation charge}$$

$4,000 × 16 = $64,000 current total depreciation

CAPITALIZATION

Capitalization is the process of converting the net operating income expected from a property into an estimated value. The capitalization rate is the rate of return on the investment.

You may use the following formula to solve a capitalization problem:

$$\frac{I}{RV}$$

FIGURE 12.8

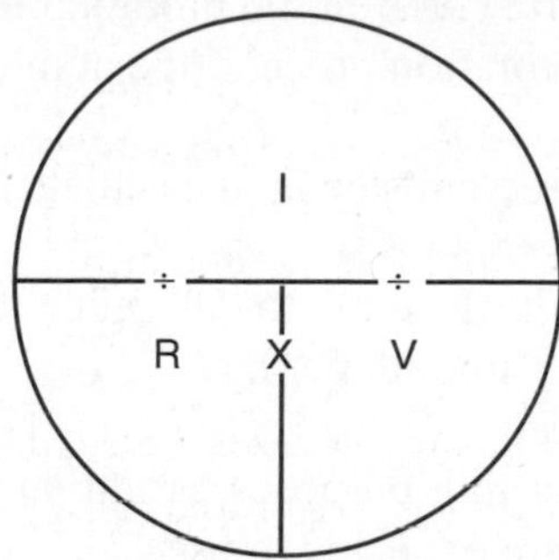

I = part or net operating income
R = capitalization rate
V = value of investment

To solve a capitalization problem, use one of the following formulas:

$$\frac{I}{R} = V \qquad \frac{I}{V} = R \qquad R \times V = I$$

What is the value of an office building expected to produce a net annual income of \$30,000, if the owner estimates that he should receive a return of 12% on his investment?

$$I \div R = V$$

$$\$30,000 \div 12\% = \$250,000 \text{ estimated value}$$

The circle formula above helps reinforce the concept.

PRORATIONS

When closing a real estate transaction, it generally is necessary to divide the financial responsibility between the buyer and seller for items such as taxes, loan interest, fuel bills, and rents. Prorations provide for an equitable distribution of income and expenses between the seller and the buyer. Accrued items such as real estate taxes are owed by the seller but will be paid at a later date by the buyer. The seller pays for accrued items by giving the buyer a credit at closing. A prepaid item—such as fuel oil that has not been used—requires a credit to the seller at closing.

Proration may be done through the day prior to closing or through the day of closing. The sales contract or custom of the area (offer to purchase) will generally determine whether the buyer or seller will pay for the actual day of closing. For example, if real estate taxes are prorated through the day of closing, the seller will pay the taxes for the day of closing.

Prorations may be calculated on either a 360-day year (12 months of 30 days each) or a 365-day year. The 365-day year requires determination of the daily charge multiplied by the actual number of days in the proration period. All prorations should be computed by carrying the division to four decimal places. The third and fourth decimal places should not be rounded off to cents until the final proration figure has been determined.

The first step in the proration process is to determine the time period involved in the proration process (the number of days charged to or through the closing date).

The second step is to calculate the dollar amount per day.

The third step is to determine the proration by multiplying the time period by the dollar amount per day.

For testing purposes, proration problems will state the number of days in a month you are expected to use.

I. General Guidelines for Prorations

A. Because property taxes are paid in arrears, the taxes are prorated through either the day prior to closing or the day of closing. The prorated tax will be credited to the buyer and debited (charged) to the seller.

B. If a buyer assumes a seller's existing loan, the balance of the loan will be credited to the buyer and debited to the seller. Because interest on the loan is paid in arrears, the amount of interest owed from the day of the last payment through the day of closing will be debited to the seller.

C. Because a water bill is prepaid, the prepaid time must be computed. The amount of this prepaid item will be debited to the buyer and credited to the seller.

D. The broker's commission is normally debited to the seller.

E. Items credited to the seller and debited to the buyer generally include
   1. The sales price
   2. Any tax and insurance reserve in the case of a buyer assuming the seller's loan
   3. Prepaid real estate taxes
   4. Any fuel oil remaining in the storage tank on the day of closing

F. Items credited to the buyer and debited to the seller include
   1. Unpaid utility bills
   2. The buyer's earnest money
   3. Tenants' security deposits and any statutory interest due thereon
   4. The unearned portion of rent collected in advance

Example
Using a 365-day year, prorate the taxes for a December 14 closing, if the annual tax bill is $1,224 and is prorated through the day of closing.
Solution
First, determine the time period during which taxes have accrued.

Jan—31 days	May—31 days	Sept—30 days
Feb—28 days	June—30 days	Oct—31 days
Mar—31 days	July—31 days	Nov—30 days
Apr—30 days	Aug—31days	Dec—14 days
		Total = 348 days

Second, divide the annual tax by the days in the year to determine the amount per day.

$1,224 ÷ 365 days = $3.3534 per day

Finally, multiply the time period by the amount per day.

$3.3534 × 348 = $1,166.99 debit to the seller and credit to the buyer (rounded)

AMORTIZATION

The majority of mortgage and deed-of-trust loans are amortized loans. Regular payments are made for up to 30 years with each payment being applied first to interest owed and the balance deducted from the principal. The amount of interest due on a specific payment date is determined by calculating the total yearly interest based on the unpaid loan balance and dividing that figure by the number of payments each year. For example, if the current outstanding loan balance is $100,000 with interest at the rate of 8 percent per year and constant payments of $769, the interest and principal due on the next payment would be calculated as shown below.

$$\$100{,}000 \times .08 = \$8{,}000$$

$$\$8{,}000 \div 12 = \$666.666 \text{ (round to \$666.67)}$$

$769.00	monthly payment
−666.67	month's interest
$102.33	month's principal

All interest due and the full amount of principal due will be paid at the end of the term.

Lenders generally use the fully amortized loan plan in which the borrower pays a constant amount that usually is monthly. Each payment is credited first to the interest due with the balance of the payment being applied to the principal amount of the loan. A prepared mortgage payment book or a mortgage factor chart is used to determine the amount of the constant payment. The mortgage factor chart indicates the amount of monthly payment per $1,000 of loan depending on the term and interest rate. The factor is multiplied by the number of thousands (and fractions thereof) of the amount being borrowed. The monthly payment (mortgage) chart is shown below.

Monthly Payment Factors (Per $1,000)

Rate	15 Years	30 Years
7.00%	$8.99	$6.65
7.25%	9.13	6.82
7.50%	9.27	6.99
7.75%	9.41	7.16
8.00%	9.56	7.34
8.25%	9.70	7.51
8.50%	9.85	7.69
8.75%	10.00	7.87
9.00%	10.15	8.05
9.25%	10.30	8.23
9.50%	10.45	8.41
9.75%	10.60	8.60
10.00%	10.75	8.78
10.25%	10.90	8.97
10.50%	11.06	9.15
10.75%	11.21	9.34
11.00%	11.37	9.53
11.25%	11.53	9.72
11.50%	11.69	9.91
11.75%	11.85	10.10
12.00%	12.01	10.29
12.25%	12.17	10.48
12.50%	12.33	10.68
12.75%	12.49	10.87
13.00%	12.66	11.07

Example

What is the monthly payment on a $60,000 loan at 9 percent for 30 years?

Solution

Refer to the monthly payment factors chart above. Move down the "Rate" column to 9%. Then move to the right to the column headed "30 years" to find the payment on a $1,000 loan ($8.05). To find the monthly payment on the $60,000 loan:

$$\text{monthly payment} = \frac{\text{amount of mortgage}}{\$1{,}000} \times \begin{array}{c}\text{payment for \$1,000 loan} \\ \text{(from monthly payment} \\ \text{factors chart)}\end{array}$$

$$\frac{\$60{,}000}{\$1{,}000} \times \$8.05 = 60 \times \$8.05 = \$483.00$$

The $483 monthly payment is for the principal and interest only. The lender might add an amount for homeowner insurance premiums and for real estate taxes.

If you know how much a borrower has available to spend on a monthly loan payment, you can use the mortgage factor chart to determine the amount of the loan that the borrower can afford.

Assume that a prospective buyer can afford $800 per month for principal and interest and the lender will make a loan for 30 years at 8 percent. To find the amount of the loan, move down column 1, "Rate," to find the interest rate; then move to the right to find where the rate and the 30-year column meet; you will find $7.34. Every $7.34 of monthly payment will support a loan of $1,000.

amount borrower has available to spend each month for
amount of loan = principal and interest = $800 ÷ $7.34 monthly
payment per $1,000

108.9918 thousands or $108,992

The mortgage factor chart also can be used to determine how much interest will be paid over the life of the loan.

Using the $800 monthly payment figure, what is the total interest paid over the life of this loan?

$800 (monthly payment) × 360 months = $288,000

$288,000 (total principal and interest)
–108,991 (amount of principal)
$179,009 (total interest paid over life of loan)

CALCULATOR FINANCING

Financial calculators allow real estate practitioners to quickly compute PI payments as well as loan amounts. If you have one, you'll notice four financial keys that symbolically represent

N = number of payments (30 years = 360 payments)
%I = percentage of interest
PMT= PI payment
PV = present value

Financial calculators require the user to enter three of the four variables, and the calculator solves the fourth. For example, in order to solve for a PMT, the user must know three variables and enter them into the appropriate keys.

Because financial calculators work with at least nine (internal) digits to the right of the decimal, they are more accurate than rate sheets that work with two digits to the right of the decimal.

Using the previous amortization problem, compute the PMT for a $108,991 loan, amortized over 30 years at 8%.

Step 1	360 is entered into the	N key
Step 2	8 is entered into the	%I key
Step 3	108,991 is entered into the	PV key
Step 4	To solve, touch the	PMT key (some calculators require that a compute key be used prior to touching the PMT key)

The solution for the PMT is $799.74

MATH REVIEW TEST

1. A broker sold a home for $62,000. The broker charged the seller a 7 percent commission and will pay 25 percent of that amount to the listing salesperson and 30 percent to the selling salesperson. What amount of commission will the listing salesperson receive from the sale of the home?
   1. $1,085
   2. $1,302
   3. $4,340
   4. None of the above

2. A man signed an agreement to purchase a home. The contract stipulated that the seller replace the damaged bedroom carpet. The carpet the buyer has chosen costs $14.95 per square yard plus $3.50 per square yard for installation. If the bedroom dimensions are as illustrated in Figure 12.9, how much will the seller have to pay for the job?
   1. $164.45
   2. $173.62
   3. $222.50
   4. $256.27

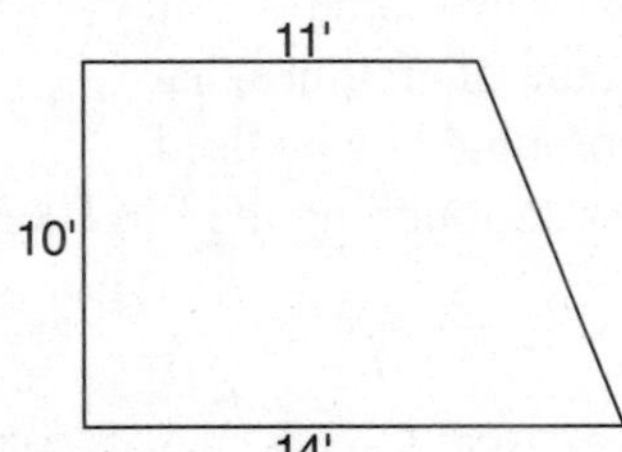

FIGURE 12.9

3. Three investors decided to pool their savings and purchase some commercial real estate for $150,000. If one invested $40,000 and the second contributed $20,000, what percentage of ownership was left for the third investor, if ownership interests were allocated on the basis of capital investment?
   1. 60 percent
   2. 40 percent
   3. 26 percent
   4. 13 percent

4. A father is curious to know how much money his son and daughter-in-law still owe on their mortgage loan. The father knows that the interest portion of their last monthly payment was $582.84. If they are paying interest at the rate of 12 percent, what was the approximate outstanding balance of their loan before the last payment was made?
   1. $48,520
   2. $58,284
   3. $63,583
   4. $69,941

5. You bought a house one year ago for $102,900. Property in your neighborhood is said to be increasing in value at a rate of 4 percent annually. If this is true, what is the current market value of your real estate?
   1. $171,600
   2. $170,160
   3. $107,188
   4. $107,016

6. You own a home valued at $75,000. Property in your area is assessed at 80 percent of its value and the local tax rate is $32.50 per $1,000. What is the amount of your monthly taxes?
   1. $1,950.00
   2. $243.75
   3. $195.00
   4. $162.50

7. You are planning to construct a patio in your backyard. An illustration of the surface area to be paved appears in Figure 12.10. If the cement is to be poured as a six-inch slab, how many cubic feet of cement will be poured in your patio?
   1. 64 cubic feet
   2. 244 cubic feet
   3. 384 cubic feet
   4. None of the above

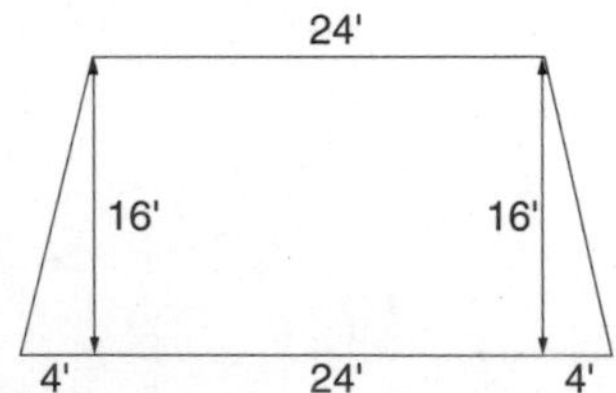

FIGURE 12.10

8. You receive a monthly salary of $500 plus 3 percent commission on all of your listings that sell and 2.5 percent on all of your sales. None of the listings you took sold last month, but you received $7,350 in salary and commission. What was the value of the property you sold?
   1. $245,000
   2. $247,000
   3. $274,000
   4. $294,000

9. A residence has proved difficult to sell. The salesperson suggests that it might sell faster if the owners enclosed a portion of the backyard with a privacy fence. If the area to be enclosed is as illustrated in Figure 12.11, how much would the fence cost at $7.25 per linear foot?
   1. $1,051.25
   2. $1,232.50
   3. $1,486.25
   4. $1,667.50

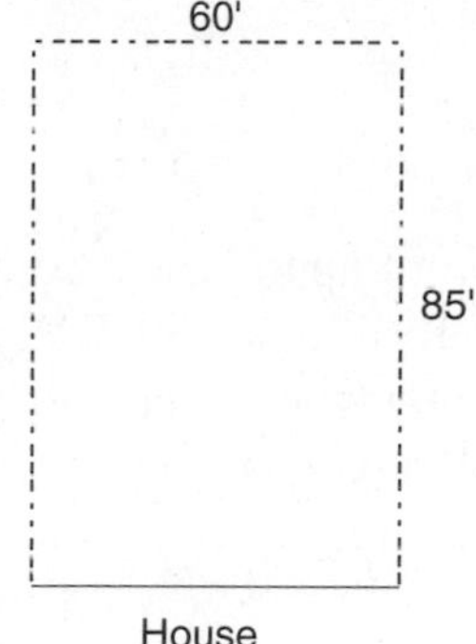

FIGURE 12.11

10. An owner leases the 24 apartments in his building for a total monthly rental of $6,000. If this figure represents a 9 percent annual return on the owner's investment, what was the original cost of the property?
    1. $800,000
    2. $720,000
    3. $666,667
    4. None of the above

For the following questions regarding closing statement prorations, base your calculations on a 30-day month. Carry all computations to three decimal places and round off after all computations have been made.

11. A sale is to be closed on April 15. Real estate taxes for the current year are $1,860 and have not been paid. What amount of the real estate tax proration will be credited to the buyer?
    1. $434
    2. $542.51
    3. $1,317.49
    4. $1,860

12. You sell your house to a married couple. They are assuming your 11 percent interest rate loan, which has a $65,400 mortgage balance. Your house payment is paid in arrears each month and you made your last payment on September 1. You expect to close on September 14. What amount of prorated interest will be debited against you at closing? (Use a 360-day year.)
    1. $279.77
    2. $319.74
    3. $419.74
    4. $599.50

13. Your brother sells a home on October 10. At the closing, the buyer assumes a three-year prepaid waste disposal contract, which is due to expire at the end of May of the next year. The original cost of the contract was $740. What proration amount will be charged to the buyer at closing? (Use a 360-day year.)
    1. $144.76
    2. $158.28
    3. $255.49
    4. None of the above

14. In a sale of residential property, real estate taxes for the current year amounted to $1,630 and already have been paid by the seller. The sale is to be closed on November 4. What is the settlement sheet entry for the tax proration?
    1. $237.19 debit to seller; $237.19 credit to buyer
    2. $253.56 credit to seller; $253.56 debit to buyer
    3. $1,476.05 debit to seller; $153.95 credit to buyer
    4. $253.56 credit to seller only

15. You are buying a house and assuming the seller's mortgage. The unpaid balance after the most recent payment (August 1, the first of the month) was $64,750. Interest is paid in arrears each month at an annual rate of 12 percent. The sale is to be closed on August 18. What is the amount of the mortgage interest proration to be credited to you at the closing?
    1. $140.72
    2. $388.49
    3. $539.19
    4. None of the above

16. A 200-acre farm is divided into house lots. The streets require one-eighth of the whole farm, and there are 220 lots. How many square feet are there in each lot?
    1. 34,650 square feet
    2. 39,784 square feet
    3. 43,916 square feet
    4. None of the above

17. The taxes of $2,140 have been paid for the entire calendar year. The seller sells on November 1. What is the amount of the remaining prepaid proration through the day prior to closing?
    1. $1,961.67
    2. $1,783.30
    3. $356.67
    4. $178.33

18. A broker received a $28,000 commission check for the sale of a house. The broker's commission was 6 percent of the total sale price. What was the total sale price of the house?
    1. $560,000
    2. $466,667
    3. $297,872
    4. 168,000

19. A seller wants to sell his house and realize $80,000 from the sale. If his only cost of selling is a 7 percent commission, what is the minimum amount he could sell his house for and realize his desired net?
    1. $85,600
    2. $86,022
    3. $87,400
    4. None of the above

20. You have been making constant payments of $623 per month on your mortgage. The balance after your last payment was $59,200. The interest rate on your mortgage is 7 percent. What will be the balance of your mortgage after your next payment?
    1. $55,056
    2. $58,577
    3. $58,922.33
    4. None of the above

21. Using the mortgage factor chart on page 135, what is the monthly payment for a $150,000 loan at 11.5 percent for 30 years?
    1. $1,429.50
    2. $1,486.50
    3. $1,525.50
    4. $1,543.50

22. Using the numbers in question 21, what is the total interest paid over the life of the loan?
    1. $150,000
    2. $385,140
    3. $533,653
    4. None of the above

23. A young couple want to purchase a home and feel that they can afford to pay $990 PI per month on a loan. They have saved enough to make a $14,000 down payment and pay closing costs. If lenders are offering 30-year loans at 8.25 percent interest, what is the maximum amount this couple can pay for a home using the loan factor of $7.51 per thousand?
    1. $131,800
    2. $141,300
    3. $145,824
    4. $155,400

24. An appraiser has estimated the replacement cost of an office building at $300,000. The building is 18 years old and has an estimated useful life of 50 years. What is the current total depreciation of the property?
    1. $96,000
    2. $102,000
    3. $108,000
    4. $114,000

25. What is the value of an apartment building that is expected to produce a net annual income of $40,000, if the owner estimates that she should receive a return of 9 percent on her investment?
    1. $444,444
    2. $500,000
    3. $571,428
    4. $666,666

26. If the current interest rate of 7% is bought down to 6½%, how much more money can someone who can afford a $1,500 PI payment borrow? (Use the amortization rate of $6.65 per thousand for 7% amortized over 30 years, and $6.32 per thousand for 6½% amortized over 30 years; and then round to the nearest dollar.)
   1. $11,778
   2. $225,564
   3. $237,342
   4. None of the above

27. How much is the PI payment on a 6%, $200,000 mortgage, amortized over 30 years using the amortization factor of 6.00?
   1. $1,200
   2. $1,800
   3. $3,333
   4. None of the above

28. On a 30-year amortized loan of $200,000, what is the principal portion of the first payment, if the interest rate is 6% and the PI payment is $1,200?
   1. $150
   2. $200
   3. $600
   4. $1,000

29. A homeowner makes a monthly PI payment of $900. Property taxes, homeowner's insurance, and private mortgage insurance add another $380 per month. What percentage of the PI payment does it take to cover the additional $380? (Round to 0.1%.)
   1. 32.2%
   2. 42.2%
   3. 52.2%
   4. 58.2%

30. A borrower makes $5,000 a month and has $750 in monthly recurring debt. If the borrower is allowed to use 36% of the monthly income minus the recurring debt, how much money is available for a house payment?
   1. $1,050
   2. $1,500
   3. $1,800
   4. $2,550

31. If a person qualifies to make a PI payment of $700, how much can he afford to borrow at 7% amortized over 30 years using a per thousand factor of 6.65? (Round to the closest dollar.)
   1. $66,500
   2. $70,000
   3. $105,263
   4. $205,263

32. A house payment is referred to as principal, interest, taxes, and
   1. recurring debt.
   2. life insurance.
   3. maintenance reserves.
   4. homeowner's insurance.

33. If a person is allowed to use 75% of an $1,800 PITI payment for PI, how much can be spent on PI?
   1. $1,350
   2. $1,400
   3. $1,500
   4. $1,700

34. How much total interest is paid on a $100,000 loan amortized over 30 years at 7% interest, using a factor of $6.65 per thousand?
   1. $66,500
   2. $100,000
   3. $139,400
   4. $239,400

35. How much total interest is paid on a $100,000 loan amortized over 15 years at 7% interest, using a factor of $8.98 per thousand?
   1. $61,640
   2. $89,800
   3. $161,640
   4. $171,640

36. A buyer falls in love with a house and needs $200,000 in order to afford the transaction. If the buyer qualifies for a $1,300 PI payment and the current interest rate is 7% amortized over 30 years ($6.65 factor), how much money is the buyer eligible to borrow? (Round to the nearest dollar.)
   1. $66,500
   2. $133,000
   3. $195,489
   4. $200,000

37. A buyer asks a seller to pay some discount points in order to lower the existing 7% interest rate to 6¾%. If the buyer can afford a $1,300 PI payment, using a factor of $6.49 (6¾% amortized over 30 years), how much money is the buyer eligible to borrow? (Round to the nearest dollar.)
   1. $87,750
   2. $133,000
   3. $200,308
   4. None of the above

38. A buyer made a 10% down payment of $15,000. The buyer was then required to purchase private mortgage insurance and pay an annual premium of 0.52% of the loan. What was the buyer's monthly PMI payment?
   1. $58.50
   2. $150
   3. $702
   4. $880

39. If the VA charges a 2% financed funding fee on a $200,000 VA guaranteed loan, how much is the funding fee?
    1. $200
    2. $400
    3. $2,000
    4. $4,000

40. FHA charges an upfront insurance premium of 1.5%, which is financed into the loan. On a $135,000 FHA-insured loan, how much is the upfront insurance premium?
    1. $1,500
    2. $1,350
    3. $2,030
    4. $2,025

MATCHING QUIZ

The column on the right contains brief memory links to important terms in Chapter 10. *Write the letter of the matching term on the appropriate line.*

A. $A = \pi\ (3.14) \times R^2$

B. $A = L \times W$

C. $A = ½\ (B \times H)$

D. $A = \frac{(B1 + B2) \times H}{2}$

E. diameter × π (3.14)

F. L × W × H

G. part divided by total

H. part divided by percent

I. total × percent

J. Amount charged for real estate services

K. Millage

L. $\frac{\text{replacement cost}}{\text{years of useful life}}$

M. (net) income/rate

N. (net) income/value

O. (cap) rate × value

P. loan divided by 1,000 × amortization factor

Q. $\frac{\text{numerator}}{\text{denominator}}$

1. ______ Circumference of a circle
2. ______ Volume of a cube
3. ______ Area of a circle
4. ______ Area of a rectangle
5. ______ Commission
6. ______ Area of a triangle
7. ______ A word that is equated with tax rate
8. ______ Formula to find monthly PI
9. ______ Area of a trapezoid
10. ______ A fraction
11. ______ Formula to find part
12. ______ Formula used to arrive at net operating income
13. ______ Formula used to find total
14. ______ Formula used to find %
15. ______ Straight-line depreciation formula
16. ______ Formula used to arrive at value
17. ______ Formula used to find cap rate

ANSWER KEY WITH EXPLANATIONS

1. \$62,000 sales price × 7% commission = \$62,000 × 0.07 = \$4,340, broker's commission

   \$4,340 × 25% = \$4,340 × 0.25 = \$1,085

   Correct answer: **1** (127)

2. See Figure 12.12.

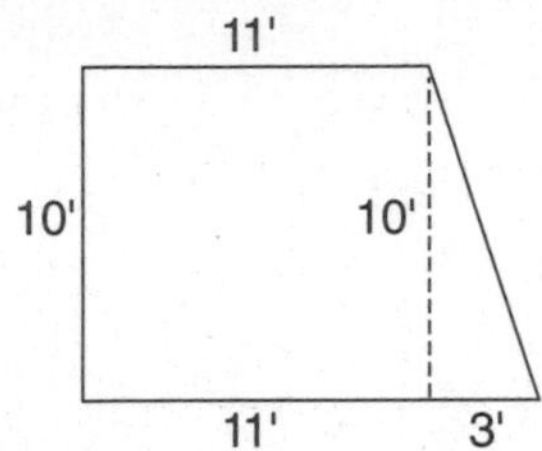

FIGURE 12.12

   11' × 10' = 110 square feet, area of rectangle

   ½ (3' × 10') = ½ (30') = 15 square feet, area of triangle

   110 + 15 = 125 square feet, total area

   Divide by 9 to convert square feet to square yards.

   125 ÷ 9 = 13.89 square yards

   \$14.95 + \$3.50 installation = \$18.45, cost per square yard

   \$18.45 × 13.89 square yards = \$256.27

   Correct answer: **4** (129–130)

3. \$40,000 first investor + \$20,000 second investor = \$60,000

   \$150,000 – \$60,000 = \$90,000 third investor's contribution

   $$\frac{\text{part}}{\text{total}} = \text{percent}$$

   \$90,000 ÷ \$150,000 = 0.60, or 60%

   Correct answer: **1** (128)

4. \$582.84 × 12 = \$6,994.08 annual interest

   $$\frac{\text{part}}{\text{percent}} = \text{total}$$

   \$6,994.08 ÷ 12% = \$6,994.08 ÷ 0.12 = \$58,284

   Correct answer: **2** (127)

5. \$102,900 × 4% = \$102,900 × 0.04 = \$4,116, annual increase in value.

   \$102,900 + \$4,116 = \$107,016, current market value

   Correct answer: **4** (128)

   Read your calculator carefully. Answer choices with the same number combinations can be misleading.

6. \$75,000 × 80% OR \$75,000 × 0.80 = \$60,000 in taxable value

   Divide by 1,000 because tax rate is stated per \$1,000.

   \$60,000 ÷ 1,000 = \$60

   \$60 × 32.50 = \$1,950, annual taxes

   Divide by 12 to get monthly taxes.

   \$1,950 ÷ 12 = \$162.50

   Correct answer: **4** (128)

7. See Figure 12.13.

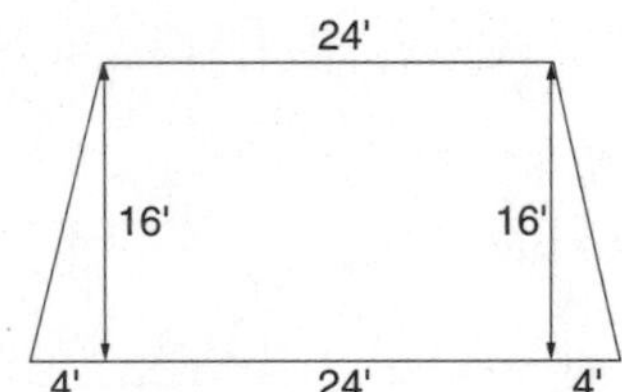

FIGURE 12.13

   24' × 16' = 384 square feet, area of rectangle

   ½ (4' × 16') = ½ (64') = 32 square feet, area of one triangle

   32 × 2 = 64 square feet, area of two triangles

   384 + 64 = 448 square feet, surface area to be paved

   6" deep = ½'

   448 × .5 = 224 cubic feet of concrete required for patio

   Correct answer: **4** (129–130)

8. $7,350 – $500 salary = $6,850 commission on sales

   $6,850 ÷ 2.5% = $6,850 ÷ 0.025 = $274,000, value of property sold

   Correct answer: **3** (127)

9. See Figure 12.14.

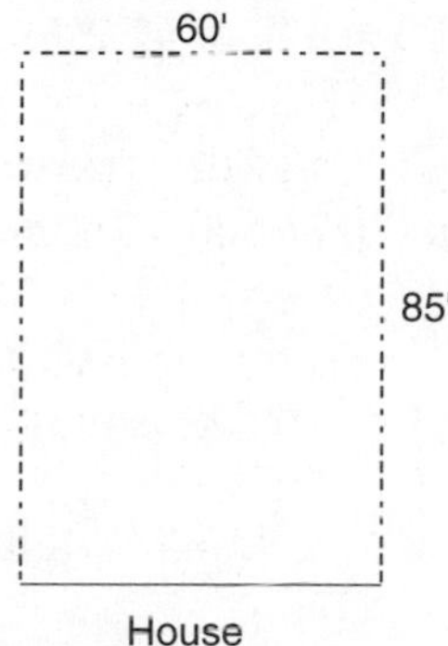

FIGURE 12.14

   Two sides of 85' plus one side of 60'

   85' × 2 = 170 feet

   170 + 60 = 230 linear feet

   230 × $7.25 = $1,667.50

   Correct answer: **4** (129–130)

10. $6,000 × 12 = $72,000 annual return

    $72,000 ÷ 9% = $72,000 ÷ 0.09 = $800,000, original cost of property

    Correct answer: **1** (132)

11. $1,860 ÷ 12 months = $155 per month

    $155 ÷ 30 days = $5.167 per day

    $155 × 3 months = $465

    $5.167 × 15 days = $77.505

    $465 + $77.505 = $542.505, rounds to $542.51

    Correct answer: **2** (133-134)

12. $65,400 × 11% OR $65,400 × 0.11 = $7,194

    $7,194 ÷ 360 days = $19.9833 per diem cost

    September 1 through 14 = 14 days

    14 days × $19.9833 = 279.7662, rounds to $279.77

    Correct answer: **1** (133–134)

13. $740 ÷ 3 years = $246.667 per year

    $246.667 ÷ 12 = $20.556 per month

    $20.556 ÷ 30 days = $.685 per day

    $20.556 × 7 months = $143.892

    $.685 × 20 days = $13.70

    $143.892 + $13.70 = $157.592, rounds to $157.59

    Correct answer: **4** (133–134)

14. $1,630 ÷ 12 months = $135.833 per month

    $135.833 ÷ 30 days = $4.528 per day

    $4.528 × 26 days = $117.728

    $135.833 + $117.728 = $253.561, rounds to $253.56

    Correct answer: **2** (133–134)

    The taxes have been paid. The seller is entitled to a refund for 1 month and 26 days. He therefore will receive a credit and the buyer will be charged (debited) for the same amount.

15. $64,750 × 12% = $64,750 × 0.12 = $7,770

    $7,770 ÷ 12 months = $647.50

    $647.50 ÷ 30 days = $21.583 per day

    $21.583 × 18 days = $388.494, rounds to $388.49

    Correct answer: **2** (133–134)

16. 43,560 square feet/acre × 200 acres = 8,712,000, total square feet

    8,712,000 square feet × $^1/_8$ = 8,712,000 × 0.125 = 1,089,000 square feet for streets

    8,712,000 – 1,089,000 = 7,623,000 square feet for lots

    7,623,000 square feet ÷ 220 lots = 34,650 square feet per lot

    Correct answer: **1** (129–130)

17. Time period: 2 months (November/December)

    $2,140 per year ÷ 12 = $178.33 per month

    $178.33 × 2 = $356.67

    Correct answer: **3** (133–134)

18. Part = $28,000, Percent = 6%

    part ÷ percent = total

    $28,000 ÷ .06 = $466,667

    Correct answer: **2** (127)

19. part ÷ percent = total

    \$80,000 ÷ 0.93 = \$86,021.5, rounds to \$86,022

    Correct answer: **2** (127)

20. \$59,200 × .07 = \$4,144.00 annual interest

    \$4,144 ÷ 12 = \$345.33 interest for one month

    \$623.00 (P&I) – 345.33 = \$277.67 principal payoff

    \$59,200 – \$277.67 = \$58,922.33 balance after next payment

    Correct answer: **3** (134–136)

21. \$1,486.50 (150,000 × 9.91)

    Correct answer: **2** (134–136)

22. \$1,486.50 × 360 months = \$535,140 (total P&I) – \$150,000 (P) = \$385,140

    Correct answer: **2** (134–136)

23. The payment chart indicates 8.25 percent loans are 7.51 per \$1,000.

    \$990 affordable monthly payment ÷ 7.51 = 131,824.23

    \$131.82423 × 1,000 = \$131,824.33 maximum loan amount

    \$131,824.33 plus down payment = \$145,824.33 maximum selling price of house.

    Correct answer: **3** (135)

24. \$300,000 ÷ 50 years = \$6,000 annual depreciation charge

    \$6,000 × 18 years = \$108,000 current total depreciation

    Correct answer: **3** (132)

25. I ÷ R = V

    \$40,000 ÷ 9% (0.09) = \$444,444

    Correct answer: **1** (132)

26. Divide \$1,500 by the 7% factor of 6.65.

    1,500 divided by 6.65 = 225.56 × 1000 = 225,564

    Next divide \$1,500 by the 6½% factor of 6.32.

    1,500 ÷ 6.32 = 237.34 × 1000 = 237,342.

    The difference is 237,342 – 225,564 = \$11,778.

    Correct answer: **1**

27. 200 (thousands) × 6.00 = \$1,200

    Correct answer: **1**

28. \$200,000 × 6% = \$12,000 divided by 12 months = \$1,000. The difference then is \$1,200 (PI) – \$1,000 (I) = \$200 (P)

    Correct answer: **2**

29. \$380 divided by \$900 = .422 or 42.2%.

    Correct answer: **4**

30. \$5,000 × 36% = \$1,800. \$1,800 – 750 = \$1,050.

    Correct answer: **1**

31. \$700 divided by 6.65 = \$105.26 × 1,000 = \$105,263

    Correct answer: **3**

32. Together these items are referred to as PITI.

    Correct answer: **4**

33. This elementary process is utilized every day in the real estate business. \$1,800 (PITI) × 75% = \$1,350 (PI)

    Correct answer: **1**

34. The payment is 100 (thousands) × 6.65 or \$665. This amount then is multiplied by 360 months to discover the total amount spent on PI payments. \$665 × 360 = \$239,400. Next, subtract the amount borrowed (\$100,000) to find the solution of \$139,400.

    Correct answer: **3**

35. The payment is 100 (thousands) × 8.98 or \$898. This amount then is multiplied by 180 months to discover the total amount spent on PI payments. \$898 × 180 = \$161,640 – \$100,000 (original loan) = \$61,640

    Correct answer: **1**

36. \$1,300 divided by 6.65 = \$195.49 × 1,000 = \$195,489

    Correct answer: **3**

37. \$1,300 divided by 6.49 = \$200.31 × 1,000 = \$200,308

    Correct answer: **3**

38. First find the loan amount. $15,000 divided by 10% = $150,000

    Then subtract the down payment of $15,000 to arrive at the loan amount of $135,000.

    $135,000 × .52% = $702 divided by 12 months = $58.50 each month for PMI.

    Correct answer: **1**

39. $200,000 × 2% = $4,000. Buyer's closing costs on a VA loan include an origination fee, the financed funding fee, and actuals. The VA waives the funding fee for disabled veterans.

    Correct answer: **4**

40. $135,000 × 1.5% = $2,025. A portion of this amount is refunded if the property is resold within seven years.

    Correct answer: **4**

ANSWER KEY: MATCHING QUIZ

1. E
2. F
3. A
4. B
5. J
6. C
7. K
8. P
9. D
10. Q
11. I
12. O
13. H
14. G
15. L
16. M
17. N

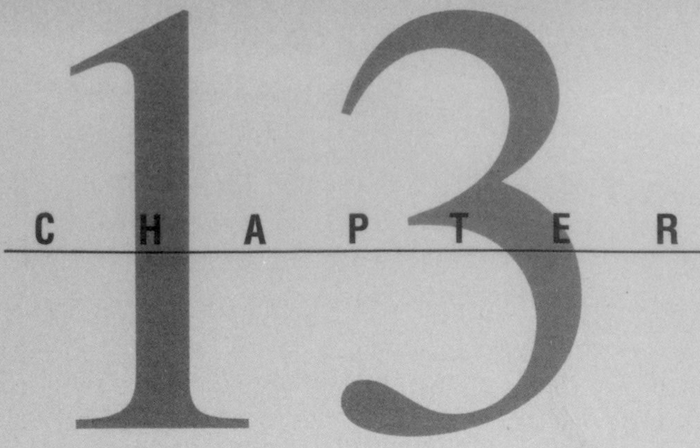

Specialty Areas

OUTLINE OF CONCEPTS

I. Property Management and Landlord/Tenant

A. A lease is a contract between the lessor (owner) and the lessee (tenant) and a transfer of possession to the tenant.

B. Leasehold estate—less-than-freehold estate involving the tenant's right to occupy the real estate during the term of the lease, usually considered personal property (nonfreehold).
   1. Estate for years—lease for a definite period of time terminating automatically without notice by either party.
   2. Periodic estate (estate from year to year)—lease for an indefinite period of time without a specific expiration date; notice must be given to terminate.
   3. Tenancy at will—lease that gives the tenant the right to possess with the consent of the landlord for an indefinite period of time; terminated by giving notice or by the death of either the landlord or the tenant.
   4. Tenancy at sufferance—tenant continues to hold possession without the consent of the landlord.

C. Types of leases
   1. Gross lease—tenant pays a fixed rent, while landlord pays all taxes, insurance, etc.
   2. Net lease—tenant pays rent plus all or part of property charges.
   3. Percentage lease—usually provides for minimum fixed rent plus a percentage of the portion of tenant's business income that exceeds a stated minimum.
   4. Graduated lease—provides for rent increase at set future dates.
   5. Index lease—allows rent to be increased or decreased periodically based on an agreed index such as change in the government cost-of-living index.

D. Requirements of a valid lease
   1. Offer and acceptance—mutual agreement of parties on contract terms.
   2. Consideration—generally takes the form of rent for right of occupancy.
   3. Capacity to contract—legal capacity.

4. Legal objectives

E. Breach of lease
   1. Tenant breach
      a. Landlord may sue tenant to obtain judgment to cover amount due.
      b. Landlord may retake possession through actual eviction.
   2. Landlord breach—tenant may terminate lease through constructive eviction, if breach causes premises to be untenantable.
   3. Death of parties or sale of property generally will not terminate a lease.

F. Management Agreement
   1. Creates an agency relationship between property manager and owner.
   2. Property manager is a general agent.
   3. Management agreement
      a. Defines manager's responsibilities.
      b. States owner's purpose.
      c. Identifies extent of manager's authority.

G. Management functions
   1. Developing an operating budget.
   2. Renting property.
   3. Selecting tenants and collecting rents.
   4. Maintaining good relations with tenants.
   5. Maintaining the property.

H. Trust Accounts
   1. Required by most state laws in order to protect the public's money.
   2. Commingling the broker's funds with his or her client's trust account funds is illegal when it exceeds the legal limits set by state law.
   3. Using a general ledger and an individual ledger provides a way to reconcile the management trust account.

II. Common Interest Ownership Properties

A. Cooperatives
   1. Title to the land and the building are held by the corporation.
   2. Each purchaser becomes a stockholder and receives a proprietary lease; each purchaser holds a personal property interest except in states that have adopted Common Interest Ownership Act, which converts this to a real estate interest.
   3. Taxes and the mortgage are liens against the corporation generally given to the shareholders.
   4. Owners-occupants may be forced to pay expenses for the shareholders who are unable to pay, to prevent foreclosure on the entire building.

B. Condominiums
   1. Generally created under a horizontal property act.
   2. The owner holds fee-simple title to one unit and a specified share in the common elements.
   3. Default in payment of taxes, mortgage payments, or monthly assessments by one unit owner may result in a foreclosure sale of that owner's unit; this does not affect the titles of the remaining owners.

C. Time-shared ownership
   1. Allows multiple buyers to buy interests in real estate with each buyer receiving the right to use the facilities for a specified period of time.
   2. Owners' use and occupancy is limited to the contractual period that was purchased.
   3. Each owner is assessed for common expenses and maintenance based on the ratio of the ownership period to the total number of ownership periods in the property.
   4. Time-share estate includes a fee-simple interest in condominium ownership or a leasehold estate.
   5. Time-share use is a contractual right under which the developer owns the real estate.

III. Subdivisions

A. Subdividers versus developers
   1. Subdivider—buys undeveloped land and divides it into smaller lots for sale.
   2. Developer—improves land, constructs buildings on land, and sells them.

B. Regulation of land development
   1. Land development plans—must comply with municipality's comprehensive plan, zoning regulations, and environmental regulations.
   2. Plats—maps that illustrate the geographic boundaries of specific lots.
      a. Plat shows block, streets, etc., in prospective subdivision.
      b. Plat must present restrictive covenants and engineering data established by deeds, declarations, etc.
      c. Plat must be approved by appropriate boards of the municipality before being recorded.
   3. Subdivision plans
      a. Lot size is generally regulated by local zoning ordinances.
      b. Plan must provide for water, sewer, and utility easements.

C. Private land-use controls
   1. Establish standards for all lots within a subdivision.
   2. Restrictive covenants control many aspects including type and construction methods.

D. Federal Interstate Land Sales Full Disclosure Act
   1. Regulates unimproved parcels sold through an interstate sale.
   2. Objective is to avoid fraudulent marketing schemes.
   3. Law requires developers to file reports with HUD prior to offering unimproved lots in interstate commerce through the mail or by telephone.
   4. The reports must contain disclosure about the properties.
   5. Buyer or lessee may be able to void contract, if not provided copy of report before signing.
   6. Law does not cover subdivisions with fewer than 25 lots or lots of 20 acres or more.

IV. Business Opportunities (brokers only)

A. Forms used

1. Inventory and equipment are personal property and are transferred by bill of sale rather than by deed.
2. A written document of assignment is used to assign accounts receivable.
3. Business sales are regulated by the Uniform Commercial Code, which governs documents and forms when personal property is used as security for a loan.
   a. The UCC requires the borrower to sign a security agreement in order for a lender to create a security interest in personal property; the security interest includes personal property that will become fixtures and must contain a complete list of the items against which the lien applies.
   b. A financing statement or UCC-1 (a short notice of the security agreement) must be filed; it identifies any real estate involved when personal property is made part of the real estate.
   c. When the financing statement has been recorded, subsequent lenders and buyers are placed on notice with regard to the security interest in fixtures and personal property.
   d. Lenders generally require that a security agreement be signed and a financing statement filed when chattels are being financed and subsequently will be affixed to the real estate.

B. Issues involved in the sale of a business

1. Contract should be comprehensive and in writing.
2. The buyer (vendee) should be aware of any representations and warranties made by the seller (vendor).
3. The offer to purchase should make the sale of the business contingent upon the issuance of the appropriate franchise (if applicable), licenses and permits, approval by vendee of existing leases, and landlord's consent, if required by terms of lease.
4. Where an ongoing business is being sold, the buyer may want the seller to commit to a covenant not to compete. The covenant should be limited as to territory and time so that the restrictive effect is no more than is necessary to protect the goodwill for which the buyer is paying. More than this is usually unenforceable in a court of law.
5. If the sale of a business includes the unpaid accounts receivable, the assignment of these accounts should be in writing and the buyer should notify the customers of the assignment and that all payments should be made to the buyer. Prior thereto the buyer should determine the authenticity of such account receivables.
6. If the seller has a lease, the buyer will generally want a new lease or an assignment of the existing lease; the buyer's preference should be a contingency in the offer to purchase.
7. If the sale includes fixtures, the buyer should check to be sure that they belong to the seller.
8. If the sale includes a building, the buyer should be sure that the business complies with zoning codes, building codes, and other governmental laws and regulations such as environmental laws, as well as marketable title.

C. Bulk transfers
   1. The sale of a business must comply with the Uniform Commercial Code (UCC). If just the business is being sold, a licensed agent may not be necessary to find a buyer. For the sale of just the business an unlicensed business broker may be hired to find a new owner. However, if the business brokerage transaction includes the transfer of real property, a licensed agent would be required.
   2. The UCC applies whenever an owner sells a substantial portion of his or her inventory.
   3. If the buyer fails to comply with the law, the buyer's title to equipment and inventory may be subject to the claims of the creditors created while the seller operated the business.

V. Commercial Property/Income Property

A. Advantages of real estate investment
   1. Serves as a hedge against inflation.
   2. Rates of return exceed the average rate of return.
   3. Leverage—using other people's money to finance an investment.

B. Disadvantages of real estate investment
   1. Lack of liquidity.
   2. Investing is generally expensive.
   3. Requires active management.
   4. Involves substantial risk.

C. Investment objectives
   1. Appreciation in value of investment.
   2. Cash flow—spendable income generated by income properties.
   3. Leverage—financing an investment by using borrowed money.
   4. Equity buildup resulting from paying off mortgage plus increase in property value.
   5. Pyramiding—using currently owned property as a catalyst to purchase additional properties through either sale or refinance of currently owned property.

D. Tax benefits
   1. Capital gains—difference between net selling price and adjusted basis of property; a portion of capital gains is excluded from income tax.
   2. Exchanges (IRS tax ruling 1031)
      a. A method of deferring taxation of capital gains.
      b. Property involved in a tax-deferred exchange must be like-kind—real estate for real estate of equal value.
      c. Any additional personal property or capital needed to even out the exchange is called boot.
      d. Boot is taxed at the time of the exchange.
   3. Depreciation
      a. Allows investor to recover cost of asset through tax deductions over useful life of asset.
      b. Depreciation may be deducted only if property produces income or is used in trade or business.
      c. Land may not be depreciated.
      d. Straight-line depreciation takes equal periodic amounts over an asset's useful life.

4. Deductions
   a. Losses may be deducted by investors in certain circumstances.
   b. Tax credits (direct reduction) are allowed for renovation of older buildings, historic properties, etc.
5. Installment sales
   a. Payments received are taxed only on profit portion.
   b. Interest received is taxed as ordinary income.

VI. Agricultural Property (broker only)

A. Property types
1. General farming properties
2. Irrigated—includes orchard, vineyard, pasture, and raw cropland.
3. Livestock ranches—used for grazing livestock.
   a. Ranch—business enterprise that depends mainly on range forage for production of livestock and related products.
4. Range—includes all grasslands and shrub lands and those forest lands that will continually or periodically, naturally or through management, support vegetation that provides forage for grazing and browsing animals.
5. Dairy farms—improvements generally contribute significantly to the value of the operating dairy farm.
6. Permanent plantings: orchards and vineyards
   a. Vary in size from small family-owned and operated grove or vineyard to large agribusiness endeavors.
   b. Require substantial knowledge about the particular varieties of trees or vines.
   c. Generally have a high value per acre, dependent on quality of management the permanent plantings have received over a period of time.
   d. Require a startup period of several years before a cash flow is realized.
7. Crop farming—growing crops that are produced annually through the tenant's own care like corn and soybeans and that he or she is entitled to take away after the tenancy is ended (called emblements).
8. Timberland
   a. Considered agricultural because it produces a crop-merchantable timber that is periodically harvested.
   b. Timber crop is harvested every 20 to 80 years, unlike other farm properties, which usually have an annual crop to harvest.
   c. Standing timber is legally considered to be real property, but once severed, becomes personal property.
9. Value of agricultural real estate is affected by
   a. Climatic conditions
   b. Management expertise
   c. Productivity

DIAGNOSTIC TEST

1. A man signed a lease for six months. This is an example of a(n)
   1. estate for years.
   2. periodic estate.
   3. tenancy at will.
   4. tenancy at sufferance.
2. You purchased the right to live in an apartment in a resort for the 32nd complete week of each calendar year for the next 30 years. The type of interest you have is called a(n)
   1. joint tenancy.
   2. time-share estate.
   3. tenancy in common.
   4. estate for years.
3. An owner in a condominium project does not
   1. hold a fee-simple title on his or her unit.
   2. have an undivided proportionate interest in the common elements.
   3. have to pay mortgages, taxes, and assessments that are liens against other units in the project.
   4. have a real property interest.
4. Which of the following statements does NOT correctly describe a cooperative development?
   1. Title to the land and building is owned by a corporation.
   2. Mortgage and taxes are liens against the corporation.
   3. Each buyer of an apartment becomes a shareholder in the corporation.
   4. The buyer holds a real property interest.
5. You have entered into a lease that requires you to pay all or part of the landlord's operating expenses. You have signed a(n)
   1. index lease.
   2. gross lease.
   3. net lease.
   4. graduated lease.
6. A woman's two-year lease had expired when she decided to continue living in her apartment without the consent of her landlord. The woman now has a(n)
   1. estate for years.
   2. periodic estate.
   3. tenancy at will.
   4. tenancy at sufferance.
7. A man bought undeveloped land and divided it into smaller lots for sale. The man would be classified as a(n)
   1. appraiser.
   2. broker.
   3. developer.
   4. subdivider.
8. Which of the following statements does NOT correctly describe the Interstate Land Sales Full Disclosure Act?
   1. It regulates unimproved parcels sold through an interstate sale.
   2. It is aimed at avoiding fraudulent marketing schemes.
   3. It covers subdivisions with fewer than 25 lots.
   4. It requires developers to file reports with HUD prior to offering unimproved lots in interstate commerce by telephone.
9. Which of the following is NOT an advantage of investing in real estate?
   1. It serves as a hedge against inflation.
   2. It does not require active management.
   3. It allows for leverage.
   4. It produces a rate of return that exceeds the average rate of return.
10. The term *boot* is related to
    1. appreciation in the value of an investment.
    2. cash flow generated by income property.
    3. pyramiding.
    4. an exchange.

11. Using borrowed money to finance an investment is known as
    1. appreciation.
    2. cash flowing.
    3. leverage
    4. pyramiding.

12. Which of the following may NOT be depreciated?
    1. A motel
    2. Land
    3. An office building
    4. An apartment building

13. Inventory and equipment sold as part of a business would be transferred to the buyer by a
    1. bargain and sale deed.
    2. bill of sale.
    3. quitclaim deed.
    4. warranty deed.

14. The law that governs documents and forms when personal property is used as security for a loan is the
    1. Interstate Land Sales Full Disclosure Act.
    2. Horizontal Property Act.
    3. Real Estate Settlement Procedures Act.
    4. Uniform Commercial Code.

15. Standing timber is legally considered to be
    1. emblements.
    2. chattels.
    3. real property.
    4. personal property.

16. At the time of harvest, crops such as corn and soybeans that require annual planting and harvesting are considered personal property and are called
    1. codicils.
    2. laches.
    3. emblements.
    4. future interest.

17. What government law regulates the sale of an actual business and its personal property apart from the real estate?
    1. FTC
    2. FCC
    3. UCC
    4. DNR

MATCHING QUIZ

The column on the right contains brief memory links to important terms in Chapter 13. *Write the letter of the matching term on the appropriate line.*

A. Estate for years	1. ______Fee-simple ownership and a specified share in the common elements
B. General agent	2. ______Tenant pays rent but no operating expenses
C. Tenancy at sufferance	3. ______A lease for a definite period of time
D. Cooperative	4. ______A landlord fails to repair a defective furnace making the leased premises unusable, therefore the tenant has the right to abandon the lease
E. Gross lease	5. ______The owner/tenant is also a stockholder
F. Condominium	6. ______A property manager
G. Net lease	7. ______Possession without the landlord's consent
H. Percentage lease	8. ______Tenant pays all of the landlord's operating expenses
I. Constructive eviction	9. ______Rent arrangement includes a percentage of tenant's income
J. Time shares	10. ______Government laws that regulate lot sizes
K. Subdivider	11. ______Multiple owners owning the same parcel of real estate but at different time intervals
L. Zoning ordinances	12. ______Buys undeveloped land and divides it into smaller tracts
M. UCC	13. ______Personal property
N. Chattel	14. ______Regulates the sale of goods or tangible personal property apart from the real estate
O. Leverage	15. ______Crops that require annual planting and harvesting
P. Capital gain	16. ______Something that doesn't depreciate
Q. Land	17. ______Financing an investment by using borrowed funds
R. Emblements	18. ______The difference between a property's net adjusted basis and selling price

ANSWER KEY WITH EXPLANATIONS: DIAGNOSTIC TEST

1. **(1)** An estate for years is a lease with a definite duration. (148)
2. **(2)** A time-share use is a right under which the developer owns the real estate; a time-share estate is a fee-simple or leasehold interest in condominium ownership. (150)
3. **(3)** The financial hazard of having to pay liens against other units exists in a cooperative development. (149)
4. **(4)** The buyer of a cooperative unit receives stock in the a corporation that actually owns the unit. The owner/tenant has a proprietary lease, and it is considered a personal property interest. (149)
5. **(3)** The lessee is responsible for paying all or part of the landlord's expense. (148)
6. **(4)** In a tenancy at sufferance, the tenant is a trespasser. (148)
7. **(4)** A developer improves land, constructs buildings on the land, and sells them. (150)
8. **(3)** The Interstate Land Sales Full Disclosure Act covers subdivisions with 25 or more lots. (150)
9. **(2)** Real estate investments require active management. (152)
10. **(4)** Boot is any additional cash or personal property needed to even out an exchange. (152)
11. **(3)** Cash flow refers to spendable income generated by an income property. Pyramiding is selling or refinancing currently owned properties in order to purchase additional properties. (152)
12. **(2)** Buildings are depreciated. It is assumed that land value will be recovered at the end of the economic life of the property. (152)
13. **(2)** A deed is used to convey title to real property; personal property is often conveyed by a bill of sale. (150)
14. **(4)** The Horizontal Property Act is related to condominium development. (151)
15. **(3)** Emblements and chattels are considered to be personal property. (153)
16. **(3)** Emblements are considered personal property and therefore the property of the entity that planted them regardless of any change in ownership. (153)
17. **(3)** The Uniform Commercial Code is the governmental law that regulates commercial law business transactions including chattel mortgages and bulk transfers (i.e., all trade fixtures, chattels, and merchandise). (151–152)

TEST SCORE

SPECIALTY AREAS			
Rating	**Range**	**Your Score**	
Good = 80% to 100%	14–17	Total Number	17
Fair = 70% to 79%	12–13	Total Wrong	–
Needs improvement = Lower than 70%	11 or less	Total Right	

Passing Requirement: 12 or Better

ANSWER KEY: MATCHING QUIZ

1. F
2. E
3. A
4. I
5. D
6. B
7. C
8. G
9. H
10. L
11. J
12. K
13. N
14. M
15. R
16. Q
17. O
18. P

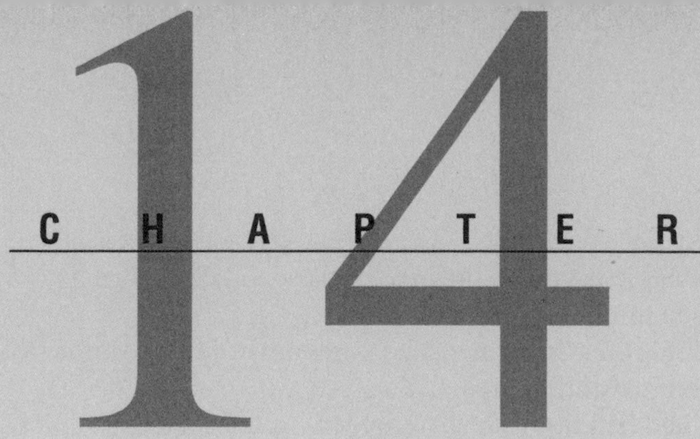

Brokerage Management

OUTLINE OF CONCEPTS

I. Types of Ownership

A. Sole proprietorship
   1. Provides broker with flexibility and control, while trading off protection against personal liability.
   2. Appropriate for the broker who desires a small operation and sales staff.

B. Joint or multiple ownership—appropriate for the broker interested in growth and expansion as well as joint ownership. There are five primary forms of multiple ownership:
   1. Corporations
      a. Advantages
         (1) Limited liability—any liability incurred by a corporation through judgments, bankruptcies, etc., limited to the investment of a shareholder in a corporation; does not affect a shareholder's personal assets.
         (2) Centralized management—shareholders elect a board of directors, who elect officers to manage the company; a licensed broker-director is responsible for the real estate brokerage phase of the business.
         (3) Continuity of life—a corporation is a legal entity that never dies; its officers may be continually replaced if necessary.
         (4) No income limitations—no upper limit on the amount of income a corporation may earn or the number of shareholders it may have.
         (5) Transferability—corporate stock may be freely transferred from one shareholder to another.
      b. Disadvantages
         (1) Double taxation—profits taxed at both the corporate and individual levels.
         (2) Treatment of losses—corporation losses may not be passed on to shareholders; they may be applied to future earnings of the corporation.
         (3) Capital gains—passed on to shareholders as ordinary income.

2. S corporations
   a. Advantages
      (1) No double taxation—income, losses, and capital gains passed directly to the shareholders.
      (2) Centralized management and continuity of life—similar to the typical corporation.
      (3) Limited liability with shareholders' interests freely transferable.
   b. Disadvantages
      (1) Ownership limited to 35 shareholders.
      (2) Not more than 20 percent of income may be from passive investments, that is, investments that are income-related, such as stock dividends or interest from deposits.
3. General partnership
   a. Advantages
      (1) No double taxation—income directly taxable to each partner.
      (2) Capital gains or losses pass directly to the partners.
   b. Disadvantages
      (1) Problems arising from the death, bankruptcy, etc., of the partner(s).
      (2) Personal liability.
      (3) Ownership not freely transferable.
4. Limited partnerships
   a. Rarely used in an active brokerage firm.
   b. Used primarily to acquire investments such as syndicates, joint ventures.
   c. One or more general partners have unlimited liability; are responsible for the operation of the business.
   d. Limited partners generally have no say in the business operation.
   e. Limited partners' liability is limited to the amount of the investment, unless the partners take an active role in management.
5. Limited liability companies
   a. Offer advantages of the single-level taxation of a partnership and the limited liability of a corporation.
   b. Avoid some of the restrictions that are imposed on an S corporation.
   c. Must generally have at least one member; members may be corporations, individuals, limited or general partnerships, a trust, or foreign persons.
   d. May be directly managed by members, or responsibility may be delegated to a property manager.

C. Franchises and alternatives—the broker may choose among various types of operations.
   1. Remain independent—provides pride of ownership.
   2. Become a member of a referral system.
   3. Franchise membership—for example, Century 21 and Electronic Realty Associates (ERA).

a. Advantages
   (1) Approaches to management and marketing—members pay an initial fee and a percentage of the profits in return for franchise "expertise."
   (2) Client referral system.
   (3) Economics of volume purchasing of equipment, signs, etc.
   (4) National advertising and promotion.
b. Disadvantages
   (1) Loss of individual identity.
   (2) High initial fees and franchise fees.
   (3) Possibly limited geographic area.

4. Quasi-franchise membership—for example, GMAC and Gallery of Homes.
   a. The broker may retain the name as part of the firm identification.
   b. Offer varied services that are less extensive than those of a franchise operation—for example, Help-U-Sell.
   c. The owner is guided by a broker on how to sell property.
   d. The seller takes on part of the broker's responsibility such as showing the property.
   e. The seller generally pays a commission less than that charged by a traditional broker.
   f. Advantages
      (1) The broker's monetary investment and time are less.
      (2) Greater exposure to FSBOs (For Sale by Owner).
   g. Disadvantages
      (1) Lower fees require increased business activity.
      (2) Increased pressure to earn a profit.
      (3) May retain offices while pooling advertising outlays and sharing in the profits of the cooperative.
5. Membership in broker association—single office composed of a group of individual brokers who share office space and expenses.
6. 100-percent commission office
   a. Landlord-broker owns the office and facilities; rents the office to other brokers or associates on a per-desk basis.
   b. Each broker or associate pays a monthly fee to cover the landlord's office expenses and a small percentage of the commission for the benefit of all the brokers and associates; the 100-percent concept often is used in combination with other forms of operation.

D. Internal structure of organization
   1. One-person organization
   2. One-agent to ten-agent organization
      a. A small, centralized operation in which the capacity for doing business grows as the size of the organization grows.
      b. Management responsibility, as well as the need for office space and equipment, will increase the cost of doing business.
   3. Monolithic organization
      a. Functions as single unit, though it normally consists of a number of work groups.
      b. There is a single source of authority at the top of the organization.

4. Decentralized organization—fewer levels of management, thus the managers have the authority to operate essentially as individual business units.

II. Sales Associate Relationship

A. Independent contractor
   1. The salesperson is under limited supervision.
   2. The salesperson contracts with the broker to produce specific outcomes—for example, leasing commissions and real estate sales.
   3. The process by which a salesperson produces a commission cannot be controlled by the broker except within the guidelines of the contract.
   4. The broker may not unduly restrict the methods that the associate may use.
   5. The broker may not withhold federal and state income taxes, Social Security taxes, or state unemployment insurance from commissions.
   6. The broker may not provide health insurance or pension plans.
   7. The salesperson must pay his or her own license fees and board dues.
   8. The salesperson is responsible for car and transportation expenses.
   9. The salesperson may not be required to attend sales meetings.
   10. The salesperson may not be required to follow a set work schedule.

B. Employee
   1. The broker can employ, guide the activities of, maintain the standards of conduct of, or terminate an employee at will.
   2. The broker is required to withhold federal and state income taxes, pay an employee's share of Social Security taxes, and withhold state unemployment insurance from commissions.
   3. The broker may choose to provide fringe benefits such as health insurance.
   4. The broker may require attendance at sales meetings.

C. Federal income tax requirements to be classified as an independent contractor—see "VII. IRS regulations," in Outline of Concepts for Chapter 10.

III. Agent Supervision (broker only)

A. A broker is responsible for supervising the activities of any salesperson employed by the broker.

B. Supervision includes but is not limited to the following:
   1. Reviewing all documents related to transactions.
   2. Providing all licensed employees with written statement of procedures under which the office and employees shall operate with respect to handling documents related to transactions.
   3. Assuming responsibility for preparation, custody, safety, and correctness of all entities on real estate forms, closing statements, and other records, even though another entity may have those responsibilities.

C. Antitrust guidelines include but are not limited to the following:
   1. Broker should provide ongoing education on antitrust.

2. Salespeople must promote company and base fees of services provided rather than comparison with competitive forms.
3. Salespeople must avoid communication with competing forms that might be interpreted as boycotts or price fixing.
4. Policy and procedures manual must include policies for antitrust compliance.

D. Fair housing guidelines include but are not limited to the following:
1. Broker should provide ongoing education on fair housing.
2. Broker should be sure that salespeople do not provide assistance reluctantly to members of protected classes.
3. Salespeople should not differentiate in the quality of service offered to members of protected classes.
4. Salespeople should not falsely represent that a property is sold or refuse to write an offer for members of protected classes.
5. Salespeople should not suggest that members of protected classes would not be comfortable in a neighborhood.

E. Americans with Disabilities Act guidelines include but are not limited to the following:
1. Salespeople should avoid referring to a person's disability.
2. Avoid using the word *special* in dealing with someone who is disabled.
3. Avoid patronizing people with disabilities.
4. Brokers should make sure office is accessible to those with disabilities.
5. Be able to communicate with people with hearing deficits.

IV. Developing Plans

A. Purpose—to commit broker's financial and human resources to those activities that will produce the highest return on investment.
1. Plans tell what broker's company wants to accomplish and provide general framework for how organization will follow through.
2. The broker must have specific goals for the company to accomplish.

B. Business plan—generally a three-year to five-year blueprint for the organization.

C. Short-range plan—tells company what it should be doing in the coming year.

D. Mission statement—states what a company's purpose is for doing business, specifically, what the business does and where the company intends to be in the future.

V. Risk Management

A. Management styles
1. Dictatorial style—the manager has total control over the organization.
2. Autocratic style—managers are authoritarian but more benevolent than dictatorial managers.
3. Participative style—more democratic than above styles; utilizes talents of people to a greater extent than is common in other styles of management.
4. Laissez-faire—manager doesn't exercise any authority; style characterized by nonintervention and indifference.

B. Benefits of training program

1. Reputation—reputation for good program attracts new salespeople.
2. Supervision—need for close supervision reduced.
3. Selection—helps the broker select the most promising salespeople.
4. Motivation—motivates salespeople to try out what they have learned.
5. Morale—aids the retention of salespeople by helping them to be productive as quickly as possible.
6. Less turnover—provides the knowledge that is necessary for salespeople to succeed, thus reducing the need to terminate the unproductive.

C. Objectives of a training program
   1. Good habits—primary objective to develop good working habits in trainees.
   2. Increased profits—provides well-chosen salespeople with greater profits.
   3. Better production—providing salespeople with training as well as attention increases their productivity.
   4. Better time management—lessens the need for salespeople to depend on brokers, thus allowing greater sales production.
   5. Learning from mistakes—makes salespeople aware of the need to learn from mistakes.

D. Personal assistants
   1. Personal assistants may handle the non–sales-related aspects of real estate transactions.
   2. Personal assistants have enhanced the productivity of salespeople as well as the profitability of brokerage firms.
   3. State licensing laws may address the numerous issues posed by the use of personal assistants.
   4. Personal assistants generally are hired and supervised by a salesperson.
   5. The broker's policies and procedures should define how salespersons' assistants are handled in an organization.

E. Recordkeeping
   1. Method of keeping financial records
      a. Cash method—records income as received and expenses when actually paid.
      b. Accrual method—records income when earned and expenses when incurred (Most firms begin operating under the cash method because the accrual method is more complicated.)
   2. Financial analysis guidelines
      a. Provides standardized method of classifying income and expenses; accounting functions are becoming computerized.
      b. After expense categories have been established and income categories assigned, the coding of deposit slips and checks written can provide the basis for the development of financial statements, balance sheets, and profit-and-loss statements.
   3. Typical bookkeeping system
      a. Records of income—can be entered on a general ledger page as in a checkbook register or on a computer and on individual ledgers to reconcile the trust account.

   b. Record of payments—carbon copy of entries, duplicate of check, or computer record is sufficient.
   c. Accounts payable—list all the bills received and the date of payment in the file or book.
   d. Payroll card—shows the gross and net salaries plus the federal and state tax deductions for all employees.
   e. Commission records—indicate the amounts of all commissions paid to each salesperson, with each transaction identified.
   f. Advertising—newspaper, Internet, cable TV, etc., ads are checked for accuracy and charted to keep track of calls received.
   g. Telephone—outgoing personal calls should be discouraged as much as possible by logging incoming and outgoing calls or by computer printouts.
   h. Supplies—a sign-in/sign-out sheet should be used to keep track of such items as lawn signs and lock boxes.
4. Miscellaneous
   a. Licensing requirements—brokers should make sure that salespeople are licensed properly.
   b. Contracts—each person in the office should sign the contract; this is essential for the independent contractor.
   c. Policy manual—the office policy and procedure manual should be ready when a brokerage office is opened.
   d. Legal advice—brokers should retain good attorneys for sound legal advice.

VI. Trust Accounts

A. Commingling business monies with escrow monies is illegal.
B. Trust account records must be kept of the names of parties for whose benefit the trust account is created; most brokers maintain trust account records on computer.
C. Notation of the date of receipt of any sum and the record of the date and manner of disbursement of funds held in trust should be maintained.
D. All disbursement notations should include the check number and the name of the payee.
E. Trust funds should be deposited in a checking account maintained especially for this purpose.

VII. Basic Financial Concepts

A. Cash flow—net spendable income from the investment calculated by deducting all the operating and fixed expenses from the gross income.
B. Company dollar—amount of income that remains after subtracting all the commissions from the gross income.
C. Gross income—revenue earned from all sources, including sales, appraisals, management fees, etc.
D. Budget—a quantified business plan.
E. Budgeting process—mechanism through which a broker can design a firm's activities and assign dollar costs and anticipated revenues to their implementation.

F. Zero-base budgeting—requires that all budgeted costs for the planning period be justified each time a new budget is developed.
G. Desk cost—the cost of providing the opportunity for salespeople to conduct business is calculated by dividing the total operating expenses of the firm (including salaries, rent, insurance, etc.) by the number of salespeople. (The number of desks is not considered in the calculation. For example, if the broker's annual overhead is $60,000 and there are two desks, each accommodating two salespeople, the desk cost for the firm is $15,000. On a 50/50 split, each salesperson does not begin to earn a profit for the broker until each has brought in a total of $30,000 in gross commissions for the year.)

DIAGNOSTIC TEST

1. Ownership in S corporations is limited to
   1. 20 stockholders.
   2. 25 stockholders.
   3. 35 stockholders.
   4. 100 stockholders.

2. Which of the following is NOT an advantage of the corporation form of ownership?
   1. Limited liability
   2. Centralized management
   3. No income limitations
   4. Double taxation

3. Which of the following statements does NOT correctly describe a limited partnership?
   1. A limited partnership is a popular form of ownership for active brokerage firms.
   2. Limited partners generally have no say in business operations.
   3. The general partner has unlimited liability.
   4. Limited partnerships are used primarily to acquire investments such as syndicates.

4. Which of the following is NOT a real estate franchise?
   1. Electronic Realty Associates (ERA)
   2. Fannie Mae
   3. Century 21
   4. Re/Max

5. A landlord-broker generally would be found in a
   1. sole proprietorship.
   2. limited partnership.
   3. general partnership.
   4. 100-percent commission office.

6. Which of the following statements does NOT correctly describe the independent contractor relationship?
   1. The salesperson is under limited supervision.
   2. The salesperson is responsible for car and transportation expenses.
   3. The broker must provide health insurance.
   4. The broker may not withhold federal income taxes from commissions.

7. A broker has an annual overhead of $300,000, and there are ten desks, each accommodating two salespeople. The broker's desk cost is
   1. $15,000.
   2. $20,000.
   3. $25,000.
   4. $30,000.

8. The person who manages your brokerage firm exercises total control over the organization. This type of management style would be called
   1. autocratic.
   2. dictatorial.
   3. participative.
   4. laissez-faire.

9. Which of the following statements does NOT correctly describe the methods of keeping financial records?
   1. The cash method records income as it is received.
   2. The accrual method records income when it is earned.
   3. Most firms begin operating under the accrual method.
   4. The accrual method records expenses when they are incurred.

10. Which of the following is NOT an objective of a training program?
    1. Increased profits
    2. Better time management
    3. Good habits
    4. Preparation for passing the license exam

11. Which of the following is NOT a benefit of a training program?
    1. Supervision
    2. Motivation
    3. Morale
    4. Handling of personal problems

12. Which of the following is NOT included in a typical bookkeeping system?
    1. Records of income
    2. Accounts payable
    3. Payroll cards
    4. A policy manual

13. Which of the following is NOT included in trust account notations?
    1. The receipt of any monies belonging to others
    2. A record of the date of the disbursement of the funds
    3. The manner in which the funds are disbursed
    4. A record of appointments to show homes

14. Which of the following statements does NOT correctly describe trust accounts?
    1. Commingling of business funds with escrow funds is illegal.
    2. Trust funds should be deposited in a business account.
    3. Trust account records must be kept of the names of the parties for whose benefit the trust account is created.
    4. All disbursement notations should include the check number and the name of payee.

15. Which of the following is NOT a part of a broker's miscellaneous record?
    1. Providing a policy manual.
    2. Ensuring that salespeople are properly licensed.
    3. Retaining an attorney to provide sound legal advice.
    4. Ensuring that salespeople are staying up-to-date in their field of expertise.

MATCHING QUIZ

The column on the right contains brief memory links to important terms in Chapter 14.
Write the letter of the matching term on the appropriate line.

A. Corporation	1. ______ Every partner has personal liability exposure
B. S corporation	2. ______ Ownership is limited to 35 shareholders
C. General Partnership	3. ______ A legal entity that never dies
D. Limited Partnership	4. ______ Members pay a percentage of their earnings for professional expertise and/or branding
E. Franchise	5. ______ One or more partners have unlimited liability while the rest are limited to the amount of their investment
F. 100% commission plan	6. ______ "To exceed our customer's expectations"
G. Independent contractor	7. ______ The person who is responsible for the direct supervision of a brokerage firm
H. Employee	8. ______ Someone who is told on the job what to do and how to do it
I. Broker	9. ______ Act that prohibits price fixing
J. Sherman antitrust act	10. ______ Someone who contracts to work with a broker to produce specific outcomes without being told exactly how to do the job
K. ADA	11. ______ The law that makes sure an office is accessible to those with disabilities
L. Mission statement	12. ______ A method for recording business income when received and expenses when paid
M. High morale	13. ______ A benefit of good training
N. Personal assistants	14. ______ If unlicensed, the duties of these agent helpers must be defined in the broker's policy and procedures manual
O. Cash method	15. ______ A checking account in the name of the brokerage, but the deposits belong to clients and customers
P. Unlawful commingling	16. ______ Gross income minus all commissions
Q. Trust account	17. ______ Dividing total operating expenses by the number of active salespeople
R. Company dollar	18. ______ Mixing the broker's personal funds beyond any state-allowed limit for the maintenance of the account
S. Desk cost	19. ______ Arrived at by deducting all expenses from gross income
T. Cash flow	20. ______ An office that rents desk space to agents and gives most of the commission to the agent

ANSWER KEY WITH EXPLANATIONS: DIAGNOSTIC TEST

1. **(3)** This is a disadvantage of S corporations as compared to limited liability companies. (160)
2. **(4)** Other disadvantages of a corporation include how capital gains and losses are treated. (159)
3. **(1)** The limited partners liability is limited to the amount of the investment. (160)
4. **(2)** ERA, Century 21, and RE/MAX are all franchises. Fannie Mae is a strong player in the secondary mortgage market. (160–161)
5. **(4)** The landlord-broker owns the office and rents the space to other brokers on a per-desk basis. (161)
6. **(3)** The broker may not provide fringe benefits such as health insurance or pension plans. (162)
7. **(1)** 10 desks × 2 salespeople = 20 salespeople

   \$300,000 annual overhead ÷ 20 salespeople = \$15,000 (165–166)
8. **(2)** Laissez-faire is the least authoritarian management style. (163)
9. **(3)** The accrual method is more complicated than the cash method. (164)
10. **(4)** Some of the larger firms maintain prelicensing classes from which they recruit salespeople. (164)
11. **(4)** Personal problems are handled by the manager or owner on an individual basis. (164)
12. **(4)** The policy and procedure manual must be made available to new salespeople. (164–165)
13. **(4)** Maintaining a record of showings would be included in the policy and procedures manual. (165)
14. **(2)** Trust funds must be deposited in a special checking account. (165)
15. **(4)** Brokers generally provide periodic meetings to present information allowing salespeople to stay up-to-date in their field. This type of material could also be included in advanced training programs. (165)

TEST SCORE

BROKERAGE MANAGEMENT			
Rating	**Range**	**Your Score**	
Good = 80% to 100%	12–15	Total Number	15
Fair = 70% to 79%	10–11	Total Wrong	–
Needs improvement = Lower than 70%	9 or less	Total Right	

Passing Requirement: 10 or Better

ANSWER KEY: MATCHING QUIZ

1. C	**6.** L	**11.** K	**16.** R
2. B	**7.** I	**12.** O	**17.** S
3. A	**8.** H	**13.** M	**18.** P
4. E	**9.** J	**14.** N	**19.** T
5. D	**10.** G	**15.** Q	**20.** F

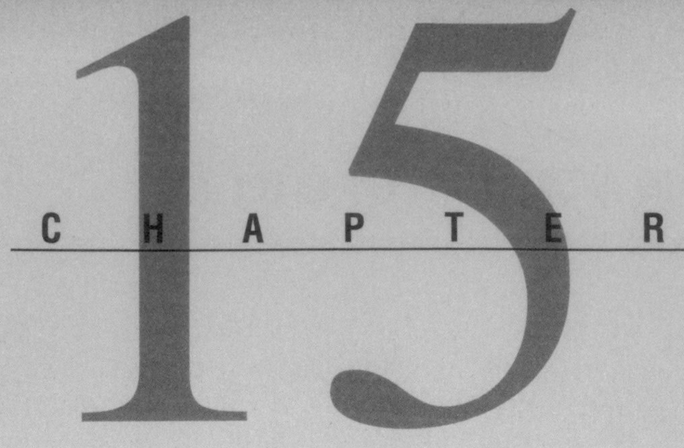

Salesperson Examinations

The sample examinations that follow evaluate your general real estate knowledge and test-taking ability. Simulate as closely as possible the actual test conditions (see Chapter 1, "Use of the Manual"); avoid distractions; and use only those tools permitted by your state. These exams contain 80 or 100 questions. Circle your answer for each question. Remember that the PSI exam includes an additional 40- to 50-question portion that tests your knowledge of your state's real estate laws and specific real estate practices.

After completing and grading the sample exams, carefully analyze your results. Did you complete all the questions in the allotted time? Did you answer a minimum of 65 or 81 questions correctly? It will be useful to mark in the answer key all the questions you missed. The answers and explanations are keyed to pages in the concepts-to-understand outlines for each part. The pattern of your errors should immediately suggest which areas require additional study.

As a final check, you may wish to review all the exam questions in the *Guide* that relate to a specific topic. Feel free to test and retest yourself. The greater your familiarity with the scope and style of the PSI exam, the better you are likely to perform.

SALESPERSON EXAMINATION I

1. Which of the following would NOT be considered real property?
   1. Mineral rights
   2. A leasehold estate
   3. Fixtures
   4. Air

2. The servient estate in an easement appurtenant is the property
   1. owned by the landlord.
   2. on which the easement is placed.
   3. owned by the tenant.
   4. that benefits from the easement.

3. Which of the following statements concerning encumbrances is NOT true?
   1. All encumbrances are liens.
   2. All liens are encumbrances.
   3. Restrictions beneficial to the grantee are encumbrances.
   4. An easement is a physical encumbrance.

4. Which of the following is NOT a specific lien?
   1. Mortgage lien
   2. State inheritance taxes
   3. Real estate taxes
   4. Mechanic's lien

5. You have entered into a lease that requires you to pay 20 percent of the owner's expenses. Your lease would be an example of a
   1. variable lease.
   2. net lease.
   3. percentage lease.
   4. gross lease.

6. If a husband and wife own an apartment building and the husband owns an undivided three-fourths interest and the wife owns a one-fourth interest, what type of tenancy exists?
   1. Leasehold estate
   2. Joint tenancy
   3. Tenancy in common
   4. Tenancy by the entirety

7. The highest form of ownership interest a person may hold in real estate is
   1. life estate
   2. fee simple.
   3. legal life estate.
   4. base fee.

8. Two unrelated people own a three-unit apartment building as tenants in common. One wants to sell but the other does not. Which of the following statements describes the legal rights of the party who wants to sell?
   1. The party may request a court to partition the building.
   2. The party may require the co-owner to sell.
   3. The party may record a lis pendens on the property.
   4. The party may refinance the mortgage in her or his own name, thus eliminating the co-owner's interest in the property.

9. Your aunt died intestate and you inherited her house. The way in which you acquired the title to her house is by
   1. curtesy.
   2. descent.
   3. escheat.
   4. laches.

10. Which of the following statements does NOT correctly describe a legal life estate?
    1. During his or her life estate the life tenant is generally answerable to the holder of the future interest.
    2. The life tenant may not commit any acts that would permanently injure the property.
    3. There may be a reversionary interest.
    4. There may be a remainder interest.

11. Which of the following is NOT a leasehold estate?
    1. An estate for years
    2. Periodic estate
    3. Time-share estate
    4. Estate from year to year

12. You are married and own a house under a form of ownership that prohibits you from selling it without the signature of your spouse. Your form of ownership is LEAST likely to be:
    1. in severalty.
    2. a joint tenancy.
    3. a tenancy in common.
    4. a tenancy by the entirety.

13. A state wants to build a publicly owned convention center to attract private development in its largest city. Can the state use eminent domain to acquire the land?
    1. No, because private investments would not be allowed.
    2. Yes, if just compensation is paid to the owners of the land.
    3. No, because eminent domain can only be used for highway expansion.
    4. Yes, if the owners hold fee-simple interest in the land.
14. Which of the following grants zoning authority to municipal governments?
    1. Eminent domain
    2. State enabling acts
    3. Laches
    4. Escheat
15. The city in which you live has a zoning ordinance. The basis for the city to have such an ordinance is
    1. eminent domain.
    2. escheat.
    3. police power
    4. riparian right
16. Which of the following terms are NOT related?
    1. Freehold estate–fee simple
    2. Grantor–person conveying title
    3. Leasehold estate–personal property
    4. Police power–deed restriction
17. Strict liability under Superfund means that
    1. each of the individual owners is personally responsible for the damages in whole.
    2. the owner is responsible to the injured party without excuse.
    3. the liability is not limited to the person who currently owns the property but also includes people who have owned the site in the past.
    4. the owner is not responsible to the injured party unless it can be proved that the owner was aware of the problem.
18. Which of the following does NOT correctly describe how real estate licensees should handle the possibility of hazardous substances on a property being sold?
    1. Clients should be asked about the possibility of hazardous substances on the property.
    2. Licensees should consider the consequences of potential liability.
    3. Licensees should be scrupulous in considering environmental issues.
    4. Licensees should not disclose the problem because it might harm the seller.
19. Sources of groundwater contamination do NOT include:
    1. waste disposal sites.
    2. underground storage tanks.
    3. use of pesticides in farming communities.
    4. radon.
20. Your neighbor has given you revocable permission to go hunting on his farm. You have a(n):
    1. leasehold estate.
    2. easement appurtenant.
    3. license.
    4. defeasible fee estate.
21. A claim based on adverse possession of property must NOT be
    1. notorious.
    2. open.
    3. hostile.
    4. secretive.
22. A man gives his friend the right to go hunting on his property for just one day. This is an example of:
    1. a license.
    2. an easement in gross.
    3. an easement appurtenant.
    4. an easement by prescription.
23. A person who receives real property by will is called a
    1. trustee.
    2. devisee.
    3. testator.
    4. hypothecator.
24. Riparian rights would exist in a
    1. condominium on a bay.
    2. house on a bay.
    3. hotel whose land abuts a large lake.
    4. cooperative on a river.
25. A developer was able to buy two adjoining single-family lots for $20,000 each. He combined the lots into one parcel with a value of $90,000. The developer's action reflects the process of
    1. accession.
    2. attachment.
    3. exchange.
    4. plottage.

26. A restaurant opened in a neighborhood and was enjoying substantial profits. Within a year another restaurant was built across the street and resulted in the first restaurant losing, in the next year, 30 percent of its profits. This is an example of the principle of
    1. competition.
    2. conformity.
    3. highest and best use.
    4. progression.

27. A meatpacking plant has just been built one block from your house. The strong odors are lowering property values in your neighborhood. The loss in value would be classified as
    1. functional obsolescence.
    2. physical deterioration.
    3. the principle of change.
    4. external obsolescence.

28. In the appraisal of a public building, an appraiser would use the
    1. cost approach.
    2. income capitalization approach.
    3. sale comparison approach.
    4. gross rent multiplier.

29. A four-bedroom house with one bathroom would be an example of
    1. physical deterioration.
    2. functional obsolescence.
    3. economic obsolescence.
    4. environmental obsolescence.

30. Which of the following is NOT a stage in the appraisal process?
    1. State the problem.
    2. Analyze the tax consequences of the property owner.
    3. Reconcile the data for the final value estimate.
    4. Analyze and interpret the data.

31. An appraiser uses the cost approach in appraising a home. The appraiser should NOT use which of the following types of information?
    1. Physical deterioration
    2. Cost of replacement of house
    3. Depreciation of land
    4. Economic obsolescence

32. A house that is the least expensive in its neighborhood has nevertheless grown significantly in value over the years because of an increasing number of larger, more expensive houses being built nearby. This growth in value is an example of the principle of
    1. regression.
    2. competition.
    3. progression.
    4. highest and best use.

33. You are preparing a competitive market analysis on a house that you hope to list for sale. Which of the following approaches to value will be used in the development of the estimated value?
    1. Cost approach
    2. Gross rent multiplier
    3. Income approach
    4. Sales comparison approach

34. A competitive market analysis reflects the use of the:
    1. cost approach.
    2. income approach.
    3. sales-comparison approach.
    4. gross-rent-multiplier method.

35. Bank *A* holds a lien on a home on which Bank *B* already had a lien. The lenders subsequently entered into an agreement in which Bank *A* moved into a first lien position. This is an example of a(n)
    1. hypothecation agreement.
    2. disintermediation agreement.
    3. reverse annuity mortgage.
    4. subordination agreement.

36. If the Federal Reserve Board raises its discount rate, which of the following is likely to occur?
    1. Mortgage money will become more available.
    2. Interest rates will stay the same.
    3. Mortgage money will become less available.
    4. Interest rates will decline.

37. You have a mortgage in which you make the same payment each month for principal and interest, with the principal payment increasing and the interest payment decreasing from month-to-month. This is called a(n)
    1. amortized mortgage.
    2. term mortgage.
    3. reverse annuity mortgage.
    4. partially amortized mortgage.

38. Which agency is involved in purchasing government-related loans?
    1. Fannie Mae
    2. Ginnie Mae
    3. Freddie Mac
    4. The "Fed"

39. Which of the following agencies is NOT included in the secondary mortgage market?
    1. FHA
    2. FNMA
    3. GNMA
    4. FHLMC

40. All loans subject to the Real Estate Settlement Procedures Act (RESPA) require lenders to
    1. charge the seller for all loan discount points.
    2. document any reason for declining credit to a loan applicant.
    3. deliver a Uniform Settlement Statement (HUD-1) form to both buyer and seller.
    4. allow the buyer to rescind the contract any time prior to the first payment due date.

41. You mortgaged your property and just made the final payment. Recording which of the following documents will provide notice that the mortgage lien has been removed?
    1. Reconveyance deed
    2. Satisfaction of mortgage
    3. Alienation of the mortgage instrument
    4. Reversion of the "deed"

42. When a loan is subject to the provisions of the Real Estate Settlement Procedures Act (RESPA), which of the following elements of a real estate transaction need NOT observe RESPA guidelines?
    1. The commission structure for licensees
    2. The type of settlement statement used at the closing
    3. Who receives a good-faith estimate of closing costs
    4. The payment of referral fees to licensees by providers of closing-related services

43. Regulation Z of the Truth-in-Lending Act provides which of the following penalties for licensees who willfully fail to comply with its advertising guidelines for real estate financing?
    1. Fines only
    2. License revocation
    3. Fines and/or imprisonment
    4. None; all violations of Regulation Z are referred to state licensing agencies

44. Salesperson *A* for broker *B* has listed a home. Salesperson *C* for broker *D* is acting as a buyer's agent and trying to sell the same home to his buyer. Salesperson *C* is primarily responsible to
    1. his own buyer.
    2. salesperson *A*.
    3. broker *B*.
    4. broker *D*.

45. In most states, the listing broker has a fiduciary duty with
    1. the customer.
    2. the listing salesperson.
    3. the client.
    4. the buyer.

46. A broker was employed by an owner to sell her home. Which of the following statements does NOT correctly describe the broker's relationship to the owner?
    1. The broker has become the seller's agent.
    2. The broker owes fiduciary duty to the seller.
    3. The broker is a special agent.
    4. The broker is a general agent.

47. You are a licensee holding an open house on one of your listings. An old friend sees the sign and stops in, and ultimately asks you to write an offer to purchase. At this point, without any discussion about agency, which of the following statements about agency is correct?
    1. Your friend is your customer.
    2. Your position as seller's agent prohibits you from writing the offer.
    3. The request automatically creates an express dual agency relationship.
    4. The relationship with your friend presents an irreconcilable conflict of interest.

48. You listed a home that was subsequently shown by six cooperating outside brokers. How many seller-agency relationships are involved in this transaction?
    1. One
    2. Six
    3. Seven
    4. None of the above

49. A salesperson listed a home for sale and transferred to another brokerage firm two weeks later. Which of the following statements describes the status of the listing?
   1. The listing is terminated.
   2. The listing is transferred to the new broker.
   3. The two brokers will negotiate to decide who will hold the listing.
   4. The listing will stay with the former broker of the salesperson.

50. A salesperson presented an offer that was accepted and received an earnest money payment for $2,000. The salesperson should:
   1. hold the payment until the buyer has received a financing commitment.
   2. give the earnest money to his broker.
   3. open up a trust account and deposit the payment in it.
   4. deposit the payment in the seller's checking account.

51. You are working as a buyer's broker for a client. Which of the following would NOT describe your role as a buyer's broker?
   1. You should show the buyer properties only in which your commission is protected.
   2. You should counsel the buyer about developing accurate objectives.
   3. You should search for the best properties for your buyer to inspect, widening the marketplace to include homes for sale by owners (FSBOs).
   4. You should help the buyer prepare the strongest offer.

52. According to the law of agency, a real estate broker does NOT owe the principal the duty of
   1. exercising reasonable care.
   2. acting in good faith.
   3. conforming with the principal's legal instructions.
   4. offering legal advice.

53. A broker acting as the agent of a seller
   1. can agree to a change in the listing price without the principal's approval.
   2. may share her commission with the salesperson of another broker.
   3. must report all offers to the principal unless instructed otherwise.
   4. must maintain as confidential all information the principal says not to disclose.

54. A broker listed a residential property under a valid written listing agreement. After the sale was completed, the owner refused to pay the broker's fee. Which of the following can the broker do?
   1. She can take the seller to court and sue for the commission.
   2. She is entitled to a lien on the seller's property for the amount of the commission.
   3. She can go to court and stop the transaction until she is paid.
   4. She can collect the commission from the buyer.

55. Commissions and fees paid by the seller to a listing agency are determined by
   1. standards promulgated by the local board of REALTORS®.
   2. negotiations between the seller and the listing licensee.
   3. applying the prevailing customary fees charged in that area.
   4. an industry index computed monthly from multiple-listing service data.

56. A listing broker is MOST likely to have earned a commission from a principal when which of the following events occur?
   1. An offer to purchase has been presented to the client.
   2. Title has been transferred to the buyer.
   3. The seller accepts and signs an offer to purchase.
   4. A "ready, willing, and able buyer" signs a noncontingent or cash offer that meets the terms of the listing contract.

57. A broker listed an owner's home and later received an offer from another licensee that met all of the listing terms and conditions. After considering the offer, the owner informed the broker that the owner no longer wished to sell, and asked to be released from the listing agreement immediately. Which of the following is a TRUE statement about the broker's position in this situation?
   1. The broker must release the owner without obligation.
   2. The broker must tell the owner that the offeror may sue for specific performance.
   3. The broker may succeed in collecting an earned commission from the owner.
   4. The broker may keep the earnest money that accompanied the offer as liquidated damages.

58. On July 1 an owner and a salesperson entered into a six-month exclusive-right-to-sell agreement for a residential property. On July 15 the owner rejected a low offer and fired the listing agent. On August 1 there was a house fire that required extensive kitchen repairs. On September 12 the owner entered into another exclusive-right-to-sell agreement with a salesperson from a different agency. On January 1 the property was still unsold. On which date was the first listing agreement MOST likely to terminate and why?
   1. July 15, because the salesperson was dismissed
   2. August 1, because the listed property suffered material damage
   3. September 12, because the owner breached the first listing agreement by signing a second
   4. January 1, because the first listing agreement ended at midnight on December 31

59. An option, prior to being exercised, is an example of
   1. an assignable contract.
   2. a unilateral contract.
   3. a bilateral contract.
   4. an executed contract.

60. Which of the following is a similarity between an exclusive-right-to-sell listing and an exclusive-agency listing?
   1. Under both, the seller avoids paying the broker a commission if the seller sells the property without the help of the broker.
   2. Both give the responsibility of representing the seller to just one broker.
   3. Both are net listings.
   4. Under both, the seller authorizes one specific salesperson to show the property.

61. A buyer has entered into an agency agreement with more than one buyer's agent but only owes compensation to the one who puts an actual transaction together. This arrangement is known as a(n)
   1. multiple-listing agreement.
   2. exclusive right agreement.
   3. exclusive agency agreement.
   4. nonexclusive agency agreement.

62. Which of the following types of clauses governs the right of a listing broker to collect a commission from an owner who waits until the listing period expires and then personally contracts to sell the property to a party the broker had shown the property to during the listing period?
   1. Alienation
   2. Protection
   3. Defeasance
   4. Habendum

63. You wrote an offer on a house for $214,000. The seller gave you a counteroffer for $218,000. The seller may withdraw the counteroffer any time
   1. within 72 hours after acceptance.
   2. prior to the buyer's acceptance.
   3. prior to removal of all contingencies in the offer.
   4. prior to closing.

64. You signed a lease for one year and took possession of an apartment. When the lease expired, you continued to live in the apartment without the owner's consent. Your tenancy would be considered to be a(n)
   1. estate for years.
   2. estate from year to year.
   3. tenancy at will.
   4. tenancy at sufferance.

65. A commercial lease that allows rent to be increased or decreased periodically based on changes in economic indicators is a(n)
   1. graduated lease.
   2. gross lease.
   3. percentage lease.
   4. index lease.

66. In theory, which of the following types of deeds gives a property buyer the MOST protection against problems that may arise with the title?
   1. Quitclaim
   2. Bargain and sale
   3. Special warranty
   4. General warranty

67. You have entered into an installment land contract for the sale of your home. Which of the following is NOT correct?
    1. The buyer is the vendee.
    2. The buyer will take possession when the contract is signed by both parties, if the contract so provides.
    3. The buyer will hold legal title during the term of the contract.
    4. The buyer will hold equitable title during the term of the contract.

68. Personal property is generally conveyed by a
    1. bill of sale.
    2. certificate of title.
    3. quitclaim deed.
    4. trust deed.

69. The movement of land caused by an earthquake would be an example of
    1. accretion.
    2. avulsion.
    3. erosion.
    4. hypothecation.

70. When property transfers from one party to another, recording the deed provides what is called
    1. validation of the agreement between the parties.
    2. a writ of attachment.
    3. certificate of title.
    4. constructive notice.

71. The IRS has how many requirements for establishing an independent contractor status?
    1. One
    2. Two
    3. Three
    4. Four

72. Brokers who violate the Sherman Antitrust Act may be punished by a maximum fine of
    1. $10,000.
    2. $25,000.
    3. $50,000.
    4. $100,000.

73. Which of the following is NOT a violation of antitrust laws?
    1. Two brokers agree that they both will pay 2.5 percent of the sales price to cooperating brokers on all listings published in an MLS after the date of the specified agreement.
    2. Two brokers agree to pay just $40 to the Reliance Title Company for closings.
    3. Two brokers agree not to cooperate with a flat-fee broker.
    4. A broker refuses to cooperate with a flat-fee broker.

74. The Civil Rights Act of 1866 prohibits discrimination based on
    1. handicap.
    2. familial status.
    3. race.
    4. sex.

75. Broker *X* is showing buyer *Y*, an Asian, homes only in Asian neighborhoods. The broker may be guilty of
    1. arbitrage.
    2. blockbusting.
    3. redlining.
    4. steering.

76. Which of the following is NOT a category protected by federal fair housing laws against discrimination in housing?
    1. Race
    2. National origin
    3. Sexual orientation
    4. Familial status

77. You sign an agreement to purchase a home. The contract requires that the seller replace the damaged living room carpet. The carpet you have chosen costs $16.95 per square yard plus $4.50 per square yard for installation. If the living room dimensions are as illustrated in Figure 15.1, how much will the seller have to pay for the job?
    1. $357.50
    2. $314.60
    3. $353.93
    4. None of the above

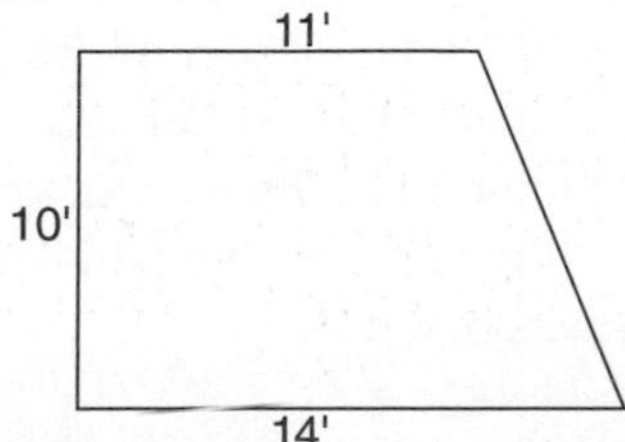

FIGURE 15.1

78. A house has been difficult to sell. The salesperson suggests it might sell faster if the owner enclosed a portion of the backyard with a privacy fence. If the area to be enclosed is as illustrated in Figure 15.2, how much would the fence cost at $8.40 per linear foot?
   1. $546
   2. $1,512
   3. $2,058
   4. None of the above

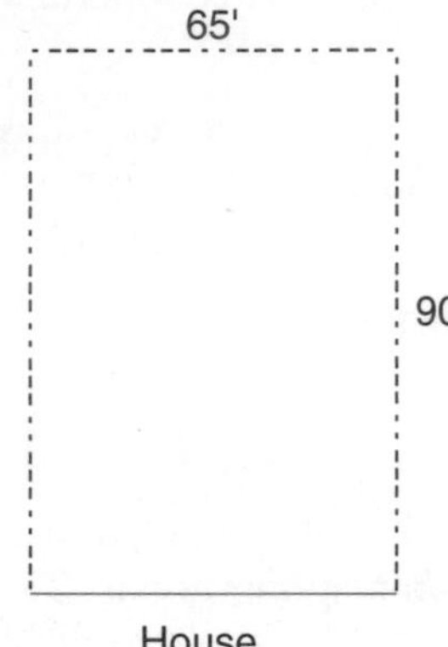

FIGURE 15.2

79. A sale is to close on June 23. Real estate taxes of $2,640 for the current year have NOT been paid. What is the amount of the real estate tax proration to be credited to the buyer? (Use a 30-day month for calculation.)
   1. $168.67
   2. $868.67
   3. $1,268.66
   4. None of the above

80. A home is valued at $92,000. Property in this city is assessed at 70 percent of its value and the local tax rate is $3.40 per $100. What is the amount of the owner's monthly taxes?
   1. $182.47
   2. $260.67
   3. $2,189.60
   4. None of the above

81. A mother wants to know how much money her son owes on his mortgage loan. The mother knows that the interest part of the last monthly payment was $473.26. If her son is paying interest at the rate of 9 percent, what was the outstanding balance of the loan before the last payment was made?
   1. $52,584.44
   2. $55,921.03
   3. $63,101.33
   4. None of the above

82. You are selling your house and a buyer is assuming your outstanding mortgage, which has an unpaid balance of $58,700 after the last payment on August 1. If the annual interest rate is 9 percent and interest is paid in arrears each month, what is the amount of mortgage interest to be debited against you at closing, using a closing date of August 18?
   1. $161.43
   2. $176.10
   3. $190.78
   4. $264.15

83. Using $9.91 as a mortgage factor, what is the monthly payment for a $150,000 loan at 11.5 percent for 30 years?
   1. $1,429.50
   2. $1,486.50
   3. $1,525.50
   4. $1,581.00

84. Using the information in question 83, what is the total interest paid over the life of the loan?
   1. $297,300
   2. $371,625
   3. $535,140
   4. None of the above

85. A broker sold a home for $146,000. The broker charged the owner 6 percent commission and will pay 25 percent of that amount to the listing salesperson and 30 percent to the selling salesperson. What amount of commission will the listing salesperson receive from the sale?
   1. $2,058
   2. $2,190
   3. $2,628
   4. None of the above

86. You receive a monthly salary of $600 plus 3.5 percent commission on all of your listings that sell and 2.5 percent on all of your sales. None of the listings that you took sold last month, but you receive $8,460 in salary and commission. What was the value of the property you sold?
   1. $131,000
   2. $224,571
   3. $314,400
   4. None of the above

87. You bought a home one year ago for $83,500. Property in your neighborhood is said to be increasing in value at a rate of 6 percent annually. If this is true, what is the current value of your real estate?
   1. $86,840
   2. $87,675
   3. $88,510
   4. None of the above

88. What is the actual value of your property if the annual taxes are $2,880 and real estate is assessed at 30 percent of actual value? (Figure a levy of 4.8%, or 48 mills, or $4.80 per 100.)
    1. $86,400
    2. $120,000
    3. $200,000
    4. None of the above

89. Three investors decided to pool their savings and buy some commercial real estate for $180,000. If one invested $60,000 and the second invested $40,000, what percentage of ownership was left for the third investor, if the percentage is based on capital investment rather than services rendered?
    1. 22.2 percent
    2. 33 percent
    3. 44.4 percent
    4. None of the above

90. A farmer was unable to secure credit from other sources, so he probably got a mortgage loan from which of the following?
    1. FHA
    2. Savings and loan
    3. Farm Service Agency
    4. Commercial bank

91. *A* and *B*, a married couple, bought a principal residence in 1991 for $200,000. They sold the property in 1999 with a capital gain of $150,000. Capital gains tax on their profit will be
    1. nothing.
    2. $50,000.
    3. $150,000.
    4. $200,000.

92. If a buyer puts 20% down and borrows $200,000, what is the purchase price of her new home?
    1. $210,000
    2. $220,000
    3. $240,000
    4. $250,000

93. Which of the following home-related expenses would NOT generally be tax-deductible for a homeowner?
    1. Interest paid on a second mortgage
    2. Penalties for late payment of real estate taxes
    3. Prepayment penalties on loans
    4. Real estate taxes

94. Which of the following types of loans would be considered conventional?
    1. A privately insured loan
    2. An FHA loan
    3. A Freddie Mac loan
    4. A VA loan

95. Which of the following is NOT an agency that purchases loans on the secondary mortgage market?
    1. FDIC
    2. FNMA
    3. FHLMC
    4. GNMA

96. A margin is added to an index to determine the interest rate in which of the following types of mortgage?
    1. Adjustable rate
    2. Blanket
    3. Graduated payment
    4. Package

97. Which of the following statements would NOT be a material fact to be disclosed by a seller's agent?
    1. Presentation of all offers
    2. A relationship that the agent has with the buyer
    3. Buyer's ability to make a lower offer
    4. Discussion of disadvantages of an offer

98. Under the new capital gains tax law, a single person may take up to $250,000 in capital gains tax-free on the sale of a home if that person has lived in the house for at least
    1. the past year.
    2. two of the past five years.
    3. one of the past three years.
    4. two of the last four years.

99. Losing a right to the court's injunction by inaction is an example of the doctrine of
    1. accession.
    2. eminent domain.
    3. annexation.
    4. laches.

100. *A* gave *B* a deed with no express or implied warranty. The deed was most likely a
    1. general warranty deed.
    2. special warranty deed.
    3. bargain and sale deed.
    4. quitclaim deed.

ANSWER KEY WITH EXPLANATIONS

NOTE: The number in parentheses at the end of each explanation refers to the page number where this material is discussed.

1. **(2)** A leasehold estate is a non-freehold estate involving the tenant's right to occupy the real estate during the term of the lease. (148)
2. **(2)** A servient estate also is referred to as a servient tenement. The property that benefits from the easement is known as the dominant tenement. (20)
3. **(1)** Encumbrances may be liens, which affect the title, or physical encumbrances, which affect the condition of the land. However, an easement is an example of an encumbrance that is not a lien. Therefore, not all encumbrances are liens but it is true that all liens are encumbrances. (20)
4. **(2)** State inheritance taxes are a general lien and affect all the debtor's property. (20)
5. **(2)** A tenant in a net lease pays rent plus all or part of the property charges. A tenant in a gross lease pays a fixed rent, while the landlord pays all his or her own expenses. (148)
6. **(3)** Tenancy in common allows for percentage differences in ownership. A leasehold estate is a personal property interest. Joint tenancy and tenancy by the entirety require equal percentages of interests in most states. (22–23)
7. **(2)** A fee simple is the highest form of interest. A base fee is subject to certain limitations imposed by the owner. A life estate is limited to the life of an owner or some other person. Legal life estates are created by state law. (21)
8. **(1)** Tenants in common may partition the property by agreement and, if no agreement, by judicial determination. (22–23)
9. **(2)** When a person dies intestate, the decedent's real estate and personal property pass to his or her heirs according to the statutes. (103)
10. **(1)** The life tenant generally is not answerable to the holder of the future interest. (22)
11. **(3)** A time-share estate may include a fee-simple interest in condominium ownership. (150)
12. **(1)** Severalty refers to one owner. Joint tenants and tenants in common may convey individual interests; to transfer title normally requires both signatures. Tenancy by the entirety requires both signatures too. (22–23)
13. **(2)** The government has the right to acquire private property for public use while paying just compensation to the owner. The convention center would attract private development of hotels and retail establishments. The type of estate held by owners would not prevent the state from acquiring the land. (34)
14. **(2)** Eminent domain, laches, and escheat were defined earlier. (34)
15. **(3)** Police power is the power of the state to establish legislation to protect public health and safety and promote general welfare. (34)
16. **(4)** Police power is a public-land-use control; a deed restriction is a private-land-use control. (34)
17. **(2)** Joint and several liability means that each owner is personally responsible for the damages in whole; if only one owner is financially able to handle the total damage, that individual owner will have to pay all and attempt to collect from the other owners their proportionate shares. Retroactive liability means that liability also extends to people who have owned the site in the past. (40)
18. **(4)** The first three answers describe how licensees should handle that type of transaction. (41)
19. **(4)** Radon is an odorless radioactive gas released from rocks under the earth's surface that finds its way to the surface; it usually is released into the atmosphere. (37)

20. **(3)** License is permission to enter the land of another for a specific purpose, and the owner of the property may revoke it at any time. (21)

21. **(4)** A claim based on adverse possession must be notorious, open, and hostile. (103)

22. **(1)** A license is considered to be revocable permission. An easement in gross is a right to use the land of another. An easement appurtenant requires two tracts of land with one of the tracts benefiting from the easement. An easement by necessity is used where the owner is landlocked, and an easement by prescription is created by the hostile use of another's land. (21)

23. **(2)** A testator is a person who makes a will. Devise refers to a transfer of real property under a will. (103)

24. **(4)** Riparian rights are water rights granted to owners along a river or stream. (34)

25. **(4)** Accession refers to acquiring title to real property through the annexation of a fixture. Attachment is the act of placing a lien upon a person's property by a court. An exchange is a transaction in which part or all of the consideration is the transfer of like-kind property. (48)

26. **(1)** The principle of competition states that excess profits create ruinous competition. (48)

27. **(4)** Functional obsolescence and physical deterioration refer to a loss of value within the property, while external obsolescence refers to a loss of value outside the property. (49)

28. **(1)** The cost approach is considered most reliable in the appraisal of special-purpose buildings such as churches and schools. (49–50)

29. **(2)** Functional obsolescence is a loss in the value of a property resulting from a deficiency in the floor plan of a house. One bathroom would be inadequate for a four-bedroom house. (49)

30. **(2)** Tax consequences would be analyzed in a feasibility study exploring the potential for profitability in a proposed project. (51)

31. **(3)** Depreciation generally is applied to a wasting asset such as a building. Land is not considered a wasting asset. (49)

32. **(3)** The answer is progression. The principle of regression states that the value of the most expensive home in a neighborhood will be lessened by the presence of less expensive homes being built nearby. The principle of competition states that excess profits create ruinous competition. Highest and best use states that each parcel of land should be developed to its most profitable use subject to legal constraints such as zoning. (48)

33. **(4)** The cost approach is most applicable to the appraisal of special-purpose properties such as a church. The gross rent multiplier is used as a substitute for the income approach in the valuation of a single-family home. The income approach is, of course, used in the appraisal of an income-producing property. (50)

34. **(3)** The sales-comparison approach relies on comparable sales as well as sales that involve willing buyers and sellers, with neither under abnormal pressure. (50–51)

35. **(4)** Hypothecation refers to the pledging of property as security for a loan in which the borrower retains possession of the property pledged as security. Disintermediation results in less availability of mortgage money for lenders. A reverse annuity mortgage allows the borrower to receive periodic payments from the lender on the equity in the home. (66)

36. **(3)** Raising the discount rate would increase the interest rates and make mortgage money less available because of the increased cost of borrowing. (64)

37. **(1)** A term mortgage allows for payment of interest only with a lump-sum payment at maturity. A partially amortized loan also involves a lump-sum or balloon payment at maturity. (59)

38. **(2)** Ginnie Mae purchases FHA-insured, VA-guaranteed, and Rural Development loans on the secondary mortgage market. (65)

39. **(1)** The FHA insures mortgages made in the primary mortgage market. FNMA, GNMA, and FHLMC are major warehousing agencies in the secondary mortgage market. (61, 65)

40. **(3)** RESPA provides for use of a HUD-1 form. (106)

41. **(2)** An alienation clause states that if the borrower sells the property, the lender has the choice of either declaring the entire debt due and payable or allowing the buyer to assume the loan. A reconveyance clause is used in a trust deed. A reversion clause could be used in a deed and stipulates that if not complied with, the property reverts to the owner. (60)

42. **(1)** The commission agreement between the broker and client is negotiable and not subject to RESPA. (106)

43. **(3)** *Willful* violation is a misdemeanor punishable by a fine of up to $5,000, one year of imprisonment, or both. (119)

44. **(4)** Salesperson *C* is primarily responsible to his broker *D*. As an exclusive buyer's agent a vicarious agency relationship would exist between the broker and the buyer because all exclusive buyer-agency agreements are the property of the broker. (75)

45. **(3)** The fiduciary relationship of trust and confidence exists between the agent and the principal (client). The listing broker does not automatically have a fiduciary duty to the buyer or customer. (73)

46. **(4)** A real estate broker is a special agent authorized to represent the principal in one specific transaction. (73–74)

47. **(1)** The seller is your client. The customer is a third party for whom a service is provided. (73)

48. **(1)** In the absence of state law, the six cooperating brokers are not agents of the seller. In 1996 the National Association of REALTORS® eliminated the offering of subagency between cooperating brokers. Cooperating brokers may extend compensation and cooperation to outside brokers, but the offering of subagency is not sanctioned by the NAR. (73)

49. **(4)** The salesperson's listing of the home created an agency relationship between the seller and the salesperson's broker. The listing belongs to the broker. (75)

50. **(2)** Earnest money must be placed in the broker's trust account. (74)

51. **(1)** The buyer's broker has a fiduciary relationship with the buyer. (73)

52. **(4)** The broker may not offer legal advice—only a licensed attorney may do so. (73)

53. **(3)** Unless instructed otherwise, the broker is responsible for submitting all offers to his or her principal. (74)

54. **(1)** In most states, the broker has no lien on a property for a commission due on negotiating the sale of that property. Accordingly, the broker may not go to court to stop the transaction. The broker cannot collect the commission from the buyer because the buyer is not in the agency relationship between the seller and broker. In some states a broker may place a lien on property if in compliance with the statute. (74)

55. **(2)** The broker is not required to charge a commission; the commission is negotiable. (74)

56. **(4)** The broker generally earns the commission when he or she produces a "ready, willing, and able" buyer. (74)

57. **(3)** The owner has the power to terminate the listing contract but not necessarily the right; the broker may be able to sue the owner for damages. The offeror would not be able to sue for specific performance because the offer was not accepted; the owner is not obligated to accept the offer. The broker would not be entitled to the earnest money because the offer was never accepted; the earnest money would have to be returned to the offeror. Finally, the point at which a commission is earned is no longer an absolute in all jurisdictions. (74)

58. **(3)** Dismissal of the salesperson does not affect the listing because the broker, not the salesperson, is a party to the contract. Material damage is not destruction. Signing a second listing while the first listing is in effect is a clear breach of contract.

(Note, though, that the first listing broker may have some recourse against the seller for expenses). Expiration of the listing was too late, in light of the second listing having been signed. (74)

59. **(2)** An option is an example of a unilateral contract. An option is a promise to keep open for a specified period an offer to sell or purchase property. When the optionee exercises an option, it becomes a bilateral contract. (94)

60. **(2)** The exclusive-agency listing allows the seller to sell his or her own house without paying the broker a commission. The broker under an exclusive-right-to-sell listing receives a commission regardless of who sells the property. Either type is given to only one broker. (92)

61. **(4)** The buyer–nonexclusive agency agreement is similar to an open listing–seller agreement. (92)

62. **(2)** Standard listings contain a clause that stipulates that if the property is sold to someone who was introduced to the property by the broker, even after the listing has expired, the broker is entitled to a commission. Usually, there is a time period written into the clause. This is called the protection clause. Alienation and defeasance are related to mortgages; the habendum clause is found in a deed. (75)

63. **(2)** Any offer or counteroffer may be withdrawn at any time prior to acceptance by the offeree. (95)

64. **(4)** A tenant at sufferance continues to hold possession without consent of the landlord. (148)

65. **(4)** An index lease is adjusted periodically based on changes in an agreed cost-of-living index. (148)

66. **(4)** A general warranty deed with title insurance provides the grantee with the most protection. A special warranty deed only promises to warrant against title defects during the grantor's time of ownership. However, with title insurance this is a good deed. The quitclaim deed is the least protective because it makes no expressed or implied warranties. (104)

67. **(3)** The buyer (vendee) will not receive the deed to the property until the entire land contract has been paid in full. (94–95)

68. **(1)** Real property is conveyed by deed. (18)

69. **(2)** Erosion is the wearing away of land by natural forces such as wind; avulsion is the sudden removal of soil by an act of nature. (41)

70. **(4)** Deeds are recorded to establish priority and provide protection against third parities. (106)

71. **(3)** The three IRS requirements for establishing independent contractor status are: (1) the individual must have a current real estate license; (2) the individual must have a written contract with broker that states that the salesperson will not be treated as an employee for federal tax purposes; and 3.) ninety (90) percent or more of the individual's income as a licensee must be based on sales production rather than the number of hours worked. (107)

72. **(4)** In addition to the maximum fine, the broker may have to serve up to three years in prison. (76)

73. **(4)** The first two responses are examples of illegal price fixing, and the third is considered illegal boycotting. However, the last is an independent business decision and does not violate antitrust laws. (76)

74. **(3)** As part of the Fair Housing Act of 1968 sex became a protected class in 1974; familial status and disability became protected classes in 1988. (114)

75. **(4)** Blockbusting, racial steering, and redlining are violations of the Federal Fair Housing Act of 1968, which was discussed. Arbitrage refers to an increase in return created by the difference between interest rates charged in financing arrangements. (117)

76. **(3)** The federal fair housing laws do not include age, martial status, or sexual orientation in their protected arrangements. (114)

77. **(4)** See Figure 15.3.

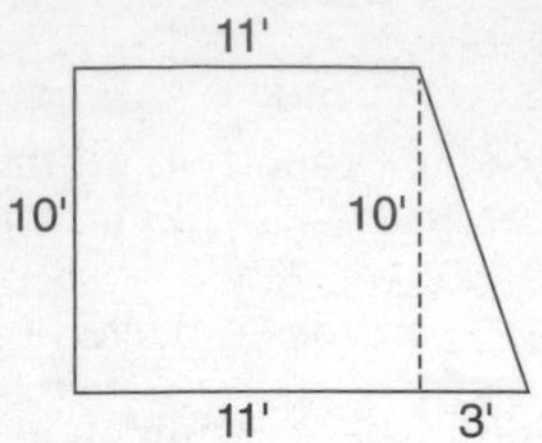

FIGURE 15.3

11' × 10' = 110 square feet, area of rectangle

½ (3' × 10') = ½ (30') = 15 square feet, area of triangle

110 + 15 = 125 square feet

To convert square feet to square yards, divide by 9

125 ÷ 9 = 13.888 square yards

$16.95 + $4.50 installation = $21.45, cost per square yard

$21.45 × 13.888 square yards = $297.92 (129–130)

78. **(3)** See Figure 15.4

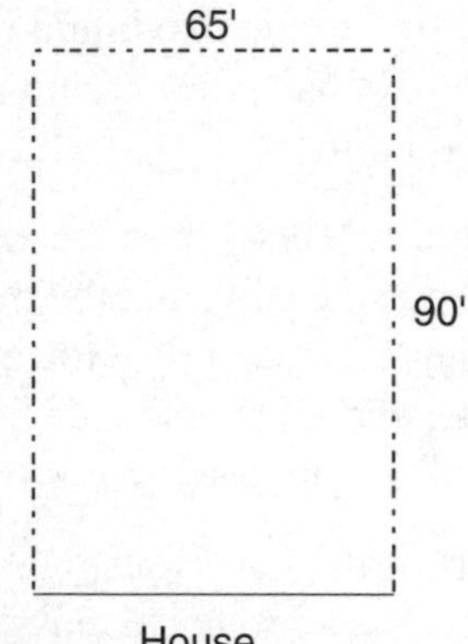

FIGURE 15.4

2 sides of 90' + one side of 65'

180' + 65' = 245 linear feet

245 × $8.40 = $2,058 (129)

79. **(3)** $2,640 ÷ 12 months = $220 per month

$220 ÷ 30 days = $7.333 per day

$220 × 5 months = $1,100

$7.333 × 23 days = $168.66

$1,100 + $168 = $1,268.66 (133–134)

80. **(1)** $92,000 × 70% (0.70) = $64,400 assessed value

Divide by 100 because the tax rate is stated per $100

$64,400 ÷ 100 = $644

$644 × $3.40 = $2,189.60, annual taxes

Divide by 12 to get the monthly taxes

$2,189.60 ÷ 12 = $182.47 (128)

81. **(3)** $473.26 × 12 = $5,679.12 annual interest

part ÷ percent = total

$5,679.12 ÷ 9% (0.09) = $63,101.33 (127)

82. **(4)** $58,700 × 9% (0.09) = $5,283

$5,283 ÷ 12 months = $440.25 per month

$440.25 ÷ 30 days = $14.675 per day

18 days × $14.675 = $264.15 (133–134)

83. **(2)** $150,000 ÷ 1,000 = $150 × 9.91 = $1,486.50 (134–137)

84. **(4)** $1,486.50 × 360 months =

$535,140 (total principal and interest) – $150,000 Amount of loan =

$385,140, total interest paid over the life of the loan (134–137)

85. **(2)** $146,000 sales price × 6% commission

$146,000 × 0.06 = $8,760 × 0.25 = $2,190 (126–128)

86. **(3)** $8,460 – $600 = $7,860, commission on sales

$7,860 ÷ 2.5% (0.025) = $314,400, value of property sold (126–128)

87. **(3)** $83,500 × 6% (0.06) = $5,010, annual increase in value

$83,500 + $5,010 = $88,510, current market value (126–128)

88. **(3)** $2,880 ÷ 0.048 = $60,000, assessed value

$60,000 ÷ 30% (0.30) = $200,000, market value (126–128)

89. **(3)** $60,000 first investor + $40,000 second investor = $100,000

$180,000 – $100,000 = $80,000, third investor's contribution

part ÷ total = percent

$80,000 ÷ $180,000 = 44.4% (126–128)

90. **(3)** The Farm Service Agency provides loans in communities of 10,000 or fewer. (62)

91. **(1)** A married couple may exclude $500,000 from capital gains tax for profits on the sale of a principal residence if they file jointly. (106)

92. **(4)** 200,000 divided by 80% = $250,000 (127)

93. **(2)** Real estate taxes, but not penalties for late payments of taxes, are deductible. (107)

94. **(1)** A conventional loan is neither insured nor guaranteed by the government agency. (61)

95. **(1)** FDIC is insurance paid by lenders to protect their customer's deposits up to $100,000. The others are members of the secondary mortgage market. (65)

96. **(1)** Most of the indexes used in adjustable rate mortgages are related to U.S. Treasury securities. The margin reflects the lender's cost of doing business. (63)

97. **(3)** A seller's agent would disclose, in most states, that the buyer was able to make a higher offer. (73–74)

98. **(2)** A single person may take up to $250,000 and a married couple may take up to $500,000 in capital gains tax-free, provided that the principal residence is occupied for at least two out of the last five years. (106)

99. **(4)** Accession and annexation relate to personal property's becoming real property. Eminent domain allows the government to take private property for public use while paying just compensation to the owner. (25)

100. **(4)** Warranty deeds contain promises or covenants; the quitclaim deed provides no promises or covenants of warranty. In a quitclaim deed, the grantor is only releasing or quitting an interest possessed; no warranty is provided to the grantee. (104)

SALESPERSON EXAMINATION II

1. A grantor wishes to convey title to a grantee in a deed that creates the least protection for the grantee. The grantor should give the grantee a
   1. bargain and sale deed.
   2. quitclaim deed.
   3. general warranty deed.
   4. special warranty deed.

2. Of the following liens, which generally would be given the highest priority?
   1. A judgment issued last year
   2. A mortgage recorded four years ago
   3. A special assessment
   4. A mechanic's lien for work begun two months ago

3. You are showing a property described as being in the "nicest neighborhood in town" when, in fact, other neighborhoods are arguably as nice. A statement such as this is MOST likely to be categorized as
   1. fraud.
   2. puffing or puffery.
   3. misrepresentation.
   4. professional negligence.

4. You are chairperson of the Democratic party in your state, and you also own an eight-unit apartment building you currently rent out. You are taking a rental application from a prospective tenant when she informs you that she works for the Republican party of your state. You inform her that all the apartments have been rented even though you know they have not been rented. Which of the following statements correctly describes this unethical situation?
   1. You have violated Regulation Z.
   2. You have violated the federal fair housing law.
   3. You have exercised your rights as an owner of private property to discriminate.
   4. You have violated RESPA.

5. When a listing agreement includes a broker protection clause, the clause
   1. protects the broker against any lawsuits filed by the client.
   2. allows the broker to buy the listed property if the broker is unable to sell it.
   3. automatically extends the listing for six months if the broker is unable to see the property.
   4. states that the owner will pay a commission to the listing broker if the property is sold to a buyer with whom the broker negotiated during the listing term within a specific time after the listing expires.

6. Which of the following would not be considered to be real property?
   1. Trees
   2. Buildings
   3. Trade fixtures
   4. Water rights

7. A sale is to be closed on June 23. Real estate taxes of $3,760 for the current year have NOT been paid. What is the amount of real estate tax proration to be credited to the buyer? (Use a 30-day month for calculation.)
   1. $1,566.65
   2. $1,806.86
   3. $1,879.98
   4. None of the above

8. The giver of an option is called the
   1. vendor.
   2. optionor.
   3. vendee.
   4. optionee.

9. Which of the following types of depreciation is generally incurable?
   1. Physical deterioration
   2. Economic or external obsolescence
   3. Functional obsolescence
   4. Physical depreciation

10. Three investors decided to pool their savings and buy a motel for $330,000. If one invested $90,000 and the second contributed $50,000, what percentage of ownership was left for the third investor?
    1. 14.1
    2. 27.3
    3. 57.6
    4. None of the above

11. Which of the following clauses gives a lender the right to declare the entire debt due and payable if the mortgaged property is either assumed without lender approval or sold on contract without lender approval?
    1. Acceleration clause
    2. Equitable redemption
    3. Defeasance clause
    4. Alienation clause

12. A woman owns a tract of land that also is a servient tenement. The easement over, through, or under the tract is a(n)
    1. lien.
    2. encumbrance.
    3. license.
    4. encroachment.

13. In an exclusive-right-to-sell listing agreement, how many agents are involved?
    1. Two
    2. One
    3. As many as the owner/lister chooses
    4. As many salespeople as the broker has in his or her office

14. The broker has listed an owner's home. This agreement will be terminated by all of the following **EXCEPT**
    1. death of the listing salesperson.
    2. death of the owner.
    3. death of the broker.
    4. bankruptcy of the broker.

15. A drunken man signed an offer to purchase. The contract that he signed is
    1. valid.
    2. void.
    3. voidable.
    4. unenforceable.

16. You sign an agreement to purchase a home. The contract requires that the seller replace the damaged living room carpet. The carpet you have chosen costs $18.95 per square yard plus $5.50 per square yard for installation. If the living room dimensions are as illustrated in Figure 15.5, how much will the seller have to pay for the job?
    1. $315.82
    2. $407.34
    3. $490.81
    4. None of the above

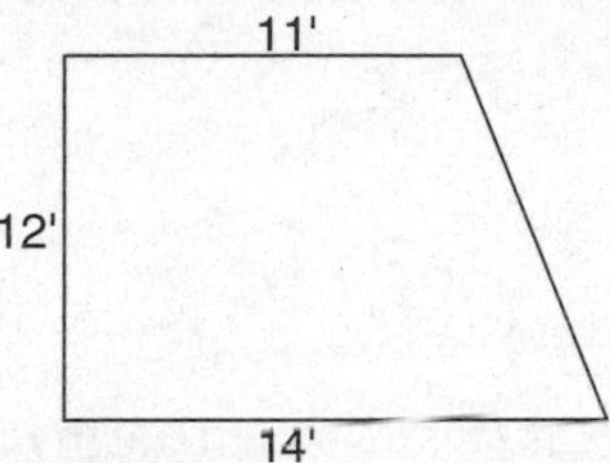

FIGURE 15.5

17. All of the following agency relationships could be used to describe a cooperating broker in a real estate transaction **EXCEPT**
    1. a subagent.
    2. an exclusive buyer's broker.
    3. a selling broker.
    4. a non-exclusive buyer's broker.

18. An appraiser is trying to determine the value of an income property by capitalizing the income stream. Which of the following factors will the appraiser use?
    1. Mortgage interest
    2. Net income
    3. Replacement cost
    4. Income taxes

19. A partial release clause generally is found in a
    1. construction mortgage
    2. package mortgage
    3. blanket mortgage
    4. wraparound mortgage

20. Which of the following scenarios would NOT be considered discriminatory under federal fair housing laws?
    1. A man owns and lives in his four-unit apartment building, and he refuses to rent to families with children.
    2. A landlord charges higher security deposits to tenants with children.
    3. A landlord places all families in selected buildings in his apartment complex.
    4. A landlord refuses to rent to a pregnant woman.

21. Which of the following is a requirement for a valid deed?
    1. The grantee must sign the deed.
    2. The consideration must be in dollars.
    3. It must contain a subordination clause.
    4. It must contain a granting clause.

22. You bought a home one year ago for $115,900. Property in your neighborhood is said to be increasing in value at a rate of 8 percent annually. If this is true, what is the current value of your real estate?
    1. $125,172
    2. $134,444
    3. $144,063
    4. None of the above

23. An enforceable contract may contain any of the following as consideration **EXCEPT**
    1. money.
    2. love.
    3. affection.
    4. duress.

24. Which of the following is an economic characteristic of land?
    1. Immobility
    2. Situs
    3. Nonhomogeneity
    4. Indestructibility

25. You have just given an option to buy your restaurant to a friend. Which of the following statements is NOT correct?
    1. Your friend is the optionee.
    2. You are the optionor.
    3. Your friend is obligated to buy your restaurant.
    4. Your friend must pay a fee of some kind for the option right.

26. A broker listed a home under the condition that the owner receive $210,000 from the sale, with the broker being able to sell the property for as much as possible and keep the difference as the commission. This unethical if not illegal agreement is an example of
    1. an exclusive-agency listing.
    2. an exclusive-right-to-sell listing.
    3. a net listing.
    4. an option listing.

27. A broker was offered a listing by homeowners who stated that they would not sell to a minority. The broker should
    1. accept the listing and allow the owners the right to choose the buyer.
    2. file a complaint with the local board of REALTORS®.
    3. accept the listing and make sure that no minorities are shown the property.
    4. refuse to accept the listing based on this condition.

28. All of the following would be public land use controls **EXCEPT**
    1. zoning.
    2. environmental protection laws.
    3. subdivision regulations.
    4. deed restrictions.

29. A home is valued at $103,000. Property in this city is assessed at 80 percent of its value and the local tax rate is $3.60 per $100. What is the amount of the owner's monthly taxes?
    1. $247.20
    2. $824
    3. $2,966.40
    4. None of the above

30. Who of the following persons would NOT be protected under the familial status definition according to the federal fair housing law?
    1. A 19-year-old girl living with her mother
    2. A 17-year-old boy living with his father
    3. A 14-year-old girl living with a person who is seeking legal custody of her
    4. A 21-year old woman who is pregnant

31. You are working as a salesperson for a broker and have just sold a home. You will receive your share of the commission on the sale from:
    1. the cooperating broker.
    2. the seller.
    3. your broker.
    4. the buyer.

32. You have been given oral permission to park in a friend's driveway while attending a football game. Their permission is a(n)
    1. easement appurtenant.
    2. encroachment.
    3. license.
    4. littoral right.

33. Charging a rate of interest in excess of the maximum rate allowed by law is
    1. novation.
    2. subordination.
    3. laches.
    4. usury.

34. Which of the following categories represents the FIRST one to be protected by federal law against discrimination in housing?
    1. Familial status
    2. Sex
    3. Race
    4. Sexual orientation

35. Using a mortgage factor of $7.69, what is the monthly payment for a $170,000 loan at 8.5 percent for 30 years?
    1. $1,247.80
    2. $1,276.70
    3. $1,307.30
    4. $1,337.90

36. Using the information in question 35 above, what is the total interest paid over the life of the loan?
    1. $279,208
    2. $300,628
    3. $311,644
    4. None of the above

37. A broker listed a home for sale under an exclusive-right-to-sell listing. A second broker cooperated with the listing broker and sold the home. The house was sold, and the commission was split between the listing broker and the selling broker. Which of the following is FALSE?
    1. The selling broker is not an agent of the listing broker.
    2. The listing broker is an agent of the seller.
    3. The seller is a customer of the selling broker.
    4. A broker who is not the seller's agent cannot receive any part of the commission.

38. The requirement that a lender use the Uniform Settlement Statement form (HUD-1) for certain government-related loans is a requirement of
    1. IRS regulations.
    2. RESPA.
    3. Regulation Z.
    4. Federal Housing Administration (FHA) regulations.

39. All of the following would be considered a lien except a(n)
    1. encroachment.
    2. judgment.
    3. mechanic's lien.
    4. mortgage.

40. The borrower under a note secured by a mortgage is the
    1. mortgagor.
    2. trustee.
    3. mortgagee.
    4. vendee.

41. Which of the following licensees is MOST likely to act as a general agent for a client?
    1. Broker
    2. Property manager
    3. Cooperative broker
    4. Listing salesperson

42. The relationship of trust and confidence that a broker has with a principal is called a(n)
    1. fiduciary relationship.
    2. hypothecation.
    3. escrow.
    4. trustor relationship.

43. You received a real estate loan from a bank in which the lender was privately insured against loss in the event of default and foreclosure. The loan would have been which of the following?
    1. Conventional insured
    2. Federal Housing Authority (FHA)
    3. Veterans Administration (VA)
    4. Rural development

44. A 500-acre farm is divided into house lots. The streets require one-eighth of the whole farm, and there are 300 lots. How many square feet are in each lot?
    1. 48,636
    2. 55,584
    3. 63,525
    4. 72,600

45. Which of the following real estate loans is guaranteed against loss by the government?
    1. Conventional
    2. Veterans Administration (VA)
    3. Federal Housing Authority (FHA)
    4. Seller carries back in excess of $100,000

46. The agency that serves as the nation's banker and fiscal manager is the
    1. United States Treasury.
    2. Federal Reserve System.
    3. Federal National Mortgage Association (FNMA), or "Fannie Mae."
    4. Federal Home Loan Mortgage Corporation (FHLMC), or "Freddie Mac."

47. You receive a monthly salary of $1,200 plus a 3 percent commission on all of your listings that sell and 2.5 percent on all of your sales. None of the listings that you took sold last month, but you receive $6,300 in salary and commission. What is the value of the property that sold?
    1. $170,000
    2. $204,000
    3. $252,000
    4. None of the above

48. A mortgage in which the lender receives an equity position as well as interest on the mortgage is a(n):
    1. adjustable-rate mortgage.
    2. participation mortgage.
    3. reverse annuity mortgage.
    4. wraparound mortgage.

49. A sale closed on July 21. Real estate taxes of $3,420 for the current year have not been paid. What is the settlement sheet entry for the proration of the real estate taxes?
    1. Credit seller, $1,985.50; debit buyer, $1,988.50
    2. Debit seller, $1,995; credit buyer, $1,995
    3. Debit seller, $1,909.50; credit buyer, $1,909.50
    4. Debit buyer, $00.00; credit seller, $1,710

50. *A,* who works for broker *C* on a 50-50 basis, sold a house listed by broker *E* for $193,950. The seller agreed to pay a 6 percent commission but stipulated in the listing that 60 percent was to go to the selling broker. How much commission (to the nearest dollar) will *A* make on this sale?
    1. $2,327.40
    2. $2,909.25
    3. $3,491.10
    4. $4,189.32

51. You tore out an old furnace and installed a new furnace with central air conditioning in your home. This newly installed personal property becomes a
    1. trade fixture.
    2. chattel fixture.
    3. fixture.
    4. physical trade fixture.

52. An easement would generally be utilized in which of the following?
    1. Accession
    2. Novation
    3. Partition
    4. Right of way

53. You had an exclusive-right-to-sell listing with a seller and you showed the property to a prospective buyer during the listing term. The seller openly negotiated with this prospective buyer and asked him to wait until the listing had expired to buy the property so there would be a commission savings on the transaction. You found out that the property was sold to the prospective buyer within a month of the time the listing expired. Are you entitled to a commission? Why or why not?
    1. No; because the entire transaction occurred after the listing expired.
    2. No; because exclusive right-to-sell listings allow the seller to sell the property themselves without owing a commission.
    3. Yes; because you were the procuring cause of the sale.
    4. Yes; because you are entitled to a commission if the property is sold by anyone within a year of the listing period.

54. Which of the following would NOT be an example of economic or external obsolescence?
    1. Changing land uses in a neighborhood.
    2. The major employer in the city going out of business.
    3. A poor floor plan.
    4. A nearby landfill contaminating the ground waste.

55. A lender that refuses to provide loans on properties located in a minority neighborhood regardless of the ethnicity of the applicant would be engaged in a discriminatory practice known as
    1. steering.
    2. redlining.
    3. blockbusting.
    4. hypothecating.

56. A house located next to an airport would be an example of
    1. functional obsolescence.
    2. economic or external obsolescence.
    3. physical deterioration.
    4. physical depreciation.

57. You have sold your home and taken back a mortgage from the buyer for part of the balance due. The type of mortgage you hold is a
    1. blanket mortgage.
    2. purchase money mortgage.
    3. participation mortgage.
    4. wraparound mortgage.

58. An odorless radioactive gas produced by the decay of other radioactive materials in rocks under the earth's surface is which of the following?
    1. Asbestos
    2. UFFI
    3. Lead
    4. Radon

59. Within the field of real estate finance, what does the *secondary mortgage market* refer to?
    1. Placing of junior liens
    2. Transferability of mortgages among mortgagees
    3. Transferability of mortgages among mortgagors
    4. None of the above

60. Which of the following types of depreciation contains elements that are incurable only?
    1. Physical deterioration
    2. Economic or external obsolescence
    3. Functional obsolescence
    4. Physical depreciation

61. A woman wants to know how much money she owes on her mortgage loan. She knows that the interest part of the last monthly payment was $647.91. If she was paying an interest rate of 9 percent, what was the outstanding balance of her loan before the last payment was made?
    1. $64,791.10
    2. $77,749.20
    3. $86,388
    4. $97,186.50

62. Which of the following types of listings establishes a broker-compensation arrangement whereby the broker gets to keep all proceeds in excess of a stated minimum sales price? (This is considered to be an unethical or illegal listing arrangement.)
    1. Net
    2. Open
    3. Exclusive agency
    4. Exclusive-right-to-sell

63. Which of the following factors would NOT be considered by an appraiser in conducting a neighborhood analysis?
    1. Relation to the rest of the community
    2. Rent levels
    3. Racial characteristics of the residents
    4. Zoning

64. A contract in which the intentions of the parties are shown by their conduct is
    1. an express contract.
    2. an implied contract.
    3. a bilateral contract.
    4. an executory contract.

65. Who of the following is NOT considered an agent?
    1. A broker who has listed an owner's home for sale
    2. A property manager, managing property for others for a fee
    3. A salesperson employed by a broker
    4. A nonlicensed personal assistant of an agent

66. A swollen, rushing river sweeps away an outcropping of land with several trees on it. The term that most accurately identifies this kind of property loss is
    1. erosion.
    2. avulsion.
    3. accretion.
    4. disenfranchisement.

67. You have purchased three lots and combined them into one large parcel to build an apartment building. This is an example of
    1. the principle of progression.
    2. assemblage.
    3. the principle of substitution.
    4. plottage value.

68. A summary of all the recorded instruments affecting the title to a property is called a(n):
    1. abstract of title.
    2. certificate of title.
    3. escrow.
    4. title insurance policy.

69. A contract in which one party promises to do something if the other party performs a specific act is a(n)
    1. unenforceable contract.
    2. unilateral contract.
    3. void contract.
    4. bilateral contract.

70. Federal fair housing laws prohibit housing discrimination against all of the following groups of people **EXCEPT**
    1. women.
    2. college students.
    3. ethnic minorities.
    4. families with minor children.

71. The form of listing that provides the most protection to the broker is the
    1. exclusive agency.
    2. exclusive-right-to-sell.
    3. net listing.
    4. open listing.

72. All of the following represent environmental hazards that may affect the marketability of a residential property **EXCEPT**
    1. xenon.
    2. radon gas.
    3. lead-based paint.
    4. underground storage tanks.

73. Brokers who violate the Sherman Antitrust Act may be punished by a maximum prison term of
    1. one year
    2. two years
    3. three years
    4. five years

74. *M,* a real estate broker, was renting *P*'s apartments as *P*'s property manager. *M* showed the remaining vacant apartment to *S,* an African-American woman. *M* checked *S*'s job, credit, and housing references and was about to inform *S* that she would be able to sign a lease when *P* called and inquired about *S*'s color. *M* should
    1. tell *P* because *M* has a fiduciary responsibility of loyalty to *P.*
    2. tell *P* only on the condition that *P* keeps the information in confidence.
    3. not tell *P* because it is not a material fact.
    4. not tell *P* because *S* is a member of a protected class.

75. An appraiser has estimated the replacement cost of an office building at $300,000. The building is 22 years old and has an estimated useful life of 60 years. What is the current total depreciation of the building?
    1. $90,000
    2. $110,000
    3. $130,000
    4. None of the above

76. What is the value of an apartment building that is expected to produce a net annual income of $20,000, if the owner estimates that she should receive a return of 8 percent on her investment?
    1. $120,000
    2. $160,000
    3. $200,000
    4. $250,000

77. *A* and *B,* a married couple, sold their principal residence in 1999 and made a profit on the sale of $600,000. *A* and *B* had lived in that property since 1987. *A* and *B* will have to pay capital gains tax on
    1. $100,000.
    2. $250,000.
    3. $500,000.
    4. $600,000.

78. First-time homebuyers may make penalty-free withdrawals from their tax-deferred IRAs up to
    1. $5,000.
    2. $10,000.
    3. $20,000.
    4. $50,000.

79. A portion of *A*'s land is protected from judgment for unsecured debts. *A*'s protection is based on
    1. riparian rights.
    2. dower rights.
    3. littoral rights.
    4. homestead rights.

80. *A* has given *B* permission to park in *A*'s driveway during the month of July. *B* has
    1. an easement appurtenant.
    2. a life estate.
    3. a license.
    4. an easement by prescription.

ANSWER KEY WITH EXPLANATIONS

NOTE: The information in parentheses at the end of each explanation refers to the page number where this material is discussed.

1. **(2)** The general warranty and special warranty deed contain express warranties. A bargain and sale deed has an implied warranty. A quitclaim deed contains no warranty. (104)
2. **(3)** Special assessments and real estate taxes take priority over all other liens, regardless of the date of recording. (20)
3. **(2)** Your opinion would be an example of puffing. (75)
4. **(3)** Political belief is not a protected class under the federal fair housing laws. (117)
5. **(4)** The broker protection clause refers to the broker's commission. The broker protection clause does not exist in Connecticut. In addition, the automatic extension of listing agreements is against the law in most states. (75)
6. **(3)** Trade fixtures are items installed by a tenant for conducting a business. (18)
7. **(2)** \$3,760 ÷ 12 months = \$313.33 per month

   \$313.33 ÷ 30 days = \$10.444 per day

   \$313.33 × 5 months = \$1,566.65

   \$10.444 × 23 = \$240.21

   \$1,566.65 + \$240.21 = \$1,806.86 (133–134)
8. **(2)** The giver of an option is the optionor; the buyer is the optionee. The vendor is a seller of realty; the vendee is the purchaser of realty. (94)
9. **(2)** Functional obsolescence and physical deterioration and depreciation may be incurable. Economic obsolescence generally is incurable. (50)
10. **(3)** \$90,000 (first investor) + \$50,000 (second investor) = \$140,000

    \$330,000 – \$140,000 = \$190,000, third investor's contribution

    part ÷ total = percent

    \$190,000 ÷ \$330,000 = 0.5757 or 57.6% (127–128)
11. **(4)** An acceleration clause states that if the borrower defaults, the lender has the right to declare the entire debt due and payable. The defeasance clause requires the lender to execute a satisfaction of mortgage when the note is fully paid. Equitable redemption refers to the right of borrowers to redeem this interest in their property prior to a public foreclosure sale. (60)
12. **(2)** The tract of land over which an easement appurtenant runs is the servient tenement; an easement appurtenant is an encumbrance, as are the lien, license, and encroachment. (20)
13. **(2)** In an exclusive-right-to-sell listing, there is only one agent. Regardless of who procures a buyer, the exclusive-right-to-sell broker receives a commission. (92)
14. **(1)** The listing salesperson is a subagent whose death will not affect the listing contract. (93–94)
15. **(3)** A voidable contract may be disaffirmed because one of the parties signed when under duress. (91–92)

16. **(2)** See Figure 15.6.

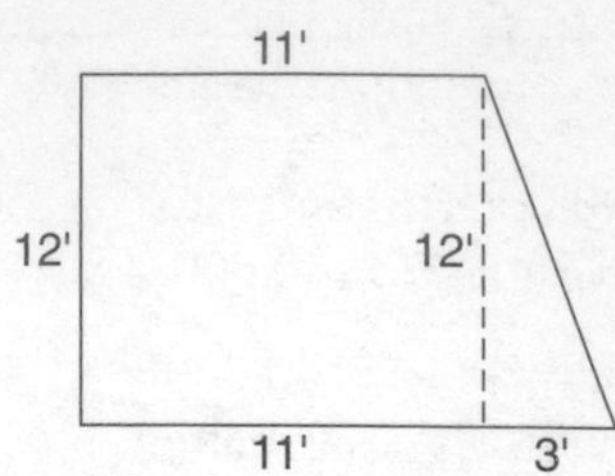

FIGURE 15.6

11' × 12' = 132' = 132 square feet, area of rectangle

½ (3' × 12') = ½ (36') = 18 square feet, area of triangle

132 + 18 = 150 square feet

To convert square feet to square yards, divide number of square feet by 9.

150 ÷ 9 = 16.666 square yards

$18.95 + $5.50 = $24.45, cost per square yard

$24.45 × 16.66 square yards = $407.34 (129–130)

17. **(4)** The listing broker would be the only agent of the seller, and none of the cooperating brokers could legally represent the seller, because the offering of subagency to outside brokers is against public policy. (73–75)

18. **(2)** The net income in an operating statement does not reflect interest and taxes. (50–51)

19. **(3)** A blanket mortgage covers more than one property or lot; it is typically used to finance the development of a subdivision. (62)

20. **(1)** Rentals of rooms in an owner-occupied one to four-family dwelling are exempt from federal fair housing laws. (117)

21. **(4)** The grantor must sign the deed. Consideration can be monetary or nonmonetary. Subordination clauses are used in mortgages.
(104–105)

22. **(1)** $115,900 × 8% (0.08) = $9,272 annual increase in value

$115,900 + $9,272 = $125,172 current market value (127)

23. **(4)** A valid contract must be based on good and valuable consideration. If duress is involved, however, there would not be a meeting of the minds; the contract would thus not be valid. (91)

24. **(2)** Immobility, nonhomogeneity, and indestructibility are physical characteristics of land. (18)

25. **(3)** The optionee (prospective buyer) pays for the option right but assumes no obligation to make any other payments until she decides whether or not to exercise her option right. (94)

26. **(3)** The other listings would include a commission agreed on in advance in terms of a percentage dollar amount. (92)

27. **(4)** Federal fair housing laws provide that it is unlawful to discriminate on the basis of race when selling residential property. The broker must refuse to accept the listing based on this condition. (114)

28. **(4)** Zoning, environmental protection laws, and subdivision regulations are public land-use controls. (34–35)

29. **(1)** $103,000 × 80% (0.80) = $82,400 assessed value

Divide by 100 because the tax rate is stated per $100.

$82,400 ÷ 100 = $824.00

$824 × $3.60 = $2,966.40, annual tax

$2,966.40 ÷ 12 = $247.20 (36)

30. **(1)** Under certain circumstances the familial status category protects individuals who have not reached the age of 18. (114)

31. **(3)** A salesperson can only receive compensation from the broker for whom she works. (75)

32. **(3)** A license provides permission to enter the land of another for a specific purpose. Littoral rights involve water rights. An encroachment is an illegal extension of the building beyond the land of its owner. An easement appurtenant requires two tracts of land. (21)

33. **(4)** Charging a rate of interest in excess of the maximum rate allowed by law is known as usury. Novation refers to an agreement in which a new debtor is accepted in place of an old one. Laches is a court doctrine used to bar a legal claim because of undue delay in asserting the claim. Subordination refers to an agreement that changes the order of priority of liens between two creditors. (66)

34. **(3)** Race became a protected class in 1968; sex in 1974. Sexual orientation is not a protected class under federal fair housing laws. (114)

35. **(3)** $170,000 ÷ 1,000 = 170 × 7.69 = $1,307.30 (13) (134–137)

36. **(2)** $1,307.30 × 360 months = $470,628
Total principal and interest –170,000
Amount of loan $300,628
Total interest paid over life of the loan (134–137)

37. **(4)** A broker need not be the seller's agent to receive part of the commission. In most markets cooperation and compensation are extended to other members of the multiple-listing system. (92)

38. **(2)** The other choices do not deal with a closing forms. (106)

39. **(1)** An encroachment is an encumbrance. (20)

40. **(1)** The borrower under a note secured by a mortgage is a mortgagor. The lender is a mortgagee. The trustee holds the real estate as a security for the loan under a trust deed. The vendee is the buyer in a real estate contract. (59)

41. **(2)** Often a property manager has multiple duties to perform for the principal. The broker is considered a special agent because the broker's task is often singular (procure a buyer or find a property). (73–74)

42. **(1)** Hypothecation is the pledging of property as security for a loan without losing possession of it. Escrow is a third-party agreement; the trustor is the borrower in a trust deed. (73)

43. **(1)** Privately insured loans are conventional loans. All non-FHA and non-DVA loans are conventional loans. (61)

44. **(3)** 43,560 sq. ft. per acre × 500 acres

21,780,000 × (0.125) = 2,772,500 sq. ft. for streets

21,780,000 – 2,722,500 = 19,057,500 sq. ft. for lots

19,057,500 sq. ft. ÷ 300 lots = 63,525 sq. ft. per lot (19)

45. **(2)** The Department of Veterans Affairs (DVA) loan provides a guarantee to the lender. There is no insurance premium for a guaranteed loan. However, an FHA loan is insured by the federal government, and an insurance premium is charged. (61–62)

46. **(1)** The U.S. Treasury is responsible for supervising the daily fiscal operations of the federal government. FHLMC and FNMA are warehousing agencies in the secondary mortgage market. The Federal Reserve regulates the flow of money through member banks. (64)

47. **(2)** $6,300 – $1,200 = $5,100, commission on sales

$5,100 ÷ 2.5% (0.025) = $204,000, value of property sold (127)

48. **(2)** A participation mortgage provides the lender with a percentage of cash flow beyond the interest paid by the borrower. (63)

49. **(3)** $3,420 ÷ 12 months = $285 per month

$285 ÷ 30 days = $9.50 per day

$285 × 6 months = $1,710

$9.50 × 21 days = $199.50

$1,710 + $199.50 = $1,909.50

The taxes for the year have not been paid. When they are paid, the buyer will be in possession and will have to pay the bill. The seller, therefore, must pay (be debited) for the portion of the year that she occupied the property. The buyer receives a credit for the same amount. (133–134)

50. **(3)** \$193,950 sales price × 6% (0.06) commission = \$11,637, broker commission

    \$11,637 × 60% (0.60) = \$6,982.20 × 0.05 = \$3,491.10, selling salesperson's commission (126–127)

51. **(3)** A trade fixture is attached to real property for the purpose of carrying on a business. A chattel fixture is an item of personal property. (18)

52. **(4)** An easement gives the dominant tenant a right-of-way. (20)

53. **(3)** The broker's commission would be protected by the broker protection clause in the listing contract. (74)

54. **(3)** A poor floor plan is considered functional obsolescence. Economic or external obsolescence is a loss in value due to factors outside the property. (50)

55. **(2)** Redlining refers to discriminatory denial of loans to people in selected areas, regardless of their qualifications. (117)

56. **(2)** Economic or external obsolescence is a loss in value resulting from an environmental factor outside of the property's boundaries, such as being located next to an airport. (50)

57. **(2)** A purchase money mortgage involves seller financing in which the legal title passes to the buyer. (62)

58. **(4)** Asbestos is a material used for many years as insulation on heating pipes and ducts. Prior to 1978, UFFI was used to insulate buildings; because of its toxic outgassing, it was removed from the market. Lead is a material used to impede water flow. (37)

59. **(2)** The secondary mortgage market deals only with the first mortgages of mortgagors (borrowers) transferred among mortgagees (lenders). (65)

60. **(2)** Economic obsolescence occurs outside the property. (50)

61. **(3)** \$647.91 × 12 = \$7,774.92

    \$7,774.92 ÷ 9% (0.09) = \$86,388 (127)

62. **(1)** Under a net listing, the broker may retain as compensation all money received in excess of the "net" set by the seller; the compensation is not definitely specified. This type of listing is either prohibited or discouraged by licensing authorities in many states. (92)

63. **(3)** Appraisers are not allowed to discuss racial characteristics in an appraisal report. (51–52)

64. **(2)** A contract in which the parties show their intentions by conduct is an implied contract; intention is shown by words in an expressed contract. Promises are exchanged in a bilateral contract. Something remains to be performed in an executory contract. (91)

65. **(4)** A nonlicensed personal assistant working for an agent would not be considered an agent. The personal assistant could act either as an employee or independent contractor for the licensed agent. (73–75)

66. **(2)** Avulsion is the *sudden* tearing away of land by action of nature while erosion is the *gradual* wearing away of land by natural forces of water and wind. (41)

67. **(2)** Plottage is the value increment resulting from assemblage. (49)

68. **(1)** A buyer's attorney examines the abstract for flaws and prepares a written opinion of the condition of ownership. (104)

69. **(2)** An unenforceable contract appears to be valid but neither party may sue the other to force performance. A void contract lacks an essential element of a valid contract and thus has no legal effect. A bilateral contract is a contract in which both parties promise to do something. (91)

70. **(2)** Sex, race, and familial status are protected classes under federal fair housing laws. (114)

71. **(2)** Under an exclusive-right-to-sell listing, the broker receives the commission regardless of who sells the property. (92)

72. **(1)** Xenon is an inert gas and trace element in air. (37–40)

73. **(3)** The Sherman Antitrust Act also provides for a maximum $100,000 fine. (76)

74. **(4)** A licensee may not disclose that a prospective tenant is a member of a protected class. (114)

75. **(2)** $300,000 ÷ 60 = $5,000, annual depreciation charge

    $5,000 × 22 = $110,000, current total depreciation (132)

76. **(4)** I ÷ R = V

    $20,000 ÷ .08 = $250,000, estimated value (132)

77. **(1)** *A* and *B* would be entitled to an exclusion of $500,000. (106)

78. **(2)** The withdrawals must be used for down payments on their homes. (107)

79. **(4)** Riparian and littoral rights are water rights, while dower rights are a legal life estate. (22)

80. **(3)** An easement appurtenant requires a dominant tenement while an easement by prescription requires use without the owner's approval. A life estate is limited to the lifetime of the owner of the life estate or the lifetime of another (pur autre vie). (21)

SALESPERSON EXAMINATION III

1. Which of the following terms would include the interests, benefits, and rights inherent in the ownership of real estate?
   1. Chattel
   2. Personal property
   3. Real property
   4. Trade fixtures
2. Which of the following is a physical characteristic of land?
   1. Scarcity
   2. Situs
   3. Permanence of investment
   4. Immobility
3. *C* and *D* held title as joint tenants. Which of the following statements would NOT correctly describe the requirements for them to own as joint tenants?
   1. *C* and *D* have the right of survivorship.
   2. *C* and *D* must have equal interests.
   3. *C* and *D* must be married.
   4. *C* and *D* may partition the land.
4. Which of the following statements would NOT correctly describe easements?
   1. An easement is an encumbrance.
   2. An easement appurtenant must have a dominant tenement and a servient tenement.
   3. An easement in gross must have a dominant tenement.
   4. An easement constitutes an interest in land.
5. *D* has a property that is a servient tenement in an easement appurtenant. *D* is considering selling his property to *F.* Which of the following statements would NOT correctly describe their potential transaction?
   1. The easement is an encumbrance.
   2. The easement may have a negative effect on the value of the property.
   3. The easement is very likely to prevent *D* from selling his property to *F*.
   4. The easement may have an impact on *F*'s use of the property.
6. Contractor *R* replaced the roof on *T*'s house. If *T* refuses to pay *R* for the work, *R* has the right to
   1. remove the roof.
   2. take *T*'s personal property and hold it as compensation should the lien be unpaid.
   3. file a mechanic's lien.
   4. record a judgment.
7. The local utility company holds an easement to install power lines on a vacant lot. This is an easement
   1. appurtenant.
   2. in gross.
   3. by necessity.
   4. by prescription.
8. A wife and husband may NOT hold title to their home as
   1. tenants by the entirety.
   2. tenants at will.
   3. tenants in common.
   4. joint tenants.
9. *L, M,* and *P* are joint tenants. If *L* dies
   1. *L*'s interest will go to his surviving spouse.
   2. *L*'s interest will go to *M* or *P* depending on the terms of *L*'s will.
   3. *L*'s interest will escheat to the state.
   4. *L*'s interest will go to *M* and *P.*
10. The SE ¼ of the SW ¼ of the NE ¼ of Section 23 contains
    1. 10 acres.
    2. 40 acres.
    3. 160 acres.
    4. 320 acres.
11. *V* has been informed that her land is being taken by the state for the development of a new highway. The state will pay *V* for her land. This process illustrates the right of
    1. escheat.
    2. police power.
    3. taxation.
    4. eminent domain.

12. Which of the following would NOT be a governmental restriction on land?
    1. Police power
    2. Deed restriction
    3. Eminent domain
    4. Taxation

13. *K* builds an office building on commercially zoned land that is subsequently rezoned by the city to residential. *K* will
    1. have to close his office building.
    2. have to get his land rezoned by the city to continue operating his building.
    3. need a conditional use permit to continue operating his property.
    4. be able to continue with his office building which is now a nonconforming use.

14. *T* wants to build a medical clinic in a neighborhood that is zoned residential. *T* will need to obtain a
    1. nonconforming use.
    2. downzoning.
    3. variance.
    4. conditional use permit.

15. Electromagnetic fields (EMFs) are created by
    1. peeling paint.
    2. the movement of electrical currents.
    3. contaminated groundwater.
    4. the decay of radioactive materials in rocks under the earth's surface.

16. Which of the following hazardous substances enters a house through the basement floor of a house?
    1. Asbestos
    2. Radon
    3. Lead
    4. Urea-formaldehyde foam insulation

17. *C* objected to the violation of a deed restriction in her subdivision but waited one year to request a court injunction to enforce the restriction. The judge subsequently ruled that *C* had waited too long to request court action. The judge would not issue the injunction. *C*'s loss is an example of
    1. accession.
    2. reliction.
    3. annexation.
    4. laches.

18. The water rights of a landowner adjacent to a stream are known as
    1. equitable rights.
    2. littoral rights.
    3. riparian rights.
    4. prior appropriation rights.

19. A Holiday Inn was developed just outside a city and within six months was operating at 95 percent occupancy. One year later a Marriott was built across the street. This would be an example of the principle of
    1. competition.
    2. contribution.
    3. progression.
    4. increasing and decreasing returns.

20. A four-bedroom house with only one bathroom is an example of
    1. physical deterioration.
    2. functional obsolescence.
    3. environmental obsolescence.
    4. locational obsolescence.

21. The most reliable approach for appraising a single-family home would be the
    1. cost approach.
    2. income approach.
    3. sales comparison approach.
    4. gross income multiplier.

22. Which of the following statements correctly describes how effective gross income is calculated in the operating statement?
    1. Annual potential gross income minus annual operating expenses
    2. Annual potential gross income minus vacancy and rent loss
    3. Annual potential gross income ÷ the capitalization rate
    4. Annual potential gross income ÷ annual operating expenses

23. An example of a governmental action to consider in a neighborhood analysis would be
    1. the street pattern.
    2. new construction.
    3. population density.
    4. special assessments.

24. Which of the following would NOT be a characteristic of value?
    1. Effective demand
    2. Utility
    3. Plottage
    4. Scarcity

25. Deposits in commercial banks are insured by
    1. BIF.
    2. SAIF.
    3. FNMA.
    4. GNMA.

26. Which of the following statements does NOT correctly describe the secondary mortgage market?
    1. FNMA buys conventional, FHA, and VA loans.
    2. GNMA works with FNMA in the tandem plan.
    3. FHLMC administers special assistance programs.
    4. FNMA sells government guaranteed bonds.

27. Deposits in commercial banks are insured for up to
    1. $10,000.
    2. $20,000.
    3. $50,000.
    4. $100,000.

28. Which of the following does NOT provide its own money for loans on real estate?
    1. Commercial banks
    2. Mortgage brokers
    3. Savings and loan associations
    4. Life insurance companies

29. A trust deed generally is released by a(n)
    1. satisfaction document.
    2. release document.
    3. reconveyance document.
    4. acceleration document.

30. Using the mortgage factor of 10.45, what is the monthly payment for a $200,000 loan at 9.5 percent for 15 years?
    1. $1,682
    2. $2,060
    3. $2,090
    4. $2,120

31. Using the information in question 30, what is the total interest paid over the life of the loan?
    1. $176,200
    2. $181,600
    3. $463,200
    4. $552,400

32. Which of the following mortgages includes real and personal property?
    1. Blanket mortgage
    2. Package mortgage
    3. Wraparound mortgage
    4. Participation mortgage

33. Which of the following laws would utilize an advertising "trigger"?
    1. Statute of limitations
    2. Regulation Z
    3. RESPA
    4. Statute of frauds

34. Reserve requirements for banks are controlled by the
    1. BIF.
    2. FDIC.
    3. FED.
    4. U.S. Treasury.

35. The agency relationship between the broker and his or her seller-client is
    1. universal.
    2. general.
    3. specific.
    4. special.

36. Broker *P* listed *S*'s house. *P* has the authority to
    1. modify the listing price.
    2. accept an offer for *S*.
    3. encourage prospective buyers to make an offer at less than list price.
    4. market the property.

37. Broker *Q* listed *W*'s house, which was sold by a broker from another company, *Y*. Which of the following would NOT describe *Y*'s role in the transaction?
    1. *Y* was the buyer's agent.
    2. *Y* was a cooperating broker.
    3. *Y* was expecting some compensation.
    4. *Y* was a subagent of the seller.

38. You listed a home that was subsequently shown by four different cooperating brokers. How many seller-agents are involved in this transaction?
    1. One
    2. Two
    3. Four
    4. Five

39. You listed a home for $200,000 and agreed to a 7 percent commission on the selling price. You and the seller subsequently amended the list price to $190,000 with a commission of6 percent of the selling price. The house sold two weeks later for $180,000. Your commission was
    1. $10,800
    2. $11,400
    3. $12,600
    4. $14,000

40. Broker *A* listed *B*'s house for sale. The next day, *A* was contacted by *C* and *D* about the availability of homes in the city. On the following day, *A* showed *B*'s house to *C* and *D*. Which of the following statements correctly describes this situation?
    1. *A* has created a fiduciary relationship with *B, C,* and *D*.
    2. When *A* showed *B*'s house to *C* and *D, A* was entering into a dual agency.
    3. *B, C,* and *D* are *A*'s customers.
    4. *B* is a client of *A,* and *C* and *D* are *A*'s customers.

41. Broker *M* listed the home of owner *V* who indicated that she was very anxious to sell her house. *M* may
    1. disclose to prospective buyers that the seller will take less than the list price.
    2. not disclose the seller's motivation unless he has the owner's permission to do so, in writing.
    3. not disclose the seller's motivation under any condition.
    4. disclose the seller's motivation only if he is showing *V*'s house to a buyer with whom he has a buyer-agency agreement.

42. Which of the following statements would NOT be a violation of the antitrust law?
    1. Two brokers agreeing to boycott by not sharing listings with a third broker.
    2. A broker in a listing presentation informs a prospective client that she would have to receive a 7 percent commission because it was the local board rate.
    3. A broker refuses to sell his listed house to a customer unless the customer lists her present home with the broker.
    4. A broker refuses to give another broker the same MLS commission as she offered to the rest of the brokers on MLS.

43. *Y,* who works for broker *T* on a 50-50 basis, sold a house listed by broker *S* for $206,000. The seller agreed to pay a 7 percent commission but stipulated in the listing that 55 percent was to go to the selling broker. How much commission (to the nearest dollar) will *Y* make on this sale?
    1. $3,966
    2. $7,931
    3. $14,420
    4. None of the above

44. Which of the following would not be classified as a latent defect?
    1. Nonconforming use of property
    2. Inadequate electrical outlets
    3. Exposed floor joists charred from a kitchen fire
    4. An inadequate furnace

45. Which of the following statements correctly describes the status of dual agency?
    1. Dual agency is always allowed as long as the broker tells the parties.
    2. Dual agency is legal in every state.
    3. Disclosure of dual agency should be made subsequent to completing an offer to purchase.
    4. Dual agency is not allowed unless all parties agree to it.

46. Assuming single agency, which of the following statements best describes a material fact to be disclosed by a seller's agent back to the seller?
    1. Presentation of lower offers
    2. The buyer's ability to make a higher offer
    3. Disclosure of the property's deficiencies
    4. Disclosure of how long the property has been listed

47. Broker *F* listed owner *Z*'s house with the condition that *F*'s commission would be the excess received over $160,000. *F* has a(n)
    1. exclusive agency listing.
    2. exclusive-right-to-sell listing.
    3. open listing.
    4. net listing.

48. *P* signed an offer to purchase in a state of obvious drunkenness. The next morning he realized what he had done and told the broker that he did not want to be bound by the terms of the contract. This would be an example of a(n)
    1. valid contract.
    2. void contract.
    3. voidable contract.
    4. unenforceable contract.

49. Which of the following would NOT terminate a listing contract?
    1. The listing broker dies
    2. The salesperson dies
    3. The listed property is destroyed
    4. Bankruptcy of the owner of the listed property

50. *G* and *J* entered into a contract to purchase that is subject only to *G*'s getting financing. The contract would best be described as
    1. a voidable contract.
    2. an executed contract.
    3. a unilateral contract.
    4. an executory contract.

51. Buyer *S* and seller *T* have entered into a binding offer to purchase. Which of the following would correctly describe the rights of the parties at this point in the transaction?
    1. *T* holds equitable title.
    2. *S* is entitled to immediate possession.
    3. *S* holds equitable title.
    4. *T* may terminate the contract.

52. Which of the following require certain real estate contracts to be in writing in order to be enforceable?
    1. Statute of descent and distribution
    2. Statute of frauds
    3. Statute of limitations
    4. Uniform Commercial Code

53. Seller *D* entered into an installment land contract, or contract for deed, with buyer *L*. Which of the following correctly describes the parties?
    1. *D* is the grantor; *L* is the grantee.
    2. *L* is the vendor; *D* is the vendee.
    3. *D* is the grantee; *L* is the grantor.
    4. *D* is the vendor; *L* is the vendee.

54. *A* gave *C* an option to buy her home for $225,000. *C* has 30 days to inform *A* as to whether he will exercise his option. At this point in the transaction the option contract is considered to be a(n)
    1. bilateral contract.
    2. unenforceable contract.
    3. unilateral contract.
    4. anticipatory contract.

55. *M* and *O* wish to change the closing date on their binding offer to purchase (agreement or contract). They should generally use which of the following forms to modify the language?
    1. An amendment or contractual modification
    2. A counteroffer
    3. An addendum
    4. A multiple counteroffer

56. A seller and buyer entered into an instrument of conveyance in which the buyer immediately received legal title. Which of the following instruments would have been used by the parties?
    1. An offer to purchase
    2. A deed
    3. A land contract
    4. An option

57. A man forged his wife's name on a deed and sold their home. The wife subsequently was able to have the title insurance company give her a check for one-half the market value of the home. Which type of deed would the wife usually give to the title company upon receipt of the check?
   1. A warranty deed
   2. A bargain and sale deed
   3. A special warranty deed
   4. A quitclaim deed

58. One of the covenants in a general warranty deed promises that the grantor has title and the right to convey. This is the covenant of
   1. further assurance
   2. quiet enjoyment
   3. seisin
   4. warranty forever

59. Which of the following parties must sign the deed in order for it to be a valid conveyance?
   1. The listing broker
   2. The director of the public record office
   3. The grantor
   4. The grantee

60. Which of the following requires the recorded summary of a property to be updated and an attorney to render a report about the quality of title?
   1. Abstract and opinion
   2. Torrens system
   3. Certificate of title
   4. Title insurance

61. A married couple sold their primary residence for $400,000 in 2004 after living in it for 10 years. They purchased their property in 1992 for $190,000. The balance of their mortgage when they sold was $30,000. The capital gains tax on their profit will be
   1. $42,000.
   2. $52,500.
   3. zero.
   4. $160,000.

62. Which of the following laws prohibits the payment of referral fees by lenders when no services are actually rendered?
   1. Regulation Z
   2. RESPA
   3. Statute of frauds
   4. Statute of limitations

63. *B* had been diagnosed as mentally ill when his rental application was rejected by a landlord based on his mental health problems. Which of the following statements correctly describes *B*'s status under the Federal Fair Housing Act?
   1. *B*'s illness does not provide him with protected class status.
   2. Once *B* has signed a lease, he may not be evicted because he is a member of a protected class.
   3. *B* is protected under the law but must file a complaint within one year after the alleged discriminatory housing practice.
   4. *B* is not protected unless he is currently receiving treatment for his illness.

64. Which of the following would NOT be a protected class under the Federal Equal Credit Opportunity Act?
   1. Sex
   2. Marital status
   3. Dependency on public assistance
   4. Sexual orientation

65. Which of the following would NOT be protected under the Federal Fair Housing Act?
   1. A person diagnosed as mentally ill
   2. A convicted drug dealer
   3. An alcoholic who has been diagnosed and treated and is not currently addicted
   4. A drug addict who has been diagnosed and treated and is not currently addicted

66. Which of the following laws regulate the advertising of credit terms by lenders?
   1. Regulation Z
   2. RESPA
   3. Federal Equal Credit Opportunity Act
   4. Statute of frauds

67. Which of the following properties would NOT be exempt from the Federal Fair Housing Act?
    1. The rental of an owner-occupied one-family home
    2. The Elks Club renting only to members on a nonprofit basis
    3. The Lutheran Church renting its own dwelling units on the condition that they be occupied by only Lutherans
    4. The rental of an owner-occupied five-family apartment building

68. Which of the following laws utilizes "trigger terms"?
    1. Federal Equal Credit Opportunity Act
    2. RESPA
    3. Regulation Z
    4. Statute of frauds

69. A broker sold a home for $154,000. The broker charged the seller a 6 percent commission and will pay 30 percent of that amount to the listing salesperson and 35 percent to the selling salesperson. What amount of commission will the listing salesperson receive from the sale of the home?
    1. $2,310
    2. $2,772
    3. $3,234
    4. None of the above

70. Buyer *A* bought a house for $200,000. She was required to pay her bank a discount fee of $9,600 for points on her $160,000 loan. How many points did *A* pay for the loan?
    1. 4
    2. 5
    3. 6
    4. 7

71. You want to know how much money you owe on your mortgage loan. You know that the interest portion of your last monthly payment was $619.73. If you are paying interest at the rate of 9 percent, what was the outstanding balance of your loan before the last payment was made (to the nearest dollar)?
    1. $82,631
    2. $92,960
    3. $106,239
    4. None of the above

72. You own a home valued at $146,000. Property in your area is assessed at 70 percent of its value and the local tax rate is $2.84 per $100. What is the amount of your semiannual taxes?
    1. $241.87
    2. $1,451.24
    3. $2,902.48
    4. None of the above

73. You bought a house one year ago for $172,900. Property in your neighborhood is said to be increasing at a rate of 5 percent annually. If this is true, what is the current market value of your real estate?
    1. $179,816
    2. $181,545
    3. $183,279
    4. None of the above

74. You receive a monthly salary of $600 plus 2 percent commission on all of your listings that sell and 3 percent on all of your sales. None of the listings you took sold last month, but you received $7,940 in salary and commission. What was the value of the property you sold?
    1. $146,800
    2. $244,667
    3. $367,000
    4. None of the above

75. An owner leases the 16 apartments in his building for a total monthly rental of $12,800. If this figure represents an 8 percent annual return on the owner's investment, what was the original cost of the property?
    1. $153,600
    2. $1,706,667
    3. $1,920,000
    4. $2,194,286

For the next two questions regarding closing statement prorations, base your calculations on a 30-day month. Carry all computations to three decimal places and round off after all computations have been made.

76. A sale is to be closed on March 14. Real estate taxes for the current year are $3,170 and have not been paid. What amount of the real estate tax proration will be credited to the buyer?
    1. $651.62
    2. $660.42
    3. $642.81
    4. None of the above

77. In a sale of residential property, real estate taxes for the current year amounted to $2,840 and already have been paid by the seller. The sale is to be closed on December 3. What is the settlement sheet entry for the tax proration?
    1. $220.87 debit to seller; $220.87 credit to buyer
    2. $212.98 credit to seller; $212.98 debit to buyer
    3. $2,627.02 debit to seller; $205.09 credit to buyer
    4. $212.98 credit to seller only

78. The tenant is a trespasser in which of the following leases?
    1. Estate for years
    2. Periodic estate
    3. Tenancy at will
    4. Tenancy at sufferance

79. *A* purchased a fee-simple interest in one of 40 units in a property development. *A* also received a 2 percent share of the ownership in all of the grounds and facilities outside the units. *A* owns which of the following types of property?
    1. Partnership
    2. Time-share
    3. Cooperative
    4. Condominium

80. *C* borrowed from several banks to get into an investment he could not have financed on his own. This is an example of
    1. Appreciation
    2. Leverage
    3. Equity buildup
    4. Pyramiding

ANSWER KEY WITH EXPLANATIONS

NOTE: The information in parentheses at the end of each explanation refers to the page number where the material is discussed.

1. **(3)** Chattels and trade fixtures are personal property. (18)
2. **(4)** Scarcity, situs, and performance of investment are economic characteristics. (18)
3. **(3)** Joint tenants do not have to be married. (23)
4. **(3)** An easement in gross does not have a dominant tenement; it has a servient tenement only. (20)
5. **(3)** An easement would have to be disclosed to a potential buyer but is unlikely to affect the transfer of title to the property. (20)
6. **(3)** *R* would have to give notice of the lien and then file a court suit within the time required by state law. (20)
7. **(2)** The easement held by the utility company is a commercial easement in gross. (20)
8. **(2)** In the leasehold estate known as a tenancy at will, a person continues occupancy of the real estate with the owner's permission. (22–23)
9. **(4)** *L*'s interest will automatically go to *M* and *P* under the right of survivorship. (23)
10. **(1)** $4 \times 4 \times 4 = 64$

    640 acres ÷ 64 = 10 acres (19)
11. **(4)** Escheat is a state law that provides for ownership to transfer to the state when an owner dies intestate (without a will) leaving no heirs and no will. Police power is used to enact laws such as zoning ordinances and building codes. Taxation on real estate is used to raise funds to meet the needs of the government. (103)
12. **(2)** A deed restriction is a private land-use control. The other answers were discussed in the preceding question. In the event of a conflict between a zoning ordinance and a deed restriction, the more restrictive of the two takes precedence. (41)
13. **(4)** Zoning ordinances are not retroactive; *K*'s property was appropriately zoned when he developed it, thus he can continue to operate his building. (35)
14. **(4)** A conditional-use permit allows for a use specifically permitted. Here, a commercial use is desired in a residential zone, which is not permitted. (35)
15. **(2)** EMFs are suspected of causing cancer and related diseases. (39–40)
16. **(2)** Asbestos is used in insulation. Lead was used as an ingredient in oil-based paint. Urea-formaldehyde was used primarily in building insulation. (37)
17. **(4)** Accession occurs when tenants leave their trade fixtures on the rented premises after the lease expires; the tenant's trade fixtures (personal property) become the real property of the landlord. Reliction refers to the increase in land resulting from the gradual recession of water from the usual water area. Annexation occurs when personal property such as strips of lumber are used to build the floor of the house. (25)
18. **(3)** Water rights are discussed on pages. Littoral rights are granted to owners along a large lake or ocean. (34)
19. **(1)** The principle of competition states that excess profits create ruinous competition. (48)
20. **(2)** Functional obsolescence is a loss in value due to a deficiency in the floor plan or design of a house. One bathroom in a four-bedroom home is inadequate and, therefore, functionally obsolescent. (49)

21. **(3)** The cost approach is the most applicable to the appraisal of a special-purpose property such as a school. The income approach is most reliable for income-producing property. The gross income multiplier is also used in appraising income property. (50)

22. **(2)** Annual net operating income is calculated by subtracting annual operating expenses from effective gross income. Annual net operating income is then capitalized to arrive at an estimate. (50–51)

23. **(4)** Zoning could also be a governmental factor. (51)

24. **(3)** Plottage is the additional value created by assembling parcels of land to create a higher and better use. (48)

25. **(1)** The bank insurance fund is part of the Federal Deposit Insurance Corporation. (64)

26. **(3)** Special assistance programs are administered by GNMA. (65)

27. **(4)** Deposits in commercial banks are insured by BIF. (64)

28. **(2)** Mortgage brokers generally originate loans for other lenders; they do not use their own money. (64)

29. **(3)** Mortgages are released by a satisfaction or release of mortgage documents; an acceleration clause is used in a mortgage to deal with default on the part of the borrower. (59)

30. **(3)** $200,000 ÷ 1,000 = 200 × 10.45 = $2,090 (134–137)

31. **(1)** $2,090 × 180 months = $376,200 – $200,000 = $176,200, total interest paid on the life of the loan (134–137)

32. **(2)** A package mortgage includes both real and personal property, such as a loan to purchase a motel. (63)

33. **(2)** Regulation Z regulates real estate ads relating to mortgage financing terms. Specific credit terms such as down payment are referred to as "trigger" terms and may not be advertised unless the ad includes five categories of information including cash price and required down payment. (118–119)

34. **(3)** The Federal Reserve controls reserve requirements of member banks as part of its monetary policy authority. (64)

35. **(4)** The relationship is known as special agency. (73–74)

36. **(4)** *P* is a special agent responsible for finding a buyer for the seller's property. (73–74)

37. **(4)** *Y* represents the buyer as an agent. According to the National Association of Realtors, *Y* cannot represent the seller if he works for a different real estate company. The reason is because the offering of subagency to an outside firm places a menacing contingent liability on the cooperating broker. (73–74)

38. **(1)** According to the National Association of REALTORS®, cooperating brokers from outside firms cannot be subagents of another brokerage firm's seller. Therefore, only the listing broker represents the seller. (73–74)

39. **(1)** $180,000 × .06 = $10,800 (127)

40. **(4)** *A* has not entered into a fiduciary relationship with *C* and *D;* there cannot be a dual agency. (73)

41. **(2)** The listing broker has a fiduciary relationship with the seller, including loyalty. A buyer-agency relationship would not affect the listing broker's loyalty to the seller. (73)

42. **(4)** An individual broker can react negatively to another broker; this is not a violation of the antitrust law. (76)

43. **(1)** $206,000 sales price × 7% (0.07) commission = $14,420 broker commission

$14,420 × 55% (0.55) = $7,931
$7,931 × 0.50 = $3,966. (127)

44. **(1)** A latent defect is a structural defect that may not be discovered by an ordinary inspection. (84)

45. **(4)** The risks of dual agency have resulted in the practice being illegal in some states. Disclosure alerts the parties that they may have to assume greater responsibility for protecting their interests than would be the case if they had agents representing only their own interests. (74)

46. **(2)** Material facts refer to relevant information that the seller's agent knows or should be aware of and communicated to the seller. Obviously the seller's agent has a fiduciary duty to present all offers. The buyer's agent is concerned about disclosing the property's deficiencies and how long it has been on the market. (73–74)

47. **(4)** Net listing is either illegal or discouraged in most states because of the potential conflict of interest between broker's profit motive and broker's fiduciary responsibility to this seller. (92)

48. **(3)** *P* did not have the mental capacity to be bound by the terms of a binding contract, thus he may disaffirm it if he wishes. *P* has a voidable contract. (92)

49. **(2)** The salesperson is not a party to the listing contract. (92)

50. **(4)** In an executory contract something remains to be done by one or both parties. (91)

51. **(3)** *S* receives equitable title and will receive legal title at closing. (95)

52. **(2)** According to the statute of frauds, certain contracts must be in writing to be enforceable by the courts. (94)

53. **(4)** The vendee receives possession and equitable title and agrees to pay real estate taxes, insurance premiums, and expenses for maintaining the property. The vendee will not receive legal title until the land contract has been paid in full. (94–95)

54. **(3)** The option becomes a bilateral contract if the optionee chooses to exercise the option right. (94)

55. **(1)** The addendum adds additional language to the approved forms. The counteroffer and multiple counteroffer can only modify language prior to the offer becoming binding on all parties. (95)

56. **(2)** The seller withholds legal title to the property until the terms of the contract are fulfilled in a land contract, offer to purchase, and option. (104)

57. **(4)** A quitclaim deed contains no warranties; the grantor simply quits or releases any claim she has against the property. (104)

58. **(3)** The covenant of seisin also promises that the grantor has possession. (104)

59. **(3)** The grantee has to be identified but does not have to sign the deed for it to be valid. (105)

60. **(1)** In abstract states, the abstract is brought up to date and an attorney renders an opinion to the buyer about the quality of the seller's title. In title insurance states, the title company does an internal search. (104)

61. **(3)** A married couple may exclude up to $500,000 from capital gains on the sale of their principal residence if they file jointly. The couple must have occupied the property as their residence for at least two of the past five years. (106–107)

62. **(2)** Referral fee would take the form of anything of value for services, such as mortgage loans or title insurance. (106)

63. **(3)** Mentally ill people do not have to be currently receiving treatment to be protected under the law. However, they would have to file their complaint within the one year period to be protected under the law. (114–115)

64. **(4)** Sexual orientation is not a protected class under the Federal Fair Housing Act. (117)

65. **(2)** Convicted drug dealers are not protected under the federal fair housing laws under any condition. (114–115)

66. **(1)** Regulation Z requires full disclosure of the true cost of financing including the annual percentage rate (APR) before the completion of a transaction. (118–119)

67. **(4)** The rental of an owner-occupied apartment building of four units or less is exempt from the Federal Fair Housing Act. (117)

68. **(3)** The statute of frauds is a law that requires certain contracts to be in writing in order to be enforceable. (119)

69. **(2)** $154,000 × 6% (0.06) commission = $9,240 broker's commission

$9,240 × 30% (0.30) = $2,772 (127)

70. **(3)** $9,600 ÷ $160,000 = .06 or 6 percent
1 point equals 1 percent of the loan amount
6 percent = 6 points (61)

71. **(1)** $619.73 × 12 = $7,436.76 annual interest

$$\frac{\text{part}}{\text{percent}} = \text{total}$$

$7,436.76 ÷ 9% (0.09) = $82,630.67, rounds to $82,631 (127)

72. **(2)** $146,000 × 70 percent (0.70) = $102,200 assessed value

Divide by100 because tax rate is stated per $100

$102,200 ÷ 100 = $1,022

$1,022 × $2.84 = $2,902.48 annual taxes

Divide by 2 to get semiannual taxes

$2,902.48 ÷ 2 = $1,451.24 (35–36)

73. **(2)** $172,900 × 5% (0.05) = $8,645 annual increase in value

$172,900 + $8,645 = $181,545 current market value (127)

74. **(2)** $7,940 – $600 salary = $7,340 commission sales

$7,340 ÷ 3% (0.03) = $244,667 value of property sold (127)

75. **(3)** $12,800 × 12 = $153,600 annual return

$153,600 ÷ 8% (0.08) = $1,920,000 original cost of property (127)

76. **(1)** $3,170 ÷ 12 months = $264.166 per month

$264.166 ÷ 30 days = $8.806 per day

$264.166 × 2 months = $528.332

$8.806 × 14 days = $123.284

$528.332 + 123.284 = $651.616, rounds to $651.62 (133–134)

77. **(2)** $2,840 ÷ 12 months = $236.666 per month

$236.666 ÷ 30 days = $7.888 per day

$7.888 × 27 days = $212.976, rounds to $212.98

The taxes have been paid. The seller is entitled to a refund for 27 days. He, therefore, will receive a credit, and the buyer will be charged (debited) for the same amount. (133–134)

78. **(4)** The other leases allow the tenant to possess with the landlord's consent. (24)

79. **(4)** An owner of a condominium unit holds fee-simple title to the unit and a specified share (as a tenant in common) in the common elements. (149)

80. **(2)** Leverage is using borrowed money to finance an investment. The amount of leverage used by an investor is in direct proportion to the risk. (152)

Broker Examinations

The PSI broker examination, like the salesperson exam, consists of two parts a national exam and a state exam.

The national portion of the broker examination contains questions that closely resemble the national salesperson exam in that (with the exception of broker management) both exams cover the same categories. The differences between the two exams involve slight variations in weighing of categories, math and brokerage management. The subject area and number of questions in each area varies from state to state.

The two sample broker examinations that follow evaluate your general real estate knowledge and your test taking ability.

BROKER EXAMINATION I

1. Which of the following would be considered to be real property?
   1. A leasehold estate
   2. Fixtures
   3. Chattels
   4. Trade fixtures
2. Your uncle died without a will, and you inherited his real estate. The way in which you would acquire his estate is by
   1. accession.
   2. the statute of descent and distribution.
   3. escheat.
   4. novation.
3. Loans to low-income people in rural areas are made and guaranteed by
   1. The Federal Home Loan Mortgage Corporation (FHLMC).
   2. Rural Development.
   3. Farm Service Agency.
   4. The Federal Housing Administration (FHA).
4. A man receives possession of property under a deed that states that he will own the property as long as the present building standing on the property is not torn down. The type of estate the man holds is which of the following?
   1. Life estate
   2. Nondestructible estate
   3. Fee-simple estate
   4. Determinable fee estate
5. You would like to hire more than one broker to sell your house and be able to sell the house yourself without paying a commission to a broker. Which of the following listing agreements should you choose?
   1. Net
   2. Open
   3. Exclusive agency
   4. Exclusive-right-to-sell
6. Which of the following is responsible for investigating and prosecuting violations of federal fair housing laws?
   1. National Association of REALTORS® (NAR)
   2. Equal Employment Opportunity Commission (EEOC)
   3. Department of Housing and Urban Development (HUD)
   4. Associate of Real Estate License Law Officials (ARELLO)
7. You have been making constant payments of $653.00 per month on your mortgage. The balance after your last payment was $80,300. The interest rate on your mortgage is 8 percent. What will the balance of your mortgage be after your next payment?
   1. $79,647.00
   2. $80,067.32
   3. $80,182.33
   4. $80,300.00
8. Using the mortgage factor of 6.65, what is the monthly payment for $121,000 at 7 percent for 30 years?
   1. $733.19
   2. $804.65
   3. $816.75
   4. $847.00
9. Using the numbers in question 8, what is the total interest paid over the life of the loan?
   1. $166,709.23
   2. $167,514.74
   3. $168,319.46
   4. $168,674.00
10. Which of the following statements correctly identifies a defining characteristic of conventional mortgages?
    1. They are assumable.
    2. There is no down payment.
    3. They are guaranteed by the federal government.
    4. Their interest rates are set by the lender.

11. A home valued at $92,000 is assessed at 70 percent of its value and is taxed at a rate of $3.40 per $100. What are the semiannual taxes on this property?
    1. $1,094.80
    2. $1,564.80
    3. $2,189.60
    4. None of the above

12. A broker has been showing homes to some prospects. The prospects have learned of a home for sale by its owner, which they are interested in visiting. The broker calls the owner to arrange a showing, although the owner will not list with the broker. The broker shows the home and writes the offer to purchase, which is accepted by the owner. Which of the following statements correctly describes this situation?
    1. The owner is legally bound to pay the broker a commission.
    2. The prospects are responsible for paying a commission to the broker.
    3. The owner and the prospects are legally bound to pay a commission to the broker.
    4. Neither the owner nor the prospects are legally bound to pay a commission to the broker.

13. A veteran wishes to receive a loan for $70,000 to buy a home. The home has been appraised by the VA at $68,000. Which of the following statements most accurately describes the veteran's situation?
    1. The veteran may buy the home with a VA loan only if he is able to lower the price to $68,000.
    2. The veteran may buy the home with a VA loan if the seller agrees to hold a second mortgage of $2,000.
    3. The veteran may buy the home with a VA loan if he makes a down payment of $2,000.
    4. The veteran may not buy the home.

14. You are paying interest on a $75,000 mortgage for three years after which the entire loan is due. This is called a(n)
    1. amortized mortgage.
    2. graduated payment mortgage.
    3. purchase-money mortgage.
    4. term mortgage.

15. A farmer is unable to pay the county taxes on his farm. The delinquent taxes would be considered
    1. a lien.
    2. an attachment.
    3. an easement.
    4. an appurtenance.

16. A licensee's relative asks the licensee for information about one of the licensee's listings. After reviewing it, the relative arranges to see the property with the licensee. Two weeks later, the relative submitted an offer through another agency on the licensee's listing. Which of the following statements about this situation is CORRECT?
    1. The listing licensee should disclose the family relationship with the buyer to the seller.
    2. The selling licensee should refuse to continue with the transaction if the buyer mentions the listing licensee's family status.
    3. The buyer has breached an express agency relationship with the listing licensee and must resubmit the offer using the listing licensee.
    4. The listing licensee is entitled to a portion of the selling licensee's compensation for having introduced the buyer to the property.

17. Which of the following Internal Revenue Service (IRS) forms is used to report commissions paid to salespeople by brokers?
    1. W-9
    2. 1031
    3. 1040
    4. 1099 Misc.

18. A retired woman owns her home free and clear and is looking for a mortgage that would provide her with monthly payments until she dies. This type of mortgage is called a
    1. guaranteed payment mortgage.
    2. blanket mortgage.
    3. participation mortgage.
    4. reverse annuity mortgage.

19. A man leased a store with the agreement that he would pay a fixed rent and the landlord would pay all operating expenses. This is an example of a
   1. gross lease.
   2. graduated lease.
   3. net lease.
   4. percentage lease.

20. You have entered into a land contract for the sale of your home. Which of the following statements is NOT correct?
   1. The seller is the vendor.
   2. The buyer is the vendee.
   3. The seller will hold legal title during the term of the contract.
   4. The seller will retain possession during the term of the contract.

21. Which of the following terms identifies the practice of charging loan interest rates in excess of the maximum allowed by law?
   1. Usury
   2. Leverage
   3. Arbitrage
   4. Novation

22. Which of the following statements correctly describes the way in which a listing broker should represent her client?
   1. The listing broker can tell a prospective buyer the lowest price her client will accept.
   2. The listing broker may choose which offers to present to her client.
   3. The listing broker with two offers may hold back on presenting the second offer until her client has responded to the first offer.
   4. The listing broker must present all offers to her client promptly when received.

23. Which of the following is true as it relates to an easement appurtenant?
   1. This easement may be acquired by prescription only.
   2. The easement right cannot be terminated.
   3. The dominant tenement owner pays taxes only on the dominant estate.
   4. The easement right reverts to the owner of the servient estate on the death of the owner of the dominant estate.

24. *A* died and left a will that transferred one-half of his 36-unit apartment building to his wife, one-fourth to his son, and one-fourth to his daughter. The devisees will be holding title as
   1. tenants in common.
   2. tenants by the entirety.
   3. joint tenants.
   4. tenants at will.

25. A licensee has entered into a written buyer-broker agreement with a client whereby the licensee will be compensated if the client buys a property of the type described in the agreement within the agreement period, regardless of whether or not the licensee located the property for the buyer. This type of agreement is known as
   1. dual agency.
   2. open-buyer agency.
   3. exclusive-buyer agency.
   4. exclusive-agency buyer agency.

26. A mortgage is all of the following **EXCEPT**
   1. an encumbrance.
   2. a lien on real property.
   3. a recordable legal document.
   4. an example of involuntary alienation.

27. Three investors decided to pool their savings and buy an office building for $200,000. If one invested $70,000 and the second contributed $40,000, what percentage of ownership was left for the third investor?
   1. 20 percent
   2. 35 percent
   3. 45 percent
   4. None of the above

28. A broker is selling a home for $85,900. The owner tells the broker that the roof needs repair, the basement leaks, and the house is a nonconforming use and that she will accept an offer well below $85,900. The broker now is negotiating with a prospect for the sale of the home. The broker should NOT tell the prospect that the
   1. roof needs repair.
   2. basement leaks.
   3. house is a nonconforming use.
   4. seller will accept an offer well below $85,900.

29. You listed a home for sale under an exclusive-right-to-sell agreement and showed the property to a person who wrote an offer with an earnest money check that was subsequently rejected by the owner. What should happen to the earnest money check?
    1. It should be deposited into the broker's trust account.
    2. It should just be returned to the buyer.
    3. It should be returned to the buyer only after the seller signs a release form.
    4. It should be given to the seller.

30. An investor finds that the cost of installing an air-conditioning system in an office building is greater than is justified by the rental increase that might result from the improvement of the property. However, the investor installs the air-conditioning to avoid having tenants move to comparable office space nearby that is air-conditioned. The investor's decision is most reflective of the principle of
    1. anticipation.
    2. competition.
    3. contribution.
    4. highest and best use.

31. *A* loaned money to her sister and in return took a mortgage as security for the debt. She immediately recorded the mortgage. Thereafter, *B* loaned money to the same sister, took a mortgage, and recorded it. The sister later defaulted, and a court determined that *B*'s interest had priority over *A*'s interest. Under these circumstances, chances are that
    1. *A* knew *B* was going to make a loan before *A* made her own loan.
    2. *B*'s loan was larger than *A*'s loan.
    3. *A* had signed a subordination agreement in favor of *B*.
    4. *B* had signed a satisfaction.

32. A sale closed on July 29. Real estate taxes of $2,380 for the current year have not been paid. What is the settlement sheet entry for the proration of real estate taxes?
    1. Credit seller $1,381.70; debit buyer $1,381.70
    2. Debit seller $998.30; credit buyer $1,381.70
    3. Debit seller $1,381.70; credit buyer $1,381.70
    4. Debit buyer $00.00; credit seller $2,380.00

33. You receive a monthly salary of $600 plus 3 percent commission on all your listings that sell and 3.5 percent on all of your sales. None of the listings that you took sold last month, but you received $4,100 in salary and commission. What was the value of the property you sold?
    1. $100,000
    2. $116,666
    3. $117,142
    4. None of the above

34. A broker has been asked to serve as an agent of a friend who wishes to sell his home. Prior to listing the friend's home, the broker is asked by another friend to serve as her agent in finding a home. Relatives of the two friends also have asked the broker to serve as their agent in helping them find homes. Which of the following statements is correct?
    1. The broker is not allowed to work with the relatives because he would have a conflict of interest.
    2. The broker may not serve as agent to the various parties unless he gets permission from all of the parties.
    3. The broker may serve only as an agent of the seller.
    4. The broker may serve as agent for any of the buyers and sellers.

35. Which of the following types of depreciation is incurable?
    1. A leaky roof
    2. A worn-out water heater
    3. A zoning variance of the neighbor's property for commercial use
    4. Warped doors

36. A salesperson would like to be classified as an independent contractor by her broker. What percentage of her income must be based on sales production for her to qualify for independent-contractor status?
    1. 60 percent
    2. 70 percent
    3. 80 percent
    4. 90 percent

37. A couple is interested in buying a property located in an economically distressed section of town. Although the couple has an excellent credit history, they have been refused a loan by three different lenders. The MOST LIKELY statement regarding these lenders is that they are
    1. engaging in illegal redlining.
    2. violating antitrust laws by all making the same decision.
    3. violating the requirements of the Equal Credit Opportunity Act (ECOA).
    4. not engaging in illegal activities, as the rejections are based on independently made economic-based property reviews.

38. You have listed a property. The seller told you that he must net at least $14,000 after all fees and expenses are paid. You estimate the seller's closing cost to be $3,500, and he must pay off an existing loan of $108,750. In addition, you are going to charge 7 percent commission on the sale. What is the least amount that the property can sell for to return the seller's desired net?
    1. $126,250
    2. $134,310
    3. $135,088
    4. $135,752.69

39. Which approach to value is an appraiser most likely to emphasize in the appraisal of a single-family home?
    1. Cost approach
    2. Gross income multiplier approach
    3. Income capitalization approach
    4. Sales comparison approach

40. Which of the following installment sales amounts is NOT covered by the imputed interest law?
    1. $2,000
    2. $4,000
    3. $9,000
    4. $10,000

41. The tax on the profit realized from an IRS 1031 exchange is
    1. ordinary income in the year of the exchange.
    2. deferred.
    3. eliminated.
    4. None of the above

42. You own an apartment building that provides you with a gross income of $40,000 a year. Your annual expenses are $10,000 a year. The value of your real estate if you need a 12 percent return on your investment is
    1. $83,333.
    2. $250,000.
    3. $333,333.
    4. $444,444.

43. Which of the following statements does NOT correctly describe joint tenancy?
    1. It is a form of co-ownership.
    2. Owners have the right of survivorship.
    3. Owners must be husband and wife.
    4. Owners may partition the property.

44. Which of the following statements does NOT correctly describe radon gas?
    1. As radon is released from the rocks, it finds its way to the surface and usually is released into the atmosphere.
    2. Radon enters a house through the roof vents.
    3. Radon can become concentrated in the crawlspace.
    4. Long-term exposure to radon gas is said to cause lung cancer.

45. Strict liability under Superfund means that
    1. each individual owner is personally responsible for the damages in whole.
    2. the owner is responsible to the injured party without excuse.
    3. the liability is not limited to the person who currently owns the property but also includes people who have owned the site in the past.
    4. anyone who has been involved in the transaction will be liable for damages.

46. Which of the following may NOT be governed by deed restrictions?
    1. Height of a building
    2. Ethnicity of tenants
    3. Use of a residence as a business
    4. Types of pets that can be housed within the subdivision

47. The business ownership structure of an S corporation provides which of the following benefits over the standard corporation structure?
    1. Profits are not taxed.
    2. The requirements for incorporation are simpler.
    3. The liability of individual owners for losses is removed.
    4. The investor's membership list does not have to be disclosed to the Internal Revenue Service (IRS).

48. The rent on a house is $400 a month, or $4,800 a year, and the house recently sold for $52,000. The gross rent multiplier on the house was
    1. 10.8.
    2. 108.
    3. 130.
    4. 130.8.

49. The rate of return an investor will require to invest in real estate is called a(n)
    1. gross rent multiplier.
    2. gross income multiplier.
    3. capitalization rate.
    4. assemblage.

50. National advertising and economies of volume purchasing are advantages for
    1. franchises.
    2. quasi-franchises.
    3. broker cooperatives.
    4. broker associations.

51. A broker requires that all budgeted costs for the planning period be justified each time a new budget is developed. This requirement reflects
    1. the cash method of keeping financial records.
    2. the concept of cash flow.
    3. the concept of desk cost.
    4. the concept of zero-base budgeting.

52. Which of the following statements does NOT correctly describe the independent-contractor relationship?
    1. The salesperson contracts with a broker to produce specific outcomes such as commission.
    2. The broker may not tell salespeople how to sell real estate.
    3. The broker must provide a pension plan.
    4. The salesperson must pay his or her board dues.

53. A salesperson works for a broker. The salesperson may
    1. work for the broker as an independent contractor.
    2. place an ad without identifying the broker.
    3. receive a commission directly from a seller.
    4. receive a commission directly from another broker.

54. A broker has listed a home. The broker generally will earn her commission when
    1. she submits an offer to purchase to the seller.
    2. the seller indicates that he thinks an offer to purchase is acceptable.
    3. she finds a "buyer ready, willing, and able" to buy on the terms of the listing.
    4. the closing takes place.

55. A Hispanic buyer has asked a broker to show her homes in a white neighborhood. The broker's response to the buyer should be
    1. "I think you would be happier in a neighborhood with people of similar background."
    2. "I don't think you would be comfortable with the people in that neighborhood because they do not welcome outsiders."
    3. "I'll be happy to show you homes in that neighborhood, but I think you could do better than that."
    4. "I'll be happy to show you homes in that neighborhood or any other neighborhood."

56. During a listing presentation, the seller tells the broker that she will not sell to Hispanics. Should the broker follow the seller's instructions?
    1. Yes. The owner has a right to choose prospective buyers.
    2. Yes. The broker is the seller's agent and must honor his fiduciary responsibility.
    3. No. The broker might lose any commission by limiting potential buyers.
    4. No. The broker should not accept the listing.

57. You are preparing a competitive market analysis (CMA) on a two-story, three-bedroom house with one bathroom on the first floor and all of the bedrooms on the second floor. The appraisal term that BEST identifies how this affects the list price is
   1. physical deterioration.
   2. deferred maintenance.
   3. functional obsolescence.
   4. economic obsolescence.

58. Which of the following is NOT an example of real property?
   1. A neighbor's strawberry bush, which she calls "fructus naturales"
   2. Percolating water
   3. Unexcavated clay
   4. The clay bricks that you will use to build your patio wall

59. A listing broker acting as a single agent in the course of selling the property would be in violation of the broker's fiduciary duties to the seller by
   1. telling a prospective buyer the lowest price the seller will accept below the list price.
   2. paying for a property appraisal during the course of helping the owner set the list price.
   3. accepting a commission that is lower than usual for marketing similar properties in the area.
   4. allowing prospective buyers to prepare and submit offers through buyer-brokers instead of subagents of the seller.

60. A CORRECT statement about a competitive market analysis (CMA) is that it
   1. must be performed by a licensed appraiser.
   2. must be reviewed by an employing broker in order to be valid.
   3. is based on the sales comparison (market data) approach to value.
   4. will develop a final assessment of value by averaging three bank appraisals.

61. Which of the following forms of ownership is characterized by double taxation?
   1. Corporation
   2. Sole proprietorship
   3. S corporation
   4. General proprietorship

62. A man wants to know how much money he owes on his mortgage loan. He knows that the interest part of the last monthly payment was $608.52. If he was paying interest at the rate of 10 percent, what was the outstanding balance of his loan before that last payment was made?
   1. $60,852.20
   2. $66,937.20
   3. $73,022.40
   4. $77,942.26

63. Your aunt bought her house one year ago for $62,400. Property in her neighborhood is said to be increasing at a rate of 7 percent annually. If this is true, what is the current market value of your aunt's real estate?
   1. $65,520
   2. $66,144
   3. $66,768
   4. $66,971

64. Your home is valued at $104,000. Property in your city is assessed at 70 percent of its value, and the local tax rate is $3.35 per $100. What is the amount of your monthly taxes?
   1. $192.86
   2. $203.23
   3. $290.33
   4. $331.64

65. In the cost approach, an appraiser makes use of which of the following?
   1. Sales prices of similar properties
   2. The owner's original cost of construction
   3. An estimate of the building's replacement cost
   4. Multiplying the net income by the capitalization rate

66. An appraisal of a church probably would be based on the
   1. market/data approach.
   2. cost approach.
   3. income approach.
   4. capitalization approach.

67. With an FHA loan, the buyer will NOT be required to
   1. pay a 20 percent down payment.
   2. find an approved lender willing to make the loan.
   3. buy a house that meets minimum FHA safety standards.
   4. buy mortgage insurance to protect the lender.

68. Which of the following statements regarding points is true?
   1. Points must be charged to the seller.
   2. One point equals 1 percent of the loan.
   3. Points must be charged to the buyer.
   4. One point equals 1/4 percent of the loan.

69. *X*, who works for broker *Y* on a 50-50 basis, sold a house listed by broker *Z* for $167,750. The seller agreed to pay a 7 percent commission, but stipulated in the listing that 65 percent was to go to the selling broker. How much commission will *X* make on the sale (to the nearest dollar)?
   1. $2,054
   2. $3,816
   3. $4,110
   4. $7,633

70. The net spendable income from an investment is known as the
   1. budget.
   2. cash flow.
   3. company dollar.
   4. gross income.

71. A broker has calculated the amount of income remaining after deducting all of the firm's commissions from the firm's gross income. The broker has calculated the
   1. budget.
   2. cash flow.
   3. company dollar.
   4. desk cost.

72. A broker has an annual overhead of $200,000; there are ten desks, each accommodating two salespeople. The broker's desk cost is
   1. $5,000.
   2. $10,000.
   3. $15,000.
   4. $20,000.

73. The discriminatory practice of guiding ethnic minorities toward available housing in neighborhoods made up of residents of the same ethnic group is referred to as
   1. puffing.
   2. steering.
   3. redlining.
   4. blockbusting.

74. Which of the following statements does NOT apply to both purchase money mortgages and land contracts?
   1. The seller is financing the transaction.
   2. The buyer takes possession when the contract is executed.
   3. The buyer gives the seller a down payment.
   4. The buyer has equitable title during the life of the contract.

75. Which of the following is covered by Regulation Z?
   1. A personal property credit transaction for $20,000
   2. A loan with three installments
   3. A real estate purchase agreement
   4. An agricultural loan for $29,000

76. Which of the following is exempted from the Federal Fair Housing Act?
   1. The rental of rooms in an owner-occupied, four-family dwelling
   2. The rental of rooms in an owner-occupied, five-family dwelling
   3. The rental of a single-family home when a broker is used
   4. The lodgings of a private club when the lodgings are operated commercially

77. You purchased a residence and neither took possession nor recorded the deed. Which of the following statements BEST describes the status of your property ownership?
   1. You have given actual notice of ownership.
   2. You do not have a valid deed from the previous owner.
   3. You have not provided constructive notice of ownership.
   4. You will have to go to court to assert your ownership rights prior to reselling the property.

78. The relationship of the broker to the listing owner who hired him or her is that of a(n)
   1. attorney-in-fact.
   2. strawman.
   3. trustee.
   4. fiduciary.

79. Which of the following would NOT be deposited in your trust account?
    1. The commission you earn on a transaction
    2. Earnest money received on a transaction
    3. The down payment for a land contract transaction
    4. An amount sufficient to cover the bank service charges on the account

80. Which of the following statements does NOT correctly describe a limited liability company?
    1. It offers the single-level taxation of a partnership.
    2. It may not be directly managed by members.
    3. It offers the limited liability of a corporation.
    4. It must have at least one member.

81. In order to represent legally all parties in the same real estate transaction, a licensee MUST
    1. hold a securities license.
    2. agree to receive compensation from only one of the principals.
    3. ensure that all documents that the licensee signs are notarized.
    4. obtain the informed consent to dual agency from all principals.

82. You are working as an agent for a prospective buyer. The buyer buys a house listed on the multiple-listing service (MLS) of which you are a member. Which of the following statements does NOT correctly describe the situation?
    1. You acted as a disclosed dual agent.
    2. You will be entitled to a commission from the buyer.
    3. You could be paid by the seller if the parties agree.
    4. The listing broker is an agent of the seller.

83. Tenancy in common is distinguished by which of the following characteristics?
    1. The co-owners have right of survivorship.
    2. Ownership interests must be equal.
    3. A co-owner cannot will his or her interest in a property.
    4. Each co-owner's interest may be conveyed separately.

84. A plumbing company installed a new furnace and filed a lien for nonpayment immediately on completion. This was most likely a
    1. voluntary lien.
    2. general lien.
    3. novation.
    4. specific lien.

85. Which of the following is NOT an example of functional obsolescence?
    1. A five-bedroom house with one bathroom
    2. Outdated plumbing fixtures
    3. A roof that leaks
    4. A poor floor plan

86. A broker listed and sold a seller's home. The broker most likely earned her commission when
    1. the transaction was closed.
    2. she found a buyer "ready, willing, and able" to buy on the terms of the listing.
    3. the buyer's financing contingency was removed from the offer to purchase.
    4. the buyer's check cleared the bank after closing.

87. A salesperson has taken a four-month exclusive-right-to-sell listing on a house. Prior to the expiration of the listing, the salesperson leaves the state and inactivates her license. Which of the following correctly describes the status of the listing?
    1. The listing automatically terminates when the salesperson leaves the state and inactivates her license.
    2. The seller may terminate the listing once the salesperson has left the state.
    3. The broker will have to negotiate with the seller to retain the listing.
    4. The listing will continue as a valid contract between the seller and the broker.

88. A parcel of property that measures ⅛ mile by ⅛ mile is equal to
    1. 10 acres.
    2. 40 acres.
    3. 160 acres.
    4. 320 acres.

89. Which of the following is NOT an advantage of the FHA-insured loan?
    1. low down payment
    2. Buyer protection with FHA insurance
    3. Enables cash-short buyers to enter real estate market
    4. Protects lender with FHA insurance

90. Which of the following is NOT a legal requirement of an option?
    1. A purchase price and how it will be determined
    2. Consideration
    3. The date on which the option will expire
    4. The exercise of the option by the optionee

91. A 300-acre farm is divided into house lots. The streets require one-eighth of the whole farm and there are 280 lots. How many square feet are in each lot?
    1. 38,115
    2. 40,838
    3. 46,671
    4. None of the above

92. The process of reviewing the various approaches to value in order to arrive at a final estimate of market value is called
    1. assemblage.
    2. capitalization.
    3. balance.
    4. reconciliation.

93. A broker and a seller have just signed a listing contract for the sale of the seller's house. Which of the following statements does NOT correctly describe their situation?
    1. A fiduciary relationship now exists between the broker and seller.
    2. The broker has become a general agent for the seller.
    3. The broker is an agent and the seller is the principal.
    4. The broker has become a special agent for the seller.

94. The Americans with Disabilities Act (ADA) requires that an employer with a MINIMUM of how many employees must comply with the ADA requirements?
    1. 3
    2. 5
    3. 10
    4. 15

95. You have just listed a property, and the owner has informed you that the roof leaks and the fourth bedroom was added without a building permit being issued. Which of the following best describes the type of disclosure you should make to potential buyers?
    1. You should disclose that the roof leaks.
    2. You do not have to disclose that the bedroom was added without a permit because the project has already been completed.
    3. You do not have to disclose either unless you are instructed to do so by the seller.
    4. You must disclose both the roof leak and the lack of a building permit.

96. *A* agreed to lease *D*'s house on a month-to-month basis. This lease is an example of a(n)
    1. tenancy at will.
    2. estate for years.
    3. tenancy at sufferance.
    4. periodic estate.

97. According to federal fair housing laws, parties who feel that they have been aggrieved by a discriminatory housing practice have a MAXIMUM of how long after the event to file a complaint?
    1. Thirty days
    2. Sixty days
    3. Six months
    4. One year

98. You lease the 36 apartments in your building for a total monthly rental of $8,000. If this figure represents an 8 percent annual return on your investment, what was the original cost of the property?
    1. $100,000
    2. $236,000
    3. $1,200,000
    4. $2,360,000

99. *P* bought a house for $160,000 five years ago. His mortgage was for $128,000. Today *P*'s house is valued at $200,000, and his mortgage balance is $123,000. What is *P*'s equity in the property?
    1. $32,000
    2. $37,000
    3. $72,000
    4. $77,000

100. The county zoo holds title to the land that includes a condition that the zoo will hold title so long as it does not charge an admission fee. This is an example of a
    1. fee-simple estate.
    2. defeasible-fee estate.
    3. conventional life estate.
    4. tenancy at will.

ANSWER KEY WITH EXPLANATIONS

NOTE: The number in parentheses at the end of each explanation refers to the page number and the outline reference where this material is discussed.

1. **(2)** A leasehold estate, chattels, and trade fixtures are classified as personal property. (18)

2. **(2)** When persons die intestate, their real estate and personal property pass on to their heirs according to statute. (103)

3. **(2)** Rural Development makes and guarantees loans to low-income people in rural areas. FHLMC is a warehousing agency in the secondary mortgage market. FHA insures home mortgages. Farm Service Agency makes and guarantees loans to farmers and ranchers. (62)

4. **(4)** The words *as long as* are key to the creation of a determinable fee, sometimes referred to as a qualified fee, conditional fee, or base-fee estate. (21)

5. **(2)** Under an open listing, if the seller personally sells the property without the aid of any broker, the seller is not obligated to pay the commission. (92)

6. **(3)** NAR is the REALTOR® trade association. EEOC deals with discrimination in employment, while ARELLO works with license law issues. (114)

7. **(3)** $80,300 × .08 = $6,424 annual interest

   $6,424 ÷ 12 = $535.33 interest for one month

   $653.00 P&I – $535.33 = $117.67 principal payoff

   $80,300 – $117.67 = $80,182.33 balance after next payment (134–135)

8. **(2)** $804.65 ($121,000 × 6.65) (134–136)

9. **(4)** $804.65 × 360 months = $289,674

$289,674	total P&I
–121,000	loan
$168,674	total interest (134–136)

10. **(4)** A conventional mortgage is neither insured nor guaranteed by the government. A down payment generally is higher than with insured and guaranteed loans. (61)

11. **(1)** $92,000 × 70% (0.70) = $64,400, assessed value ÷ 100 = $644

    $644 × $3.40 = $2,189.60 annual tax

    Divide by 2 to get the semiannual tax

    $2,189.60 ÷ 2 = $1,094.80 (35–36)

12. **(4)** The broker is not entitled to a commission because he had no contractual agreement with the buyer or the seller. (92)

13. **(3)** The loan amount cannot exceed the DVA appraisal on a DVA loan. The veteran must pay the difference between the appraised value and the purchase price in cash. (61–62)

14. **(4)** Payments on an amortized mortgage include principal and interest. A purchase-money mortgage involves seller financing. A graduated payment mortgage has low initial payments that increase over time. (59)

15. **(1)** Attachment refers to the act of taking a person's property into legal custody or placing a lien thereon by court or judicial order to hold it available for application to that person's debt to a creditor. An easement is the right to use the land of another for a specific purpose. An appurtenance is a right, privilege, or improvement that belongs to and passes with the transfer of the property but is not necessarily a part of the real property. (20)

16. **(1)** The relationship of the buyer to the listing licensee is of no concern to the selling licensee. Showing a property to a customer does not create an express agency. Introducing the property to the buyer does not necessarily entitle the listing licensee to a portion of the selling licensee's compensation. (73–74)

17. **(4)** Brokers must report details of a closing to the IRS on Form 1099S; Section 1031 of the Internal Revenue Code deals with a tax-deferred exchange. (107)

18. **(4)** A reverse annuity mortgage becomes due on a specific date, the sale of the property, or the death of the borrower. (63)

19. **(1)** A graduated lease provides for rent increase at set future dates, while a percentage lease provides for minimum fixed rent plus a percentage of the business income. Under a net lease, the tenant pays rent plus all or part of the property charges. (148)

20. **(4)** The vendee (buyer) takes possession when the contract is executed. (94–95)

21. **(1)** Leverage is using other people's money to finance an investment. Arbitrage refers to buying and selling credit instruments to profit from differences in prices. Novation occurs when a new obligation is substituted for an old one. (66)

22. **(4)** The listing broker is required to prepare as well as submit all offers unless otherwise instructed. The broker does not have the authority to accept or reject those offers for the seller. (73–74)

23. **(3)** The dominant tenement owner may terminate the easement right but does not pay the real estate taxes on the servient tenement. The dominant tenement owner may acquire his or her rights under an easement appurtenant by means other than by prescription. (20)

24. **(1)** Tenants by the entirety must be husband and wife. Joint tenancy requires the interest to be equal. (22–23)

25. **(3)** The different types of buyer brokerage agreements are discussed on pages 74–75.

26. **(4)** A mortgage is a voluntary act, not involuntary. (59, 103)

27. **(3)** $70,000 (first investor) + $40,000 (second investor) = $110,000

$200,000 × $110,000 = $90,000, third investor's contribution

$$\frac{\text{part}}{\text{total}} = \text{percent}$$

$90,000 ÷ $200,000 = 0.45, or 45% (127)

28. **(4)** The broker is responsible for disclosing physical defects in the house, but to disclose that the seller would take less than the list price would be a violation of the broker's fiduciary responsibilities to the seller. (73)

29. **(2)** The offer was not accepted and therefore not ratified. The earnest money was returned before it was even deposited into the broker's trust account. (74)

30. **(2)** If the air-conditioning system is installed because of saleability, it would be contribution. In this case, the installation was due to the market availability of air-conditioned space. (49)

31. **(3)** Neither *A*'s knowledge of *B*'s making a loan nor the size of such a loan would affect the priority of claims. The court could not rule in favor of *B* if *B* had signed a satisfaction. A subordination clause is a clause in which the mortgagee (*A*) permits a subsequent mortgage (*B*'s loan) to take priority. (60)

32. **(3)** $2,380 ÷ 12 months = $198.333 per month

$198.33 ÷ 30 days = $6.611 per day

$198.33 × 6 months = $1,189.98

$6.611 × 29 days = $197.719

$1,189.88 + $191.719 = $1,381.699 or $1,381.70

The taxes for the year have not been paid, and when they are, the buyer will be in possession and have to pay the bill. The seller, therefore, must pay (be debited) for the portion of the year that he occupied the property. The buyer receives a credit for the same amount. (133–134)

33. **(1)** $4,100 – $600 salary = $3,500, commission sales

$3,500 ÷ 3.5% (0.035) = $100,000 value of property sold (127)

34. **(4)** The broker may serve as an agent of the seller or any of the buyers. The broker could even represent a buyer and a seller in the same transaction, provided that he or she had the knowledge and consent of all parties involved. (73)

35. **(3)** A zoning variance for commercial use is economic or locational obsolescence, which would be incurable. (49)

36. **(4)** An individual must also have a current real estate license and have a written contract with the broker that states that the individual will not be treated as an employee for tax purposes. (107)

37. **(4)** What is described in the question could be looked on as "legal" redlining. The lenders refused to loan because of the depressed economic conditions of the neighborhood, not because of the racial or ethnic makeup of the area. (116)

38. **(4)** Start by adding the desired net $14,000 PLUS existing loan payoff of $108,750 and closing costs of $3,500 = $126,250, the minimum that the seller must receive.

    If the selling price is 100 percent, the commission is 7 percent and the net to the seller is 93 percent.

    $126,250 is 93 percent of the selling price.

    Therefore, $126,250 ÷ 93% (0.93) = selling price of $135,752.69. (127–128)

39. **(4)** The sales comparison approach is considered the most reliable of the three approaches in appraising residential property. (50)

40. **(1)** Installment sales of less than $3,000 are not covered by the imputed interest law. (108)

41. **(2)** Under Section 1031 of the Internal Revenue Code, real estate investors can defer taxation of capital gains by making a property exchange. Property involved in the exchange must be of like kind—real estate for real estate. (108)

42. **(2)** $40,000 gross income – $10,000 expenses = $30,000 net annual income

    $30,000 net annual income ÷ 12% (0.12) = $250,000 value of real estate (50)

43. **(3)** The owners must be husband and wife in tenancy by the entirety. (23)

44. **(2)** Radon generally enters the house through the basement foundation as well as through the crawlspace. (37)

45. **(2)** Liability under the Superfund is also considered to be retroactive, meaning that the liability is not limited to the current owner but includes previous owners of the site. (40–41)

46. **(2)** Deed restrictions (private land-use controls) may not be used to discriminate against members of protected classes; they may be terminated by a quitclaim deed executed by the necessary parties. (41)

47. **(1)** There is no double taxation as in a corporation. In other words, income losses and capital gains are passed directly to the shareholders. (160)

48. **(3)** The gross rent multiplier (GRM) relates to *monthly* income, not annual.

    $52,000 sale price ÷ $400 monthly rent = 130 gross multiplier (50)

49. **(3)** The gross rent and gross income multipliers are used as substitutes for the income approach. Assemblage is the joining of two or more properties. (50)

50. **(1)** Other advantages of a franchise include management expertise and a client referral system. Disadvantages include loss of individual identity and high initial fees and franchise fees. (161)

51. **(4)** Cash flow refers to net spendable income; company dollar is the amount of income that remains after subtracting all the commissions from the gross income. The cash method records income as received and expenses when actually paid. (165)

52. **(3)** The broker may not provide fringe benefits such as health insurance. In addition, the broker may not withhold federal and state income taxes, social security taxes, or state unemployment insurance from commissions. (162)

53. **(1)** A salesperson cannot place blind ads. The salesperson may not receive monetary compensation for a real estate transaction from anyone other than the broker for whom he or she is working. (162)

54. **(3)** It is important to distinguish between earning and receiving a commission. (74)

55. **(4)** The broker must not restrict the buyer's freedom of choice. (114–116)

56. **(4)** It is illegal under federal fair housing laws to accept a listing that involves discrimination, such as refusing to sell to members of a protected class. (114–116)

57. **(3)** Functional obsolescence is a loss in value due to a deficiency in the floor plan or design of the house. (49)

58. **(4)** Real property refers to physical land and appurtenances, including easements, water rights, mineral rights, and fixtures. Strawberry bushes are perennial plants and would be considered real property. Percolating water and unexcavated clay would also be considered real property. Personal property refers to anything that can be moved. (18)

59. **(1)** Disclosing the lowest price that the seller will accept is a violation of the fiduciary relationship. (73–75)

60. **(3)** A competitive market analysis is based on the sales comparison approach to value. (48)

61. **(1)** Double taxation is a primary disadvantage of the corporation form of ownership. (159)

62. **(3)** $608.52 × 12 = $7,302.24

    $7,302.24 ÷ 10% (0.10) = $73,022.40 (127)

63. **(3)** $62,400 × 7% (0.07) = $4,368

    $62,400 + $4,368 = $66,768, or

    $62,400 × 107% (1.07) = $66,768 (127)

64. **(2)** $104,000 × 70% (0.70) = $72,800 assessed value

    Divide by 100 because the tax rate is stated per $100

    $72,800 ÷ 100 = $728

    $728 × $3.35 = $2,438.80 annual taxes

    Divide by 12 to get monthly payments

    $2,438.80 ÷ 12 = $203.23 (34–35)

65. **(3)** Sales prices of similar properties are used in the market/data approach. The net income and capitalization rate are used in the income approach. The owner's original cost of construction would be irrelevant, because in the cost approach the appraiser is concerned with the current replacement cost of the structure. (49–50)

66. **(2)** The market/data approach is considered most reliable when appraising a single-family home. The income approach and capitalization approach are stressed in appraising commercial and industrial properties. (49–50)

67. **(1)** The buyer's down payment on an FHA loan is 3 percent plus closing costs. (61)

68. **(2)** One point equals 1 percent of the loan. (61, 66)

69. **(2)** $167,750 sales price × 7% (0.07) = $11,742.50 broker's commission

    $11,742.50 × 65% = $7,632.63 × 0.50 = $3,816 selling salesperson's commission (127)

70. **(2)** The budget is the quantified business plan; company dollars is the amount of income remaining after subtracting all the commissions from the gross income. Gross income is the revenue earned from all the sources in a brokerage firm such as sales and management fees. (165)

71. **(3)** Budget and company dollar were defined previously. Desk cost is the cost of providing the opportunity for salespeople to conduct their business. (165)

72. **(2)** $200,000 annual overhead ÷ 20 (10 desks × 2 salespeople each) = $10,000 desk cost (165–166)

73. **(2)** Puffing is sales psychology. Redlining is selecting specific areas and choosing not to make loans in that area; the areas generally are composed of members of protected classes. Blockbusting is panic peddling. (117)

74. **(4)** The vendee in a land contract holds equitable title until the land contract is paid in full, while the mortgagor receives legal title at closing. (62, 94–95)

75. **(1)** Loans with five or more installments would be covered. An agricultural loan for less than $25,000 would also be covered. (118–119)

76. **(1)** Rental of rooms in an owner-occupied dwelling of five units or more is not exempted. (117)

77. **(3)** An unrecorded deed is valid between the parties, but constructive notice must be given to protect against subsequent buyers of the property. (106)

78. **(4)** An attorney-in-fact is a competent, disinterested person authorized by another person to act in his or her place. A strawman is one who buys property for someone else to conceal the identity of the real buyer. A trustee holds property in trust for another to secure the performance of an obligation. (73–74)

79. **(1)** A broker may not commingle his or her personal funds with those of clients in a trust account. (165)

80. **(2)** Limited liability companies may be directly managed by members, or responsibility may be delegated to a property manager. (159)

81. **(4)** Brokers generally are prohibited from representing and collecting compensations from both parties to a transaction unless both parties receive prior knowledge and give mutual consent. (74)

82. **(1)** In this situation you are the agent of the buyer and the listing broker is the agent of the seller. (74)

83. **(4)** Answers 1, 2, and 3 are all characteristics of joint tenancy. (22–23)

84. **(4)** A voluntary lien is a mortgage lien such as a lien created by an owner who obtains a mortgage loan. A general lien usually affects all the property of a debtor, both real and personal. A specific lien usually is secured by a specific property. (20)

85. **(3)** A roof that leaks would be an example of physical deterioration. (50)

86. **(2)** The broker is entitled to a commission when she is employed by the seller and finds a "ready, willing, and able" buyer. (74)

87. **(4)** The salesperson is an agent of the broker. When the salesperson no longer is employed by the broker, the broker retains any unsold or unexpired listings. The status of the listings remains unchanged. (75)

88. **(1)** 8 × 8 = 64
640 acres ÷ 64 = 10 acres (19)

89. **(2)** FHA insurance is provided as protection for the lender. (61)

90. **(4)** When an option is given, the optionee gives the optionor consideration, the price is determined, and the time is set. The optionee does not have to exercise the option. (94)

91. **(2)** 43,560 square feet per acre × 300 acres = 13,068,000 square feet
13,068,000 square feet × (0.125) = 1,633,500 square feet for streets
13,068,000 – 1,633,500 = 11,434,400 sq. ft. for lots
11,434,500 square feet ÷ 280 lots = 40,838 square feet per lot (127)

92. **(4)** Reconciliation is the next-to-last step in the appraisal process. (51–52)

93. **(2)** The listing agreement is an employment contract. The broker is "employed" to do only one thing, and that is to find a "ready, willing, and able" buyer. The broker, therefore, is a special agent, not a general agent. (73–74)

94. **(4)** ADA requires that any employer with 15 or more employees must adopt nondiscriminatory employment procedures and make reasonable accommodations to enable an individual with a disability to perform in his or her employment. (117–118)

95. **(4)** The broker is obligated to disclose to the buyer the material facts relating to property. (73)

96. **(1)** A tenancy at will gives the lessee the right to possession until either party decides to terminate. An estate for years is a lease for a definite duration, whereas a periodic estate has an indefinite duration. (148)

97. **(4)** The statute of limitations for initiating administrative proceedings is one year after the alleged discriminatory housing practice. (116)

98. **(3)** $8,000 × 12 = $96,000 annual return
$96,000 ÷ 8% (0.08) = $1,200,000 original cost of property (127)

99. **(4)** $200,000 current value – $123,000 current mortgage = $77,000 equity (127)

100. **(2)** A defeasible-fee estate continues for an indefinite period. The period of ownership may be based on either a certain or uncertain event. The words *so long as* indicate that the estate will be extinguished on the occurrence of the designated event; for example, the charging of admission to the zoo. (21)

BROKER EXAMINATION II

1. You have hauled your heavy farm equipment across some vacant land of your neighbor's for years with your neighbor's knowledge, but not permission. Now your neighbor wants to make improvements on the property and tells you to stop using it. Assuming you meet the required statutory period for having used the property, you may be able to get the courts to grant you the right to continue using the land, even if it means your neighbor's plans have to be abandoned. Which of the following terms BEST identifies the right described above?
   1. License
   2. Adverse possession
   3. An easement appurtenant
   4. An easement by prescription

2. The basic reason for choosing among a general warranty, a special warranty, or a quitclaim deed is to
   1. avoid the need for a habendum clause.
   2. verify the kind of estate the grantee will receive.
   3. explain any restrictions or limitations on the title.
   4. define the covenants by which the grantor is bound.

3. Under their mother's will, a woman and her brother inherited title to a house as tenants in common. The woman married and had title to her share put in joint tenancy with her husband. Her brother is now
   1. a joint tenant with his sister and her husband.
   2. sole owner of the property.
   3. a tenant in common, owning an undivided ⅓ interest.
   4. a tenant in common, owning an undivided ½ interest.

4. With permission, a tenant is going to place a window air conditioner in a rented space. In order to purchase the right size air conditioner, the tenant must compute the cubic feet of a room that is 90' × 60' × 10'. What is the cubic feet of this room?
   1. 5,400
   2. 9,600
   3. 54,000
   4. 96,000

5. You are taking a listing on a property and notice that a neighboring building appears to have a roof overhang encroaching on the property line. The seller has never noticed this, even though the building has been there for several decades. Which of the following statements BEST identifies this situation?
   1. The seller must record a party wall easement prior to transferring title.
   2. The seller must perform a title search to discover if this represents a cloud on the title.
   3. The neighbor may be entitled to a prescription easement guaranteeing the right to leave the building as is.
   4. The neighbor may claim ownership of the property under the roof under the doctrine of prior appropriation.

6. Broker *C* is renting apartments for landlord *M*. *C* shows an apartment to an African-American couple. Prior to informing the couple that they may have the apartment, he receives a call from the landlord who asks about the race of the prospective tenants. Which of the following statements correctly describes how *C* should respond to *M*'s question concerning the race of the prospective tenants?
   1. *C* should tell the owner that the prospective tenants are African-American.
   2. *C* should tell the landlord that he cannot answer that question.
   3. *C* should state that he will answer the question only if the owner promises to keep the information confidential.
   4. *C* should provide the race of the prospects only if he tells the landlord it is illegal, but he must respond because he owes loyalty to the landlord.

7. The state needs your farm to build a highway. You have rejected their offer. The state may obtain your property by exercising its right of
   1. adverse possession.
   2. eminent domain.
   3. escheat.
   4. police power.

8. Keeping which of the following types of funds in a broker's trust account is MOST likely to be illegal?
   1. Rents on an apartment building you are managing
   2. Earnest money deposits
   3. Commission earned on previous sales
   4. Security deposits on properties you are managing

9. *X* owns a life estate, and *Y* hold the future interest in the life estate. When *X* dies
   1. *X*'s wife will become the owner under her dower interest.
   2. *X*'s life estate will pass to his heirs according to the terms of his will.
   3. *X* and *Y* will hold title as tenants in common.
   4. *Y* will hold title to the property.

10. *A* has had an offer to purchase accepted by *B*. Prior to closing, *A* will hold
    1. fee-simple title.
    2. defeasible title.
    3. legal title.
    4. equitable title.

11. A zoning ordinance would NOT regulate
    1. land use.
    2. height of the building.
    3. use of the building.
    4. construction standards.

12. When the owner of a property sold for back taxes or mortgage default is granted a period of time after the sale to buy the property back, this is referred to as the owner's
    1. lien priority.
    2. homestead rights.
    3. statutory right of redemption.
    4. deed in lieu of foreclosure.

13. You have pledged your home as security for a mortgage without giving up possession. This is called
    1. hypothecation.
    2. abstract.
    3. subordination.
    4. release of mortgage.

14. Which of the following statements does NOT correctly describe the relationship of a salesperson working for a broker as an employee?
    1. The broker may choose to provide fringe benefits.
    2. The broker may not tell salespeople how to list property.
    3. The broker may require attendance at sales meetings.
    4. The broker is required to withhold federal and state income taxes from commissions.

15. The rent on a house is $900 a month, or $10,800 a year, and the house recently sold for $126,000. The gross rent multiplier on the house was
    1. 11.67.
    2. 14.
    3. 111.7.
    4. 140.

16. A broker has been found guilty of discrimination under the Federal Fair Housing Act for the third time in the past seven years. The broker will be subject to a civil penalty not exceeding
    1. $10,000.
    2. $25,000.
    3. $50,000.
    4. $100,000.

17. An earthquake tore away some of the land on your farm recently. This is an example of
    1. accession.
    2. accretion.
    3. avulsion.
    4. erosion.

18. Which of the following practices does NOT constitute a discriminatory act under the Federal Fair Housing Act?
    1. The owner-occupant of a duplex refuses to rent to a family with children.
    2. A lender uses one type of application for whites and another for African-Americans.
    3. A white broker refers Hispanic prospects only to Hispanic brokers.
    4. A property manager requires a higher security deposit for African-Americans than whites.

19. In the sales comparison approach to value, if a feature in the comparable property is inferior to that of the subject property, a
    1. plus adjustment must be made to the price of the subject.
    2. minus adjustment must be made to the price of the comparable.
    3. plus adjustment must be made to the price of the comparable.
    4. minus adjustment must be made to the price of the subject.
20. If you give your land to your brother for the balance of his life and at his death the land is to go to your sister, his interest or estate is called a
    1. reversion.
    2. curtesy.
    3. base fee.
    4. life estate.
21. Buyer *A* purchased a home for $148,000 with the help of a mortgage for 90 percent of the selling price. Four years later, the balance of the mortgage was $129,000. An appraisal of the house at that same time estimated the value of *A*'s home at $163,000. *A*'s equity in the home is
    1. $14,800.
    2. $19,000.
    3. $34,000.
    4. None of the above.
22. A property manager renting units for an apartment owner is an example of a
    1. special agent.
    2. general agent.
    3. subagent.
    4. dual agent.
23. Which of the following situations may be unethical but would NOT be prohibited under the Federal Fair Housing Act?
    1. A broker makes a profit by inducing owners to sell because of prospective entry of minorities into the neighborhood.
    2. A broker encourages minorities to live in areas of minorities.
    3. A lender refuses to make mortgage loans in a minority neighborhood.
    4. A broker refuses to show a house to a potential buyer based on the buyer's sexual orientation.
24. The relationship of trust and confidence that a broker has with a client is a(n)
    1. escrow relationship.
    2. subordination agreement.
    3. fiduciary relationship.
    4. trustee relationship.
25. A salesperson may legally accept a cash bonus directly from
    1. a seller for whom she did an excellent job.
    2. an appreciative buyer.
    3. a grateful title company.
    4. a broker/employer.
26. A broker knowingly misled a potential buyer on the boundary lines of a property. The buyer discovered the problem after buying the property. Is the broker guilty of fraudulent misrepresentation?
    1. Yes, because the broker should have had the property surveyed before commenting on the property boundary lines.
    2. Yes, because the broker intentionally misled the buyer.
    3. No, because the broker is not a surveyor.
    4. No, because the broker did not provide any misrepresentation in writing.
27. You own a defeasible fee estate and sell it on a land contract. Until the land contract has been paid in full, the buyer will hold a(n)
    1. leasehold estate.
    2. life estate.
    3. equitable title.
    4. fee-simple title.
28. A broker sold a home for $183,000. The broker charged the owner a 7 percent commission and will pay 30 percent of that amount to the listing salesperson and 25 percent to the selling salesperson. What amount of commission will the listing salesperson receive from the sale?
    1. $3,202.50
    2. $3,843
    3. $4,483.50
    4. $12,810

29. A seller asks a listing licensee to drop the price of the property to $105,000 from $120,000 in order to spur a quick sale. The licensee then prepares a new competitive market analysis (CMA), which indicates the property may be worth $115,000. In this situation, the licensee's BEST course as a fiduciary for the seller is to
    1. offer to buy the property for $105,000.
    2. follow instructions and drop the price immediately.
    3. encourage the seller to hold the price up for negotiation room.
    4. disclose to the seller that the home is worth $115,000 before proceeding with a list-price change.

30. You have just given an option to buy your house to your friend. Which of the following statements does NOT correctly describe your agreement?
    1. Your friend is the optionee.
    2. Your friend is not obligated to buy your house.
    3. You are the optionor.
    4. You will have to return the fee for the option right to your friend if he chooses not to buy your house.

31. Which of the following facts would not need to be disclosed by a broker?
    1. There is water in the basement.
    2. There is an underground storage tank in the backyard.
    3. There is asbestos wrap on the heating pipes.
    4. The seller has AIDS.

32. A broker was listing a man's house for sale when the man informed her that he was Catholic and could not sell the house to anyone who was not Catholic. The broker should
    1. take the listing but state that she could not promise that she could get a Catholic buyer.
    2. get the request in writing on the listing contract and then attempt to find a Catholic buyer.
    3. take the listing but tell the owner that she would have to check with the state licensing board to make sure it was appropriate.
    4. not take the listing.

33. A broker has entered into a listing contract with a client in which the broker will receive a commission regardless of who sells the property during the term of the listing contract. The broker's listing is a(n)
    1. exclusive-right-to-sell listing.
    2. net listing.
    3. open listing.
    4. exclusive-agency listing.

34. Three investors decided to pool their savings and buy an office building for $250,000. If one invested $80,000 and the second investor contributed $50,000, what percentage of ownership was left for the third investor?
    1. 20 percent
    2. 32 percent
    3. 48 percent
    4. None of the above

35. You own an apartment building that provides you with a gross income of $50,000 a year. Your annual expenses are $12,000. The value of your real estate if you receive a 14 percent return on your investment is
    1. $85,714.
    2. $170,928.
    3. $271,429.
    4. $325,143.

36. In order to permanently buy down a buyer's interest rate, an owner agrees to pay two points amounting to $3,500. How much money did the buyer borrow?
    1. $175,000
    2. $350,000
    3. $700,000
    4. None of the above

37. *K* owns his home in fee simple. This means that *K* has
    1. a legal life estate.
    2. a personal property interest.
    3. a tenancy by the entirety.
    4. the highest type of interest in real estate.

38. Your home is valued at $143,000. Property in your city is assessed at 80 percent of its value, and the local tax rate is $3.65 per $100. What is the amount of your monthly taxes?
    1. $319.37
    2. $347.96
    3. $352.73
    4. $357.50

39. Which of the following represents the MOST likely recourse for a lender who has foreclosed on a property and does not recover enough from the sale to cover the outstanding loan amount due?
    1. Sue the borrower for a deficiency judgment
    2. Apply to the appropriate federal agency for the difference
    3. Seek compensation from the borrower's title insurance company
    4. Initiate proceedings to recover the difference from homestead exemption funds

40. You own a home on a block that is zoned residential; however, there is a retail store on the lot next door to you. The retail store
    1. is an example of downzoning.
    2. is a nonconforming use.
    3. will have to close if you file a complaint with the planning commission.
    4. is a buffer zone.

41. Which of the following statements is CORRECT about an exclusive agency listing? It authorizes
    1. the listing agent to sign offers on behalf of the seller.
    2. the listing agent to be the only licensee to show the property.
    3. the seller to find a buyer and not be obligated to pay a sales commission.
    4. the seller to demand that the listing firm purchase the property if it remains unsold at the end of the listing period.

42. A doctor built a $400,000 home in a neighborhood of $200,000 homes. This situation reflects the principle of
    1. competition.
    2. conformity.
    3. progression.
    4. regression.

43. You purchased a home with an FHA-insured loan. At closing, the seller was charged the five discount points for the loan. This money will be paid to
    1. the broker.
    2. the lending institution.
    3. the FHA.
    4. you.

44. A doctrine of law that gives title to property to a buyer under a binding offer to purchase under certain conditions is known as
    1. accession.
    2. equitable conversion.
    3. laches.
    4. partition.

45. You have just purchased a business including the inventory and equipment. Title to the inventory and equipment will be transferred to you by means of a
    1. bargain and sale deed.
    2. bill of sale.
    3. quitclaim deed.
    4. warranty deed.

46. You have listed a property. The seller told you that she must net at least $18,000 after all fees and expenses are paid. You estimate the seller's closing costs to be $5,200, and she must pay off an existing loan of $104,600. In addition you are going to charge a 6 percent commission on the sale. What is the least amount that the property can sell for to return the seller's desired net?
    1. $111,277
    2. $130,425
    3. $137,419
    4. None of the above

47. Six months after a real estate transaction closes, one of the parties discovers information about the transaction that raises the possibility that he was the victim of fraud. Which of the following terms BEST identifies the legal principle governing whether or not the aggrieved party can still bring a lawsuit this long after closing?
    1. Laches
    2. Equity of redemption
    3. Statute of frauds
    4. Statute of limitations

48. Legislation that has helped resurrect once deserted, defunct, and derelict toxic industrial sites is known as
    1. DNR.
    2. waste field.
    3. due diligences.
    4. Brownfields.

49. A commercial real estate agent needs to determine the number of acres in a vacant parcel of land that measures 800' × 1200'. How many acres are in this area?
    1. 22.04
    2. 62.04
    3. 2,000
    4. 960,000

50. Which of the following responsibilities would NOT be considered part of the licensee's fiduciary duties to a client?
    1. Procuring a buyer for a seller-client
    2. Presenting all offers promptly to the client
    3. Advising a buyer-client how to take title to the property
    4. Ensuring that earnest monies are placed in a trust account

51. Standing timber is legally considered to be
    1. emblements.
    2. personal property.
    3. real property.
    4. trade fixtures.

52. Which of the following governs the disclosures required when advertising financing terms for real estate?
    1. Regulation Z
    2. Sherman Antitrust Act
    3. Equal Credit Opportunity Act (ECOA)
    4. Real Estate Settlement Procedures Act (RESPA)

53. Title of the land and building in a cooperative is held by a
    1. corporation.
    2. general partnership.
    3. homeowners association.
    4. syndicate.

54. Which of the following would be required for a deed to be valid?
    1. The grantee must sign the deed.
    2. The deed must be recorded by the grantor.
    3. The grantor must sign the deed.
    4. The deed must be recorded by the grantee.

55. A broker has an accepted offer to purchase a property and would like to change the language to reflect the desire of the buyer and seller to revise the contract. The broker will accomplish this by means of a(n)
    1. addendum.
    2. amendment.
    3. counteroffer.
    4. rescission.

56. The major employer in your city has decided to relocate to another state, resulting in a substantial decline in housing prices. This would be an example of
    1. the principle of regression.
    2. functional obsolescence.
    3. physical deterioration.
    4. economic obsolescence.

57. Which of the following is a physical characteristic of land?
    1. Scarcity
    2. Situs
    3. Immobility
    4. Improvements

58. If an owner listed a property for $300,000 but accepted an offer for $275,000, what was the percent of change between the asking price and the actual selling price?
    1. 2.75%
    2. 3.00%
    3. 5.50%
    4. 8.25%

59. A correct statement about an easement in gross is that it
    1. benefits the dominant tenement.
    2. has only a dominant tenement.
    3. has only a servient tenement.
    4. has both a dominant and a servient tenement.

60. Ownership is freely transferable in all of the following forms of ownership EXCEPT
    1. a sole proprietorship.
    2. a corporation.
    3. an S corporation.
    4. a general partnership.

61. Using the mortgage factor of $7.34, what is the monthly payment for $129,000 at 8 percent for 30 years?
    1. $923.64
    2. $946.86
    3. $968.79
    4. $99.01

62. Using the numbers in question 61, what is the total interest paid over the life of the loan?
    1. $209,975.88
    2. $210,922.74
    3. $211,869.60
    4. $212,816.46

63. You and your brother have purchased an apartment building as joint tenants. Which of the following statements does NOT correctly describe your situation?
    1. You and your brother hold the right of survivorship.
    2. Owners must be related in order to own joint tenancy.
    3. The unities of title, time, interest, and possession are required to create a valid joint tenancy.
    4. Either you or your brother may partition the land.

64. You and your husband live in a community property state. Which of the following assets owned by you would be considered community property?
    1. A car given to you after your marriage.
    2. A duplex that you and your husband purchased after your marriage.
    3. Stock inherited by your husband after your marriage.
    4. A house that you owned before you were married.

65. Limited liability companies must have a MINIMUM of how many members?
    1. 1 member
    2. 10 members
    3. 35 members
    4. 75 members

66. You have listed a property. The seller told you that he must net at least $26,000 after all fees and expenses are paid. You estimate the seller's closing cost to be $5,000 and he must pay off an existing loan of $119,600. In addition, you are going to charge 6 percent commission on the sale. What is the least amount that the property can sell for to return the seller's desired net (to the nearest dollar)?
    1. $127,234
    2. $154,893
    3. $169,825
    4. $160,213

67. The use of lead-based paint in residential properties was banned for health reasons in which year?
    1. 1972
    2. 1978
    3. 1977
    4. 1991

68. A father wants to know how much money his daughter owes on her mortgage loan. The father knows that the interest part of the last monthly payment was $526.49. If his daughter is paying interest at 8 percent, what was the outstanding balance of the loan before the last payment was made?
    1. $70,198.67
    2. $78,973.50
    3. $90,255.42
    4. None of the above

69. A difference between an individual's ownership interest in a cooperative and a condominium is that in a cooperative, the owner
    1. is not subject to real estate taxes.
    2. holds fee-simple title, whereas a condominium owner holds a proprietary lease.
    3. is not responsible for unpaid real estate taxes of other owners, whereas a condominium owner is.
    4. holds a personal property interest, whereas a condominium owner holds a real property interest.

70. A CORRECT statement about agency relationships when a salesperson lists a property is that
    1. the licensee becomes a principal.
    2. the licensee's broker becomes the agent of the seller.
    3. the seller is entitled to subagency from all licensees who show the property.
    4. the seller must sign a dual-agency relationship agreement with all prospective buyers.

71. The denial of a loan by a lender is a violation of the Federal Fair Housing Act if such denial is based on
    1. lack of income.
    2. familial status.
    3. public beliefs.
    4. sexual preference.

72. Which of the following does NOT represent a pair of individuals in which the first person has fiduciary responsibilities to the second?
    1. Listing broker to seller
    2. Buyer-broker to buyer
    3. Mortgagor to mortgagee
    4. Appraiser to client

73. A married couple owned their home as tenants by the entirety. They then separated, and the husband continued to live in the house. If the husband decides to sell the home, can he do so without the wife's consent?
    1. Yes, because the wife relinquished her interest when she moved out of the house
    2. Yes, because under tenancy by the entirety either party may sell the house without the consent of the other party
    3. No, because the wife holds a dower interest that will not be extinguished upon the sale of the house
    4. No, because under tenancy by the entirety title may be conveyed only by a deed signed by both parties

74. A salesperson working as an independent contractor
    1. is required to attend sales meetings.
    2. may not be required to follow any set work schedule.
    3. is not responsible for transportation expenses.
    4. may receive fringe benefits if the broker agrees.

75. A broker has met with a customer and declined to work with the person in finding a home. It is legal for the broker to decline the opportunity, if the decision is based on the customer's
    1. familial status.
    2. income.
    3. race.
    4. religion.

76. A borrower's three-day right of rescission for a residential real estate loan transaction is based on the provisions of
    1. Regulation Z.
    2. the Federal Fair Housing Act.
    3. the Equal Credit Opportunity Act (ECOA).
    4. the Real Estate Settlement Procedures Act (RESPA).

77. You have listed your house with only one licensed broker but reserved the right to sell the property yourself without owing a commission. This relationship is called a(n)
    1. net listing.
    2. open listing.
    3. exclusive-agency listing.
    4. exclusive-right-to-sell listing.

78. A woman owns a four-unit apartment building but does not live there. She is currently advertising for Lutheran tenants only. Is her advertising policy legal?
    1. Yes, because the property contains four units
    2. Yes, because no real estate agent is involved in the marketing of the property
    3. No, because four-unit properties are not exempted from the Federal Fair Housing Act
    4. No, because she is not living in the apartment building

79. The civil penalty for a first violation of the Americans with Disabilities Act (ADA) is up to
    1. $10,000.
    2. $25,000.
    3. $50,000.
    4. $100,000.

80. You own an apartment building in which one of your tenants subsequent to his lease expiring has continued to live in his unit without a new lease. However, the tenant has continued to pay the same agreed rent, and you have accepted it. This type of tenancy is a(n)
    1. estate for years.
    2. estate from period to period.
    3. tenancy at will.
    4. tenancy at sufferance.

ANSWER KEY WITH EXPLANATIONS

1. **(4)** A license may be canceled by the licensor. Adverse possession would result in a change of ownership. An easement appurtenant requires a dominant tenement. (20–21)

2. **(4)** The habendum clause follows the granting clause when it is necessary to define the ownership to be enjoyed by the grantee. Any type of deed should explain any restrictions and limitations on the title. (104)

3. **(4)** The sister and her husband jointly own an undivided one-half interest as tenants in common with the brother. (22–23)

4. **(3)** Cubic feet is computed by multiplying 90' × 60' × 10' = 54,000 sq. ft. (130)

5. **(3)** A title search would not reveal the existence of an encroachment. Prior appropriation relates to water rights. A party wall easement would be appropriate if that was the case and could be negotiated with the neighbor. (21)

6. **(2)** A broker may not disclose that a prospective tenant is a member of a protected class. (114–117)

7. **(2)** Eminent domain is the right of the government to acquire private property for public use while paying just compensation to the owner. (103)

8. **(3)** A broker may not commingle his funds with those of his clients in his trust account. (165)

9. **(4)** When the life tenant dies, the life estate is terminated. On the death of the life estate owner, full ownership will pass to the owner of the future interest. (22)

10. **(4)** After both the buyer and the seller have executed the offer to purchase contract, the buyer acquires equitable title. (94–95)

11. **(4)** Construction standards are regulated by building codes. (35)

12. **(3)** Lien priority and homestead rights refer to the rights of creditors. A deed in lieu of foreclosure is an alternative to a process of foreclosure. (60)

13. **(1)** Hypothecation is pledging of property as security for a loan without losing possession of it. Arbitrage, subordination, and release of mortgage were discussed above. (66)

14. **(2)** The broker may guide activities and maintain standards of conduct for a salesperson working as an employee. (162)

15. **(4)** The gross rent multiplier (GRM) relates to monthly rental income, not annual.

    $126,000 sale price ÷ $900 monthly rent = 140 gross rent multiplier (50)

16. **(3)** Specific penalties under the Federal Fair Housing Act are discussed in Part 12. (116)

17. **(3)** Erosion is the gradual wearing away of land by the action of natural forces. Accession and accretion were discussed above. (41)

18. **(1)** Treating people differently because they are members of a protected class is a violation of the Federal Fair Housing Act. There is, however, an exemption covering rentals if the rooms or units are in an owner-occupied one-family to four-family dwelling. (114–117)

19. **(3)** You should use the three steps for making adjustments in the value comparison approach to value:
    1. Always work from the price of the comparable to the subject property.
    2. C.B.S.—comparable better subtract.
    3. S.B.A.—subject better add. (49–50)

20. **(4)** Your brother's interest is a life estate because it is limited to your brother's life. A reversion would exist only if the land reverted to you. A base fee may be inherited. Curtesy refers to the life estate of a husband.

21. **(3)** $163,000 (current appraised value) – $129,000 (current mortgage balance) = $34,000, *A's* equity in the home (22)

22. **(2)** A broker employed to sell an owner's home would be a special agent. Cooperating brokers under a multiple-listing service (MLS) would be subagents. Dual agency occurs when a broker represents both the seller and the buyer in a transaction. (73–74)

23. **(4)** Sexual orientation is not a protected class under the Federal Fair Housing Act. (115–117)

24. **(3)** An escrow relationship refers to a third-party agreement such as an escrow agent who does a closing for the buyer and seller. A subordination agreement changes the order of lien priority between the two creditors. A trustee acts as an agent and is generally responsible for handling money or holding title to land. (73)

25. **(4)** A salesperson may accept financial compensation for completing a real estate transaction only from her employing broker. (75)

26. **(2)** This is clearly a case of intentional misrepresentation, which is considered fraudulent. (75)

27. **(3)** The fact that you own a defeasible fee estate does not affect the vendee's interest of equitable title in the estate. (94–95)

28. **(2)** \$183,000 sales price × 7% (0.07) = \$12,810 × 0.30 = \$3,843 (127)

29. **(4)** The broker has a fiduciary responsibility to the seller, which requires that she disclose her fair opinion of value to the principal. (73)

30. **(4)** The fee for the option right belongs to the owner (optionor) regardless of the outcome of the transaction. (94)

31. **(4)** Persons who have AIDS are protected under the Federal Fair Housing Act. (114)

32. **(4)** Religion is a protected class under the Federal Fair Housing Act. (114)

33. **(1)** In an exclusive-agency or open listing, the sellers have the right to sell their property on their own without having to pay the broker a commission. A net listing is based on the net price the seller will receive if the property is sold; the broker receives any amount received above the net price. The net listing is prohibited or discouraged in most states. (92)

34. **(3)** \$80,000 (first investor) + \$50,000 (second investor) = \$130,000

    \$250,000 – \$130,000 = \$120,000 third investor's contribution

    $$\frac{\text{part}}{\text{percent}} = \text{total}$$

    \$120,000 ÷ \$250,000 = 0.48, or 48% (127)

35. **(3)** \$50,000 gross income – \$12,000 expenses = \$38,000 net annual income

    \$38,000 net annual income ÷ 14% (0.14) = \$271,429 value of real estate (127)

36. **(1)** Divide the discount points by 2%. \$3,500 divided by 2% = \$175,000 (66)

37. **(4)** A fee simple is a real property interest, while a legal life estate is a spouse's estate in all the inheritable real estate of the deceased spouse. Tenancy by the entirety is a unit form of ownership in which the owners must be husband and wife. (21)

38. **(2)** \$143,000 × 80% (0.80) = \$140,000 assessed value

    Divide by 100 because the tax rate is stated per \$100

    \$1,144 × \$3.65 = \$4,175.60 annual taxes

    Divide by 12 to get monthly taxes

    \$4,175.60 ÷ 12 = \$347.96 (35–36)

39. **(1)** Deficiency judgments may be obtained for any deficiency. (61)

40. **(2)** Downzoning refers to a situation where the zoning for a parcel of land is changed from a dense to a less dense usage. The planning commission cannot close the retail store. A nonconforming use generally is removed if it suffers 50 percent or more damage and is not rebuilt within one year. A buffer zone is a land area that separates one land use from another. (75)

41. **(3)** Only one broker is authorized to act as an exclusive agent of the seller, but the sellers may sell the property themselves. Brokers generally enter into exclusive-right-to-sell listings. (92)

42. **(4)** The principle of regression states that the value of the better property is affected adversely by the presence of the lesser quality properties. (49)

43. **(2)** Discount points usually are charged by and paid to the lender when the FHA interest rate is less than the conventional, or market, rate of interest. (61)

44. **(2)** Accession refers to a way in which personal property can become real property. Laches and partition are described above. (106)

45. **(2)** Inventory and equipment are considered to be personal property. (18)

46. **(4)** Add the desired net, $18,000, plus the existing loan payoff, $104,600, and the closing costs, $5,200. $127,800 is the minimum that the seller must receive. The correct answer is $127,800 ÷ 0.94 (100% – 6%) = $135,957. (127)

47. **(4)** Laches is a doctrine whereby one is unable to assert a legal right because of waiting too long to enforce it. Equity of redemption refers to the time period for foreclosure during which the buyer may redeem his property. The statute of frauds requires certain contracts to be in writing in order to be enforceable. (25)

48. **(4)** Brownfields legislation promotes the cleanup and reuse of thousands of defunct, derelict, and abandoned industrial sites. Often clustered near prime real estate areas, these once contaminated sites can very easily be converted into tax revenue sites. (85)

49. **(1)** The problem is solved by multiplying 800 × 1200 = 960,000, divided by 43,560 = 22.04. (126)

50. **(3)** A broker may not offer legal advice; only a licensed attorney may do so. (73–75)

51. **(3)** All of the alternative answers refer to personal property. (18)

52. **(1)** Regulation Z required disclosure of cost in a credit transaction as well as the advertising of financing terms. The Sherman Antitrust Act deals with antitrust violations such as boycotting. ECOA prohibits discrimination against protected classes with regard to loan applications. (118–119)

53. **(1)** Each buyer in the cooperative becomes a shareholder and receives a proprietary lease. (149)

54. **(3)** The grantee must be identified in the deed. Unrecorded deeds are valid between the parties. However, the deed should be recorded in order to provide constructive notice. (104–106)

55. **(2)** An amendment changes the language of a contract; an addendum adds additional terms. (95)

56. **(4)** Functional obsolescence and physical deterioration are losses in value that occur within the property, while economic obsolescence occurs outside the property. The principle of regression was discussed above. (50)

57. **(3)** Scarcity, situs, and improvements are economic characteristics of land. (18)

58. **(4)** The solution is found by subtracting the difference and then dividing by the difference by 300,000. Next convert the solution from a decimal to a percent. 300,000 – 275,000 = 25,000 divided by 300,000 = 0.825, or 8.25% (127)

59. **(3)** An easement in gross does not have a dominant tenement. (20)

60. **(4)** A general partnership also is exposed to the problems arising from the health or bankruptcy of the partner(s). (160)

61. **(2)** 946.86 ($129,000 × 7.34) (134–136)

62. **(3)** $946.86 × 360 months = $340,869.60

$340,869.60	total P & I
– $129,000.00	loan
$211,869.60	total interest (134–136)

63. **(2)** Owners in joint tenancy do not have to be related. (22–23)

64. **(2)** Community property includes real and personal property acquired by either spouse during the marriage. Separate property (real or personal) is that owned individually by either spouse before the marriage. Separate property also includes any property acquired by inheritance or gift during the marriage or purchased with separate funds during the marriage. (23)

65. **(1)** Members of limited liability companies may be individuals, corporations, trusts, general or limited partnerships, or foreign persons. (160)

66. **(4)** Add the desired net, \$26,000, plus the existing loan payoff, \$119,600, and the closing cost, \$5,000. \$150,600 is the minimum that the seller must receive.

    If the selling price is 100 percent and the commission is 6 percent, the net to seller is 94 percent.

    \$150,600 is 94 percent of the selling price. Therefore, \$150,600 ÷ 94% (0.94) = selling price of \$160,212.76, rounds to \$160,213. (127)

67. **(2)** Licensees involved in the sales, financing, appraisal, or management of properties built prior to 1978 face potential liability for any personal injury suffered by occupants resulting from exposure to lead-based paint. (38)

68. **(2)** \$526.49 × 12 = \$6,317.88 annual interest

    part ÷ percent = total

    \$6,317.88 ÷ 8% (0.08) = \$78,973.50 (127)

69. **(4)** Each buyer receives a proprietary lease and becomes a stockholder. However, a cooperative is converted to a real estate interest in those states that have adopted the Common Interest Ownership Act. (149)

70. **(2)** The broker is the agent of the seller. The salesperson is the agent of the broker and subagent (not agent) of the seller. (73–74)

71. **(2)** Familial status was added in 1988. (114)

72. **(3)** Mortgagees have a fiduciary relationship with investors who place money in their lending institutions. (59)

73. **(4)** Tenancy by the entirety is a unit ownership of the property. (23)

74. **(2)** Independent contractors work under limited supervision from the broker. (162)

75. **(2)** Familial status, race, and religion are protected classes under the Federal Fair Housing Act.

76. **(1)** The three-day right of rescission covers a home equity loan or the refinancing of a home mortgage. It does not cover owner-occupied residential purchase-money as first mortgage or deed of trust loans. (114)

77. **(3)** A net listing is based on the amount of money the seller will receive if the property is sold. In the open listing, the seller retains the right to employ any number of brokers to act as his or her agents. In an exclusive-right-to-sell listing, the seller gives up the right to sell the property himself or herself and thus avoids paying the broker's commission. (92)

78. **(4)** The Federal Fair Housing Act exempts the rental of units in an owner-occupied one-family to four-family dwelling. (117)

79. **(3)** A penalty of up to \$100,000 may be assessed for any subsequent violation of ADA. (118)

80. **(2)** A periodic estate is a lease for an indefinite period of time without a specific expiration date; notice must be given to terminate. (148)

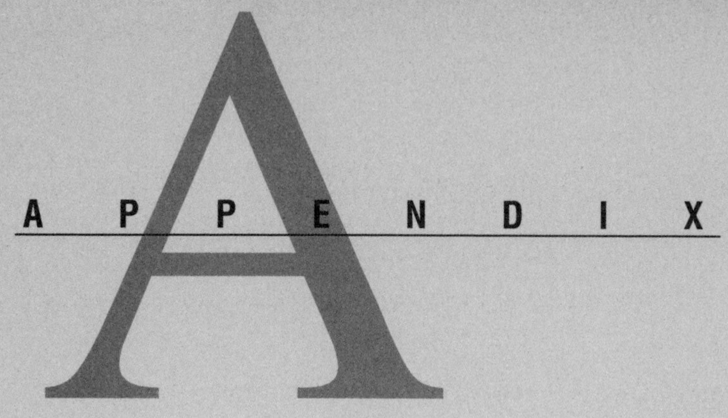

MATHEMATICAL FORMULAS AT A GLANCE

1. Area of a circle	$A = \pi\ (3.14) \times r^2$
2. Area of a rectangle	$A = L \times W$
3. Area of a triangle	$A = \frac{1}{2}\ (B \times H)$
4. Area of a trapezoid	$A = \dfrac{(B1 + B2) \times H}{2}$
5. Circumference of a circle	Diameter × π (3.14)
6. Volume of a cube	$V = L \times W \times H$
7. Pythagorean Theorem	The length of the hypotenuse in a right triangle is equal to the square root of the sum of the squares of the lengths of the other two sides.
8. Formula used to find %	part divided by total
9. Formula used to find total	part divided by percent
10. Formula used to find part	total × percent
11. Commission	selling price × commission rate charged for real estate services
12. A percentage of assessed value used to compute property tax	millage rate
13. Formula used to compute straight-line depreciation	$\dfrac{\text{replacement cost}}{\text{years of useful life}}$

14. Formula used to compute value	I/R
15. Formula used to compute cap rate	I/V
16. Formula used to compute NOI	R × V
17. Formula used to compute PI	loan amount divided by 1,000 × amortization factor
18. Formula used to compute approximate loan amount	PI divided by amortization factor × 1,000
19. Formula to create a fraction	$\frac{\text{numerator}}{\text{denominator}}$
20. Number of square feet in one acre	43,560 square feet

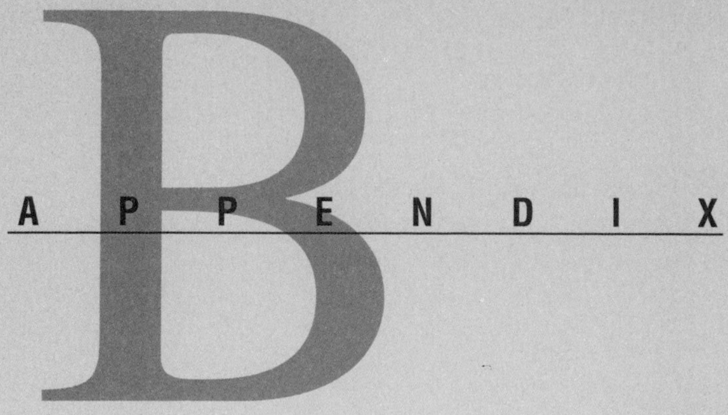

MATHEMATICS PRACTICE AND REVIEW

Broker questions are marked with an asterisk (*)

Mathematics is a tool that real estate practitioners use on a daily basis. Most real estate agents use calculators and partner with knowledgeable loan originators to provide answers to today's financial questions. However, a fundamental knowledge of basic math, algebra, and geometry may be required to provide customers and clients with real-time information. It's important to remember that those empowered with math's secrets can add value to any transaction.

Let's examine some basic problems that real estate agents encounter and discover math's role in solving them.

1. How much will it cost a homeowner to replace carpet and pad in a 20' × 14' room, if carpet is $20 a square yard and pad is $2.25 a square yard?

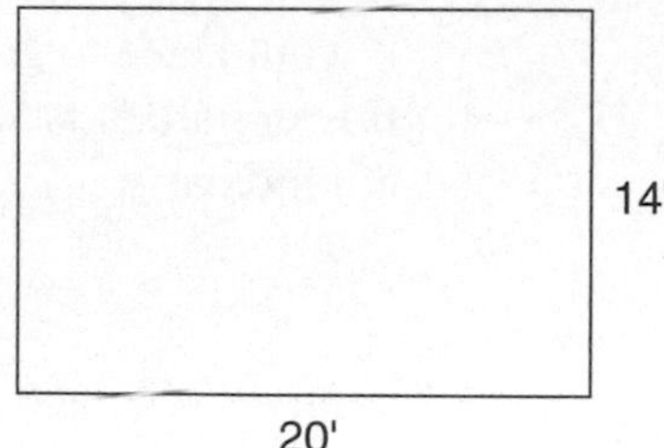

FIG. A

2.* Using π = 3.14, how many square feet of decorative rock would it take to fill in a circular garden that has a radius of 6'?

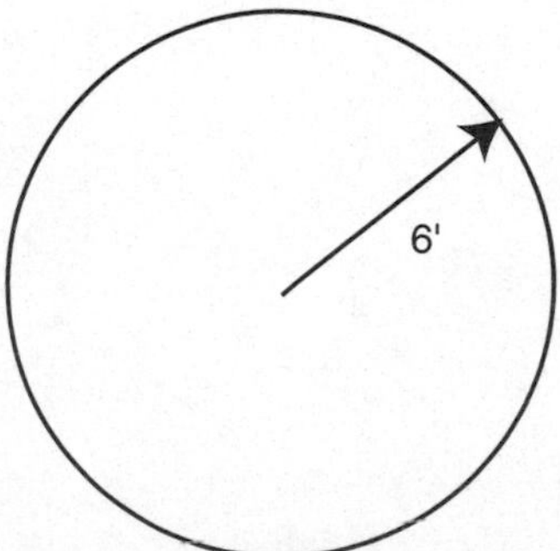

FIG. B

3.* Before listing, the owner of an A-frame decided to repaint the front of her house. If the triangular-shaped area has a base of 26 feet and a height of 30 feet, how many square feet need to be repainted?

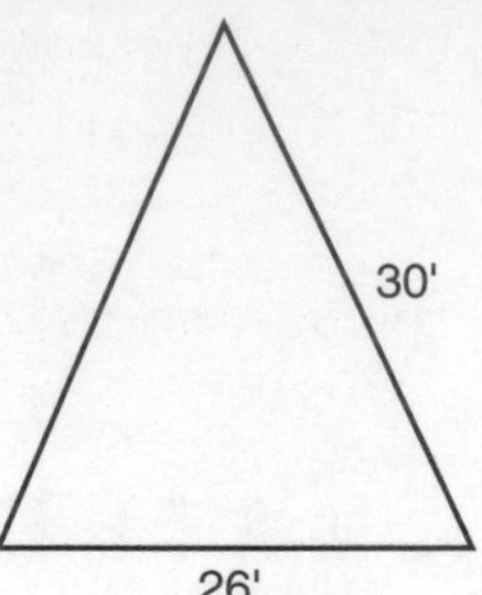

FIG. C

4.* A homeowner hires a roofing contractor to replace the shingles on the backside of his hip roof. The area that needs to be replaced is shaped like a trapezoid. The bottom parallel line is 38', the top parallel line is 24', and the distance between the parallel lines is 16'. How many square feet need to be reshingled?

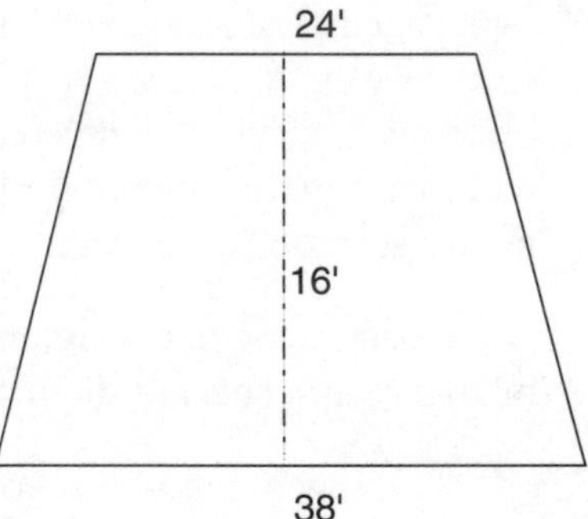

FIG. D

5.* In a house offered for sale, a buyer asks an agent how many feet of edging it would take to go around a circular flower garden. If the diameter of the flower garden is 10 feet, how many feet of edging is necessary to go around the area?

6.* A buyer is concerned about safety and decides to run a new chain-link fence along the creek side of her new home. If the property resembles a 90-degree triangle and the two other sides (as diagrammed) are 80' and 120', what is the distance between points A and B?

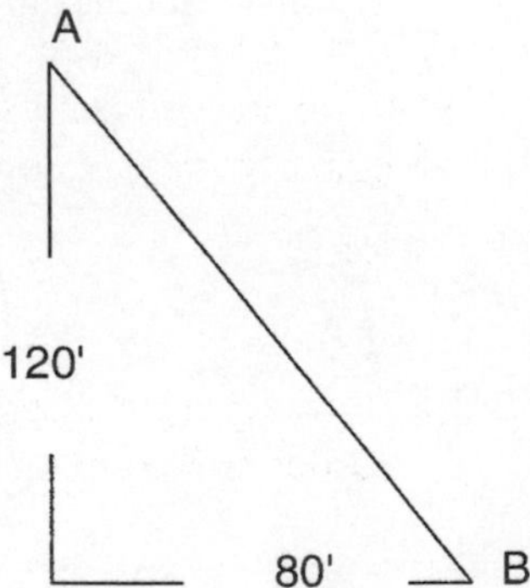

FIG. E

7.* With permission, a tenant is going to place a window air conditioner in a rented area. In order to purchase the right size, the tenant asks the agent to compute the room's cubic square feet. If the room size is 60' × 25' and the height of the room is 9', what is the cubic area?

8. A commercial real estate agent needs to determine for a client the number of acres in a vacant parcel. If it measures 800' × 1,100', how many acres are there?

9. A tenant signed a percentage lease with a landlord. After reaching an agreed break-even threshold, the tenant needs to pay the landlord 5% of the gross income above the threshold amount. If the tenant made an additional $22,000, how much additional rent is due?

10. A tenant signed a percentage lease with a landlord. After reaching an agreed break-even threshold, the tenant is required to pay the landlord an additional 5% each month. However, included in one month's additional gross income is a 6% sales tax. What is the additional rent owed to the landlord after removing the sales tax from $22,000 in additional income?

11. In order to buy down a buyer's interest rate, an owner agrees to pay (on the buyer's behalf) two discount points amounting to $2,800. Discount points are based on the loan amount. How much money did the buyer borrow?

12. If a buyer has a 20% down payment and borrows $140,000, what is the purchase price of the new home?

13. If a broker charges 6% commission and then splits the commission with cooperative brokers, how much commission would a cooperative broker expect to receive on a $300,000 sale?

14. If a cooperative broker received $9,000 and that amount was 50% of an earned 6% commission, what was the selling price of the property sold?

15. If a 1000' × 2000' commercially zoned property is divided into thirds for the building envelope, parking spaces, and green space, how many acres are available for parking spaces?

16. On an income tax form, a homeowner reported $13,240 in paid mortgage interest. If the homeowner's mortgage interest rate for the previous year was 5.5%, what was her approximate loan balance?

17. If a homeowner purchased a $300,000 home and then two years later sells it for $330,000, what is the percentage increase from the initial purchase?

18. A $300,000 residentially assessed property is taxed at 55%. If the tax rate is 35 mills, what is the monthly property tax?

19. A homeowner pays $481.25 in monthly tax, in a tax district that uses 35 mills and 55% of the property's assessed value. What is the assessed value of the property?

20. An agent pays a broker $1,400 each month for desk costs as well as a monthly 5% franchise fee on all earned commissions. If the agent's gross earnings for one month are $13,800, how much will the agent net after paying for desk costs and the franchise fee?

21. A seller decides to paint the front of his ranch style home and wants to determine the exact square footage in order to purchase enough paint. If the front of the house is 38' × 10' and there is a picture window that measures 5' × 4' and a door opening that measures 3' × 7', what is the remaining square footage?

22. A property manager leases 50 apartments in a building complex. Twenty-five tenants pay $800 a month for their three-bedroom units, and the other twenty-five tenants pay $600 a month for their two-bedroom units. Using a 5% vacancy and collection factor, what is the effective gross income?

23. An appraiser has determined the effective gross income of a property to be $399,000. If annual operating expenses are $199,000 and the cap rate is 11.5%, what is the value of the property?

24. If an investor wanted a 9% return on an income property that had an NOI of $200,000, what amount should the investor offer?

25. A buyer purchased a duplex. The current owner lived in one side and rented out the other for $800 a month. The owner collected rent at the beginning of the month, and the closing took place on the 10th of a 30-day month. How many dollars should be prorated to the buyer?

26. An owner decides to sell her house and pay a 5% commission, provided that she nets $325,000 from the sale. What does the asking price have to be to net the owner $325,000?

27. If a relocation company is paid a 30% referral fee based on 50% of a 6% commission, how much would the company receive on a $300,000 transaction?

28. If an owner decides to list his property and wants to net $325,000 after paying a 7% commission, what should be the listed price (rounded to the nearest dollar)?

29. A real estate agent is preparing a CMA and found a comparable that sold for $220,000 one year earlier. Using a 4.5% annual appreciation factor, what is the dollar increase for the time adjustment?

30. A borrower signed a $200,000 note for a 7.00%, 30-year amortized loan. Using an amortization factor of $6.65, what is the monthly PI payment?
    a. $1,230
    b. $1,350
    c. $1,430
    d. None of the above

31. A 30-year, 7.00% amortized loan has a dollar per thousand factor of $6.65. Using this factor, what is the borrowing power of someone who can afford a monthly PI payment of $1,330?

32. A buyer asks a seller to pay 2 discount points in order to permanently buy down her interest rate to 6.75% ($6.49 per thousand). The buyer can afford a $1,330 PI payment. What is the amount due for discount points?

33. In addition to a 10% down payment, a borrower needs 3% for closing costs. How much money does the borrower need to bring to closing if the purchase price of his new home is $180,000?

34. In a real estate transaction a seller agrees to pay three discount points in order to help a buyer qualify for a loan. If the discount points paid by the seller amounted to $4,000, how much money did the buyer borrow?

35. An appraiser used the market, cost, and income approach to determine the value of a property. She reconciled the three approaches by using 50% of the $180,000 market approach; 30% of the $190,000 cost approach; and 20% of the $195,000 income approach. Using these data, what is the appraiser's reconciliation figure for value?

36. An owner listed a property for $280,000 but accepted an offer for $274,000. What was the percent of change between the asking price and the actual selling price?

37.*A broker has 14 full-time sales agents, and total expenses for the office are $235,000. What is the broker's desk cost?

38.*A broker has 14 full-time sales agents, and the brokerage's NOI is $125,000. What is each agent's desk worth?

39. An agent's production goal is $4,000,000, and the office goal is $32,000,000. What percent of the office goal is the agent's goal?

40. A vacant lot measures 80' × 120'. The building setback requirements are 10' for the side yard and 25' for the front- and backyard setbacks. What are the dimensions of the building envelope?

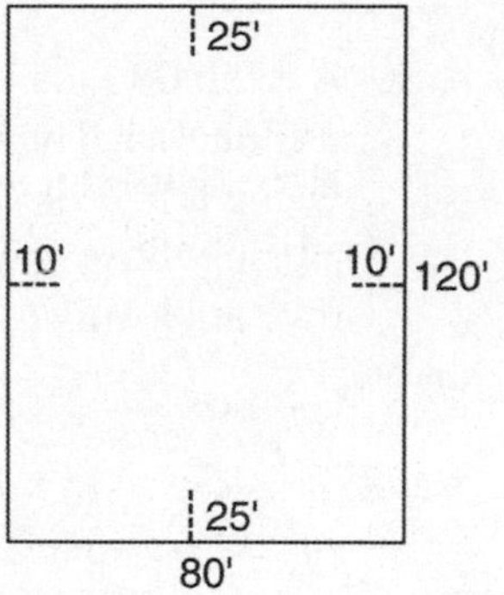

41.*If 30% was added to a monthly PI payment for property taxes and homeowner's insurance, then the PI + TI = 130%, or 1.30. What is the reciprocal (multiplication factor) of 1.30?

42. What is the decimal equivalent of 1/8?

43. What is the decimal equivalent of 3/8?

44. What is the decimal equivalent of 5/8?

45. What is the decimal equivalent of 7/8?

46. If a farmer buys the W ½ of the NW ¼ of Section 5 for $2,500 an acre, how much did he pay for the property?

47. How many acres are there in the NE ¼ of the SW ¼ and the W ½ of the SE ¼ of Section 5?

48. A 100-acre parcel is divided into equal-sized building lots. If the streets take up 1/4 of the area and there are 140 lots, what percent of an acre is each lot?

49. How much money is owed on a 6%, interest-only $20,000 loan that is paid off six months early?

50. A $250,000 loan that was amortized over 30 years at 7% interest closed on June 16. The first payment is due August 1 for the month of July. Using a 360-day year and assuming that interest is paid for the day of closing, how much of an interest adjustment payment does the borrower owe at closing?

ANSWER KEY WITH EXPLANATIONS

1. The room size is L × W = A. 20' × 14' = 280 square feet

   The carpet and pad need to be added together. \$20 + \$2.25 = \$22.25

   If 280 sq. ft. is divided by 9 sq. ft. (the number of square feet in one square yard), then the resulting number of sq. yds. could be multiplied by \$22.25.

   280 sq. ft. ÷ 9 sq. ft. = 31.11 sq. yds. × \$22.25/ sq. yd. = \$692.22

2. The formula for the area of a circle is $A = \pi \times r^2$.

   The radius is 6; 6^2 is (6 × 6) = 36 sq. ft.
   36 sq. ft. × (π)3.14 = 113.04 square feet

3. The formula for a triangle is A = ½B × H. The base is 26'. 26' divided by 2 = 13. 13' × 30' height = 390 sq. ft.

   (If a gallon of paint covers approximately 200 square feet, then the owner needs to purchase 2 gallons of paint.)

4. The formula for a trapezoid is

   $$A = \frac{(B1 + B2) \times H}{2}$$

   Add base 1 to base 2. 38' + 24' = 62' × 16' (height) = 992'

   Next, divide 992' by 2 = 496 sq. ft.

   (Shingles are purchased in squares [one square equals 100 sq. ft.].

   Therefore, the owner needs approximately 5 squares of shingles.)

5. The formula for circumference is diameter × π (3.14).

   10' × 3.14 = 314' of edging

6. The formula is the Pythagorean Theorem, which is calculated by determining the square root of the sum of the squares.

   To solve this problem requires a calculator with a square root key. $\sqrt{\ }$

   First multiply 80 × 80 = 6,400

   Then, multiply 120 × 120 = 14,400

   Add these squared numbers, 6,400 + 14,400 = 20,800 and then locate and enter 20,800 into the square root key.

   The result is 144.22 feet.

   (If the fencing cost per running foot was \$15, then the buyer could estimate his or her costs to be 144.22 feet × \$15 a foot = \$2,163.33.)

7. cubic area (volume) = L × W × H

   60' × 25' = 1,500' × 9' = 13,500 cubic square feet

   (Empowered with this information, the tenant can more intelligently purchase the right air-conditioning unit.)

8. area = L × W; divide that by 43,560 (number of sq. ft. in an acre)

   800 × 1,100 = 880,000 ÷ 43,560 = 20.20 acres

9. part = total × percentage
   \$22,000 × 5% = \$1,100, or \$22,000 × .05 = \$1,100.

10. \$22,000 is 106% of the total. The \$22,000 includes the gross rent and a 6% sales tax. To remove the sales tax requires this mathematical formula:

    $$\frac{\text{part}}{\text{percentage}} = \text{total}$$

    \$22,000 is 106% of the total. Therefore, \$22,000 ÷ 106%, or 1.06 = \$20,754.72. This is the amount that the tenant uses to multiply the 5% percentage lease agreement. \$20,754.72 × 5% (.05) = \$1,037.74

    It is always wise to check an answer by working the problem backwards.

    So, if the tenant's 5% of the gross income is \$1,037.74, then \$1,037.74 should be divided by 5%, or .05 = \$20,754.72. If we add 6% for sales tax, we will arrive back at \$22,000. Our solution is correct.

11. $\frac{\text{part}}{\text{percentage}} = \text{total}$

$2,800 is 2%, or .02, of the total. Simply stated, divide any number by its percentage of the whole and you'll discover the whole number.

$2,800 divided by 2% = $140,000. (140,000 × 2% = $2,800)

12. In this problem the $140,000 = 80% of the total because the borrower made a 20% down payment (100% – 20% = 80%). Therefore, 140,000 ÷ 80% = $175,000.

Working backwards, 175,000 × 80% = $140,000. Solution is correct.

13. The solution is 300,000 × 6% × 50%.

300,000 × 6% = 18,000 × 50% = $9,000.

14. The solution requires discovery of the part. $9,000 divided by 50% = $18,000. Next, the $18,000 must be divided by its percentage of the total. $18,000 divided by 6% = $300,000.

15. area = L × W; divide that by the number of square feet in acre (43,560).

1,000 × 2,000 = 2,000,000 divided by 43,560 = 45.91 acres

Then divide 45.91 acres by 3 to arrive at 15.30 acres for parking.

16. $\frac{\text{part}}{\text{percentage}} = \text{total}$

$13,240 divided by 5.5%, or .055 = $240,727.27 total

17. Initially, the solution requires subtraction in order to determine the dollar difference between the two numbers. Then a fraction is required to solve. $330,000 – $300,000 is $30,000. Divide 30,000 by the initial purchase price of 300,000 = .10. Convert .10 into a percent, and 10% is the answer.

18. This requires only simple math. 300,000 × 55%, or .55 = $165,000

$165,000 is the taxable value.

Multiply the taxable value of 165,000 × 3.5% (millage) and the annual solution is $5,775. However, the question asks for the monthly amount: $5,775 ÷ 12 = $481.25.

19. This requires simple division. The part that we start with is the monthly tax that must be multiplied by 12. $481.25 × 12 = $5,775

This annual amount is 3.5% of the total (taxable value).

$5,775 ÷ 3.5%, or .035 (millage) = $165,000.

Since the property is taxed at 55%, then the $165,000 is 55% of the total (assessed value). $165,000 divided by 55%, or .55 = $300,000.

20. The solution requires that the $13,800 be multiplied by 95% to remove the 5% franchise fee on all earned commissions. $13,800 × 95% = 13,110. Next, the monthly desk cost is subtracted: $13,110 – $1,400 = $11,710.

Worked backwards, $11,710 + $1,400 = $13,110 divided by 95% = $13,800.

21. area = L × W

38' × 10' = 380 square feet
380 sq. ft. – 41 sq. ft ([5 × 4] = 20 + [3 × 7] = 21) = 339 square feet

22. Using the income approach, the appraiser determines the annual gross income and then determines the effective gross income by subtracting expected vacancy and "rubber check" losses from gross income.

$800 × 25 = $20,000 × 12 = $240,000 annual income

$600 × 25 = $15,000 × 12 = $180,000 annual income

$420,000 × 95% = $399,000
OR $420,000 × .95 = $399,000
OR $420,000 – 5% = $399,000

Note: Most financial calculators allow the user to subtract percents (%).

Try the one you're using. Type in 420,000 and then touch the minus (–) key. Next, touch 5 and then the % key. With some calculators you have to touch the = key to complete the equation; other calculators eliminate this step and go right for the answer.

23. Net operating income (NOI) is determined by subtracting operating expenses from effective gross. Then the IRV formula kicks into place.

    I (Net Operating Income) divided by R (Capitalization Rate) = V (Value)

    $399,000 – $199,000 = $200,000 divided by 11.5%, or .115 = $1,739,130.43

24. IRV formula: I/R = V

    200,000 divided by 9%, or. 09 = $2,222,222.22

25. In proration problems, first determine who has the money. In this problem, the seller has all of the rent for the entire month. However, the seller isn't going to be the owner after the 10th; therefore, the buyer is entitled to the rent from the date of the closing to the end of the month. If you include the 10th, it is 21 days.

    The 10th through the 30th is 21 days.

    $800 divided by 30 days = $26.67 × 21 days = $560

26. What percent of the total does the homeowner expect to receive?

    $325,000 divided by 95% = $342,105.26

    Working backwards, what is $342,105.26 – 5%? Answer = $325,000

    Note: When taking any math exam that gives you four solutions, one of them has to be correct. If you can't figure out the proper way to solve a math problem, it's OK to use the answer key in an attempt to work backwards.

27. This is a multiplication problem. $300,000 × 6%, or (.06) = $18,000

    $18,000 × 50%, or (.50) = $9,000 × 30%, or (.30) = $2,700

    Referral companies get paid based on either the listing side or the selling side of a transaction. Normally these two sides are divided 50-50. In this problem the broker paid a 30% referral fee based on the selling half of the transaction.

28. $\dfrac{\text{part}}{\text{percentage}} = \text{total}$

    $325,000 divided by 93%, or .93 = $349,462.37, rounds to $349,462.

29. Multiplying the one-year-old sale by a 4.5% annual appreciation rate solves this problem.

    $220,000 × 4.5%, or .045 = $9,900.

30. None of the above.

    The solution is $200,000 divided by 1,000 = 200 × $6.65 = $1,330.

31. The solution requires division. $1,330 divided by 6.65 = $200 × 1,000 = $200,000. In this problem you are expected to solve for the number of thousands that one could borrow. As noted, $6.65 (dollars per thousand) divided into the affordable PI payment of $1,330 is 200. In other words, the borrower qualifies for a 200 thousand loan, or 200 × 1,000 = $200,000.

32. The solution requires division.

    First, $1,330 needs to be divided by $6.49 to discover the number of thousands that can be borrowed.

    $1,330 divided by $6.49 = $204.93 × 1,000 = $204,930. This is the loan amount.

    Discount points are computed by multiplying the loan amount by the discount percentage. $204,930 × 2% = $4,098.60.

33. Simple math is necessary to solve this problem. $180,000 × (10% + 3%) 13%, or .13 = $23,400

34. $\dfrac{\text{part}}{\text{percentage}} = \text{total}$

    $4,000 divided by 3%, or .03 = $133,333.34

35. To solve this problem requires an understanding of a weighted average. The most common average is a statistical mean, but that isn't the kind used in the reconciliation process. In a statistical mean all three of these variables would be added together and then divided by three. However, in the reconciliation process the appraiser uses three different percentages that total 100%. Based on the appraiser's experience and knowledge of the marketplace, a weighted average is used as follows.

Market approach	180,000× 50% =	90,000
Cost approach	190,000× 30% =	57,000
Income approach	195,000× 20% =	39,000
	100%	$186,000

The appraised value is $186,000.

36. To solve a percent-of-change problem, you must first determine the difference between the two numbers.
Step 1. 280,000 – 274,000 = 6,000
Step 2. Divide the difference by the original asking price.

$\frac{\text{part}}{\text{total}}$ = percentage

6,000 ÷ 280,000 = .0214, or 2.14%

37. Simple division computes the broker's desk cost.

Total expenses divided by number of full-time agents = desk cost

$235,000 (total expense) ÷ 14 (number of full-time agents' desks) = $16,785.71

38. Simple division computes the broker's desk worth.

NOI divided by number of full-time agents = desk worth

$125,000 (NOI) divided by 14 (number of full-time agent's desks) = $8,928.57

39. $\frac{\text{part}}{\text{total}}$ = percentage

4,000,000 divided by 32,000,000 = .01250, or 12.5%

40. This is a simple math problem.

Side 80' – (10' + 10') = 60'
Front and back 120' – (25' + 25') = 70'

The dimensions are 60' × 70'.

41. Reciprocals are determined by dividing the 1.30 factor into the number 1. 1 ÷ 1.30 = .7692, or 76.92%

If a buyer wanted to purchase a home and is curious to know how much of her $1,500 house payment is eligible for PI, then the agent can do one of two things.

1. 1,500 ÷ 1.30 = $1,154 (rounded) OR
2. 1,500 × 76.92% = $1,154 (rounded)

Reciprocals are very helpful. Continuing with this same problem, the buyer wants to know how much she could afford to borrow with a PI payment of $1,154. Using a 7% interest rate, amortized over thirty years, the dollar per 1,000 factor would be $6.65. $1,154 divided by 6.65 = $173.53 × 1,000 = $173,534. Now the buyer can start looking for homes she can afford.

42. 1 ÷ 8 = .125

43. 3 ÷ 8 = .375

44. 5 ÷ 8 = .625

45. 7 ÷ 8 = .875

46. In rectangular survey, this problem is solved by multiplying the denominators and dividing the resulting number into the total area of a section, which is 640 acres.

2 × 4 = 8 640 ÷ 8 = 80 acres
80 × 2,500 = $200,000

47. The word *and* means that there are two different areas; therefore, the two parcels must each be computed separately and then added together.

4 × 4 = 640 ÷ 16 = 40 acres
2 × 4 = 640 ÷ 8 = 80 acres
120 acres

48. The solution requires that a fraction be set up.

100 acres × 75% = 75 acres, the amount reserved for building lots.

Take those 75 acres × 43,560 square feet (per acre) = 3,267,000 sq. ft.

3,267,000 sq. ft. ÷ 140 lots = 23,335.71 square feet per lot

23,335.71 ÷ 43,560 (sq. ft. per acre) = .5357, or 53.57% of an acre

49. 20,000 × 6% = $1,200 × 50% (one half of a year) = $600.

50. First compute the simple interest. 250,000 × 7% = $17,500. Then, divide the 17,500 by 360 days = $48.61 interest per diem. Finally, multiply the per diem amount by the remaining number of days in June (June 16 – 30). $48.61 × 15 days = $729.15

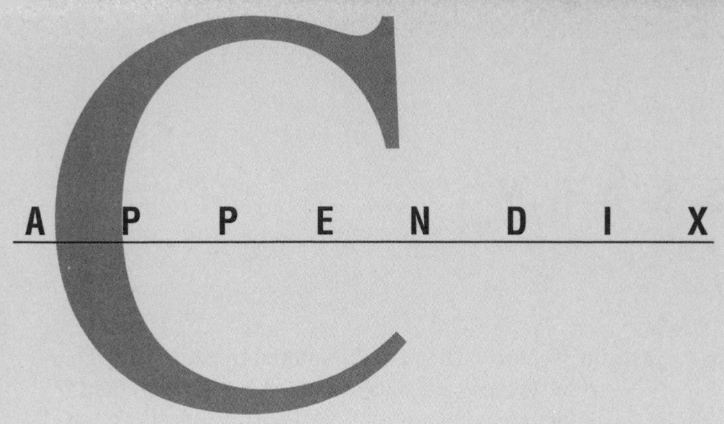

APPENDIX C

WEB SITE AND PALM DIRECTORY

With the advent of the personal digital assistant (Palm Pilot) came a revolution of shared programs for the Palm Pilot. A good site to get connected for palm programs is www.palmone.com; a good site for shareware is www.shareware.com. **PZ calc** and **Loan Wizard Pro** are two examples of excellent financial palm software tools for real estate agents, and www.realdata.com is a helpful software site for financial calculations.

Search engines that can help you include:

- www.altavista.com
- www.askjeeves.com
- www.dogpile.com
- www.excite.com
- www.lycos.com
- www.google.com
- www.yahoo.com

Following are some general Web sites that may also be helpful:

American Society of Home Inspectors	www.ashi.com
Appraisal Institute	www.appraisalinstitute.org
Federal Housing Administration	www.hud.gov/offices/hsg/index.cfm
Fair Housing Act	www.hud.gov/groups/fairhousing.cfm
Financial calculations	www.realdata.com
Government forms	www.hudclips.org
Landlord tenant	www.law.cornell.edu/topics/landlord tenant.html
Lead Safe USA	www.leadsafeusa.com/
National Association of Home Builders	www.nahb.com
National Association of REALTORS®	www realtors.com
General real estate news	www.inman.com; www.realttimes.com
U.S. Department of Housing and Urban Development	www.hud.gov
U.S. Department of Veterans Affairs	www.va.gov
U.S. Environmental Protection Agency	www.epa.gov

GLOSSARY

abandonment The voluntary and permanent cessation of use or enjoyment with no intention to resume or reclaim one's possession or interest. May pertain to an easement of a property.

abstract of title A condensed version of the history of a title to a particular parcel of real estate as recorded in the county clerk's records; consists of a summary of the original grant and all subsequent conveyances and encumbrances affecting the property.

abutting The joining, reaching, or touching of adjoining land. Abutting parcels of land have a common boundary.

accelerated depreciation A method of calculating for tax purposes the depreciation of income property at a faster rate than would be achieved using the straight-line method. Note that any depreciation taken in excess of what would be claimed using the straight-line rate is subject to recapture as ordinary income to the extent of the gain resulting from the sale. *See also* straight-line method.

acceleration clause A provision in a written mortgage, note, bond, or conditional sales contract that in the event of default, the whole amount of the principal and the interest may be declared due and payable at once.

accession Title to improvements or additions to real property is acquired as a result of the accretion of alluvial deposits along the banks of streams or as a result of the annexation of fixtures.

accretion An increase or addition to land by the deposit of sand or soil washed up naturally from a river, lake, or sea.

accrued depreciation The actual depreciation that has occurred to a property at any given date; the difference between the cost of replacement new (as of the date of the appraisal) and the present appraised value.

acknowledgment A declaration made by a person to a notary public or other public official authorized to take acknowledgments that an instrument was executed by him or her as a free and voluntary act.

actual eviction The result of legal action originated by a lessor, by which a defaulted tenant is physically ousted from the rented property pursuant to a court order. *See also* constructive eviction.

actual notice Express information or fact; that which is known; actual knowledge.

administrator The party appointed by the county court to settle the estate of a deceased person who died without leaving a will.

ad valorem tax A tax levied according to value; generally used to refer to real estate tax. Also called general tax.

adverse possession The actual, visible, hostile, notorious, exclusive, and continuous possession of another's land under a claim to title. Possession for a statutory period may be a means of acquiring title.

affidavit A written statement signed and sworn to before a person authorized to administer an oath.

agent One who represents or has the power to act for another person (called the principal). The authorization may be express, implied, or apparent. A fiduciary relationship is created under the law of agency when a property owner, as the principal, executes a listing agreement or management contract authorizing a licensed real estate broker to be her or his agent.

agreement of sale A written agreement by which the purchaser agrees to buy certain real estate and the seller agrees to sell, on the terms and conditions set forth in the agreement.

air lot A designated airspace over a piece of land. Air lots, like surface property, may be transferred.

air rights The right to use the open space above one's property. It can be sold to build a skywalk or for a utility company to erect power lines.

alienation The act of transferring property to another. Alienation may be voluntary, such as by sale, or involuntary, such as through eminent domain.

alienation clause (due-on-sale clause) Clause in a mortgage instrument that does not allow the borrower to sell (without lender approval) on assumption or contract-for-deed. If an attempt is made to do so without prior approval, all of the mortgaged balance becomes due on the sale of the property. Also known as the *due-on-sale clause*.

alluvion The actual soil increase resulting from accretion.

amenities Neighborhood facilities and services that enhance a property's value. They are always outside of the property. Swimming pools, three-car garages, decks, etc. that are on the property are called *features*.

Americans with Disabilities Act (ADA) A federal law, effective in 1992, designed to eliminate discrimination against individuals with disabilities.

amortization The liquidation of a financial burden by installment payments, which include principal and interest.

amortized loan A loan in which the principal and interest are payable in monthly or other periodic installments over the term of the loan.

antitrust laws The laws designed to preserve the free enterprise of the open marketplace by making illegal certain private conspiracies and combinations formed to minimize competition. Violation of antitrust laws in the real estate business generally involves either price fixing (brokers conspiring to set fixed compensation rates) or allocation of customers or markets (brokers agreeing to limit their trades or dealings to certain areas or properties).

appraisal An estimate of the quantity, quality, or value of something. The process through which conclusions about property value are obtained; also refers to the report that sets forth the process of estimation and conclusion of value.

appraised value An estimate of a property's present worth.

appreciation An increase in the worth or value of a property, due to economic or related causes, which may prove to be either temporary or permanent; opposite of depreciation.

appurtenant Belonging to; incident to; annexed to. For example, a garage is appurtenant to a house, and the common interest in the common elements of a condominium is appurtenant to each apartment. Appurtenances pass with the land when the property is transferred.

arbitration A means of settling a controversy between two parties through the medium of an impartial third party whose decision on the controversy (if agreed upon) will be final and binding.

assessment The imposition of a tax, charge, or levy, usually according to established rates.

assignment The transfer in writing of rights or interest in a bond, mortgage, lease, or other instrument.

assumed name statute (fictitious name statute) The law, in effect in most states, that stipulates that no person shall conduct a business under any name other than his or her own individual name, unless such person files the desired name with the county clerk in each county where the business is conducted. In the case of brokers and salespeople, statement of such filing should be submitted to the state's real estate commission.

assumption of mortgage The transfer of title to property to a grantee, by which the grantee assumes liability for payment of an existing note secured by a mortgage against the property. Should the mortgage be foreclosed and the property sold for a lesser amount than that due, the grantee/purchaser who has assumed and agreed to pay the debt secured by the mortgage is personally liable for the deficiency. Before a seller may be relieved of liability under the existing mortgage, the lender must accept the transfer of liability for payment of the note.

attorney-in-fact The holder of a power of attorney.

attorney's opinion of title An instrument written and signed by the attorney who examines the title, stating her or his opinion as to whether a seller may convey good title.

avulsion A sudden tearing away of land by the action of natural forces.

balloon payment The final payment of a mortgage loan that is considerably larger than the required periodic payments because the loan amount was not fully amortized.

bargain and sale deed A deed that carries with it no warranties against liens or other encumbrances but that does imply the grantor has the right to convey title. Note that the grantor may add warranties to the deed at his or her discretion.

base fee A determinable fee estate that may be inherited.

base line One of a set of imaginary lines running east and west and crossing a principal meridian at a definite point. Base lines are used by surveyors for reference in locating and describing land under the rectangular survey system (or government survey method) of property description.

benchmark A permanent reference mark or point established for use by surveyors when measuring differences in elevation.

beneficiary 1. The person for whom a trust operates or in whose behalf the income from a trust estate is drawn. 2. A lender who lends money on real estate and takes back a note and deed of trust from the borrower.

bequest A provision in a will providing for the distribution of personal property.

bilateral contract A contract in which each party promises to perform an act in exchange for the other party's promise to perform.

bill of sale A written instrument given to pass title to personal property.

binder An agreement that may accompany an earnest money deposit for the purchase of real property as evidence of the purchaser's good faith and intent to complete the transaction.

blanket mortgage A mortgage that covers more than one parcel of real estate and provides for each parcel's partial release from the mortgage lien on repayment of a definite portion of the debt.

blockbusting The illegal practice of inducing homeowners to sell their properties by making representations regarding the entry or prospective entry of minority persons into the neighborhood. Sometimes referred to as *panic peddling.*

blue-sky laws The common name for state and federal laws that regulate the registration and sale of investment securities.

boycotting Two or more businesses conspire against other businesses to reduce competition.

branch office A secondary place of business apart from the principal or main office from which real estate business is conducted. A branch office generally must be run by a licensed real estate broker, broker salesperson, or associate broker working on behalf of the broker operating the principal office.

breach of contract The failure, without legal excuse, of one of the parties to a contract to perform according to the contract.

bridge loan A loan that bridges the sale of property. For example, a homeowner borrows from the bank the equity from her current home to use as a down payment on a new home. Then, when her current home sells, she uses her equity to repay a bridge loan.

broker One who buys and sells for another for a commission. *See also* real estate broker.

brokerage The business of buying and selling for another for a commission.

broker/salesperson A person who has passed the broker's licensing examination but is licensed to work only on behalf of a licensed broker and who may be allowed to manage an office. In many states, known as (and licensed as) associate broker or broker/associate.

brownfields Deserted, defunct, and derelict toxic industrial sites in need of renewal. Federal legislation has diminished the innocent landowner's liability exposure and provided the landowner the opportunity to expense cleanup costs rather than capitalize them.

budget loan A loan in which the monthly payments made by the borrower cover not only interest and a payment on the principal but also 1/12 of such expenses as taxes, insurance, assessments, private mortgage insurance premiums, and similar charges.

buffer zone A strip of land that separates one land use from another.

building code An ordinance specifying minimum standards of construction of buildings for the protection of public safety and health.

building line A line fixed at a certain distance from the front and/or sides of a lot beyond which no structure can project; a setback line used to ensure a degree of uniformity in the appearance of buildings and unobstructed light, air, and view.

building restrictions The limitations on the size or type of property improvements established by zoning acts or by deed or lease restrictions. Building restrictions are considered encumbrances, and violations render the title unmarketable.

bundle of legal rights The theory that land ownership involves ownership of all legal rights to the land, such as possession, control within the law, and enjoyment, rather than ownership of the land itself.

business plan A three- to five-year blueprint for an organizational or individual real estate practitioner.

buydown A payment made, often by the seller, to help the buyer qualify for the loan.

canvassing The practice of making telephone calls or visiting from door to door to seek prospective buyers or sellers; in the real estate business, generally associated with acquired listings in a given area.

capacity of parties The legal ability of persons to enter into a valid contract. Most persons have full capacity to contract and are said to be **competent parties.**

capital gain Profit earned from the sale of an asset.

capital investment The initial capital and the long-term expenditures made to establish and maintain a business or investment property.

capitalization The process of converting into present value (or obtaining the present worth of) a series of anticipated future periodic installments of net income. In real estate appraisal, it usually takes the form of discounting. The formula is expressed as income/rate = value.

capitalization rate The rate of return a property will produce on the owner's investment.

cash flow The net spendable income from an investment, determined by deducting all operating and fixed expenses from the gross income. If expenses exceed income, a negative cash flow is the result.

casualty insurance A type of insurance policy that protects a property owner or other person from loss or injury sustained as a result of theft, vandalism, or similar occurrences.

caveat emptor A Latin phrase meaning, "Let the buyer beware."

certificate of sale The document generally given to a purchaser at a tax foreclosure sale. A certificate of sale does not convey title; generally, it is an instrument certifying that the holder may receive title to the property after the redemption period has passed and that the holder paid the property taxes for that interim period.

certificate of title The statement of opinion on the status of the title to a parcel of real property, based on an examination of specified public records.

chain of title The succession of conveyances from some accepted starting point by which the present holder of real property derives her or his title.

chattels Personal property.

city planning commission A local governmental organization designed to direct and control the development of land within a municipality.

claim of right Used as a factor in determining adverse possession claims. Adversely occupying another's real estate for a statutory period of time may create a claim of right.

cloud on title A claim or encumbrance that may affect the title to land.

CLUE An insurance company repository for reported claim activity and previous property damage. CLUE is an acronym for Comprehensive Loss Underwriting Exchange. Insurers use the report to ascertain patterns of possible future claims and adjust their insurance premiums according to risk.

codicil A testamentary disposition subsequent to a will that alters, explains, adds to, or confirms the will, but does not revoke it.

coinsurance clause A clause in insurance policies covering real property that requires the policyholder to maintain fire insurance coverage generally equal to at least 80 percent of the property's actual replacement cost.

collateral Something of value given or pledged to a lender as a security for a debt or obligation.

color of title Used as a factor in an adverse possession claim when the occupying party actually received title but by a defective or incorrect deed (color of title).

commercial property A classification of real estate that includes income-producing property such as office buildings, restaurants, shopping centers, hotels, and stores.

commingled property Property of a married couple that is so mixed or commingled that it is difficult to determine whether it is separate or community property. Commingled property becomes community property.

commingling The illegal act of a real estate broker who mixes the money of other people with that of his or her own; brokers are required by law to maintain a separate trust account for other parties' funds held temporarily by the broker.

commission The payment made to a broker for services rendered, such as in the sale or purchase of real property; usually a percentage of the selling price of the property.

common elements The parts of a property that are necessary or convenient to the existence, maintenance, and safety of a condominium or that are normally in common use by all of the condominium residents. All condominium owners have an undivided ownership interest in the common elements.

common law A body of law based on custom, usage, and court decisions.

community property A system of property ownership based on the theory that each spouse has an equal interest in the property acquired by the efforts of either spouse during marriage.

comparables The sold properties, listed in an appraisal report, which are substantially equivalent to the subject property.

competent parties Persons who are recognized by law as being able to contract with others; usually those of legal age and sound mind. *See also* capacity of parties.

composite depreciation A method of determining the depreciation of a multibuilding property using the average rate at which all the buildings are depreciating.

condemnation A judicial or administrative proceeding or process to exercise the power of **eminent domain.**

condominium The absolute ownership of an apartment or a unit, generally in a multiunit building, based on a legal description of the airspace the unit actually occupies, plus an undivided interest in the ownership of the common elements, which are owned together with the other condominium unit owners. The entire tract of real estate included in a condominium development is called a *parcel* or *development parcel.* One apartment or space in a condominium or a part of a property intended for independent use and having lawful access to the public way is called a *unit.* Ownership of one unit also includes a definite undivided interest in the common elements.

conformity *See* principle of conformity.

consideration Something of value that induces one to enter into a contract. Consideration may be "valuable" (money or commodity) or "good" (love and affection). Also, an act of forbearance, or the promise thereof, given by one party in exchange for something from the other. Forbearance is a promise *not* to do something.

constructive eviction 1. Acts by the landlord that so materially disturb or impair the tenant's enjoyment of the leased premises that the tenant is effectively forced to move out and terminate the lease without liability for any further rent. 2. A purchaser's inability to obtain clear title.

constructive notice Notice given to the world by recorded documents. All persons are charged with knowledge of such documents and their contents, whether or not they have actually examined them. Possession of property also is considered constructive notice that the person in possession has an interest in the property.

contingencies A provision or condition in the purchase of real estate requiring a certain act to be done or an event to happen before the contract becomes binding.

contract An agreement entered into by two or more legally competent parties by the terms of which one or more of the parties, for a consideration, undertakes to do or to refrain from doing some legal act or acts. A contract may be either **unilateral,** where only one party is bound to act, or **bilateral,** where all parties to the instrument are legally bound to act as prescribed.

contract for deed A contract for the sale of real estate under which the sale price is paid in periodic installments by the purchaser, who is in possession and holds equitable title although actual title is retained by the seller until final payment. Also called an *installment contract* or *land contract.*

contract for exchange of real estate A contract for sale of real estate in which the consideration is paid wholly or partly in property.

conventional loan A loan that is not insured or guaranteed by a government agency.

conveyance A written instrument that evidences transfer of some interest in real property from one person to another.

cooperative A residential multiunit building whose title is held by a trust or corporation that is owned by and operated for the benefit of persons living within the building. These persons are the beneficial owners of the trust or the shareholders of the corporation, each having a proprietary lease.

corporation An entity or organization created by operation of law whose rights of doing business are essentially the same as those of an individual. The entity has continuous existence until dissolved according to legal procedures.

correction lines The horizontal provisions in the rectangular survey system (government survey method) made to compensate for the curvature of the earth's surface. Every fourth township line (at 24-mile intervals) is used as a correction line on which the intervals between the north and south range lines are remeasured and corrected to a full six miles.

cost approach The process of estimating the value of a property by adding the appraiser's estimate of the reproduction or replacement cost of the building, less depreciation, to the estimated land value.

counseling The business of providing people with expert advice on a subject, based on the counselor's extensive, expert knowledge of the subject.

counteroffer A new offer made as a reply to an offer received, having the effect of rejecting the original offer. The original offer cannot be accepted thereafter unless revived by the offeror repeating it.

credit scoring A three-digit score that assesses a borrower's credit risk and the probability of default based on his or her past pay performances, outstanding credit balances, credit mix, time on file, and number of search inquiries.

cul-de-sac A dead-end street that widens sufficiently at the end to permit an automobile to make a U-turn.

curtesy A life estate, usually a fractional interest, given by some states to the surviving husband in real estate owned by his deceased wife. Most states have abolished curtesy.

cycle A recurring sequence of events that regularly follow one another, generally within a fixed interval of time.

datum A horizontal plane from which heights and depths are measured.

dba Doing business as.

debenture A note or bond given as evidence of debt and issued without security.

debt Something owed to another; an obligation to pay or return something.

declining balance method An accounting method of calculating depreciation for tax purposes designed to provide large deductions in the early years of ownership. *See also* accelerated depreciation.

decreasing returns See diminishing returns.

deed A written instrument that when executed and delivered conveys title to or an interest in real estate.

deed in lieu of foreclosure A process by which the mortgagor can avoid foreclosure. Mortgagor gives a deed to mortgagee when mortgagor is in default according to terms of mortgage.

deed of reconveyance The instrument used to reconvey title to a trustor under a deed of trust once the debt has been satisfied; also called a *reconveyance deed.*

deed of trust An instrument used to create a lien by which the mortgagor conveys her or his title to a trustee, who holds it as security for the benefit of the noteholder (the lender); also called a *trust deed.*

deed restrictions The clauses in a deed limiting the future uses of the property. Deed restrictions may impose a variety of limitations and conditions, such as limiting the density of buildings, dictating the types of structures that can be erected, and preventing buildings from being used for specific purposes or from being used at all.

default The nonperformance of a duty, whether arising under a contract or otherwise; failure to meet an obligation when due.

defeasance clause A clause used in leases or mortgages that cancels a specified right on the occurrence of a certain condition, such as cancellation of a mortgage on repayment of the mortgage loan.

deficiency judgment A personal judgment levied against the mortgagor when a foreclosure sale does not produce sufficient funds to pay the mortgage debt in full.

delinquent taxes Unpaid taxes that are past due.

delivery The legal act of transferring ownership. Documents such as deeds and purchase agreements must be delivered and accepted to be valid.

delivery in escrow Delivery of a deed to a third person until the performance of some act or condition by one of the parties.

demand The willingness of persons to buy available goods at a given price; often coupled with **supply.**

density zoning The zoning ordinances that restrict the average maximum number of houses per acre that may be built within a particular area, generally a subdivision.

depreciation 1. In appraisal, a loss of value in property due to all causes, including physical deterioration, functional obsolescence, and economic obsolescence. 2. In real estate investment, an expense deduction for tax purposes taken over the period of ownership of the income property.

descent The hereditary succession of an heir to the property of a relative who dies intestate.

determinable fee estate A fee-simple estate in which the property automatically reverts to the grantor on the occurrence of a specified event or condition.

devise A transfer of real estate by will or last testament. The donor is the devisor and the recipient is the devisee.

diminishing returns The principle that applies when a given parcel of land reaches its maximum percentage return on investment and further expenditures for improving the property yield a decreasing return.

discount points An added loan fee charged by a lender to make the yield on a lower-than-market-value loan competitive with higher-interest loans. *See also* point.

discount rate The rate of interest a commercial bank must pay when it borrows from its federal reserve bank. Consequently, the discount rate is the rate of interest the banking system carries within its own framework. Member banks may take certain promissory notes that they have received from customers and sell them to their district federal reserve bank for less than face value. With the funds received, the banks can make further loans. Changes in the discount rate may cause banks and other lenders to reexamine credit policies and conditions.

dispossess To oust from land by legal process.

dominant tenement A property that includes in its ownership the appurtenant right to use an easement over another's property for a specific purpose.

dower The legal right or interest recognized in some states that a wife acquires in the property her husband held or acquired during their marriage. During the lifetime of the husband, the right is only a possibility of an interest; on his death it can become an interest in land.

due-on-sale clause *See* alienation clause.

duress The use of unlawful constraint that forces action or inaction against a person's will.

DVA loan A mortgage loan on approved property made to a qualified veteran by an authorized lender and guaranteed by the Department of Veterans Affairs to limit possible loss by the lender. Also called a *GI-guaranteed mortgage.*

earnest money deposit An amount of money deposited by a buyer under the terms of a contract. In the event that the buyer, for no valid or legal reason, backs out of the transaction, earnest money is sometimes used as liquidated damages.

easement A right to use the land of another for a specific purpose, such as for a right-of-way or utilities;

an incorporeal interest in land. An easement appurtenant passes with the land when conveyed.

easement by necessity An easement allowed by law as necessary for the full enjoyment of a parcel of real estate; for example, a right of ingress and egress over a grantor's land.

easement by prescription An easement acquired by continuous, open, uninterrupted, exclusive, and adverse use of the property for the period of time prescribed by state law.

easement in gross An easement that is not created for the benefit of any land owned by the owner of the easement but that attaches personally to the easement owner. For example, the right to an easement granted by *A* to *B* to use a portion of *A*'s property for the rest of *B*'s life would be an easement in gross.

economic life The period of time over which an improved property will earn an income adequate to justify its continued existence.

economic obsolescence The impairment of desirability or useful life arising from factors external to the property, such as economic forces or environmental changes, that affect supply-demand relationships in the market. Loss in the use and value of a property arising from the factors of economic obsolescence is to be distinguished from loss in value from physical deterioration and functional obsolescence, both of which are inherent in the property. Also referred to as *locational obsolescence* or *environmental obsolescence.*

emblements Growing crops that are produced annually through the tenant's own care and labor and that she or he is entitled to take away after the tenancy is ended. Emblements are regarded as personal property even prior to harvest, so if the landlord terminates the lease, the tenant still may reenter the land and remove such crops. If the tenant terminates the tenancy voluntarily, however, he or she generally is not entitled to the emblements.

eminent domain The right of a government or municipal quasi-public body to acquire property for public use through a court action called **condemnation,** in which the court determines that the use is a public use and determines the price or compensation to be paid to the owner.

employee status The status of one who works as a direct employee of an employer. An employer is obligated to withhold income taxes and Social Security taxes from the compensation of his or her employees. *See also* independent contractor.

employment contract A document evidencing formal employment between the employer and the employee or between the principal and the agent. In the real estate business, this generally takes the form of a listing or management agreement.

encroachment A fixture or structure, such as a wall or fence, that invades a portion of a property belonging to another.

encumbrance Any lien that may diminish the value of the property, such as a mortgage, tax, or judgment lien; easement; restriction on the use of the land; or an outstanding dower right.

endorsement The act of writing one's name, either with or without additional words, on a negotiable instrument or on a paper attached to such instrument.

equalization The raising or lowering of assessed values for tax purposes in a particular county or taxing district to make them equal to assessments in other counties or districts.

equitable title The interest held by a vendee under a contract for deed or an installment contract; the equitable right to obtain absolute ownership to property when legal title is held in another's name. (Insurable interest)

equity The interest or value that an owner has in a property over and above any mortgage indebtedness.

erosion The gradual wearing away of land by water, wind, and general weather conditions; the diminishing of property caused by the elements.

errors and omissions insurance Insurance coverage for real estate agents against claims for innocent and negligent misrepresentation.

escheat The reversion of property to the state in the event that its owner dies without leaving a will and has no heirs to whom the property may pass by lawful descent.

escrow The closing of a transaction through a third party called an escrow agent, or *escrowee,* who receives certain funds and documents to be delivered on the performance of certain conditions in the escrow agreement.

estate for years An interest for a certain, exact period of time in property leased for a specified consideration.

estate in land The degree, quantity, nature, and extent of interest that a person has in real property.

estate in severalty An estate owned by one person.

estoppel certificate A legal instrument executed by a mortgagor showing the amount of the unpaid balance due on a mortgage and stating that the mortgagor has no defenses or offsets against the mortgagee at the time of execution of the certificate. Also called a *certificate of no defense.*

estovers Legally allowed necessities such as the right of a tenant to use timber on leased property to support a minimum need for fuel or repairs.

ethical Conduct conforming to professional standards.

et al Latin, meaning "and others."

et ux The Latin abbreviation for *et uxor,* meaning "and wife."

et vir Latin, meaning "and husband."

eviction A legal process to oust a person from possession of real estate.

evidence of title A proof of ownership of property, which is commonly a certificate of title, a title insurance policy, an abstract of title with lawyer's opinion, or a Torrens registration certificate. *See also* Torrens system.

exchange A transaction in which all or part of the consideration for the purchase of real property is the transfer of like-kind property (that is, real estate for real estate). *See* IRS 1031 on page 108.

exclusive-agency listing A listing contract under which the owner appoints a real estate broker as his or her exclusive agent for a designated period of time to sell the property on the owner's stated terms for a commission. The owner, however, reserves the right to sell without paying anyone a commission by selling to a prospect who has not been introduced or claimed by the broker.

exclusive-right-to-sell listing A listing contract under which the owner appoints a real estate broker as his or her exclusive agent for a designated period of time to sell the property on the owner's stated terms and agrees to pay the broker a commission when the property is sold, whether by the broker, the owner, or another broker.

executed contract A contract in which all parties have fulfilled their promises and thus performed the contract.

execution The signing and delivery of an instrument. Also, a legal order directing an official to enforce a judgment against the property of a debtor.

executor The person designated in a will to handle the state of the deceased. The probate court must approve any sale of property by the executor.

executory contract A contract under which something remains to be done by one or more of the parties.

expenses The short-term costs that are deducted from an investment property's income, such as minor repairs, regular maintenance, and renting costs.

expressed contract An oral or written contract in which the parties state their terms and express their intentions in words.

Fair Housing Act of 1968 The term for Title VIII of the Civil Rights Act of 1968 as amended, which prohibits discrimination based on race, color, sex, religion, national origin, handicaps, and familial status in the sale and rental of residential property.

Federal Home Loan Mortgage Corporation (FHLMC) A federally chartered corporation created to provide a secondary mortgage market for conventional loans (Freddie Mac).

Federal Housing Administration (FHA) A federal administrative body created by the National Housing Act in 1934 to encourage improvement in housing standards and conditions, to provide an adequate home-financing system through the insurance of housing mortgages and credit, and to exert a stabilizing influence on the mortgage market.

federal income tax An annual tax based on income, including monies derived from the lease, use, or operation of real estate.

Federal National Mortgage Association (FNMA) "Fannie Mae" is the popular name for this federally chartered corporation, which creates a secondary market for existing mortgages. FNMA does not loan money directly, but rather buys DVA, FHA, and conventional loans.

fee-simple estate The maximum possible estate or right of ownership of real property continuing forever. Sometimes called a *fee* or *fee-simple absolute.*

FHA appraisal An FHA evaluation of a property as security for a loan. Includes the study of the physical characteristics of the property and surroundings, and the location of the property.

FHA loan A loan insured by the FHA and made by an approved lender in accordance with FHA regulations.

fiduciary relationship A relationship of trust and confidence, as between trustee and beneficiary, attorney and client, principal and agent.

financing statement *See* Uniform Commercial Code.

first mortgage A mortgage that creates a superior voluntary lien on the property mortgaged relative to other charges or encumbrances against the property.

fiscal policy The government's policy in regard to taxation and spending programs. The balance between these two areas determines the amount of money the government will withdraw or feed into the economy in an attempt to counter economic peaks and slumps.

fixture An article that was once personal property but has been so affixed to real estate that it has become real property.

forcible entry and detainer A summary proceeding for restoring to possession of land one who is wrongfully kept out or has been wrongfully deprived of the possession.

foreclosure A legal procedure by which property used as security for a debt is sold to satisfy the debt in the event of default in payment of the mortgage note or default of other terms in the mortgage document. The foreclosure procedure brings the rights of all parties to a conclusion and passes the title in the mortgaged property either to the holder of the mortgage or to a third party who may purchase the realty at the foreclosure sale, free of all encumbrances affecting the property subsequent to the mortgage.

foreign acknowledgment An acknowledgment taken outside of the state in which the land lies.

franchise A private contractual agreement to run a business using a designated trade name and operating procedures.

fraud A misstatement of a material fact made with intent to deceive or made with reckless disregard of the truth and that actually does deceive.

freehold estate An estate in land in which ownership is for an indeterminate length of time, in contrast to a **leasehold estate.**

functional obsolescence The impairment of functional capacity or efficiency; the inability of a structure to perform adequately the function for which it currently is employed. Functional obsolescence reflects the loss in value brought about by factors that affect the property, such as overcapacity, inadequacy, or changes in the art.

future interest A person's present right to an interest in real property that will not result in possession or enjoyment until some time in the future, such as a **reversion** or right of reentry.

gap A defect in the chain of title of a particular parcel of real estate; a missing document or conveyance that raises doubt as to the present ownership of the land.

general contractor A construction specialist who enters into a formal construction contract with a landowner or master lessee to construct a real estate building or project. The general contractor often contracts with several subcontractors specializing in various aspects of the building process to perform individual jobs.

general lien A lien on all real and personal property owned by a debtor.

general partnership *See* partnership.

general tax *See ad valorem tax.*

general warranty deed A deed that states that the title conveyed therein is good from the sovereignty of the soil to the grantee therein and that no one else can successfully claim the property. This type of deed contains several specific warranties sometimes referred to as the English Covenants of Title.

GI-guaranteed mortgage See DVA loan.

government lots Fractional sections in the rectangular survey system (government survey method) that are less than one full quarter-section in area.

Government National Mortgage Association (GNMA) "Ginnie Mae," a federal agency and division of HUD that operates special assistance aspects of federally aided housing programs and participates in the secondary market through its mortgage-backed securities pools.

graduated lease Lease that provides for rent increases at set future dates.

graduated payment mortgage A mortgage loan for which the initial payments are low but increase over the life of the loan.

grant The act of conveying or transferring title to real property.

grant deed A type of deed that includes three basic warranties: (1) the owner warrants that she or he has the right to convey the property; (2) the owner warrants that the property is not encumbered other than with those encumbrances listed in the deed; and (3) the owner promises to convey any after-acquired title to the property. Grant deeds are popular in states that rely heavily on title insurance.

grantee A person to whom real estate is conveyed; the buyer.

grantor A person who conveys real estate by deed; the seller.

gross lease A lease or property under which a landlord pays all property charges regularly incurred through ownership, such as repairs, taxes, insurance, and operating expenses. Most residential leases are gross leases.

gross national product (GNP) The total value of all goods and services produced in the United States in a year.

gross rent multiplier (GRM) A figure used as a multiplier of the gross monthly rental income of a property to produce an estimate of the property's value.

ground lease A lease of land only, on which the tenant usually owns a building or is required to build her or his own building as specified in the lease. Such leases are usually long-term net leases; a tenant's rights and obligations continue until the lease expires or is terminated through default.

guaranteed sale plan An agreement between the broker and the seller that if the seller's real property is not sold before a certain date, the broker will purchase it for a specified price.

guardian One who guards or cares for another person's rights and properties. A guardian has legal custody of the affairs of a minor or a person incapable of taking care of his or her own interests, called a *ward.*

habendum clause The deed clause beginning "to have and to hold," which defines or limits the extent of ownership in the estate granted by the deed.

heir One who might inherit or succeed to an interest in land under the state law of descent when the owner dies without leaving a valid will.

hereditaments Every kind of inheritable property, including personal, real corporeal, and incorporeal.

highest and best use The possible use of land that will produce the greatest net income and thus develop the highest land value.

holdover tenancy A tenancy by which a lessee retains possession of leased property after her or his lease has expired and the landlord, by continuing to accept rent from the tenant, agrees to the tenant's continued occupancy as defined by state law.

holographic will A will that is written, dated, and signed in the handwriting of the maker.

homeowner's insurance policy A standardized package insurance policy that covers a residential real estate owner against financial loss from fire, theft, public liability, and other common risks.

homeowner's warranty program An insurance program offered to buyers by some brokerages, warranting the property against certain defects for a specified period of time.

homestead protection The land and the improvements thereon designated by the owner as his or her homestead and, therefore, protected by state law, either in whole or in part, from forced sale by certain creditors of the owner.

HUD The Department of Housing and Urban Development; regulates FHA and GNMA.

hypothecation The pledge of property as security of a loan in which the borrower maintains possession of the property while it is pledged as security.

implied contract A contract under which the agreement of the parties is demonstrated by their acts and conduct.

implied grant A method of creating an easement. One party may be using another's property for the benefit of both parties—for example, a sewer on a property that serves two or more properties. Sometimes referred to as an *easement by implication.*

improvement 1. Improvements *on* land: any structure, usually privately owned, erected on a site to enhance the value of the property; for example, buildings, fences, and driveways. 2. Improvements *to* land: usually a publicly owned structure; for example, curbs, sidewalks, and sewers.

inchoate right Incomplete right, such as a wife's dower interest in her husband's property during his life.

income approach The process of estimating the value of an income-producing property by capitalization of the annual net income expected to be produced by the property during its remaining useful life.

incorporeal right A nonpossessory right in real estate; for example, an **easement** or right-of-way.

increasing returns The principle that applies when increased expenditures for improvements to a given parcel of land yield an increasing percentage return on investment.

independent contractor One who is retained to perform a certain act but who is subject to the control and direction of another only as to the end result, and not as to how he or she performs the act. Unlike an employee, an independent contractor pays all of his or her expenses, pays his or her income and Social Security taxes, and receives no employee benefits. Many real estate salespeople are independent contractors.

index lease Lease that allows the rent to be increased or decreased periodically, based on changes in a selected economic index, such as the Consumer Price Index.

industrial property All land and buildings used or suited for use in the production, storage, or distribution of tangible goods.

installment contract *See* contract for deed.

installment sale A method of reporting gain received from the sale of real estate when the sale price is paid in two or more installments over two or more years. If the sale meets certain requirements, a taxpayer can spread recognition of the reportable gain over more than one year, which may result in tax savings.

insurable title A title to land that a title company will insure.

insurance The indemnification against loss from a specific hazard or peril through a contract (called a policy) and for a consideration (called a premium).

interest A charge made by a lender for the use of money.

interim financing A short-term loan usually made during the construction phase of a building project, often referred to as a *construction loan.*

intestate The condition of a property owner who dies without leaving a will. Title to such property passes to his or her heirs as provided in the state law of descent.

invalid Having no force or effect.

invalidate To render null and void.

investment Money directed toward the purchase, improvement, and development of an asset in expectation of income or profits. A good financial investment has the following characteristics: safety, regularity of yield, marketability, acceptable denominations, valuable collateral, acceptable duration, required attention, and potential appreciation.

joint tenancy The ownership of real estate by two or more parties who have been named in one conveyance as joint tenants. On the death of a joint tenant, her or his interest passes to the surviving joint tenant or tenants by the right of survivorship.

joint venture The joining of two or more people to conduct a specific business enterprise. A joint venture is *similar* to a partnership in that it must be created by agreement between the parties to share in the losses and profits of the venture. It is *unlike* a partnership in that the venture is for one specific project only, rather than for a continuing business relationship.

judgment The official and authentic decision of a court on the respective rights and claims of the parties to an action or suit. When a judgment is entered and recorded with the county recorder, it usually becomes a general lien on the property of the defendant for a ten-year period.

judgment clause A provision that may be included in notes, leases, and contracts by which the debtor, lessee, or obligor authorizes any attorney to go into court to confess a judgment against him or her for a default in payment. Also called a *cognovit.*

laches An equitable doctrine used by the courts to bar a legal claim or prevent the assertion of a right because of undue delay, negligence, or failure to assert the claim or right. *See also statute of limitations.*

land The earth's surface extending downward to the center of the earth and upward infinitely into space.

land contract *See* contract for deed.

law of agency *See* agent.

lawyer's opinion of title *See* attorney's opinion of title.

lease A contract between a landlord (the lessor) and a tenant (the lessee) transferring the right to exclusive possession and use of the landlord's real property to the lessee for a specified period of time and for a stated consideration (rent). By state law, leases for longer than a certain period of time (generally one year) must be in writing to be enforceable.

leasehold estate A tenant's right to occupy real estate during the term of a lease, generally considered to be a personal property interest.

legacy A disposition of money or personal property by will.

legal description A description of a specific parcel of real estate sufficient for an independent surveyor to locate and identify it. The most common forms of legal description are **rectangular survey, metes and bounds,** and subdivision **lot and block (plat).**

legality of object An element that must be present in a valid contract. If a contract has for its object an act that violates the laws of the United States or the laws of a state to which the parties are subject, it is illegal, invalid, and not recognized by the courts.

lessee The tenant who leases a property.

lessor One who leases property to a tenant.

leverage The use of borrowed money to finance the bulk of an investment.

levy To assess, seize, or collect. To levy a tax is to assess a property and set the rate of taxation. To levy an execution is to seize officially the property of a person to satisfy an obligation.

license 1. A privilege or right granted to a person by a state to operate as a real estate broker or salesperson. 2. The revocable permission for a temporary use of land—a personal right that cannot be sold.

lien A right given by law to certain creditors to have their debt paid out of the property of a defaulting debtor, usually by means of a court sale.

life estate An interest in real or personal property that is limited in duration to the lifetime of its owner or some other designated person.

life tenant A person in possession of a life estate.

liquidated damages Liquidated damages occur when, by contractual agreement, defaulted earnest money becomes the personal property of the seller.

liquidity The ability to sell an asset and convert it into cash at a price close to its true value.

lis pendens A public notice that a lawsuit affecting title to or possession, use, and enjoyment of a parcel of real estate has been filed in either a state or federal court.

listing agreement A contract between a landowner (as principal) and a licensed real estate broker (as agent) by which the broker is employed as agent to list and sell real estate on the owner's terms within a given time, for which service the landowner agrees to pay a commission.

listing broker The broker in a multiple-listing situation from whose office a listing agreement is initiated, as opposed to the selling broker, from whose office negotiations leading to a sale are initiated. The listing broker and the selling broker may, of course, be the same person. *See also* multiple listing.

littoral rights 1. A landowner's claim to use water in large lakes and oceans adjacent to her or his property. 2. The ownership rights to land bordering these bodies of water up to the high-water mark.

lot and block description A description of real property that identifies a parcel of land by reference to lot and block numbers within a subdivision, as identified on a subdivided **plat** duly recorded in the county recorder's office.

management agreement A contract between the owner of income property and a management firm or individual property manager outlining the scope of the manager's authority.

marginal lease A lease agreement that barely covers the costs of operation for the property.

marginal real estate Land that barely covers the costs of operation.

marketable title A good or clear salable title reasonably free from risk of litigation over possible defects; also called a *merchantable title.*

market/data approach A method of appraising or evaluating real property based on the proposition that an informed purchaser would pay no more for a property than the cost to him or her of acquiring an existing property with the same utility. This approach is applicable when an active market provides sufficient quantities of reliable data that can be verified from authoritative sources. The approach is relatively unreliable in an inactive market or in estimating the value of properties for which no real comparable sales data are available. It is also questionable when sales data cannot be verified with principals to the transaction. Also referred to as the *market comparison* or *direct sales comparison approach.*

market price The actual selling price of a property.

market value The most profitable price a property will bring in a competitive and open market under all conditions requisite to a fair sale. The price at which a buyer would buy and a seller would sell, each acting prudently and knowledgeably, and assuming the price is not affected by undue stimulus.

mechanic's lien A statutory lien created in favor of contractors, laborers, and materialmen or material suppliers who have performed work or furnished materials in improving real property.

metes-and-bounds description A legal description of a parcel of land that begins at a well-marked point and follows the boundaries, using direction and distances around the tract, back to the **point of beginning.**

mill A tax rate used by municipalities to compute property tax. For example, 50 mills = 5% of the taxable value, or it can be computed by thinking of millage as $50 per $1000 of taxable value.

A. 200,000 taxable value × 5% = $10,000

B. 200,000/1000 = 200 × $50 = $10,000

millage rate A property tax rate obtained by dividing the total assessed value of all the property in the tax district into the total amount of revenue needed by the taxing district. This millage rate then is applied to the taxable value of each property in the district to determine individual taxes.

misrepresentation To represent falsely; to give an untrue idea of a property. May be accomplished by omission or concealment of a material fact.

monetary policy The government regulation of the amount of money in circulation through such institutions as the Federal Reserve Board.

money judgment A court judgment ordering payment of money rather than specific performance of a certain action. *See also* judgment.

money market Those institutions, such as banks, savings-and-loan associations, and life insurance companies, who supply money and credit to borrowers.

month-to-month tenancy A periodic tenancy—the tenant rents for one period at a time. In the absence of a rental agreement (oral or written), a tenancy generally is considered to be from month to month.

monument Fixed natural or artificial objects, used in metes-and-bounds description, to establish the boundaries; located at the corners.

mortgage A conditional transfer or pledge of real estate as security for a loan. Also, the document creating a **mortgage lien.**

mortgage lien A lien or charge on a mortgagor's property that secures the underlying debt obligations.

mortgagor One who, having all or part of title to property, pledges that property as security for a debt; the borrower.

multiple listing An exclusive listing (generally, an exclusive right to sell) with the additional authority and obligation on the part of the listing broker to distribute the listing to other brokers in the multiple-listing organization.

municipal ordinances The laws, regulations, and codes enacted by the governing body of a municipality.

mutual rescission The act of putting an end to a contract by mutual agreement of the parties.

negligence Carelessness and inattentiveness resulting in violation of trust. Failure to do what is required.

net income The gross income of the property minus vacancy, collection losses, and operating expenses (not including debt service).

net lease A lease requiring the tenant to pay not only rent but also costs incurred in maintaining the property, including taxes, insurance, utilities, and repairs. If the tenant pays for everything, it is referred to as a triple net lease.

nonconforming use A use of property that is permitted to continue after a zoning ordinance prohibiting it has been established for the area.

nonhomogeneity A lack of uniformity; dissimilarity. Because no two parcels of land are geographically alike, real estate is said to be nonhomogeneous, or heterogeneous.

notarize To certify or attest to a document, as by a **notary public.**

notary public A public official authorized to certify and attest to documents, take affidavits, take acknowledgments, administer oaths, and perform other such acts.

note An instrument of credit given to attest a debt.

novation Acceptance by parties to an agreement to replace an old debtor with a new one. A novation releases liability.

offer and notification of acceptance The two components of a valid contract; a "meeting of the minds."

officer's deed A deed by sheriffs, trustees, guardians, etc.

one hundred percent commission plan A salesperson compensation plan by which the salesperson pays his or her broker a monthly service charge to cover the costs of office expenses and receives 100 percent of the commissions from the sales that he or she negotiates.

open-end mortgage A mortgage loan expandable by increments up to a maximum dollar amount, all of which is secured by the same original mortgage.

open listing A listing contract under which the broker's commission is contingent on the broker producing a **"ready, willing, and able" buyer** before the property is sold by the seller or another broker; the principal (owner) reserves the right to list the property with other brokers.

option The right to purchase property within a definite time at a specified price. No obligation to purchase exists, but the seller is obligated to sell if the option holder exercises the right to purchase.

optionee The party that receives and holds an option.

optionor The party that grants or gives an option.

ownership The exclusive right to hold, possess or control, and dispose of a tangible or intangible thing. Ownerships may be held by a person, corporation, or governmental entity.

package mortgage A method of financing in which the purchase of the land also finances the purchase of certain personal property items. Take, for example, the purchase of a motel, in which washers, dryers, refrigerators, beds, and linen are packaged together.

parol evidence rule A law that states that no prior or contemporary oral or extraneously written agreement can change the terms of a contract.

partial eviction A case in which the landlord's negligence deprives the tenant of the use of all or part of the premises.

participation financing A mortgage in which the lender participates in the income of the mortgaged venture beyond a fixed return, or receives a yield on the loan in addition to the straight interest rate.

partition The division of cotenants' interests in real property when the parties do not all voluntarily agree to terminate the co-ownership; takes place through court procedures.

partnership An association of two or more individuals who carry on a continuing business for profit as co-owners. Under the law, a partnership is regarded as a group of individuals rather than as a single entity. A general partnership is a typical form of joint venture in which each general partner shares in the administration, profits, and losses of the operation. A limited partnership is a business arrangement by which the operation is administered by one or more general partners and funded by limited or silent partners, who are by law responsible for losses only to the extent of their investment.

party wall easement A wall that is located on or at a boundary line between two adjoining parcels for the use of the owners of both properties.

payee The party that receives payment.

payor The party that makes payment to another.

percentage lease A lease commonly used for retail property in which the rental is based on the tenant's gross sales at the premises; often stipulates a base monthly rental plus a percentage of any gross sales above a certain amount.

performance bond A binding agreement, often accompanied by surety and usually posted by one who is to perform work for another, that assures that a project or undertaking will be completed as per the agreement or contract.

periodic estate An interest in leased property that continues from period to period—week to week, month to month, or year to year.

permanent reference marker Referred to as a PRM, it is a fixed object that leads the surveyor to the point of beginning (POB). In most surveys, two different PRMs are used to locate the POB.

personal assistant An individual working for a broker or salesperson who handles non–sales-related aspects of real estate transactions. However, if the personal assistant is licensed, then he or she can also handle the sales-related aspects of the transaction.

personal property Items, called **chattels,** that do not fit into the definition of real property; movable objects.

physical deterioration A reduction in utility resulting from an impairment of physical condition. For purposes of appraisal analysis, it is most common and convenient to divide physical deterioration into curable and incurable components.

plat A map of a town, section, or subdivision indicating the location and boundaries of individual properties.

plat book A book containing recorded subdivisions of land.

point A unit of measurement used for various loan charges; one point equals one percent of the amount of the loan. *See also* discount points.

point of beginning The starting point of the survey situated in one corner of the parcel in a **metes-and-bounds description.** All metes-and-bounds descriptions must follow the boundaries of the parcel back to the point of beginning.

police power The government's right to impose laws, statutes, and ordinances to protect the public health, safety, and welfare, including zoning ordinances and building codes.

power of attorney A written instrument authorizing a person (the attorney-in-fact) to act on behalf of the maker to the extent indicated in the instrument.

premises The specific section of a deed that states the names of the parties, recital of consideration, operative words of conveyance, legal property description, and appurtenance provisions.

prepayment clause In a mortgage, the statement of the terms on which the mortgagor may pay the entire or stated amount of the mortgage principal at some time prior to the due date.

prepayment penalty A charge imposed on a borrower by a lender for early payment of the loan principal to compensate the lender for interest and other charges that would otherwise be lost.

price fixing *See* antitrust laws.

primary mortgage market *See* secondary mortgage market.

principal 1. A sum lent or employed as a fund or investment, as distinguished from its income or profits. 2. The original amount (as in a loan) of the total due and payable at a certain date. 3. A main party to a transaction—the person for whom the agent works.

principal meridian One of 35 north and south survey lines established and defined as part of the rectangular survey system (government survey method).

principle of conformity The appraisal theory stating that buildings that are similar in design, construction, and age to other buildings in the area have a higher value than they would have in a neighborhood of dissimilar buildings.

priority The order of position or time. The priority of liens generally is determined by the chronological order in which the lien documents are recorded; tax liens (like special assessments), however, have priority, even over previously recorded liens.

probate The formal judicial proceeding to prove or confirm the validity of a will or proof of heirship and to settle the affairs of the deceased.

procuring cause The effort that brings about the desired result. Under an open listing, the broker who is the procuring cause of the sale receives the commission.

property disclosure acts State mandated seller's property disclosure reports. These reports place the burden of defect disclosure on the seller. Agents are not required to discover property defects, but are required to disclose them if they are known.

property management The operation of the property of another for compensation. Includes marketing space; advertising and rental activities; collecting, recording, and remitting rents; maintaining the property; tenant relations; hiring employees; keeping proper accounts; and rendering periodic reports to the owner.

property tax Taxes levied by the government against either real or personal property. The right to tax real property in the United States rests exclusively with the states, not with the federal government.

proration The proportional division or distribution of expenses of property ownership between two or more parties. Closing statement prorations generally include taxes, rents, insurance, interest charges, and assessments.

prospectus A printed advertisement, usually in pamphlet form, presenting a new development, subdivision, business venture, or stock issue.

public utility easement A right granted by a property owner to a public utility company to erect and maintain poles, wires, and conduits on, across, or under her or his land for telephone, electric power, gas, water, or sewer installation.

pur autre vie A Latin term meaning "for the life of another." A life estate pur autre vie is a life estate measured by the life of a person other than the grantee. Also spelled *per autrie vie.*

purchase-money mortgage A note secured by a mortgage or deed of trust given by a buyer, as a mortgagor, to a seller, as a mortgagee, as part of the purchase price of the real estate.

qualifying The act of determining a prospect's motivation, then matching his or her needs with the available inventory.

quitclaim deed A conveyance by which the grantor transfers whatever interest he or she has in the real estate without warranties or obligations.

range A six-mile strip of land measured east and west from the meridian lines.

"ready, willing, and able" buyer One who is prepared to buy property on the seller's terms and is ready to take positive steps to consummate the transaction.

real estate Land; a portion of the earth's surface extending downward to the center of the earth and upward infinitely into space, including all things permanently attached thereto, whether by nature or by man.

real estate broker Any person, partnership, association, or corporation that sells (or offers to sell), buys (or offers to buy), or negotiates the purchase, sale, or exchange of real estate, or that leases (or offers to lease) or rents (or offers to rent) any real estate or the improvements thereon for others and for a compensation or valuable consideration. A real estate broker may not conduct business without a real estate broker's license.

Real Estate Settlement Procedures Act (RESPA) The federal law ensuring that the buyer and seller in a real estate transaction have knowledge of all the settlement costs when the purchase of a one to four-family residential dwelling is financed by a federally related mortgage loan. Prohibits kickbacks.

reality of consent An element of all valid contracts. Offer and acceptance in a contract usually are taken to mean that reality of consent also is present. This is not the case, however, if any of the following are present: mistake, misrepresentation, fraud, undue influence, or duress.

real property Real property consists of land, anything affixed to it so as to be regarded as a permanent part of the land, that which is appurtenant to the land, and that which is immovable by law, including all rights and interests.

REALTOR® A registered trademark term reserved for the sole use of active members of local REALTORS® boards affiliated with the National Association of REALTORS®.

recapture *See* accelerated depreciation.

receiver The court-appointed custodian of property involved in litigation, pending final disposition of the matter before the court.

reconciliation The final step in the appraisal process in which the appraiser reconciles the estimates of value received from the market/data, cost, and income approaches to arrive at a final estimate of market value for the subject property.

recording The act of entering or recording documents affecting or conveying interests in real estate in the recorder's office established in each county. Until recorded, a deed or mortgage generally is not effective against subsequent purchases or mortgage liens.

recovery fund A fund established in some states from real estate license funds to cover claims of aggrieved parties who have suffered monetary damage through the actions of a real estate licensee. To protect the public, some states mandate **errors and omissions insurance** as a requirement for licensure.

rectangular survey system A system established in 1785 by the federal government that provides for surveying and describing land by reference to principal meridians and base lines.

redemption period A period of time established by state law during which a property owner has the right to redeem her or his real estate from a foreclosure or tax sale by paying the sales price, interest, and costs. Many states do not have mortgage redemption laws.

redlining The illegal practice of denying loans or restricting their number for certain areas of a community.

Regulation Z A regulation of the Federal Reserve Board designed to ensure that borrowers and customers in need of consumer credit are given meaningful information with respect to the cost of credit.

release To relinquish an interest in or claim to a parcel of property.

relocation service An organization that aids a person in selling a property in one area and buying another property in another area.

remainder The remnant of an estate that has been conveyed to take effect and be enjoyed after the termination of a prior estate, such as when an owner conveys a life estate to one party and the remainder to another.

renegotiable rate mortgage A mortgage loan that is granted for a term of 3 to 5 years and secured by a long-term mortgage of up to 30 years with the interest rate being renegotiated or adjusted each period.

rent A fixed, periodic payment made by a tenant of a property to the owner for possession and use, usually by prior agreement of the parties.

rent schedule A statement of proposed rental rates, determined by the owner or the property manager or both, based on a building's estimated expenses, market supply and demand, and the owner's long-range goals for the property.

replacement cost The cost of construction at current prices of a building having utility equivalent to the building being appraised but built with modern materials and according to current standards, designs, and layout.

reproduction cost The cost of construction at current prices of an exact duplicate or replica using the same materials, construction standards, design, layout, and quality of workmanship and embodying all the deficiencies, superadequacies, and obsolescences of the subject building.

rescission The termination of a contract by mutual agreement of the parties.

reservation in a deed The creation by a deed to property of a new right in favor of the grantor. Usually involves an **easement,** a **life estate,** or a mineral interest.

restriction A limitation on the use of real property, generally originated by the owner or subdivider in a deed.

reverse annuity mortgage A mortgage loan that allows the owner to receive periodic payments based on the equity in the home.

reversion The remnant of an estate that the grantor holds after he or she has granted a life estate to another person; the estate will return or revert to the grantor. Also called a *reverter.*

reversionary right An owner's right to regain possession of leased property on termination of the lease agreement.

rezoning The process involved in changing the existing zoning of a property or area.

right of first refusal A person's right to have the first opportunity to either lease or purchase real property.

right of survivorship *See* joint tenancy.

riparian rights An owner's rights in land that borders flowing water such as a stream or river. These rights include access to and use of the water.

Rural Development A federal agency of the U.S. Department of Agriculture that channels credit to farmers and rural residents and communities; formerly known as the Farm Service Agency and Farmer's Home Administration (FmHA).

sale and leaseback A transaction in which an owner sells her or his improved property and, as part of the same transaction, signs a long-term lease to remain in possession of the premises.

sales contract A contract containing the complete terms of the agreement between buyer and seller for the sale of a particular parcel or parcels of real estate.

salesperson A person who performs real estate activities while employed by or associated with a licensed real estate broker.

satisfaction A document acknowledging the payment of a debt. Once filed, the collateral pledged (mortgage) is returned to the mortgagor for a "mortgage burning party."

secondary mortgage market A market for the purchase and sale of existing mortgages, designed to provide greater liquidity for mortgages; also called the *secondary money market.* Mortgages are originated in the primary mortgage market.

section A portion of a township under the **rectangular survey system** (government survey method). A township is divided into 36 sections numbered 1 to 36. A section is a square with mile-long sides and an area of one square mile, or 640 acres.

self-proving will A will in which the witnesses give their testimony at the time of signing. This testimony is preserved in a notarized affidavit to eliminate the problem of finding the witnesses at the maker's death and to assist in the probating procedure.

selling broker *See* listing broker.

separate property The real property owned by a husband or wife prior to their marriage.

servient tenement The land on which an easement exists in favor of an adjacent property; also called a *servient estate.*

setback The amount of space local zoning regulations require between a lot line and a building line.

severalty The ownership of real property by one person only; also called *sole ownership.*

situs The personal preference of people for one area of land over another, not necessarily based on objective facts and knowledge.

sole ownership *See* severalty.

sovereignty of the soil The beginning of the record of ownership of land by conveyance from the sovereign or the state. Historically this is known also as a *patent*.

special assessment A tax or levy customarily imposed against only those specific parcels of real estate that will benefit from a proposed public improvement, such as a street or sewer.

special warranty deed A deed in which the grantor warrants or guarantees the title only against defects arising during the period of his or her tenure and ownership of the property and not against defects existing before that time, generally using the language "by, through, or under the grantor but not otherwise."

specific lien A lien affecting or attaching only to a certain, specific parcel of land or piece of property.

specific performance suit A legal action brought in a court of equity in special cases to compel a party to carry out the terms of a contract. The basis for an equity court's jurisdiction in breach of a real estate contract is that land is unique, and mere legal damages would not adequately compensate the buyer for the seller's breach.

sponsoring broker A duly licensed real estate broker who employs a salesperson. Under law, the broker is responsible for the acts of her or his salespeople.

squatter's rights Those rights acquired through adverse possession. By "squatting" on land for a certain statutory period under prescribed conditions, one may acquire title by limitations. If an **easement** only is acquired, instead of the title to the land itself, one has title by prescription, or **easement by prescription.**

statute of frauds The part of a state law that requires certain instruments such as deeds, real estate sales contracts, and certain leases to be in writing to be legally enforceable.

statute of limitations That law pertaining to the period of time within which certain actions must be brought to court.

statutory lien A lien imposed on property by statute, for example, a tax lien; in contrast to a voluntary lien, which an owner places on his or her own real estate, for example, a mortgage lien.

steering The illegal practice of channeling home seekers to particular areas or avoiding specific areas, either to maintain or to change the character of an area, or to create a speculative situation.

straight-line method A method of calculating depreciation for tax purposes computed by dividing the adjusted basis of a property less its estimated salvage value by the estimated number of years of remaining useful life.

subcontractor *See* general contractor.

subagency An agent appoints a subagent to help the agent in a specified transaction and to act on the principal's behalf.

subdivision A tract of land divided by the owner, known as the subdivider, into blocks, building lots, and streets according to a recorded subdivision plat that must comply with local ordinances and regulations.

subletting The leasing of premises by a lessee to a third party for part of the lessee's remaining term. *See also* assignment.

subordination A relegation to a lesser position, usually in respect to a right or security.

subordination agreement An agreement that changes the order of priority of liens between two creditors.

subrogation The substitution of one creditor for another, with the substituted person succeeding to the legal rights and claims of the original claimant. Subrogation is used by title insurers to acquire the right to sue from the injured party to recover any claims they have paid.

substitution An appraisal principle stating that the maximum value of a property tends to be set by the cost of purchasing an equally desirable and valuable substitute property, assuming that no costly delay is encountered in making the substitution.

suit for possession A court suit initiated by a landlord to evict a tenant from leased premises after the tenant has breached one of the terms of the lease or has held possession of the property after the lease's expiration.

suit for specific performance A legal action brought by either a buyer or a seller to enforce performance of the terms of a contract.

suit (bill) to quiet title A legal action intended to establish or settle the title to a particular property, especially when there is a cloud on the title.

summation appraisal An approach under which value equals estimated land value plus reproduction costs of any improvements after depreciation has been subtracted.

supply The amount of goods available in the market to be sold at a given price. The term often is coupled with **demand.**

surety bond An agreement by an insurance or bonding company to be responsible for certain possible defaults, debts, or obligations contracted for by an insured party; in essence, a policy insuring one's personal and/or financial integrity. In the real estate business, a surety bond generally is used to ensure that a particular project will be completed at a certain date or that a contract will be performed as stated.

survey The process by which boundaries are measured and land areas are determined; the on-site measurement of lot lines, dimensions, and positions of buildings on a lot, including the determination of any existing **encroachments** or **easements.**

syndicate A combination of two or more persons or firms to accomplish a joint venture of mutual interest. Syndicates dissolve when the specific purpose for which they were created has been accomplished.

taxation The process by which a government or municipal quasi-public body raises monies to fund its operation.

tax lien A charge against property created by the operation of law. Tax liens and assessments take priority over all other liens.

tax rate The rate at which real property is taxed in a tax district or county. For example, in a certain county, a home is taxed at a rate of 50 mills, or $50 per 1,000, or 5.0% of the taxable value.

tax sale A court-ordered sale of real property to raise money to cover delinquent taxes.

tenancy at sufferance The tenancy of a lessee who lawfully comes into possession of a landlord's real estate but who continues to occupy the premises improperly after her or his lease rights have expired.

tenancy at will An estate that gives the lessee the right to possession until the estate is terminated by either party; the term of this estate is indefinite.

tenancy by the entirety The joint ownership, recognized in some states, of property acquired by husband and wife during marriage. On the death of one spouse, the survivor becomes the owner of the property.

tenancy in common A form of co-ownership by which each owner holds an undivided interest in real property as if he or she were the sole owner. Each individual has the right to partition. Unlike a joint tenancy, there is no right of survivorship between tenants in common, and owners may have unequal interests.

tenant One who holds or possesses lands or tenements by any kind of right of title.

tenement Everything that may be occupied under a lease by a tenant.

termination (lease) The cancellation of a lease by the action of either party. A lease may be terminated by expiration of the term, surrender and acceptance, constructive eviction by lessor, or option, when provided in the lease for breach of covenants.

termination (listing) The cancellation of a broker-principal employment contract. A listing may be terminated by death or insanity of either party, expiration of listing period, mutual agreement, sufficient written notice, or the completion of performance under the agreement.

testate Having made and left a valid will.

testator A will maker.

"time is of the essence" A phrase in a contract that requires the performance of a certain act within a stated period of time.

title insurance Insurance designed to indemnify the holder for loss sustained by reason of defects in a title, up to and including the policy limits.

Torrens system A method of evidencing title by registration with the proper public authority, generally called the registrar. Named for its founder, Sir Robert Torrens.

township The principal unit of the **rectangular survey system** (government survey method). A township is a square with six-mile sides and an area of 36 square miles.

township lines The horizontal lines running at six-mile intervals parallel to the base lines in the rectangular survey system (government survey method).

trade fixtures The articles installed by a tenant under the terms of a lease and removable by the tenant before the lease expires.

trust A fiduciary arrangement by which property is conveyed to a person or institution, called a trustee, and held and administered on behalf of another person, called a beneficiary.

trust deed An instrument used to create a lien by which the trustor conveys his or her title to a trustee, who holds it as security for the benefit of the note holder (the lender); also called a **deed of trust.**

trustee One who as agent for others handles money or holds title to their land.

trustee's deed A deed executed by a trustee conveying land held in a trust to the beneficiary.

undivided interest *See* tenancy in common.

unearned increment An increase in the value of a property caused by increased population, development, or demand for which the owner is not responsible.

Uniform Commercial Code A codification of commercial law, adopted in most states, that attempts to make uniform laws relating to commercial transactions, including chattel mortgages and bulk transfers. Security interests in chattels are created by an instrument known as a security agreement. Article 6 of the code regulates bulk transfers, that is, the sale of a business as a whole, including all fixtures, chattels, and merchandise.

unilateral contract A one-sided contract by which one party makes a promise to induce a second party to do something. The second party is not legally bound to perform; if the second party does comply, however, the first party is obligated to keep the promise.

unity of ownership The four unities traditionally needed to create a joint tenancy—unity of title, unity of time, unity of interest, unity of possession.

urban renewal The acquisition of run-down city areas for purposes of redevelopment.

useful life In real estate investment, the number of years a property will be useful to the investors.

usury The practice of charging more than the rate of interest allowed by law.

valid contract A contract that complies with all the essential elements of a contract and is binding and enforceable on all parties to it.

valid lease An enforceable lease that has the following essential parts: lessor and lessee with contractual capacity, offer and acceptance, legality of object, description of the premises, consideration, signatures, and delivery. Leases for more than one year also must be in writing.

value The present worth of future benefits arising from the ownership of real property. To have value, a property must have utility, scarcity, effective demand, and transferability.

variable rate mortgage A mortgage loan that contains an interest rate provision related to a selected index. Under this provision, the interest rate may be adjusted annually either up or down.

variance An exception from the zoning ordinances; permission granted by zoning authorities to build a structure or conduct a use that is expressly prohibited by zoning ordinance.

writ of attachment The method by which a debtor's property is placed in the custody of the law and held as security, pending the outcome of a creditor's suit.

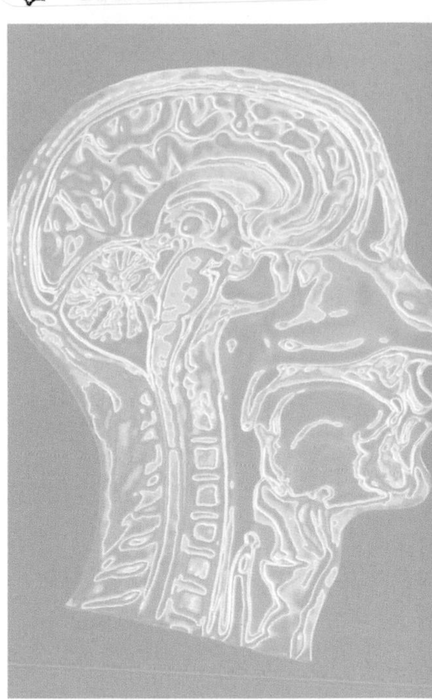

INVENTIONS FOR EVERYONE 1901–1950 172

INFORMATION & UNCERTAINTY 1951 ONWARD.................... 212

INDEX OF INVENTIONS & DISCOVERIES 252

INDEX OF INVENTORS & DISCOVERERS 254

PICTURE CREDITS & ACKNOWLEDGMENTS 256

This American Edition, 2020
First American Edition, 2002
Published in the United States by DK Publishing
1450 Broadway, Suite 801, New York, NY 10018

Copyright © 2002, 2006, 2014, 2018, 2020
Dorling Kindersley Limited
DK, a Division of Penguin Random House LLC
20 21 22 23 24 10 9 8 7 6 5 4 3 2 1
001–316678–Jul/2020

All rights reserved. Without limiting the rights under the copyright reserved above, no part of this publication may be reproduced, stored in or introduced into a retrieval system, or transmitted, in any form, or by any means (electronic, mechanical, photocopying, recording, or otherwise), without the prior written permission of the copyright owner.
Published in Great Britain by Dorling Kindersley Limited

A catalog record of this book is available from the Library of Congress
ISBN 978-1-4654-9435-1

DK books are available at special discounts when purchased in bulk for sales promotions, premiums, fund-raising, or educational use. For details, contact: DK Publishing Special Markets, 1450 Broadway, Suite 801, New York, NY 10018
SpecialSales@dk.com

Printed and bound in China

For the curious

www.dk.com

Smithsonian

Established in 1846, the Smithsonian is the world's largest museum and research complex, dedicated to public education, national service, and scholarship in the arts, sciences, and history. It includes 19 museums and galleries and the National Zoological Park. The total number of artifacts, works of art, and specimens in the Smithsonian's collection is estimated at 156 million.

Introduction

Three million years of creativity and curiosity have produced tens of thousands of inventions and discoveries. Those that successfully met basic human needs—from the need to survive to the need to know—have played a big part in shaping our world.

Our world is very different from the world of our ancestors. Tens of thousands of inventions and discoveries have transformed the way we do things and the way we think. An invention is something new, created by arranging things in some novel way. A discovery is a thing or principle that already existed, needing only to be found. But it is often difficult to tell where invention ends and discovery begins. Whatever they are, few inventions or discoveries are made overnight. There is usually a period of preparation before they emerge. Even then, they take time to act. An invention may take years to displace existing methods. A discovery may take generations to change habits of thought.

It is often difficult to tell where invention ends and discovery begins, and neither happens overnight.

When did it happen?

This is not a book of "firsts." I have listed most inventions and discoveries under the date when they were first made public. But some dates relate to the beginning of something that only later became well known, or to a later stage of something that took time to influence people. It can also be difficult to say exactly who invented or discovered something. Often, when the time is right, many people come up with the same idea. And making an idea work can be more important than simply thinking of it. At the top of each invention or discovery, I have named the people who I think contributed most to it.

Below, where possible, I have mentioned others who helped or attempted something similar. Some stories are too interesting to squeeze into a small space. I have given these either a separate box or two whole pages. These longer stories show how complicated inventing or discovering can be and how it can change people's lives. Other aspects of these lives appear at the foot of most pages in a timeline, which records events in the wider world.

We may soon know enough to control the machinery of life itself, making the future less certain.

FASTER AND FASTER

Over the centuries, inventions and discoveries followed two main trends. Ancient ideas became modern science as measurement and mathematics improved on observation and argument, and the way things were made changed radically as scientific techniques displaced traditional crafts. These trends continue at an ever greater rate today. You may notice that while the first section of the book covers nearly three million years, the last covers only fifty. Despite this rapid change, many inventions and discoveries have had a lasting effect. Some, such as windmills or the theory of continental drift, vanished for a while but were born again. Others, such as pottery, have never been replaced. Inventions and discoveries like these were used or remembered because they met basic human needs. Until recently, these needs have not changed. But we may soon know enough to control the machinery of life itself, changing our basic needs and making the future less certain. I hope that this book will help you understand how we got where we are now, and maybe even help you guess where we are going next.

Roger Bridgman

LEARNING THE BASICS

BY MAKING TOOLS that either change their environment or help them to cope with it, human beings can survive where other animals cannot. It took hundreds of thousands of years for people to make the basic inventions and discoveries that underpin what we now call technology.

Stone tools

c.3,000,000 BCE

The main difference between ourselves and most other animals is that we use tools. The oldest known tools, found in Africa, were made more than two million years ago. They are simply lumps of stone that have been shattered with another stone to make a sharp edge for chopping meat or wood. The people who made them would also have made tools from wood, but none have survived.

Hand ax *The best stone for tools was flint. This flint hand ax, from about 1000–5000 BCE, was found in Saint Acheul, near Amiens, France.*

If flakes are chipped off, flint naturally forms sharp edges

Hand ax

c.1,800,000 BCE

Over a period of more than one million years, the first crude stone tools evolved into beautifully shaped blades. Their makers flaked away the surfaces of a large flint pebble until its sides were sharp, for cutting or scraping, and one end was pointed, for piercing. The remaining blunt end fitted snugly into the hand, which is why the blades are called hand axes.

Use of fire

c.1,400,000 BCE

People discovered the value of fire long before they found out how to make it. Fires can be started naturally by friction, lightning, or sunlight striking through a drop of water. The first people to use fire simply kept these natural flames going. They used fire for warmth and to cook food. Better still, fire could be used to clear away bushes and trees so that the grass grew thicker, attracting animals for people to catch and eat.

Mining

c.40,000 BCE

Early people made full use of everything around them, including rocks, which they used to make tools and to extract minerals. After a time, the good rocks on the surface were all used up, and people had to start digging to find what they wanted. The first mines were just shallow pits, but miners were eventually forced underground. One of the minerals they wanted was red ochre, which was used as a pigment for ritual purposes and for cave paintings. The oldest known underground mine was used for collecting red ochre. It is at Bomvu Ridge in Swaziland, Africa.

Cord attached to the ends of the crosspiece is also fixed to, and wrapped around, the shaft

Wooden crosspiece was pumped downward to turn the shaft via the cord

Stone weight was used to apply more pressure to the bit

Drill shaft, the end of which was equipped with a cast-iron bit

Drill *The bow drill (right) is Egyptian. The drill (left) is a recent pump drill from New Guinea, which was used to drill holes in wood.*

Drill was kept upright by a piece of wood or stone held on top of it

Drill

c.35,000 BCE

The earliest drills were probably pointed stones that people spun between the palms of their hands. Later, sticks were spun like this to make fire (✻ *see* **page 11**). People also discovered that they could spin the drill faster by wrapping a cord around it, tying the ends of the cord to a wooden bow and pushing this back and forth. This bow drill was used in some parts of the world until recent times.

c.1,600,000 BCE
Earth enters its most recent ice age. Ice will eventually cover northern Europe and North America. Most of it will have gone by 10,000 BCE, leaving behind a changed landscape.

c.50,000 BCE
A huge meteorite, the size of a building, falls on Earth in what is now Arizona, The rock weighs about 440,000 tons and forms a huge crater 0.75 miles (1.2 km) wide and 490 ft (150 m) deep.

FISH HOOK *This modern fish hook from Hawaii was made in much the same way as the first fish hooks.*

Engraving tool

c.35,000 BCE

As long as 40,000 years ago, people were making delicate objects and works of art using stone engraving tools called burins. Made by forming a sharp edge on a flake of flint, a burin could be used to scratch lines and cut grooves in bone or wood. This allowed people to create more precise tools, such as needles, and to engrave decoration on larger objects.

Fish hook

c.35,000 BCE

The earliest method of catching a fish was with a piece of stone, pointed at both ends, baited, and tied to a line. This gorge, as it is called, simply jammed in the fish's throat. The first real fish hooks were developed by the earliest "modern" humans, the Cro-Magnons. They caught their fish using a barbed bone hook, one of the many small, specialized tools they made using the versatile burin that they had perfected.

Handles for tools

c.35,000 BCE

Attaching a wooden handle to a blade may not sound like a breakthrough, but it was. People could not hit things very hard with a tool held in their hands because it hurt. Nor could they swing the tool very quickly because their arms were too short. A handle, or haft, helped them overcome both these limitations, protecting their arms from impact and increasing the length of their swing. Hand axes (✱ *see* **page 7**) could be used to clear away bushes, but axes with hafts could be used to chop down trees.

Spear thrower

c.35,000 BCE

By creeping along quietly, early hunters could often get close enough to an animal to throw a spear at it and kill it. But sometimes the animal would run away. What the hunters needed was a way of throwing spears from farther away. The spear thrower was a piece of wood or antler with a notch at one end to hold the spear. It enabled hunters to hurl their weapons farther and increased their chances of killing their prey.

Bow and arrow

c.30,000 BCE

Bows and arrows were depicted in cave paintings from 30,000 BCE onward, but no actual examples survive today. By 18,000 BCE, arrows were equipped with flint points, making them deadly to animals. Later, the bow came into use as a major military weapon and became deadly to people, too.

Cave painting

c.30,000 BCE

Dramatic paintings made by people living more than 30,000 years ago lay forgotten until 1879, when a little girl, Maria de Sautuola, visited the

HOUSE *After 20,000 years of development, houses began to be made of brick. This is a model of a house from the 6th century* BCE.

c.35,000 BCE The first people to enter the Americas travel over a land bridge between Siberia and Alaska, which is exposed by the low sea level. The bridge will later disappear as ice melts worldwide.

c.27,000 BCE In what will become Germany, an unknown sculptor carves the Venus of Willendorf, one of the earliest known sculptures of a human. It has exaggerated female proportions and is painted red.

caves at Altamira in Spain with her father. She noticed the huge paintings of animals high above her head. Since then, even earlier paintings have been discovered at Chauvet in France. The artists of these early paintings had to invent paint, brushes, scaffolding, and even artificial lighting before they could begin painting.

Paintbrush

c.30,000 BCE

The artists who created the cave paintings at Altamira in Spain, Lascaux in France, and in other places, probably put color on to the walls in several different ways, including spitting it out. Some of the effects they produced must have needed a paintbrush. At its simplest, this could have been a twig chewed at one end to separate the fibers, but the world's first interior decorators may also have used bunches of feathers or bristles.

Rope

c.30,000 BCE

It is difficult to say exactly when people first started to make rope because few early examples have survived, except in bogs, where the acid water has stopped it from rotting. But some early drawings and sculptures show it in use. It has also sometimes been preserved as an impression in clay, as in the caves of Lascaux, where archaeologists found evidence of a rope braided from three plant fibers. One early use of rope was for making nets and snares for catching food.

House

c.28,000 BCE

People started to build houses about 30,000 years ago, but most people lived in shelters or caves. They also built simple huts, in which they probably lived for some time before moving on to find food. At Dolnì Vestonice in the Czech Republic, archaeologists have found the remains of houses built from stone, wood, and mammoth bones, dating from about 25,000 BCE.

Boomerang

c.19,000 BCE

Used by hunters in Africa, India, and Australia, the boomerang was originally just a heavy stick thrown at an animal to injure it and make it easier to catch. Over the centuries, the stick was reshaped so that it would fly farther and faster, and even return to its thrower. The first known boomerang was found in a cave in southern Poland, and it is probably about 21,000 years old. The Australian boomerang was in use by 8000 BCE.

Pottery

c.13,000 BCE

Having harnessed the power of fire, people were able to make pottery. The first potters needed only to find some soft clay, shape it, and then heat it in a fire. Because an ordinary fire did not heat the clay very evenly, the resulting pots were fragile and not completely waterproof, but they still proved extremely useful. Pottery from about 15,000 years ago has been found in Japan.

Doorway supported by a large branch

Roof and walls plastered with mud

c.23,000 BCE
Ice tightens its grip on Earth as the ice age reaches its peak. As more water is locked up in glaciers, the sea level continues to fall. By this time, it is 300 ft (90 m) below its level today.

c.18,000 BCE
People in Australia cover rocks with thousands of elaborate engraved designs. They also create images in color. For red, they use a rock called red ocher, or sometimes human blood.

Cutting holes in the skull

c.10,000 BCE

People once thought that disease was caused by demons getting inside a person's head or gods stealing their soul. Their answer was to cut a hole in the head to let the demons out or the soul back in. Trephining probably took place as early as 10,000 BCE, and a skull from about 5000 BCE, found at Ensisheim in France, shows clear evidence of the operation. Other skulls show that people survived it—bone around the hole has grown, proving that the patient lived.

Whistle

c.10,000 BCE

The whistle could be the earliest musical instrument. Archaeologists have found examples more than 12,000 years old. People in China were using whistles with more than one note at least 9,000 years ago. We don't know exactly how the whistle was invented, but it is likely that the first step was when someone blew across the end of a natural tube, such as bamboo or bone.

Agriculture

c.9000 BCE

See **pages 12–13** for the story of how hunters became farmers.

Oven

c.9000 BCE

The earliest method of cooking was to put food over an open fire and turn it occasionally. But this wasted fuel and someone had to do the turning. It was more efficient to put the fire inside a stone or clay chamber—an oven. Once the oven was hot, the cook could rake out the fire, put the food in, and seal it up until the food was ready. The first known ovens were found in the city of Jericho in ancient Palestine, where people have been living for more than 10,000 years.

Skull shows four circular holes, or trephinings

Bone shows signs of healing, indicating that this individual survived the process of trephining

Cutting holes in the skull *This skull was trephined in 2200–2000 BCE.*

Flint mining *This prehistoric pick is made from a deer's antler.*

Flint mining

c.8000 BCE

For hundreds of thousands of years, people made tools from the stones they found around them. As the need for tools grew, toolmakers began to dig for suitable stones like flints. Fortunately, flints are found in soft chalk, which miners could cut away with picks made from antlers. Early flint miners in Britain and France sank complex mining shafts and galleries that went as deep as 40 ft (13 m).

c.11,000 BCE People now occupy most of the Americas, except the northern parts covered by glaciers. Using stone-tipped spears, they hunt mastodons and mammoths (both similar to elephants) and even camels.

c.8300 BCE A period of change known as the Middle Stone Age begins. World temperatures rise sharply and the great ice sheet covering Europe starts to shrink, opening up huge areas of land for people to occupy.

Sheep

c.8000 BCE

About 10,000 years ago, sheep lived wild in western Asia and around the Mediterranean. They are now found in more countries than any other domestic animal. The first farmers may have favored sheep because they tended to follow a leader, which made them easy to herd. They were also small and hardy and produced valuable wool as well as meat and milk.

Wheat and barley

c.7500 BCE

Wheat and barley are basically just types of grasses. Modern varieties are the result of a continuous process of selection, which started when the first farmers chose to cultivate the plants with the most plentiful and largest seeds. The first crops were probably cultivated

somewhere in the Middle East, perhaps near Jericho, which had a large population to feed. Traces of wheat and barley seeds have been found buried under the modern town.

Sheep *Images of farmers with sheep and cows made 4,500 years ago in the city of Ur, Mesopotamia.*

Chisel

c.7000 BCE

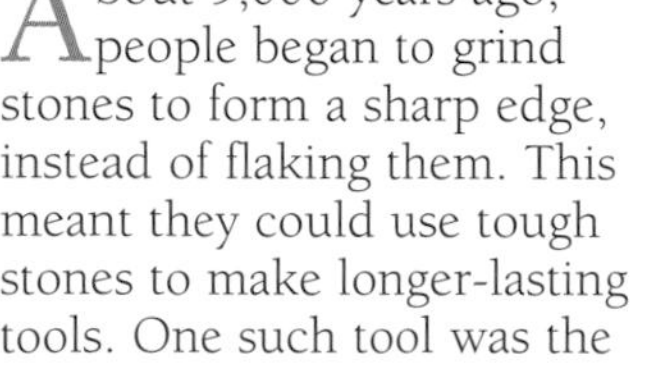

About 9,000 years ago, people began to grind stones to form a sharp edge, instead of flaking them. This meant they could use tough stones to make longer-lasting tools. One such tool was the chisel, a blade sharpened at the end, not the side. It gave better control for carving objects from wood or other soft materials.

Making fire

c.7000 BCE

People have used fire for more than a million years but discovered how to make it only about 9,000 years ago. Two main methods were used. One was to hit a rock called pyrites with a flint, which produced sparks that could be used to start a fire. The other method was to spin a stick called a fire drill against a piece of wood until sparks flew. Archaeologists have found the equipment used for both methods throughout Europe.

Flax

c.7000 BCE

By about 9,000 years ago, people were growing plants to make their fibers into rope and cloth. The first plant to be cultivated for this reason was flax, a tall plant with blue flowers. Fibers extracted from its stems were spun into a thread called linen, which we still use today because it is much stronger than cotton. Archaeologists have found early flax plants and linen fishing nets and fabrics in Switzerland. The ancient Egyptians also used linen to wrap mummies.

c.8300 BCE The saber-toothed tiger, a large ferocious cat with fangs, finally becomes extinct. Well equipped to hunt and kill large animals such as the mastodon, it cannot survive since this and many other prey die out.

c.8000 BCE After occupying many parts of the world for more than a million years, lions begin to disappear. By this time, they have become extinct in North America. In another 8,000 years, there will be none left in Europe.

GOING FOR GROWTH

No going back as hunters become farmers

Flint blade (c.4000–2300 BCE) in a modern handle

Ears of einkorn wheat

EARLY HARVEST
The first farmers grew einkorn, a type of wheat, and other crops. They harvested the wheat with a sickle, made by attaching a flint blade to a wooden handle. The sickle made it easy to cut down the tall, strong stems.

Carbonized wheat, barley, fig seeds, and grape seeds from an archaeological site in Jordan

Some time after 10,000 BCE, people made the first real attempt to control the world they lived in, through agriculture. Over thousands of years, they began to depend less on what they could hunt or gather from the wild and more on animals they had tamed and crops they had sown. The abundant food that agriculture provided allowed small villages to grow into great cities.

It is not clear why people changed their lifestyle like this. We can only guess at what inspired them to try herding sheep or planting wheat. Whatever the reasons, there was no going back. Farming produced more food per person than hunting and gathering, so people were able to raise more children. And, as more children were born, more food was needed. Agriculture gave people their first experience of the power of technology to change lives.

Some of the first people to become farmers lived in a huge, sunny, well-watered area in the Middle East called the Fertile Crescent (now Iran, Iraq, Israel, Jordan, Syria, and Turkey), where the conditions were ideal for crops and livestock. But the story of the dawn of agriculture was repeated over and over again throughout the world. People invented agriculture independently

THRESHING AND WINNOWING
Large-scale growing demanded efficient ways of processing the harvest. Wheat or barley was first threshed—beaten with flails to separate the grains from the husks. Then it was winnowed—thrown into the air so that the wind blew the husks away while the valuable grains fell to the ground.

in places as far apart as China and South America. They may have started because people noticed that the grains they gathered sometimes sprouted or that sheep liked to stick together and were easy to control.

By about 6000 BCE, people had discovered that the best cereals to grow were wheat and barley and that pigs, cows, and sheep returned the effort involved in rearing them by providing meat, milk, leather, and wool. Later, they used oxen for pulling plows. People learned to work with the seasons, planting at the right time and, in dry areas, making use of annual floods to irrigate their fields. They also invented granaries where the harvest could be stored.

This style of farming lasted for another 8,000 years. Then, with the rise of science, changes began. New methods meant that fewer people were needed in farming. In the last century or so, these changes have accelerated. New power machinery, artificial fertilizers, and pesticides have now totally transformed a way of life that started in the Stone Age.

Harvesting today
Cereals are still harvested in the "Fertile Crescent" today. The principles of harvesting grain have not changed over the centuries, but in many areas the farmers now use machines like this combine harvester in Syria. This huge machine cuts, threshes, and winnows the crop.

As well as changing people's lives, agriculture gradually changed the landscape as farmers began to plow fields and channel water to their crops.

Mortise and tenon joint

c.7000 BCE

Having learned how to make good tools, people could start to do precise woodwork. But first they had to solve the problem of how they could join together two pieces of wood. One method was with the mortise and tenon joint, in which one piece of wood has a tongue shape at the end, which fits into a matching hole in the other piece of wood. This joining method was also used for stone structures like Stonehenge and is still the most widely used wood joint.

Sickle

c.7000 BCE

Soon after people began to grow crops, they developed special tools for harvesting them. The first was a short, straight blade known as a sickle. Dating from about 7000 BCE onward, flint sickles were one of the inventions that made agriculture possible (✷ *see* **pages 12–13**). A later development was a curved blade, which could cut several stems at once. The curved sickle is still in use today in some places but with a steel blade instead of a stone one.

COPPER *This copper is pure enough to be used almost as it is.*

TRADERS AND THEIR TRADES

SEVERAL EARLY settlements, such as Çatal Hüyük in Turkey (6500–5400 BCE) and San Lorenzo in South America (1150–900 BCE), owed their growth to trade. Çatal Hüyük's population grew to about 5,000 at its height because it had access to the valuable material obsidian. Trading was also important for island dwellers, who could rarely find everything they needed locally but were able to produce specialized crops such as spices.

Cinnamon

OBSIDIAN
A natural glass formed by volcanoes, obsidian could be used to make much sharper cutting tools than flint or other stones. People living in what is now Turkey had plenty of this material but lacked precious metals, so they traded one for the other. Obsidian from this area has been found in ancient Palestine, 550 miles (900 km) away.

SPICES
Trading in spices such as cinnamon, cloves, ginger, and pepper goes back to 2000 BCE or earlier. The spices originated in the East, and traders who knew where to get them made large profits by bringing them westward. The traders kept their sources—places like the Spice Islands (now part of the Moluccas group of islands in Indonesia)—strictly secret.

Peppercorns

Ginger

Copper

c.6500 BCE

The person who discovered copper, the first widely used metal, must have been thrilled. It is one of the few metals found in metallic form. People in Turkey were using it for small, precious objects by 6500 BCE. By 3000 BCE, with the development of ways to extract the metal from its ore, copper was in use all over the Middle East and the Mediterranean.

Lead

c.6500 BCE

Lead is one of the most ancient metals. As with copper, people started to use it in about 6500 BCE in Turkey. Unlike copper, lead is rarely found as a pure metal and has to be extracted from its ore by roasting it in a hot fire to release the metal. The earliest known objects made of lead are beads, suggesting that at first people considered lead a precious material and used it only for display.

Painted pottery

c.6500 BCE

Although early methods of firing were not very effective, even the earliest potters tried to make their wares look beautiful. Pots found in the ancient city of Çatal Hüyük, Anatolia (now Çumra in Turkey), dating from about 6500 BCE, had been washed over with a thin layer of cream clay called slip and decorated with the natural pigment red ocher.

The ends face upward, away from the water

BOAT
This boat from Lake Titicaca in the Andes mountains is made of reeds. The Egyptians were making boats from reeds by about 4000 BCE.

c.6800 BCE Methods of farming improve in villages in the Middle East. Farmers grow a wider range of crops and use land more efficiently. They domesticate what will become one of the most important farm animals—the pig.

c.6000 BCE Britain becomes cut off from Europe as the land link between what are now England and France is finally broken. Melting of the great glaciers has caused the sea to rise by hundreds of feet.

Trading

c.6500 BCE

Few communities are able to produce everything they need. Trading allows people to exchange things they have too much of for things they lack, and probably make a profit at the same time. Trading became common when the first cities were established, and the profits from trading helped many cities to grow. As transportation improved, trading spread more widely, exposing previously isolated groups of people to each other's knowledge and customs. (✱ *See also* **Traders and Their Trades.**)

DRUM *This Sumerian vase from the end of the 4th century BCE shows a musician playing a drum made from animal skin stretched across a wooden frame.*

Ax

c.6000 BCE

From about 6000 BCE, stone ax heads with a straight edge and heavy base began to appear, the earliest of which have been found in Sweden. Another basic tool, the adze, developed at about the same time. It was like an ax but with the blade turned around to strike across, not along, the direction of swing. It was used to shape heavy woods.

Drum

c.6000 BCE

The remains of drums have been found dating from 6000 BCE onward. Drums have always had religious, political, or military significance, and the urge to influence a crowd with noise and rhythm has led people to develop the drum into many forms. The first drums were skins stretched over anything hollow, but now there are hundreds of varieties, such as African talking drums, classical kettle drums, and tambourines.

Boat

c.6000 BCE

The first "boat" was probably just a dead tree on which someone hitched a ride downstream. But once tool makers had perfected stone axes, people used them to shape and hollow tree trunks to make real boats—dugout canoes. Boat builders also covered wooden frames with animal skins to make lighter boats like the coracle, which is still used today. Later, people in ancient Egypt made boats by lashing reeds together.

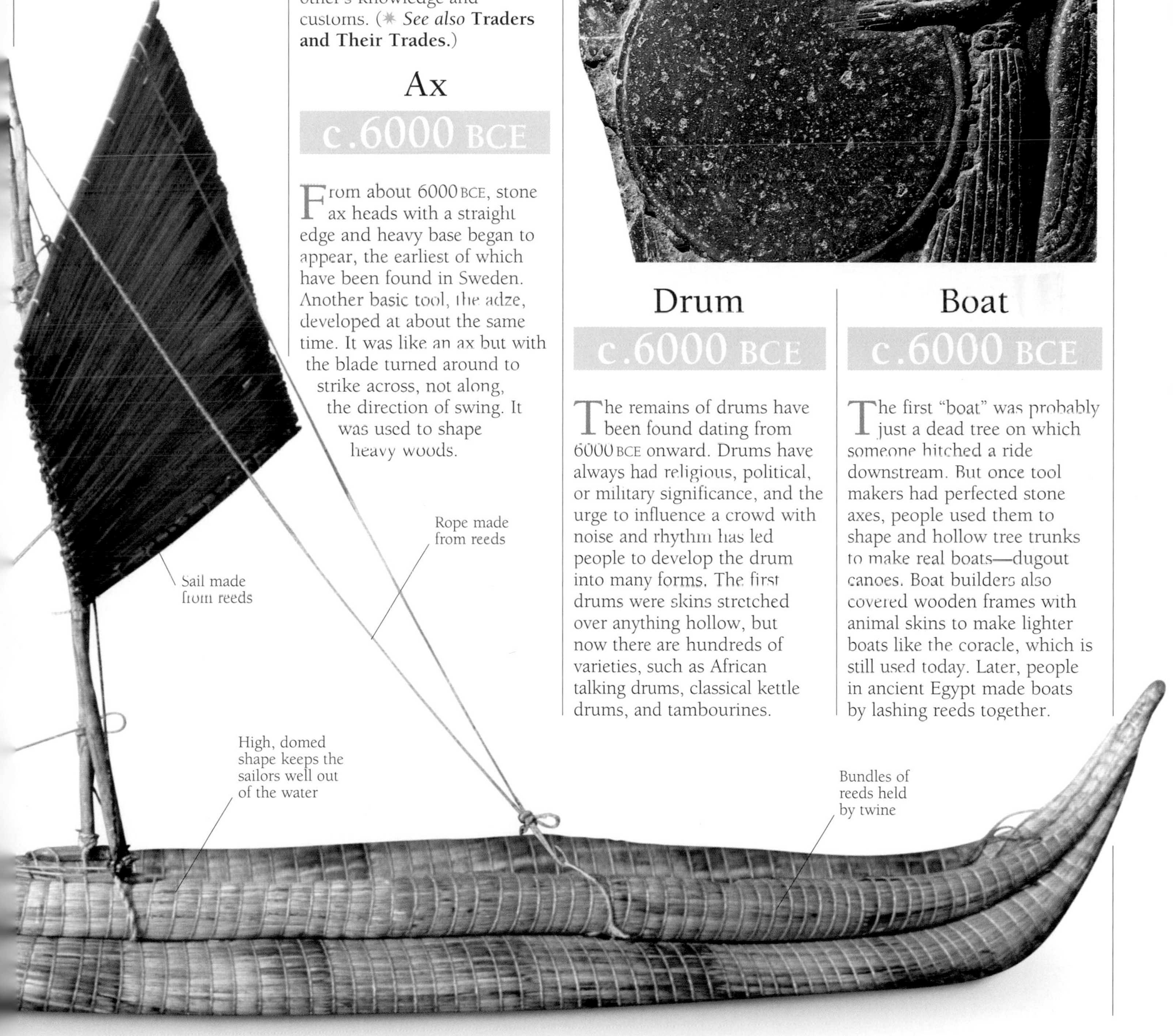

Sail made from reeds

Rope made from reeds

High, domed shape keeps the sailors well out of the water

Bundles of reeds held by twine

c.6000 BCE The city of Çatal Hüyük, in what is now Turkey, becomes one of the largest settlements of the Near East, after about 500 years of occupation. Its mud-brick buildings will survive for another 500 years.

c.6000 BCE Chinese painters extend their range of pigments by heating mixtures of organic and inorganic materials to create new colors. They make these into paint with gum, egg white, gelatine, or beeswax.

Basket weaving

c.5500 BCE

Basket weaving and cloth making were both common by 5000 BCE. Baskets probably came first because weaving a basket was easier than weaving cloth. No loom was needed, and weavers could use whole plant stems instead of having to spin plant fibers into thread. Baskets were made using split bamboo in China, flax and straw in the Middle East, and willow in Europe. People in these areas also used the same materials to weave matting.

Leather

c.5000 BCE

Early hunters knew that animal skins would be useful if they could stop them from decomposing. By about 5000 BCE, they had figured out various ways of turning skin into leather. They started by drying the skin then applied a range of substances, including urine. By about 800 BCE, people in the ancient state of Assyria in northern Mesopotamia (Iraq) had developed a better process. They soaked the skin in a solution containing the chemical alum and vegetable extracts that were rich in the chemical tannin.

Loom

c.5000 BCE

To weave cloth, a thread called the weft is passed under and over alternate threads called the warp. The earliest weavers may have used a needle, but by 5000 BCE, most looms allowed the weaver to avoid going under-and-over by lifting half the warp threads for the weft to pass straight through, then lifting the other half for the weft to pass back.

Plow

c.5000 BCE

Seeds grow best in soil that has been broken up and turned over. Early farmers used sticks to prepare the soil. The plow, developed later, did the job better, although early plows did not turn the soil over. The first plows were pulled or pushed by people, but by 4000 BCE, oxen were doing the pulling and the farmer had only to steer.

Seal

c.4500 BCE

The seal was the first security device used to protect goods and sign documents. In 4500 BCE, people in Mesopotamia sealed packages by tying them with string, putting clay around the knot, and squashing the clay with a stone carrying their mark. A thousand years later, when people started writing on clay tablets, they signed their documents in a similar way.

GRINDSTONE *This quern was used to make flour by grinding grain between the two stones.*

Grindstone

c.5000 BCE

Cereal grains are difficult to digest unless they are cracked open. At first, people did this by pounding them with rocks. Then they used two stones, one on the ground and one in the hands. The flour produced was more nutritious than whole grains and could be made into bread. This type of grindstone is sometimes called a saddle quern because the lower stone gets ground into a saddle shape with use.

Irrigation

c.5000 BCE

Irrigation is a means of getting water to plants so that they can grow, even when the land is dry. From about 5000 BCE, the ancient Egyptians practiced irrigation on a grand scale. Every year, the Nile River flooded, and the Egyptians used sluices and ponds to trap the water and its valuable nutrient, and send it to where it was needed.

PLOW *This model plow was found in an Egyptian tomb of 2000 BCE.*

c.5500 BCE Chinese people begin to grow rice in the Huang He (Yellow River) valley in eastern China. Within five centuries, this small beginning will develop into a fully agricultural way of life.

c.5000 BCE The fertile land to the north of the Persian Gulf is settled by the Ubaidians, the first of many occupants of the area that will become Sumer. They develop a rich culture that includes pottery and sculpture.

Scales

c.4000 BCE

The simplest device for weighing things is the beam balance, a length of wood or metal hung from its center with a pan hung from each end. The object to be weighed, in one pan, is balanced against weights in the other. It was developed in about 4000 BCE in Mesopotamia. By 1500 BCE, the ancient Egyptians had improved the accuracy of these early scales by passing the cords for the pans over the ends of the beam instead of through holes in it.

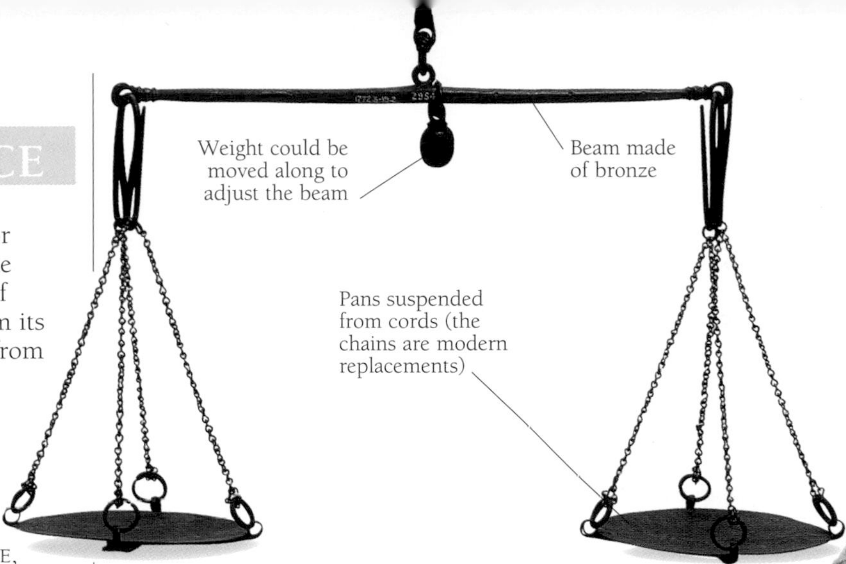

Weight could be moved along to adjust the beam

Beam made of bronze

Pans suspended from cords (the chains are modern replacements)

SCALES *These ancient Roman scales use the same principle as Mesopotamian scales. They are simple and very accurate. Similar ones remained in use until modern times.*

BRICK *Made in Mesopotamia in about 2500 BCE, this mud brick was partly fired.*

Edges formed by the wooden mold

Silver

c.4000 BCE

Silver is often found naturally with copper and lead, but it is more difficult to extract so it came into use rather later. Archaeologists have found silver ornaments buried in tombs dating from 4000 BCE. By 2500 BCE, silver mines were in full production in the area now called Turkey. From the beginning, silver was valued for its rarity and beauty. It was used as money, and this remained its main use until recent times, when it became the essential ingredient of photographic film.

Brick

c.3500 BCE

People made the first bricks from mud. They mixed the mud with straw to reinforce it, then shaped the bricks in wooden molds and dried them in the sun. Builders were using bricks of this kind 7,000 years ago, but they were not very good because heavy rain could turn them back into mud. More practical bricks began to be made in the Middle East in about 3500 BCE. They were made of clay and fired by heating them in a kiln, which made them as hard and as waterproof as pottery.

Oxen provide the power

c.4500 BCE Farmers from southwest Asia migrate up the valley of the Danube River in Germany, mixing with people still only hunting for food. They settle here, build large wooden houses, and trade for tools.

c.3900 BCE The Yangshao culture emerges in eastern China. Its people keep animals, practice simple farming, and later discover the secret of silkworms. Their other specialty is pottery painted in red, white, and black.

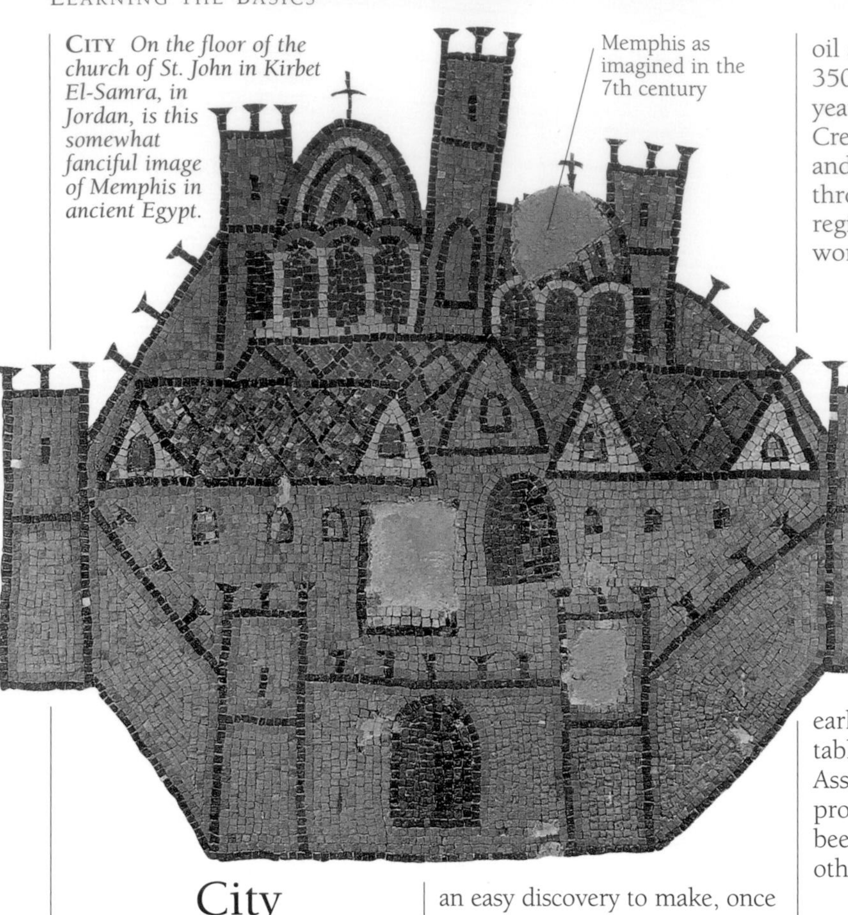

CITY *On the floor of the church of St. John in Kirbet El-Samra, in Jordan, is this somewhat fanciful image of Memphis in ancient Egypt.*

City

c.3500 BCE

Because farming (✱ *see* **pages 12–13**) meant that fewer members of each community were needed to produce food, other members were free to develop cities. They were places where people gathered for security and to exchange goods and ideas and were the foundations of civilization. The earliest large settlement was Jericho in the Middle East, which dates from about 7000 BCE, but the first real cities, with streets and public buildings, were Thebes and Memphis in Egypt, both of which existed by 3500 BCE.

Metal casting

c.3500 BCE

Casting is a way of making objects by letting molten metal solidify in a mold. It was an easy discovery to make, once people had learned to melt metals, because any metal they spilled would have been shaped by what it fell on. The first known castings are ax heads made of copper from the Balkan region of southeast Europe. They were made between 4000 BCE and 3000 BCE. Later, copper was replaced by bronze (✱ *see* **page 20**), which is easier to cast and is much harder.

Olive

c.3500 BCE

People on the island of Crete in the Mediterranean Sea were growing olive trees and harvesting olives for their oil and as a food by about 3500 BCE. More than 5,000 years later, olives are still Crete's most important crop, and olive growing has spread throughout the Mediterranean region and to other parts of the world with a similar climate.

Opium

c.3500 BCE

Opium is a substance made from the unripe seed heads of poppies. It has been in use for more than 5,000 years to relieve pain and help people sleep. Some of the earliest known writings—clay tablets of about 3000 BCE from Assyria—refer to its medical properties. Since then, it has been used to make several other drugs, notably morphine, discovered by German chemist F. W. A. Sertürner in 1806, which is still one of the most potent painkillers available.

Donkey

c.3500 BCE

Wheels are not always the best way to move things from place to place. In certain conditions, goods may travel more safely strapped to an animal. The first beast of burden was the donkey, domesticated from the African wild ass. In Sudan, in northwest Africa, people were using pack animals, as they are often called, as early as 4000 BCE, long before wheeled vehicles were invented. They probably chose the donkey because it is easy to tame, stands up well to harsh treatment, and can carry a load of up to 132 lb (60 kg).

METAL CASTING *Metalworkers discovered that bronze was easy to melt and cast into objects.*

c.3500 BCE People in Europe begin to bury their dead in long barrows. These earth mounds are typically 230 ft (70 m) long and point east-west. An entire high-status family would be buried in a chamber at the east end.

c.3500 BCE Sculptors in the Mesopotamian city of Uruk make outstanding items, such as a goddess's head in white limestone inlaid with other materials. They also carve vases from alabaster, a translucent stone.

Potter's wheel

c.3500 BCE

People made the first pots with their bare hands. Later, they built up pots from a "worm" of clay. Neither method produced perfectly round pots. By about 3500 BCE, potters were molding clay on a turntable, possibly made from a round stone, which helped them shape their pots more uniformly. Before long, they were using a heavy stone on an axle, which they spun with their feet. This left their hands free to work the clay on a smaller turntable above, and the potter's wheel was born.

Kiln-fired pottery

c.3500 BCE

Clay heated in a fire does not get hot enough to change into really strong pottery. By about 3500 BCE, potters had developed kilns, often fueled with charcoal, in which hot gases rushed up through a stack of pots. Clay placed in such a kiln produced better pottery. Because kilns were expensive to run, potters who used them needed plenty of customers and usually operated in cities.

Road

c.3500 BCE

Early roads were not surfaced like modern roads, but they could be just as long. The Persian Royal Road, built in about 3500 BCE, stretched for 1,785 miles (2,857 km) between the Persian Gulf and the Aegean Sea. By 1050 BCE, the Chinese were traveling on the Silk Road, which remained the world's longest road for 2,000 years. Great roads were also built by the Incas in South America and by the ancient Egyptians, who needed to transport building materials for their pyramids.

KILN-FIRED POTTERY *This beaker was made between 2500 and 1800 BCE.*

Sail

c.3500 BCE

Early boat users, noticing that the wind sometimes helped their progress, stretched skins or matting between poles to make the most of it. Sails made of cloth came later. They first appear in ancient Egyptian art from about 3300 BCE. Whatever they were made of, early sails worked only when the wind was behind them. Sails that could catch wind from the side, making sailors less dependent on the weather, were not invented for another 1,500 years.

Wheel

c.3500 BCE

Wheels were first used to move things around in Mesopotamia. It seems unlikely that the idea came from logs used as rollers, because the earliest wheels don't look anything like logs. People made them from planks, even in countries with trees that were large enough to slice into wheels. The wheel is more likely to have started life as an aid to potters in their quest to make perfectly rounded pots.

Wheeled vehicle

c.3500 BCE

The first record of anything with wheels is a pictograph (picture writing) found in Sumeria, an ancient civilization in southern Mesopotamia. It dates from about 3500 BCE. The same pictograph shows that earlier vehicles had runners like a sled. Within 500 years, wheeled vehicles were almost everywhere. They have been found in tombs and bogs and appear in wall paintings and carvings. In China, vehicles have been found dating from 2600 BCE onward.

c.3500 BCE The first pottery in the Americas is made in Ecuador and Colombia. The idea spreads northward as new crops, such as beans, demand better storage. Pottery making will reach Mexico by 2300 BCE.

c.3500 BCE Corn, or maize, a basic Central American crop, begins to be grown on a large scale, displacing a more established cereal, millet. Beans and hot chile peppers are already being grown in many places.

KINDS OF CALENDARS

A CALENDAR is like a clock that tells you what time of year it is, instead of what time of day. All calendars have to allow for the fact that a year does not contain a whole number of days or lunar months. Early calendars tended to run fast or slow, because their year was shorter or longer than the actual time it takes for Earth to go around the sun.

LUNISOLAR CALENDARS
These calendars were based on the lunar month, during which the moon goes from new to full and back. This has no connection with the solar year, the time Earth takes to go exactly once around the sun. So people using lunisolar calendars had to throw in an extra month every now and then to keep their months in step with the years.

Sun god surrounded by the 20 days of a month

THE EGYPTIAN CALENDAR
The Egyptians ignored the moon and used 12 months of exactly 30 days each, plus 5 days at the end of the year, which didn't belong to any month. It was a simple method, but because this calendar gave a year of exactly 365 days, one-quarter of a day shorter than the true solar year, it gained 25 days in every 100 years.

This is an Aztec calendar stone. The Aztecs ruled most of Mexico in the 15th century. The calendar was based partly on a ritual cycle of 260 days.

Writing numbers in tens

c.3400 BCE

People were counting their possessions long before they began writing words. One way they did this was by cutting notches in a stick. Early counting methods like this gradually evolved into writing numbers. At first, people wrote 24 marks to represent the number 24. By about 3400 BCE, the Egyptians had a more efficient system, with different symbols for 1, 10, 100, and so on. Using this system, they could write 24 using just six marks: two 10s and four 1s.

Bronze

c.3300 BCE

People began to use metal instead of stone for the production of their tools in about 3500 BCE. This happened when they discovered that copper could be extracted from certain rocks. Bronze, a harder metal, which was made by mixing copper with tin, was discovered several hundred years later. Easily shaped by casting (melting and pouring into a mold), and tougher than any stone, the discovery of bronze had a huge impact on human development.

Writing

c.3100 BCE

See **pages 22–23** for the story of how Middle Eastern traders created the first permanent records.

Candle

c.3000 BCE

Cave painters were using burning torches and crude oil lamps 30,000 years ago. Candles were better than these because their fuel did not spill, making them easy to carry around, and their wick gave a controlled flame. Candlesticks

CANDLE
Candles were originally formed from wax made by bees.

Ripples in wax caused because candle was hand-dipped

Tapered shape produced by dipping the wick repeatedly in molten wax

c.3200 BCE In England, work starts on a monument that will be known as Stonehenge. At this stage, it does not have much stone but is simply a "henge"—a sacred place surrounded by a bank and a ditch.

c.3200 BCE New people begin to arrive in the area to the north of the Persian Gulf. They speak a different language from the people already there, but together they form the Sumerian civilization.

dating from 3000 BCE have been found in both Crete and Egypt. The candles they once held were made by dipping thin cords into molten wax.

Lubricants

c.3000 BCE

The first wheeled vehicles needed lubrication because a wooden wheel rubbing on a wooden axle created a lot of heat. Any sort of oil or fat eased the problem for a while but quickly burned away. The Egyptians, in about 1500 BCE, were perhaps the first people to mix fat with lime and other substances, making lubricants that lasted.

Boat built from planks

c.3000 BCE

The first boats built from planks are thought to have come from ancient Egypt. At Abydos, south of Cairo, archaeologists found 14 large boats, which had been made, almost 5,000 years ago, by "sewing" planks together with ropes. The buried fleet was probably intended for use in the afterlife by a pharaoh. The boats' construction shows that the Egyptians still had a lot to learn—the boats had no frame and kept out water with reeds put between the planks.

Calendar

c.3000 BCE

The first calendars appeared in Babylonia, an ancient state in southern Mesopotamia. They were not very accurate because they were based on the moon as well as the sun and kept getting out of line with the seasons. The Egyptians, who had to know when to expect the annual flooding of the Nile, were the first to make a calendar based only on the sun. (✱ *See also* **Kinds of Calendars.**)

COTTON *The textile fiber comes from various species of the plant* Gossypium.

Cosmetics

c.3000 BCE

People often feel the need to make themselves look more attractive or more frightening, and cosmetics have been used for these purposes since the earliest times. The oldest known cosmetics were found in ancient Egyptian tombs dating from about 3000 BCE. They include perfume, skin cream (used by men as well as women), eye shadow, and mascara. Different minerals were ground to make different colors, such as iron oxide for red and malachite for green. About 1,000 years later, Britons daubed themselves with a blue dye called woad to frighten their enemies.

Cotton

c.3000 BCE

Cotton fabric starts out as a mass of silky fibers attached to the seeds of a plant belonging to the mallow family. It was probably discovered about 5,000 years ago by people in the valley of the Indus River, in what is now called Pakistan. They discovered that the cotton seed fibers could be woven into much finer fabrics than flax fibers could (✱ *see* **page 11**). News of the discovery soon spread west into Mesopotamia, where the Assyrians welcomed cotton fabric as a substitute for rough wool. It then spread eastward into China.

c.3000 BCE On a group of islands in the Aegean Sea, the Cycladic culture emerges. Although based on seafaring and metalworking, the culture will be remembered for its simplified marble sculptures of females.

c.3000 BCE The first known vet begins practicing in the state of Mesopotamia (now mainly Iraq). His name is Urlugaledinna. He treats all kinds of animals, and in many cases he uses herbal medicines to cure them.

PUTTING IT IN WRITING

Middle Eastern traders create the first permanent records

Clay signature
Clay was used to carry information long before real writing began. People in Mesopotamia sealed packages with clay, then used a stone seal to impress their personal mark on it.

Writing, like so many inventions, came about by accident, and this one happened on the back of an envelope. About 6,000 years ago in Mesopotamia, a group of people known as the Sumerians invented a new way of keeping track of trade. They made clay tokens shaped like animals, jars, and other goods and recorded deals by wrapping the tokens up in clay envelopes. Once they'd sealed an envelope, they could no longer see what was inside it. So, using a pointed stick, they marked the soft clay with signs that showed its contents.

It didn't take them long to realize that, once they'd done this, they didn't need the tokens any more: just the marked envelope would do. So by about 3100 BCE, the envelopes had turned into simple squares of clay recording trade deals in symbols. Writing had begun.

At first, the Sumerians used marks that were simplified pictures. To speed things up, they started jabbing the clay with the end of a reed instead of drawing with a stick. The pictures stopped looking like real things and became true writing. Archaeologists call it cuneiform. It was used for 3,000 years.

There are some problems with writing in this way. Every time a new word is invented, someone has to invent a new mark. Some

Writing with a reed
The first "pencil and paper" was a stiff piece of reed and a soft piece of clay. The end of the reed was cut and used to make marks in the clay.

Cuneiform writing
Writing in Sumeria speeded up as curved lines gradually developed into wedges or triangles with short, straight sides. Later, signs were written from left to right, without any spaces between words.

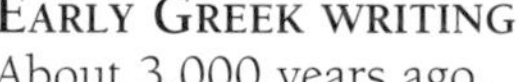

Early Greek writing
About 3,000 years ago, people on the island of Crete used three different kinds of writing. In the 1950s, British architect Michael Ventris discovered how to read the kind seen here, called Linear B. The other two remain a mystery.

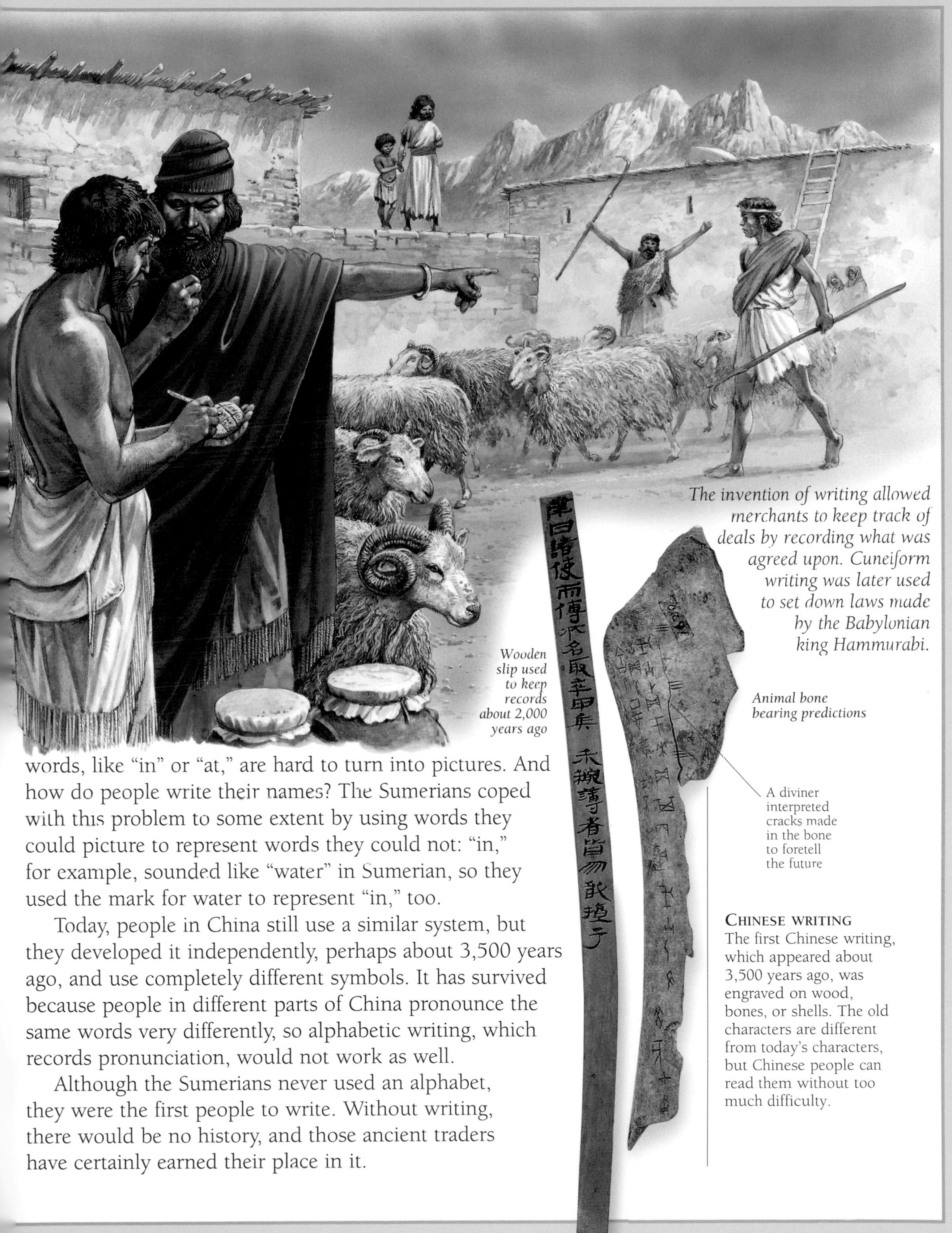

The invention of writing allowed merchants to keep track of deals by recording what was agreed upon. Cuneiform writing was later used to set down laws made by the Babylonian king Hammurabi.

Wooden slip used to keep records about 2,000 years ago

Animal bone bearing predictions

A diviner interpreted cracks made in the bone to foretell the future

words, like "in" or "at," are hard to turn into pictures. And how do people write their names? The Sumerians coped with this problem to some extent by using words they could picture to represent words they could not: "in," for example, sounded like "water" in Sumerian, so they used the mark for water to represent "in," too.

Today, people in China still use a similar system, but they developed it independently, perhaps about 3,500 years ago, and use completely different symbols. It has survived because people in different parts of China pronounce the same words very differently, so alphabetic writing, which records pronunciation, would not work as well.

Although the Sumerians never used an alphabet, they were the first people to write. Without writing, there would be no history, and those ancient traders have certainly earned their place in it.

Chinese writing
The first Chinese writing, which appeared about 3,500 years ago, was engraved on wood, bones, or shells. The old characters are different from today's characters, but Chinese people can read them without too much difficulty.

Ramp

c.3000 BCE

By about 3000 BCE, people were using the basic elements of machines: wheels, levers, and inclined planes, known as ramps. The inclined plane makes it easier to raise a heavy object by allowing it to be pushed or pulled gradually up a slope, instead of lifting it straight up. The 2-ton stone blocks of Egypt's Great Pyramid of Giza were put into place in about 2500 BCE by workers pulling them up ramps.

Lathe

c.3000 BCE

The lathe, perhaps 5,000 years old, allows its user to form a piece of material into a circular shape by spinning it against a cutting edge. The mechanism of the earliest lathes was like that of early drills (✱ *see* **page** 7). A cord was wrapped around the piece to be shaped and pulled back and forth by a bow to make it rotate. Marble vases turned on a lathe, dating from before 2000 BCE, have been found on some islands in the Aegean Sea.

Harp

c.3000 BCE

The harp is one of the oldest musical instruments. It first appeared in Sumeria and Egypt about 5,000 years ago. Early harps resembled bows used to fire arrows but had several strings stretched across instead of one. These were plucked to sound notes. Although the harp has developed over the centuries into something almost as complicated as a piano, it is still played in its simplest form in parts of Africa and Afghanistan.

Lever

c.3000 BCE

A simple lever is a rod or bar that turns over a pivot point called a fulcrum. It changes the force exerted on one end into a greater force, but with smaller movement, at the other end. People were using levers by 3000 BCE, and probably long before that. They may have discovered that a rock that was impossible to lift directly could be levered up with a tree branch resting on a smaller stone, which acted as the fulcrum. It wasn't until about 250 BCE that Archimedes came up with a full explanation of how levers worked.

Lyre

c.3000 BCE

The lyre is a musical instrument that is closely related to the harp. The strings are stretched between two arms attached to a box or bowl. People were playing lyres in Sumeria by 2800 BCE. The instrument remained a favorite with the ancient Greeks, who linked it to the god Apollo, a handsome and gifted musician. Unlike the harp, the lyre did not make it into the modern orchestra.

Decorated base strengthens the sound

Harp *A harpist of c.2500 BCE is shown here in a picture from Ur in Mesopotamia.*

Papyrus

c.3000 BCE

The ancient Egyptians used papyrus much like we use paper. They made it by squashing and drying a mat of reed fibers until they stuck together, then polishing them with a stone to form a smooth sheet. Papyrus was too stiff to fold, so the Egyptians joined the sheets together to make long scrolls. It was on these scrolls that they wrote and drew much of what we now know about ancient Egypt from about 2600 BCE onward.

Painting with wax

c.3000 BCE

The ancient Egyptians liked art. By about 3000 BCE, they had developed a new technique of painting on walls, using a mixture of pigments and melted beeswax. When the painting was complete, they heated it to make it melt into the surface of the wall. This method is called encaustic painting. The result was rich and colorful, and many of the paintings can still be seen today. The technique was revived by US artist Jasper Johns in the 1960s.

Stone buildings

c.3000 BCE

In 2600 BCE, the Egyptian pharaoh Djoser and his architect Imhotep created the step pyramid at Sakkara—the first pyramid to be made entirely of stone. It was designed to be Djoser's tomb and rose in six steps to a height of 200 ft (60 m). At that time, nearly all buildings were made of bricks or wood. Small stone buildings did exist, but Djoser's gigantic pile of square-cut stone blocks must have seemed truly

c.3000 BCE The Egyptians establish the first widely used unit of length, the cubit. It is the distance between the elbow and the end of the middle finger, usually about 18 in (450 mm) but sometimes longer.

c.3000 BCE Merchants in the state of Babylonia begin to use bottomry, a form of insurance. They take out a loan to equip a ship. The interest rate is steep, but if the ship sinks, they don't have to pay the money back.

amazing. The pyramids of Egypt are still some of the world's most impressive stone buildings. The tallest one is the Great Pyramid of Khufu at Giza. It is made from about two million huge blocks of limestone and stands 482 ft (147 m) high.

Venus

c.3000 BCE

Since Venus is close to the sun, it is never visible in the middle of the night, but it is often the brightest object in the evening or morning sky. So it is not surprising that it was one of the first heavenly bodies to be studied. It features in the ancient astronomical records of China, Egypt, Greece, and South America, and the Babylonians made records of its movements as early as 3000 BCE.

Dam

c.2900 BCE

Dams are among the largest constructions that ancient people built. Probably the earliest was a 49 ft (15 m) mound raised beside the Nile River in Egypt in about 2900 BCE. It was built to protect the city of Memphis from flooding. The remains of another dam almost as old can still be seen today at Wadi Gerrawi in Egypt. Instead of providing protection from floods, this one was built in 2500 BCE to catch the seasonal flood in a dry river bed feeding the Nile. It is 295 ft (90 m) thick.

Papyrus *Artists working on papyrus could include fine detail. In this ancient Egyptian illustration, the heart of a dead person is being weighed to see if he is worthy of eternal life.*

Clay tablet book

c.2800 BCE

The first books were not made of paper. Instead, their writers, working in Mesopotamia in about 2800 BCE, used rectangles of soft clay called tablets. One tablet could contain quite a lot of information, but not enough to be called a book. To write something longer, people did exactly what we do today. They used several tablets and numbered them to keep them in the right order.

c.2800 BCE People in northern Europe start to switch from mass burials in "houses for the dead" to graves that hold only one person. Not just anyone gets a grave to themselves. They are confined to high-ranking men.

c.2800 BCE Tree-lined walks and ponds with water birds appear in ancient Egypt as the first garden designers get started. Working for wealthy clients, they use a system of rectangular walled enclosures and include small pavilions.

ACUPUNCTURE *This set of eight acupuncture needles and their protective case are from 19th-century China.*

Needles made of steel

Protective case made of mahogany

Lost-wax casting

c.2800 BCE

Lost-wax casting is a way of making hollow objects. A lump of clay is covered with wax, which is then modeled and covered with plaster. When the mold is heated, the wax runs out, leaving a gap between the clay and plaster. Molten metal is poured into the gap and left to cool. This process is thought to have been invented by the Sumerians. The ancient Egyptians, who probably learned the technique from them, were using it by 2200 BCE, and it is still used today.

Tea

c.2700 BCE

Shen Nong

Tradition says that the Chinese emperor Shen Nong was boiling water beneath a camellia tree in about 2700 BCE when a leaf fell in, creating the first cup of tea. The new drink, however, was not mentioned in a book until about 800 CE, and it took another 800 years for tea to reach Europe. By 1657, the first "cuppa" had been sold in London, and tea became wildly fashionable.

Acupuncture

c.2700 BCE

Sticking needles into certain places in the body can relieve pain and may restore health. Acupuncture was developed in China before 2500 BCE and has changed little, except that stone needles have now been replaced by stainless steel. Acupuncture is based on the idea that the life force, or *chi*, of the body flows in certain channels, which can become blocked. Twirling a needle in the right place is thought to make the *chi* start flowing smoothly again.

Chair

c.2600 BCE

People were probably sitting on chairs well before 2600 BCE, but the first chairs we actually know about were found in the tombs of ancient Egyptian kings. Placed there for their owner's comfort in the afterlife, these chairs had soft, padded seats and legs carved in the shapes of animals. The Egyptians also used folding stools of a design that can still be bought today.

Leavened bread

c.2600 BCE

The first bread was rather hard to chew because it wasn't made lighter, or leavened, with yeast or other agents. The ancient Egyptians were the first people to produce leavened bread. They kept a stock of

Gilded bust of a woman on each side of the seat

The goddess Taweret flanked by two representations of the god Bes

Chair made of reddish wood, covered with silver and gold

Feet take the shape of a cat's paws

CHAIR *This ancient Egyptian chair is known as the chair of Sitamun, who was the daughter of the pharaoh Amenhotep III.*

Low, silver-covered supports may have been designed to lift up the elaborately carved legs, away from possible damage

c.2800 BCE Cannabis, or hemp, begins to be grown in China. It is valued for its oily seeds and as a source of fibers for cloth and ropes, rather than as a drug. Centuries pass before it is grown in the Western world.

c.2700 BCE Egyptian farmers dance to make the rains come and are recorded in paintings placed in tombs. Their dances are intended to bring the community not only rain but also health and plenty of children.

"sour dough," in which fermenting organisms were at work, and mixed in some of this whenever they made fresh dough. As the organisms from the sour dough multiplied, they produced bubbles of carbon dioxide gas, making the finished bread much lighter.

Silk

c.2600 BCE

Silk is still considered to be the most desirable of fabrics. It was first made in China about 46 centuries ago, and its origin was a closely guarded secret. The silkworm and the luxurious, fibrous covering of its cocoon are said to have been discovered by a 14-year-old girl named Xilingshi, who was the wife of the emperor Huang Di. Nearly 3,000 years passed before the secret was revealed, spreading to India, Japan, and eventually Europe.

Arch

c.2500 BCE

Without arches, the only way to hold up doorways and roofs is with straight beams. An arch can span a greater distance than a straight beam, allowing wall openings to be larger. The first arches, built in India and Mesopotamia in about 2500 BCE, were produced simply by building the top of the walls out toward each other until they met. By 100 BCE, Roman builders were using semicircular arches in almost all their buildings.

Carpet

c.2500 BCE

The ancient Egyptians were weaving carpets of a sort by about 2500 BCE, but nomadic tribes in eastern countries, such as Turkestan, soon became the greatest carpet makers. One carpet found preserved by the cold in Siberia had been buried with a nomad chieftain 2,500 years previously, showing that carpets were highly prized. Carpets have often been associated with magic and romance. In 48 BCE, the Egyptian queen Cleopatra introduced herself to the Roman emperor Julius Caesar by jumping out of a rolled-up carpet.

Glass

c.2500 BCE

Glass had humble beginnings. It was probably discovered by accident. Made by heating sand with limestone and wood ash, it first appeared in the form of small ornamental beads in about 2500 BCE. The basic formula may have been discovered in Mesopotamia, but it was the ancient Egyptians who began to develop it into the material we know today. By 1450 BCE, they were making glass bottles in molds, and over the next 1,000 years, their techniques spread to Europe and the East.

Ink

c.2500 BCE

The first ink came in the form of a solid block made from soot mixed with glue and had to be wetted before it could be used for writing. The ancient Egyptians wrote on papyrus with ink and a pen made from a reed, using a flowing style of writing called hieratic. In China, scribes wrote their characters with a brush. You can still buy blocks of Chinese ink exactly like those made 4,500 years ago.

Mirror *The reflecting surface of this ancient Roman mirror is polished silver. The handle is in the form of the club and lion skin of the ancient Greek mythical hero Hercules.*

Mirror

c.2500 BCE

Humans look at themselves in the mirror every day. This began four or five thousand years ago using discs of polished copper or bronze. A hand mirror was an essential fashion accessory in ancient Egypt, and the Romans gazed at themselves in mirrors made of silver. The first glass mirrors, requiring a reflective material on one side such as silver, were made by Venetian craftsmen in about 1300 CE.

c.2700 BCE A Chinese book of herbal medicine describes one of the first laxatives—rhubarb. It is taken as the powdered root of the plant. Rhubarb will not be cultivated for this purpose in the West until the 18th century CE.

c.2500 BCE A colossal pyramid is built in Egypt by the pharaoh Khufu. Future generations will know the Great Pyramid of Giza, near Cairo, as one of the most amazing structures in the history of architecture around the world.

Potato

c.2500 BCE

Farmers in Peru, South America, were cultivating potatoes in the high Andes mountains more than 4,000 years before Spanish invaders discovered the strange new vegetable and took it back to Europe. Potatoes ceased to be important in Peru but became a major crop elsewhere. By the middle of the 19th century, Ireland was so dependent on the potato that a series of crop failures led to famine.

Skis

c.2500 BCE

As people in the northern hemisphere spread north toward the Arctic, they had to learn to cope with deep snow. Skis started out as something more like snow shoes: short, wide, wooden frames covered in leather. In time, they became the longer, more rigid devices we know today. The oldest known skis, found in the bogs of Finland and Sweden, date from about 2500 BCE, and a Norwegian rock carving from about the same date clearly shows people using skis.

SKIS *There is plenty of snow in Scandinavia, so it was an obvious place for skis to develop. Both the Vikings and Lapps used them.*

Welding

c.2500 BCE

Welding is the process of joining metal parts together using pressure or heat, and sometimes using a filler metal for a stronger weld. Used today for making cars and ships, it was first used with jewelry. Queen Pu-abi of Sumeria was buried about 4,500 years ago with all her finery. This included some exquisite necklaces, the pieces of which, unlike earlier jewelry, were welded together. They are still in one piece today.

Parchment

c.2400 BCE

Parchment is a smooth, white leather on which people write. It is supposed to have been invented in 200 BCE, when King Ptolemy of Egypt banned exports of papyrus, forcing the ruler of a rival kingdom, Eumenes of Pergamum, to find a substitute. Although the word "parchment" is derived from "Pergamum," parchment books are known to have existed well before this alleged incident, and ancient Egyptians had been writing on something very similar since 2400 BCE.

Horse

c.2300 BCE

Horses, more wild and willful than sheep or pigs, took time to tame. The first people to get them under control lived in eastern Europe, around the area that is now called Ukraine. We don't know exactly when horses were domesticated, but by 2000 BCE they were being used in Babylonia. Three hundred years later, they were also being used in Syria and ancient Palestine. They arrived in Egypt when a tribe of nomads, the Hyksos, used horse-drawn chariots to capture the city of Memphis and eventually most of Egypt.

c.2500 BCE People in northern Peru build downward and live in stone-lined pits. They know nothing of pottery but weave baskets for containers. They also grow gourds (hollow fruits) and store things in these.

c.2400 BCE On the island of Malta, a complex "cult of the dead" develops. It starts with shared tombs cut into the rock near Xagra and Zurrieq and ends with an amazing underground burial chamber near Rahal Gdid.

Barrel vault

c.2000 BCE

Once builders had discovered how to make arches, they were soon using them to hold up the most crucial and awkward part of any building—the roof. By building a row of arches one behind the other, they created a strong, tunnel-shaped structure. Because of its shape, this is called a barrel vault. It was in use soon after the arch was invented and remained a favorite feature with builders until modern times.

Bathroom

c.2000 BCE

A bathroom was considered essential by some builders as long as 4,000 years ago. Even relatively humble houses excavated at Mohenjo-Daro in the Indus Valley (in what is now Pakistan), and dating from about 2000 BCE, had bathrooms with drains. Some even had toilets, of a sort, with seats to sit on. Further west, in about 1700 BCE, the wealthier Minoans of ancient Crete had more lavish bathrooms to which they could sneak off for a quiet soak.

Bell chime

c.2000 BCE

Clocks that chime use an idea that started in China before 2000 BCE. Bells or blocks of stone tuned to musical notes were hung from a frame. They were hit with hammers to add music to religious ceremonies or simply to play tunes. The idea spread to Japan, India, and the West, where monks were playing rows of bells by about 850 CE. Five hundred years later, the idea was adapted for public timekeeping, with the monks replaced by clockwork.

Chariot

c.2000 BCE

Four-wheeled battle wagons were in use in Mesopotamia by 3000 BCE. They developed from lumbering oxcarts, and although clumsy, they gave the Mesopotamian armies an advantage over their enemies. With the introduction of horses, and a switch to two wheels instead of four, the chariot, with its high-speed mobility, was born in about 2000 BCE. (✳ *See also* **Wheels of War.**)

WHEELS OF WAR

AS WITH many inventions, military commanders were pioneers in the development of wheeled transportation. Large vehicles were probably first used for royal funerals, but soldiers soon saw that wheels could deliver men and materials to the battle front more quickly than feet or pack animals. It was only later that chariots were used for fighting. Eventually, as soldiers became more skillful at riding horses, chariots went out of use.

Chariots were used for sports as well as war. Here, Assyrian king Ashurnasirpal II hunts lions.

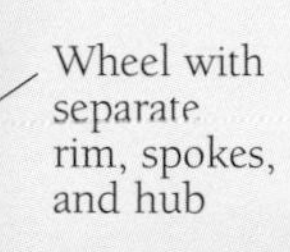

Wheel with separate rim, spokes, and hub

Pole for attaching horses

Fast, maneuverable Roman chariots were highly developed fighting and racing vehicles.

CHARIOTS AS TRANSPORTATION

The first chariots had heavy bodies made of wood and leather and four solid wooden wheels. The front axle pivoted for mobility and was attached to a long pole, to which two oxen were attached by a wooden yoke. The charioteer rode in a raised section at the front that pivoted with the axle.

THE FIGHTING CHARIOT

The introduction of horses and a lighter construction, including spoked wheels (✳ *see* **page 31**), made the chariot into a formidable fighting platform for one or two soldiers. It had only two wheels, allowing it to take sharp turns but could be pulled by as many as four horses. These lightweight chariots helped win many battles.

c.2300 BCE The Sumerian Empire, weakened by internal strife, is taken over by an invader, Sargon I. He founds a new city, Agade. It becomes the wealthiest in the world, and the Sumerians become the Akkadians.

c.2250 BCE In the ancient Mesopotamian city of Ur, the world's first recorded author and poet, Enheduanna, writes hymns and poetry. She is also a high priestess, an extremely important political role.

Iron

c.2000 BCE

When iron was first discovered in southeast Asia, about 4,000 years ago, it was considered more valuable than gold. As ways of extracting it and working it improved, people were able to make better use of its strength and flexibility. By about 1200 BCE, the Iron Age had begun, pushing humanity faster than ever toward the modern world. Because iron is hard to melt, early users had to invent new techniques, such as shaping it by hammering rather than casting.

Paved road

c.2000 BCE

The first road known to have been surfaced and drained so that it was usable in all weather was built by the Minoans on the Mediterranean island of Crete in about 2000 BCE. It was paved with stone and made higher in the center so that water would drain to the edges, which had gutters in some places. One feature of this road seems odd today: the pedestrian walkway was in the middle, not at the sides.

Dice

c.2000 BCE

It is thought that the ancient Egyptians were the first people to play with dice like the ones we use now. Before dice were given their spots in about 2000 BCE, they existed in many other forms. People originally threw dice to try to predict the future, using objects such as bones or teeth. Perhaps it was inevitable that prediction soon led to gambling. Today, people still place bets on the roll of dice.

Lock

c.2000 BCE

Most locks today are based on an idea from about 2000 BCE. The ancient Egyptians invented a wooden lock in which a bolt was held by pins that dropped into holes in it. Only a key shaped to push all the pins out of the way would free the bolt. Modern Yale locks and keys work in much the same way (✻ *see* **page 144**).

Saw

c.2000 BCE

Unlike an ax or knife, a saw can cut cleanly through any thickness of

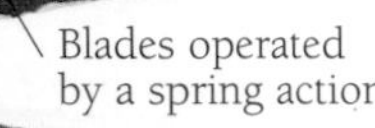

IRON *Suitably treated iron is springy and takes a sharp edge—ideal for making shears like these from ancient Rome.*

Square sail

Mast and sail on the model were missing upon discovery but were replaced by replicas based on other ships of the same time

Sailor at the bow with a plumb line to test the depth of the water

Men pull the rope to adjust the position of the sail

SHIP *Ancient Egyptian ships, like this model found in a tomb of c.2000 BCE, needed paddles to help the sails propel the craft through the water. It was a common custom to place models of boats in the tombs of kings and nobles, for their transportation in the afterlife.*

c.2000 BCE People of the Celtic race build "beehive" houses in Scotland and Ireland. The houses, constructed from rough stone blocks, are circular in shape and rise to a point in the center like a straw beehive.

c.2000 BCE The world's first written language, Sumerian, ceases to be spoken because the Sumerians, now the Akkadians, switch to the language of their conquerors. Sumerian will live on in written form for 2,000 years.

wood. Its angled teeth cut in easy stages and create a gap wide enough for the blade to pass right through. The invention of the saw was made possible by the discovery of copper and, by 1500 BCE, the ancient Egyptians were sawing planks. Western saws cut on the push stroke, but to stop them from buckling, early saws worked the other way around.

Sexagesimal number system

c.2000 BCE

Our 60-minute hour and 60-second minute come from a system devised about 4,000 years ago by the Babylonians. It was the first to use a basic feature of the decimal system we use today—the value of each digit depended on where it was placed. The Babylonians based their system on 60 instead of 10, so a 1 in the first position meant 1, but in the second position it meant 1 × 60, or 60, and in the third position it meant 1 × 60 × 60, or 3,600.

Male and female plants

c.2000 BCE

The Babylonians were expert farmers and gardeners. They found out early on that some kinds of plants can, like people, be either male or female. The female plant produces fruit but only when fertilized by pollen from a male plant. Illustrations on Babylonian seals show fertilization being done artificially, and by 1800 BCE, people were buying and selling male date-palm flowers for this purpose.

Sling *The young Israelite David challenges the Philistine giant Goliath with his trusty sling.*

Support for steering oar

Passengers seated at the stern

Large oar used for steering

The Egyptians used planks of cedar wood for the best real ships

Ship

c.2000 BCE

It is hard to say when a boat becomes a ship, but a ship needs to be large enough to cross open water safely. The ancient Egyptians built the first ships well suited to the sea about 4,000 years ago. They had already discovered how to arrange their sails to cope with winds coming from the side. To deal with winds coming from in front of them, they kept paddles on board, too.

Tongs

c.2000 BCE

Tongs were probably first made for handling hot metal. They could have appeared at any time after people started melting metals, from about 3000 BCE onward. The earliest evidence is an ancient Egyptian wall painting from about 1450 BCE. It shows a metalworker blowing through a tube to make a fire hot while he holds an object over it with an unmistakable pair of tongs.

Sling

c.2000 BCE

A sling is a weapon made from a piece of leather with two cords attached. Its user puts a stone onto the leather, whirls the sling around with the cords, then releases one cord to launch the stone. It was with a sling that David famously killed Goliath in the Old Testament Bible story. The Old Testament was written in about 1000 BCE, so the sling must date back to before then. It was used by the ancient Egyptian army in about 750 BCE and can still be seen today.

Spoked wheel

c.2000 BCE

The first wheels were solid and heavy, but it didn't take vehicle builders long to figure out that the important parts were the rim and the hub. They made the rest of the wheel lighter by cutting holes in it, forming crude spokes. Stronger spokes, usually four, made from separate pieces of wood, were being used in Mesopotamia by 2000 BCE, but it was another 1,000 years before this type of wheel reached northern Europe.

c.2000 BCE The Aleutian Islands, off the coast of Alaska, are colonized by people from the mainland. They build villages on the seashore near fresh water, travel in skin boats, and hunt seals and bears.

c.2000 BCE An event similar to throwing the hammer starts at the Tailteann Games in Ireland, but with a chariot wheel, not a hammer. Celtic hero Chulainn grabs the wheel by the axle and hurls it as far as he can.

Corset

c.1900 BCE

People have never been satisfied with the shape of their bodies. Four thousand years ago, Minoan women living on the island of Crete in the Mediterranean Sea were wearing corsets to pinch in their waists. And it may not just have been the women who wanted to accentuate their curves: wall paintings from about 1500 BCE, excavated at the palace of King Minos, also show Minoan men looking suspiciously wasp-waisted.

Running water

c.1700 BCE

The ancient bathrooms of Mohenjo-Daro in the Indus valley had everything but running water. This wasn't good enough for wealthy Minoans on Crete. They wanted their water on tap, and excavations show that they got it. Pipes and drains ran throughout the great palace of King Minos at Knossos, making bath time more of a pleasure than a chore.

Child's swing

c.1600 BCE

Nobody really knows when the swing was invented or, more probably, developed from a dangling creeper. But a swing was found in excavations of Minoan Crete dating back to 1600 BCE. The swing is just one of the ancient amusements, like jacks (fivestones) or blindman's buff, that have kept children happy for countless generations.

Brass

c.1500 BCE

Brass is an alloy, or mixture, of copper and zinc. Its strength, bright color, and resistance to corrosion make it a good material for many objects. Its early history is difficult to trace because it was often confused with bronze. As late as the 18th century, many people used brass that was made by a method dating back to its discovery. In this process, copper and zinc ore were heated together, producing brass. Because the zinc ore that they used was called calamine, the product was known as calamine brass.

Flag

c.1500 BCE

We don't treat flags with such great respect today, but when they were invented in China, they had life-and-death significance and played a vital part in battles. If a leader's flag was captured by the enemy, it was all over. Strangely enough, the first important flag we know about, which belonged to the first ruler of the Zhou Dynasty in about 1100 BCE, was white—a color that people in the West now associate with surrender and defeat.

Gloves

c.1500 BCE

Although the weather does sometimes get cold in Egypt, the fine linen gloves found in the tomb of the boy king Tutankhamun were probably more ceremonial than practical. They show, however, that even in this generally hot country, some people were wearing gloves by 1350 BCE. People in colder places must have worn them, too, but we do not have any evidence of this before about 700 CE.

Secret writing

c.1500 BCE

As soon as people began to write, they started to worry that the wrong people would read what they had written. Secret writing, or encryption, has a long history. The first known example is in ancient Egyptian hieroglyphs of about 1500 BCE. It may have been

c.1900 BCE Interior decorators are hard at work for wealthy people in Egypt. They paint patterns on plaster, hang textured matting screens, add red, white, and black striped dados, and install painted wooden ceilings.

c.1750 BCE The best-known ruler of the 1st dynasty of Babylon, Hammurabi, records his laws on tablets. The "Code of Hammurabi" is probably the first promulgation of laws in human history.

CORSET *Elegant women appear to be wearing corsets in this wall painting of about 1800 BCE. The painting is in the Minoan palace at Knossos on the island of Crete.*

Trumpet

c.1500 BCE

A trumpet is any kind of tube that you sound by squeezing air into it through your lips. The Australian didgeridoo is technically a trumpet, as is the shofar, made from a ram's horn, which is still used in Jewish rituals. The earliest existing silver trumpet dates from about 1500 BCE and comes from ancient Egypt. It was probably used for ritual purposes. The Romans developed trumpets for use in battle, but it was another 1,000 years before the trumpet really began to develop into the musical instrument that is played today.

Armor

c.1100 BCE

Body armor was worn in battle until the 17th century, when improved weapons made it useless. It developed little by little—helmets, belts, reinforced shirts—over thousands of years. In about 1100 BCE, Chinese soldiers were wearing armor made from layers of rhinoceros hide. By 800 BCE, Greek warriors were wearing substantial bronze helmets, metal shin guards, and bronze items called cuirasses, which totally covered their chest.

TRUMPET *The Australian didgeridoo, made from a eucalyptus branch, produces a deep droning sound. It is usually about 5 ft (1.5 m) long.*

intended to amuse rather than conceal. But some writers of books in the Old Testament in the Bible did try to hide the meaning of their text by reversing the entire alphabet.

Shoes

c.1500 BCE

The earliest shoes were sandals, but by about 1500 BCE, in Mesopotamia, people were wearing shoes that completely enclosed their feet. They were similar to what we would now call moccasins—single pieces of soft leather drawn up around the ankles with a rawhide thong. At about the same time, the Minoans of Crete were stepping into calf-length boots for winter wear.

Clepsydra

c.1500 BCE

The Egyptians usually told the time from the sun but were also using a clock called a clepsydra by about 1500 BCE. The basic model was just a pot of water with a hole near the bottom and marks down the side. As the water ran out, its level showed the time. The flow slowed as the pot emptied, so the marks had to be closer together near the bottom, making them hard to read. An improved model, invented in about 270 BCE, worked the other way around: water ran into the pot, moving a pointer to show the time.

CLEPSYDRA *This is a cast of a clepsydra found at the ancient Egyptian temple at Karnak. The clepsydra dates from 1415–1380 BCE.*

c.1600 BCE A scribe in Egypt prepares a new edition of a 1,500-year-old medical manual. The papyrus scroll gives instructions for examining patients with a range of conditions and details the treatment for each case.

c.1400 BCE Greek people begin to write their language, using a script quite unlike the alphabet they will develop later. In 3,350 years' time, a cryptographer will decipher it, and it will be called Linear B.

ICE SKATES *This skate is made from a leg bone of a horse. Dating from about 1200 CE, it was inexpensive and did not rust.*

Oars

c.1100 BCE

Oars of various kinds are as old as boats but were probably perfected by the Phoenicians, seafarers who came from an area that is now mainly Lebanon. By 1100 BCE, they were the greatest traders in the eastern Mediterranean, and by 700 BCE, they had developed the bireme, a ship with an extra deck to allow for twice as many oars. Later, the Greeks developed this into the formidable trireme, a fighting ship with oars on three levels.

Camel

c.1000 BCE

The ancient Egyptians knew about camels as early as 3000 BCE, but they do not seem to have used them to carry anything. The idea of loading this unfriendly but almost desert-proof beast with up to 1,100 lb of goods came from Mesopotamia about 2,000 years later. The people here also bred the camel into a lighter, faster animal for riding.

Ice skates

c.1000 BCE

You would expect ice skates to come from somewhere with plenty of ice, and it does seem likely that skating began in Scandinavia about 3,000 years ago. Metals were a luxury there, so the first ice skates were made from bones of animals such as reindeer and horses. Developed as a practical necessity, skating eventually became a sport, with the canals of the Netherlands providing ideal ice rinks from medieval times.

Knitting

c.1000 BCE

A disadvantage of woven fabrics is that people need a loom to make them. Although early looms were portable, clothes that could be made using nothing but a pair of needles had obvious appeal to nomadic people. So it is likely that knitting originated among the nomads of the deserts of north Africa in about 1000 BCE. It seems to have reached Europe by way of Egypt, where archaeologists have found knitted items dating from about 450 BCE.

Magnet

c.1000 BCE

Some time before 800 BCE, the Greeks discovered a curious black rock in the plains of northern Greece. Thales of Miletus may later have written about the rock's strange attraction to iron, but the Greeks do not seem to have discovered its ability to indicate north/south. Chinese explorers discovered this some 300 years later (✱ *see* **page 37**). The place where it was first found, Magnesia, gave its name to the mineral (magnetite) and to anything with the same property (a magnet).

OARS *This is a model of a Phoenician bireme of c.700 BCE.*

c.1100 BCE The circle of stones now known as Stonehenge is still in use. It gets a face-lift in the shape of a much longer entrance avenue, stretching 1.7 miles (2.8 km) east and then southeast to the Avon River.

c.1000 BCE A new Hindu calendar is adopted in India. Its year is 12 Moon months. An actual year is longer than this, so one extra month is added in every 30. The calendar will still be in use 3,000 years later.

Iron-tipped plowshare

c.900 BCE

The part of a plow that lifts and turns the soil, the plowshare, wore away quickly when it was made of wood or bronze. Iron is harder than bronze but was an expensive material in ancient times. The answer was to continue to use a wooden plowshare but use iron to protect the tip. Plows of this type were probably being used in ancient Palestine by 900 BCE.

Alphabet

c.900 BCE

An alphabet contains symbols for individual speech sounds. Early writers did not use an alphabet; their symbols stood for whole words or, later, syllables. An alphabet with symbols for consonants appeared in Syria or ancient Palestine in about 1600 BCE. By about 900 BCE, the Greeks had adapted this to their own language by adding vowels. This was the first alphabet that recorded speech accurately, and it became the ancestor of several others, including the alphabet used for English.

Socks

c.800 BCE

Once they started wearing shoes, people must have felt the need for socks. We don't know when they first started wearing them, but the earliest mention of socks was in a poem by the Greek poet Hesiod, who was working in about 700 BCE. These early socks were probably made of felt rather than knitted, so they wouldn't have been very comfortable.

Oil lamp

c.700 BCE

People have been making artificial light by burning oil sucked up by plant fibers for at least 30,000 years. But true oil lamps, with a reservoir that could be refilled and a fibrous wick that gave a controlled flame without burning away itself, came much later. Simple lamps, with a spike or channel to hold a wick, existed in ancient China and Egypt, but the first really practical lamps—they even had handles—appeared in ancient Greece in about 700 BCE. They usually ran on olive or nut oil. None of these early lamps gave out enough light for detailed work after dark. (✱ *See also* **New Lamps for Old.**)

NEW LAMPS FOR OLD

TO MAKE a successful lamp, three things have to be just right: the fuel, the fuel reservoir, and the wick. Oil burns with less smoke than fat. The reservoir should be easy to fill and convenient to carry. The wick is needed to spread the oil into a thin film so that it will vaporize and burn. A good wick will feed the flame without burning away rapidly itself.

This ornate bronze oil lamp was used by rich people in the late 900s CE in the Afghan empire of central Asia.

THE FIRST LAMPS
The first cave painters may have worked by the light of burning branches. It is possible that while they were cooking they noticed that a branch burned for longer if it was soaked in fat. From there, it would have been a short step to the first lamp—a container of moss or twigs dipped in fat or oil. Moss or twigs spread the oil, but they tended to burn away.

LATER OIL LAMPS
Improving on the fat-soaked bunch of twigs, called a lampas, the ancient Greeks developed oil lamps shaped like a teapot with a fibrous wick in the spout. No great improvements were made until 1784 when Swiss inventor Aimé Argand produced a lamp with a cylindrical wick and a glass chimney.

c.1000 BCE A big, white, shaggy breed of dog known as the great Pyrenees or Pyrenean mountain dog reaches Europe from Asia. It is used to guard sheep from wolves and bears, which are common in the region.

800 BCE The population of China reaches 14 million as the country continues to grow. Over the next 800 years, it will increase more than fourfold to 60 million, and after a further 2,000 years, it will be about one billion.

Shadow clock

c.700 BCE

People knew at least 3,500 years ago that the shadow cast by a vertical pole could be used to indicate the time. By 700 BCE, at the latest, the ancient Egyptians had developed the shadow clock. It had a straight scale of hours, probably with a raised part at one end to cast a shadow on the scale, and it had to be turned to point the opposite way after half a day. Astronomers, including Berosus from Babylonia, made curved sundials several hundred years later.

Archimedean screw

c.600 BCE

The Archimedean screw is a kind of pump that is still used today for irrigating the land (✱ *see* **page 16**). A cylinder with a large screw inside has its bottom end dipping into water. As the screw is turned, it pushes water up the cylinder in the same way that a wood screw is pulled into wood. Archimedes did not invent the screw himself, but he wrote about it, probably after seeing one being used in Egypt in about 260 BCE. The date of the screw's actual invention is uncertain.

Rotary quern

c.600 BCE

After 3,000 years in which generations of people laboriously ground corn by hand between two stones, an improvement, known as the rotary quern, was developed. It had a heavy, circular top stone that fit snugly into a hole in a stone base. Grain was fed through a hole in the center of the top stone, which was turned around and around with a wooden handle. The two stones crushed the grain between them,

Cobalt blue

c.650 BCE

The deep blue color known as cobalt blue, still widely used on pottery, seems to have been discovered by the Assyrians in about 650 BCE. The use of minerals containing cobalt to give a blue color is part of one of their glass recipes. They knew nothing, of course, about the chemical element cobalt, which was not discovered until 1742. Although cobalt blue is used to decorate Chinese porcelain today, Chinese potters did not begin to use it until 800 CE at the earliest.

c.700 BCE People in Assyria (now mainly northern Iraq) hunt with hawks and falcons. All kinds of hunting are popular with royalty. The Assyrian king Ashurbanipal has himself portrayed in stone with the words, "I killed the lion."

c.650 BCE After a humiliating defeat by Argos, Sparta's new ruler, Lycurgus, rebuilds the city focusing solely on warfare. Over the next century, Sparta's warriors will conquer surrounding territory and most of southwest Greece.

grinding it into flour. The flour came out of the narrow gap around the edge of the top stone. This useful device was probably invented before 500 BCE, but nobody really knows where.

Metal coins

c.600 BCE

Before about 600 BCE, people often exchanged pieces of precious metal in return for goods. It was easy to cheat by handing over impure metal or too small a quantity, so traders wasted time checking the quality and weight of all the different pieces. The Lydians, from what is now western Turkey, had an idea. They standardized the quality and weight of the pieces and stamped them with the king's mark as proof of their value. They had invented coins.

Store

c.600 BCE

According to the Greek historian Herodotus, who lived in about 450 BCE, the people who invented coins also invented stores. The Lydians certainly had a talent for making money. Their capital city, Sardis, was known for its magnificence, and one of their kings gave his name to the expression "rich as Croesus," which means very rich indeed.

Attraction of objects to amber

c.600 BCE

Thales of Miletus

The history of electricity starts with a yellow fossil resin called amber. In about 600 BCE, the Greek philosopher Thales observed that amber rubbed on cloth attracted small, light objects. What he saw was the result of static electricity, but it was more than 2,000 years before an English doctor, William Gilbert, investigated this thoroughly (✳ *see* **page 85**). He coined the term "electric," for the attracting effect, from the Greek word "elektron" meaning "amber."

MAGNETIC COMPASS *This Chinese sundial includes a built-in compass.*

Magnetic compass

c.500 BCE

When and where the compass was invented depends on what is meant by compass. The properties of the magnetic rock called lodestone (or magnetite) were used hundreds of years before a magnetized needle was pivoted in a case to make a compass. The earliest records are from China in about 500 BCE, where pieces of lodestone were used to guide mineral prospectors. The first real compass did not appear until 1100 CE or later.

WRITING BRUSH *Used in 19th-century Japan, this writing brush is made of hair set in a bamboo shaft.*

Fixing post holds the screw in place

ARCHIMEDEAN SCREW *The cylinder is cut away in this model of an Archimedean screw to show how the screw lifts water as it turns.*

Musical ratios

c.520 BCE

Pythagoras

See **pages 38–39** for the story of how Pythagoras and his followers discovered the harmony of the universe.

Pythagoras's theorem

c.520 BCE

Pythagoras

Pythagoras's theorem states that in a right-angled triangle, the square of the longest side is equal to the sum of the squares of the other two sides. Pythagoras may not have thought of it himself—it could have been any member of the group he founded in Italy in about 530 BCE (✳ *see* **pages 38–39**). But no matter who invented it, the theorem often crops up in the mathematics of the modern world, and we couldn't get by without it.

Writing brush

c.500 BCE

Before the invention of the writing brush, in about 500 BCE, people in China wrote on bamboo with a stiff stylus. The writing brush, with its pencil-sized bamboo shaft and pointed tip, could be used on silk. A brush is well suited to the complexities of Chinese script. It came into its own two or three hundred years later, when it was used for ***li-shu***, the first writing to make full use of the elegant brush strokes we now associate with Chinese calligraphy (✳ *see* **page 50**).

c.600 BCE Seafarers from Phoenicia (now Lebanon) regularly make the 3,750 mile (6,000 km) journey to Britain to collect tin from Cornwall. To do so, they have to figure out ways to navigate the open ocean.

c.500 BCE The last Irish elk, a type of deer similar to a moose, dies out. With it go the largest antlers ever known. The Irish elk's antlers measured up to 13 ft (4 m) across and had sharp points all around the edge.

THE MUSIC OF NUMBERS

Pythagoras and his followers search for the harmony of the universe

ANCIENT JOURNEY
Pythagoras was born on the island of Samos in the Aegean Sea. In about 530 BCE, he sailed westward to Crotona, in the south of what is now Italy.

Two and a half thousand years ago, a small town in Italy was home to an extraordinary group of thinkers. They discovered facts about music and mathematics that we still use today, but more important, they came to believe that the world around us is based on mathematical rules

The Greek philosopher Pythagoras was about 50 years old when he crossed the Ionian Sea to settle in Crotona (now Crotone) and gather his students around him. Bound by vows of loyalty and secrecy, the Pythagoreans held beliefs that amounted to a mathematical religion—but they also believed in some things, like reincarnation, that had nothing to do with mathematics.

Pythagoras is best known for the theorem that bears his name, but this was just one of many relationships that his group found between numbers. The Pythagoreans were fascinated by the fact that 1 + 2 + 3 + 4 = 10, and that these numbers can be arranged into a triangle, which they called the *tetraktys*. Their belief that the whole universe was based on a mystic order, or *kosmos*, was strengthened when they discovered what appeared to be a link between the *tetraktys* and music.

Starting with a musical string that had a length of one unit, they found that dividing it into two, three, or four parts produced new notes that all harmonized perfectly with each other. This doesn't explain how complex music works, but for the simple instruments that the Pythagoreans used, it worked. This discovery not only laid the foundations of the science of music but also encouraged the Pythagoreans' belief that mathematics was the key to understanding the universe.

FAULTY SCIENCE
The study of music was often confused by dependence on Pythagoras's rules. This 1490 woodcut is meant to show his principles, but it wouldn't have worked! He experimented only with strings and never thought about music made with more than one instrument.

SECRETIVE PHILOSOPHER
This bust portrays Pythagoras as a great mathematician and philosopher, but neither he nor most of his followers published their work.

The Pythagoreans were among the first thinkers to contemplate an Earth not at the center of everything. They speculated that the planets revolved around a "central fire"—although they probably didn't think of Earth as one of the planets. Some of Pythagoras's followers speculated on a mystical "music of the spheres" created by movements of mathematically spaced planets. But this beautiful theory was based on speculation, not facts.

We have moved on since Pythagoras's time. We have learned that mathematics is a powerful tool to describe how the world works but that simple explanations not based on facts often lead us into mistakes. Pythagoras assumed that there was a mathematical order in the universe—a single "theory" that could explain everything. While scientists have made progress in exploring and describing the physical universe, such a philosophical understanding has not yet been reached.

The debater
This detail from a frieze at the University of Athens probably shows an accurate view of how the Pythagoreans tested their theories, basing them on belief and argument, not experiment. Their mathematics was limited to what we now call geometry.

The tetraktys *was a triangle figure made of 10 dots. It included the numbers 4, 3, 2, and 1, like their theory of music. The Pythagoreans tried to describe everything in the world with just a few ideas.*

The mathematician
We don't know what Pythagoras looked like, but many artists through the ages have used their imagination to portray him as a man fascinated by his mystic symbols and books.

THE AGE OF AUTHORITY

MANY NEW DISCOVERIES and inventions were made between 500 BCE and 1400 CE, a period that also saw the flowering of ancient Greece and Rome and of the world's great religions. But most people's thoughts remained bound by tradition, by accepted belief, and by the authority of those in power.

Iron in building *This is the Temple of Concord, one of about 20 temples in Agrigento dating from the 5th and 6th centuries* BCE.

Sturdy column with a flat top, or capital, known as the Doric style

Ancient Greek buildings may have been inspired by earlier buildings whose roofs were supported by tree trunks

Iron in building

c.470 BCE

The Victorians are usually thought of as being the first people to use iron as a structural material. But 2,300 years before Queen Victoria, ancient Greek builders in Agrigentum (now Agrigento, Sicily) installed a huge iron beam 16 ft (5 m) long in one of the city's many temples. The ancient Greeks were also using other, smaller beams and all kinds of iron fixtures to hold their blocks of stone together.

Theater scenery

458 BCE

Aeschylus

The word "scenery" comes from the dressing room, or "skene," once used by actors in ancient Greece. It was in a building at the back of the stage, and, by the time of the playwright Aeschylus, it was also being used to support colored panels, which formed a background for the actors. For the first performance of his trilogy of plays the *Oresteia*, Aeschylus created an even better background. He had the plain panels painted with colorful pictures to create what we now call scenery.

Central heating *The Greeks may have circulated hot air around these pillars in the ruined city of Phaselis to heat the room above.*

Cause of solar eclipses

c.450 BCE

Anaxagoras

Even the sophisticated people of Athens regarded eclipses of the sun with fear, until the Greek philosopher Anaxagoras explained them. Anaxagoras came to Athens from what is now Turkey. He said that a solar eclipse was just the moon getting in the way of the sun. This was true, but he also thought that the sun was a white-hot rock less than half the size of Greece.

Central heating

c.450 BCE

Most people think the Romans were the first builders of central heating systems, but the Greeks may have built them first. The Romans called their under-floor hot air system a hypocaust, and "hypocaust" is actually a Greek word meaning "burning below." The ruined Greek city of Phaselis, now in Turkey, has buildings with hollow floors, just like a Roman hypocaust. This suggests that the Greeks were using central heating as early as 450 BCE.

Earth, air, fire, and water

c.450 BCE

Empedocles

Ancient Greek philosophers spent centuries wondering what the universe was made of. By about 350 BCE, most of them had accepted a theory put forward by the statesman and poet Empedocles about 100 years earlier. He said that everything was made of earth, air, fire, and water mixed in various proportions. His theory may seem funny to us, but it was the first one that suggested the existence of chemical elements, and it eventually led to modern chemistry.

490 BCE The first ever marathon is run in Greece when a soldier staggers 26 miles (42 km) from Marathon to Athens to bring news of a victory over the Persians. A race of this distance will become a sporting event 2,386 years later.

450 BCE Responding to popular demand, the Romans move toward more open government by writing down and publishing their laws. Before this, the laws were known only to a select few, so justice was rarely carried out.

Signs of the zodiac

c.450 BCE

It was probably the Babylonians who devised the signs of the zodiac. These represent the 12 groupings of stars through which the sun seems to travel during the year. A cuneiform tablet dated 419 BCE carries a horoscope using the signs. It was the ancient Greeks, however, who named the band of sky that contains the Ram, the Bull, and the other constellations. They called it *"zodiakos kyklos,"* or "circle of animals."

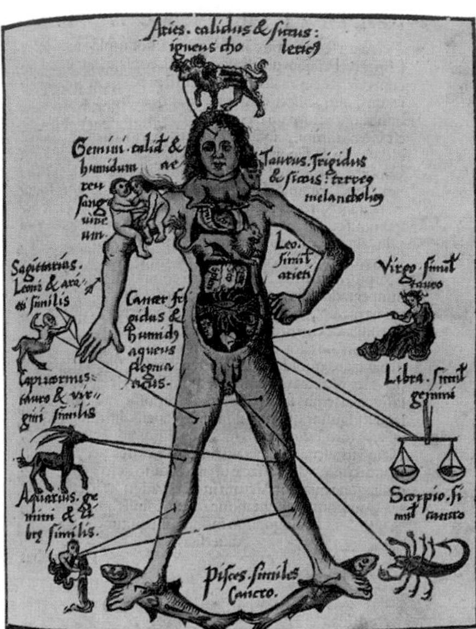

SIGNS OF THE ZODIAC
This 16th-century woodcut gives one of many theories that developed linking the zodiac with the body.

Flying actor

c.450 BCE

Sophocles

When an ancient Greek playwright got into an impossible tangle with a plot, the usual way out was to have a god descend from heaven and fix the mess. The god was played by an actor hoisted into the air with a crane. The same device, called a mechane, was also useful for comic effects: a character in one play by Aristophanes flies up to heaven on a dung beetle.

Planned city

c.450 BCE

Hippodamus of Miletus

Many ancient cities have some kind of regular grid plan, but Hippodamus of Miletus was the first real town planner. He was a colorful and influential character who believed that buildings should be grouped according to their function. He put his thoughts into practice when he became involved in the rebuilding of the Greek port of Piraeus and the construction of a new Greek settlement in southern Italy.

Knitted socks

c.450 BCE

After enduring scratchy felt socks for centuries, feet finally got some loving care in the shape of knitted socks. Knitting is ideal for making snugly shaped garments like gloves and socks and allows them to be made in one piece instead of being stitched together from separate pieces of cloth. Some wealthy ancient Egyptians were buried in their knitted socks in about 450 BCE, and 800 years later, people in Saudi Arabia wore knitted socks with their sandals.

Mule

c.450 BCE

Horses are not well suited to hot, dry climates. Donkeys are better suited but are often too small and slow. We don't know who came up with the idea of crossing a horse with a donkey to get the best of both, or whether it occurred naturally, but it probably happened in or around Turkey. The result was the tough, strong mule, an animal that was first recorded by the ancient Greek historian Herodotus in about 450 BCE.

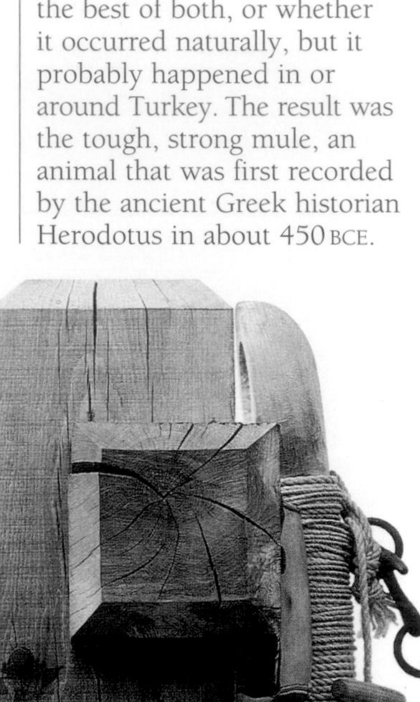

c.450 BCE Chinese military expert Sunzi writes the first book on spying. It shows how to organize intelligence and counterintelligence systems with secret agents, including double agents who spy for both sides.

443 BCE Censorship begins in Rome with the appointment of the first censor. At first, his job is just to count people, but it soon gets extended to looking after public morality and suppressing unwanted publications.

University

c.450 BCE

If we take a university to be any center of learning, then the world's first university was probably Nalanda in the north of India's Bihar state. This Buddhist monastic institution may have been in existence while Gautama the Buddha, founder of the Buddhist religion, was still alive. It survived until after 1100, when invaders from Turkey destroyed it.

Coded correspondence

c.410 BCE

The first secret messages were exchanged by the Spartan army chiefs of ancient Greece, using a tapered rod called a scytale. They wound a strip of leather around the rod, then wrote on the leather. When unwrapped, the strip displayed a meaningless jumble, but when wrapped around an identical scytale, it revealed what had been written. It was thanks to a scytale message that Lysander of Sparta avoided defeat by the Persians in 404 BCE.

Catapult

c.400 BCE

Long before gunpowder was invented, huge wooden catapults were used to hurl missiles, such as iron-tipped darts or boulders. The first examples may have been used in 399 BCE in the war between Rome and the ancient empire of Carthage in north Africa. A pair of arms were swung back to hold the missile, twisting and tightening cords made of animal sinews. When the tension in the cords was released, the arms sprang forward, launching the missile up to 1,640 ft (500 m) away, but not very accurately.

Crossbow

c.400 BCE

A soldier could shoot an arrow farther with a crossbow than with an ordinary bow. The first crossbow was the gastrophetes—a stiff bow of ancient Greece. The "gastro" part of its name means "stomach," because the soldier had to rest one end of the bow in the pit of his stomach. He rested the other end on the ground and bent the bow into the firing position, ready to be released by a trigger. It was a deadly weapon, as long as there was time to load it.

CROSSBOW *By the 15th century, the crossbow had developed into a long-range weapon that was aimed like a rifle.*

Improved Babylonian calendar

c.380 BCE

The early Babylonian calendar started a new month with every new moon (✱ *see* **page 21**). To keep it in step with the seasons, extra months had to be added now and then. Confusingly, different cities added months at different times. Some might even add two months in the same year. In 541 BCE, everyone was ordered to add months at the same times, but it was not until about 380 BCE that astronomers worked out a cycle of extra months that really kept the calendar on track. Then, for a while, the Babylonian calendar became the best in the world.

CATAPULT *The catapult was still used as a weapon in the Middle Ages. It was useful if there was time to get it into place and the target was easy to hit.*

c.430 BCE A giant statue of the Greek god Zeus is completed by Phidias. Nearly 40 ft (12 m) high, it shows Zeus on a throne encrusted with gold and precious stones. It becomes one of the Seven Wonders of the World.

390 BCE The Gauls, a Celtic race living in what is now northern Italy and France, sweep down the valley of the Po River and overwhelm Rome. The city is ransacked, but after a payoff of gold, the invaders depart.

Pen tip

c.380 BCE

Scribes in ancient Egypt wrote on papyrus (✳ *see* **page 24**) with a pen made from a reed. This had a soft point, rather like a modern felt-tip. The first pens with a hard tip, split at the end to channel the ink, came from ancient Greece. They were still made from reeds, but scribes could produce finer writing with them. With the introduction of parchment (✳ *see* **page 28**), which was smoother than papyrus, most writers eventually switched to using the more flexible quill pens, which were made from long feathers.

Reed cut and split at the end to hold the ink

PEN TIP *Early Greek documents were written with pens made from stiff reeds. Scribes often kept their pens in a wooden case. This one has a space for ink at one end.*

Automaton

c.370 BCE

Archytas of Tarentum

An automaton is a machine that imitates the actions of a living creature. The earliest known was a pigeon built in about 370 BCE by the Greek philosopher Archytas of Tarentum. It "flew" around on an arm driven by steam or air. Influenced by Pythagoras, much of Archytas's work involved music. But he was also interested in the mathematics of mechanical devices, which may explain why he designed the pigeon.

CELESTIAL SPHERES *In this 16th-century view of the universe, Atlas holds up Earth surrounded by the planets on their spheres.*

Celestial spheres

c.360 BCE

Eudoxus of Cnidus

Planets and other celestial bodies seem to move irregularly against a smoothly revolving background of stars. The ancient Greek astronomer Eudoxus offered the first explanation for this. He said that everything astronomers saw was carried around Earth on 27 spheres. The outermost sphere held the stars, while the sun, the moon, and the planets had several spheres each. Their combined steady motions created the observed irregular motion. Despite numerous flaws, Eudoxus's theory was, with some refinements, the best available for 2,000 years.

c.350 BCE Greek philosopher Aristotle puts forward six arguments for a spherical Earth. His reasoning is generally accepted, putting an end to centuries of speculation about the shape of the world.

330 BCE As the final act of his conquest of the Persian Empire, the Macedonian king Alexander the Great burns down the palace in the city of Persepolis. From now on, Greek culture will begin to influence the Middle East.

Atomic theory

c.350 BCE

Democritus

The ancient Greek philosopher Democritus held views that have influenced the whole of modern science. He was probably the first person to put forward the idea that the world is made of atoms, the smallest things that can exist. He said that there were countless numbers of them, all made of the same stuff, but with different shapes. They could be arranged in different ways to produce everything in the world. This theory is close to what we now believe—not bad for someone who lived about 2,400 years ago.

Cookbook

c.350 BCE

Archestratus

Throughout history, people have tried to improve the ways of preparing food. As long ago as 350 BCE, the ancient Greek writer Archestratus produced a book about the joy of food called *Pleasant Living*. About 200 years later, an enthusiast named Athenaeus produced a book containing, among other things, several recipes for cheesecake.

Coal

c.350 BCE

Archaeologists believe that coal may have been burned in Wales as long as 4,000 years ago. But the first written record of coal is a mention by the ancient Greek philosopher Aristotle in a book he wrote on geology in about 350 BCE. His interest in coal came from his theories about Earth. Later people, from the Romans onward, were more interested in coal as a source of heat or for use in smelting metals. In about 1200, a monk named Reinier of Liège wrote about metalworkers using a black earth similar to charcoal.

Iced dessert

c.350 BCE

The ancient Romans enjoyed their food, especially anything cold and sweet. Sugar was a rarity and refrigeration unknown, but from the 4th century onward, they used natural ice and honey. This was a problem in summer, so the emperor Nero had snow brought from the mountains and served with sweetened fruit juice. Meanwhile, people in China were eating ice cream, invented there in about 2000 BCE. This reached Europe in about 1300, when the Italian traveler Marco Polo returned with recipes from the Far East.

Mercury

c.350 BCE

Mercury, the only metal that is liquid at room temperature,was used by the Chinese in attempts to achieve immortality. Probably known to the ancient Egyptians, it was definitely being mined and refined by about 350 BCE. Its seemingly magical properties made it a key ingredient in alchemy, in which people tried to make gold out of cheaper metals. It was also used in early medicine, although people knew it could be poisonous.

Formal logic

c.350 BCE

Aristotle

Everyone needs to know how to argue logically. The ancient Greek philosopher Aristotle was the first to set out clear rules for argument. He pointed out, for example, that an argument like "Fish can swim; I can swim, so I am a fish" is false. (A true statement would be "Fish can swim; I am a fish, so I can swim.") He also pointed out that all knowledge depends on a set of principles that can be accepted as true without proof. His rules were so good that, for centuries, people believed he had said all there was to say on the subject. Many of his ideas are still essential to science and philosophy.

Euclidean geometry

c.300 BCE

Euclid of Alexandria

Euclid was possibly the greatest math teacher ever. His way of explaining geometry in about 300 BCE was still being used in the 20th century. He collected earlier texts and rearranged them with his own work so that they made more sense. His book, *The Elements*, takes readers on a journey from basic ideas to surprising outcomes. Its clarity is still hard to beat. Many of Euclid's ideas are in math books used today.

Lead pipe

c.300 BCE

Plumbers get their name from "plumbum, " which was the Roman word for lead. Roman engineers brought water from the surrounding hills into their cities, then sent it to where it was needed through pipes. They sometimes made these from wood but more often used lead because it lasted longer and was soft and easy to roll up into tubes. Lead pipes were still in use in the early 20th century, but most have now been replaced because, unfortunately, as the Roman engineer Vitruvius pointed out, too much lead is poisonous.

Lead pipe *In ancient Rome, city dwellers often had their name put on their own lead water pipes.*

320 BCE Cities continue to grow, and with them the problem of waste disposal. In Athens, a law is passed preventing people from throwing their garbage into the streets. The first waste collection systems are also organized.

c.304 BCE In Rome, Gnaeus Flavius erects a permanent calendar showing the days on which legal business can be conducted. Before this, the days were just read out each month, making justice uncertain.

MOSAIC *A tessera mosaic made between 250 and 50 BCE shows how well this seemingly rigid technique could show detail and movement.*

Mosaic

c.300 BCE

Mosaics are pictures made up using small pieces of colored stone or glass cemented to walls or floors. The first mosaics were probably made using natural pebbles. By 300 BCE, the "tessera" technique had been invented, in which tiny tiles cut from stone or glass were used to give fine detail and rich color. This beautiful, hard-wearing form of interior decoration went down well with the Romans. Many of their mosaics still exist today.

Scientific botany

c.300 BCE

Theophrastus

After thousands of years spent using and cultivating plants, people began to wonder where the plants came from and how they worked. The scientific study of plants is called botany, and the ancient Greek philosopher Theophrastus was the first real botanist. Between about 320 and 280 BCE, he wrote more than 200 books on the subject. Only two, which deal with the origin and growth of plants, have survived. Modern botanists no longer use his work, but without him they might never have gotten started.

Saddle

c.300 BCE

The first horse riders rode bareback, clinging on without the help of saddle or stirrups. They sat on some kind of blanket or cloth, and this eventually evolved into the padded leather saddle used today. Chinese riders were using saddles by about 50 BCE, but it is thought that saddles were invented at least 250 years earlier than this by a group of nomads called the Scythians, who lived in what is now mostly Ukraine.

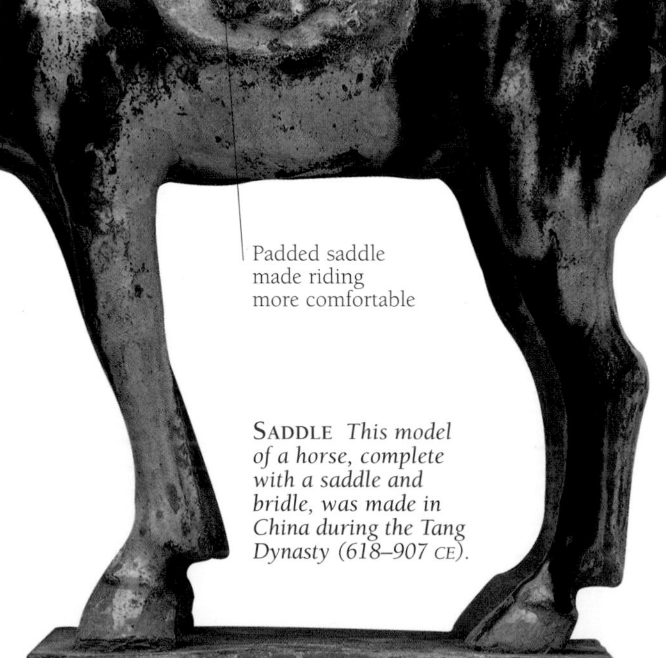

Padded saddle made riding more comfortable

SADDLE *This model of a horse, complete with a saddle and bridle, was made in China during the Tang Dynasty (618–907 CE).*

Lighthouse

c.280 BCE

Sostratus of Cnidus

Ancient mariners often relied on fires to guide them into harbor. These showed smoke by day and a light to aim for at night and were simply placed on hilltops. The first real lighthouse was created in Egypt, on the island of Pharos, off Alexandria. When its Greek engineer Sostratus of Cnidus finished it in about 280 BCE, it was probably about 410 ft (125 m) high—almost as high as the pyramids (✱ *see* **page 24**). It had stairs inside, and fuel for its fire was hoisted up by pulley.

Compressed air

c.270 BCE

Ctesibius of Alexandria

Ctesibius of Alexandria discovered that air can be compressed and will then exert a force. He may have done this by plunging a pot into water with its mouth downward and noticing that this required some force. Seeing that the inside of the pot stayed dry, he would have realized that

c.300 BCE Geographer Pytheas becomes the first Greek to describe northern Europe after sailing to Land's End in England and exploring much of Britain on foot. On the way, he enjoys the local honey-based drink, mead.

293 BCE Hygeia, the goddess of health, reaches Rome. With her husband Asclepius, the god of medicine, she will watch over the well-being of Roman citizens. She is depicted giving her snake a drink from a saucer.

the air inside was pushing the water out. We do know that Ctesibius used his discovery in several air-powered inventions.

Bridge for boarding ships

c.260 BCE

Gaius Duilius

Military leaders have always been called upon to solve practical problems. World War II soldiers erected "instant" steel bridges to help them get across rivers, and the Roman commander Gaius Duilius used wooden bridges more than 2,000 years before. In 260 BCE, he found himself fighting a battle at sea with soldiers trained to fight on land. So he brought some "land" on to his ships in the form of wooden bridges that hooked on to the enemy ships. His soldiers could then rush across and fight as usual. They won the battle.

Archimedes's principle

c.250 BCE

Archimedes

See **pages 48–49** for the story of how Archimedes solved a weighty problem and discovered how things float.

Size of Earth

c.250 BCE

Eratosthenes of Cyrene

The astronomer Eratosthenes of Cyrene (now Shahhat in Libya) was the first person to figure out the size of Earth. He found that on midsummer's day, at noon, the sun shone straight down a well at Aswan, in Egypt, so the sun there was directly overhead. But at exactly the same time, the shadow of a vertical stick about 500 miles (800 km) north at Alexandria showed that the sun was not overhead but angled at about 7 degrees from the vertical. Eratosthenes realized that the difference was caused by the curvature of Earth. Using the idea that there were 360 degrees in a circle, and knowing the distance between Aswan and Alexandria, he was able to calculate Earth's circumference as the distance between Aswan and Alexandria × 360 ÷ 7. Eratosthenes's calculation came up with the answer of about 25,700 miles (41,143 km). The true value is about 25,000 miles (40,000 km), so he wasn't too far off.

Compound pulley

c.250 BCE

Archimedes

A simple pulley is a rope passed around a wheel, and it is useful for lifting things vertically. One end of the rope is attached to the load and the other end of the rope is pulled to lift the load. Greek inventor Archimedes developed the compound pulley from the simple pulley by wrapping the rope around several wheels instead of one, which enabled people to lift heavier loads. It meant pulling the rope farther but took less effort at any one time. Compound pulleys, using chains rather than ropes, are still used for heavy lifting jobs.

Heart valves

c.250 BCE

Erasistratus of Ceos

An ancient Greek doctor called Erasistratus of Ceos was one of the first people to think about how the human body works. Although we have different theories today, his ideas did make sense. He gave the first correct account of how valves inside the heart prevent blood from flowing backward. His name for one of the valves, the tricuspid, is still used today.

Diaphragm separates the thorax from the abdomen

Model shows the internal organs of a female

Human anatomy based on dissection

c.250 BCE

Herophilus of Chalcedon

Anatomy is the study of the structure of bodies. Early anatomists were often forbidden to cut open dead bodies, so some of their descriptions and diagrams of the internal organs of humans were based on guesswork. The ancient Greek doctor Herophilus was one of the first scientists to base his anatomy on real observations, and he accurately described the brain, nerves, blood vessels, eyes, and other parts of the body.

HUMAN ANATOMY BASED ON DISSECTION *This 15th-century model for teaching anatomy probably shows more detail than was known to Heophilus.*

c.287 BCE The ordinary people of Rome, the plebeians, gain a great victory in their campaign for recognition, as plebeian Quintus Hortensius becomes "dictator." He decrees that plebeian laws must apply to rich people, too.

282 BCE After 12 years' work, Greek sculptor Chares of Lyndus completes a 105 ft (32 m) high bronze statue of the sun god Helios, on the island of Rhodes. An earthquake destroys it within 60 years, and it is sold for scrap.

DOING SCIENCE IN THE BATH

Archimedes solves a weighty problem and discovers how things float

Golden leaves used to adorn a religious statue

GOLD FOR GODS AND KINGS
Ancient craft workers fashioned gold into decorations that not only were beautiful but also indicated the importance of the wearer. That is why Hieron wanted to make sure that his wreath was made of pure gold.

Why do some things float and others sink? This is an important question for ship designers, but the ancient Greek scientist Archimedes may have found the answer while he was checking the quality of a king's jewelry.

Archimedes was born in Syracuse, Sicily, in about 290 BCE. He was related to the king, Hieron II, so had plenty of time to think and write about mathematics and mechanics. Hieron often called upon Archimedes to help him with problems. He had a gold wreath that he thought contained some silver, and he asked Archimedes to find out exactly how much. Archimedes knew he could check the wreath if he could measure its density (its mass in relation to its volume) because silver is less dense than gold. The obvious way to find the density of something is to measure its weight (which is proportional to its mass) and volume, but Archimedes didn't know how to measure the volume of the wreath.

One day, he noticed the water rising as he got into his bath. He realized that he could fill a bathtub to the top, lower Hieron's wreath into it to make the water overflow, then take the wreath out and see how much water was needed to fill the bathtub again. That would be the volume of the wreath.

Archimedes may also have noticed that he felt lighter in his bath. Left to itself, bath water doesn't rise or fall, so every part of it must get an upward push that balances its own weight. The same force must push on anything placed in the water. When anything is immersed in a fluid, even partly, it feels an upward

EUREKA!
It is said that Archimedes was so excited by his discovery that he leaped out of his bath and ran naked through the streets shouting "Eureka!" ("I've found it!"). This probably never happened, but people still shout "Eureka!" at moments of discovery.

TESTING THE PRINCIPLE
Two identical containers filled to the brim with water will balance exactly. When an apple is carefully lowered into one of them, so that the container stays full, the balance is unchanged. Archimedes's principle says that the floating apple will push its own weight of water out of the container, making the total weight the same as before.

Identical containers on an accurate set of scales

push equal to the weight of fluid it displaces. We now call this Archimedes's principle. Using this, Archimedes could have immersed the wreath in water and noted how much weight it lost, then have figured out how much silver the wreath contained, without measuring its volume at all.

Archimedes probably didn't do this. Nevertheless, he had solved Hieron's problem. He may also have discovered why things float or sink. Objects placed in water move downward until their weight is balanced by the weight of the water they displace, then stay at that level. If their average density is more than that of water, they cannot float. They sink.

Later, Hieron had more serious problems. When Archimedes was an old man, the Romans besieged Syracuse. Once again, he was called upon. He used his scientific knowledge to design ships, catapults, and even, it is said, giant mirrors to burn Roman ships with the sun's rays. In 211 BCE, the city was eventually captured. The Roman soldiers rampaged through it, burning and killing. Sadly, one of their victims was Archimedes, the genius who did science in his bath.

Greek trireme of about 450 BCE

Greek warship
The magnificent trireme, a Greek ship with three layers of oars, showed how much importance the Greeks attached to winning battles at sea. It was extremely fast and could sink an enemy ship with its built-in battering ram. Fighting techniques moved on, and the trireme evolved into a ship that could carry large numbers of heavily armed soldiers.

Archimedes was a genius who needed only the simplest of equipment to make profound discoveries.

Pipe organ

c.250 BCE

Ctesibius of Alexandria

The Greek inventor Ctesibius was the first person to put together all three parts of an organ: pipes, a keyboard, and a supply of air. To get a steady sound from the pipes, Ctesibius realized that he needed to supply air to them at a steady pressure. So he attached them to a large container, open at the bottom and standing in a tank of water. As he pumped air into the container, the weight of water pressing on the air kept the pressure fairly constant, even though the amount of air in the container varied. His organ, called a hydrolos because of the water (from *hydro*, the Greek word for "water"), was loud enough to play outdoors.

Safety pin

c.250 BCE

The modern safety pin was invented in 1849 by US mechanic Walter Hunt, but this useful fastener has a much longer history. A clothing clasp called a fibula is thought to have been invented by a group of people called the Phrygians in about 1100 BCE. It was worn by the ancient Greeks and Romans, often in elaborately decorated form. By 250 BCE, the pin had become recognizable as the object that Hunt reinvented more than 2,000 years later.

Simple pattern carved in the bronze clasp

SAFETY PIN *This Hungarian brooch dates from about 50 BCE. It fastens using the same principle as a safety pin.*

SAFETY PIN *This type of early pin of about 750 BCE was found in Italy. It is a brooch that was probably worn by someone of high rank.*

Front of brooch made from glass discs

Spring mechanism

Surface area and volume of a sphere

c.250 BCE

Archimedes

The formulas for calculating the surface area and volume of a sphere are used throughout science. The first person to work them out was the Greek mathematician Archimedes. He proved that a sphere has four times the surface area of a circle the same size. He also proved that a sphere has two-thirds the volume of the cylinder that just contains it. These are easy problems to solve using modern mathematical tools, but Archimedes had to use imaginary spheres, which he sliced, weighed, and measured in his imagination to get the answers. His methods, lost for centuries, anticipated 17th-century calculus (✳ *see* **page 96**).

Standardized Chinese writing

c.220 BCE

Shi Huangdi

In Chinese writing, each pictorial character stands for a word, not a sound. It works like numbers in Western languages. People in different Western countries all understand the symbol "2" but pronounce it "two," "deux," and so on, depending on their language. This principle is useful in China, because speakers of its many local dialects can all read the same writing, but only if the same characters are used everywhere. The standardization of Chinese writing was just one of the many reforms that the forceful emperor Shi Huangdi introduced in about 220 BCE, as part of his plan to turn the separate states of China into one nation.

Streetcar

c.220 BCE

Shi Huangdi

Today, electric streetcars run in many of the world's cities. Chinese emperor Shi Huangdi did not have electricity in 220 BCE, but he saw the need for orderly, smoothly flowing traffic. He decreed that all carts should have their wheels the same distance apart and had matching grooves put in the streets. This may have been the world's first streetcar system.

222 BCE After four centuries of occupation by Celtic tribes, the city of Mediolanum in the north of Italy is overrun by Romans from the south and becomes part of their empire. It will eventually be known as Milan.

218 BCE Using elephants to carry heavy equipment, Carthaginian general Hannibal leads 40,000 soldiers over the snowbound Alps into Italy in an attempt to conquer Rome. He wins some battles but fails in the end.

Standardized Chinese writing *Each Chinese character consists of a number of lines. Early Chinese characters were simplified pictures, but they gradually evolved into the shapes of today. These characters mean "soccer."*

Soccer

c.200 BCE

Soccer began in China more than 2,000 years ago as a game called ***cuju***, originally used as a form of exercise for soldiers. Players competed by kicking a ball into a net and were not allowed to touch it with their hands—rules that still exist in today's version of the game.

Punctuation

c.200 BCE

Aristophanes of Byzantium

The rules of punctuation can make writing more complicated, but punctuation does make life easier for readers. The idea came to us through Greek and Latin. Early Greek writers used hardly any punctuation, and didn't even put spaces between words. Aristophanes of Byzantium, who was librarian of the library of Alexandria in about 200 BCE, was the first to remedy this. By adding punctuation to Greek text, he began the trend that led to modern punctuation, including one mark that has a Greek name—the apostrophe.

Chain mail

c.200 BCE

The ancient Greek warrior's bronze chest protector, or cuirass, was heavy and restricted its wearer's movement. From perhaps 200 BCE onward, Greek soldiers increasingly wore chain mail in battle, and soldiers in Sumeria may already have been using it a few years earlier. Made of thousands of iron rings looped together over a leather or cloth backing, chain mail offered protection against swords and spears. It was more flexible than a cuirass so it was relatively comfortable, although a shirt could weigh 22 lb (10 kg). Chain mail eventually became standard equipment for Roman legionnaires.

Chain store

c.200 BCE

A chain store is a shop that is part of a group run by the same company and selling the same goods. They became a prominent feature of towns and cities everywhere in the 20th century. But the Hudson's Bay Company was operating a chain of stores in the US before 1750, and the earliest-known chain stores were selling their wares in China as long ago as 200 BCE.

Flute

c.200 BCE

Flute *Almost any tube can form a flute. This bone was made into a musical instrument by a 10th-century Viking.*

The flute that musicians play today is held sideways rather than lengthwise. This "transverse" flute may have developed independently in both China and Europe. Pipes played sideways were used in China as early as the 9th century BCE, but the instrument now known in China as the ***di***, or ***dizi***, was not perfected until about 200 BCE. It has six finger holes, plus an extra hole, with a thin piece of bamboo or reed over it. When a musician blows into the pipe, the bamboo vibrates to create the plaintive sound typical of Chinese flute music. At about the time that this pipe began to be heard, musicians in what is now Tuscany, in Italy, also seem to have taken up the transverse flute. In Germany, it was used in military bands from about 1100 CE.

215 BCE Rome passes laws ruling that women must not wear more than half an ounce of gold jewelry or have tunics of more than one color. The laws also limit the number of guests at banquets and prevent men from wearing silk.

213 BCE Wise men repeatedly tell Chinese emperor Shi Huangdi that he is a fool to look for alchemists or magicians who can give him eternal life. The emperor gets even by having all their books burned.

Sari

c.200 BCE

Indian women were wearing the elegant sari as long ago as 200 BCE. This single piece of fine cloth, worn wrapped around the body and sometimes over the head, appears in Indian sculptures dating from about 150 BCE. Women depicted in the sculptures from this period are typically shown wearing a sari, a head scarf, and lots of jewelry. Today, saris are made from synthetic fabrics as well as traditional silk or cotton.

Steel

c.200 BCE

Once people had discovered iron, they accidentally made steel, which is iron containing a little carbon. It is much stronger than pure iron. The carbon could have come from the charcoal the people burned with iron ore to extract the iron. Steel making started in several places at about the same time. China and India had real steel industries from about 200 BCE. They heated iron with charcoal to get carbon into it, then reheated and hammered the metal until the carbon was mixed throughout.

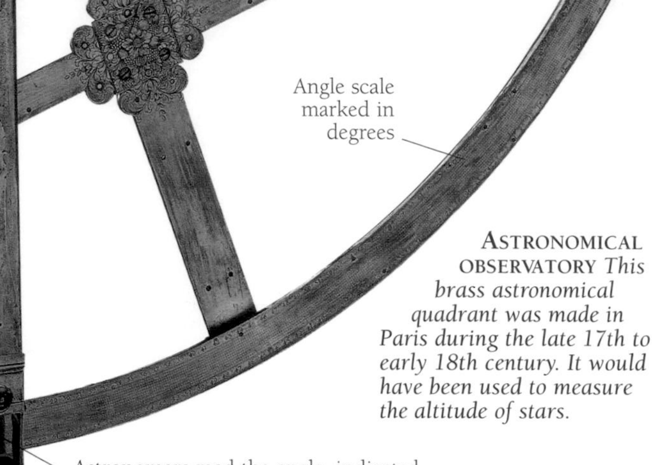

ASTRONOMICAL OBSERVATORY *This brass astronomical quadrant was made in Paris during the late 17th to early 18th century. It would have been used to measure the altitude of stars.*

Piston

c.150 BCE

Pistons working in cylinders drive many machines today, using compressed air or fuel. Pistons are difficult to make accurately enough to stop leaks, so early inventors tried to avoid them. For example, the pumps that blew air into metalworking furnaces from about 1000 BCE were usually just bellows. But as early as 150 BCE, or even earlier, some metalworkers were using better air pumps using the piston-and-cylinder principle.

PISTON *Early water pumps often used pistons because the water acted as a lubricant, and leaks didn't matter very much.*

Astronomical observatory

c.150 BCE

Hipparchus

Basic astronomical observatories existed in Babylonia in 2500 BCE, but they did not have any instruments. A great observatory built at Alexandria in Egypt in about 300 BCE did not have many instruments either. The first observatory with fairly accurate instruments for measuring star positions was probably on the Greek island of Rhodes, where the astronomer Hipparchus worked between about 134 and 129 BCE. Much later, in the 9th or 10th centuries, great new observatories were established at Damascus and Baghdad.

c.200 BCE Rome suffers from success as the city's population grows out of control. Poorer people are packed into wooden buildings three floors high, which often collapse or catch fire. Within 20 years, plague sweeps the city.

c.150 BCE Wealthy Romans become convinced that dancing is a shameful and dangerous activity. To protect their children from what they see as its anti-Roman influence, they order that all dancing schools should close.

Horseshoes

c.150 BCE

People were riding horses by 2000 BCE, but it was 150 BCE before they began to think of ways to protect horses' feet so they could ride them on rocky ground and roads. Shoes for horses and mules were developed by the people in eastern Europe who had first tamed the horse. Most early shoes were made of leather. Metal shoes, nailed to the hoof, were being used in western Europe by about 450 CE.

Precession of the equinoxes

c.150 BCE

Hipparchus

The equinoxes are the times of the year when day and night are the same length. Their dates shift slightly each year—an effect called precession. This was discovered by the Greek astronomer Hipparchus, who noticed that his star positions had all moved by the same amount from those measured by earlier Greek and Babylonian astronomers. With a little scientific detective work, he found out that the change was caused by a very slow shifting of Earth's axis of rotation.

Trigonometry

c.150 BCE

Hipparchus

Trigonometry is a branch of mathematics that studies the relationships between the angles and sides of different figures or the distance of objects from each other. This relationship can be useful if you want to determine the size or distance of far away objects. Hipparchus, a mathematician and astronomer, used his knowledge of trigonometry to measure the distances of the sun and moon more accurately than ever before, even though, today, we know his measurements were much too small. His research filled 12 books, and he became known as the founder of modern trigonometry.

Stirrups

c.150 BCE

Stirrups, those useful footrests for riders, were almost certainly invented by people from the same area—modern Ukraine—as those who tamed the horse in the first place (✳ *see* **page 28**). This simple invention made a huge difference to the way horses were used in war. It is very hard to stay on a galloping horse without stirrups, let alone fight for your life at the same time.

Star magnitudes

c.130 BCE

Hipparchus

Some stars look brighter than others, so astronomers classify them on a magnitude scale, which records their brightness as seen from Earth. The astronomer Hipparchus began this system when compiling a star catalogue. Working on the island of Rhodes, he listed 850 stars so accurately that his observations were useful until as late as the 17th century.

Groin vault

c.100 BCE

The barrel vault, a tunnel-like structure made from a series of arches, could be used to create buildings of any length. But unfortunately, its walls could contain only small openings. Large ones made the arches collapse. The Romans, masters of the arch, found a solution: they made each opening into the start of another barrel vault. In this way, they could make buildings of any size from a grid of vaults crossing each other to form self-supporting "groin vaults."

Iron plowshare

c.100 BCE

We don't know whether the Romans used iron plowshares in the light soils of southern Europe, but the implements were ideal for cutting through the heavier soils found in the north. While some people in the north continued with wooden plows, others, including the invading Romans and local people such as the Celts, switched to iron. Efficient agriculture may have been one of the things that helped the Celts build a strong culture—and make themselves a nuisance, if not a threat, to the Romans.

STIRRUPS *These stirrups were used by Vikings between 850 and 1050 CE.*

c.150 BCE Philosopher Crates of Mallus takes time off from his usual work on Greek grammar to make one of the first ever geographical globes. It shows that by this time the Greeks are convinced the world is round.

124 BCE Two scholars, Gonsun Hong and Dong Zhongshu, found China's first university. Its job will be to teach civil servants how to run the Chinese empire, including skills like interpreting portents and omens.

SCREW PRESS *This small wooden press was used to crush grapes for wine or olives for oil.*

Screw press

c.100 BCE

The screw press used a large wooden screw to squeeze things between two boards. It was probably invented by the Greeks in about 100 BCE for pressing olives or grapes. The Greeks and the Romans also used it to press their clothes. Its real importance, however, comes from what it was used for 1,500 years later: pressing type onto paper to print books (✳ *see* **pages 76–77**).

Waterwheel

c.100 BCE

Grinding corn in a hand-powered mill, or quern, (✳ *see* **page 36**) was tiring work and was often left to women. Ancient Greek women must have welcomed the first water-powered quern in about 100 BCE. The top stone was connected to horizontal paddles turned by a fast-flowing stream. Within 70 years, the Romans were building large vertical water-wheels like those seen today.

Tin can

c.100 BCE

Cans made from tin-coated steel were first used to preserve food in 1810. But about 2,000 years earlier, the Romans already knew that tin was ideal for lining metal food containers because it was resistant to corrosion and easy to apply. They made their tin containers from copper and used them for cooking, not storage. Tin-lined copper pans can still be bought today.

Shorthand

63 BCE

Marcus Tiro

Politicians like their words to be remembered, and the great Roman statesman Cicero was no exception. In 63 BCE, he

Woodworking plane

c.100 BCE

The traditional way to get a flat surface on wood is with a plane. A plane is a block of wood or metal with a blade set into it sticking out slightly. The blade takes a thin shaving off the surface of the wood as the plane is pushed across it. The origin of the plane is a mystery, but the Romans used them. Planes that were very much like modern ones were found at Pompeii, an ancient city in southern Italy, which the Romans colonized in 80 BCE and which was buried by the eruption of Mount Vesuvius in 79 CE.

WATERWHEEL *These water-wheels of the late 16th century were used to power a mill grinding corn into flour.*

100 BCE China's Silk Road extends westward to reach the Roman Empire as Chinese emperor Wudi conquers or makes alliances with large areas of central Asia. Ideas and luxury goods will travel the 3,700 mile (6,000 km) route.

67 BCE After decades in which its citizens have seen their coinage fall in value, Rome solves the problem by introducing a gold coin, the aureus. Seventy years later, Emperor Nero will steal the gold to prop up his empire.

asked his friend Marcus Tiro to invent a shorthand system so that the important speeches he made in the senate could be recorded forever. Tiro did a good job. His system was still in use centuries after the Roman Empire had collapsed.

News bulletin

59 BCE

There has always been a demand for news. Without printing, the only way to get it to people was to write it out and pin it up where everyone could see it. *Acta Diurna* (Daily Acts) was started by Julius Caesar in 59 BCE as an official propaganda sheet. It quickly expanded and was soon offering the latest news on births, marriages, horoscopes, and public executions.

Paper

c.50 BCE

It is easy to forget what marvelous stuff paper is. Light, strong, and cheap, it quickly displaced other writing materials as it spread from China to the West. The story is that a Chinese courtier invented it in 105 CE as a substitute for silk, but archaeologists have found paper dating from 49 BCE in the Shanxi district of China. Paper has been a key component of many later inventions, from printing to tea bags. (✱ *See also* **The Papermakers.**)

THE PAPERMAKERS

TRADITIONAL PAPERMAKERS dip a frame with a mesh bottom into a vat containing water and plant fibers. As the water drains away, the fibers cling together on top of the mesh. Further drying and pressing form the paper into a sheet. Modern paper is made from wood fibers using huge machines, but the first paper was handmade with fibers from Chinese hemp and ramie plants.

A worker uses traditional Chinese methods to make paper in a workshop in Tantou, China.

PAPER AND PRINTING
The invention of letterpress printing in about 1450 made it easier for people to produce multiple copies of a book. But if books had continued to be printed on vellum (a kind of leather), they would have remained expensive. Paper arrived just in time to turn a good invention into a great one.

HOW PAPER REACHED THE WEST
It took 12 centuries for papermaking to complete its journey from China to Europe. Spreading first to Korea, it reached Japan in about 650 CE. Paper mills in Syria were exporting to Europe by the 8th century, but Europeans did not start making their own paper until about 400 years later.

Julian calendar

45 BCE

Julius Caesar

By 45 BCE, the Roman Empire's calendar was in a mess. Extra days were added in a confusing way and dates were counted backward from certain special days. When officials began mismanaging it to suit themselves, reform became urgent. Julius Caesar introduced a year of 365 days with a leap year every fourth year. While he was at it, he rearranged the months, naming July after himself and August after Augustus, who was later to be his successor. The result was very close to the calendar we use now.

Glassblowing

c.10 BCE

Centuries after the ancient Egyptians had discovered how to shape glass by blowing it into molds (✱ *see* **page 27**), people still did not realize that it could be shaped using air alone. It was in Syria, probably in about 10 BCE, that someone first put a blob of molten glass onto the end of a tube, blew hard, and watched the glass swell into a bubble without any mold to shape it. For some time, most glassworkers continued to shape glass in molds, but the glassblowing process eventually became as important as molding. The resulting smooth, rounded vessels were shipped all over the Roman Empire.

44 BCE On March 15, a group of senators including Gaius Cassius and Marcus Brutus kill Julius Caesar as he enters the senate house in Rome. His assassins believe that he wants to make himself king, destroying Rome as a republic.

c.19 BCE Roman engineers in the south of France complete a huge aqueduct with three layers of arches. It channels water over the Gard River to the city of Nimes. The Pont du Gard will survive for more than 2,000 years.

Dome

c.50 CE

A dome is just an arch that arches in all directions. Sumerian builders were building rudimentary domes more than 4,000 years ago, but the first great dome builders were the Romans. They made extensive use of concrete. One of their earliest domes, which roofed a palace for the emperor Nero in 68 CE, was 50 ft (15 m) in diameter. The dome of the Pantheon in Rome, which was completed 60 years later and still stands today, is nearly three times as wide.

Bolt

c.50 CE

A screw thread can exert a large force when turned with a small force, making bolts and screws ideal for holding things together. The thread is very difficult to make, especially the female thread on the inside of a nut, which is used in conjunction with the male thread on a bolt. By about 50 CE, a tool for cutting these, called a tap, was in use. At about the same time, the Greek scientist and inventor Hero of Alexandria was writing about machines with parts that had to be held together with well-made bolts.

Street lamp

c.50 CE

People in large cities today depend on good street lighting. By about 50 CE, some public places in Rome had lighting after dark. It cannot have been very bright. The street lamps were just giant, metal versions of the teapot-shaped pottery oil lamps invented in Greece about 750 years earlier (✱ *see* **page 35**).

Topiary

c.50 CE

Topiary, the art of clipping or growing shrubs into geometric shapes, was a fashionable pastime in Rome in about 50 CE. It is most likely to have begun as some pruning that got out of hand, although a friend of the emperor Augustus claimed to have invented it. As well as being interesting in its own right, Roman topiary also suggests that the Romans had developed a form of shears suitable for use in the garden.

Wheelbarrow

c.50 CE

The wheelbarrow should have been an obvious invention once the wheel had arrived (✱ *see* **page 19**), but it appears that no one thought of it for another 3,500 years. Chinese laborers were trundling barrows around from about 50 CE onward, but people still didn't catch on in the West. The earliest evidence we have of European builders and miners using this versatile one-wheeled vehicle are depictions of some in medieval illustrations.

Vending machine

c.60 CE

Hero of Alexandria

The first known vending machine was designed by the Greek inventor Hero of Alexandria in about 60 CE. The idea was that when someone dropped in a coin the machine would release a shot of holy water. Hero described his machine in a book. We don't know whether he ever built one—or if it would have been reliable!

60 CE The leader of the British Celtic Iceni tribe, Boudicca, leads a rebellion against the Romans with her daughters. After early successes, she is defeated near Towcester by the Roman army under Suetonius Paullinus.

64 CE After 10 years under the tyrannical Roman emperor Nero, a fire sweeps through Rome. Although Nero probably started the fire himself, he blames it on the Christians and uses it as an excuse to persecute them.

DOME *The dome of the Pantheon in Rome was the world's largest until modern times.*

Formula for the area of a triangle

c.60 CE

Hero of Alexandria

There is a well-known formula for figuring out the area of a triangle—half of the base times the height—but if the height isn't known, it has to be calculated before the formula can be applied. Nearly 2,000 years ago, Hero of Alexandria discovered a different formula that doesn't involve knowing the height of the triangle, just the length of its three sides. His formula is: area = $\sqrt{[s(s-a)(s-b)(s-c)]}$—where a, b, and c are the sides and s is half of the perimeter. Despite its simplicity, the formula is not widely used.

Steam aeolipyle

c.60 CE

Hero of Alexandria

Often said to be the first steam engine, the aeolipyle was built by Hero of Alexandria and was really just a toy. It was a metal ball set on a hollow spindle. Steam rushed into the ball through the spindle and out again through two nozzles at the sides. These acted like little rockets and made the ball spin around. Probably named after Aeolus, the Greek god of the winds, the aeolipyle didn't do anything useful, but it did demonstrate the power of steam. It would be another 17 centuries before this power was unleashed.

Steam escaped through vents, forcing the ball to rotate

Water was heated in the boiler

STEAM AEOLIPYLE *This is a modern reconstruction of Hero of Alexandria's toy.*

Scissors

c.100 CE

Scissors are ideal for cutting soft things such as cloth, paper, or hair. The scissor principle was known in 3000 BCE, but scissors like those used today, with two separate blades pivoted at the center, were invented by the Romans in about 100 CE. Until steel became cheaper in the 16th century, scissors remained a specialized tool used only by professionals like tailors and barbers.

Truss bridge

c.100 CE

When someone stands on a plank laid across a gap, only the top and bottom of it do much to hold them up. The wood in the middle adds weight but not strength. A truss, which is a framework with most of its strength at the top and bottom, is more efficient at bearing weight. The Romans had grasped this concept by 100 CE and were using truss bridges to get their armies across rivers. By 300 CE, they were also using trusses to support roofs up to 75 ft (23 m) wide.

Earthquake detector

c.130 CE

Chang Heng

It is obvious when a major earthquake is happening, but smaller warning shocks can go unnoticed without the help of a detector, or seismoscope. In about 130 CE, Chinese scientist Chang Heng invented what may have been the first of these—certainly one of the strangest. It had eight bronze dragons arranged in a circle, each holding a ball in its mouth, with eight bronze frogs directly below each with their mouths pointing upward. Due to the way the dragons were arranged, at least one of them would feel the slightest tremor. When this happened, its ball would drop, clanging into the mouth of the frog below, raising the alarm and supposedly indicating the direction of the earthquake.

79 CE After an earlier earthquake, the southern Italian city of Pompeii is destroyed by the eruption of nearby Mount Vesuvius. Its inhabitants, including wealthy Roman vacationers, are buried alive in ash and lava.

115 CE Chinese scholar, poet, and single mother Ban Zhao dies at the age of 70. Her career, following marriage at 14 and the early death of her husband, included completing a history of the Han Dynasty and writing many poems.

Epicyclic universe

c.140 CE

Ptolemy

Ptolemy was an astronomer and mathematician who lived in ancient Egypt. Five centuries before him, the Greek astronomer Eudoxus had explained the movements of the stars and planets with his theory of celestial spheres (✳ *see* **page 44**), but this did not account for all the details of the planets' movements or why they sometimes changed brightness. It became clear that the motions of the planets could not be explained with the simple idea that they moved in circles. Ptolemy solved the problem by suggesting that each heavenly body moved in small circles, or epicycles, at the same time as it orbited Earth in a large circle, generally accepted as the truth by astronomers for the next 1,500 years.

Crank

c.150 CE

A crank converts a to-and-fro movement into a rotary movement. For example, bicycle pedals convert the up- and-down motion of the legs into the rotary motion of the wheels. The date for when the crank was invented depends on how it is defined. The first rotary querns (✳ *see* **page 36**) could qualify as early cranks, and they go back to 600 BCE, but it is not until 150 CE that there is evidence of the first "bent rod" crank being used. One is depicted in a Chinese tomb model of a winnowing machine.

Bucket was found at Pompeii, Italy

SOAP *The image on this Roman bucket shows the goddess Venus using soap to wash her hair.*

Soap

c.150 CE

People seem to have made soap from about 1000 BCE onward, by boiling fat with wood ash. Soap was originally used for medicinal purposes and was not really the kind of soap that makes a good lather. It was probably the Romans, in about 150 CE, who first started using soap to wash things, and Roman women were using a kind of soap as a shampoo one hundred years earlier.

Sympathetic nervous system

c.170 CE

Galen

Many parts of the body are not under conscious control but are operated by the sympathetic nervous system. This system automatically readies us for action by, among other things, speeding up the heart and shutting down the digestion. The influential Greek physician Galen studied the human body extensively, including its nerves. Some of the nerves he identified in about 170 CE are now known to form part of the sympathetic nervous system.

Cataract operation

c.200 CE

Cataracts is a condition of the eye in which the lens becomes cloudy, leading to impaired vision and even blindness. Surgeons today can usually restore sight by replacing the damaged lens. Amazingly, cataract surgery was being done about 2,000 years ago. An Indian medical encyclopedia, the *Susruta-samhita*, which is thought to have been compiled by an Indian surgeon named Susruta, gives detailed instructions for the procedure. The only method he suggested for anaesthetizing patients seems to have been to give them alcohol.

Algebra

c.250 CE

Diophantus of Alexandria, al-Khwarizmi

No single person invented algebra. The art of doing arithmetic without actual numbers developed slowly, starting in Babylonia and ancient Egypt, with calculations expressed entirely in words. When Diophantus wrote his book *Arithmetica* in about 250 CE, he introduced symbols to replace some of the words. Nearly 600 years later, Persian scholar al-Khwarizmi clarified the idea of an equation and also showed how to solve quadratic equations. The word "algebra" comes from the Arabic "al-jabr."

136 CE The Roman emperor Hadrian completes a great wall to keep out barbarians from the north of Britain. It stretches 73 miles (118 km) from Bowness on the Solway Firth to Segedunum (now Wallsend) on the Tyne River.

184 CE The Yellow Turbans, a religious peasant movement in northeast China, start a rebellion that will cause the collapse of the Han Dynasty. They aim to replace the Han "Green Heaven" with a "Yellow Heaven" of perfect peace.

Book with pages

c.350 CE

The first books had no pages—they were written on a continuous scroll. Roman emperor Julius Caesar is sometimes credited with having been the first to fold a scroll into pages instead of rolling it, making it easier for a messenger to carry. Both the ancient Greeks and the Romans had ring-bound notebooks with wooden pages, but it wasn't until about 350 CE that the book with pages, or codex, became the standard way of storing words. The early Christians found the more compact codex useful for hiding their forbidden texts under their clothes. (✳ *See also* **Birth of the Book.**)

BIRTH OF THE BOOK

FROM ABOUT 50 BCE, books, particularly religious texts, started getting longer and the codex gradually became more attractive. Papyrus, the usual writing material at that time (✳ *see* **page 24**), tended to crack when folded into pages, so most of the new codexes were made from parchment (✳ *see* **page 28**), a material that was known in 2400 BCE but had been little used.

A page from a Greek Bible of the 4th century CE.

WHY PAGES WON

As well as being a handy shape, a codex allows people to turn to any section instantly or flip the pages to scan the contents. Because the pages of books can have writing on both sides, it is also possible to pack in twice as many words as on a scroll of the same size.

THE OLDEST CODEXES

The oldest surviving book with pages is a Greek Bible written between 300 and 400 CE. It is known as the Codex Sinaiticus because it was found near Mount Sinai, Egypt. Another Bible, the Codex Alexandrinus, was written a century later. Both are kept in the British Museum.

Jointed fishing rod

c.350 CE

Fishing rods have probably been around nearly as long as fish hooks (✳ *see* **page 8**). It was only when wealthy Romans began to take up fishing as a pastime in the 4th century CE that rods more than about 3 ft 3 in (1 in) long came into use. They were made of wood, and because they were long, they had to be made in several sections. So they looked a bit like a modern, jointed fishing rod.

JOINTED FISHING ROD
This floor mosaic was found in the Roman town of Leptis Magna, now in Libya, Africa. It clearly shows people fishing with rods.

250 CE The Roman Catholic Church creates a new class of priests known as exorcists. Their job is to persuade demons to leave people or places thought to be under their power, especially as a preliminary to baptism.

330 CE In Constantinople (now Istanbul), the world's largest racetrack is finally completed after 127 years. With room for 60,000 spectators, this "hippodrome" will host chariot races, political rallies, and public executions.

Public hospital

c.397 CE

St. Fabiola

Temples may have been used as refuges for the sick as long ago as 4000 BCE, but it is thought that the first public hospital opened in Rome in about 397 CE. It was founded by a woman who did so much good that she was made a saint. Fabiola was a highly educated Roman aristocrat who became a Christian. She created several hospitals and also gave help to monasteries. The monks in turn started more hospitals.

Plow with wheels

c.500 CE

A basic plow doesn't have wheels. The person doing the plowing holds it upright as an animal pulls it along. This is fine on light soils, but in the heavy soils of northern Europe, something sturdier was needed. In about 500 CE, heavy wheels were added to the basic plow, making it easier to handle and stable enough to be pulled by several animals.

Horse collar

c.500 CE

The first animals used for hauling things were oxen, which pushed on a wooden bar, or yoke. This didn't suit horses. The yoke pressed on their throats so they couldn't pull very hard. A padded collar that fitted around the neck was better. Its origins are not clear, but it may have been invented in China in about 500 CE. Horse collars were being used in the West by the 12th century.

ASTROLABE *This invention let people find their latitude or local time by studying the stars' position.*

Quill pen

c.500 CE

Quill pens came into use in about 500 CE and were in common use until the 19th century. They were usually made from one of the larger wing feathers of a goose. The feather was prepared by cutting the tip to a sharp point then making a slit to channel the ink. The hollow quill held enough ink for a line or two of writing.

BC and AD dates

525 CE

Dionysius Exiguus

The year numbers used today were laid down by the Christian Church: BC means "before Christ" and AD stands for *anno Domini*, meaning "in the year of the Lord." In 525 CE, a monk named Dionysius Exiguus had the idea of using the birth of Christ as a starting point (AD 1), and calculated that this was 754 years after the founding of Rome. Today, BCE and CE are often used instead, meaning "before common era" and "common era," respectively.

Astrolabe

c.550 CE

The astrolabe was an astronomical calculator and star finder. Its star map would be turned to match the sky at any time, and adjustable sights allowed stars to be located accurately. The earliest surviving examples were made in the Middle East in the 6th century CE. By the mid-15th century, wealthy travelers might have owned an astrolabe.

Block printed book

c.600 CE

Books were being printed in China long before movable type was perfected (✳ *see* **pages 66–67**). The printers wrote their

books by hand on thin paper, then stuck each page face down on a block of wood. The writing, visible through the paper, showed them where to carve the wood to leave text standing proud. They inked the block and pressed paper

BLOCK PRINTED BOOK *Patterns and symbols are carved into this wooden printing block.*

400 CE The first inhabitants of Hawaii reach the island from the Marquesas Islands more than 2,000 miles (3,200 km) away. They bring with them no written language but a rich oral culture of myth and practical knowledge.

415 CE The earliest-known female mathematician, Hypatia, is brutally murdered in Alexandria, Egypt. The leading mathematician and astronomer of her time, she was a prolific teacher and worked on geometry and number theory.

Decorated fan *This late 19th-century Japanese folding fan is made of a wooden frame covered in gilded paper. It is decorated with a painting of a bird and chrysanthemums.*

on it to create copies of the original writing. Things were printed in this way from about 600 CE onward.

Tapestry

c.600 CE

True tapestries are woven on a loom using different colored threads. The first tapestries were made in China about 1,500 years ago. Some, made of fine silk, looked almost like painted pictures. Others, designed as wall hangings, were coarser but larger. Tapestry was invented independently in Europe possibly in the 8th century. The famous French Bayeux tapestry, which tells the story of the invasion of Britain by William the Conqueror in 1066, is not a tapestry at all—it's a piece of embroidery, which is fabric decorated with needlework.

Windmill

c.600 CE

The first known windmill, invented in 7th-century Persia, was a simple wheel with cloth sails used to drive a millstone to grind grain. The wheel was mounted on a vertical shaft directly above a millstone mounted on the same shaft. These windmills were giant, upside-down versions of the early waterwheels invented seven centuries before (✱ *see* **page 54**). They developed into today's wind turbines, used to generate an environmentally friendly and renewable source of electricity.

Folding fan

c.650 CE

Folding fans, as opposed to rigid ones, were invented in Japan in the 7th century. This clever accessory became especially popular in medieval China and Japan, where there was more to fans than simply keeping cool—they were important social items, used by both men and women and often lavishly decorated. In 18th-century Europe, where all things Chinese were fashionable, folding fans became popular and were carried by wealthy women.

Zero to represent nothing

c.650 CE

Brahmagupta

Zero is a difficult idea. How can you count something that isn't there? It was a long time before mathematicians could accept a number that stood for nothing. One of the first scholars to accept the concept was the great Hindu astronomer Brahmagupta, who worked in the 7th century. The English word "zero" comes, in a roundabout way, from the Hindu word "*sunya,*" meaning "empty." Hindu mathematicians wrote zero as a circle, the same symbol that is used today.

476 CE The Western Roman empire comes to an end. German chieftain Odoacer deposes its last emperor, Romulus Augustulus, 66 years after the city of Rome was overrun by the Germanic people known as the Visigoths.

529 CE As part of a drive to rid his empire of non-Christian thinking, Byzantine emperor Justinian closes the 900-year-old Academy in Athens, a center of thought and learning founded by the great Greek philosopher Plato.

Flamethrower

c.670 CE

Callinicus of Heliopolis

Setting fire to an enemy's property usually means having to get close to it, but a weapon that shoots a jet of flame can do damage at a distance. The first people to try this were the Byzantines from Constantinople (present-day Istanbul in Turkey) in the 7th century CE. Possibly invented by a Syrian architect named Callinicus, "Greek fire"—a sticky, flaming liquid thrown in pots or squirted from tubes—was much feared by their enemies. Greek fire helped the Byzantines defeat a Saracen (Arab) fleet in 673 CE.

Paddle wheel

c.780 CE

Ships with paddle wheels have a long history. They may have existed toward the end of the 5th century CE, but the first clear description of one is given by the writer Li Kao in about 780 CE. It was a Chinese warship with twin paddle wheels turned by sailors walking on treadmills. It was said to be as fast as a sailing ship. In 1130, Chinese peasant Yang Yao led a revolt backed up by paddle warships. In 1838, British engineer Isambard Brunel launched the first transatlantic steamship service with the paddle-powered *Great Western*.

PADDLE WHEEL *This is a model of the giant wheels that drove Brunel's ship the* Great Eastern, *launched in 1858.*

STAINED-GLASS WINDOW *This window was created in about 1330.*

Kimono

c.700 CE

The Japanese kimono—a long, wide-sleeved robe—dates from about 700 CE. It has no buttons or other fastenings and is simply wrapped around the body in a particular way and tied with a sash, which is called an *obi*. The kimono developed from a similar garment worn by courtiers in China as early as 200 BCE. By the 17th century, 1,000 years of further development had turned it into the beautiful garment we know today.

Porcelain

c.800 CE

Porcelain is no ordinary pottery. It is pure white, translucent, and very strong. Its secret ingredient is a mineral called petuntse, which is a kind of granite. When mixed with china clay and fired at a high temperature, it turns to glass. Porcelain was discovered in China in about 800 CE and was perfected by about 1300 CE. From then on, China exported vast quantities to the West, where potters struggled to imitate it.

Stained-glass window

c.800 CE

In the 7th century, large sheets of glass did not exist, so builders had to make church windows by joining many small pieces of glass together. By the end of the century, they were using colored glass but did not make pictures with this until the 9th century. The glorious stained glass of Europe's Gothic cathedrals was in place by the 12th century, and painted glass appeared 200 years later.

Systematic use of zero

c.820 CE

Muhammad al-Khwarizmi

It is accepted today that a zero at the end of a number makes it 10 times bigger, e.g., 20 is 10 times bigger than 2. But early number systems were rather vague about using zero in this way. They used it to show that the tens column, for example, had nothing in it, but rarely used it in the units column. The first mathematician to use zero in

691 CE Caliph Abd al-Malik finishes the Dome of the Rock, a shrine in Jerusalem. It stands where it is said Muhammad, founder of Islam, ascended into heaven and Abraham, ancestor of the Jews, prepared to sacrifice his son.

750 CE At Tegernsee, on the Isar River in Germany, a Benedictine monastery is founded. It becomes known as München, meaning "home of the monks." It will grow to become Germany's third largest city, Munich.

today's systematic way was Muhammad al-Khwarizmi, in about 820 CE. His ideas reached the West through the efforts of the French scholar Gerbert of Aurillac, who became Pope in 999 CE.

Diagnosing smallpox

c.900 CE

Smallpox and the less dangerous disease measles have similar early symptoms. Persian physician ar-Razi, known in the West as Rhazes, told doctors how to tell the difference in about 900 CE. He said that "inquietude, nausea, and anxiety are more frequent in the Measles than in the Smallpox; while the pain in the back is more peculiar to the Smallpox than to the measles."

Cyrillic alphabet

c.900 CE

Russian and some related languages are written with the Cyrillic alphabet. It was named after St. Cyril, one of the people who preached Christianity in eastern Europe in the 9th and 10th centuries. Like the rather different alphabet used for English, it is derived from the Greek alphabet that St. Cyril knew but has several extra letters, which were needed to represent the speech sounds of the region.

Gunpowder

c.900 CE

Gunpowder was the first known substance that would burn when packed into a tube. In about 900 CE, Chinese alchemists were surprised to discover that when three well-known ingredients were mixed in the right proportions, they could produce an intense flame or explosion. They put their discovery to work in fireworks for fun and rockets for war. From the 14th century onward, Europeans used gunpowder in cannons and firearms and this changed the whole nature of warfare. Gunpowder remained the only known explosive until the 17th century. (✷ *See also* **Explosive Events.**)

EXPLOSIVE EVENTS

THE HISTORY OF GUNPOWDER is not clear. The secret was certainly known first in China, but nobody is sure whether people in the West learned it from the East or discovered it for themselves. English scientist Roger Bacon recorded the formula for making gunpowder in the 13th century, but it is possible that he discovered it by studying the works of Arabs, who had themselves learned it from the Chinese.

Medieval engraving of workers packing gunpowder into a tube

CANNONS AND ROCKETS
Gunpowder packed into a tube burns so intensely that it can throw objects out of the tube, forming a crude cannon, or propel the tube itself through the air as a rocket. Chinese scientists used both of these effects for military purposes and may also have used gunpowder to make bombs.

FIREWORKS
Gunpowder was probably first used in fireworks. Even an inaccurate rocket made a good display, experimental cannons could throw decorative balls of fire, and the explosive properties could provide fun in firecrackers.

12th-century Chinese emperor Wu-Wang entertains guests with gunpowder.

837 CE Planet Earth has a near miss on April 9 as Halley's comet makes its closest ever approach. The wandering ball of dust and ice strays to within 310,000 miles (494,000 km) of the planet. It will return in about 76 years.

874 CE Ingólfr Arnarson reaches Iceland from Norway and becomes its first inhabitant. He starts a farm, which he calls Reykjavík, meaning "smoky," because of the steam from nearby hot springs. It will become Iceland's capital.

PAPER MONEY *13th-century Mongol emperor Kublai Khan watches as officials pay his bills with paper money.*

Paper money

c.900 CE

As China grew wealthier, increasing amounts of cash were needed to keep trade going. Paper money was used occasionally before 900 CE, but it became common really only when merchants in the great trading city of Chengdu began to use it in the 10th century. Within 300 years, under the rule of the Mongol emperor Kublai Khan, China had practically replaced metal coins with paper money.

Mental hospital

918 CE

Attitudes toward mental illness have varied from place to place and time to time. In many countries, people have often put unusual behavior down to possession by demons or treated disturbed people like animals. But the people of 10th-century Baghdad (now the capital of Iraq) thought differently. Despite being constantly under attack from their enemies, they managed to set up the first known mental hospital in 918 CE. Their policy was to treat disturbed people with respect.

Andromeda galaxy

965 CE

as-Sufi

A galaxy is a system of stars. Our sun is just one star among hundreds of millions in the Milky Way galaxy. The Andromeda galaxy is 2.3 million light-years away. Islamic astronomer as-Sufi recorded it in 965 CE. Although it is very easy to see, it was not recorded again until 1612, after observation with a telescope.

Theory of vision

c.1000

Alhazen

See **pages 66–67** for the story of how an Arab scientist faked insanity to found modern optics.

Fireworks

c.1000

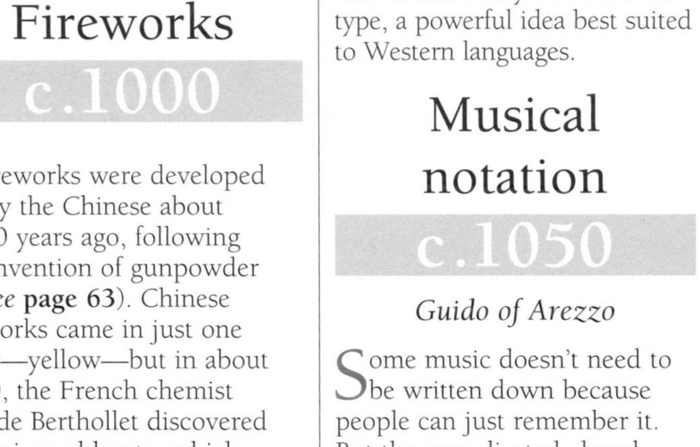

Fireworks were developed by the Chinese about 1,000 years ago, following the invention of gunpowder (✳ *see* **page 63**). Chinese fireworks came in just one color—yellow—but in about 1800, the French chemist Claude Berthollet discovered potassium chlorate, which made multicolored fireworks possible. Firework makers eventually discovered that strontium compounds produce crimson, while barium compounds produce green.

FIREWORKS *A Chinese family honors its kitchen god with a shower of sparks.*

Movable type

1045

Bi Sheng

Printing with movable type—separate letter blocks that can be assembled to form text—revolutionized Western communication in the 15th century (✳ *see* **pages 76–77**), but as early as 1045, Chinese alchemist Bi Sheng was molding types from clay and glue, then assembling them by sticking them down with resin. The types could even be reused by heating the resin to release them. Unfortunately, Chinese uses thousands of characters and doesn't really suit movable type, a powerful idea best suited to Western languages.

Musical notation

c.1050

Guido of Arezzo

Some music doesn't need to be written down because people can just remember it. But the complicated choral music of 9th-century Europe needed to be written down to

968 CE On December 22, Byzantine historian Leo the Deacon observes a total eclipse of the sun. Writing a description of what he sees, he is the first to record the glow, or corona, that surrounds the sun at totality.

986 CE Bjarni Herjulfsson from Greenland is the first European to sight the mainland of North America when his ship is blown off course in a storm. He sails along what is now the Atlantic coast of Canada before returning home.

indicate where voices should rise and fall. The squiggles people used at the time didn't look much like music until about 1050, when Guido of Arezzo, a Benedictine monk and music teacher, placed the marks on a grid of five lines, or staff. It was, however, another 500 years before people were writing music as we do today.

Mechanical clock

1088

Su Sung, Henry De Vick

The first recorded mechanical clock, built in 1088, did not use clockwork. Its Chinese inventor, Su Sung, designed a waterwheel that paused to empty a bucket after it filled, marking intervals of time. The first clockwork clock was put in the Palais de Justice, Paris, by Henry De Vick in about 1360. It had only one hand and, with errors of up to two hours a day, was probably less accurate than Su Sung's clock.

Three-field system

c.1100

The same crop grown year after year in the same field will eventually exhaust the soil. Early farmers just moved on and used new land, but this was impossible in medieval Europe because farmers had to stay in one place. From about 1100, European farmers began using a three-field system. They planted one-third of their land in the fall, another third in spring, and left the rest unplanted for a year to recover, rotating the use of the patches of land each year. In this way, the farmers got two harvests a year, and by planting a spring crop of peas or beans, which increase nitrogen in the soil, they increased the fertility of the land as well.

Gothic arch

c.1140

The pointed Gothic arches in cathedrals made these medieval buildings lighter and more spacious than earlier ones. Roman arches were semicircular, so tall arches had to be wide, which created design problems. They also needed heavy walls to stop them from spreading. Gothic arches could be made taller without making them wider, and their sideways push was smaller so walls could be thinner and windows larger.

Fireplace

c.1150

The first fireplaces were just fire pits in the middle of the floor, and smoke went out through a hole in the roof. A few fireplaces with tall chimneys appeared in the 12th century. They carried smoke away and created a draught to make the fire burn well. With a raised iron grate, which let air reach the fire from below as well as from above, they made a dent in the winter chill.

Mechanical clock
This is a model of Su Sung's mechanical clock tower.

c.1000 Murasaki Shikibu writes *The Tale of Genji*, considered to be the world's first-ever novel and one of the greatest works of Japanese literature. She is also a poet as well as a lady-in-waiting in Japan's imperial court.

1066 On Wednesday, September 27, William, Duke of Normandy, invades England with about 6,000 soldiers. He travels east toward Hastings, where on October 14, he will defeat Harold II's army and change English history.

VISION OF THE FUTURE

Arab scientist Alhazen fakes insanity to found modern optics

CITY OF CAIRO
Cairo, the capital of Egypt, is on the Nile River, 100 miles (160 km) south of the Mediterranean coast. In the 10th century, it became a walled city, one of the greatest of the medieval world. Its name comes from the Arabic words *al-Qahhirah*, which mean "victorious."

Photography, modern telephones, and television are just a few of the inventions that depend on optics—the science of light. For hundreds of years, the subject was in confusion. Then, about 1,000 years ago, a "crazy" Arab scientist named Alhazen helped everyone see things more clearly.

The story is that Alhazen went to Cairo, Egypt's fastest-growing city, to advise the notoriously cruel ruler al-Hakim on how to control the flow of the all-important Nile River. But Alhazen's ideas didn't work, and the Nile flowed on as usual. He thought that the only way to escape the wrath of the terrifying leader—who had once had all the dogs in Cairo killed just to stop them from barking—was to pretend to be insane. Fortunately, his idea worked, and al-Hakim let him get on with his studies of mathematics and physics.

Alhazen stopped thinking about water and started thinking about light. What happened when he saw something? Did feathery feelers come out of his eyes to explore the surface of objects, as Pythagoras had thought? Or was ancient Greek philosopher Epicurus right to think that light, from a source like the sun, bounced off objects and entered the eye?

To a scientist like Alhazen, Pythagoras's ideas seemed ridiculous. If they were true, why couldn't people see in the dark? So he sided with Epicurus but took his ideas a lot further. Using his mathematical skills, Alhazen figured out much of what is known today about the way light is reflected by flat and curved mirrors and bent by glass or the atmosphere. He even explained why two eyes work better than one.

Greek philosopher and mathematician Pythagoras.

SENSE OF SIGHT
Pythagoras, who lived from about 580 to 500 BCE, was one of the first people to think about how the eye worked. About 200 years later, Epicurus realized that sight was caused by light entering the eye.

Epicurus (c.341–c.270 BCE) was, like Pythagoras, born on the Greek island of Samos.

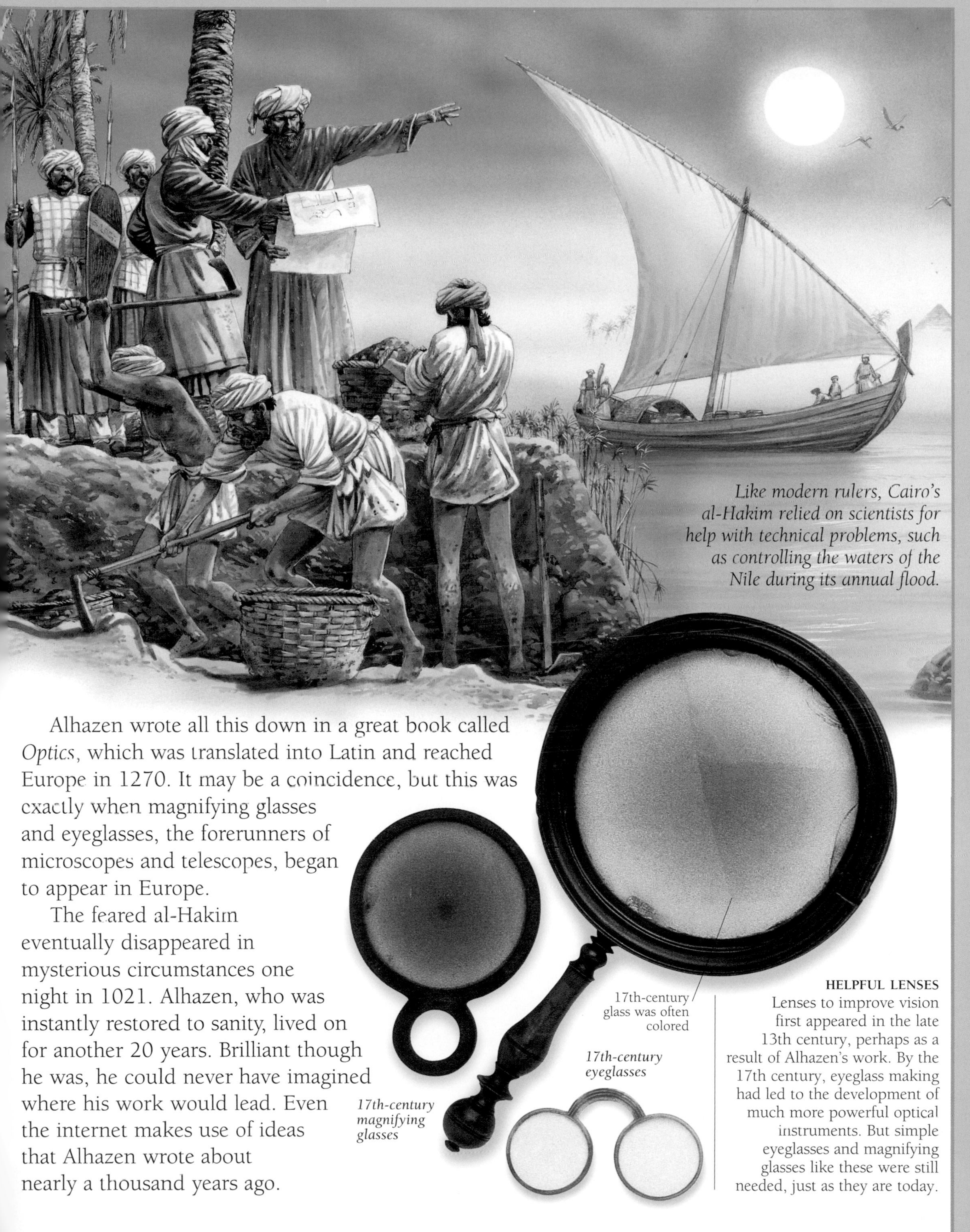

Like modern rulers, Cairo's al-Hakim relied on scientists for help with technical problems, such as controlling the waters of the Nile during its annual flood.

Alhazen wrote all this down in a great book called *Optics*, which was translated into Latin and reached Europe in 1270. It may be a coincidence, but this was exactly when magnifying glasses and eyeglasses, the forerunners of microscopes and telescopes, began to appear in Europe.

The feared al-Hakim eventually disappeared in mysterious circumstances one night in 1021. Alhazen, who was instantly restored to sanity, lived on for another 20 years. Brilliant though he was, he could never have imagined where his work would lead. Even the internet makes use of ideas that Alhazen wrote about nearly a thousand years ago.

17th-century glass was often colored

17th-century eyeglasses

17th-century magnifying glasses

HELPFUL LENSES
Lenses to improve vision first appeared in the late 13th century, perhaps as a result of Alhazen's work. By the 17th century, eyeglass making had led to the development of much more powerful optical instruments. But simple eyeglasses and magnifying glasses like these were still needed, just as they are today.

RUDDER *This model of an English ship of about 1430 has a fully developed rudder. Copied from a small image, it does not show the tiller that would have been used to control it.*

Rudder

c.1200

It is thought that some early Chinese boats were steered with simple rudders, but until about 1200 CE, most boats around the world were steered by sailors trailing oars over the side. The modern rudder arrived in stages. First, a large steering oar was attached near the back, or stern, of the boat. In about 1200, it was moved right to the stern to become a simple rudder. By about 1300, a long steering lever, called the tiller, had been added to complete the rudder.

Modern numerals

1202

Leonardo Pisano

The modern number system arrived in the West after a long, slow trip from India. The system, which was started in the 6th or 7th centuries in India, was taken up by Arab mathematicians in the 9th century and reached the West during the 10th century. It made little impact until Leonardo Pisano wrote *Liber Abaci* (Book of the Abacus) in 1202. The book explained everything about Arabic numerals, from how to write them to the mysteries of hundreds, tens, and units. The new system made calculations much easier.

Propaganda dropped from the air

1232

Military commanders have often tried to win battles with words instead of weapons. One way is to drop leaflets from the air. This tactic was tried as early as 1232, when the Mongols (nomads of central Asia) besieged the Chinese city of K'ai-feng. They used kites to drop leaflets on the people inside. It is not known whether any of the citizens read the leaflets, but by 1234 the Mongols had taken over the city.

1215 Supported by the Archbishop of Canterbury, England's barons demand a declaration of rights from King John. The Magna Carta (great charter) is drafted at Runnymede, near Windsor, and sealed by John on June 15.

1225 On the Île de la Cité in the center of Paris, the great cathedral of Notre Dame (Our Lady) is completed after 65 years' work. It sets a new standard for cathedrals and will become one of the world's most visited buildings.

Buttonhole

c.1250

You might think that buttons and buttonholes were invented together, but buttons actually came first. The ancient Greeks and Romans used buttons to fasten their clothes at the shoulder, but these went through loops, not holes. Buttonholes were invented in Europe in the 13th century. They made buttons so popular that laws were passed to limit the number that people could have, to prevent rich people from having too many.

Magnetic poles

1269

Petrus Peregrinus de Maricourt

French engineer Petrus Peregrinus de Maricourt did the first known scientific experiment on a magnet. He put a sliver of iron in various places on a round lump of magnetic rock called lodestone and marked the stone to show how the iron positioned itself each time. His lines converged at opposite sides of the stone. The marked stone looked like a globe with lines of longitude radiating from the north and south poles. He called these points the magnetic poles, a term that is still used today.

Eyeglasses

c.1280

Eyeglasses, in the form of a pair of lenses clipped on to the nose, appeared in the 13th century, but nobody is sure where they came from. The English scientist Roger Bacon described a magnifying glass for reading small print in 1268, but this is not quite the same thing. In Italy, where eyeglass making was established by 1301, two men from Florence, Alessandro di Spina and Salvino degli Armati, have been credited with the invention. But, like so much else at this time, eyeglasses may have been invented in China as early as the 10th century.

EYEGLASSES *Medieval eyeglasses were pivoted to grip the nose.*

Mathematics of the rainbow

c.1280

Qutb ash-Shirazi, Kamal Farisi

Figuring out what's going on when we see a rainbow requires advanced trigonometry (✱ *see* **page 53**), and by about 1280, Muslim astronomers had created the math they needed. At an observatory financed by a grandson of the 13th century Mongol ruler Genghis Khan, two students, Qutb ash-Shirazi and Kamal Farisi, applied the new math to the optical theories of Alhazen (✱ *see* **pages 66–67**) to offer an explanation of the way rain bends sunlight into a multicolored circle.

Rocket

c.1300

Although the Chinese may have made simple rockets as fireworks soon after the invention of gunpowder, serious military use came only later. "Arrows of flying fire" were used when the Mongols besieged the Chinese city of Kai-feng in 1232, but these were probably just fireworks tied to arrows. Chinese soldiers are not thought to have begun using rockets as weapons until 1300 at the earliest, but by 1330, rockets were equipped with explosive warheads and were no longer toys.

Shoe sizes

c.1305

The earliest system of standard shoe sizes may possibly date back to 1305, when King Edward I of England decided that the inch should be fixed at the length of three barleycorns. This made the official barleycorn one-third of an inch long. It has been said that children's shoes then began to be based on this barleycorn measure. As a large child's foot at that time was about 13 barleycorns (4.33 in/ 11 cm) long, a shoe to fit it was called size 13.

NAVIGATION CHART *This 1375 chart centers on the Mediterranean Sea. The many straight lines aided navigation.*

Navigation chart

1311

Petrus Vesconte

World maps were mostly used as book illustrations prior to the 12th century. Petrus Vesconte of Genoa, Italy, was one of the first to make navigation charts—maps useful to sailors. A 1311 chart made by him, drawn mostly from information he collected from sailors, rather than careful measurements, is the oldest known.

Printer's type case

c.1313

Wang Chen

Unaware of Bi Sheng's failure with movable type in 1045 (✱ *see* **page 64**), Chinese magistrate Wang Chen tried something similar in about 1313. He needed 60,000 wooden Chinese characters to print a book. To store these, he invented the first printer's type case, which had a compartment for each character. Because he needed so many cases, Wang Chen stacked them in layers on a spindle so that he could swivel one out as needed.

1275 Venetian explorer Marco Polo crosses Asia's Gobi Desert into China, where he travels to the court of Kublai Khan, ruler of China and lands beyond. Polo will later recount this meeting, and more, in *The Travels of Marco Polo*.

1306 A small town protected by a dam on the Amstel River in the Netherlands finally gets official recognition after being granted privileges in 1275. Its name, Amsterdam, from "Amstel dam," will become familiar to millions.

CANNON *This French print shows highly developed cannons being used during the siege of Paris by the German Empire, 1870–1871.*

Practical manual of anatomy

1316

Mondino de' Luzzi

Much of what doctors now know about the human body originally came from early examinations of the dead. An Italian doctor, Mondino de' Luzzi, did a lot of this and often gave public lectures while he dissected corpses. Although he tended to see what his predecessor Galen (✱ *see* **page 58**) told him he should, his 1316 book *Anathomia Mundini* was the first European anatomy book since ancient times that was based on observation of human bodies. It was the first systematic guide to human dissection and remained the standard manual until 1543, when Andreas Vesalius's manual was published (✱ *see* **page 80**).

Cannon

c.1320

The Chinese made cannons (large guns that stand on the ground) soon after they invented gunpowder (✱ *see* **page 63**), but because they were made only of bamboo, they were really just oversized fireworks. Only cannon barrels made of bronze or iron were strong enough to withstand a powerful explosion. They were not made until about 1320, when techniques for casting and boring them were perfected. The new weapons were rushed into action all over Europe. By the 15th century, the cannon had grown into a monster that could fire balls weighing more than 55 lb (25 kg).

Alchemy textbook

c.1320

Geber

The first popular books on alchemy—the study of base metals and theories for turning them into gold—were published in 1320 under a false name. By 1300, several books written by 8th-century Arab alchemist Jabir ibn Hayyan had been translated into Latin. The books had made Jabir famous, so an unknown alchemist pretended to be Jabir when he wrote *De Investigatione Perfectionis* (The Study of Perfection) to make people read it. He wrote several other books under the name Geber (his version of Jabir), but he could really have used his own name. His books were so good that alchemists everywhere used them anyway.

Striking clock

1335

Early clocks just rang a bell to mark the beginning of each hour. The first clock to sound out the actual time was built in Milan, Italy, and started striking in 1335. It was a major achievement for medieval technology—a machine that could count. The Milan clock was quickly followed by others throughout Europe, including one in Salisbury cathedral, England, which was installed in 1386 and is still working today.

Chromatic keyboard

c.1350

The first keyboard instrument was the organ, but it couldn't play all the different

1321 Italian poet Dante Alighieri dies on September 14 at the age of 56. His *Divine Comedy*, written in Italian, not Latin, describes a journey through hell, purgatory, and paradise. It is one of the greatest poems in all literature.

1333 A catastrophic flood sweeps through the Italian city of Florence as the Arno River overflows its banks. All of the city's bridges are destroyed. Despite this, Florence grows and prospers, becoming one of Italy's finest cities.

sharps and flats, or semitones. It was therefore a great step forward when, in about 1350, organs in Europe began to have chromatic keyboards. These had semitones as well as whole tones, allowing them to play in more than one key. But the keyboards were designed for chubby fingers, and it was the end of the 15th century before organ keys slimmed down to their present size.

Firearms

c.1350

Cannons were fairly easy to design, but figuring out how smaller, portable weapons could be charged with powder, aimed, and fired proved more difficult. The earliest attempts, used in Europe from about 1350, had no triggers and were held under the arm, making it impossible to aim them accurately. The first firearm that looked anything like a modern weapon was the harquebus. This didn't reach the battlefield until about 1470, and it was useless against fast, accurate bows and arrows.

Clavichord

c.1360

The clavichord is a distant ancestor of the piano. The first reference to what was probably a clavichord is in a French ledger of about 1360, although the musical instrument did not get its modern name until later. The clavichord's mechanism is very simple: when a key is pushed down, a thin metal blade strikes the string. The note sounds until the key is released, giving the player great control over the sound—a definite advantage for musicians who like to practice at night.

Canal lock

c.1373

Canal locks are pieces of medieval technology that can still be seen in action. They move boats up and down between stretches of canal with different water levels, trapping boats in a basin that fills to raise them or empties to lower them. The first is said to have been built at Vreeswijk in the Netherlands, in 1373, but there were certainly locks at Viterbo, Italy, by 1481.

Woodcut

c.1400

A woodcut is a picture carved on a piece of fine-grained wood, which is then used for printing. Whole books were being printed from wood blocks in China by 600 CE, but the woodcut has a different history. It began to be used in about 1400, especially for the production of playing cards. But it really came into its own after 1450, when printing from movable types had been perfected. Readers wanted to see the same kind of pictures they had always had in handwritten books, and the woodcut was there to provide them.

Players used a bat resembling a modern tennis racket

Tennis

c.1400

Tennis today is a very different game from the French pastime *jeu de paume* (palm game) that started it all. As the name suggests, the French game was played with hands, not rackets. By about 1400, wooden bats had replaced hands, and a game resembling tennis emerged. In the 16th century, it was played indoors with rackets. Then, about 300 years later, a British army officer, Walter Wingfield, adapted the game to outdoors, creating "lawn" tennis as it is now known.

TENNIS *The game of* jeu de paume *was popular in 18th-century France.*

Carpenter's brace

c.1400

A type of drill invented in about 1400, the brace is also the ancestor of the car-engine crankshaft. It is a rod with a U shape in the middle, a handrest at the top, and a drill bit at the bottom. The carpenter steadies it with the handrest, grasps the U, and moves his arm, making the same action as a piston in a car.

1347 Germ warfare hits Europe as soldiers from the East catapult corpses infected with Black Death into a trading post in southern Ukraine. The virulent disease spreads rapidly, killing a third of Europe's population in four years.

1362 For the first time since 1066, English court proceedings are conducted in English instead of Latin or Norman French. The Statute of Pleadings, which makes this possible, says that proceedings must still be recorded in Latin.

NEW WORLDS, NEW IDEAS

HUMAN UNDERSTANDING of the world grew enormously between 1400 and 1750. Our planet ceased to be seen as the center of the universe and seemed to grow as explorers reached new lands. New discoveries, and new means to communicate them, led to an age of reason and the beginnings of modern science.

METAL MOVABLE TYPE *These casts are from Korean bronze type used in about 1406.*

Metal movable type

1403

Htai Tjong

People in Korea started working on movable metal types in the 14th century, and in 1403, King Htai Tjong of Korea had the first true font of metal type made. One hundred thousand bronze characters were cast, and that was just the start. The king had two more complete fonts ready long before movable type was perfected in Germany (✱ *see* **pages 75 and 76–77**).

Water-powered ironworks

1408

Walter Skirlaw

Medieval ironworkers heated iron ore with charcoal in a furnace to produce a spongy lump of iron called a bloom. The hotter the fire was, the better the furnace worked, so air was pumped in with bellows to feed the flames. As demand for iron grew and furnaces got larger, something more than muscle power was needed to work the bellows. In England, which would become the largest iron producer in the world, the problem was tackled by Walter Skirlaw, the Bishop of Durham. He set up a water-powered bloomery in 1408.

Code breaking

1412

al-Kalka-shandi

Early attempts at secret writing were not effective, but by the late 14th century, Arab code writers and breakers, called cryptographers, were getting serious. They invented systems for changing each letter into a different one and used the fact that some letters occur more often than others to decipher supposedly secret messages. These tricks of the trade were published in 1412 by Egyptian scholar al-Kalka-shandi, forming the first reliable set of instructions for code makers and breakers.

Perspective

c.1412

Filippo Brunelleschi, Leon Alberti

The Italian architect and artist Filippo Brunelleschi discovered linear perspective—the art of drawing objects in a way that gives an impression of their size and relative position—between 1410 and 1415. The discovery revolutionized the way artists drew pictures. Until he discovered the "vanishing point," to which all parallel lines converge, pictures were built up from flat shapes. Twenty years later, his friend Leon Alberti wrote a book giving detailed instructions on how to create the correct perspective. This enabled painters to produce pictures with a realism that was unsurpassed until 19th-century photography.

Tower windmill

c.1420

One problem with windmills is that the wind doesn't always blow from the same direction. Early windmills contained their entire mechanism in a huge wooden box mounted on a pivot, so it was difficult to swing the sails into the wind. The tower mill, invented in about 1420, had all its heavy machinery in a fixed tower.

Only the sails, which were mounted on a movable cap, had to be moved to track the wind—a much easier task.

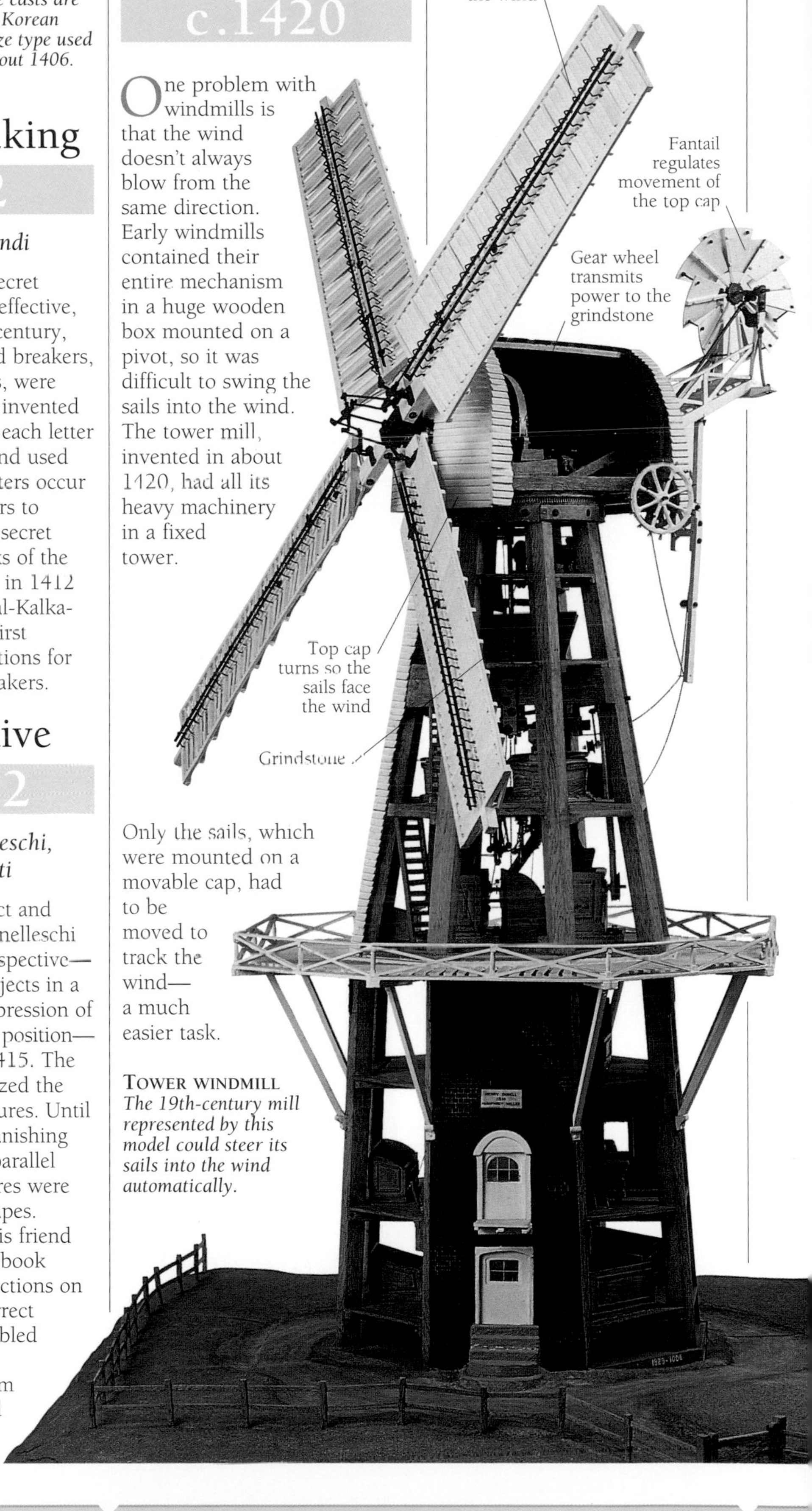

TOWER WINDMILL *The 19th-century mill represented by this model could steer its sails into the wind automatically.*

1405 Chinese admiral Zheng He ends China's isolation with the first of a series of missions to countries around the South China Sea, which he knows as the Western Oceans. Sixty-two ships reach Indochina, Java, and Sri Lanka.

1418 Italian architect Filippo Brunelleschi is asked to design the dome of Florence's cathedral. His highly original solution, octagonal in form, with its white structural ribs exposed on the outside, will dominate the city's skyline.

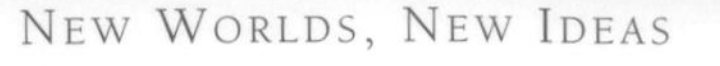

Flywheel

c.1430

A car engine (✱ *see* **page 150**) wouldn't work without its flywheel, a heavy wheel that stores energy during the brief bursts of burning inside the cylinders, then releases it to keep the engine running smoothly. Although early devices like the potter's wheel incorporated a kind of flywheel action, separate flywheels first appeared in the early 15th century. They evened out the jerky rhythm of machines powered by feet moving up and down on a treadle.

Oil painting

1430

Robert Campin, Jan van Eyck

Although the Romans knew about oil paint, it was the French and Flemish painters Robert Campin and Jan van Eyck who perfected its use in art. Both were attracted by the realism that oil paint allowed. Earlier paints, such as tempera, which was made with eggs, couldn't produce the same smoothly graded tones. Using the new paint and the new laws of perspective (✱ *see* **page 73**), van Eyck painted pictures with a realism never seen before.

Peep show

1437

Leon Alberti

Having studied perspective, Leon Alberti realized that he could apply the same laws to a miniature scene to make it more realistic. The peep show was a box with a hole in one end. Inside was a three-dimensional scene modeled in perspective. When the model was viewed through the hole, it leapt to life with startling realism. Alberti made his first peep shows in 1437. He even painted the scenery on glass to allow for lighting effects.

HARPSICHORD *This harpsichord was made in Belgium in about 1600. It has two keyboards, known as manuals.*

Beautifully decorated case indicates the status of the harpsichord's owner

Harpsichord

c.1450

The harpsichord was king of the keyboards from about 1500 until well after the piano was invented in 1709 (✱ *see* **page 100**). Unlike the piano, its strings are plucked, not struck with hammers, as the keys are pressed. Because of this, it is not possible to vary the loudness of a note by striking the key with more or less force. Some harpsichords have several sets of strings so that pieces of music can be played at different volumes. The instrument was first described in about 1450. It spread rapidly throughout Europe and is still played today.

Anemometer

c.1450

Leon Alberti

Weather watchers measure the speed of the wind with an anemometer (from the Greek word "*anemos*," meaning "wind"). The type with cups attached to a vertical shaft dates from about 1850, but the first anemometer was devised 400 years earlier. Italian artist and mathematician Leon Alberti's instrument was much simpler—just a rectangular metal plate, hinged at the top. When the wind blew, the plate tilted, giving a rough indication of the speed. Alberti described it in about 1450 in his book *The Pleasures of Mathematics*. As British scientist Robert Hooke was reinventing a more accurate form of anemometer, Mayans were building "windtowers."

Trombone

c.1450

Originally called the sackbut, the trombone was invented in France in about 1450. It is basically a tube that produces sound from vibration of the lips. The simplest instruments of this type can play only a few notes because their length is fixed. A trombone can play a full range of notes because its length can be changed with tubes that slide in and out. The modern trombone has not changed much since the original instrument was designed more than 550 years ago.

1431 French military leader Joan of Arc is convicted of denying true religion, after she hears voices that guide her to incite the French to expel the English. On Wednesday, May 30, the English burn her at the stake in Rouen.

1435 Italian sculptor Donatello completes a nearly life-size bronze statue of the biblical hero David, the first nude figure made since ancient times. People are astonished by the expressive realism of this freestanding work of art.

Metal printing plate

c.1455

Woodcuts, made in Europe from about 1400 (✱ *see* **page 71**), could not produce as finely detailed pictures, but metal plates could. An artist engraved the required lines on the plate, usually made of copper, with a sharp tool called a graver. The plate was then covered with greasy ink and the surface wiped clean again, leaving ink only in the engraved lines. When damp paper was pressed hard onto the plate, it picked up the ink from the lines, forming a print. This process, known as intaglio, was first used in about 1455. It required more pressure than normal printing, so printers still used woodcuts in books containing text printed with type.

Letterpress printing

1455

Johann Gutenberg

See **pages 76–77** for the story of how Gutenberg died in poverty as printing changed the world.

Dance notation

c.1460

People who teach dance or develop dances have often needed to write down the movements they want the dancers to make. The ancient Egyptians did this to some extent with hieroglyphs, but the earliest written system appeared in Spain in about 1460, using letters to represent movements. In other parts of Europe, shortened words were used for the same purpose in instruction books for dancers, such as two found in the library of Margaret of Austria: *The Book of Low Dances* (c.1460) and *The Art and Teaching of Fine Dancing* (c.1488).

Roman type *This title page from a 16th-century philosophical work shows the elegant type at its best.*

Roman type

1464

Adolf Rusch

The first printed books used heavy, spiked letters. Printers soon wanted lighter letters better suited to the new printing technique. They chose an alphabet they thought was Roman, but which had actually been designed by a 9th-century English monk. The first "roman" type was used by German printer Adolf Rusch in 1464. In 1465, two other German printers, Sweynheim and Pannartz, used a type even closer to today's roman type, which is what you are reading.

MARGA-
RITA PHILOSOPHICA, RATI-
onalis, Moralis philoſophiæ principia, duodecim libris dialogice cõple-
ctens, olim ab ipſo autore recognita:
nuper aũt ab Orontio Fineo Delphi
nate caſtigata & aucta, unà cum ap-
pendicibus itidem emẽdatis, & quã
plurimis additionibus & figuris, ab
eodem inſignitis. Quorũ omni-
um copioſus index, uerſa
continetur pagella.

Vireſcit uulnere uirtus.

BASILEAE 1535.

1436 The first of two laws limiting trade in grain is passed in England. The aim of the Corn Laws is to make England self-sufficient in grain by restricting both imports and exports. The effect is widespread starvation as prices rocket.

1452 The cathedral in Florence receives the last of three pairs of bronze doors by sculptor Lorenzo Ghiberti. They show *Old Testament* scenes modeled in deep, naturalistic relief. Centuries later, people will still flock to see them.

THE POWER OF THE PRESS

Inventor Johann Gutenberg dies in poverty as printing changes the world

JOHANN GUTENBERG
Little is known about Johann Gutenberg, not even his date of birth. His skill as a jeweler must have helped him perfect the metal types he needed.

Fifteenth-century Europe was itching for change. For more than 1,000 years, it had been dominated by the Church and a society that valued traditional wisdom. Now new ideas were in the air. But with only pen and parchment to spread the word, that was where they were likely to stay.

In the German city of Strasburg, a young jeweler named Johann Gutenberg was acting very strangely. He was borrowing money from his friends to buy materials that had nothing to do with jewelry. He wouldn't say why he needed them or why they cost so much. In the end, his friends refused to lend him any more money until he came clean. His secret astonished them. He was working on an invention that would allow books to be mass-produced instead of copied out by hand.

Gutenberg's new movable type, oil-based ink, and printing press looked as if they had a future, and in 1438, the friends formed a partnership. But things began to go wrong. One partner died and his children wanted a share in the partnership. They took Gutenberg to court. They lost, but the secret of Gutenberg's work got out, and the race to print a book was on.

Gutenberg returned to his home city, Mainz, to perfect his invention. Still desperate for money,

Printer pulls this bar to bring the platen down on the type

Paper is held on this tympan, which is folded down on top of the type

A form of type is placed on the press bed

Platen

Coffin moves under the platen

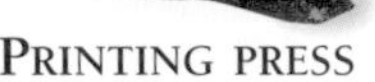

PRINTING PRESS
The printing press developed from winemaking and bookbinding presses. The inked type faced upward and paper was pressed down on it.

MAKING A MATRIX
Each letter was carved on a steel punch, which was then hammered into a piece of copper to form a matrix. This was clamped into a mold, and molten metal was poured in, filling the shape punched into the matrix to form the type.

Steel punches have a letter carved on the end

Punch hammered into soft copper

Copper matrices carry an impression of the letter

he persuaded businessman Johann Fust to make him two large loans. By 1455, Gutenberg's first book was ready. He showed it off at the trade fair in nearby Frankfurt, where visitors commented on the book's clarity.

Early printing was hard work. Type was set and inked by hand, and it took two or three people to produce each page.

It was then that Fust suggested it was time he got his money back. But Gutenberg couldn't or wouldn't pay. Once again, he found himself facing a judge in court. This time, he didn't win. Fust got control of everything. Pausing only to steal Gutenberg's best assistant, he set himself up as the world's first successful printer.

Fust didn't keep his lead for long. Within 25 years, there were printers all over Europe. By 1500, they had printed 30,000 books, spreading new ideas far and wide and helping launch the age we call the Renaissance.

And Johann Gutenberg? He kept on printing but didn't make much money. The Archbishop of Mainz gave him food and clothing, but by 1468, Gutenberg was dead. The future he had helped create was on its way without him.

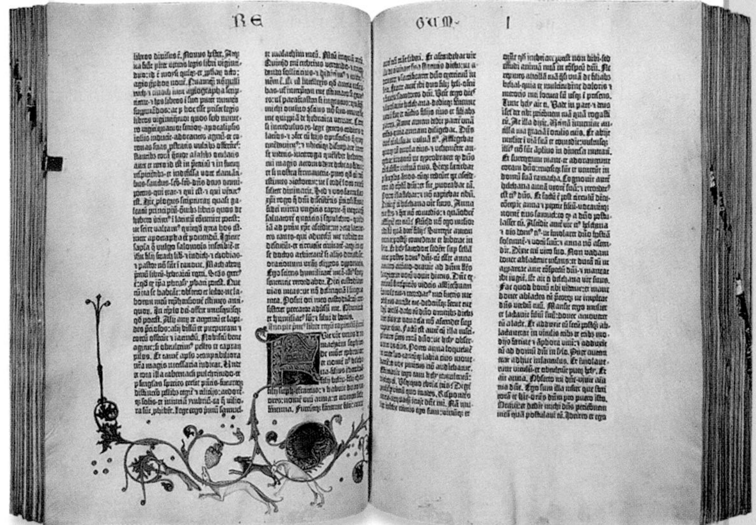

First books
The first books, like this Gutenberg Bible, were designed to imitate handwritten work. The printed letters were often embellished by hand with elaborate colored decoration.

Cryptographic frequency table

1465

Leon Alberti

A frequency table shows how often each letter of the alphabet is used. With this table, anyone can crack a simple substitution cipher. For example, in English, "e" is the most often used letter. If "k" is the most common letter in a ciphered document, it must represent "e." The first frequency table was published in 1465 by the Italian architect Leon Alberti. Because it made simple ciphers useless, Alberti also invented a cipher wheel that encrypted messages more securely.

Carillon

c.1480

Visitors to the Netherlands and Belgium can still enjoy the haunting sound of the carillon, a set of bells that plays tunes. Developed from earlier devices that produced simple clock chimes, it appeared around 1480. The secret of the carillon lies in the careful shaping of the bells. If this is not done correctly, they generate discordant tones that ruin the music.

Stove

1490

An open fire wastes energy, so people put their fires in stone, tile, or brick ovens. The first recorded stove was built in Alsace, France, in 1490, trapping heat before it went up the chimney. Later stoves had iron fins to regulate the flow of the smoke and extract heat from it. In Russia, it was often part of the building, with flues heating all the rooms.

The New World

1492

Christopher Columbus

In the 15th century, a young Italian sailor made a miscalculation that led him to the Americas. Christopher Columbus thought the Earth was smaller than it really is. Because it was round, he said a quicker way of getting to China and India in the east would be to sail westward. Most people did not believe him, but in 1492, Queen Isabella of Spain sponsored a voyage to try out his idea. He never reached India but landed instead in the West Indies. Columbus made four voyages to this "New World" and reached South America, at what is now Venezuela, on his third voyage, in 1498. Although he failed to find a new route to Asia, his discovery brought the New World and Europe together, changing both forever.
(✳ *See also* **Columbus in the Americas**)

America
Columbus sailed westward on August 3, 1492, in this ship, the Santa Maria.

Square sails carried on the main mast and foremast

The *Santa Maria* was a caravel from northern Spain

Short, stocky body

Automatic keyboard instrument

c.1500

Before about 1500, musicians were needed to make instruments play music. Then instruments that played themselves began to appear. One had a cylinder the width of the keyboard with pins sticking out of it, one for each note to be played. Someone turned a handle to make the cylinder revolve, and the pins worked the keys to make them play harpsichord or organ music. King Henry VIII of England had an automatic keyboard instrument, and street entertainers are still using them in the 21st century.

1455 The Wars of the Roses, a series of civil wars fought over who should rule England, begins with a battle at St. Albans. On this occasion, York, whose emblem is a white rose, defeats Lancaster, with their emblem of a red rose.

1475 In Bruges, Flanders, William Caxton publishes the first book to be printed in English. Having learned about printing in Germany, he uses it to produce *Recuyell of the Historyes of Troye*, which he has translated from French.

COLUMBUS IN THE AMERICAS

When Columbus arrived in the Americas, both the north and south continents were already inhabited by people who had lived there for thousands of years and built advanced civilizations of their own. Columbus and his men brutally suppressed the indigenous peoples, killing and enslaving many of them, and decimating their populations. Soon after, European immigrants began to flood to the "New World," changing the continent forever.

Columbus meets native inhabitants of the New World

The medieval world
Before Columbus sailed west, the entire world known to Europeans consisted of Asia, Africa, and Europe. China dominated Asia, while power in Europe was shared by many countries, including England, France, and Spain.

Columbus's big idea
Trade with the East was important in the 15th century, but getting there was difficult. Columbus thought he could reach the East by sailing west. Expert sailors told him he was wrong but failed to stop him from attempting it.

Unfair exchange
Europeans brought new plants, animals, and ideas to the Americas, in return acquiring new foods such as corn and potatoes. These newcomers were often bad news for native people, attacking them, enslaving them, and bringing disease.

Pineapple *A pineapple's fruit is formed by a number of separate flowers fusing together.*

Pineapple

c.1500

The pineapple, a native of South America, was unknown to Europeans before Columbus' discovery of America in 1498. Europeans then began to transport the fruit and grow the plants elsewhere. By 1502, Portuguese explorers had found pineapples in the West Indies. They were soon growing them 4,400 miles (7,000 km) away on St. Helena, an island in the South Atlantic, which was trading with Europe by 1590. By this time, the English adventurer Sir Walter Raleigh had discovered the pineapple on one of his voyages to North and South America.

Watch

1500

Peter Henlein

The first watch was the size of a hamburger. Invented by German locksmith Peter Henlein, it used a spring instead of weights to drive clockwork inside. Henlein's "Nuremberg egg"' had a metal cover, which had to be lifted to see the time, and no minute hand. Despite these shortcomings, people could at last carry the time with them.

Halftone woodblock print

1510

Lucas Cranach, Hans Burgkmair

Early printing could produce pictures only in stark black and white. Cross-hatching could be used to suggest in-between tones, but it was not very convincing. Two German artists, Lucas Cranach and Hans Burgkmair, were the first to solve this problem. They made several woodcuts for each picture, one for black, one for gray, one for a lighter gray, and so on. Printed on top of each other, they gave realistic results.

1478 King Ferdinand V and Queen Isabella of Spain, tell Pope Sixtus VI to set up the Spanish Inquisition. Its aim is to seek out and destroy enemies of the Roman Catholic Church. It will become notorious for its use of torture.

1510 In the Netherlands, painter Hieronymus Bosch completes his strange and disturbing triptych (picture in three sections) called The *Garden of Earthly Delights*. Its nightmare symbolism will influence painters 400 years later.

Laudanum

c.1520

Paracelcus

From the early 16th century, doctors used laudanum as a painkiller, until other drugs became popular nearly 400 years later. Made by dissolving opium in alcohol, it was introduced by Paracelcus, a Swiss physician. In England, Thomas Sydenham pioneered its use about a century after Paracelcus. Laudanum was widely used as a painkiller in the 18th and 19th centuries, and many patients became addicted to it.

LAUDANUM *These laudanum bottles were essential items in the 19th-century medicine chest.*

Music type

c.1525

Pierre Attaignant

Printing music from movable type was, to begin with, done in two steps: first the five-line staff, then the notes. By 1525, French printer Pierre Attaignant had invented a better system. Each note carried a bit of staff, so lines and notes were printed together. Within 10 years, Attaignant was printing music by every leading composer.

Fluorspar

1529

Georgius Bauer

As well as being a beautiful crystal, fluorspar, or fluorite, is important in making steel and aluminum. It is a compound of calcium and fluorine, often found near hot springs. The German scholar and scientist Georgius Bauer, usually known as Agricola, described it first in 1529. He regarded it as a fossil, the term that scientists used then for anything found in the earth.

Scientific study of human anatomy

1543

Andreas Vesalius

For centuries, what doctors knew about the structure of the human body was largely based on the work of the Greek physician Galen (✱ *see* **page 58**). Then, Flemish physician Andreas Vesalius took a fresh look at human anatomy. From his own dissections, he discovered that Galen had based his work on animals, not humans. In 1543, Vesalius produced a book describing human anatomy in detail. It showed what could be done by daring to dissect.

Solar system

1543

Nicolaus Copernicus

In the 16th century, most people believed that the planet Earth stood still at the center of a moving universe.

SOLAR SYSTEM *Users turned the handle of this 18th-century orrery to show the annual rotation of the Earth around the sun and the moon's rotation around Earth.*

When Nicolaus Copernicus published a book in 1543 saying that Earth orbits the sun and revolves daily on its own axis, few believed him. By the late 17th century, however, most scientists in Britain, France, Denmark, and the Netherlands agreed with Copernicus, and in 1758, the Roman Catholic Church finally allowed its members to read what he had written.

Botanical garden

1543

Botanical gardens are not just places to stroll. They are also living libraries of scientific knowledge, often gathered over centuries. The first public botanical garden was opened at Pisa, Italy, in 1543. Two years later, another was opened by the University of Padua in Italy. Modern botanical gardens, such as Kew Gardens in England, maintain seed banks to help save plants from extinction.

Complex numbers

1545

Gerolamo Cardano

Complex numbers are used in advanced mathematics. Without them, problems that involve the square root of a negative number cannot be solved. This is because the squares of negative numbers are always positive, so there is

1535 French explorer Jacques Cartier, trying to find a route to China through North America, sails up a river he names the St. Lawrence to a hill he calls Mont Réal and a village that will become Quebec. It is the beginning of Canada.

1535 The Inca Empire of Peru is destroyed by Spanish conqueror Francisco Pizarro. Having executed chieftain Atahualpa two years earlier, he sacks Cuzco, capital of the Inca Empire, and founds the modern city of Lima.

no "real" number that can be a square root of a negative number. In 1545, Italian mathematician Gerolamo Cardano swept this difficulty aside by inventing a new number to represent the square root of –1. Combined with ordinary numbers, it gave what are now called complex numbers, providing the solution to a wide range of mathematical problems.

Stage lighting

1545

Sebastiano Serlio

In the early 16th century, the stages of most theaters in Europe were lit by daylight, but Italian architects were hoping to create a type of theatrical lighting to control stage effects. In 1545, Sebastiano Serlio suggested placing a globe of colored water in front of a torch or candle to tint and concentrate the light.

Railroads in mines

c.1550

Trains pulled by locomotives did not appear until the 19th century, but transportation by rail was used earlier. Wheels roll more easily on rails than on a road, which allows heavier loads to be pulled. Railroads first appeared in mines, where tons of rock had to be moved through narrow tunnels. The earliest was built in France in about 1550. Similar railroads existed in England by 1605.

Occupational disease

1556

Georgius Bauer

People are not designed to work in mines and factories, where dust and chemicals can attack them at close quarters and make them ill. One of the first people to recognize this was Georgius Bauer, better known as Agricola. In his great book *De Re Metallica* (About Metallurgy), he described the appalling conditions that existed in 16th-century mines and the occupational diseases, such as "difficulty in breathing and destruction of the lungs," that miners suffered.

Camera obscura

1558

Giambattista della Porta

The term "camera obscura" means "a dark room," and the modern camera started as a darkened room with a tiny hole in it. On the wall opposite the hole, a faithful, though upside-down, image of the outside world appeared. It was fuzzy and dim until 1558, when Italian physicist Giambattista della Porta suggested changing the hole to a lens. The lens let in more light and focused it to a sharp image, which an artist could trace accurately.

Botanical garden *The Jardin des Plantes, Paris, was opened to the public in 1650.*

1536 When the Roman Catholic Church will not allow him to divorce his wife, King Henry VIII of England says that he will no longer obey the Pope. He closes down nunneries, monasteries, and similar places and confiscates their property.

1555 French astrologer and doctor Nostradamus publishes his book *Centuries*. Its verses, written in language that can be interpreted in different ways, are said to predict the future. One says the end of the world will be in 3797.

Pulmonary circulation

1564

Matteo Colombo

Long before William Harvey showed that blood circulates around the body (✳ *see* **page 89**), Italian surgeon Matteo Colombo showed its circulation through the lungs. In a book published in 1559, he described how blood was pumped by the heart to the lungs, where it mixed with a "spirit" (oxygen), became bright red, and was then returned to the heart.

Pencil

1565

Conrad Gesner

Conrad Gesner, a German-Swiss naturalist, was the first person to identify graphite as a distinct mineral. And he was also the first to think of using this soft, slippery form of carbon for writing. In 1565, he had the idea of placing it in a wooden holder to form a writing instrument. An abundant source of graphite was discovered in England at about this time, but pencils as we know them, with their "lead" glued into place, were not made until 1812.

Mercator map projection

1568

Gerhard Mercator

Mapmakers have to show the curved Earth on flat paper, called a projection, so they cannot avoid distorting it in some way. The Flemish geographer Gerhard Mercator was the first person to tackle this systematically. He knew that for easy navigation, sailors needed a map that showed constant compass directions as straight lines. His way of representing the world does this. Although it makes countries near the poles look much too big, it is still used for many maps today.

Supernova

1572

Tycho Brahe

A central point of the teachings of Aristotle was that the stars never changed. So the Danish astronomer Tycho Brahe got a big shock on November 11, 1572, when he noticed that the constellation of Cassiopeia had acquired a bright new star. We know now that it was a supernova—a star destroying itself in a massive explosion. Tycho confirmed that the star was beyond the moon, therefore in the realm of the "fixed" stars. When he published this observation in 1573, his reputation was made. His star had exploded those ancient beliefs.

Gregorian calendar *This 18th-century perpetual calendar gives the date of Easter each year either in the Julian or Gregorian calendar.*

Instructions for finding the date of Easter are given on the back

Bottle cork

c.1580

For centuries, wine came in jars or barrels, which did not usually have corks. When bottles appeared, their stoppers were often made of cork. It is not clear when this material became widely used, but in about 1600 Shakespeare wrote his play *As You Like It*. One character says to another, "Take the cork out of thy mouth, that I may drink thy tidings," showing that Shakespeare's audience must have been familiar with the invention.

Gregorian calendar

1582

Pope Gregory XIII

Although Julius Caesar improved the calendar enormously in 45 BCE (✳ *see* **page 55**), by 1582 it had fallen behind the seasons again. The reason was that an Earth year is 365.242 days, not 365.25 as Caesar had assumed. Pope Gregory XIII sorted things out once and for all. First, he chopped out 10 days to reset the calendar. Then, by decreeing that one leap year should disappear in three out of every four centuries, he corrected the error, creating the calendar we use today.

Constant swing of a pendulum

c.1583

Galileo Galilei

The time a pendulum takes to swing from side to side is the same whatever the size of the swing, provided it is not too large. The great Italian scientist Galileo was the first to notice this in about 1583, supposedly while watching a lamp swinging in Pisa cathedral during a boring service. The problem of accurate time-keeping was solved in principle, but a practical pendulum clock was not available until Christiaan Huygens of the Netherlands built one in 1657 (✳ *see* **page 92**).

1564 On April 26, a baby who will become the world's most famous writer is christened in Stratford-upon-Avon, England. His father, merchant John Shakespeare, and mother, Mary Arden, call their first son William.

1570 A new architecture based on clean, classical lines and simple layout is born in Italy as Andrea Palladio completes the Villa Rotunda in Vincenza. Thousands of "Palladian" buildings will appear in the centuries to come.

CONSTANT SWING OF A PENDULUM *Galileo designed his pendulum machine in the 16th century. This model of it was built in 1883.*

Infinity of the universe

1584

Giordano Bruno

Astronomical references in the Bible reflect the current beliefs of the time, that Earth is the centre of the universe. The Italian philosopher and poet Giordano Bruno had other ideas, and was burned at the stake in 1600 for views that now seem normal. It was bad enough that he believed that Earth orbited the Sun. It was unforgivable of him to say that the universe contained an infinity of worlds like our own. What really sealed his fate was his statement that the Bible should guide morality, not astronomy.

INFINITY OF THE UNIVERSE *The universe is much bigger than early astronomers, such as Hipparchus, once thought.*

Decimals

1585

Simon Stevin

The idea of decimals was known but not much used until the Flemish mathematician Simon Stevin published a little pamphlet called *La Thiende* (The Tenth) in 1585. He proposed a complicated way of writing decimal fractions, which we no longer use. He also advocated the use of decimal coins, measures, and weights—a suggestion that has been taken up, with varying degrees of enthusiasm, almost everywhere.

Triangle of forces

1586

Simon Stevin

A problem in mechanics is how an object will move when pulled or pushed in two directions at once. We can solve it with something called a parallelogram of forces, in which the strength and direction of forces acting on an object are represented by the sides of a parallelogram. This technique was developed from the slightly simpler triangle of forces invented by Simon Stevin in 1586. It was a new departure at the time, as were many of Stevin's discoveries, some of which put him ahead of the more famous Galileo.

Book carousel

1588

Agostino Ramelli

These days, we can access a range of information without leaving our seats, using mobile apps and the internet. This is not a new idea. In 1588, Italian engineer Agostino Ramelli realized that readers were natural couch potatoes and designed a large wooden gadget like a fairground Ferris wheel, with shelves that stayed horizontal as the wheel turned. Users could stay seated while they spun the wheel to consult any one of 10 volumes. Ramelli recommended it particularly for "those who are suffering from indisposition."

1577 El Greco, a painter with a unique, almost mystical style, arrives in Toledo, Spain. The Cretan-born artist expresses his spirituality by crowding his pictures with elongated figures stretching toward heaven.

1588 In May, Philip II of Spain sends a heavily armed fleet of 130 ships—the Spanish Armada—to invade Elizabeth I's England. After a rousing speech by the queen, English naval forces defeat the Spanish invaders.

KNITTING MACHINE *This 19th-century machine is a development of Lee's design.*

Knitting machine

1589

William Lee

When English clergyman William Lee realized that his girlfriend liked hand knitting more than him, he set out to change this. He designed a knitting machine in 1589, which remained in use until the 19th century. Some of its principles are still used today. Lee asked Queen Elizabeth I to protect his ideas. First she said the machine was no good, and then she said it was too good and would ruin hand knitters. Lee died in poverty.

Flush toilet

1591

John Harington

Toilet humor goes back to the inventor of the flush toilet, or water closet, John Harington. He was a famous wit at the court of the English queen Elizabeth I, and he published his design under the title *The Metamorphosis of Ajax*, a pun on the word "jakes"—Elizabethan slang for a toilet. Harington installed the first water closet in England at Richmond Palace, but his invention was not much used before the late 18th century, when the U-bend and cistern were invented.

Modern algebraic notation

1591

François Viète

The first person to write algebra more or less as we do today was the French mathematician François Viète. His book *Introduction to the Analytical Arts* was the first to use letters consistently for mathematical quantities. Viète also introduced the plus and minus signs and used words such as "quadratus" instead of signs.

Thermoscope

1592

Galileo Galilei

Galileo is famous for revolutionizing physics with his experiments and for insisting that the Earth orbited the sun. He also made several useful inventions, including the thermoscope. Noticing that air expanded when it got warm, he dipped the neck of a bottle into liquid. As the air in the bottle warmed or cooled, the liquid was pushed out or sucked in, indicating the temperature.

Wind-driven sawmill

1592

Cornelis Cornelisz

Windmills for grinding grain and windmills for pumping water—that was about it until a Dutch painter with the memorable name of Cornelis Cornelisz thought of applying wind power to another industrial task: sawing wood. Like other mills, the one he built in 1592 needed to be turned to face the wind. It was so big that he had to float it on a raft to make this possible.

Southern star constellations

1595

Pieter Keyser

From any one point on Earth, only half of the stars are visible. Earth gets in the way of the rest. So until Western explorers ventured south of the equator,

Water-filled globe focuses flame on to lens below

Reservoir of oil

Oil lamp used to light specimen

Lens to focus light on specimen

Objective lens

Microscope was turned up and down a screw thread to focus the image

COMPOUND MICROSCOPE *During the 1660s, Englishman Robert Hooke made compound microscopes, such as this one, containing two or sometimes three lenses.*

1591 The Rialto Bridge, one of the best-loved bridges in Venice, Italy, is completed, replacing an earlier bridge. Antonio da Ponte, who won a competition with his design, gives it a single stone arch and a double row of shops.

1597 One of the greatest singer-songwriters of the Elizabethan age, John Dowland, publishes his *First Book of Songs or Ayres*. It will be the bestselling song book of its time. Many of the lyrics express unbearable sadness.

European astronomers knew nothing about large areas of the heavens. In 1595, Pieter Keyser, a Dutch navigator, named 12 new constellations, which he had discovered while he was sailing to the East Indies. By 1603, these had found their way into the latest celestial globes and atlases.

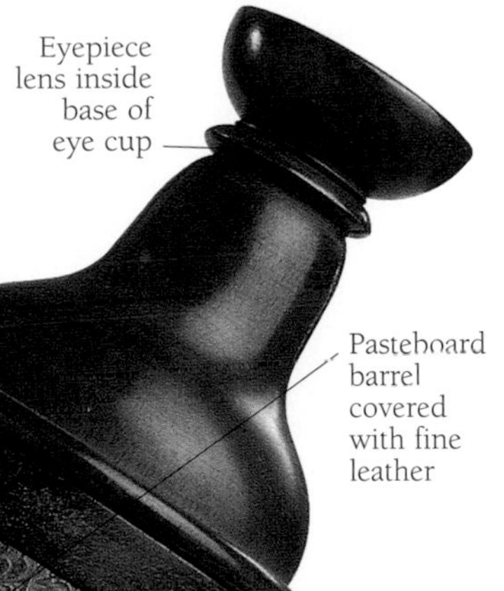

Compound microscope

c.1600

Hans Janssen

It's possible to magnify things with a single lens, but in theory, it's better with two. The first microscope with two lenses, called a compound microscope, was built in about 1600, possibly by Dutch eyeglass maker Hans Janssen. Hampered by poor lenses, early compound microscopes didn't give such clear images as the single-lens instruments created later by Dutch naturalist Antoni van Leeuwenhoek.

Magnetism of Earth

1600

William Gilbert

Magnetism was a complete mystery until the English physician William Gilbert started his experiments. He published the results in 1600. His book on the magnet took the first steps toward modern electromagnetic theory and also contained many observations about the magnetism of Earth. Gilbert concluded that compass needles point north because Earth itself is a giant magnet whose north and south poles roughly coincide with its geographic poles. In an age without Newton's theory of gravity (✱ *see* **pages 98–99**), Gilbert was not the only scientist who speculated that the whole universe was held together by magnetic attraction. (✱ *See also* **Magnetic Planet**.)

MAGNETIC PLANET

William Gilbert believed that the Earth contained a huge bar magnet, but in reality its core is too hot to allow this. The modern theory is that electric currents circulating in its liquid iron core create the magnetic field. However this field arises, navigators have been using it for centuries whenever they use a magnetic compass to guide them. We now know that its influence extends far beyond Earth.

William Gilbert (1544–1603)

The magnetic compass

The principle of the compass may first have been used by the Chinese for land exploration and in their *feng shui* philosophy for checking the orientation of buildings. The difference between magnetic and geographic north was known by 1050, and compasses with iron needles floating on water were in use at sea by the 12th century.

The northern lights

Early sailors would have been familiar with the northern lights—eerie, dancing curtains of light that sometimes appear in the night sky of the far north and south. But they would not have connected them with the behavior of their compasses. In fact, both reveal the existence of Earth's magnetic field.

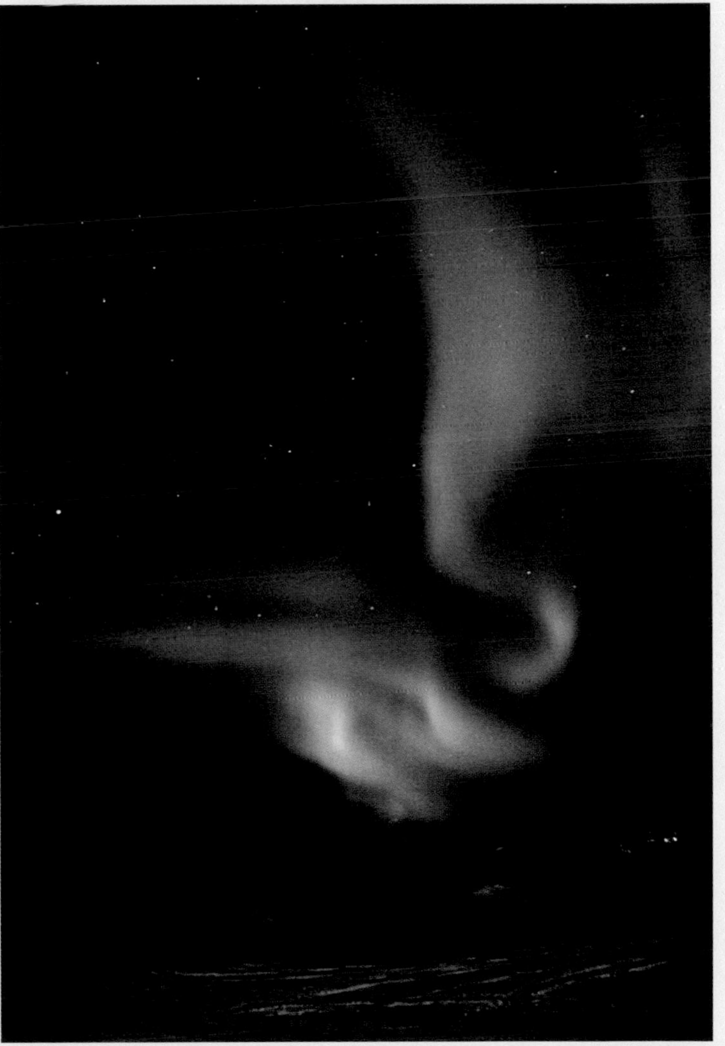

Lights, or auroras, like this can be seen near both north and south poles.

1598 In England, the Poor Laws are passed to deal with people who are old, sick, or have no money. The laws provide money for them but say that if people can work, they must go into a workhouse—often little better than going to prison.

1599 The Globe Theatre opens near the Thames River in south London with a performance by the Chamberlain's Men. The company's leading playwright is William Shakespeare, who has shares in the theater.

NAMING OF STARS *Before Bayer published* Uranometria, *there was no systematic way of naming the stars. The book's ornate title page is typical of the period.*

Naming of stars

1603

Johann Bayer

Thousands of stars can be seen without a telescope, so astronomers need a system for naming them all. The standard way is to label the stars in each constellation with Greek letters; our nearest star (actually three stars close together) is called alpha Centauri because it is the brightest star in the Centaurus constellation and alpha is the first letter of the Greek alphabet. This system was invented by German lawyer Johann Bayer for a guide to the stars, *Uranometria,* which was published in 1603. It was the first really accurate star atlas. Where there were more visible stars than letters in the Greek alphabet, Bayer continued with Latin characters. His system has since been extended to cover about 1,300 stars.

Valves in the veins

1603

Hieronymus Fabricius ab Aquapendente

Once blood has done its job of transporting important substances around the body, it goes back through the veins to the heart to be pumped around again. But gravity and friction are against it. Without one-way valves in veins, it might go the wrong way. In 1603, the Italian surgeon Hieronymus Fabricius ab Aquapendente published details of the valves that he had discovered in human veins. He didn't quite understand why they were there, but his observation helped William Harvey prove that blood circulates (✷ *see* **page 89**).

Theory of shadows

1604

Johannes Kepler

The recording of light and shade, so easily done by the camera today, demanded

Convex objective lens gathers light and bends it to form an upside-down image

TELESCOPE *This is a replica of one of Galileo's telescopes, which he made in 1610.*

Thermostat

c.1600

Cornelis Drebbel

A thermostat keeps something at a constant temperature by turning the heat up and down. In about 1600, Dutch inventor Cornelis Drebbel made a mechanical thermostat by coupling the damper of a furnace, which regulates the flow of air, with a thermometer. This was significant because it was one of the first examples of a feedback control system.

1600 Shakespeare writes what will become one of his greatest plays, *Hamlet.* With 10 years of experience behind him, he produces a tragedy that presents, like no other play, the highs and lows of human existence.

1605 Spanish writer Miguel de Cervantes publishes his book *Don Quixote de la Mancha.* It will become the most translated book in the world. Its main character, Don Quixote, and his servant Sancho Panza, overcome many imaginary foes.

careful thought from 16th-century artists. The key is that light travels in straight lines, illuminating some areas but being blocked from others. Much of the theory of shadows was figured out by Leonardo da Vinci, the Renaissance genius, but it was a German astronomer, Johannes Kepler, who produced a coherent theory of light rays in 1604.

Telescope

1608

Hans Lippershey

In 1608, Dutch spectacle maker Hans Lippershey discovered that if you look through the right pair of lenses, distant objects appear bigger. Possibly the first to invent the telescope, he may also have invented a microscope, which, like the telescope, involves looking through two lenses. He offered his telescope, or "looker," as he called it, to the government, but they said they would prefer binoculars. However, within a year, the Italian scientist Galileo had recognized the importance of the telescope and was using his own to make startling discoveries about our galaxy.

Newspaper

1609

Johann Carolus

Newspapers started as private newsletters circulated between company offices. They gradually turned into publications of political news. Either of two German papers that started in 1609 could have been the world's first: the *Relation* published by Johann Carolus, or the *Avisa Relation oder Zeitung*. By 1650, all the major cities in Europe had newspapers, usually only a single sheet without headlines or pictures.

Moon craters

1609

Galileo Galilei

Everyone believed the Greek philosopher Aristotle's theory that the moon was a perfect sphere—until 1610, when Galileo pointed a telescope at it. He saw that the Moon was far from perfect, being pockmarked with clearly visible craters. It was just one of many observations that began to shake the certainties of the ancient world.

Moons of Jupiter

1610

Galileo Galilei, Simon Marius

Galileo became expert at making telescopes and eventually built one that made objects look 20 times bigger. In January 1610, he trained it on Jupiter and saw the planet's four largest moons. He published this observation, and much else revealed by the telescope, in a book called *The Starry Messenger*. The moons were named—Io, Europa, Ganymede, and Callisto—by the German astronomer Simon Marius.

Orion nebula

1610

Nicolas de Peiresc

Stargazing became a popular occupation once the telescope was invented. In 1610, a French scholar, Nicolas de Peiresc, aimed his telescope at the constellation of Orion and was the first to notice what looked like a cloud. We now know this to be a mass of glowing gas containing new stars, which we call a nebula. It is strange that nobody recorded the Orion nebula before, because it is visible without a telescope.

Math for fun

1612

Claude-Gaspar de Méziriac

One of the first and most successful puzzle makers was the French mathematician Claude-Gaspar de Méziriac, with his 1612 book *Pleasing and Delightful Number Problems*. As well as the usual brain-teasers involving weighing things with strange sets of weights and getting awkward combinations of objects across rivers, it included a number of intriguing card tricks. Its last reprint was in 1959.

Flintlock musket

c.1612

The first portable firearms were made in the 14th century, but it was not until the 17th century that the first really effective ones appeared. They used a trigger mechanism to set off the powder, allowing a soldier to hold the weapon with both hands and aim it accurately. The best of them was the flintlock musket. The first true flintlock may have been made by a French gunmaker named Marin de Bourgeoys for Louis XIII of France, in about 1612. Its trigger released a spring-loaded flint, which struck a steel plate, creating sparks to light the gunpowder and fire a bullet. By 1630, the flintlock musket was being used throughout Europe.

Wooden stock

Spiral grooving, or rifling, cut inside the musket barrel spins the musket ball so that it flies in a straight line

FLINTLOCK MUSKET *The flintlock musket was loaded from the front. It was slow in action but remained the standard long-range firearm until cartridges preloaded with powder and a bullet made it obsolete.*

1607 On Thursday, May 14, colonists found Jamestown, on an island in the James River, Virginia. It is the first permanent English settlement in the Americas. The colonists have been led there by a guide, Christopher Newport.

1612 Englishman John Rolfe discovers a new method for curing tobacco. This enables large quantities of tobacco to be exported and sold. By 1630, as much as 1.5m lb (0.7m kg) of tobacco will have been exported to England.

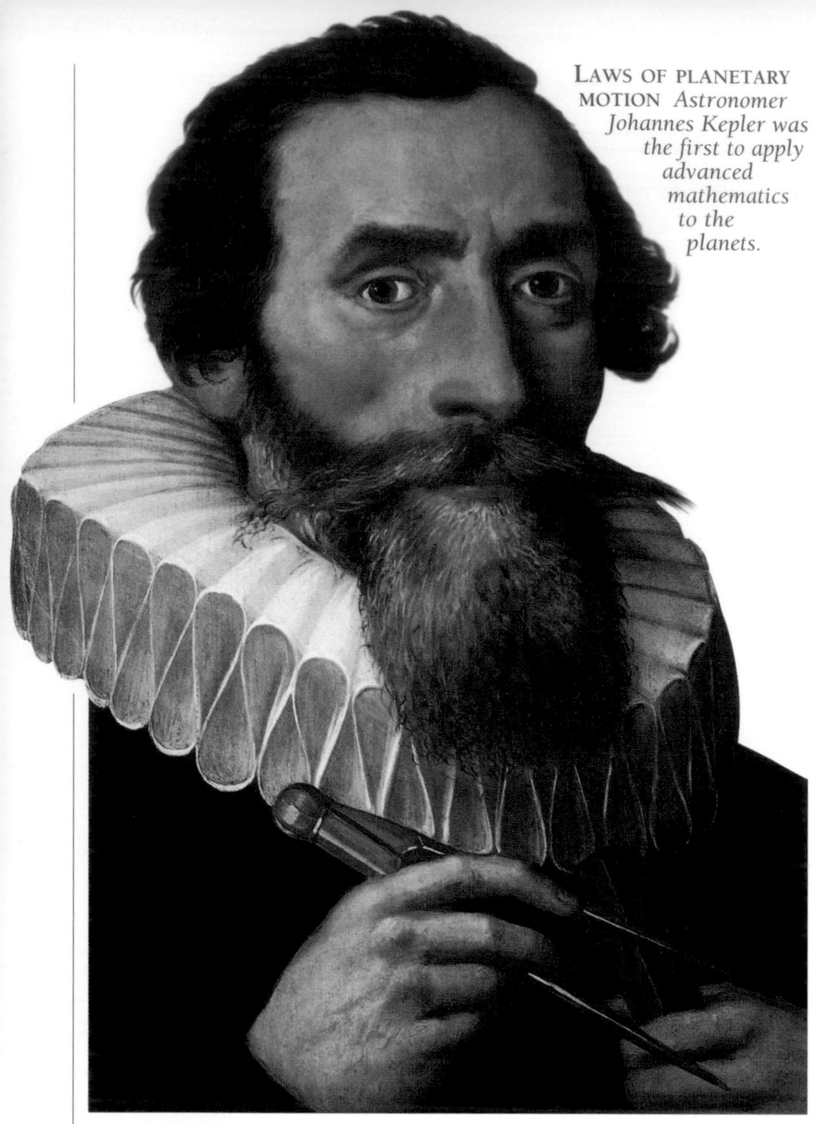

LAWS OF PLANETARY MOTION *Astronomer Johannes Kepler was the first to apply advanced mathematics to the planets.*

Systematic study of metabolism

1614

Santorio Santorio

Italian physician Santorio Santorio was trying to find out whether the solids and liquids leaving the body weighed the same as the food and drink being consumed. To do this, he sat on a pair of scales weighing his solid and liquid intake and outtake. He found that they didn't; there was something missing. We now know the missing ingredient is carbon dioxide, but Santorio called it "insensible perspiration." His 30-year experiment was the first in which detailed measurements of the body's metabolism were made.

Logarithms

1614

John Napier, Joost Bürgi

Logarithms simplify calculations by converting multiplication and division into addition and subtraction. Scottish mathematician John Napier started working on the idea in about 1594 and published it in 1614. Further details followed in another book that came out two years after his death. Swiss mathematician Joost Bürgi published the same idea independently in 1620.

Index to a book

1614

Antonio Zara

A book without an index is like a website without a search engine. This applies especially to large, factual books, so it's not surprising that the first index was compiled by an encyclopedia maker. When Antonio Zara, Bishop of Petina, now in Croatia, compiled his *Anatomy of the Arts and Sciences* in 1614, he took pity on his readers and included a list of words and where to find them.

Laws of planetary motion

1619

Johannes Kepler

In the early 17th century, people accepted Copernicus's theory that the planets orbited the sun at a constant speed and in perfect circles. Then the astronomer Johannes Kepler showed that they didn't. Using the excellent data gathered by his former employer Tycho Brahe, he calculated that the planets' paths were ovals, or ellipses, not circles, and that their speed was not constant. The universe was turning out to be more complicated than people thought.

Structure of a candle flame

1620

Francis Bacon

The English statesman and philosopher Francis Bacon believed that people could learn more about nature by observing things and thinking about them than by reading books and making hasty judgments. In 1620, he published details of a revealing observation he had made: a candle flame has a distinct structure, with a dark center and a bright edge. This simple fact eventually helped scientists to understand combustion. Bacon's way of thinking about observations has become a key method of science.

Submarine

1620

Cornelis Drebbel

English mathematician William Bourne described a submarine in 1578, but Dutch engraver Cornelis Drebbel was the first person to build one. His "diving boat" of 1620 was made of wood and covered in greased leather to stop leaks. Powered by 12 oarsmen, it made trips up and down the Thames River at a depth of about 15 ft (4.5 m). Passengers breathed through tubes held up on the surface of the water by floats. The passengers once included the man who paid for the invention, King James I.

Law of refraction

1621

Willebrord Snell

Light normally travels in straight lines, but when it enters something like glass, its direction can change—an effect called refraction. In 1621, Dutch astronomer Willebrord Snell discovered the law that describes this change in direction. Once people knew the law, scientists eventually began to use it to design more effective lenses. Later, French mathematician Pierre de Fermat showed that Snell's law amounted to saying that light always takes the quickest route.

1614 Native American woman Pocahontas, daughter of Chief Powhatan, marries English colonist John Rolfe in Virginia. She had been captured by the English and had converted to Christianity, changing her name to Rebecca.

1616 Architect Mehmet Aga completes a splendid new mosque in Constantinople (now Istanbul) for Sultan Ahmet I. Its interior is decorated with blue tiles, which will in the future give it its popular name, the Blue Mosque.

Smelting iron with coke *Flames light the sky as coal is heated to make coke for smelting iron in 18th-century Britain.*

Smelting iron with coke

1621

Dud Dudley

Iron is made by heating its ore with carbon, and until the 17th century, the carbon came from wood charcoal. By 1620, trees were getting scarce, so English iron maker Dud Dudley began to experiment with coal. Coal contains a lot of sulfur, which would ruin the iron, so Dudley devised a way of removing the sulfur and other unwanted elements by roasting the coal. The solid that remained, which we call coke, was almost pure carbon. Dudley got a patent for his process in 1621, but coke was not widely used in smelting iron until 1709, when English iron master Abraham Darby started using it on a large scale.

Dictionary

1623

Henry Cockeram

The first dictionary actually called a dictionary was published by an Englishman, Henry Cockeram, in 1623. His *English Dictionarie* contained only "hard" words. He didn't see the point of listing words that everybody knew. John Kersey, however, in his *New English Dictionary* of 1702, did give definitions of everyday words, creating one of the first modern dictionaries.

Convection heating

1624

Louis Savot

The Romans used warm air for heating, but it traveled under the floor, not inside the room. The alternative method of heating was an open fire, which sent most of its warm air up the chimney. French architect Louis Savot thought he could combine both ideas to heat rooms. In 1624, he designed a fireplace that drew in air under the floor, heated it, then wafted it into the room. He published the idea in 1685.

Circulation of the blood

1628

William Harvey

In 1628, English physician William Harvey made one of the most important discoveries in the history of medicine. Through observation and experiment, he proved that our blood circulates. Before this, doctors believed that blood was made in the liver and then turned into flesh. Harvey's idea seems obvious today, but that's only because we live in the era of scientific medicine that he helped create.

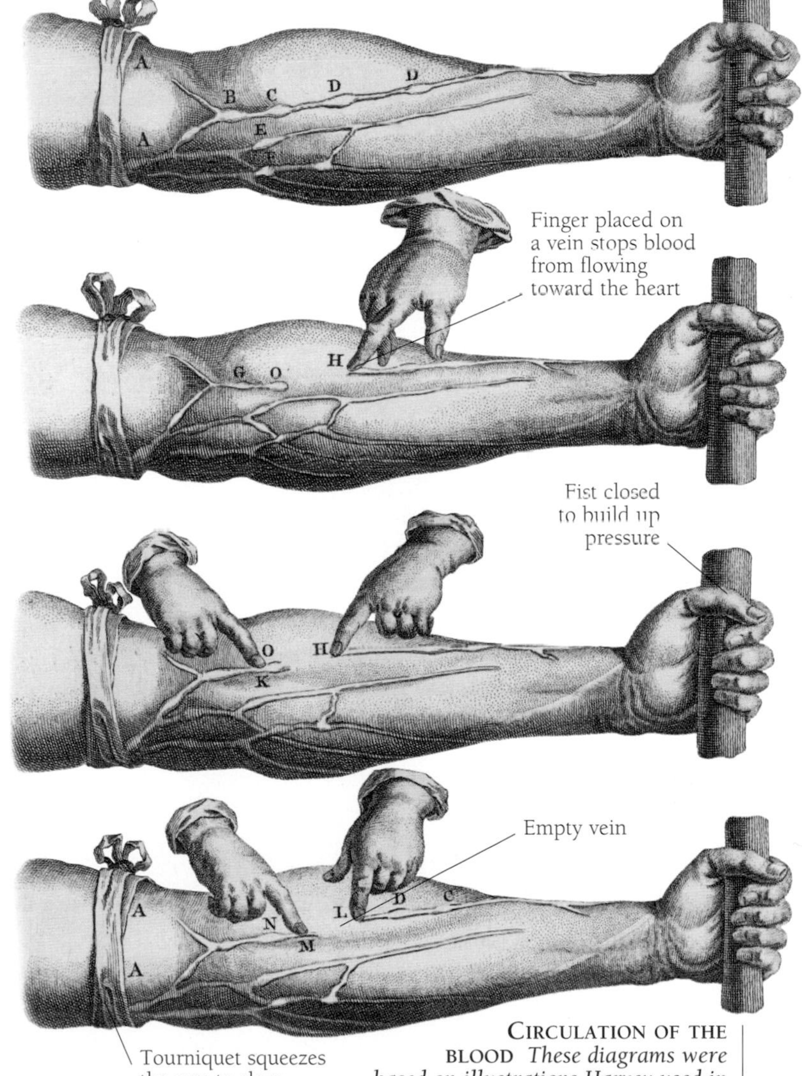

Circulation of the blood *These diagrams were based on illustrations Harvey used in 1628 to explain blood circulation.*

1620 One hundred Puritans escape persecution by leaving England for America. The Pilgrim Fathers, as they will be known, set sail from Plymouth on September 16, heading for Virginia, but get lost and settle at Cape Cod.

1624 Dutch painter Frans Hals, a master of the quick, bold brushstroke, paints his best-known picture, *The Laughing Cavalier*. Unusually, its subject—an extravagantly dressed soldier—is smiling, as if for a photograph.

Vernier scale

1631

Pierre Vernier

Readings from a graduated scale can be inaccurate because the position of a pointer has to be estimated by eye. In 1631, French civil servant Pierre Vernier invented an improved scale, which is still used today. Instead of a simple pointer, it has a second smaller scale with slightly narrower divisions than the main scale. By noting which of these lines up exactly with the main scale, its user can obtain a much more precise readout.

Slide rule

1633

William Oughtred

An English minister, William Oughtred, turned math into mechanics in 1633 by making two scales showing the logarithms of numbers (✻ *see* **page 88**). Users could multiply and divide by sliding the scales to a certain position and reading off the answer. Robert Bissaker improved the sliding action in 1654, and the slide rule became a basic tool for scientists and engineers until the invention of calculators made it obsolete.

X–Y coordinates

1637

René Descartes

Graphs turn pairs of numbers represented by *x* and *y* into meaningful shapes. This idea was invented by the French philosopher René Descartes, who is perhaps more famous for saying "I think, therefore I am." It allowed people to solve geometric problems with algebra and algebraic problems with geometry. Descartes also started the convention of using letters from the end of the alphabet to represent unknown quantities and letters from the beginning of the alphabet to represent known ones.

Umbrella

1637

The first rainproof umbrella dates from 1637. King Louis XIII of France was reported as having sunshades and "umbrellas of oiled cloth." These would probably have looked like traditional Chinese and Japanese parasols, with a folding wooden frame. The steel-ribbed device we use now was invented by Samuel Fox of England in 1852.

Parabolic path of a projectile

1638

Galileo Galilei

Until the 17th century, people believed that things kept moving only if something kept pushing them. Galileo

TRANSIT OF VENUS *This model, made in about 1760, shows how Venus can seem to move across the Sun.*

1632 The famous Japanese sumo wrestler Akashi Shiganosuke forces his opponent out of the ring to become the world's first Yokozuna, or grand champion of Sumo, after the revival of public matches 32 years earlier.

1642 The great Dutch artist Rembrandt van Rijn paints a huge group portrait called *The Night Watch*. The painting shows an army company marching out from its headquarters in the shadowy gloom of early morning.

showed that this was untrue—a moving object keeps moving until something stops it. Objects in the real world slow down and stop because of friction or gravity. Galileo did more experiments that proved that a falling object speeds up as it falls. He went on to study projectiles—objects that are thrown into the air. He deduced that a projectile moves forward at a constant speed but accelerates downward. It therefore follows a curved path called a parabola.

Transit of Venus

1639

Jeremiah Horrocks

A "transit" of Mercury or Venus occurs when one of them appears to travel across the face of the sun. Transits of Venus happen only in June or December and always in pairs eight years apart. They are very rare, the pairs occurring at intervals of well over a century. English clergyman Jeremiah Horrocks was an amateur astronomer. Using standard astronomical tables, he calculated that there would be a transit of Venus in December 1639, the first ever recorded. He also calculated a new distance for the sun.

Mezzotint engraving *Mezzotints were used to publish pictures of many celebrities, including chemist Humphry Davy.*

Mezzotint engraving

1642

Ludwig von Siegen

There was no good way of printing all the tones of a picture until Dutch artist Ludwig von Siegen invented the mezzotint, a variation on the ordinary engraving process used with metal printing plates (✱ *see* **page 75**). Instead of drawing directly on the metal plate, the artist first roughens its entire surface. Printed, this would give solid black, because the roughened surface traps the ink. By smoothing different areas of the plate to varying degrees, however, the artist can produce lighter tones where required—completely smooth areas do not print at all. Mezzotint reproductions of paintings were popular until the invention of photography.

Barometer

1643

Evangelista Torricelli

Italian physicist Evangelista Torricelli helped Galileo in the last months of the great scientist's life. Galileo suggested the experiment that made Torricelli famous. Torricelli filled a tube with mercury, then upended it in a dish. The mercury started to drop out, then stopped. Torricelli realized that the mercury was prevented from falling further by the pressure of the atmosphere. As the air pressure rose and fell, so did the mercury in the tube. Torricelli had invented the barometer, although it was French physicist Edmé Mariotte who named it in 1676.

Barometer *This is a replica of the barometer invented by Torricelli.*

Torricelli's column of mercury could reach a height of about 30 in (760 mm)

Revolving stage

1645

Giacomo Torelli

Behind every stage show is machinery that the audience never sees, including the revolve. With this huge turntable, a scene can be changed in seconds. The first revolve was probably built by an Italian architect, Giacomo Torelli. He built a theater containing one in Venice, Italy, in about 1645. He then worked at a theater in Paris, France. His work there was so good that when he returned to Italy, his successor in Paris destroyed the machinery in a fit of jealousy.

Recognition of gases as distinct from air

1648

Jan Baptista van Helmont

Jan Baptista van Helmont was an alchemist. He believed in the "philosopher's stone," which was supposed to turn ordinary metals into gold. He also made a real discovery: that the gases given off by two different processes—burning charcoal and fermenting grape juice—were actually one and the same. He recognized, too, that it was a distinct gas, not just another form of air. We now call this gas carbon dioxide. His works, published after his death in 1648, show that he also discovered another gas, nitric oxide.

1643 Louis XIV, who will later be known as the Sun King, becomes king of France. He regards himself as having absolute power over his subjects. As well as spending hugely on war, he will also be an extravagant patron of the arts.

1647 In India, the Taj Mahal is completed. Built by the emperor Shah Jahan in memory of his favorite wife, Mumtaz Mahal, it is made of white marble, inlaid with semiprecious stones. It will attract visitors for centuries to come.

Strength of a vacuum

1654

Otto von Guericke

Torricelli's barometer (✳ *see* **page 91**) showed that the atmosphere exerts a force. According to legend, Engineer Otto von Guericke of Magdeburg in Germany showed just how large that force could be. In 1654, he gave an amazing demonstration to Emperor Ferdinand III. He took two metal bowls, put them together to form a sphere, and pumped the air out with a pump he had developed. With no air inside the bowls, the air pressure on the outside held them together so strongly that teams of horses could not pull these "Magdeburg hemispheres" apart. (✳ *See also* **Working in a Vacuum**.)

Pendulum clock

1657

Christiaan Huygens

Galileo realized as early as 1583 that a pendulum would make an excellent timekeeper, but he never managed to turn it into a practical clock. The Dutch mathematician Christiaan Huygens solved the problem in 1657 when he designed a mechanism that allowed the swing of a pendulum to control the rotation of weight-driven gearwheels. He also devised a pendulum that would swing at exactly the same rate whatever the size of its swing. The pendulum improved the accuracy of timekeeping so much that it was at last worth giving clocks a minute hand.

Red blood cells *A scanning electron microscope reveals the dish shape of red blood cells.*

Red blood cells

1658

Jan Swammerdam

Blood is red because it is full of red cells. Nobody knew this until the Dutch naturalist Jan Swammerdam looked at blood under a microscope in 1658. One of the best microscopists of his day, he used the instrument to discover many new facts. Unfortunately, his father thought this was all a waste of time and stopped his allowance. Swammerdam died an unhappy man.

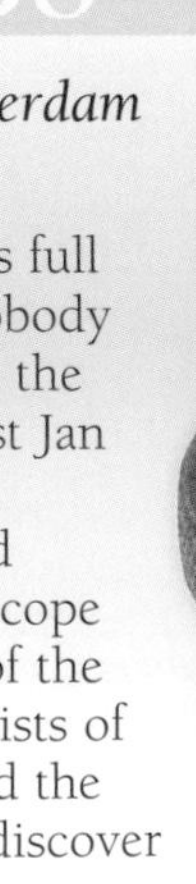

Rotation of Mars

1659

Christiaan Huygens

Squinting through what would today be considered very poor telescopes, 17th-century astronomers made many discoveries. In 1659, Christiaan Huygens managed to sketch surface features on Mars. He noticed that the features moved between his observations, and he realized that the planet was rotating. Seven years later, the Italian-born French astronomer Gian Cassini measured the length of a day on Mars—the time the planet takes to make one rotation. He found it was just 40 minutes longer than a day on Earth.

Capillaries

1661

Marcello Malpighi

The microscope helped solve many mysteries. One of them was the missing link in William Harvey's theory of the way blood

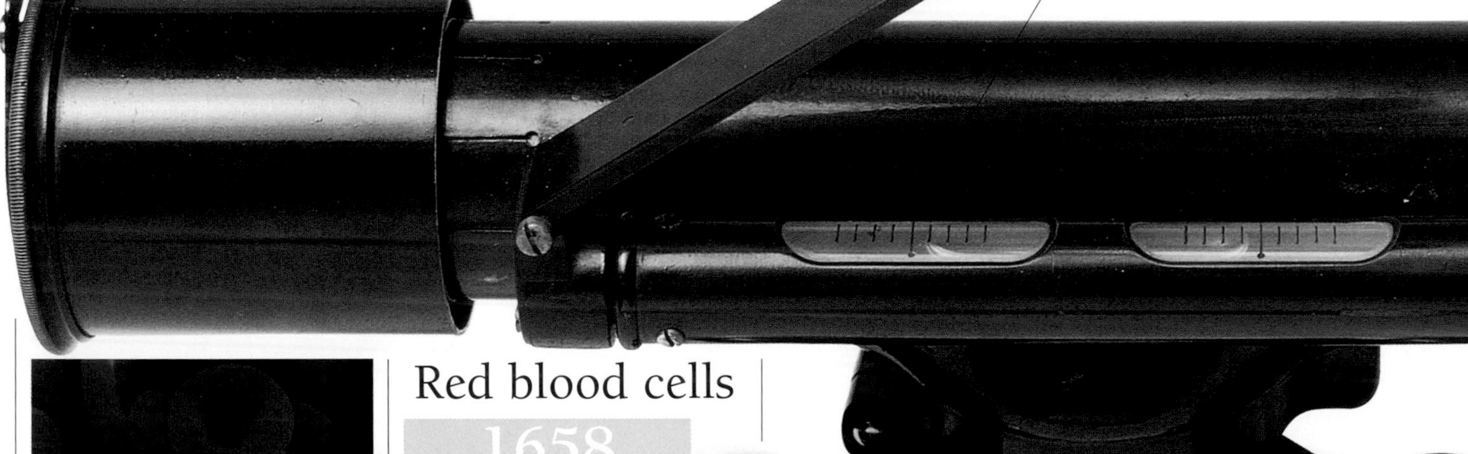

Spirit level *This early 20th-century instrument uses the principle of the spirit level to measure small changes of height of plots of land.*

1652 Dutch commander Jan Van Riebeeck lands at Table Bay in the Cape of Good Hope to set up a supply station for Dutch ships on their way to the Dutch East Indies. The country of South Africa will develop from this settlement.

1655 The island of Jamaica becomes an English colony. An expedition led by Admiral William Penn and General Robert Venables overwhelms the Spanish settlers who have been there since the time of Christopher Columbus.

circulates (✳ *see* **page 89**). How did blood get from arteries to veins? Marcello Malpighi, working in Bologna, Italy, in 1661, found the answer. The blood traveled through tiny vessels, which were visible only under a microscope: capillaries.

pressure is raised and vice versa. In France, this principle is called Mariotte's law, because Edmé Mariotte not only discovered it for himself but also noted that the law does not hold if the temperature changes.

Level

1661

Anything affected by gravity can be used to check whether something is level. The best thing is a bubble in a liquid, which always rises to the highest point. In a slightly curved-shape tube, this is in the center when the tube is level. If the tube is mounted in a suitable holder, the user has to only place it on an object and center the bubble to ensure the object is level. This gadget, the level, first appeared in 1661, and builders still use levels today.

Life table

1662

John Graunt

People who study population are known as demographers. They use statistics, such as how many people live in an area and how many births and deaths per thousand. English shopkeeper John Graunt founded the subject by studying death records. In 1662, he published tables showing the probability that someone of a given age would live to some greater age. "Life tables" like these are now the basis of life insurance.

WORKING IN A VACUUM

THE ANCIENT PHYSICS OF ARISTOTLE said that a vacuum was impossible. In the 17th century, improved technology could challenge this directly. Once Guericke had demonstrated an effective air pump, other people, such as Irish chemist Robert Boyle, built them, too. With the ability to move air around at will, they began to find out more about combustion, sound, weather, and much else.

Otto von Guericke was a great showman as well as a good scientist.

Replica Boyle-Hooke vacuum pump of 1659

Glass chamber fitted on top of this cylinder

Handle moved to force piston in or out

Rack turned by gearwheel to move piston

MAKING A VACUUM

Simple pumps use pistons to suck out air. One-way valves stop it from rushing back in. Because a piston sucks out only a fraction of the remaining air on each stroke, the vacuum is never perfect, even if the valves and seals don't leak. This did not put off early experimenters.

THE SCIENCE OF AIR

With air under control, scientists like Guericke, Boyle, and Edmé Mariotte could find out some facts about it. For example, without air, candles don't burn and there is no sound; and reducing the pressure of moist air makes clouds form. Mariotte and Boyle also discovered the law that links air pressure and volume (✳ *see* **this page**).

Boyle's law

1662

Robert Boyle, Edmé Mariotte

Robert Boyle worked with the English physicist Robert Hooke, who helped him build an effective air pump. Boyle used the new pump to make all sorts of discoveries about air, but the one everybody remembers is Boyle's law. This says that the volume of a given mass of gas varies inversely with its pressure, which means that the gas will contract if the

Reflecting telescope

1663

James Gregory

The first telescopes used lenses to refract light from a distant object before it reached the observer. The lenses produced color fringes, making the images indistinct. Mirrors didn't do this, so a telescope that used mirrors promised clearer vision. Italian astronomer Niccolò Zucchi suggested this in 1616, but the first practical design came from Scottish mathematician and astronomer James Gregory in 1663. In 1668, Isaac Newton produced his own design, which drew the reflecting telescope to the attention of scientists. Gregorian reflectors are still used. One was launched into space in 1980.

1660 Britain's premier scientific association, the Royal Society, is founded in London after 15 years of informal meetings between prominent English scientists. Two years later, it will receive a royal charter from King Charles II.

1661 King Louis XIV of France sets up the Royal Academy of Dancing to improve ballet training. Under its first director, Pierre Beauchamps, professional standards improve. Centuries later, it will become the Paris Opéra Ballet.

Polar caps of Mars

c.1666

Gian Cassini

Mars has polar ice caps like Earth—at least they look like them, but they are probably thinner and made mainly of frozen carbon dioxide. In about 1666, Gian Cassini, who made some of the earliest telescopic observations of Mars, was the first person to report the caps. In spite of his pioneering work, Cassini was somewhat old-fashioned in his approach. He later rejected Isaac Newton's theory of gravity (✱ *see* **page 98**).

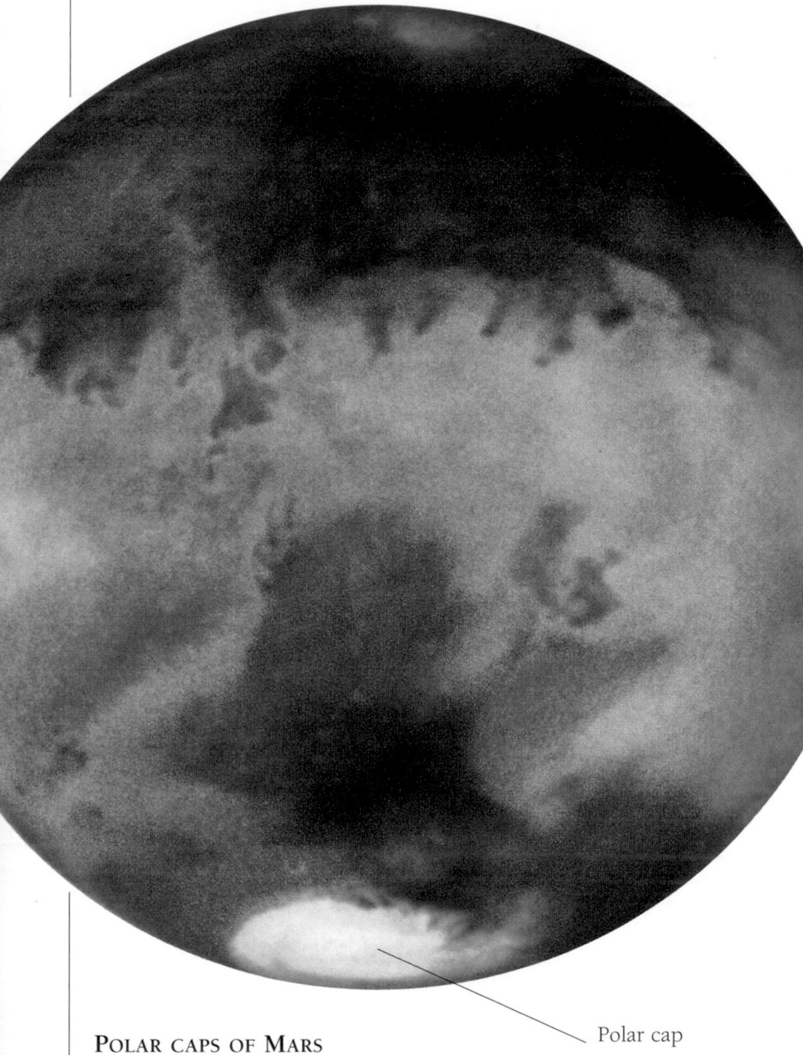

POLAR CAPS OF MARS
The Hubble Space Telescope took this photo of Mars in 1997.

Phosphorus

1669

Hennig Brand, Robert Boyle

Phosphorus makes matches burn. It is also an essential part of the chemistry of our bodies. German alchemist Hennig Brand discovered it in 1669 when, for some reason, he made an extract of his own urine. To his amazement, the extract glowed in the dark; it was phosphorus. Hennig kept his discovery secret, but in 1680, Robert Boyle also discovered the new element for himself.

Shop scales

1669

Gilles de Roberval

Old-fashioned scales with separate weights use a mechanism devised by French mathematician Gilles de Roberval in 1669. The pans are supported from below with a system of arms that makes them move vertically. Objects do not have to go exactly in the center of the pans, making the scales ideal for shops and other places where speed and simplicity matter.

Champagne

c.1670

Dom Pérignon

Winning race-car drivers cannot resist shaking the bottle of champagne they get and squirting its overflowing contents everywhere. The trick works because champagne contains carbon dioxide, which is formed by a special method of fermentation called *méthode champenoise*. It was invented, it is said, by a Benedictine monk called Dom Pérignon, in about 1670. But he was probably only one of many winemakers in the Champagne region of France who contributed to the development of this unique drink.

Diffraction of light

1672

Robert Hooke

Light travels in straight lines. This is almost true. At the edges of objects, it actually bends very slightly, so shadows are a little smaller than the simple straight-line idea would suggest. This effect is called diffraction and was discovered in 1672 by the English physicist Robert Hooke. Hooke's discovery later supported the theory that light traveled in waves (✱ *see* **page 97**) because waves would bend around objects in exactly this way.

Protozoa

1676

Antoni van Leeuwenhoek

Dutch naturalist Antoni van Leeuwenhoek was not a trained scientist, but he was lucky enough to have a job that left him plenty of spare time. He spent it making ever better lenses with which he could see ever smaller things. In 1674, he became the first person to see protozoa—tiny, single-celled creatures that swim around in ponds and rain barrels. His descriptions of the hidden world around us made a big impact on science.

Speed of light

1676

Ole Rømer

Light travels so fast that it's difficult to measure its speed. It helps if you work with light that has to travel a long way. Danish astronomer Ole Rømer found this out by accident in 1676, when he noticed that the time between eclipses of Jupiter's moons (when they are hidden behind the planet) varied throughout the year. Rømer realized that this must be because the distance from Earth to Jupiter varied throughout the year, and so did the distance that light from the moons had to travel. Rømer calculated that the speed of light was 137,000 miles (225,000 km) per second. This was 25 percent too slow, but a good start.

1666 On September 2, a small blaze in a bakery in London gets out of control, starting the Great Fire of London. Four days later, more than 13,000 houses and many public buildings, including St. Paul's Cathedral, lie in ashes.

1675 After the Great Fire of London in 1666, mathematician and architect Christopher Wren's designs of a bold new replacement for St. Paul's Cathedral are accepted. Some of the boldness is removed by his client, the Church.

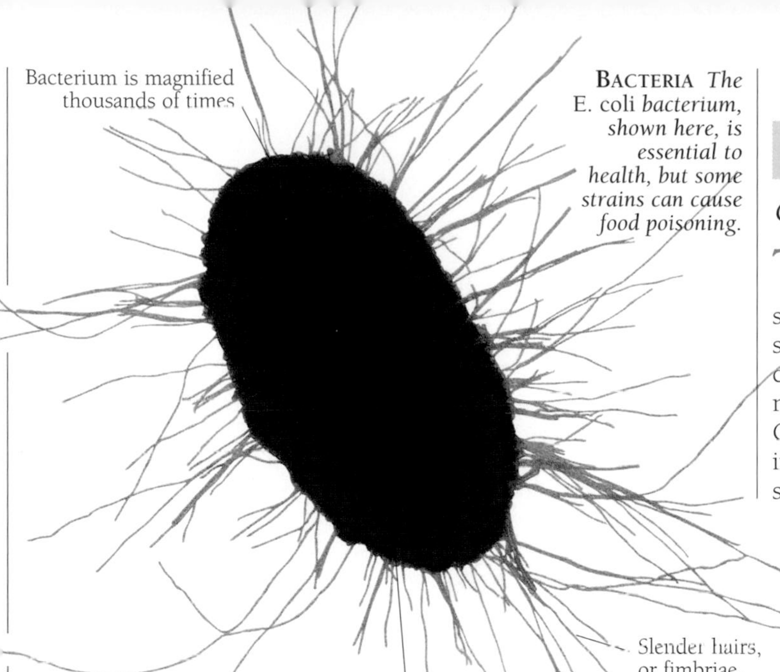

BACTERIA *The E. coli bacterium, shown here, is essential to health, but some strains can cause food poisoning.*

Bacteria

1676

Antoni van Leeuwenhoek

Bacteria are even smaller than protozoa. So it wasn't until 1676, when Antoni van Leeuwenhoek had made a lens that magnified 280 times, that he saw some of the larger types of bacteria, collected from his own mouth. To see them, he used some secret techniques, which probably included lighting his tiny subjects from the side so that they stood out sharply like dust in a sunbeam.

Lemonade

1676

Lemon juice must have been used in drinks for a very long time, but the first commercial lemonade appeared in Paris in 1676. Thirsty Parisians could buy it from roaming sellers belonging to the *Compagnie de Limonadiers*, which had an exclusive license to distribute the drink. Lemonade sellers dispensed the refreshing mixture of water, lemon juice, and honey from tanks strapped to their backs.

Binary system

1679

Gottfried Leibniz, Shao Yung

The binary system records numbers by using just two symbols, such as 0 and 1. The system is essential to modern computers, but it may go back more than 3,000 years. The Chinese classic *I Ching,* written in the 12th century BCE, showed how to make predictions from binary patterns. The 11th-century Chinese philosopher Shao Yung was influenced by the book, and it is possible that German mathematician Gottfried Leibniz was made aware of the binary system through his writings. Leibniz loved the beauty of the binary system. To him, its two digits stood for nothingness and God. He thought it could form a universal language, something that never occurred to the writer of the *I Ching*.

LEMONADE *By the 19th century, lemonade was big business. This Italian lemonade seller is no longer roaming the streets but has a permanent stall.*

1678 Puritan preacher John Bunyan writes the first part of *The Pilgrim's Progress*, the story of the journey of a soul seeking salvation. His rich, biblical prose conveys the ideas of vice and virtue through the book's human characters.

1679 The onion-shaped domes and twisted, brightly colored turrets of St. Basil's Cathedral, Moscow, are finally completed after 124 years of work. The building is a high point of Russian Orthodox Church architecture.

Repeating watch *The exquisite mechanism of this Quare repeating watch was normally hidden from its user.*

Pressure cooker

1679

Denis Papin

Food cooks more quickly in water that is hotter than its normal boiling point. In 1679, French-English physicist Denis Papin made water hotter than hot with his "digester," a closed vessel with a safety valve. When water was heated inside it, the pressure rose. The increased pressure stopped the water from boiling until it was hotter than normal.

Repeating watch

1680

Daniel Quare

Owners of early watches had to take them out of their pocket and open a protective cover before they could read the time—assuming there was enough light. In 1680, English clockmaker Daniel Quare made life easier when he invented his "repeater." Its owner had only to reach into a pocket and touch a button or move a lever to hear the approximate time ring out on a tiny bell inside the watch. This was especially useful at night.

Tunneling with explosives

1681

Pierre Riquet

The mountains of Europe are riddled with tunnels, many of which were blasted through the solid rock with the help of explosives. According to one authority, the first major tunnel made this way was for the Canal du Midi, which crosses France, linking the Atlantic Ocean and the Mediterranean Sea. Between 1666 and 1681, French engineer Pierre Riquet cleared a 515 ft (160 m) path for the canal through a sandstone hill by setting off gunpowder in hundreds of holes, which he had drilled into the rock.

Halley's comet *All comets are giant "dirty snowballs" made of ice and dust.*

Halley's comet

1682

Edmond Halley

It used to be thought that comets appeared only once. Then English astronomer Edmond Halley showed that they could orbit the sun, coming back repeatedly. He studied the path of a comet that appeared in 1682 and was able to show that this, and two earlier comets, were in fact the same comet. In 1705, he predicted that it would return again in 1758. It did and was named in his honor.

Calculus

1684

Gottfried Leibniz, Isaac Newton

Calculus is the mathematics of change: physical change, such as movement, or mathematical change, such as increasing area. It was invented independently by Gottfried Leibniz in Germany and Isaac Newton in England. Newton created a special method to solve problems in mechanics. Leibniz produced something more like modern calculus. Newton had the basics by 1666, but in 1684, Leibniz became the first to publish his work, making Newton his lifelong enemy.

Laws of motion

1687

Isaac Newton

English scientist Isaac Newton formulated three laws of motion, which he published in 1687. The laws are still used to get people to the moon. The first law states that the velocity of an object (its speed and direction) will change only if a force acts on it. This was discovered by Galileo, but the other two laws are all Newton. The second says how

1682 The Palace of Versailles is ready at last on a site just southwest of Paris, after 21 years of building that at times involved 30,000 workers. King Louis XIV moves his court into the extravagantly furnished new buildings.

1688 England's first female novelist, Aphra Behn, publishes *Oroonoko*, the story of an African prince who is made a slave. Some people do not believe a woman could have written anything so good and accuse her of copying.

much an object's velocity will be changed by a given force, while the third says that pushing on an object makes it push back equally hard in the opposite direction.

Gravity

1687

Isaac Newton

See **pages 98–99** for the story of how Newton discovered the glue that holds the universe together.

Wave theory of light

1690

Christiaan Huygens

Light has puzzled scientists since the earliest times. Although the law of refraction was known by 1621, nobody could explain why light obeyed it. Christiaan Huygens proposed the first theory that light was a stream of waves. These waves made secondary "wavelets" when passed through an object. When light hit glass at an angle, the "wavelets" produced slowed down, making the light bend. In conflict with Newton's ideas, it was not seriously considered until the 19th century.

Clarinet

c.1700

Johann Denner

The clarinet is a woodwind instrument with a wide range of notes and a smooth, distinctive tone. It was developed from an earlier musical instrument, the chalumeau, by the German musician and instrument maker Johann Denner, in about 1700. To extend the range of the chalumeau, Denner added three extra keys to bridge the awkward gap between the instrument's lower and upper registers. The lower register of a clarinet is still sometimes called the chalumeau.

Phlogiston theory of combustion

c.1700

Georg Stahl

When something burns, flames come out, so people naturally thought that combustible substances lost something when they burned. In about 1700, German chemist Georg Stahl called this "phlogiston." A problem with this theory is that things get heavier when they burn, so phlogiston would have to weigh less than nothing. By 1783, French chemist Antoine Lavoisier had substituted gain of oxygen for loss of phlogiston, which is the true explanation of burning.

Seed drill

c.1701

Jethro Tull

Seed drills sow seed in neat rows instead of scattering it. The Babylonians had them, but in about 1701, English farmer Jethro Tull invented the first automatic seed drill. It was part of a system of farming that he developed after seeing grapevines flourishing in rows with the soil between them loose and weed-free. Not all his ideas were accepted, but the benefits of precise drilling were. The successors to Tull's drill are at work in fields today.

SEED DRILL *Jethro Tull shows off his seed drill in this mural from the Science Museum in London.*

1694 The Bank of England is founded on Friday, July 27. Although private, it lends all its money—£1.2 million—to the government, and is in turn granted the right to issue currency and do all the country's company banking.

1697 "Sleeping Beauty," "Cinderella," and other fairy tales reach a wide public for the first time, as French writer Charles Perrault publishes *Tales of Mother Goose*. He has collected them from people who knew them by heart.

THE MOON IS FALLING

Isaac Newton discovers the glue that holds the universe together

Trinity College
Trinity College, Cambridge, England, was founded by King Henry VIII in 1546. Newton went there to study in 1661.

When Isaac Newton was only three years old, his father died and his mother married again. She went to live in the next village, leaving him with his grandmother. Newton was not happy. He often sat in the orchard behind his home, Woolsthorpe Manor in Lincolnshire, England, smoldering with hatred for his new stepfather. In 1653, when Newton was 10, his mother came back. She expected him to make himself useful, but he wanted only to read. In the end, she packed him off to school.

Newton didn't learn much at school except Latin, but Latin was the language of science. He certainly needed it when he got to Cambridge

Newton knew his orchard well. It was an ideal spot for the intense thought that led him to the idea of universal gravitation.

University. There was so much to read. The official teaching was old-fashioned, but Newton taught himself the new science of Galileo, Descartes, and others. "Plato is my friend, Aristotle is my friend," he wrote in his notebook, "but my best friend is truth."

No sooner had he received his degree, in 1665, than the Plague came, which forced everyone to leave Cambridge. Newton returned to Woolsthorpe. The orchard was still there, and Newton still went to sit there, his mind now full of scientific questions. One of them was, "What keeps the planets in their orbits?" A famous story tells us that as Newton pondered this among the old trees, with heavenly bodies like the moon uppermost in his thoughts, an apple fell. It took a genius like Newton to see the connection. The moon kept circling Earth because, like the apple, it was falling. Gravity made the moon curve toward Earth instead of continuing in a straight line. And what worked for the moon could work for the planets circling the sun.

Newton was able to show that the force of gravity got weaker in proportion to the square of distance. In other words, a planet twice as far from the sun as another will experience only one-quarter of the force; if it is three times as far away, the force will be one-ninth, and so on.

Other people had suggested this, but Newton went further. Using powerful new math he'd invented, together with his laws of motion, he proved that gravity could account for the orbits of all the planets. It was the glue that held the universe together.

In 1687, Newton published his book *Mathematical Principles of Natural Philosophy*, usually known as the *Principia*, a shortened form of its Latin title. In it he explained his three basic laws, which govern the way objects move, and his theory of gravity and the universe. But his personal universe was not so well ordered. Just before publication, another scientist, Robert Hooke, accused him of copying his ideas. Newton never forgave him. Just as he hated the man who stole his mother, he now despised the rival who was trying to steal his glory.

UNIVERSAL LAW
The mass of the moon is unimaginably greater than that of an apple. Yet both obey the same law of gravity.

REFLECTING TELESCOPE
Newton believed that lenses would never make a good telescope, so he designed one that used a mirror instead. It is still a popular design.

Replica of Newton's reflecting telescope

SOLAR SYSTEM
This clockwork model of the solar system was built in about 1712. Newton thought of the solar system as a giant machine. He was never sure that God would not have to intervene to keep it running.

Two separate plant groups

1703

John Ray

Plants come in two kinds: the ones that look like grasses or palms, and the rest. Scientists call them monocotyledons and dicotyledons—monocots and dicots for short. The baby seedlings in the first group have only one leaf, while the others have two. These important plant groups were first recognized by English naturalist John Ray in 1703, after a lifetime of study.

Composition of white light

1704

Isaac Newton

Long before Newton's time, it was generally known that white light passing through a prism is broken into colors. However, most people believed that it was due to some change the prism made on light—like clay being pressed through a mold. To disprove this notion, Newton showed that light is actually made up of many colors by using a second prism to recombine light back into white. Although he made this discovery in 1670, he waited until 1704 to publish his findings in his book *Opticks*.

Piano

1709

Bartolomeo Cristofori

Today, most keyboard instruments play louder when the keys are struck harder. The best keyboard of 300 years ago, the harpsichord, did not do this because it plucked its strings with a mechanism that was unaffected by the force applied. Italian harpsichord builder Bartolomeo Cristofori invented touch sensitivity in 1709 with his *gravicembalo col piano e forte* (harpsichord with soft and loud), which eventually became the piano. Cristofori's keyboard instrument hit its strings with small hammers, giving more control over the sound.

STEAM ENGINE *The piston of a Newcomen engine was connected to the rods of a water pump by a rocking beam.*

Steam engine

c.1710

Thomas Newcomen, John Calley

English engineer Thomas Newcomen designed his steam engine in about 1710 and built the first one in 1712. It was based on an earlier pump invented by Thomas Savery, which used the vacuum created by condensing steam to suck water out of mines. Working at first with another inventor, John Calley, Newcomen made the vacuum move a piston, which then drove a separate pump to remove the water. Although incredibly inefficient, the Newcomen engine remained the best available for 50 years.

Laws of chance

1713

Jakob Bernoulli, Abraham de Moivre

Guessing and gambling might not suggest the precision of mathematics, but top mathematicians like Pierre de Fermat and Blaise Pascal were studying the laws of chance as early as the 17th century. The first important book on the subject came from Swiss mathematician Jakob Bernoulli and was published in 1713. Then, in 1718, came another by French mathematician Abraham de Moivre, which revealed most of today's basic probability theory.

MERCURY THERMOMETER *This early English thermometer has its tube attached to a scale marked on a separate piece of wood.*

1703 Peter the Great, the tsar of Russia, founds the city of St. Petersburg, which he calls his "window on Europe." Thousands of Russian serfs die in the building of the city, which, in 1712, will become Russia's capital for two centuries.

1707 England and Scotland become the Kingdom of Great Britain with the passing of the Act of Union. Scotland agrees to be governed by parliament in England but keeps it own legal system and Presbyterian Church.

Stereotype *This is a clay stereotype mold. The metal stereotype made from it is reversed.*

Mercury thermometer

1714

Daniel Fahrenheit

German physicist Daniel Fahrenheit invented two things at once: a more useful thermometer and a temperature scale, which was later named after him. Early thermometers either relied on the expansion of air or allowed alcohol to expand from a small bulb into a fine tube. Fahrenheit's thermometer, which he produced in 1714, used the second of these methods, but with mercury instead of alcohol. This allowed him to measure higher temperatures.

Diving bell

1717

Edmond Halley

A diving bell is a chamber in which people can stay under water without diving equipment. In 1687, William Phips, the future governor of the state of Massachusetts made one to recover sunken treasure in the West Indies, but his divers wouldn't use it. The first long periods spent under water were in a bell invented by English astronomer Edmond Halley. In 1717, he described how people had survived at a depth of 55 ft (17 m) for an hour and a half. He supplied air to the bell by sending it down in weighted barrels.

Stereotype

1727

William Ged

Once a book was printed, early printers broke up the type and reused it. If a reprint was needed, they had to set up the pages again. Scottish goldsmith William Ged saved labor in 1727 by inventing the stereotype, a copy of a page of type made by pouring metal into a plaster mold. French printer Gabriel Valleyre had a similar idea but used clay. With stereotypes, printers did not have to lock up tons of type.

Aberration of light

1728

James Bradley

There was no direct evidence that Earth is speeding through space until English astronomer James Bradley discovered the aberration of light in 1728. Imagine a car standing in the rain. Streaks of rain run vertically down the windows. When the car moves, the streaks slope backward. This is what Bradley saw, only the car was Earth, the rain was light from a star, and the slope was an extra tilt of his telescope.

Achromatic lens

1729

Chester Hall

Isaac Newton said that lenses would always produce images with color fringes. In 1729, English judge Chester Hall proved him wrong. By combining a convex lens of ordinary glass with a concave lens of heavy flint glass, he canceled out the fringes, creating a color-free, or achromatic, lens. English optician John Dollond later did the same. The lenses led to the first really good microscopes and telescopes.

Cobalt

1730

Georg Brandt

In the early 18th century, chemistry was shaking off the last of alchemy. Georg Brandt, a metallurgist from Sweden, used the more scientific approach. He was rewarded in 1730 with the discovery of cobalt. He later exposed alchemists claiming to make gold as frauds. Cobalt is now essential to advanced magnets and radiotherapy.

1726 Anglo-Irish writer Jonathan Swift writes *Travels into Several Remote Nations of the World*, later known as *Gulliver's Travels*. His satire about countries called Lilliput, Brobdingnag, Houyhnhnms, and Laputa will become a classic.

1729 At Oxford University, England, John Wesley, with his brother Charles, founds the Methodist Church. Preaching personal salvation through faith, Wesley's new, less formal Church appeals strongly to working people.

Sextant

c.1730

John Hadley, Thomas Godfrey

Sailors can navigate by measuring the height of the sun. Simple ways of doing this are inaccurate, and looking straight at the sun can damage the eyes. In about 1730, John Hadley in Britain and Thomas Godfrey in North America both found a better method: looking at a reflection of the sun in a movable mirror. The instruments that they invented were called octants, because the mirror swung over one-eighth of a circle. A later version, the sextant, gave even greater accuracy. When used with a chronometer to compare local time with ship time, it allowed sailors to figure out their exact position.

Index arm is moved until the mirrors appear to line up the Sun with the horizon

Index mirror reflects onto the horizon mirror below

The horizon mirror reflects the sun

Telescope allows navigator to see the horizon and sun

By reading the angle from the index arm, the sun's altitude, and hence the latitude of the ship, can be calculated

SEXTANT *Using a system of mirrors, the sextant measures the sun's altitude to an accuracy of 0.01 degrees.*

Flying shuttle

1733

John Kay

In weaving, thread on a reel in a holder called a shuttle is shot back and forth. John Kay, the son of an English woolen manufacturer, invented the flying shuttle in 1733. Before then, for wide cloth, a solitary weaver would have to walk from one side of the loom to the other to pick up the shuttle and throw it back, so it was more economical to have two weavers to throw it back and forth. Kay found a solution by adding rollers to the shuttle so that it ran on a track. It was operated by one weaver, halving the labor needed to make broad cloth. It was a key to the Industrial Revolution in Britain (✳ **see page 111**) but brought Kay neither fame nor fortune.

Measurement of blood pressure

1733

Stephen Hales

Stephen Hales was an English clergyman and also an expert scientist. He specialized in taking measurements of living things and was the first person to measure blood pressure. His technique, revealed in 1733, was brutally straightforward: he simply stuck a tube into a horse's artery and measured the height to which the blood rose. He also invented surgical forceps, among other innovations.

Rubber

1736

Charles-Marie de la Condamine

Rubber got its name in 1770 when British chemist Joseph Priestley found it would rub out pencil. Rubber trees, with their sticky sap, had been discovered earlier by the French scientist Charles-Marie de la Condamine, while he was on an expedition in South America. Rubber wasn't really new to Europeans—even Christopher Columbus knew about it—but it was Condamine's samples, sent back to France in 1736, that put this unique natural product on the scientific map.

Bernoulli effect

1738

Daniel Bernoulli

Swiss scientist Daniel Bernoulli figured out that if a stream of fluid (a gas or liquid) speeds up, its pressure drops. This "Bernoulli effect" can be seen in a popular science exhibit—a ball suspended on a stream of air from a blower. The air coming out of the blower is moving faster than the air that went in, so its pressure is lower than the surrounding air.

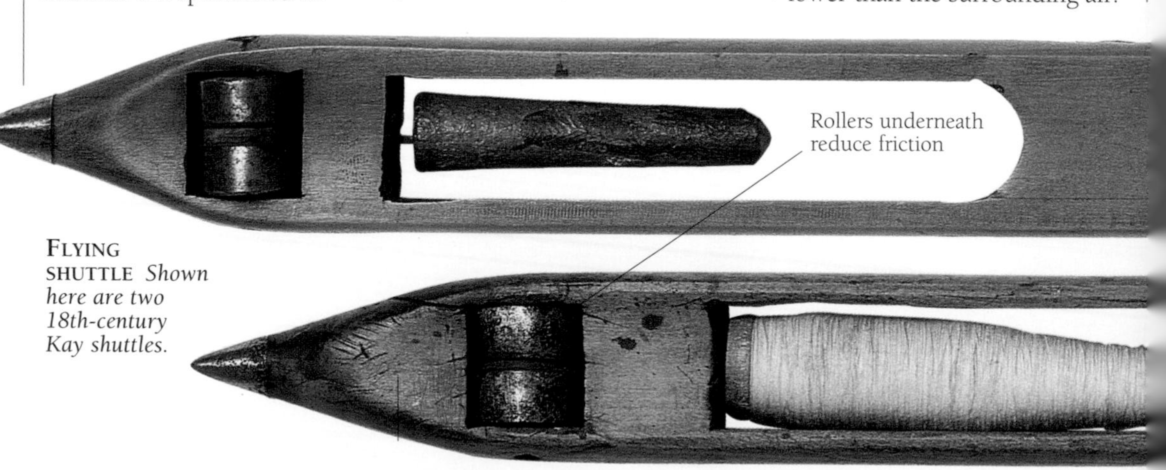

FLYING SHUTTLE *Shown here are two 18th-century Kay shuttles.*

1731 The first magazine to be called a magazine is published in Britain. At this time, magazine means "storehouse," and *The Gentleman's Magazine* is a sort of storehouse of articles collected every month from other publications.

1732 American writer and printer Benjamin Franklin begins publishing *Poor Richard's Almanac*, about a simple country dweller who becomes known for his practical proverbs and witty aphorisms. Franklin continues the *Almanac* until 1758.

If the ball moves from the air stream, the higher pressure pushes it back.

Franklin stove

1740

Benjamin Franklin

Benjamin Franklin was a writer, scientist, and diplomat, who played a leading part in creating the US. He still found time to create a simple invention that would warm thousands of homes in the republic: the Franklin stove. It was marketed as the "Pennsylvania Fireplace" and was the ancestor of the wood-burning stoves of today. Made of cast iron, it had a hinged door to enclose the fire and an adjustable ventilator to control the rate of combustion.

High-quality steel

c.1740

Benjamin Huntsman

Mass-produced steel is good enough for most things, but sometimes a more personal touch is needed. English clockmaker Benjamin Huntsman, finding that ordinary steel made poor watch springs, began to make his own steel in Sheffield in about 1740. He was the first to make steel hot enough to melt, allowing it to form a perfectly even alloy. He kept the process a secret, never patented it, and it was eventually copied by other people. Huntsman's work helped make Sheffield famous for fine steel.

Celsius scale of temperature

1742

Anders Celsius

Inventors of temperature scales hate doing the obvious. Daniel Fahrenheit set the freezing and boiling points of water at a seemingly strange 32 and 212 degrees. In 1742, Swedish astronomer Anders Celsius went decimal with a scale that ran from 0 to 100, but made freezing point 100 and boiling point 0. Eventually, his scale was turned upside down to produce the Celsius scale used today.

Silver-plated tableware

1743

Thomas Boulsover

There has always been a demand for anything that looks like solid silver but costs less. In 1743, English cutlery maker Thomas Boulsover discovered that he could make copper look and behave like silver. Working in Sheffield, Boulsover heated copper between thin sheets of silver then rolled the hot sandwich to produce Sheffield plate. It quickly pushed solid silver off all but the wealthiest tables.

Slip casting

c.1745

Ralph Daniel

Some earthenware items are made by slip casting. A suspension of clay in water, called slip, is poured into a mold. When dry, the shape is removed and fired. English potter Ralph Daniel invented the process in about 1745. He started with iron mold, but soon discovered that plaster molds worked better because they sucked out water from the slip and sped up drying.

Leyden jar

1745

Ewald von Kleist, Pieter van Musschenbroek

In the 18th century, electricity was often regarded as a fluid—something that has no definite shape but takes on the shape of its container. This may have been the thinking behind German physicist Ewald von Kleist's invention of the Leyden jar in 1745. The jar was covered with metal and made of glass so that electricity could not leak out. The following year, physicist Pieter van Musschenbroek of the University of Leiden in the Netherlands invented the jar independently. He named it and told other people about it. A charged jar could give a mighty shock. One demonstration involved 1,000 hand-holding monks. When the jar was connected to the first and last monk, all of them jumped.

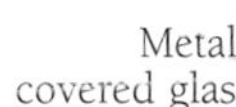

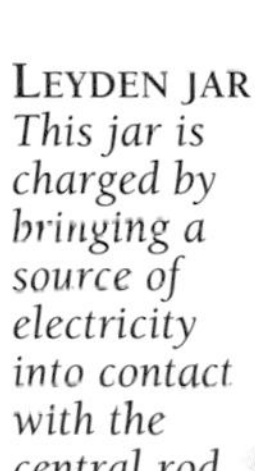

Leyden jar *This jar is charged by bringing a source of electricity into contact with the central rod.*

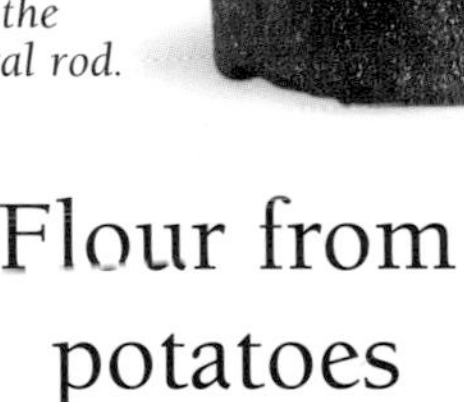

Flour from potatoes

1746

Eva Ekeblad

Food was scarce in 18th-century Sweden, but hidden in the greenhouses of its upper classes was the answer—potatoes. Swedish countess Eva Ekeblad used them to make flour and alcohol. This provided extra flour and also allowed some of the wheat, rye, and barley previously used for alcohol to go into making bread, easing the famine. The potato went from an exotic vegetable to a staple food.

1742 On April 13, in Dublin, Ireland, German composer George Frideric Handel's choral and orchestral work *Messiah* is performed for the first time. An instant success, it will be a hugely popular work for centuries to come.

1745 Charles Edward Stuart, known as Bonnie Prince Charlie, lands on the isle of Eriskay, off western Scotland, on July 25. He will lead an unsuccessful attempt to put him on the British throne in place of the German George II.

REVOLUTIONARY CHANGES

POLITICAL REVOLUTION in France and independence for the US had enormous effects on the world between 1750 and 1850. At the same time, the Industrial Revolution moved Western workers from farms to factories, and sciences such as chemistry shook off their last links with the ancient past.

Electrical nature of lightning *Thunderclouds threaten as Franklin flies his kite.*

Electrical nature of lightning

1752

Benjamin Franklin

US scientist Benjamin Franklin could have killed himself when he flew a kite in a thunderstorm. He did it to prove that lightning is caused by electricity. Electric charge from the thunderclouds passed down the string, and Franklin collected it in a Leyden jar (✻ *see* **page 103**). Amazingly, he lived to show that the charge behaved just like electricity from other sources.

Scientific names for plants

1753

Carolus Linnaeus

Until Swedish botanist Carl von Linné published his *Species Plantarum* (Kinds of Plants) in 1753, botanists described plants using very long-winded names. Linné, known as Linnaeus, classified plants into closely related groups, or genuses, then gave each one the genus name plus its own species name. For example, *Taraxacum officinale* is the dandelion. Linnaeus's system is still in use today.

Carbon dioxide

1756

Joseph Black

Carbon dioxide was recognized by the alchemist Jan Baptist van Helmont in 1648, but the first person to investigate it systematically and relate it to other chemical substances was the British chemist Joseph Black. In 1756, he announced his discovery that carbonates release what he called "fixed air" (carbon dioxide) when heated. Black's work eventually helped chemists gain a new understanding of air and also of combustion.

Prevention of scurvy

1757

James Lind

Scurvy is caused by lack of vitamin C. The gums swell, joints get stiff, and there may be bleeding beneath the skin. In 1757, British naval surgeon James Lind published a book recommending that sailors should receive rations of citrus fruits, which contain vitamin C. At that time, more British sailors died from scurvy than in battle. The navy thought about Lind's idea for 40 years, then tried it. Scurvy disappeared like magic.

Indestructible lighthouse

1759

John Smeaton

Lashed by storms off the coast of England, the Eddystone rock has been feared by sailors for centuries. The weather had destroyed two lighthouses there before British engineer John Smeaton discovered how to defy nature. He cemented together interlocking blocks of stone with concrete that would set under water. His lighthouse lasted more than 100 years. Even then it was the rock that crumbled, not the lighthouse.

Improved blast furnace

1760

John Smeaton

When Abraham Darby started using coke to smelt iron (✻ *see* **page 89**), he needed a better blast furnace. British engineer John Smeaton, one of the first to apply science to engineering, made the furnace larger and blew air through it with a fan powered by an efficient new waterwheel. Water rushed over the top of the new "overshot" wheel instead of underneath it.

Prevention of scurvy *James Lind tells sick sailors that limes are the answer to their problems.*

1752 In August, the bell that will be known as the Liberty Bell arrives in Philadelphia, from England, where it was made. It will be rung on July 8, 1776, to celebrate the first public reading of the Declaration of Independence.

1759 French writer Voltaire, a critic of those who try to restrict others' freedom of thought, writes his novel *Candide*. Its central character, Candide, fights against the stupidity of the world but is forced in the end to give up.

Spinning jenny

1764

James Hargreaves

Until the middle of the 18th century, people spun thread with a spinning wheel, which could spin only one thread at a time. James Hargreaves's spinning jenny (said to be named after his daughter) could spin several threads at once. Traditional spinners were alarmed about the machine, because it could put them out of work, but it helped to start the Industrial Revolution in Britain and brought greater prosperity in the end.

Faller wire guided the thread

Pulleys rotated the spindles

Clove helped to twist the fibers together

Creels held the fibers to be spun

Driving wheel was turned to make the spindles rotate

SPINNING JENNY *This replica of Hargreaves's machine shows that it was basically the older spinning wheel rearranged to drive several spindles.*

Latent heat

1761

Joseph Black

When water is heated, it keeps getting hotter until it turns into steam. Some of the heat doesn't actually raise the temperature but is used to change the "state" of water into steam. Likewise, when water changes into ice, heat is also released. This hidden heat was discovered by British chemist Joseph Black. Three years later, he explained the effect to James Watt, who had noticed it while working on a steam engine.

Finding longitude at sea

1761

John Harrison

Early sailors navigated by the sun and the stars. This was all right for determining their latitude (position north or south), but measuring longitude (position east or west) was difficult. One way was for them to compare the time at home, shown by a clock, with the time where they were at sea, shown by the sun. But no clock existed that would work at sea and keep accurate enough time. The government offered £20,000 to anyone who solved the longitude problem. Between 1735 and 1761, British clockmaker John Harrison built four chronometers. The fourth model was tested on a trip to Jamaica and proved accurate to within five seconds. Although Harrison had solved the problem, the government was reluctant to give him his full reward, and he was an old man before it finally paid up.

FINDING LONGITUDE AT SEA *The fourth version of Harrison's chronometer looks very much like a modern watch, only bigger. It is shown here at about two-thirds its actual size.*

1762 Ideas about education change with the publication of *Émile* by the French thinker Jean-Jacques Rousseau. His argument that true education can be built only on children's natural impulses will greatly influence later educators.

1763 The Treaty of Paris ends the Seven Years' War, also known as the French and Indian War. France gives Britain all its North American lands east of the Mississippi River, and Canada. Spain gives up Florida to Britain for Cuba.

Dividing engine

1766

Jesse Ramsden

Accurate measurements require accurately made measuring tools. Before British instrument maker Jesse Ramsden perfected his dividing engine in 1766, angles on theodolites and other instruments were made by hand by craftsmen and could be somewhat hit-or-miss. The dividing engine produced scales for scientific instruments mechanically. It was faster and more accurate than craftsmen and meant that maps, as well as astronomical and navigational measurements, were more reliable.

Hydrogen

1766

Henry Cavendish

British scientist Henry Cavendish was the first person to show that hydrogen was a distinct gas, not just a sort of air. He released hydrogen from sulfuric acid by dissolving metal in it, then measured its density. He found that it was lighter than any other gas. Later, he confirmed that hydrogen forms water when it burns. This led French chemist Lavoisier to call it hydrogen, from the Greek for "water maker."

Improved steam engine

1769

James Watt

The first steam engines were built to pump water out of coal mines. It was lucky there was plenty of coal, because the engines wasted a lot of fuel. James Watt discovered how to reduce the waste, allowing steam engines to compete with waterwheels in powering the new factories. He also invented better ways of controlling steam engines and connecting them to other machines. (✳ *See also* **The Story of Steam.**)

Steam tractor

1769

Nicolas Cugnot

Early steam engines were huge, heavy, and underpowered, but by 1769, they were good enough for Nicolas Cugnot, a French army engineer, to build a three-wheeled steam tractor. The following year, he built a bigger one to pull heavy guns. Its single front wheel, which was used for steering, was driven by a two-cylinder high-pressure steam engine. Although the later machine successfully pulled a three-ton cannon at walking speed, Cugnot never got the money he needed to solve its problems, such as how it could carry enough water to keep the engine going and how to stop the high-pressure steam from leaking out.

Water frame

1769

Richard Arkwright

Before fibers can be woven into cloth, they have to be spun into threads. To keep up with the demands of new weaving machinery, such as the flying shuttle (✳ *see* **page 102**), spinning had to speed up. In 1769, Richard Arkwright invented a high-speed spinning machine that made really strong thread. He called it a water frame because it was driven by water power.

THE STORY OF STEAM

THOMAS SAVERY'S STEAM ENGINE, which he patented in 1698, simply sucked up water with the vacuum created when steam condenses. Thomas Newcomen's engine, built in 1712, had a piston and could operate a mechanical pump but wasted fuel because its cylinder had to be warmed up from cold after every stroke. James Watt added a separate cooling chamber, allowing the main cylinder to stay hot all the time.

SAVERY'S ENGINE
Steam entered a chamber, forcing water out through a valve. The steam was then cooled, creating a vacuum that sucked water in through another valve, ready to be forced out during the next cycle.

NEWCOMEN'S ENGINE
Steam entered a cylinder, causing a piston to move upward. The steam was then cooled, creating a vacuum that allowed the atmosphere to push the piston down. This operated a pump through a rocking beam.

WATT'S ENGINES
Having added a separate cooling chamber, Watt further improved Newcomen's engine by letting steam push the piston down as well as up and adding gears that allowed the engine to drive rotating machinery.

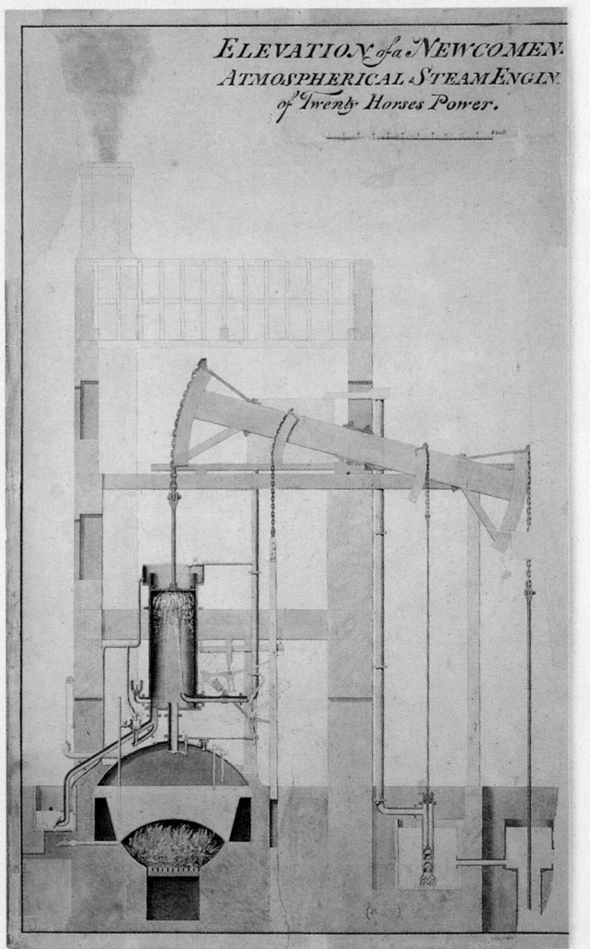

Drawing of a Newcomen engine of about 1826

1765 England enacts the Stamp Act and the Quartering Act to raise revenues in the English colonies. These two acts are widely resented by colonists and spark the independence movement in the American colonies.

1769 San Francisco Bay, one of the world's best natural harbors, is discovered by people arriving on foot. Led by Spanish explorer Gaspar de Portolá, they were sent to look for Monterey Bay but missed it and went too far north.

Factory

c.1770

Richard Arkwright

Richard Arkwright realized that his water-powered spinning machine (✱ *see* **page 107**) meant that spinners would have to gather where there was a waterwheel. In about 1770, in partnership with two local stocking makers, Samuel Need and Jedediah Strutt, he opened a water-powered mill at Cromford in Derbyshire, England. This was the first real factory and marked the start of the industrial age.

Oxygen

1772

Carl Scheele, Joseph Priestley

Oxygen has a complicated history. Swedish chemist Carl Scheele discovered it in 1772 but waited five years before publishing the fact. Meanwhile, British chemist Joseph Priestley discovered a gas in which things burned fast. Believing that burning things gave out "phlogiston" (✱ *see* **page 97**), he called it "dephlogisticated air." But the French chemist Antoine Lavoisier proved that the gas combined with burning substances rather than sucking phlogiston out. Lavoisier's new name for it, oxygen, means "acid maker," which it isn't.

Bode's Law

1772

Johann Titius, Johann Bode

There's something odd about the planets from Mercury to Uranus. There seems to be a relation between their distances from the sun. This was first noticed by German astronomer Johann Titius, and his formula was published by fellow astronomer Johann Bode in 1772. At that time, there were gaps where the formula predicted there should be planets. When later astronomers found that the asteroids and Uranus filled the gaps, it seemed to prove Bode's law. Then Neptune and Pluto were discovered, and these planets don't obey the law, so the relationship is probably just an amazing coincidence.

Carbonated drinks

1772

Joseph Priestley

The first carbonated drinks flowed out of the ground—natural carbonated water from

FACTORY *Collycroft woolen mill was built in Bedworth, England, in about 1790. It was a typical water-powered factory. This model of it is cut away to show the inside.*

1770 London's Bethlem Royal Hospital, an asylum for mentally ill people that is better known as Bedlam, shuts its doors to admission-paying spectators. The behavior of its inmates is no longer regarded as entertainment.

1772 John Fielding, chief magistrate of the Bow Street Police Court, London, starts issuing the *Quarterly Pursuit*, an information sheet detailing current stolen property and wanted persons. It will become the daily *Police Gazette*.

health-giving springs. The first to imitate them was Joseph Priestley. In 1772, he started producing "soda water" in quantity. He had found out how to make it several years earlier and in the process had made important discoveries about the gas carbon dioxide.

Precision boring machine

1775

John Wilkinson

Early steam engine builders were hampered by the difficulty of making the huge cylinders the engines required. British ironmaster John Wilkinson improved matters greatly with the precision boring machine he built in 1775 at his father's factory in Wales. It could bore deep, wide holes in large pieces of iron to form much more accurate cylinders than before. James Watt used the machine when building his later engines (✱ *see* **page 107**).

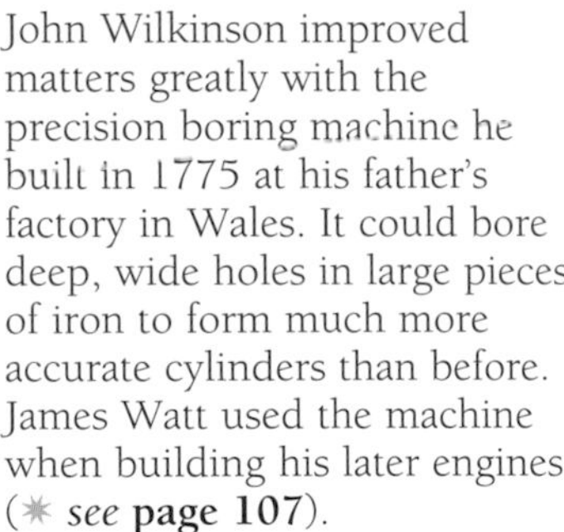

Division of labor

1776

Adam Smith

To make a sandwich, bread has to be filled and condiments added. If two people have to make a pile of sandwiches, is it quicker if both people make complete sandwiches or if one fills and the other adds condiments? The second way is quicker because doing just one job is simpler. This principle, called division of labor, was identified in 1776 by Scottish economist Adam Smith. He saw its extra productivity as the true source of prosperity.

Photosynthesis

1779

Jan Ingenhousz

In sunlight, green plants take in more carbon dioxide than they give off, and they give off more oxygen than they take in. In darkness, the reverse is true. Dutch doctor Jan Ingenhousz published this discovery in 1779 under the delightful title *Experiments Upon Vegetables, Discovering Their Great Power of Purifying the Common Air in Sunshine, and of Injuring It in the Shade and at Night*. This was the first description of the basics of photosynthesis.

Iron bridge

1779

Abraham Darby, Thomas Pritchard

A metal bridge seemed revolutionary at a time when stone, bricks, and wood were the only materials used for large structures. Abraham Darby built the world's first iron bridge in 1779 to the design of Thomas Pritchard. Its 100 ft (30.5 m) arch spans the Severn River at Coalbrookdale, Shropshire, in England. Having survived disastrous floods in 1795, Darby's bridge is still used today.

Mule spinning machine

1779

Samuel Crompton

Samuel Crompton's "mule" could draw, twist, and wind fibers into a fine thread. Unlike a hand spinner, though, it could work on a thousand reels at the same time. Like the animal of the same name, the mule was a hybrid, using ideas from Hargreaves's spinning jenny and Arkwright's water frame (✱ *see* **pages 106 and 107**). It soon replaced both of them.

Uranus

1781

William Herschel

The planet Uranus is just visible to the naked eye, but British astronomer William Herschel discovered it with a telescope. On March 13, 1781, he spotted what he thought might be a comet, but the way it moved convinced him it was a planet. He wanted to name it after the king, while French astronomers generously insisted it should be called Herschel. In the end it was decided to stick to naming planets after gods, and it became Uranus.

HOT-AIR BALLOON *The first demonstration of a Montgolfier balloon took place in June 1783.*

Hot-air balloon

1783

Joseph Montgolfier, Étienne Montgolfier

The first hot-air balloons were made by two French papermakers, Joseph and Étienne Montgolfier. In September 1783, they sent three animals on a successful 2 mile (3 km) trip in a balloon. Then, in November, they organized the first human escape from Earth's surface. Two volunteers remained aloft for 25 minutes, climbing to 1,500 ft (450 m) above Paris and traveling 5.3 miles (8.5 km). Strangely, the brothers never risked a flight themselves.

1776 On Thursday, July 4, the Declaration of Independence is approved in the US. It notes why 13 British colonies "ought to be Free and Independent States." Independence Day will later be celebrated as a national holiday.

1777 Europeans learn of the existence of New Zealand when British explorer James Cook publishes *A Voyage Towards the South Pole and Round the World*. Cook spent a year charting its islands and getting to know its Maori people.

Hydrogen balloon

1783

Jacques Charles

While the Montgolfiers were experimenting with hot air over Paris (✱ *see* **page 109**), the French scientist Jacques Charles was working with the lightest of all gases, hydrogen, to get a balloon airborne. In 1783, he ascended in a hydrogen balloon to nearly 10,000 ft (3 km). Charles is also known for a law describing how gases expand when heated.

Parachute

1783

Louis Lenormand

Frenchman Louis Lenormand invented his parachute as a means of escape from a burning building. After testing it by jumping from trees, he made his first serious trial in December 1783. He leaped from the top of the Montpelier observatory in France with a 14 ft (4.3 m) chute and landed safely on the ground. The first person to jump from the air was another Frenchman, André Garnerin, who took the plunge in 1797 after his hot-air balloon burst over Paris.

Tungsten

1783

Juan D'Elhuyar, Fausto D'Elhuyar

Tungsten is the metal that glows white-hot inside an old-fashioned light bulb. It has the highest melting point of any metal that can be made into wire, is very dense—making it good for fishing weights—and is an important ingredient of cutting tools. It was first isolated by the Spanish D'Elhuyar brothers, Juan and Fausto, in 1783, although it was already known to the Swedish chemist Carl Scheele.

Bifocal eyeglasses

1784

Benjamin Franklin

Older people can find it hard to see things close up as well as far away. Reading glasses make nearby objects clearer but make distant ones less clear. In his old age, Benjamin Franklin solved the problem with the bifocal lens. This has a section for distant vision mounted above one for near vision. When wearers of bifocal eyeglasses look down to read, they automatically see through the near vision part of the lens; when they look up, the distant vision section comes into play.

Pickproof lock

1784

Joseph Bramah

Picking a lock means opening it without the key. Some locks are harder to pick than others, but one of the hardest was invented as long ago as 1784. British engineer Joseph Bramah offered £210 to anyone who could pick his lock, but it was 67 years before anyone claimed the reward. Even then it took US locksmith A. C. Hobbs 51 hours—hardly feasible for a burglar.

Heddle raised and lowered the warp threads

Gear wheels drove cams to move the different parts

Finished cloth wound onto a roller

POWER LOOM *By the mid-19th century, the power loom had been developed into a highly effective, reliable machine. British looms like this one by Harrison and Sons produced cloth for sale worldwide.*

1784 Jedidiah Morse, father of the inventor of Morse code, publishes the US's first geography textbook, *Geography Made Easy*. It is a great success, and Morse writes several more books on US geography.

1786 On May 1, an audience in Vienna, Austria, gives a warm reception to *The Marriage of Figaro*, a new opera by Wolfgang Amadeus Mozart. Its comic scenes disguise an attack on the foolishness and corruption of the nobility.

Puddling process for wrought iron

1784

Henry Cort

Iron with too much carbon in it is brittle. Before British ironmaster Henry Cort invented his "puddling" process in 1784, the only way to produce flexible, or wrought, iron was to hammer freshly smelted iron while it was still hot, squeezing out carbon. Cort melted iron with iron oxide to form a puddle, then stirred it while hot gases burned off the carbon. The purer metal gathered into a large ball that, with just a little hammering, became wrought iron.

Power loom

1785

Edmund Cartwright

The designer of the first power loom, Edmund Cartwright, was a British country parson. He was, in his own words, "totally ignorant of the subject, having never at that time seen a person weave." He realized, though, that cheap yarn from powered spinning machines could transform cloth making. His first loom, built in 1785, was very crude, but by 1787, he had improved it enough to start a weaving factory in Doncaster. The government later awarded him £10,000 in recognition of his pioneering work. (✱ *See also* **Weaving a New World.**)

WEAVING A NEW WORLD

BETWEEN ABOUT 1750 AND 1850, in a process known as the Industrial Revolution, Britain transformed itself from a largely agricultural nation into the world's leading industrial power. The industry that led the way was cloth making. Attracted by higher wages, workers moved from farms into the new factories. These were made possible by water power, steam power, new machines, and more adventurous ways of raising money.

This 1834 drawing of a Lancashire cotton mill cannot convey the deafening noise of the many power looms.

SPEEDING UP SPINNING
Until about 1770, spinning was largely done by women in their own homes. Merchants would deliver raw wool and then collect the homemade yarn. When powered machines were introduced, spinning took place in factories instead.

LOOMING LARGER
Weaving was also done at home, mainly by men, but factories also threatened this home-based industry. Changes were slower than in spinning, but by 1825 half of British cloth was woven on power looms in factories.

FROM COUNTRY TO CITY
Early factories were noisy and dangerous but offered new opportunities for women and better wages than farm work. Even skilled craft workers, unable to compete with factory prices, were forced into industrial cities.

Stability of the solar system

1786

Pierre-Simon Laplace

Although gravity explains the way the planets move, Newton (✱ *see* **pages 98–99**) was not sure they would go on forever. He suggested that God intervened from time to time to keep them on track. A century later, people did not believe so readily in divine intervention. In 1786, French mathematician Pierre-Simon Laplace proved that Newton's theory, properly applied, does predict a stable solar system: in the long run, any wobbles cancel out.

Centrifugal governor

1787

James Watt

The governor was one of James Watt's more significant additions to the steam engine. It kept the engine's speed constant as conditions varied. Watt adapted it from a device used in windmills. Weights mounted on a spindle flew out sideways if the engine sped up, closing the steam valve and slowing down the engine. Like Cornelis Drebbel's thermostat of 1600 (✱ *see* **page 86**), it was an early example of feedback control.

CENTRIFUGAL GOVERNOR *Watt based his governor on this windmill regulator.*

1787 During the summer, the Constitution of the United States of America is written by 55 delegates meeting in Philadelphia. It defines the various parts of the US's system of government and the basic rights of its citizens.

1787 Eleven ships sail from England, carrying the first white settlers to Australia. They arrive at Botany Bay but later divert to a new site, Port Jackson. Of the 1,030 people who land there on January 26, 1788, 736 are convicts.

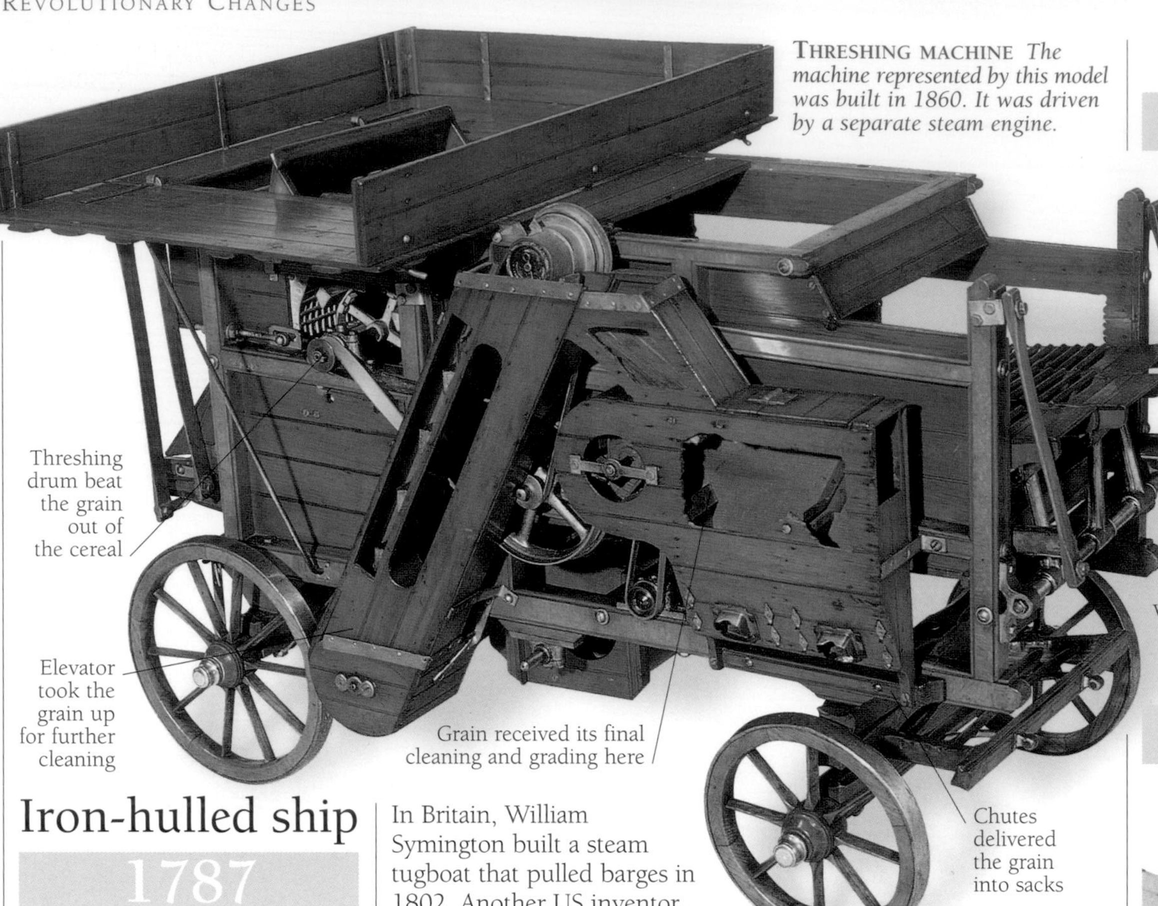

THRESHING MACHINE *The machine represented by this model was built in 1860. It was driven by a separate steam engine.*

Iron-hulled ship

1787

John Wilkinson

John Wilkinson had iron in his soul. When he was 20 years old, he built an iron furnace. Later, in addition to making a machine to bore holes in iron (✱ *see* **page 109**), he was involved in building the first iron bridge. He used his boring machine to make iron cannons and, in 1787, built an iron barge to carry them down the Severn River in Britain—the first ever iron ship. He was even buried in an iron coffin.

Steamship

1787

John Fitch, William Symington, Robert Fulton

The first working steamboat, built in France, shook to pieces in 15 minutes. In 1787, US clockmaker John Fitch built a more robust craft that made several 20 mile (30 km) trips. In Britain, William Symington built a steam tugboat that pulled barges in 1802. Another US inventor, Robert Fulton, having seen the tugboat, built the first really successful steamship, the SS *Clermont*, in 1807. With its sister ship SS *Phoenix*, it plied the Hudson River for many years.

Threshing machine

1788

Andrew Meikle

Corn was traditionally beaten, or threshed, with sticks to separate the grain from its straw and outer covering, known as chaff. The wind was then used to blow away the smaller chaff. In 1788, Scottish millwright Andrew Meikle invented a machine to do the threshing. The wheat was trapped between a rotating drum and a close-fitting cover, to strip the chaff from the grain. There was no wind inside the machine, so the mixture had to be separated afterward.

Modern chemistry

1789

Antoine Lavoisier, John Dalton

Before French chemist Antoine Lavoisier cleaned it up, chemistry was full of old-fashioned names and notions. As well as overturning mistaken theories, he and his followers renamed the known elements and compounds and established the basic naming system used today. After this, Lavoisier's 1789 *Elementary Treatise of Chemistry*, together with British schoolmaster John Dalton's 1808 *New System of Chemical Philosophy*, laid the foundations of modern chemistry. Lavoisier's brilliance did not save him from the French Revolution, though; he was guillotined in 1794.

Platinum

1789

P. F. Chabaneau

The valuable, silvery-gray metal platinum was known as long ago as 700 BCE, but only as an impurity in gold. Workable platinum was first produced in 1789 by the French physicist P. F. Chabaneau. Instead of using it for some sensible laboratory apparatus, he had it made into a decorative cup, which he gave to the Pope.

Uranium

1789

Martin Klaproth

Uranium, essential to nuclear power, was discovered in 1789

1788 After years of odd behavior, King George III of England becomes so deranged that parliament passes a bill to remove him from the throne and replace him with his son. He will recover the next year before the law comes into effect.

1789 The United States Supreme Court is established as the highest court in the land and the final court of appeal. John Jay becomes the first Chief Justice. Congress adopts the first 10 amendments to the Constitution, the Bill of Rights.

by the German chemist Martin Klaproth. He named it after the planet Uranus. Although he believed that he had isolated a new element from the mineral pitchblende, in reality he had extracted only uranium dioxide. The French chemist Eugène Péligot, realizing this in 1841, was the first to produce uranium as pure metal.

Printing ink roller

1790

William Nicholson

In the 18th century, printing ink was dabbed onto the type with leather pads. This was a slow process and required some skill to get the type inked evenly. In 1790, British engineer William Nicholson came up with an improvement that was literally revolutionary: a leather roller. When printing presses were mechanized in the 19th century, the leather on the roller was replaced by a strange but effective mixture of glue and molasses.

Speech synthesizer

1791

Wolfgang von Kempelen

If your computer can talk, it's thanks to research that goes back to the 18th century. By the 1770s, the basics were understood well enough for Hungarian engineer Wolfgang von Kempelen to start building the first speech synthesizer. He published details of his machine in 1791 in his book *The Mechanism of Human Speech and a Description of a Speaking Machine*. His machine could produce sentences, but it needed a lot of skill to "play." The original machine, with nostrils and a mouth, bellows for lungs, and a reed for the voice, is now in the Deutsches Museum, Munich, Germany.

Titanium

1791

William Gregor, Martin Klaproth

Titanium dioxide is what makes white paint white. Pure titanium and its alloys are used inside jet engines because they stand up well to the enormous heat. This versatile element was first discovered, as an ore called menachanite, by British clergyman William Gregor on a Cornish beach in 1791. Three years later, German chemist Martin Klaproth confirmed Gregor's discovery and chose the name titanium for the new element.

Ambulance

1792

Dominique Larrey

The ambulance was a military invention. Before French surgeon Dominique Larrey's work, few armies had much more than a first-aid kit for battlefield injuries. In 1792, Larrey organized the "flying ambulance"—a mobile team of paramedics supporting Napoleon's troops in battle. They carried medical supplies with them and could get some of the wounded to the hospital on a lightweight vehicle. Larrey became chief surgeon of the French army and later devised ambulances to get the wounded into field hospitals.

Gas lighting

1792

William Murdock

In the 19th and 20th centuries, coal gas was used for lighting. Early experiments were carried out in Belgium and Scotland by chemist J. P. Minckelers and the Earl of Dundonald, but the gas industry owes more to Scottish engineer William Murdock. In 1792, he lit his cottage in Cornwall, England, by heating coal in a closed vessel and piping the gas to lights. Later, he developed a complete system for making and storing gas.

AMBULANCE *By 1915, during World War I, the military ambulance really could fly. But only the favored few went by air.*

1789 The French Revolution begins in earnest on Tuesday, July 14, when the people of Paris storm the Bastille, a royal prison, and organize a people's militia. The hated King Louis XVI is forced to withdraw his troops.

1791 The Ordnance Survey of Great Britain is founded and begins to make new maps of Britain and Ireland. Its prime objective is to provide better maps for military purposes. Its work sets new standards for detail and accuracy.

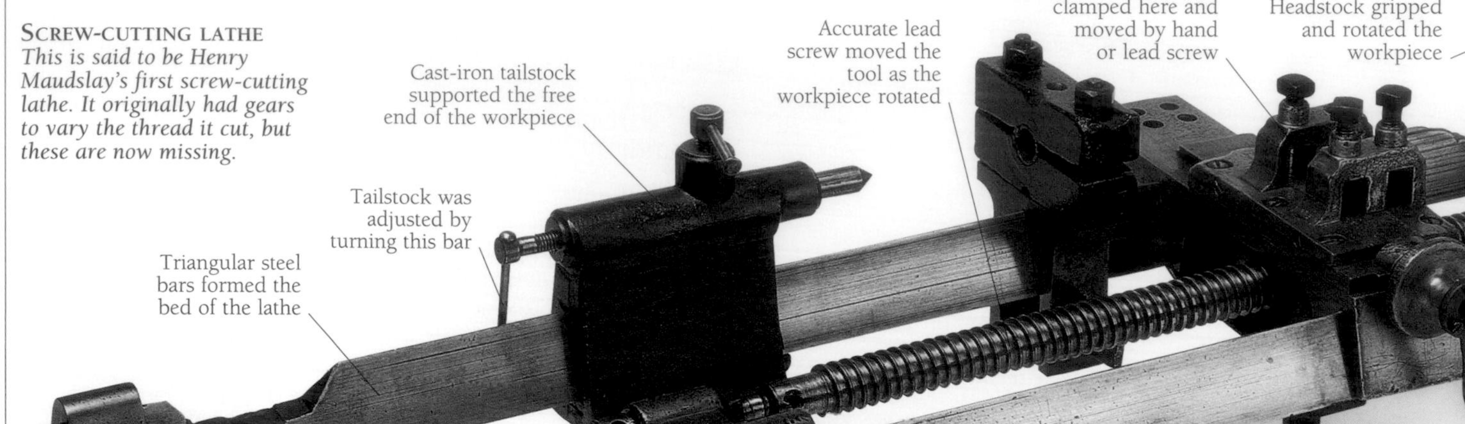

SCREW-CUTTING LATHE
This is said to be Henry Maudslay's first screw-cutting lathe. It originally had gears to vary the thread it cut, but these are now missing.

Cotton gin

1793

Eli Whitney

Cotton is the fiber attached to the seeds of the cotton plant. It cannot be used until the seeds have been removed. In 1793, US engineer Eli Whitney invented the first machine to remove the seeds—the cotton gin. A revolving cylinder covered with rows of hooks forced the cotton through a comb to rake out the seeds. It was so successful that it made the US the world's leading cotton producer, overtaking other regions such as Egypt and India. Despite this, it brought Whitney little profit.

Semaphore telegraph

1794

Claude Chappe

Between 1792 and 1814, France was usually at war with Austria. Some of the fighting was near Lille in northern France. To speed up communication with Paris, engineer Claude Chappe built a chain of towers. Each one had movable arms to signal letters and numbers, which could be seen from the next tower using a telescope. In August 1794, this semaphore telegraph sent news of a victory over a distance of 128 miles (205 km) in less than an hour.

Screw-cutting lathe

1797

Henry Maudslay, David Wilkinson

A lathe spins metal against a tool to give it a circular shape. If the tool also moves sideways, it cuts a screw thread. This could be done with a hand-operated screw mechanism, but in 1797, Henry Maudslay in Britain and David Wilkinson in the US invented lathes where the tool was driven by a screw geared to the lathe. They cut accurate threads with ease.

Chromium

1797

Nicolas Vauquelin

Chromium can prevent corrosion of other metals, either as plating or in stainless steel. French chemist Nicolas Vauquelin discovered the element in 1797 as an impurity in lead ore. He called it chromium, from the Greek word for color, because its compounds are brightly colored. This makes them especially useful in paints.

Lithography

1798

Aloys Senefelder

Most printing today relies on a process invented in 1798 by an unsuccessful German actor, Aloys Senefelder. He was trying to make printing plates from limestone, by writing on them with grease and then etching them, when he discovered that his plates would print before they were etched because the printing ink stuck to the grease but not to the wet stone. In today's lithography, the plates are metal and the image is formed photographically, but the principle remains the same.

Beryllium

1798

Nicolas Vauquelin

Perhaps the best-known beryllium compound is the green gemstone called emerald. Electrical contacts made of copper also contain beryllium, which makes the copper springy without reducing its conductivity. Beryllium was first identified as beryllium oxide by French chemist Nicolas Vauquelin in 1798. This compound conducts heat well but does not conduct electricity, making it useful today in certain electronic components. Pure beryllium metal was prepared in 1828 by German chemist Friedrich Wöhler and, independently, by French chemist Antonine Bussy. It is often used in the space and nuclear industries.

1794 What will become one of the world's best loved poems, "The Tyger," which begins "Tyger, tyger, burning bright / In the forests of the night," is printed by British artist and poet William Blake in *Songs of Innocence and Experience*.

1795 France replaces its old weights and measures with the metric system. Its basic unit, the meter, is taken to be one 40-millionth of the circumference of Earth. By the late 20th century, it will be used by most countries worldwide.

Smallpox vaccine

1798

Edward Jenner

Smallpox was a deadly viral infection common 200 years ago. British surgeon Edward Jenner noticed that people who caught cowpox, a similar but milder disease, never got smallpox. In 1796, he scratched a boy's skin, then applied fluid from a girl with cowpox. It was the first vaccine. The boy later survived deliberate smallpox infection, and in 1798 Jenner published the first book on vaccination. (✱ *See also* **Protection for Life.**)

PROTECTION FOR LIFE

EDWARD JENNER HIT ON THE PRINCIPLE by which all vaccines work. The body creates different antibodies to destroy specific viruses or other invaders. But making the right antibody takes time, so a big infection can overwhelm the system. It works better with advance warning in the shape of harmless vaccine particles resembling the unwanted guest. Then, if the real thing comes along, the body is ready for it.

Edward Jenner

Simple tools used by Jenner for his early work

Cupping horn

SMALLPOX BEFORE JENNER
Before vaccination, the only precaution against smallpox was variolation, a procedure made popular by Lady Mary Wortley Montagu. Infectious matter from a person with smallpox was applied to a scrape in the skin of someone who wanted to be protected. This risky process could produce either immunity or smallpox itself.

VACCINATION FOR ALL
Jenner's work stirred up a lot of opposition, but his ideas began to take hold as deaths from smallpox dwindled. In 1881, the French biologist Louis Pasteur created a vaccine against anthrax, a fatal disease caught from animals. Today, we can be vaccinated against a wide range of once deadly infections.

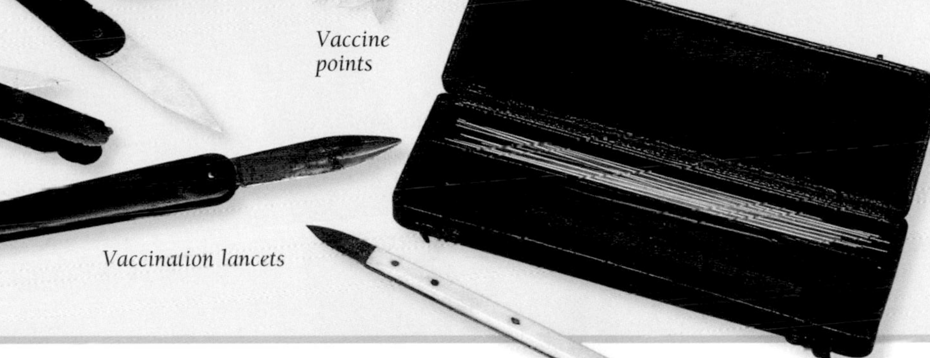

Vaccine points

Vaccination lancets

Lancet and vaccinator

Laughing gas

1799

Humphry Davy

Joseph Priestley discovered nitrous oxide in 1772, but it was 1799 before Humphry (later Sir Humphry) Davy found that the gas could make people laugh. While suggesting that it might be useful in surgery, he also liked to throw parties at which he used nitrous oxide to give his guests a good laugh.

LAUGHING GAS *In this 1802 cartoon, James Gillray suggests some comical dangers of playing with laughing gas. Davy is wielding the bellows.*

Stratigraphy

1799

William Smith

Stratigraphy, a key way to understand Earth, was developed by British surveyor William Smith. He noticed the same sequence of rock layers in different places. Tracing these over a wide area, he drew the first geological maps. He also saw that each rock had its own fossils and that those in higher layers were more complex life forms. This lets geologists group rocks by age, according to the fossils they contain.

1796 A new medical system called homeopathy is introduced by a German doctor named Samuel Hahnemann. It treats an illness with tiny doses of drugs that produce effects similar to the symptoms of that illness.

1798 British poets William Wordsworth and Samuel Taylor Coleridge together produce the slim volume *Lyrical Ballads*. It opens with Coleridge's "Rime of the Ancient Mariner" and marks the start of poetry's Romantic Movement.

Battery

1800

Alessandro Volta

In 1780, Italian doctor Luigi Galvani noticed that a frog's leg in contact with two different metals would twitch and found that the effect was electrical. His friend Alessandro Volta proved that it was the metals, not the animal tissue, that produced the electricity. In 1800, he made the first battery, a stack of silver and zinc discs separated by brine-soaked cardboard, and showed that electricity from his "pile" behaved like static electricity.

Electrolysis of water

1800

William Nicholson, Anthony Carlisle

British engineer William Nicholson and surgeon Anthony Carlisle began to use Volta's new battery. They found that bubbles formed when they put wires from the battery into salt water. Investigation revealed that the bubbles from one wire were hydrogen. Oxygen was liberated at the other wire, but it combined with the wire rather than forming bubbles. This was the start of electrochemistry, which would reveal much about the nature of chemical compounds.

Iron-framed printing press

1800

Charles Stanhope

In printing, the bigger the area of type, the greater the force needed to squeeze the paper into contact with it. Wooden presses couldn't stand the force needed to print a large sheet. Charles Stanhope, a scientifically minded aristocrat, improved things by making the first cast-iron press. Stronger than a wooden press, it could print large sheets in one pull.

CHROMATIC HARP *This French pedal harp dates from about 1810.*

Strings stretched between the neck and the sound box

Pedals for retuning the strings

Asteroid

1801

Giuseppe Piazzi

Italian astronomer Giuseppe Piazzi discovered the first asteroid in 1801 but soon lost it again as it moved into the daytime sky. It fitted just where Bode's Law said there was a missing planet (✱ *see* **page 108**). German mathematician Carl Gauss invented a way of calculating its orbit from Piazzi's few observations. Using this information, German astronomer Franz von Zach later found the missing asteroid. Piazzi named it Ceres.

Chromatic harp

c.1801

Sébastien Érard

Simple harps have one string per note and can normally play in only one key. Adding too many extra strings would make the instrument unplayable, so attempts to solve the problem have all been based on rapid retuning. The first harp that could play in every key was designed by Sébastien Érard in France between 1801 and 1810. Its double-action pedal mechanism can instantly retune any of its seven sets of strings.

Jacquard loom

1801

Jacques de Vaucanson, Joseph-Marie Jacquard

By raising and lowering the warp (lengthwise) threads on a loom in the right sequence, elaborate patterns can be woven. In the 18th century, this was done manually by a "drawboy." Inventor Jacques de Vaucanson replaced the boy with a punch-card mechanism in 1745, but this was ignored until 1801, when Joseph-Marie Jacquard turned it into the Jacquard loom. As well as weaving under the control of punch cards, it acted as an inspiration to the earliest computer pioneers.

Ultraviolet light

1801

Johann Ritter

Radio waves, X-rays, and many other kinds of radiation, including light, the only visible kind, are electromagnetic waves. They can be arranged in order of wavelength to form a spectrum. The part of the electromagnetic spectrum that we can see, the visible spectrum, has red at one end and violet at the other. In 1800, William Herschel discovered infrared radiation beyond the red end of the visible spectrum when he put a thermometer there and noted that it heated up. This made German physicist Johann Ritter have a look beyond the violet end. There, he found that silver chloride, which darkens in light, darkened more quickly, again revealing the presence of radiation—ultraviolet light.

1800 In the US, the Library of Congress is founded. Like the British Museum library, founded 41 years earlier, its goal is to collect at least one copy of everything published in the US, as a way of establishing copyright.

1801 Following a decree of the revolutionary government of France, seven years earlier, what were once the royal art collections of France at last become fully accessible to the public. They are displayed at the Louvre palace in Paris.

High-pressure steam engine

1802

Richard Trevithick, Oliver Evans

James Watt would never try steam at high pressure because he was convinced it was too dangerous. British engineer Richard Trevithick had no such fears. He made his cylinders extra thick and the pressure 10 times higher. In 1802, he patented the resulting smaller, more powerful engine, which made steam power far more versatile. At about the same time, Oliver Evans was pioneering high-pressure engines in the US, where they were taken up with even greater enthusiasm.

Mass production

1802

Marc Brunel, Henry Maudslay

Mass production reduces a complex operation to simpler operations, each carried out by a separate machine. The first true mass production system made wooden blocks for the rigging of sailing ships. It was designed by French engineer Marc Brunel and built by British engineer Henry Maudslay. Each of its 45 machines carried out a single operation, such as drilling a hole. It increased output per person by more than 10 times.

Names for clouds

1803

Luke Howard

Clouds tell us a lot about the weather, so it's not surprising that meteorologists recognize many types. Most of the names they use, such as cirrus and cumulus, were invented in 1803 by British chemist Luke Howard. His lifelong interest in the weather led him to lecture on meteorology and to publish the first book about it. In recognition of his work, he was elected to the Royal Society (a leading scientific society founded in 1660) in 1821.

Railroad locomotive

1804

Richard Trevithick

In 1804, when Richard Trevithick added wheels to his high-pressure engine and used it on a tramway, he created the first steam locomotive. It pulled 70 people and 11 tons (10 tonnes) of iron 10 miles (16 km) at a speed of 5 mph (8 km/h). Its advanced features included blowing used steam up its own chimney to make the fire burn faster. Unfortunately, the locomotive wore out the cast-iron tracks on which it ran, so Trevithick was forced to abandon it.

Railway locomotive
This is a model of Trevithick's locomotive Catch-Me-Who-Can, *which he built in 1808.*

Rods powered by the piston drove the rear wheels

Strongly built boiler

Pump fed water into the boiler

1802 After the breakup of her marriage, Marie Tussaud, an expert in wax modeling, arrives in Britain from France, with several models and two children. She will tour Britain for 33 years, then start a waxwork museum in London.

1804 Tsurya Namboku IV, chief playwright of the Kawarazaki Theatre in Japan, scores his first big hit with *Tokubei of India: Tales of Strange Lands*. Written for top actor Onoe Matsusuke I, it is full of the macabre and the grotesque.

Arc light

c.1807

Humphry Davy

By 1807, British chemist Humphry Davy had demonstrated a sensational effect to an audience at the Royal Institution of Great Britain. He brought together two carbon rods connected to a colossal 3,000-volt battery, then drew them apart to produce a blinding white flame 4 in (10 cm) long. It was another 70 years before electric generators were good enough to turn this bold experiment into practical lighting for streets and warehouses.

ARC LIGHT *In Minneapolis, the first electric arc lights were illuminated in February 1883.*

Sodium and potassium

1807

Humphry Davy

Volta's battery (✳ *see* **page 116**) brought a flurry of new discoveries. Two of them, sodium and potassium, were made by Humphry Davy at the Royal Institution. Because these elements are so reactive, they are never found uncombined. In separate experiments, Davy melted sodium hydroxide and potassium hydroxide, then connected a battery across the molten masses to extract the metals from their different compounds electrically.

Atomic weights

1808

John Dalton

In 1808, British schoolmaster John Dalton helped create the formulas and equations of modern chemistry. In his *New System of Chemical Philosophy*, he said that chemical elements consist of atoms, each element having atoms of a different weight. The ratios of these weights, and the proportions in which atoms combined, were whole numbers. Ignored for nearly 50 years, Dalton's work eventually had a great effect.

Lace-making machine

1809

John Heathcoat

Lace was originally made by clever hands manipulating lots of bobbins. Only rich people could afford to buy it. In 1809, British inventor John Heathcoat patented a machine that could imitate handmade lace. With his partner Charles Lacy, he set up a mill to turn out the new product. It was wrecked in 1816 by Luddites—organized groups of workers who tried to stop machines forcing workers into factories.

Canning

1810

Nicolas Appert, Peter Durand

Canned food started with an attempt to provide better food for French soldiers. The idea was developed by French confectioner Nicolas Appert, in 1809. He put jars of food into boiling water, then sealed them while still hot. Although Appert didn't know it, this killed bacteria and prevented reinfection. In 1810, British inventor Peter Durand replaced the jars with tin-coated iron containers, creating the first canned food. By 1820, it was feeding the British navy.

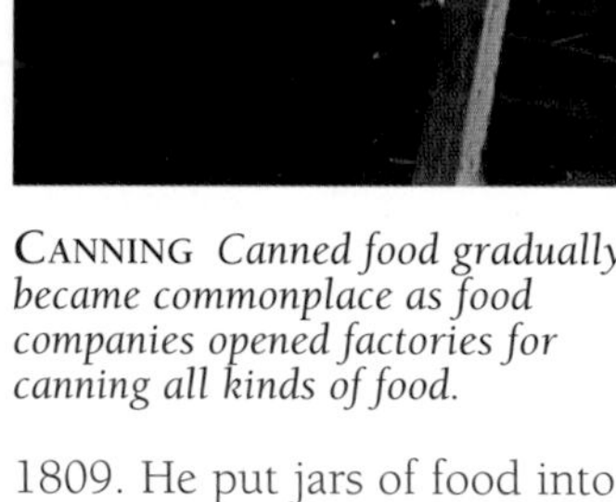

CANNING *Canned food gradually became commonplace as food companies opened factories for canning all kinds of food.*

Compound steam engine

1811

Arthur Woolf

In a high-pressure steam engine, the steam released after each stroke of the piston is still under pressure and therefore contains wasted energy. By feeding it into a second cylinder, much of this

1807 Three years after all US states north of Maryland abolish slavery, British antislavery reformers William Wilberforce and Thomas Clarkson finally succeed in making it illegal to import slaves into any British colony.

1812 In Germany, language and folklore researchers Jacob and Wilhelm Grimm publish the first of a two-volume set of folktales called *Kinder-und Hausmärchen*. The stories will appear 45 years later as *Grimms' Fairy Tales*.

can be recovered. British inventor Jonathan Hornblower patented the idea in 1781 but was prevented from developing it by James Watt, who claimed that it infringed his own steam engine patent (✳ *see* **page 107**). However, British engineer Arthur Woolf rediscovered the principle in 1804 and produced the first successful compound engine in 1811, after Watt's patent had expired.

Cylinder printing press

1811

Friedrich König, Andreas Bauer

Early 19th-century printing presses worked in much the same way as the one used by Gutenberg in 1455 (✳ *see* **page 76**). Then, with better engineering, faster machines became possible. The first was designed by German engineers Friedrich König and Andreas Bauer in 1811. The paper was wrapped around a cylinder that rotated as the type rolled under it. In 1814, a steam-driven König and Bauer at the offices of *The Times* newspaper in London hit a record-breaking total of 1,100 sheets an hour.

Sensory and motor nerve fibers

1811

Charles Bell

Scottish anatomist Charles Bell did fundamental research on the human nervous system. Working in London, he investigated the structure of the brain and spinal nerves. His biggest discovery was that there are two kinds of nerve fibers: sensory fibers that bring in messages to the spinal cord and brain, and motor fibers that send out instructions. Bell's findings were later confirmed by the French physiologist François Magendie.

Miner's safety lamp

1816

Humphry Davy, George Stephenson

See **pages 120–121** for the story of how Davy and Stephenson fought to save miners' lives.

Kaleidoscope

1816

David Brewster

In 1816, Scottish physicist David Brewster took time off work to invent the optical toy called a kaleidoscope. Multiple reflections between a pair of mirrors set at an angle to each other turn a collection of colored fragments into a constantly changing symmetrical pattern. Its name is Greek, meaning "see beautiful shapes."

KALEIDOSCOPE *Brewster's kaleidoscope was far more elaborate than today's toy.*

Tube in which colored fragments are viewed

Object plates containing loose colored fragments

Lockable case

1813 Jane Austen sees her novel *Pride and Prejudice* in print at last, 17 years after she started writing it. Austen declares the book's central character, Elizabeth Bennett, to be her favorite among the many heroines she has created.

1815 On June 18, Napoleon suffers his final defeat, at the Battle of Waterloo in Belgium. As well as making some tactical errors, he is heavily outnumbered by 133,000 men led by General von Blücher and the Duke of Wellington.

MAKING THE MAGIC LAMP

Humphry Davy and George Stephenson fight to save miners' lives

Monday, May 25, 1812, was a terrible day for the mining village of Felling, near Newcastle, England. A massive underground explosion killed 92 miners, some of them only 10 years old. It was one of a series of disasters caused by the flame in miners' lamps making "firedamp," or methane gas, explode. In the previous 10 years, 108 miners had died in the northeast alone. Now the number had risen to 200. Something had to be done.

A committee was formed to investigate the problem. It asked the advice of William Clanny, a local doctor, Humphry Davy, a chemist, and George Stephenson, a self-educated mine mechanic.

Both Clanny and Stephenson started work on a safer lamp. Clanny sealed his with water, but miners had to pump air in by hand, so it wasn't very useful. Stephenson tried letting the air in through small holes. Firedamp got in, too, and burned, but the metal around the holes cooled the flame, preventing explosions. Stephenson's lamp was tested in October 1815, and it worked.

Back in London, Davy experimented with firedamp from a mine. Like Stephenson, he fed in air through small holes, but he realized that the holes had to be very small indeed. His lamp had copper gauze around the flame. It was tested in January 1816 and was a success. The mine owners held a celebration dinner and gave Davy some silverware worth 50 times a miner's yearly pay.

The miners were not impressed. They resented a southerner getting credit for something one of their own people had already invented. Many wouldn't use Davy's lamp and stuck to their "geordie"—Stephenson's design. Davy said that

BEING A MINER A section through Bradley mine in Staffordshire, in 1808, shows the rock strata and the jobs of miners. In addition to coping with rock fall and floods, early miners worked in almost total darkness. Any light came from candles, which could cause devastating explosions.

THE COMPETITORS Humphry Davy and George Stephenson were very different people. Davy, born in the southwest of England, was a well-educated gentleman and a skilled scientist. Stephenson, who came from the northeast, was a tough, practical mine mechanic who had never been to school.

Humphry Davy was a chemist, but he turned his hand to scientific matters of many kinds.

George Stephenson pioneered the first public steam railroad as well as invented a safety lamp.

Stephenson had stolen the idea from him and that the geordie wouldn't work because it wasn't scientific.

In the end, most miners' lamps incorporated ideas from all three inventors. They had glass instead of gauze around the flame, so they gave more light than Davy's lamp, but the air was still fed in through gauze to prevent explosions. The problem was solved.

Or was it? Unfortunately, the new lamps encouraged mine owners to send miners into areas that were previously thought too dangerous. And because the lamps weren't totally safe, there were just as many deaths as before. Davy and Stephenson may have fought each other for nothing.

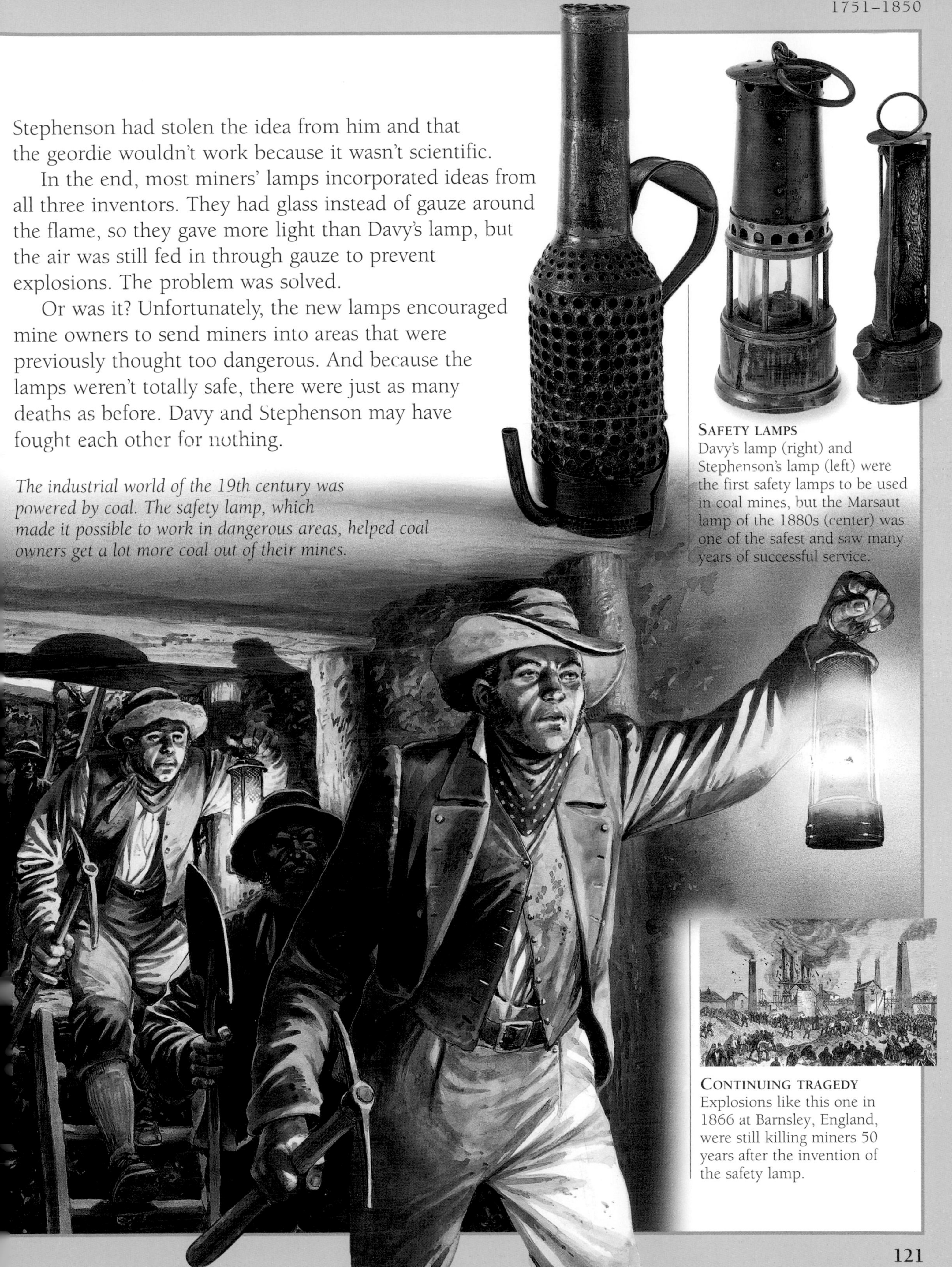

The industrial world of the 19th century was powered by coal. The safety lamp, which made it possible to work in dangerous areas, helped coal owners get a lot more coal out of their mines.

SAFETY LAMPS
Davy's lamp (right) and Stephenson's lamp (left) were the first safety lamps to be used in coal mines, but the Marsaut lamp of the 1880s (center) was one of the safest and saw many years of successful service.

CONTINUING TRAGEDY
Explosions like this one in 1866 at Barnsley, England, were still killing miners 50 years after the invention of the safety lamp.

DIVING SUIT *The heavy helmet of the 1830 Siebe suit provided a somewhat restricted view.*

Stirling engine

1816

Robert Stirling

Exploding boilers upset Scottish clergyman Robert Stirling, so he invented an engine that didn't need steam. Patented in 1816, it works by compressing a cold gas then transferring it to a heated cylinder, where it expands against a piston to do work. It is then cooled again by a radiator. The Stirling engine is quiet, clean, and efficient, but its cost and bulk limit its use.

Superphosphate fertilizer

c.1817

James Murray

Plants need phosphorus, and one source of this is fertilizer made of bones. In about 1817, Irish doctor James Murray discovered that treating bones with sulfuric acid made them soluble so that plants got their phosphorus more quickly. He called his product superphosphate. It didn't catch on, until 1843 when British farmer John Lawes started making it on a larger scale.

Tunneling shield

1818

Marc Brunel, Peter Barlow, James Greathead

Digging a tunnel under a river was impossible until French engineer Marc Brunel invented his shield in 1818. This supported the tunnel and stopped water from rushing in. As the tunnel grew, workers moved the shield forward and built a lining behind it. Brunel created the first river tunnel in 1843. Later, Peter Barlow developed a circular shield that allowed precast tunnel rings to be inserted. South African–born civil engineer James Greathead improved this in the 1860s.

Diving suit

1819

Augustus Siebe

The first practical diving suit was invented in 1819 by German engineer Augustus Siebe. Until then, underwater workers sat in a diving bell—an open-bottomed air chamber. Siebe's first suit was a jacket with an airtight helmet into which air was pumped from the surface. By 1830, he had created a totally enclosed suit.

Stethoscope

1819

René Laënnec

French doctor René Laënnec wanted to listen to his patients' lungs and hearts but was perhaps shy of putting his ear to their chests. Instead, he listened through a wooden tube and found that this *cylindre* transmitted body sounds that he could relate to various medical conditions. After he published his findings in 1819, other doctors improved on his instrument, eventually creating the device seen today.

Adding machine

1820

Thomas de Colmar

The first calculating machine that really worked was the arithmometer, patented by French insurance agent Thomas de Colmar in 1820. Although it could add, subtract, multiply, and divide, it was at first a failure, mostly because its inventor was not an engineer. By the 1850s, an improved version was beginning to be noticed, and by 1880 hundreds were in use—particularly in the insurance industry.

1816 In Rome, the opera *The Barber of Seville* by Italian composer Gioacchino Rossini has its first performance. Based on an earlier comedy by the French writer Pierre de Beaumarchais, it will become one of Rossini's most popular operas.

1818 The first science-fiction novel, *Frankenstein*, is published. It was written two years earlier by Mary Shelley while she was staying in Switzerland with the poet Byron. She was one of several guests he challenged to write a ghost story.

Electromagnetism

1820

Hans Christian Ørsted

Until Danish physicist Hans Christian Ørsted's crucial experiment of 1820, electricity and magnetism were seen as two separate subjects. The experiment was made possible by the battery, which Volta invented in 1800 (✱ *see* **page 116**). Ørsted put a compass needle near a wire then connected the wire to the terminals of a battery. The needle set itself at right angles to the current in the wire, showing that electricity could create magnetism. The two subjects were really one.

Quinine

1820

Pierre Pelletier, Joseph Caventou

Quinine is the active substance in a tree-bark extract that helps patients with malaria, a disease caused by a parasite in the blood. It was isolated in 1820 by French chemists Pierre Pelletier and Joseph Caventou and marked the start of a shift from the use of whole plant extracts toward chemically pure drugs for treating disease. The same pair of men also isolated several other well known natural chemicals, including chlorophyll.

Dry cleaning

1821

Thomas L. Jennings

A patent is a legal document that prevents other people from copying your invention. In 1821, Thomas L. Jennings became the first African American to be granted one. US Patent 3306X was registered for Jennings' "dry scouring" process, a precursor to today's modern dry cleaning. The physical copy of the patent was destroyed in a fire, so we don't know many details about his process, but we do know that it was hugely successful. It made him enough money to buy the freedom of his wife and children, who until then had been enslaved.

Non-Euclidean geometry

1823

János Bolyai, Nikolay Lobachevsky

School geometry includes Euclid's (✱ *see* **page 45**) statement that there can be only one line that passes through a given point and lies parallel to a given line. In 1823, Hungarian mathematician János Bolyai discovered that he could forget this idea and create a "non-Euclidean" geometry that made sense. Russian mathematician Nikolay Lobachevsky published the same discovery in 1829. Euclidean geometry describes the small spaces we are used to but may not be true for space as a whole. In the 1850s, German mathematician Bernhard Riemann extended non-Euclidean geometry, providing a basis for Einstein's view of gravity (✱ *see* **pages 178–179**).

Waterproof cloth

1823

Charles Macintosh

Charles Macintosh, working in rainy Glasgow, Scotland, found a way to make the first waterproof cloth. He discovered that rubber would dissolve in naphtha, a gasoline-like liquid produced in the making of coal gas. In 1823, he stuck two layers of fabric together with his rubber solution. Although at first there were problems with leaking seams and softening rubber, a "macintosh" soon became the only thing to wear in the rain.

ADDING MACHINE *Arithmometers were made by several different companies. This wood-cased brass machine dates from about 1870.*

1819 British administrator Sir Stamford Raffles founds a colonial settlement on the island of Singapore. Ideally positioned between the Indian Ocean and the South China Sea, the island will become a highly successful country.

1822 Ancient Egyptian hieroglyphs are deciphered thanks to the Rosetta Stone. Found by French troops in 1799, this has the same text in hieroglyphs and Greek, allowing French scholar Jean François Champollion to crack the code.

Maximum efficiency of a heat engine

1824

Sadi Carnot

A heat engine, such as a steam engine, turns heat, a form of energy, into mechanical work, another form of energy. The percentage of heat that gets turned into work is known as the engine's thermal efficiency. It is never anywhere near 100 percent. In 1824, French scientist Sadi Carnot discovered what limits the maximum power ouput of any given engine. It is the temperature difference between the hottest and coldest parts inside the engine: the larger the difference, the greater the power output.

Portland cement

1824

Joseph Aspdin

Portland cement is ordinary building cement. It has nothing to do with Portland, in the south of England; it was invented in the north of the country by a Yorkshire builder, Joseph Aspdin, in 1824. He burned a mixture of clay and limestone until it became so hot that it partly turned into glass. Aspdin thought his material was just as good as the fine stone quarried in Portland, hence the name.

Self-trimming candle wick

1824

J. J. Cambacères

To burn properly, a candle needs just the right length of wick. Before 1824, wicks had to be trimmed by hand, because the wax burned down but the wick didn't. French inventor Cambacères found that if the wick is braided instead of twisted, it flops over and sticks out through the flame, constantly burning away and trimming itself. All candles are now made this way.

Aluminum

1825

Hans Christian Ørsted

Although aluminum is the most common metal on Earth, nobody had seen any until Danish chemist Hans Christian Ørsted extracted some from aluminum chloride in 1825. It had already been named by Humphry Davy, who identified it in alum, used in dyeing. He called it alumium, then aluminum (now its name in North America), and finally, by its English name, aluminium, to match names like sodium. Whatever the name, it is one of the world's most useful metals.

Public steam railroad

1825

George Stephenson

George Stephenson was already building industrial locomotives when he became engineer of a proposed public tram system from Darlington to Stockton in northeast England. He thought that steam locomotives and iron rails would be better than the proposed horses and wooden rails. On September 27, 1825, a steam train ran from Darlington to Stockton. The world's first public steam railroad had opened. Both passengers and freight traveled in open cars—except the railroad's directors, who had a covered carriage. (✳ *See also* **Railroad Mania.**)

Amalgam filling

c.1826

August Taveau, Thomas Bell

Having teeth filled is no fun, but it used to be much worse. The first metal fillings had to be heated to boiling point before going into the tooth. In about 1826, August Taveau in France and Thomas Bell in Britain found that a mixture of mercury and silver formed a paste that could be inserted cold and would harden rapidly. They had invented the amalgam filling, which is still used today.

PUBLIC STEAM RAILROAD *Stephenson's* Locomotion No. 1, *seen here as a model, provided the power for the first public steam railroad.*

Water tank was carried in a waggon behind the locomotive

1824 The great German composer Ludwig van Beethoven, now totally deaf, composes his ninth symphony. Written for a large choir as well as full orchestra, its last movement contains a setting of Schiller's "Ode to Joy."

1825 The Bolshoi (Great) Theatre opens in Moscow, Russia. Taking over the dancers of its predecessor, the Petrovsky Theatre, it renames the company the Bolshoi Ballet. It will become one of the world's finest ballet companies.

RAILROAD MANIA

RAILROADS STARTED AS WOODEN TRACKS for horse-drawn traffic, but once Stephenson had proved what steam could do, steam railroads spread across Britain and the Americas with astonishing speed. Money, both public and private, poured into the new technology. By 1850, Britain had more than 6,250 miles (10,000 km) of track, while pioneers in the US had opened up the West with 9,000 miles (14,500 km) of railroads.

BRING YOUR OWN TRAIN
In Britain, the Surrey Iron Railway opened in 1803 and ran from Wandsworth on the Thames River to Merstham, south of London. It was the first to be open to everyone, but carriers had to provide their own wagons and horses.

Horses walked between the wooden tracks

A simple horse-drawn railroad speeded production at a quarry near Bath, England, in about 1730.

THE RAILROAD AGE BEGINS
At the opening of the Stockton & Darlington Railway, crowds fought to experience the new thrill of rail travel. A total of 600 people piled into the wagons, some even clinging to the outside.

GOING LIKE A ROCKET
The first all-steam railroad with its own rolling stock ran between Liverpool and Manchester in England. It opened on September 15, 1830, with a train hauled by Stephenson's *Rocket*, the clear winner of competitive trials held in 1829.

This 1949 painting by Terence Cuneo vividly captures the excitement surrounding the opening of the Stockton & Darlington Railway.

Interchangeable parts

1826

John Hall

Most products today are assembled from mass-produced parts. In the 18th century, nobody could make parts accurately enough to guarantee that they would fit together, but the US government needed guns with interchangeable parts so that weapons could be repaired quickly. In 1826, US gunmaker John Hall succeeded in making exactly what they wanted. He'd had to invent a new set of tools and techniques but, in doing so, had perfected an essential ingredient of mass production.

Reaping machine

1826

Patrick Bell, Cyrus McCormick

Without mechanical help, harvesting demands fields full of people. The first successful reaper was designed in 1826 by Scottish farmer Patrick Bell, who encouraged other farmers to copy it. A few years later, in the US, Cyrus McCormick invented a similar machine, which, like Bell's, had a revolving reel for drawing the corn into the cutter. McCormick's production models went on sale in 1840 and competed successfully with a factory-built version of the Bell reaper. McCormick sold his reapers by the thousand. His company continued until 1902, when it merged with four others to form the International Harvester Company.

Mammals from eggs

1827

Karl von Baer

Most people know that birds come from eggs, but it's not so obvious that mammals do, too. This fact was published in 1827 by Estonian naturalist Karl von Baer. A professor at Konigsburg University (now Kaliningrad in Russia), he found out more about how animals develop and created the science called comparative embryology.

1826 Japanese artist Katsushika Hokusai starts publishing a series of prints entitled *Thirty-six Views of Mount Fuji*. The series includes *The Breaking Wave off Kanagawa,* which will become the best-known Japanese print of its time.

1827 The first volume of US bird artist John Audubon's *Birds of America* is published by London engraver Robert Havell. The complete book contains 435 magnificent hand-colored illustrations and makes Audubon famous.

Greenhouse effect

1827

Joseph Fourier

The greenhouse effect is in the news as cars and power stations pump carbon dioxide into the atmosphere. Natural greenhouse effects would keep the Earth at a comfortable temperature, but the polluting gases produced by humans trap too much heat and make the Earth warmer. The existence of the effect, and its similarity to how a greenhouse works, were first suggested by the French mathematician Joseph Fourier in 1827. He didn't know how much people would worry about it 175 years later.

Match

1827

John Walker

As chemical knowledge increased, inventors began to apply it in the search for a better light. A few burned their fingers with creations like chemical-tipped wood dipped in sulfuric acid, then, in 1827, British chemist John Walker produced the first practical match. His "friction lights" lit up when rubbed on sandpaper, just like some matches today.

Match
Early matches lit as soon as they were warmed by friction so were supplied in a fireproof box in case they lit by accident. Modern matches are safer to carry.

Thin wooden spill burned easily

Head tipped with mixture containing phosphorus

Macadamized road

1827

John McAdam

Scottish engineer John McAdam realized that the best base for a road was dry soil. In 1827, he started building roads made from compacted soil with stones on top. Iron-tired cartwheels broke the stones into smaller pieces, which filled any gaps and made the surface waterproof. "Macadamized" roads were used everywhere until cars, whose pneumatic tires damaged them by sucking out the smallest stones, demanded a road surface made with tar or bitumen.

Multiple fire tube boiler

1827

Marc Séguin, George Stephenson

The first steam boilers were tanks on top of a fire. This was inefficient because little of the water was in contact with the fire. In 1827, French engineer Marc Séguin invented a boiler with tubes going through the water and hot gases from a fire going through the tubes. It heated water quickly and wasted less heat. George Stephenson used the same idea in *Rocket*, the first locomotive to run on an all-steam railroad.

Ohm's law

1827

Georg Ohm

Ohm's law is fundamental to electrical and electronic engineering. It says that electric current = voltage ÷ resistance. So when you connect a wire across a battery, if you double the length of the wire, and therefore the resistance, you will halve the current. George Ohm's scientific colleagues in Germany thought that the law was nonsense when he published it in 1827, but Ohm had the last laugh. In 1841, the Royal Society in London gave him a medal, and his name lives on as the unit of resistance.

Water turbine

1827

Claude Burdin, Benoît Fourneyron

French engineer Claude Burdin coined the word "turbine" from the Latin *turbo*, meaning "spinning top." One of his students at the St. Étienne Technical School, Benoît Fourneyron, built a working water turbine in 1827. Water fell on to a horizontal rotor and rushed through curved blades, making the rotor spin and producing as much power as six horses. He was soon building turbines that spun at 2,000 rpm (revolutions per minute) to produce 40 kW of power—ideal for generating electricity. In 1895, Fourneyron turbines were installed for this purpose at Niagara Falls on the Canada/US border.

Handles for pushing the machine

Clutch lever

Differential gear

1827

Onésiphore Pecqueur

A vehicle with both back wheels on one axle will have trouble getting around corners. This is because the wheel on the outside of the curve has to travel further, and therefore turn faster, than the wheel on the inside. This is impossible if both wheels are attached to the same shaft. Modern rear-wheel drive cars avoid this problem by having

1828 Noah Webster introduces American grammar and spelling when he publishes the *American Dictionary of the English Language*. It contains about 70,000 entries—almost half have not appeared in any earlier dictionary.

1829 Following a campaign by religious reformer Ram Mohan Roy, the rite in which a widow throws herself on her husband's funeral pyre is outlawed by the British authorities who control parts of India at this time.

each rear wheel on a separate axle, driven from the engine through an arrangement called a differential gear. This contains several gearwheels, which allow the two rear wheels to rotate at different speeds where necessary. It was invented by French engineer Onésiphore Pecquer in 1827, long before cars were thought of, for use on steam vehicles.

Braille

1829

Louis Braille

Louis Braille was blinded in an accident at the age of three. When he was 10, he went to Paris, where he was shown a way of writing messages with raised dots, designed for soldiers to use at night. Braille simplified and improved this system and, in 1829 and 1837, published his own six-dot code for blind people. It's difficult to learn but is still in use today.

Lawn mower

1830

Edwin Budding

Lawns were possible before lawn mowers, but only for people with gardeners or sheep to keep them trimmed. Edwin Budding's cylinder mower, patented in 1830, made tidy green squares available to far more people. Largely displaced by other machines for small lawns, Budding's mechanism lives on in tractor-pulled mowers for large areas of grass.

Electromagnetic induction

1831

Michael Faraday, Joseph Henry

When Hans Christian Ørsted discovered that electricity could produce magnetism (✳ *see* **page 123**), British scientist Michael Faraday guessed that magnetism might produce electricity. In 1831, he showed that it could. Plunging a magnet into a coil of wire produced a surge of current—the principle of the electric generator. Faraday also found that if two coils were wound on an iron ring, connecting or disconnecting one coil to or from a battery produced a current in the other—the principle of the transformer, which is used to change electric voltages. US scientist Joseph Henry discovered electromagnetic induction at about the same time, but Faraday published his findings first.

ELECTROMAGNETIC INDUCTION *Faraday's ring looks very much like some modern transformers.*

Cell nucleus

1831

Robert Brown

Most living cells keep their genes in a nucleus, a distinct blob in their center. This structure was first noticed and named by Scottish botanist Robert Brown in 1831, while he was investigating orchids. Although Brown didn't understand what the nucleus did, his discovery was part of a growing realization that plant cells, far from being empty, were full of life.

LAWN MOWER *Budding based his grass-cutting machine on the rotary cutter used for trimming the surface of woolen cloth in textile mills. Early Budding mowers were large machines for professional gardeners—this one was made by Ransomes of Ipswich, England—but the principle was later applied to domestic models.*

Gears turned the cutting cylinder

Cutting cylinder

Handle for a second person to help with the machine

Roller for adjusting the height of the cut

Main roller provided drive

1830 A group of British travelers, the Raleigh Travellers' Club, forms the Geographical Society of London. It supports explorations in Africa, the Arctic, and other areas and, in 1859, will become the Royal Geographical Society.

1831 Inspired by love for Irish actress Harriet Smithson, French composer Hector Berlioz writes his highly romantic *Symphonie Fantastique*. He fashions the huge orchestral work as a musical drama that ends with its hero's death.

MAGNETO *Pixii's machine was called a magneto because it used a permanent magnet to provide the changing magnetic field needed to generate current.*

Safety fuse

1831

William Bickford

Blasting out rock from mines and quarries with gunpowder is a good idea as long as nobody gets blown up. Until William Bickford's invention of the safety fuse in 1831, miners set off explosions with gunpowder laid on the ground or packed into reeds or goose quills—all highly dangerous. Bickford made his fuse from cloth wrapped around gunpowder. It burned at a predictable rate, allowing people to get away to safety before the big bang.

Steam bus

1831

Goldsworthy Gurney, Walter Hancock

Buses existed before 1831, but they were pulled by horses. The first mechanical buses appeared in Britain. Inspired by Stephenson's *Rocket* (✷ *see* **page 125**), English inventor Goldsworthy Gurney built several steam coaches that operated between Cheltenham and Gloucester. In London, Walter Hancock set up a steam omnibus service. Opposition from horse-coach owners soon forced Gurney off the road, but Hancock's service was able to survive for five years.

Magneto

1832

Hippolyte Pixii

Soon after Michael Faraday discovered that relative motion between a magnet and a wire produces electric current, Hippolyte Pixii, son of a Paris instrument maker, devised the first practical electric generator. His machine, built in 1832, rotated a magnet near a coil of wire, generating alternating current in the wire. Later, at the suggestion of physicist André Ampère, he added a switch that broke the circuit for half of each rotation, creating a pulsed direct current for experiment in electrolysis.

Electric motor

1832

William Sturgeon, Thomas Davenport

It wasn't easy to develop a useful motor from Hans Christian Ørsted's discovery that electricity could move a magnet (✷ *see* **page 123**). The vital component was the commutator, a switch that continually reverses the current to keep the motor rotating. Practical commutators were invented in 1832 by British engineer William Sturgeon and in 1834 by US blacksmith Thomas Davenport. Davenport used his motor to drive several machines, including a car.

Inductance

1832

Joseph Henry

In 1832, US scientist Joseph Henry discovered self-inductance, often called simply inductance. In this, the magnetism created by an electric current tends to maintain that current when conditions change. The effect is shown clearly when a wire is coiled up to create a stronger magnetic field. Joseph Henry discovered it when he disconnected an electromagnet and saw big sparks as the current carried on through the air instead of stopping.

1833 Oberlin College, the first college to admit both men and women, is established in Ohio. Two years later, it will be the first college to admit African Americans and, in 1841, will award academic degrees to three women.

1835 Fourteen years after his death, one of Napoleon's pet projects, the Arc de Triomphe, is completed at the top of the Champs Élysées in Paris. Built by Jean Chalgrin and Jean Raymond, it celebrates past French victories.

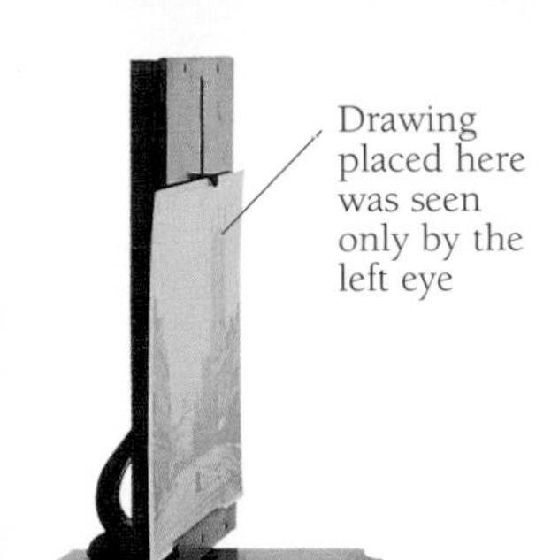

Stereoscope *Wheatstone's original device was cumbersome but useful for investigating stereoscopic vision. Brewster redesigned it without the mirrors.*

Stereoscope

1832

Charles Wheatstone

A stereoscope combines two slightly different pictures, one for each eye, into a three-dimensional image. The pictures are normally photographs, but British physicist Charles Wheatstone invented the stereoscope before photography existed. His invention was little used until David Brewster showed a simplified version at London's Great Exhibition in 1851. Queen Victoria was entranced, and stereoscopy soon became a popular craze.

Horse-drawn tram service

1832

John Stephenson, G. F. Train

The idea of using tracks for vehicles eventually spread from mines and railroads to the streets. Trams were at first drawn by horses. Probably the earliest tram builder was the Irish-US inventor John Stephenson. His trams started running on the New York and Harlem Railroad in 1832, and his company later built trams for services all over the world. The US entrepreneur G. F. Train also brought the tram to many cities. In 1860, he installed a tramway in Birkenhead, near Liverpool—the first in Britain.

Telegraph *The five-needle telegraph was easy to use but needed a six-wire connection. Pairs of needles swung left or right to point to the letters on the face.*

Telegraph

1837

William Cooke, Charles Wheatstone

Hans Christian Ørsted's discovery that a compass needle responds to electric current suggested a way of making an effective electric telegraph. In 1837, ex-soldier William Cooke and physicist Charles Wheatstone patented the first telegraph to send useful messages. Its five needles, operated by six wires, could point to 20 letters of the alphabet. By 1839, it was installed on the Great Western Railway in England and was sending the first public telegrams.

Reflex

1837

Marshall Hall

When someone pulls their finger away from a hot iron, they're using a reflex, a response that bypasses the brain for maximum speed. British physiologist Marshall Hall, seeing a headless newt respond to a pinprick, was the first to realize that nerves from the spinal cord can act independently to receive sensations and make suitable responses. British colleagues ridiculed Hall's ideas, but European scientists discovered that he was right.

Morse code

1837

Samuel Morse, Alfred Vail

See **pages 130–131** for the story of how Morse and Vail invented a new way to communicate.

1836 During its fight for independence from Mexico, the state of Texas is hit hard when the Mexicans, under Santa Anna, wipe out everyone in the fort called the Alamo. Santa Anna is later defeated by Texans shouting "Remember the Alamo!"

1837 In the United Kingdom, King William IV dies without an heir. On Tuesday, June 20, his niece Victoria, aged only 18, becomes queen. She will become one of the most important figures in British history.

WIRING THE WORLD

Samuel Morse and Alfred Vail invent a new way to communicate

MORSE'S FIRST TELEGRAPH
The first telegraph Morse built was more elaborate than the final version reengineered by Vail. Its operator did not tap out messages directly but assembled shaped pieces of metal in a holder, which moved through a switch mechanism to turn the current on and off.

This unlikely contraption was Morse's first receiver.

The Reverend Jedidiah Morse did not want his son to be an artist, but he felt it was better than having him waste time with electricity. So, after being tutored in England, Samuel Morse became a painter, one of the best in the US.

In 1832, on a ship home from Europe, Samuel heard about the newly invented electromagnet, and his interest in electricity was rekindled. With his artist's imagination, he could see it sending messages around the world.

By 1835, Morse had built an electric telegraph, using odds and ends that included one of his wooden frames for stretching artists' canvas. But how was he to convey thousands of different words along its single wire?

His first idea was to make a numbered list of words, then send the numbers, switching the current once for one,

Morse's telegraph needed only one wire, which made it easy to construct. To make the single wire work, Morse and Vail invented a code based on patterns of pulses—an idea now used for all kinds of telecommunications.

twice for two, and so on. It was terribly slow, even with an automatic switch and a better code that used short and long bursts of current—"dots" and "dashes." His homemade telegraph proved to be unreliable, too.

That might have been the end of it, but in 1837, at an unsuccessful demonstration of the telegraph in New York, Morse met the young engineer Alfred Vail. Vail took one look at Morse's amateurish efforts and offered to redesign the whole thing. He strengthened the electromagnet and replaced Morse's complicated switch with a simple, hand-operated key. He threw out Morse's word list and devised a dot-and-dash code for each letter of the alphabet. The telegraph was beginning to take shape.

In 1843, after several successful demonstrations and some political wrangling, the US government gave Morse $30,000 to build a telegraph line between Baltimore and Washington, DC. There were quite a few technical problems, because nobody had ever laid 40 miles (65 km) of wire before. But by May 24, 1844, everything was ready..

With Vail in Baltimore tending a stack of batteries and Morse in Washington looking after the politicians, the new line delivered its first message: "WHAT HATH GOD WROUGHT." Within a year, it was open to the public. Within another 30 years, telegraphs covered the globe. Thanks to Vail the engineer, the vision of Morse the artist had become a reality.

Alfred Vail
Vail met Morse soon after graduating from college. He agreed to help Morse and pay for getting patents as long as he could share in any profits. He got his father to help Morse as well.

A Morse key for sending messages

This receiver embossed dots and dashes on paper tape.

The final system
By about 1870, many refinements had been made to the telegraph. Operators could decode a message just by listening to the clicking of a sounder, leaving them free to write it down. Punched tape allowed messages to be stored, and a version of Morse code had been developed for use with underwater cables.

Not very private
A picture from a songsheet of 1860 illustrates one problem with the telegraph: every message had to be read by the operator. This could cause embarrassment, as here, with messages of an intimate nature.

Ship's propeller

1839

John Ericsson, Francis Smith

Early steamships had paddle wheels, but these did not work well in high seas. Engineers John Ericsson of Sweden and Francis Smith (later Sir Francis) of Britain both invented underwater propellers. Smith's looked like a screw, while Ericsson's was more like a fan. The British Navy wasn't interested in either, but a small ship equipped with Ericsson's propeller was shown to the US Navy. In 1839, both propellers were attached to larger ships, and trials confirmed the effectiveness of this new form of propulsion.

SHIP'S PROPELLER *This is a model of* SS Francis Smith, *which was fitted with Smith's propeller. Modern ships have their propeller further back.*

Photography

c.1839

Louis Daguerre, William Fox Talbot

In 1826, French inventor Nicéphore Niepce coated a sheet of metal with tar, put it in a box with a lens, and pointed it out of the window. Eight hours later, he had a permanent photograph. By 1839, his colleague Louis Daguerre was taking pictures in 20 minutes. A year later, William Fox Talbot announced a rival system. It allowed shorter exposures and could produce multiple prints. (✳ *See also* **Photo Pioneers.**)

Cell as the basic unit of living things

1839

Matthias Schleiden, Theodor Schwann

German lawyer Matthias Schleiden turned his hobby of botany into a full-time job and studied plants under the microscope. In 1838, he concluded that all plants are made of tiny building blocks, or cells, and they grow as the cells divide. A year later, his friend Theodor Schwann found that the same applied to animals, establishing one of the basics of biology.

Vulcanized rubber

1839

Charles Goodyear

Raw rubber gets weak and sticky when warm. In the US, rubber worker Nathaniel Hayward discovered that sulfur reduced the stickiness. Businessman Charles Goodyear, who had himself been trying to improve rubber, bought Hayward's invention. In 1839, after a series of experiments, he discovered a chemical reaction with sulfur that made the rubber harder and stronger. This way of hardening rubber is called vulcanization, and it is essential today for car tires and many other rubber items.

VULCANIZED RUBBER *By 1923, when this advertisement appeared, cars had become more common and rubber tires were big business.*

1838 US lion tamer Isaac van Amburgh comes to England and amazes Queen Victoria by putting his head in a lion's mouth. She asks artist Edwin Landseer to paint the American's portrait, complete with lions.

1839 The Grand Liverpool Steeplechase, the horse race now called the Grand National, is run for the first time at Aintree, Liverpool, in England. The winner is Lottery, a nine-year-old owned by John Elmore and ridden by Jem Mason.

PHOTO PIONEERS

MANY EARLY 19TH-CENTURY artists and scientists wanted to capture the lifelike images they saw in the camera obscura (✷ *see* **page 81**), a common drawing aid at that time. Silver salts darkened on exposure to light, but they were not really sensitive enough. Worse still, they kept what sensitivity they had after the picture was taken, so the image was soon destroyed. Daguerre and Fox Talbot both solved these problems but in completely different ways.

Plate holder

Early daguerreotype camera

Daguerreotype images

DAGUERREOTYPES
Daguerre's pictures were taken with silver iodide, formed by iodine acting on a silvered copper plate. Sitters had to be clamped in place for the extremely long exposure. After treatment with mercury vapor and fixing with salt, the delicate, silvery image was framed under glass to protect it.

Aperture rings

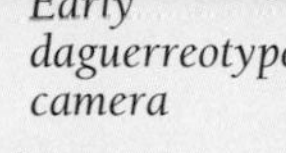

Lens and attachments

A daguerreotype camera of the 1840s

CALOTYPES
When daguerreotypes appeared, Fox Talbot hastened to perfect his calotype process. It used paper soaked in silver salts. He discovered that before these darkened visibly they formed a hidden image, which a developing solution could reveal, allowing shorter exposures. After fixing with a sodium salt, he used his paper negatives to make positive prints.

Calotype made by Fox Talbot at his home, Lacock Abbey, England, in about 1843

Fuel cell

1839

William Grove

Unlike ordinary electric batteries, fuel cells never run down—as long as they've got something to burn. A Welsh judge, William Grove, made the first one in 1839. Knowing that electricity splits water into hydrogen and oxygen, he simply reversed the process. His cell burned hydrogen in oxygen to produce water and electricity. Today, fuel cells are used in space and may soon appear in electric cars.

Polystyrene

1839

Eduard Simon

The clear plastic of CD cases is polystyrene. It is also made into a lightweight packaging material. It consists of molecules of a carbon-based chemical, styrene, linked to form chains. It was first made in 1839 by German chemist Eduard Simon but was not used because impurities made it brittle. In 1937, US chemist Robert Dreisbach made purer styrene, and within a year polystyrene was on the market.

Babbitt metal

1839

Isaac Babbitt

Rotating machinery needs bearings—holes lined with metal that can stand up to the constant rubbing of a shaft. One of the best materials for lining plain bearings is babbitt metal. It is an alloy of two soft metals, tin and lead, and two harder ones, antimony and copper. It takes oil well, will not seize up if it runs dry, and lasts a long time. It was invented by US goldsmith Isaac Babbitt in 1839.

Electroplating

c.1840

George Elkington, Auguste de La Rive

Electroplating uses electricity to coat surfaces with a layer of metal. It can make brass look like gold. The process was invented independently in about 1840 by British industrialist George Elkington and Swiss physicist Auguste de La Rive. It was Elkington who made it a success. He invented a plating bath then bought up all the rival processes so that people had to use his system.

1840 Britain gains control of New Zealand as 45 Maori chiefs sign the Treaty of Waitangi. The treaty aims to give the Maori British citizenship and protect their land, but its terms are not clear and will later lead to conflict.

1840 Canadian Samuel Cunard starts the first regular Atlantic steamship service when RMS *Britannia* sails from Liverpool to Boston. Cunard will continue to lead the way across the Atlantic with larger ships, such as *Queen Elizabeth*.

Ozone

1840

Christian Schönbein

Ozone in the stratosphere protects us from radiation, but ozone from a photocopier can be dangerous. It's a highly reactive form of oxygen, with three atoms per molecule instead of two. Ozone can be made by passing air through an electrical discharge—as in a photocopier. Discovered and named in 1840 by German chemist Christian Schönbein, many uses have since been found for it, from purifying water to bleaching food.

Postage stamp

1840

Rowland Hill

Rowland Hill believed in democracy. When he discovered that post office procedures made letters too expensive for ordinary people, he pointed out the folly of charges that were based on distance and collected on delivery. A fixed charge, he said, prepaid with an adhesive stamp, would slash costs by 75 percent. People listened in the end, and in 1840 Britain introduced the penny post. With it came the first postage stamp, the famous penny black.

Steam hammer

1840

James Nasmyth

In 1839, British engineer Isambard Kingdom Brunel started work on his ship *Great Britain.* He soon discovered that hammering out the giant shafts for its paddle wheels was beyond human ability. Scottish engineer James Nasmyth came up with the idea of a steam hammer and designed one that would hit harder than a whole gang of people. He made the first one in 1840 and patented it in 1842. By then, though, Brunel had changed his mind about his ship, deciding to use the more modern propellers instead of paddle wheels.

Dinosaurs

1841

Richard Owen

People had been finding fossilized dinosaur bones all over the place, but they didn't know what they were. Then British surgeon Richard Owen recognized that they belonged to an extinct group of reptiles unlike any now living. He named them "Dinosauria," meaning "terrible lizards," in 1841. Owen later became famous for opposing Darwin's theory of evolution and for getting the details of the earliest fossil bird completely wrong.

STEAM HAMMER *A gang of workers feeds a red-hot piece of iron through a hammer which slowly pounds it into shape.*

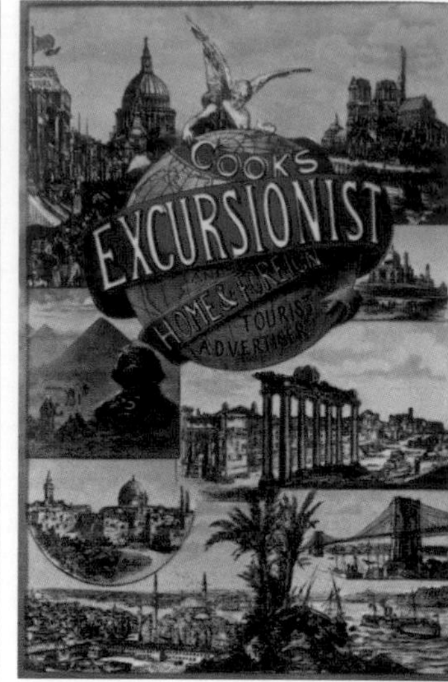

PACKAGE TOUR *By the 1870s, Cook's brochure offered package tours to wonders of the world both ancient and modern.*

Package tour

1841

Thomas Cook

A British missionary, Thomas Cook, organized the first vacation tour in 1841. It was only a train trip from Leicester to Loughborough, but it proved there was a demand. In 1855, Cook organized trips to France and then tours of Europe. His firm is now famous worldwide.

Doppler effect

1842

Christian Doppler

The sound of a speeding car falls to a lower pitch as the car passes. Austrian physicist Doppler explained this in 1842. As a sound source approaches, the waves reaching our ears are bunched up, but as it recedes they stretch out. This happens with light, too, so astronomers can tell how fast stars are approaching or receding. With radar, it enables police to check the speed of cars.

1840 Snowshoe racing becomes an organized sport in Canada with the formation of the Montreal Snowshoe Club. Racers strap broad, flat frames to their feet to stop them from sinking and run races of up to 1 mile (1.6 km).

1841 George Catlin publishes *Letters and Notes on the Manners, Customs, and Condition of the North American Indians.* He had painted over 500 works while traveling the Great Plains and visiting American Indian tribes.

CHRISTMAS CARD *John Horsley's card combined religion, good cheer, and rustic decoration.*

Conservation of energy

1842

Julius von Mayer

As early as 1806, a British doctor, Thomas Young, was using the word "energy" in its modern sense: the capacity to do work. In 1842, another doctor, Julius von Mayer of Germany, stated that energy cannot be created or destroyed. Mayer did not have much supporting evidence, and at the time, few people understood what he was saying, but this principle of conservation of energy has since become central to science. The principle was discovered independently by at least three others with more influence: William Grove in 1846, and James Joule and Hermann von Helmholtz in 1847.

Christmas card

1843

John Horsley

The first Christmas card was designed by British painter John Horsley for Henry Cole, later a founder of the Victoria & Albert Museum in London. Showing people enjoying a Christmas party, it went on sale in London in 1843.

Computer program

1843

Ada Lovelace

In the early 1800s, British inventor Charles Babbage designed his "analytical engine"—what we would now call a mechanical computer. He was assisted by Ada Lovelace, who was the first to realize that if such a machine existed, it would be able to do more than just calculations. Although the machine was never completed, Lovelace wrote an algorithm for it, the world's first computer program.

River tunnel

1843

Marc Brunel, Isambard Brunel

The first underwater tunnel was dug under the Thames River in London, from Rotherhithe to Wapping. It was started in 1825 but didn't open until 1843. Even using Marc Brunel's tunneling shield (✱ *see* **page 122**), water poured in several times during construction, once injuring Brunel's son Isambard so seriously that work stopped for several years. London Underground trains now rattle through the tunnel every day.

Sunspot cycle

1843

Samuel Schwabe

Amateurs can contribute a lot to astronomy by making regular observations. In Germany, Samuel Schwabe kept watch on the sun for 17 years, hoping to find a planet closer to the sun than Mercury. Instead, he found that the spottiness of the sun increased and decreased in an 11-year cycle. He announced the fact in 1843. It's of great importance on Earth, because sunspots can ruin radio communication.

1842 China surrenders the island of Hong Kong to Great Britain as part of the Treaty of Nanking, which ends the First Opium War. Another island will be added in 1860, and in 1898 more territory will be leased for 99 years.

1843 A new dance sensation hits Paris in the shape of the polka, a step-and-hop dance from Bohemia with a lively 2–4 rhythm. In no time at all, people in the US, Latin America, and Scandinavia will be polka-crazy, too.

Type-rotating printing press

1845

Richard Hoe

The first printing press produced a couple of sheets a minute. Modern presses print 10 whole newspapers every second, mainly because they go around and around instead of up and down. The first totally rotary press was built by US engineer Richard Hoe in 1845. It could print two sheets a second but had one snag: if all the pieces of type on its revolving cylinder were not locked in tightly, they shot out when the press started.

Anaesthetic

1846

William Morton

Anaesthetics were first used by two US dentists, Horace Wells and William Morton. Wells tried using laughing gas (✻ *see* **page 115**), unsuccessfully, in 1845 and had also tried ether as a local anaesthetic. Morton thought that he would try to get his patients to inhale ether, and he used it in a successful demonstration of anaesthetic surgery in 1846. A year later, Scottish surgeon James Simpson started using chloroform to help women through the pain of childbirth.

Lock-stitch sewing machine

1846

Walter Hunt, Elias Howe, Isaac Singer

Inventors struggled for years to mechanize sewing. The solution was to use two threads. An eye-pointed needle pushed one thread through the cloth from above while a shuttle whizzing to and fro below looped another thread through it. Walter Hunt invented this in the US in about 1843, and Elias Howe patented the same idea in 1846, but we really owe the sewing machine to US inventor Isaac Singer. He added his own ideas to Howe's and turned a raw invention into a mass-market product.

Neptune

1846

Urbain Le Verrier, Johann Galle

The discovery of the planet Neptune proved the power of physics. Astronomers knew that Uranus had an irregular orbit, and the only explanation was that it must be attracted by another planet. French astronomer Urbain Le Verrier calculated where this planet must be. When German astronomer Johann Galle looked there on September 23, 1846, he found the planet within an hour. A British mathematician, John Adams, had already done the same calculation in 1844, but British astronomers did not take this seriously.

LOCK-STITCH SEWING MACHINE
This Singer sewing machine of the 1930s shows a new addition—an electric motor. Before this, users who wanted both hands free had to power a treadle machine with their feet. The covers of this machine have been removed to show the mechanism.

1846 Founded on the bequest of English scientist James Smithson, Congress establishes the Smithsonian Institution for "the increase and diffusion of knowledge." In the 21st century, it will be the world's largest museum complex.

1847 Charlotte Brontë, one of three literary sisters living in Yorkshire, writes *Jane Eyre*. This powerful novel, with its self-willed heroine and emphasis on social psychology, will become one of the most famous in English literature.

Nitroglycerine

1846

Ascanio Sobrero

Until 1846, the only widely used explosive was gunpowder. Then Italian chemist Ascanio Sobrero discovered nitroglycerine, the first "high explosive." Much more powerful than gunpowder, it is also extremely dangerous: just dropping a container of the chemical on the floor can cause a devastating explosion. Despite this problem, nitroglycerine was used in mining even before a way was found to make it safe.

ALBUMEN PRINT *Lewis Carroll, the author of Alice, made this albumen print of two of his aunts in about 1858.*

Albumen print

c.1850

Louis Blanquart-Évrard

Those very old, brown family photos that you may have seen could have been printed on albumen paper. It was a breakthrough in its time. Before French photographer Louis Blanquart-Évrard invented it in about 1850, prints were made by Fox Talbot's original process (✳ *see* **page 132**). The new paper, with its glossy coating of egg white, gave much richer, sharper results.

ELECTRICAL NATURE OF NERVE IMPULSES *Emil Du Bois-Reymond invented this "frog pistol." He put a frog's leg inside the tube and formed a contact with the nerve ends, which made the leg muscles contract.*

Keys used to make a contact with the nerve ends in the frog's leg

Electrical nature of nerve impulses

1849

Emil Du Bois-Reymond

German physiologist Emil Du Bois-Reymond knew there was something electrical about animals when a fish gave him an electric shock. In 1849, he discovered that when nerves were stimulated, electrical waves traveled along them. Du Bois-Reymond realized that far from being channels for "animal spirits," as some people had thought, nerves were more like telegraph wires delivering messages around the body.

Laws of thermodynamics

1849

William Thomson, Rudolf Clausius

The first law of thermodynamics is just conservation of energy (✳ *see* **page 135**). The second is heat energy flows only from hot to cold. The consequences are surprising. For example, a glass of cold water contains more heat than a teaspoonful of boiling water (even though the boiling water has a higher temperature) because there is more of it. But the second law prevents this heat from doing any work. Several scientists worked on this idea from 1824 onward. William Thomson coined the term "thermodynamics" in 1849, and Rudolf Clausius published the laws in 1850. Since then, two more have been added.

Mechanical equivalent of heat

1849

James Joule

Steam engines showed that heat could turn into work. Could the opposite be true? When British physicist James Joule announced in 1847 that he had warmed water simply by stirring it, nobody believed him. After a further two years' work, Joule submitted a paper to the Royal Society called *On the Mechanical Equivalent of Heat*, which was accepted. It stated exactly how much heat was produced by a given amount of work. The unit of energy now bears his name.

Speed of nerve impulses

1850

Hermann von Helmholtz

By 1849, scientists knew that nerve impulses were electrical, making it possible to measure their speed. The German scientist Hermann von Helmholtz quickly invented the necessary equipment. In 1850, his new "myograph" showed that nerves were quicker than most other things biological. He saw impulses zipping along at about 60 mph (100 km/h).

1848 Revolution sweeps Europe as French, Germans, Italians, Poles, Czechs, Slovaks, Hungarians, Danes, and Transylvanians demand greater political rights, better government, and, where necessary, national independence.

1849 The British writer Charles Dickens starts serial publication of what he considers his best novel, *David Copperfield*. The story of a young man betrayed by his stepfather earns Dickens the amazing sum of £7,000 ($34,000).

SCIENCE TAKES CONTROL

THE LATE 19TH CENTURY saw the rise of totally new industries that could not have existed without science. Plastics, synthetic fabrics, electric light, telephones, sound recording, popular photography, cars, and radio were just a few of the inventions that would eventually transform people's lives.

Mechanism of the inner ear

1851

Alfonso Corti

Buried deep inside the ear is the organ of Corti, a delicate mechanism that turns sound into nerve impulses. It was first described in 1851 by Italian anatomist Alfonso Corti. It contains thousands of tiny hairs, which brush against a membrane suspended in fluid. When sound waves shake the fluid, the membrane ripples against the hairs, making nerve cells attached to them send signals to the brain.

Prefabricated building

1851

Joseph Paxton

In 1851, British gardener Joseph Paxton created the first large building made from prefabricated components. The Crystal Palace was built to house the Great Exhibition in London. The spectacular glass and iron structure was 1,848 ft (563 m) long, 108 ft (33 m) high, and 408 ft (124 m) at its widest point. It went up in just six months. Paxton's secret was the repeated use of basic parts that slotted together like a construction kit.

Foucault's pendulum

1851

Jean Foucault

Although early 19th-century scientists knew that the Earth must rotate on its axis, they had no direct proof. Then, in 1851, French physicist Jean Foucault hung a heavy ball on a 220 ft (67 m) wire inside a tall building in Paris, forming a large pendulum. As it swung back and forth, it appeared to be turning gradually, but it was actually Earth turning beneath it. Foucault's pendulum is a popular science exhibit today.

WET-PLATE PHOTOGRAPHY *Roving photographers had to carry all these bottles of chemicals—and a darkroom.*

REFRIGERATOR *The US General Electric "monitor top" refrigerator of 1934 had its compressor mounted on top.*

Refrigerator

1851

John Gorrie, Ferdinand Carré

Gases get hot when they are compressed and cool down when they expand. So one way to refrigerate is to compress a gas, let it cool, then lower its pressure to cool it still more. The cold gas can then cool other objects. US doctor John Gorrie found that he could produce cold air to cool feverish patients in this way and patented a refrigerator based on this principle in 1851. Eight years later, French inventor Ferdinand Carré developed a refrigerator more like those we use today. These use a working fluid that changes from liquid to gas when it expands. This makes it absorb even more heat from inside the fridge.

Wet-plate photography

1851

Frederick Archer

Although calotypes could be reprinted, their paper negatives were grainy (✳ *see* **page 133**). In 1851, British sculptor Frederick Archer made the first transparent negatives by coating glass with a light-sensitive cellulose solution. The new plates produced clearer pictures than their predecessors and needed shorter exposures, but they had to be exposed while wet and developed immediately. The results were so good that photographers did not mind, and "wet plates" quickly replaced the earlier processes.

Airship

1852

Henri Giffard

French engineer Henri Giffard's airship was the first successful powered flying machine. As in all airships, lift came from a light gas, in this case hydrogen, so its three-horsepower steam engine had only to push it along. Choosing a dead calm day, Giffard piloted the 144 ft (44 m) cigar-shaped craft over Paris at a speed of 6 mph (10 km/h) for 20 miles (30 km). It would be years before airships could cope with windy conditions.

1851 At La Fenice Theatre in Venice, Italian composer Guiseppe Verdi sees the first performance of *Rigoletto*, his 17th opera. It is a big step forward in the development of opera, with music and storytelling cleverly intertwined.

1852 One of Europe's most common birds, the house sparrow, is introduced into the US. Arriving in Brooklyn, New York, and fed partly by grain spilled by horses, the newcomer will cover the continent within a century.

Gyroscope

1852

Jean Foucault

A wheel that is spinning resists changes in the direction of its axis. Jean Foucault used this fact to confirm his earlier observation of the Earth rotating beneath a swinging pendulum (✳ *see* **page 139**). In 1852, he mounted a wheel so that its axis was free to point in any direction. He set it spinning and watched as it kept its position while the Earth turned beneath it. He called this arrangement a gyroscope, meaning "something that makes rotation visible."

Bloomers

c.1853

Amelia Bloomer

Pants for women were thought outrageous in the 19th century, which may have been why US reformer Amelia Bloomer liked them. She advocated long, baggy pants gathered at the ankle as part of a new costume that she hoped would liberate women. When she appeared in her pants in about 1853, there was more laughter than liberation. But within 35 years, a new invention made "bloomers" seem like a good idea—they were ideal for women who wanted to ride a bike.

Glider

1853

George Cayley, Otto Lillienthal

Attempts to soar like a bird came to nothing until British aristocrat George Cayley abandoned flapping wings. He figured out what was needed to lift, stabilize, and control a fixed-wing machine. Realizing that no existing engine could power an airplane, he stuck to gliders. In 1853, his coachman flew the first manned glider flight. Later, a young German named Otto Lilienthal built a series of small gliders and succeeded in making regular controlled flights in them. Cayley's and Lilienthal's work established the basics of aircraft design.

HYPODERMIC SYRINGE *This fearsome syringe of the Pravaz type was made in France.*

BLOOMERS *The new fashion, also known as Turkish trousers, was worn as early as 1849 by the actor Fanny Kemble and others, but it was Amelia Bloomer who gave it publicity, hence the name.*

Hypodermic syringe

1853

Charles Pravaz, Alexander Wood

The two parts of the hypodermic syringe, the needle and the plunger, were invented in 1853 by two different people in two different countries. In France, surgeon Charles Pravaz invented a gadget for injecting fluid into veins through a tube with a blade inside it. In Scotland, physician Alexander Wood invented the hollow needle and adapted Pravaz's device to go with it, forming the first hypodermic syringe.

Safety elevator

1853

Elisha Otis

Elisha Otis was working as a master mechanic in a US bed factory when he invented something to diminish a recurring nightmare. Knowing that people were scared of elevators, he invented a safety hoist with arms that shot out and grabbed the sides of the elevator shaft if the supporting cable broke. He sold the first safety hoist, for goods only, in 1853. Later, in New York City, he demonstrated its effectiveness by having the cable cut while he was in it. He installed his first passenger safety elevator in 1857 in a New York store. After his death, his sons, Charles and Norton, continued the business, and the name Otis is on elevators and escalators everywhere today.

Boolean algebra

1854

George Boole

Today's computers owe a lot to someone whose only math teaching came from a shoe repairer—his father. George Boole had to learn the rest himself, but by the age of 24, he was submitting work to serious mathematical journals. He thought that logic should be part of math, and in 1854 he published *An Investigation into the Laws of Thought*. It described what is now called Boolean algebra. This allows complicated logical statements to be simplified and underlies the design of much digital hardware and software.

Can opener

1855

Robert Yeates

A hammer and chisel for getting into cans were essential kitchen tools until British inventor Robert Yeates invented his can opener in 1855. It wasn't very convenient—just a sharp blade that had to be stuck into the can top and worked around the rim. But the design became popular in the US when a canned-beef company gave it a cast-iron bull's head and issued it free of charge with their cans.

Printing telegraph

1855

David Hughes

The first electric telegraphs allowed messages to be sent along a wire (✳ *see* **page 129**). The message was given to a clerk, who tapped it out in Morse code. At the other end, another clerk translated the

1854 Florence Nightingale arrives at a British Army hospital in Turkey, where more soldiers are dying from disease than from bullets in the war they are fighting. Her nursing services will make her famous worldwide.

1855 While exploring the Zambesi River in Africa, Scottish missionary David Livingstone discovers an enormous waterfall 355 ft (108 m) high and nearly 1 mile (1.6 km) wide. He loyally names it after Queen Victoria.

dots and dashes into words. Many inventors tried to bypass this with "printing telegraphs" that sent written messages directly. The first successful system was invented in 1855 by David Hughes, who taught music in the US. Its keyboard, which looked a little like a piano, sent out signals that were automatically translated and printed at the receiving end.

Condensed milk

c.1856

Gail Borden

In 1851, US inventor Gail Borden was distressed to see children becoming ill from infected milk. By 1856, he had patented a process of boiling milk under vacuum, which sterilized it without spoiling its flavor. He called it condensed milk because, knowing nothing about bacteria, he thought that it was the removal of water that made it safer to drink.

Each key sent out a different letter of the alphabet

The message was recorded on paper tape

Chain and pulley drove the rotating mechanism

Heavy weight attached to the pulley descended to power the machine

PRINTING TELEGRAPH
Hughes' "piano" keyboard would have seemed quite natural in an age without typewriters. Each key sent a differently timed pulse to a printer at the other end of the line. Good operators could send 30 words a minute.

Aniline dye

1856

William Perkin

Until 1856, natural plant extracts dominated the dye industry. This changed when a young British chemistry student, William Perkin, tried to make the drug quinine and produced an intense violet dye instead. Mauve was soon in great demand by fashionable Victorians. Many more dyes of the same type, known as aniline dyes, were to come out of different labs as Perkin's little error turned into an industry.

Transatlantic telegraph

1858

Cyrus Field, Charles Bright, William Thomson

By the 1850s, there were several short underwater telegraph lines. US financier Cyrus Field wanted to go further and link the US and Britain with a cable across the Atlantic. He recruited several brilliant engineers and scientists, including Charles Bright and William Thomson. After heroic efforts, a cable was laid in 1858 to great rejoicing on both sides. There were problems, including poor insulation, which made the cable fail within weeks, but it proved that the idea worked. A permanent link between the two countries was finally established in 1866.

1858 In Australia, voting slips and ballot boxes appear as the first secret ballots are held in Victoria and South Australia. The system will be adopted in Britain in 1872 and in the US after the 1884 presidential elections.

1858 The third and final Seminole war ends. Led by chief Oceola, the Seminole tribe has fought the US government for years to keep their native lands in Florida. Ultimately, the tribe will be forced to relocate in the West.

Evolution by natural selection

1859

Charles Darwin

In 1859, Charles Darwin, the son of a doctor, published a book that shook the world. *On the Origin of Species* presented evidence that animals and plants were not created as we see them today but evolved from earlier forms and are still evolving. Darwin's theory was based on what he called natural selection. Every member of a species is slightly different. Darwin said that the members with differences that make them more able to compete are more likely to survive and pass on these useful differences to their offspring. (✷ *See also* **Arguing About Apes.**)

Gas engine

1859

Étienne Lenoir

Burning an engine's fuel inside it rather than in a boiler promised a smaller, more efficient machine. But the first successful engine of this type was not particularly small and certainly not very efficient. Invented by French engineer Étienne Lenoir in 1859, it was basically a steam engine converted to run on gas. Its single piston sucked a mixture of gas and air into a cylinder. A spark then lit the mixture to push the piston out again. Although Lenoir's engines did not produce much power, he sold hundreds of them in France and Britain.

Lead–acid battery

1859

Gaston Planté

Even the latest cars rely on a very old type of battery. French physicist Gaston Planté knew that electrodes of lead and lead oxide immersed in sulfuric acid formed a rechargeable cell. Realizing that this would deliver more current than existing cells, he developed it into a practical battery in 1859. Commercial versions were ready just in time for the first cars.

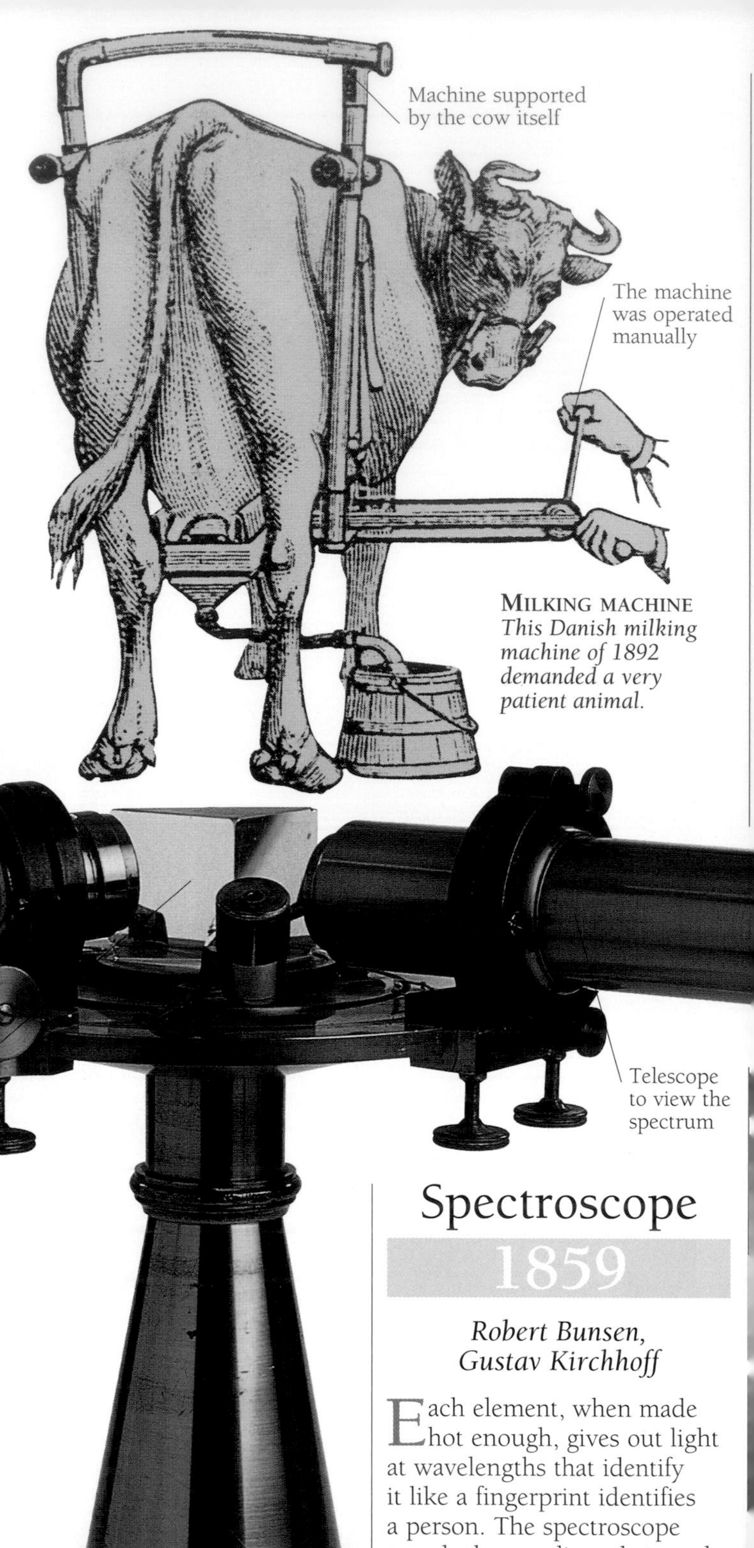

MILKING MACHINE *This Danish milking machine of 1892 demanded a very patient animal.*

SPECTROSCOPE *This 19th-century instrument, based on Bunsen's and Kirchoff's design, used a prism to split light into its colors.*

Oil well

1859

Edwin Drake, George Bissell

People originally used petroleum only for lighting and medicinal purposes. They collected it as it oozed out of a soft rock called shale. One of the best places for this was Titusville, Pennsylvania, There in 1859, Edwin Drake persuaded landowner George Bissell to let him try drilling for oil instead of just waiting for it to emerge. Only 69 ft (21 m) down, he struck lucky, creating the world's first oil well and the industry that would make the US rich.

Spectroscope

1859

Robert Bunsen, Gustav Kirchhoff

Each element, when made hot enough, gives out light at wavelengths that identify it like a fingerprint identifies a person. The spectroscope reveals these as lines that can be photographed and measured. It was invented in 1859 by German chemist Robert

1859 A clock with a huge bell known as Big Ben is installed in St. Stephen's tower at London's Houses of Parliament. The sound of Big Ben will become known all around the world when the BBC begins to broadcast it 65 years later.

1859 Rights such as self-expression, privacy, and the rights of minorities, which future generations will take for granted, are defended by British philosopher John Stuart Mill in his essay *On Liberty*. It will influence many people.

Bunsen and physicist Gustav Kirchhoff. The two scientists used their new instrument to compare lines from the sun with those from elements on Earth, giving the first analysis of the sun's atmosphere.

Milking machine

1860

L. O. Colvin

The first successful milking machine was patented by US engineer L. O. Colvin in 1860. Its big disadvantage was that it applied a constant vacuum to suck out the milk, which could damage the cow's udder. It was 1889 before Scottish engineer Alexander Shields introduced the modern type of machine, which sucks intermittently like a calf.

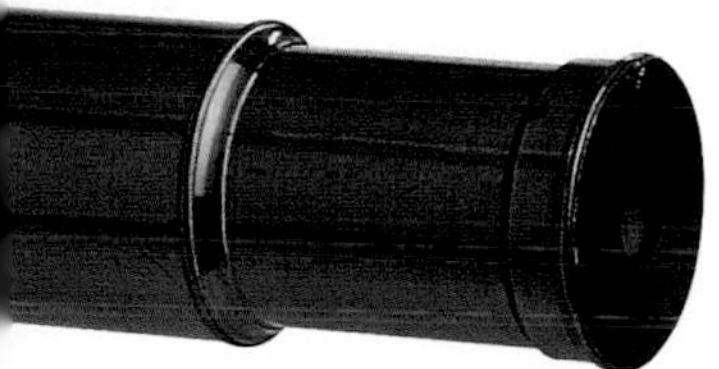

Open-hearth process for making steel

1861

William Siemens, Pierre Martin

The open-hearth process was once the most important way of making steel. It was invented by German-British engineer William Siemens in 1861 and perfected by French engineer Pierre Martin. It works by blowing a very hot flame on to a mixture of steel scrap and molten iron from a blast furnace, held in a shallow, brick-lined bath. This melts the steel and burns out excess carbon from the iron. The hot gases from the hearth are used to heat brick-lined chambers. Air to feed the flame is drawn through these chambers to preheat it. This saves fuel and also allows the flame to be made hot enough to melt steel.

Linoleum

c.1861

Frederick Walton

Linoleum, invented by British rubber manufacturer Frederick Walton, in about 1861, was the first successful smooth floor covering. Walton originally made it by coating cloth with layers of a substance containing linseed oil and other ingredients. This slowly reacted with air to form a thick, resilient coating. Linoleum is still used in areas that get heavy wear.

Speech center in the brain

1861

Paul Broca

Whenever we talk, certain parts of our brain, mostly on the left side, go into action. One of them is Broca's area, which helps us find the right words. It was identified by French surgeon and anthropologist Paul Broca in 1861. He studied people with injuries that made them speak hesitantly but did not stop them from understanding what people said. He usually found damage to an area in the front left of the brain. It was the first time that anyone had identified a part of the brain with a particular job. Other scientists, notably the German neurologist Carl Wernicke, later found areas near Broca's that were associated with other aspects of speech and language.

ARGUING ABOUT APES

ALTHOUGH MOST SCIENTISTS accepted Darwin's theory, the public and most of the Church were not so happy. As well as contradicting religious beliefs, the theory implied that living creatures were ruled entirely by physical laws. Worse still, it seemed to treat people as animals descended from apes. Fortunately for Darwin, who was a shy man, his friend, the naturalist Thomas Huxley, positively enjoyed speaking up for him in the great debate.

LIFE BEFORE DARWIN
Most people thought species were fixed or replaced occasionally by God. Some scientists had proposed theories of evolution. Jean Lamarck thought that animals could pass on changes that happened to them during their lives.

HOW DARWIN GOT HIS IDEAS
Darwin saw that finches on various Pacific islands were different. He also looked at the fossil record. The idea of natural selection came to him after he read an essay by the naturalist Thomas Malthus. Malthus said that animals compete to survive, and Darwin realized that competition could explain why animals change.

In 1874, when this cartoon was published, the idea of people having apes for ancestors still seemed strange.

NEW FORMS OF DARWINISM
Darwin's theory fits well with modern genetics, but not all scientists accept it completely. The renowned US geologist Stephen Jay Gould says that it fails to explain the way species have evolved in jumps, rather than smoothly.

1861 The tiny principality of Monaco, just east of Nice in the south of France, regains its independence after 46 years of rule by Sardinia. Its only city, Monte Carlo, opens what will rapidly become the world's best known casino.

1861 On March 17, after years of struggle, the Kingdom of Italy, with Victor Emmanuel II as its king, is proclaimed by a parliament assembled in Turin. Rome and Venice, still occupied by foreign troops, are not part of it.

Yale lock *This lock has been cut in half to show how the key moves the tumblers to the right height so that the inner cylinder can be turned.*

Yale lock

1861

Linus Yale

The Yale is probably the most widely used type of lock. It was invented in the US in 1861 and is based on a principle known to the ancient Egyptians: several pins stop the lock from moving until the right key pushes them all into the right positions. Linus Yale's father had designed a lock using this "pin tumbler" idea in 1848, but it was Linus Yale Jr. who perfected the compact revolving barrel and flat key that is used today.

Parkesine

1862

Alexander Parkes

The first plastic was based on the natural substance cellulose. British chemist Alexander Parkes discovered that if he treated cellulose with nitric acid, dissolved it in alcohol and ether, and mixed it with pigments, it formed a dough that he could mold into small articles. He won a medal for his discovery in 1862, and in 1866 the Parkesine Company went into business. It failed within two years, possibly because Parkes was too stingy to make his new material properly.

Solar hydrogen

1862

Anders Ångström

The Swedish physicist Anders Ångström was a pioneer of spectroscopy, a way of discovering the composition of things by studying the light they give out when hot. One of the things he studied was very hot—the sun. By comparing its light with light given out by hydrogen in his laboratory, he was able to show in 1862 that the sun's atmosphere contains hydrogen.

Roller skates

1863

Joseph Merlin, James Plimpton

The first person to skate without ice may have been Joseph Merlin, who lived in the 18th century in what is now Belgium. But his skates seem to have been more like in-line skates than roller skates. Four-wheeled skates were invented in 1863 by an American, James Plimpton. He started a US and British craze for roller skating, which is still popular today.

Underground railroad

1863

John Fowler

Traffic threatened mid-19th-century cities with death by choking. London fought back in 1863 with the world's first underground railroad. It wasn't very far underground: just a deep trench dug down the center of the street and roofed over so that traffic could run above it. Despite fumes from its steam locomotives, the Metropolitan Railway, engineered by John Fowler, was a great success. Electrified in 1906, the line is still in use today.

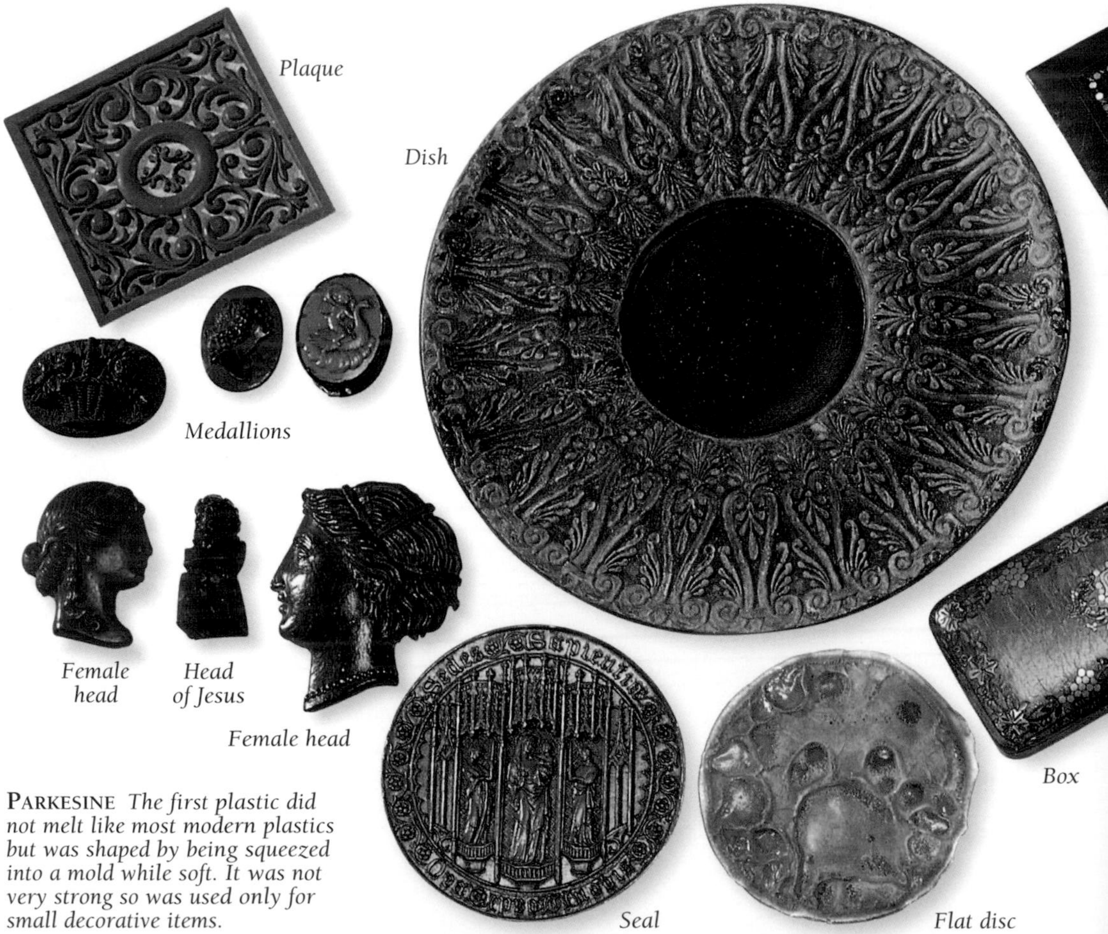
Plaque

Dish

Medallions

Female head

Head of Jesus

Female head

Box

Seal

Flat disc

Parkesine *The first plastic did not melt like most modern plastics but was shaped by being squeezed into a mold while soft. It was not very strong so was used only for small decorative items.*

1863 During this year of the Civil War, President Abraham Lincoln gives his two most famous speeches, the Emancipation Proclamation and the Gettysburg Address. Both emphasize the importance of the freedom of all men.

1863 In October, soccer's governing body, the Football Association, is founded at a meeting in London. It will standardize the rules of the game and, within eight years, organize the English championship, which will be known as the FA Cup.

Antiseptics

1865

Ignaz Semmelweis, Joseph Lister

Hungarian doctor Ignaz Semmelweis upset his boss by telling medical students at Vienna's maternity hospital to disinfect their hands. Although he proved that this made giving birth less dangerous, he was fired in 1849. Even after 1864, when Louis Pasteur's germ theory was accepted in France, most surgeons still did not even put on clean clothes before an operation. In 1865, Scottish surgeon Joseph Lister sprayed carbolic acid, a powerful germ killer, around his operating room and onto dressings, and things began to change. Lister's ideas led in the end to modern, sterile surgery.

Mercury vacuum pump

1865

Hermann Sprengel

Early 19th-century vacuum pumps moved air with pistons. But as the pressure dropped, the pistons and valves began to leak and contamination of the vacuum by lubricants became a problem. A German glassblower, Heinrich Geissler, found a solution in 1855 when he made use of the vacuum that appears above the mercury in a barometer. Then in 1865, Hermann Sprengel used falling mercury to sweep out gas molecules, producing a high-vacuum pump, which led to many further inventions, including the cathode-ray tube.

Pullman sleeping car

1865

George Pullman, Ben Field

Before air travel, it could take days to travel between cities in the US, and people usually had nowhere to sleep but in their seat on the train. Builder George Pullman realized that there was a market for something more civilized than this. Working with his friend Ben Field, he introduced the first railroad car with comfortable beds, the *Pioneer*, in 1865. The beds were arranged like bunks, with the lower bed doubling as a seat for daytime. Pullman was soon running a big organization with its own town, Pullman, to house its workers.

Clinical thermometer

1866

Thomas Allbutt

Nineteenth-century doctors knew that a patient's temperature was a good guide to their health, but until British physician Thomas Allbutt invented the clinical thermometer, there was no convenient way of measuring it. The only thermometers available could take 20 minutes to give a reading, and some of them were 12 in (30 cm) long. Allbutt reduced them to a pocket-sized instrument, which was not only more convenient to handle but also worked much faster. He usually put his thermometer under a patient's arm, not in their mouth.

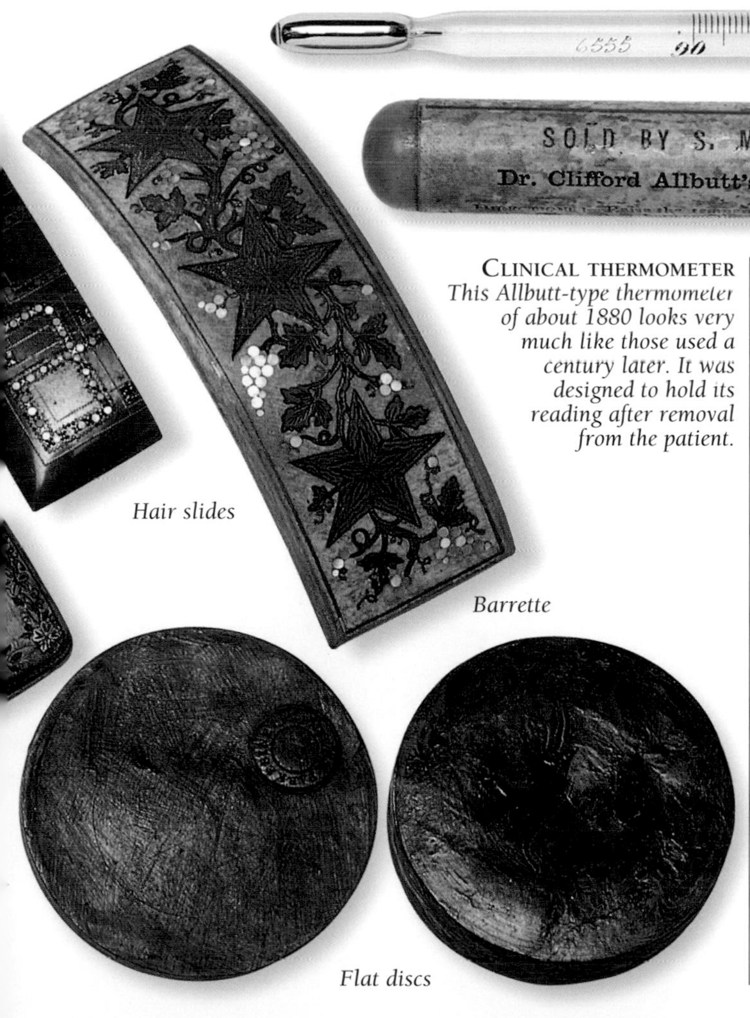

CLINICAL THERMOMETER *This Allbutt-type thermometer of about 1880 looks very much like those used a century later. It was designed to hold its reading after removal from the patient.*

Pasteurization

1865

Louis Pasteur

Pasteurization gets its name from the great French scientist Louis Pasteur, who was the first person to show that invisible organisms can spoil food and cause disease. He invented the process in 1865. It makes liquids hot enough to kill any harmful organisms without destroying their food value. For example, milk can be pasteurized by being heated to 145°F (63°C) for 30 minutes, then quickly chilled for storage. Although pasteurization increases food safety, some people prefer untreated dairy products from disease-free cows.

Laws of heredity

1866

Gregor Mendel

A man and a woman, both with brown eyes, could have a one-in-four chance of producing a child with blue eyes. Basic genetic facts like this go back to the work of an Austrian monk, Gregor Mendel. By crossing different strains of peas, he discovered that organisms inherit their characteristics in a way governed by mathematical laws. He published his results in 1866, but it was only in 1900 that Dutch botanist Hugo De Vries realized their importance to modern biology.

1865 On Friday, April 14, just days after the end of the Civil War, President Abraham Lincoln, attending a performance of *Our American Cousin* at Ford's Theater in Washington, DC, is shot. He dies the following morning.

1865 Writing as Lewis Carroll, British mathematician Charles Dodgson publishes *Alice in Wonderland.* Based on stories written for a child named Alice Liddell, and illustrated by John Tenniel, the book is an immediate success.

Leclanché cell *Liquid-filled glass cells just like this one remained in use well into the 20th century. They were ideal for powering electric door bells.*

Leclanché cell

1866

Georges Leclanché

Modern batteries started as the Leclanché cell, invented in 1866 by French engineer Georges Leclanché. The cell's negative terminal was a glass jar containing a zinc rod in a solution of ammonium chloride. A smaller pot inside the jar contained manganese dioxide and a carbon rod, forming the positive terminal. It eventually developed into today's smaller, dryer battery.

Germs

1867

Louis Pasteur

In the mid-19th century, some natural processes were still a mystery. What turned grape juice into wine, for example? Why did it sometimes go sour? French chemist Louis Pasteur proved that invisible organisms were responsible. He also proved that diseases were transmitted by microorganisms, rather than polluted air. The Academy of Sciences officially accepted his conclusions in 1864, and Pasteur was given his own laboratory at France's École Supérieure in 1867. His "germ" theory then began to be more widely accepted. By establishing the reality of germs, Pasteur revolutionized medicine and the food industry. (✳ *See also* **The Bug Hunters.**)

THE BUG HUNTERS

Others before Pasteur had thought that invasion by invisible organisms might be responsible for decay and disease. But they had not been able to prove it, so most people believed that decaying matter created life by "spontaneous generation." Even after Pasteur, many people found it hard to believe in the invisible killers. Those who did, such as Scottish surgeon Joseph Lister and German doctor Robert Koch, made great progress.

Germs before Pasteur

In 100 BCE, a Roman writer declared that disease was caused by an invisible invasion. Much later, in 1684, Francesco Redi wrote that spontaneous generation could not occur because "only life produces life." In the 19th century, Italian scientist Agostino Bassi showed that a disease of silkworms was caused by infection with invisible fungus spores.

Pasteur's legacy

German doctor Robert Koch showed that bacteria could be bred in the laboratory and established many of the techniques of bacteriology. By 1883, he had isolated the organisms that cause cholera and tuberculosis. Scientists now know that not all bacteria are bad—we depend on many microorganisms inside our bodies to keep them working properly.

Compound microscopes

Glass beaker

Silkworm cocoons

Bronze ink stand and ink wells

Pipette

Culture slide

Germs *This selection of equipment from Pasteur's laboratory shows both his tools for studying germs and one of his major concerns—the health of silkworms.*

1866 The world's first ski-jumping competition is held in Telemark, Norway. It is won by Sondre Nordheim, who made the sport possible by inventing ski bindings. He will later ski the 200 miles (322 km) from Telemark to Oslo.

1867 Russia sells Alaska to the US, prompted by a fall in demand for furs from the region and the threat of British invasion. Many Americans think the price of $7.2 million is too high, but Alaska will prove to be rich in oil.

Dynamite

1867

Alfred Nobel

The dangers of nitroglycerine were brought home to Swedish chemist Alfred Nobel in 1864 when his nitroglycerine factory blew up, killing his younger brother. Determined to tame this otherwise useful explosive, he mixed it with an absorbent material, kieselguhr, converting the dangerous liquid into a safer solid, which he patented in 1867 as dynamite. Ironically, it made him rich enough to set up the foundation that awards the Nobel Peace Prize.

Paper boat

1867

Elisha Waters, George Waters

In 1867, US carton maker Elisha Waters and his son George started making rowing boats out of paper. They glued paper over a wooden form, let it dry, then varnished it. The keel and other main members were made of wood. The light, stiff boats were ideal for sports; during 1876, US crews rowing Waters boats won no fewer than 12 major races. The Waters construction technique has since been reinvented in the modern fiberglass boat.

Helium in the sun

1868

Pierre Janssen, Norman Lockyer

The gas helium gets its name from *helios*, Greek for "sun," because that's where it was first detected. In 1868, French astronomer Pierre Janssen saw a dark line in the yellow region of the sun's spectrum. He thought it came from sodium, but British astronomer Norman Lockyer declared that it indicated an unknown element. He named it with the help of chemist Edward Frankland.

Möbius strip

1868

August Möbius

German mathematician August Möbius died without revealing his best-known discovery, the Möbius strip. It was found among his papers after his death in 1868. It is a simple strip of paper given a half twist and then glued to form a loop, and it has weird properties. For example, it has only one edge and it is impossible to make each side of it a different color because it has only one side. When cut down the center, it opens out into a single loop twice the size with a double half twist. Two Mobiüs strips zipped together form what is called a Klein bottle, which has no edges and only one surface.

Margarine

1869

Hippolyte Mège-Mouriés

Many people today prefer margarine to butter, but it's hard to believe that anybody preferred the first margarine, a mixture of beef fat, skimmed milk, cow's udder, and pig's stomach. When French inventor Hippolyte Mège-Mouriés concocted it in 1869, Napoleon III awarded him a prize for producing the first alternative to butter. It soon improved, and by 1885, it was enough of a threat to the dairy industry for the British government to stop the use of its original name, "Butterine."

CHEWING GUM *Early competition produced some unlikely advertising, such as this suggestion that gum chewing was the height of fashion.*

Air brake

1869

George Westinghouse

To stop a long train, the brakes must be applied to all the wheels, but how? US inventor George Westinghouse found the answer in 1869—use air. Unlike a mechanical linkage, air can be taken from carriage to carriage easily. Westinghouse's system also had an important safety feature. The brakes were held in the off position by air pressure and applied by releasing it, so any leaks automatically put them on.

Chewing gum

1869

Thomas Adams

The main ingredient of chewing gum is chicle, a rubbery substance from a Central American tree. Many 19th-century inventors tried to use it like rubber. One of them was US photographer Thomas Adams, who bought some from a Mexican. He failed to make rubber, but he noticed that the Mexican liked chewing chicle. In 1869, he boiled up some with flavorings and offered it to a store. Customers loved it.

1867 The British North America Act creates the Dominion of Canada from New Brunswick, Nova Scotia, and what will be Quebec and Ontario. Its government is based on British practice, and its sovereign is the British monarch.

1869 In Victoria, Australian John Deason and Richard Oates dig up Australia's largest gold nugget, weighing more than 56 lb (71 kg). They get £9,534 ($36,540) for the find, which becomes known as the "Welcome Stranger" nugget.

Synthetic alizarin

1869

Heinrich Caro, William Perkin

In 1869, Heinrich Caro in Germany and William Perkin in Britain demonstrated the power of chemistry by wiping out an entire industry. They both found a way to make alizarin, the active component of a natural red dye. It was one of the few red dyes available at the time, and thousands of people earned their living producing the natural substance—until the chemists got to work. Caro beat Perkin to the patent by one day, but Perkin still made the dye in Britain, using a cheaper method.

Periodic table

1869

Dmitry Mendeleyev

In 1866, Russian chemist Dmitry Mendeleyev listed the elements by atomic weight. He found that the list showed a pattern, with similar elements appearing at regular intervals, or periods. He published his periodic table in 1869 and in 1871 produced a version with gaps where there were breaks in the pattern. He said that the gaps represented undiscovered elements, but most chemists did not see the importance of this until at least 20 years later.

Dynamo

1870

Zénobe Gramme

Electric generators were not very effective until Belgian engineer Zénobe Gramme built his dynamo in 1870. It used an electromagnet powered by the generator itself. Several other types of dynomos already existed, but Gramme's version went further. It had a highly efficient design and a new way of connecting its generating coils. Gramme's dynamo gave a strong, steady output, making it a much better generator.

Celluloid

1870

John Hyatt

Celluloid was the first truly successful plastic. Like its unsuccessful predecessor Parkesine (✱ *see* **page 144**), it was based on cellulose. Its US inventor, John Hyatt, created the first clear, flexible material, making possible both popular photography and motion pictures. Patented in 1870, celluloid was also used for everything from dolls to shirt cuffs. Unfortunately, it was extremely flammable and caused many accidents, so it is rarely used today.

Penny-farthing bicycle

1870

James Starley, William Hillman

Bizarre though it looks, with its huge front wheel and tiny rear wheel, the penny-farthing was a serious invention by leading bicycle pioneers. British engineers James Starley and William Hillman created it in 1870 as a lighter alternative to existing velocipedes. The big front wheel did the same job as modern gears, enabling the rider to power the bike efficiently. It worked—on one long trip, a group of penny-farthing riders averaged 46 miles (74 km) a day.

CELLULOID *Basically colorless, celluloid could be made in a variety of forms, from fake ivory to mock tortoiseshell.*

"Ivory" box

"Mother of pearl" cigarette case

"Ivory" hairpin box

Marble-effect handbag

"Ivory" evening handbag

"Tortoiseshell" haircombs

"Ivory" hand mirror

1869 On November 17, after 15 years' hard negotiating and harder digging, the Suez Canal is opened. Designed by French diplomat Ferdinand de Lesseps, it provides a shortcut from the Indian Ocean to the Mediterranean Sea.

1870 German archaeologist Heinrich Schliemann discovers the city of Troy, long thought to be just the stuff of ancient Greek legends. He finds battlements, walls, and gold treasure on a mound called Hissarlik in Turkey.

Modern microscope condenser

c.1870

Ernst Abbe

The image-forming lenses of a microscope are important, but until about 1870, nobody had thought much about the optics that simply illuminate the object—the condenser. Early microscopists used condensers, but German physicist Ernst Abbe's was the first scientific design. Most microscopes now have Abbe condensers.

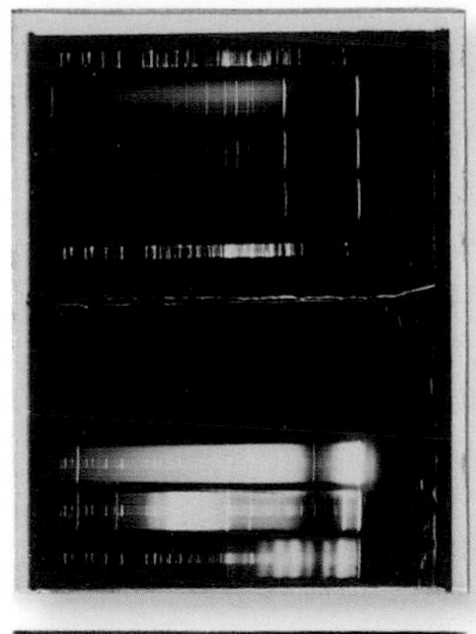

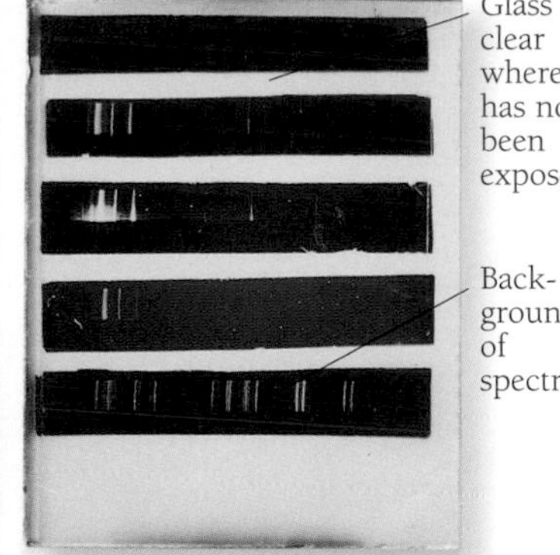

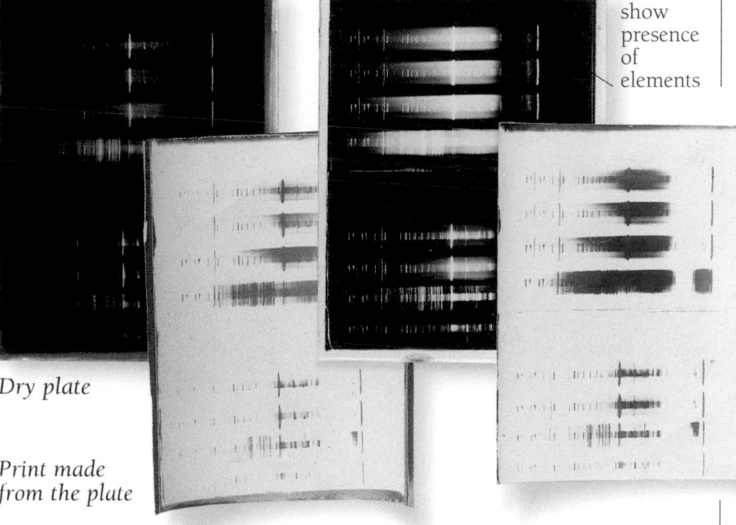

Dry plate

Print made from the plate

Dry photographic plate *Dry plates were useful to scientists. These show spark spectra (c.1915).*

Dry photographic plate

1871

Richard Maddox

Although wet plates produced excellent photographs (✳ *see* **page 139**), they were not safe or convenient. Photographers searched everywhere for the magic ingredient that would allow them to make dry plates. They eventually found it in the kitchen cabinet: gelatine.

In 1871, British doctor Richard Maddox mixed some gelatine with silver bromide and spread it on glass. When it was dry, the new coating stayed sensitive, could be developed easily, and needed shorter exposure times. Modern photography had arrived.

"Ivory" hairbrush

"Ivory" clothes brush

Cable car

1873

Andrew Hallidie

Andrew Hallidie, a wire-rope maker in the US, was shocked to see five horses killed as a horse-drawn bus slid down one of San Francisco's steep hills. So he used his ropes to create the world's first cable cars. It opened in 1873 and is still running today. Cable cars are pulled along by a constantly moving rope running in a slot in the road. To move, the cable cars grab the rope; to stop, they let go and apply their brakes.

Barbed wire

1874

Joseph Glidden

How an invention is made can matter more than what it is. Barbed wire is an example. Early types cost so much to make that few people used them. US farmer Joseph Glidden saw some barbed wire in 1873 and the following year patented a new type that could be made cheaply by machine. Soon his Barb Fence Company was turning out miles of cattle-controlling wire and helping make the US's Great Plains into great farming country.

Jeans *What we call jeans did not get their name for years. This 1910 advertisement calls them overalls.*

Jeans

1873

Jacob Davis, Levi Strauss

In the 1850s, the US's gold rush attracted people from everywhere. Levi Strauss had a business that supplied them with everything they needed, including pants. Tailor Jacob Davis started making denim pants with riveted pockets and suggested to Strauss that they could make lots of money. So Strauss provided cash to get started, Davis supplied the know-how, and in 1873 they got the first patent for jeans.

DNA

1874

Johann Miescher

DNA, the key to genetics and life, may seem like the latest thing, but it was discovered in 1874. Swiss scientist Johann Miescher was a student when he found a new substance, which he called nuclein, in the nucleus of white blood cells. He later realized that it was actually two substances. Separating out the acid part, he called it nucleic acid. It is now known as deoxyribonucleic acid, or DNA.

1872 In the US, the world's first national park is opened. The president, Ulysses S. Grant, signs a bill that preserves Yellowstone, a 3,468 sq mile (8,983 sq km) area in the Rocky Mountains, as a permanent wilderness.

1873 Canada forms a new police force to combat smuggling, horse theft, and banditry. The Northwest Mounted Police, later the Royal Canadian Mounted Police, will become famous as the Mounties, who "always get their man."

TYPEWRITER *This 1875 Sholes and Glidden machine typed in capital letters only.*

SOUND RECORDING *A phonograph from about 1885 shows recording at its simplest.*

Typewriter

1874

Christopher Sholes, Carlos Glidden, Samuel Soulé

As an ex-newspaper editor, Christopher Sholes knew exactly what a typewriter had to do: write faster than a pen. Many people had tried and failed to produce such a machine, but Sholes, helped by fellow US inventors Carlos Glidden and Samuel Soulé, succeeded. In 1873, he sold the idea to Remington, a firm of gunmakers. They launched the world's first real typewriter in 1874, after which their gun business took a back seat. The layout of the keyboard was developed to stop fast typists from jamming the keys and is still used today.

Four-stroke engine

1876

Alphonse Beau de Rochas, Nikolaus Otto

Most gasoline and diesel engines use the four-stroke cycle. Fuel and air are drawn into a cylinder, compressed, and burned, and the burned gases pumped out. The first person to think of it was French engineer Alphonse Beau de Rochas in 1862. His work was forgotten and reinvented by German engineer Nikolaus Otto in 1876. Despite de Rochas's earlier work, the cycle is still known today as the Otto cycle.

Telephone

1876

Alexander Graham Bell

See **pages 152–153** for the story of how Bell invented the telephone.

Sound recording

1877

Thomas Edison

In 1877, US inventor Thomas Edison was working on a recorder for telegraph signals. He noticed that paper indented with the signals made sounds when pulled under a needle. So he made a machine with tinfoil wrapped around a revolving cylinder and a needle connected to a thin metal disc. When he spoke, the disc vibrated and the needle indented waves on the tinfoil. Turning the cylinder again, Edison heard his own voice. He had invented sound recording. (✱ *See also* **Recording Pioneers.**)

1874 British writer Thomas Hardy establishes his reputation with his fourth novel, *Far from the Madding Crowd*. It describes the tragic relationships of heroine Bathsheba Everdene with three very different men.

1874 A group of artists including Monet, Pisarro, and Renoir, rejected by the French Academy, hold their own show. Journalist Louis Leroy, shocked by pictures that capture real light and color, dubs them the Impressionists.

Photographic motion capture

1877

Eadweard Muybridge

Eadweard Muybridge was born in Britain but worked in the US. He was the first person to record live motion photographically. A racehorse owner had asked him to settle an argument: did a galloping horse ever lift all its hooves off the ground at once? In 1877, Muybridge set up a row of cameras along a racetrack. As a horse galloped by, it tripped their shutters, making each camera record a different part of the movement. The answer to the question was "yes."

Cream separator

1878

Gustav de Laval

Skimmed milk isn't skimmed—it's spun like clothes in a washing machine. The first cream separator using this principle was invented in 1878 by Swedish engineer Gustav de Laval. In its final form, his machine poured milk on to a set of spinning discs, which forced the watery part to the outside and left the cream in the center. By 1883, Laval had built a steam-powered separator, 40 times faster than a modern washing machine.

Light bulb

1878

Thomas Edison, Joseph Swan

In 1878, both Thomas Edison in the US and the chemist Joseph Swan in Britain made light bulbs. Both of them had trouble finding a filament that would last long. Edison tried platinum but soon switched to carbon, which Swan had first tried 20 years earlier. By 1880, both inventors had produced good light bulbs, which they showed off at the 1881 Paris Electrical Exhibition. From then on, their lamps began to be used everywhere.

Microphone

1878

David Hughes

Returning to London after making a fortune in the US, David Hughes set up as a full-time inventor. In 1878, he discovered that loose electrical contacts were sensitive to sound. Two barely touching carbon rods placed on a table and connected to a battery and telephone earpiece could reveal sounds as quiet as the tramp of a fly's feet. These sounds were so tiny that Hughes called his invention a microphone. Its real future was as part of a better telephone.

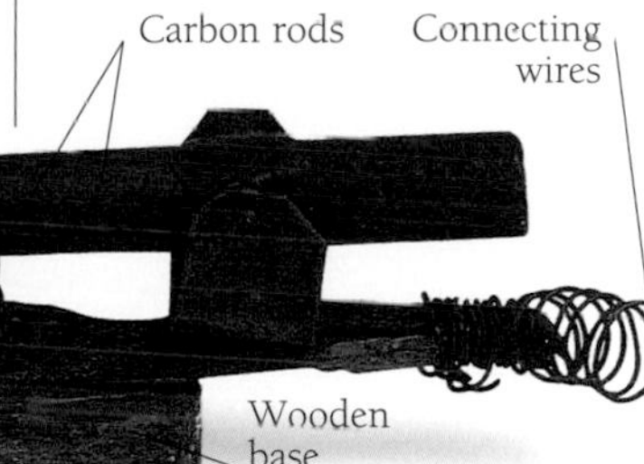

Microphone *Two carbon rods touch to form one type of Hughes microphone.*

Two-stroke engine

1879

Dugald Clerk

A two-stroke engine uses more fuel than a four-stroke engine of the same power, but it also weighs less. Its mechanism is simpler, and each of its cylinders delivers power on every revolution, not every other revolution, as in a four-stroke. The first effective two-stroke engine was invented by Scottish engineer Dugald Clerk in 1879 and patented in 1881. It was designed to run on coal gas to power workshop machinery. Two-stroke engines are now used for things like scooters and lawn mowers, where lightness matters more than efficiency.

Threaded drive axle moves the tinfoil beneath the needle

Brass cylinder—tinfoil is wrapped around this

RECORDING PIONEERS

THE EARLY RECORDING industry solved its problems step by step. Tinfoil was not a good recording medium. It was soon replaced by wax. Edison produced cylindrical records on his phonograph, but they were slow and expensive to copy. Flat discs, which could be stamped out by the thousand, dealt with that. But the problem of how to make sounds louder was not solved until the arrival of electronics in the 1920s.

The Phonograph
Edison developed his invention into a sophisticated home entertainment device that could produce surprisingly good sound. He eventually solved the problem of copying cylindrical recordings but failed to sign up many good musicians.

The Graphophone
Recordings on wax were first made by US inventors Chichester Bell and Charles Tainter. Their machine recorded on cylinders that were wax-coated. Although used mainly for dictation, it could produce excellent recordings.

Early 20th-century gramophone

The Gramophone
Flat disc records were invented in 1887 by a German engineer, Emil Berliner, working in the US. Because of their shape, they were easily mass-produced. And when renowned musicians started recording on them, their future was assured.

1875 On Wednesday, August 25, British merchant navy captain Matthew Webb becomes the first person to swim the English Channel without any buoyancy aid. He completes the 21 mile (34 km) crossing in 21 hours 45 minutes.

1876 Financed by wealthy widow Nadezhda von Meck, Russian composer Pyotr Tchaikovsky writes the ballet *Swan Lake*. In 1877, it is danced, with little success, by the Bolshoi Ballet under choreographer Wenzel Reisinger.

DOING AWAY WITH DISTANCE

Helped by Thomas Watson, Alexander Graham Bell invents the telephone

Bell's box telephone incorporated a larger magnet than others, which made it more sensitive.

Bell demonstrated this telephone to Queen Victoria.

PUBLICITY MACHINE
Bell was an expert at publicity. His crude laboratory instruments became fine objects of polished brass, rich wood, and ivory when they were to be demonstrated to someone as important as Queen Victoria. Bell made a good impression on the Queen when they met in 1878, despite making the mistake of touching her arm without permission to attract her attention to an incoming call.

It was Valentine's Day, 1876. A good day to tell the world about an invention that would help people communicate. It's lucky Alexander Graham Bell didn't leave it any longer. Two hours after he'd deposited papers describing his telephone to people at the US Patent Office, his rival, Elisha Gray, warned them that he was about to do the same. But Bell was first.

It was hard on Gray. Both men had similar ideas, but Bell had an advantage: he knew more about speech and hearing. Bell's father was a speech teacher and had invented a way to help deaf people speak. His grandfather had given speech lessons, so as Alexander grew up in Edinburgh, Scotland, he was surrounded by ideas about speech and hearing. He even got his dog to talk by making it growl then moving its mouth with his hands!

The family emigrated to Canada in 1870. Bell went to Boston, where he opened a school for teachers of the deaf. He experimented with a harmonic telegraph, which sent messages as dots and dashes similar to musical notes. Bell noticed that a strip of iron near an electromagnet mimicked the vibrations of a similar strip and electromagnet connected to it by wires. He thought he might use this to transmit speech.

With mechanic Thomas Watson, he tried hard to make electric currents imitate sound waves. The original arrangement wasn't sensitive enough, so Bell tried a needle dipping into acid. The needle was attached to a sheet of parchment stretched on a frame, with a horn to concentrate sound on to it. Sound shook the parchment, which varied the resistance of the needle's contact with the acid, which, in turn, varied the current.

Early telephone cable

WIRED FOR SOUND
As telephones became more popular, cities got choked with overhead wires, so some lines went underground. Early phone cables contained many paper-insulated wires in a lead sheath.

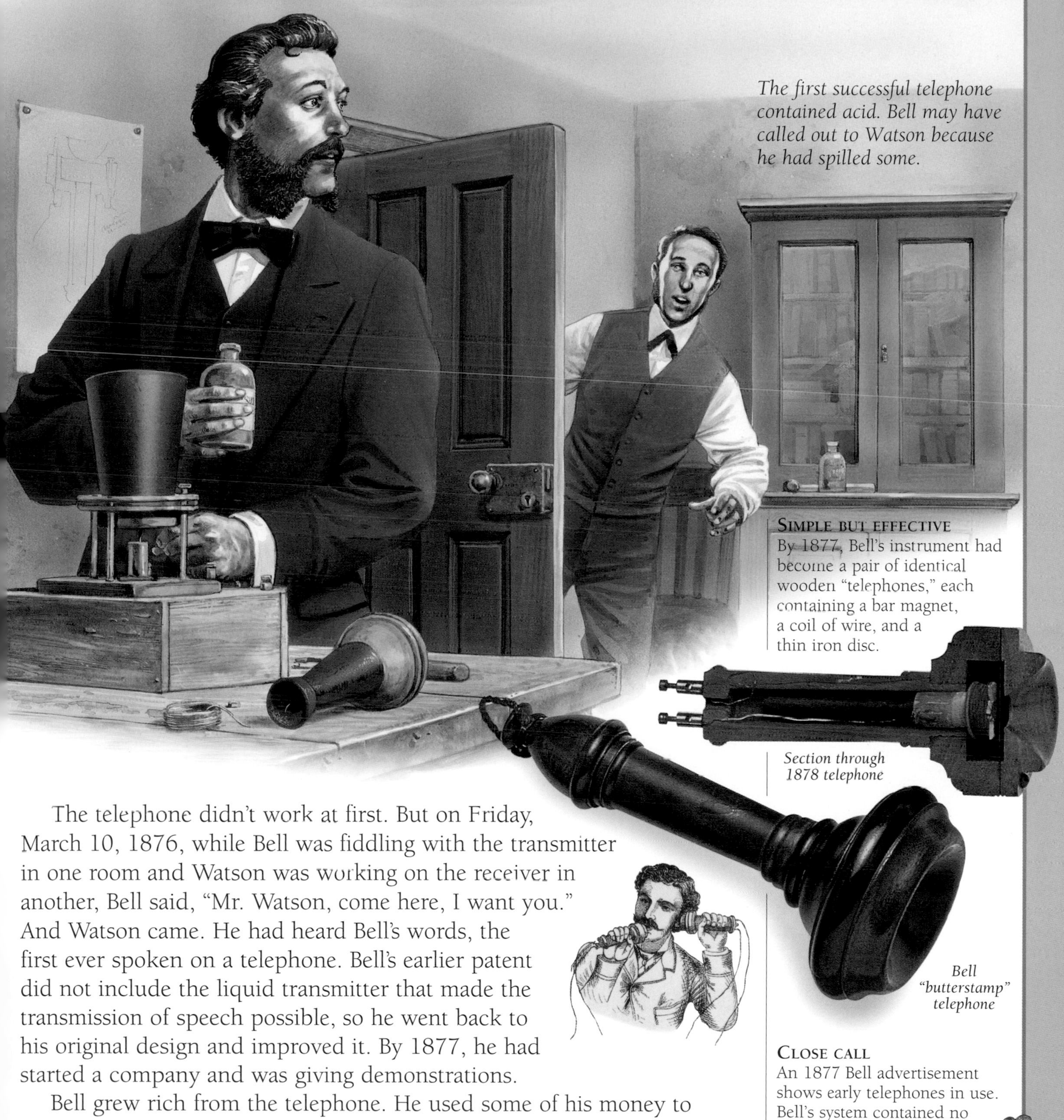

The first successful telephone contained acid. Bell may have called out to Watson because he had spilled some.

Simple but effective
By 1877, Bell's instrument had become a pair of identical wooden "telephones," each containing a bar magnet, a coil of wire, and a thin iron disc.

Section through 1878 telephone

Bell "butterstamp" telephone

The telephone didn't work at first. But on Friday, March 10, 1876, while Bell was fiddling with the transmitter in one room and Watson was working on the receiver in another, Bell said, "Mr. Watson, come here, I want you." And Watson came. He had heard Bell's words, the first ever spoken on a telephone. Bell's earlier patent did not include the liquid transmitter that made the transmission of speech possible, so he went back to his original design and improved it. By 1877, he had started a company and was giving demonstrations.

Bell grew rich from the telephone. He used some of his money to help deaf people and some to build a home in Canada. He made several more inventions and became president of the National Geographic Society, turning its magazine into the publication we know today. But Bell will always be remembered best for doing away with the distance that can separate two people who need to talk.

Close call
An 1877 Bell advertisement shows early telephones in use. Bell's system contained no amplification, making distant calls faint. This was remedied by the invention of the carbon microphone (✷ *see* **page 151**).

Cash register

1879

James Ritty, John Patterson

A cash register records every sale, preventing store clerks from putting money into their own pockets. The first one was invented by US tavern keeper James Ritty in 1879. It displayed the money paid on a dial and recorded it by punching a paper roll. It wasn't easy to use, and cash registers caught on only after coal merchant John Patterson bought the idea. As well as improving it, he set up the world's first professional sales force to sell it.

CASH REGISTER *Many early cash registers, like this one from 1935, had dials rather than keys.*

Electric train

1879

Werner von Siemens

As soon as good electric motors were available, they were used in trains. The first electric train was exhibited in Berlin, Germany, in 1879. Built by German engineer Werner von Siemens, it ran in a circle, took only 30 people, and went no faster than 4 mph (6 km/h). Within five years, real electric trains and trams were running in Germany, the US, and Britain.

Saccharin

1879

Ira Remsen, Constantin Fahlberg

Saccharin is very much sweeter than sugar and does not make people fat, so it is used a lot in food and beverages, despite its disagreeable aftertaste. US chemist Ira Remsen and his student Constantin Fahlberg discovered it by accident in 1879. They noticed that after one session in the lab, everything they touched tasted sweet. They soon tracked down the chemical responsible for this and turned it into a commercial product.

Venn diagram

1880

John Venn

Venn diagrams help with logic. They were invented in 1880 in England by a Cambridge University instructor, John Venn, and use circles to stand for different things. For example, suppose there is one circle representing cats, another black things, and a third green things. The cat circle would be drawn to overlap the black circle, but not the green circle, to show that some cats are black but no cats are green. The idea can be extended to much more complicated statements.

Public electricity supply

1882

Thomas Edison

Electric light bulbs were not much use without electricity. One of their inventors, Thomas Edison, knew this very well, so he built the first public electricity supply system. It opened in New York in September 1882, a year after Edison had demonstrated the idea in London. Edison's system provided brighter, safer lighting than gas, but it used direct current, which did not transmit over long distances. Because of this, it lost out to alternating current in the end.

Practical life raft

1882

Maria Beasley

Maria Beasley invented the first life raft that was fireproof, compact, safe, and easy to launch. It had guard rails to prevent users from falling overboard and rectangular metal floats that folded up neatly for storage. Twenty of Beasley's rafts were carried on the ill-fated RMS *Titanic*, which sank on its maiden voyage in 1912. Thanks to her invention, 706 passengers were able to float safely until help arrived.

Function of thyroid gland

1883

Victor Horsley

The thyroid gland lies in the neck, wrapped around the voice box. In 1883, Victor Horsley (later Sir Victor) proved that the gland's job is to control how fast the body burns food—called its metabolic rate. He did this by removing the thyroid glands from monkeys. We now know that the thyroid gland makes a hormone that speeds up the body's cells.

Electric streetcar

1883

Magnus Volk

A tram is an electric bus that runs on rails in the road. Many inventors created trams in the early 1880s. The German firm Siemens and Halske was operating trams between Frankfurt and Offenbach

ELECTRIC STREETCAR *This is a model of a double-decker streetcar that operated in London in about 1915. Streetcars were a feature of many large cities by 1900. Some places abandoned them; others kept them. Now some cities are bringing back this form of transportation.*

1879 In Boston, Massachusetts, religious leader Mary Baker Eddy founds the First Church of Christ, Scientist. Christian Scientists believe that humans are spiritual, not material, and value prayer above conventional medicine.

1881 P. T. Barnum, James A. Bailey, and James L. Hutchinson form the circus known as "The Greatest Show on Earth." Starring Jumbo the Elephant from April 1882, it will become the most successful circus of its time in the United States.

in 1884, but the first tramway to take paying passengers was probably one built in 1883 by British engineer Magnus Volk. Running on narrow-gauge tracks along the sea front at Brighton, England, it is still in service.

Wires collect electricity from overhead cables to power the streetcar

Metal wheels ran along rails

Car has controls at both ends so it does not have to turn around

Induction motor

1883

Nikola Tesla

An induction motor is an electric motor that has no electrical connections to the part that rotates. This makes it more reliable, because there are no sliding contacts. It was invented in 1883 by Serbian-US engineer Nikola Tesla.

INDUCTION MOTOR *Tesla's original motor did not look much like the machines of today, but its operating principle was the same.*

He figured out how to create a rotating magnetic field using stationary electrical windings. Placed in this rotating field, a conducting rotor will spin. This is because the field induces currents in the rotor, turning it into a magnet, which is pushed around as the field rotates. Induction motors now power most of the world's electrically driven machinery.

Three-phase electricity supply

1883

Nikola Tesla, George Westinghouse

A three-phase electricity supply uses three wires instead of two. It gives two different voltages from one set of wires and can create the rotating magnetic field needed in an induction motor. The idea occurred to Nikola Tesla in 1883. US engineer George Westinghouse, looking for something better than Edison's supply system, bought Tesla's idea in 1888. Today, nearly all household electricity is delivered by three-phase systems.

1882 Judo begins in Japan when Kano Jigoro learns about a samurai form of fighting called jujitsu and founds his Kodokan School. Fighters in this unarmed combat sport try to master their opponent by turning their own force against them.

1883 The volcanic island of Krakatau in Indonesia destroys itself in one of the world's biggest eruptions. The explosion is heard 3,000 miles (5,000 km) away. Thousands are killed and dust pollutes the atmosphere for years.

Artificial silk

1884

Hilaire Chardonnet, Joseph Swan

Artificial silk was the first synthetic fiber. In about 1880, both Hilaire Chardonnet in France and Joseph Swan in Britain made "silk" by squirting cellulose nitrate solution through a nozzle. The product was highly flammable, but both inventors found a way of converting it back into safer cellulose. Chardonnet got a patent for his process in 1884 and by 1891 had set up a factory at Besançon to make artificial silk commercially.

Motorcycle

1884

Edward Butler, Gottlieb Daimler

The first motorcycle had three wheels. It was designed by British engineer Edward Butler in 1884, although he didn't build it until 1887. Its engine was at the back and drove a single rear wheel. In 1885, German engineer Gottlieb Daimler designed the first two-wheeled motorcycle. He built it purely because he wanted to test a new high-speed gas engine that he had designed (✳ *see* **page 157**). It got its first outing on November 10, 1886.

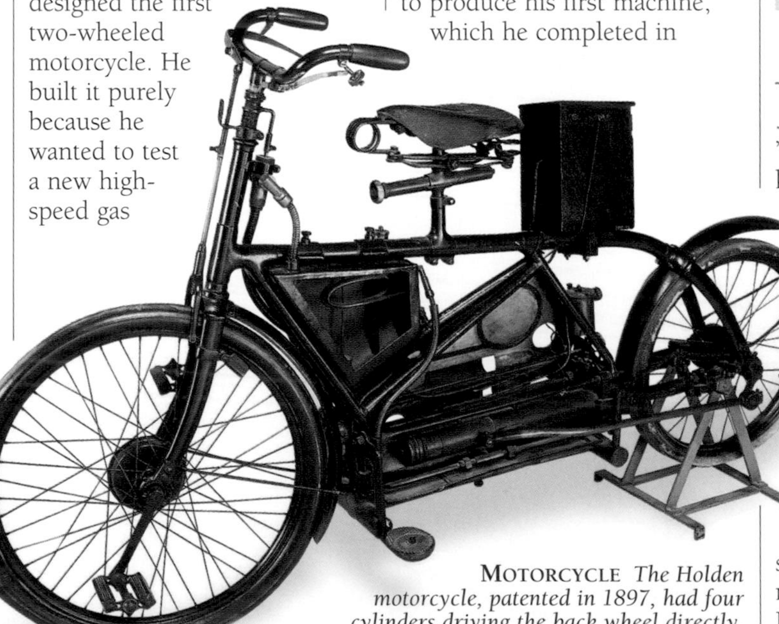

MOTORCYCLE *The Holden motorcycle, patented in 1897, had four cylinders driving the back wheel directly.*

Multistage steam turbine

1884

Charles Parsons

A steam turbine is like a fan in reverse. Steam rushes through blades, making them spin. If there were only one set of blades, most of the steam's energy would be wasted, but in 1884 British engineer Charles (later Sir Charles) Parsons invented a turbine with many sets of blades on one shaft. These were graded in size to capture most of the steam's energy. Turbines like this are now used everywhere to power ships and electric generators.

Adder-lister

1885

William Burroughs

The first adding machine that printed its calculations was created by a US inventor who left school at 15. It took William Burroughs four years to produce his first machine, which he completed in 1885. It had more than 80 keys, arranged in columns of nine, and a handle to operate the printer. The following year, Burroughs formed the American Arithmometer Company. He continued to develop his machine, but it was 1892 before it was good enough to sell.

ADDER-LISTER *The Burroughs machine had an intricate mechanism.*

Bicycle

1885

John Starley

Many inventors worked on bicycles in the 1870s and '80s. But the first design that looked like a modern bike was made by British engineer John Starley in 1885. Several makers had already produced chain-driven "safety bicycles," but Starley was the first to make both wheels about the same size, put them in a diamond-shaped frame, and slope the front forks to the correct angle to make the wheel go in a straight line. His machine's name, the Rover, lives on in the Range Rover and Land Rover.

BICYCLE *The Rover in this 1888 advertisement has all the essential features of a modern bike.*

Bicycle hub gear

1885

W. T. Shaw

Cycling uphill is easier if you can change into a lower gear. British engineer W. T. Shaw was one of the first people to help cyclists, with his "crypto-dynamic" gearing of 1885. Then, in 1902, British engineers Henry Sturmey and James Archer both invented similar gears. These were brought together by bicycle maker Frank (later Sir Frank) Bowden. Like earlier designs, the Sturmey-Archer gear was housed inside the bike's rear hub.

1884 The first women's singles tennis championship is held at the All England Croquet and Lawn Tennis Club, Wimbledon, which was founded in 1877. Maud Watson claimed the title from Lilian Watson 6-8, 6-3, 6-3.

1884 US writer Mark Twain writes his most popular book, *Huckleberry Finn*. This children's novel, a sequel to his highly successful *The Adventures of Tom Sawyer*, uses vivid language and humor to deal with violence and racism.

Gas mantle

1885

Carl Auer von Welsbach

In the late 19th century, many people used gas lamps. Electric lighting could have swept these away, but in 1885, Austrian chemist Carl Auer von Welsbach discovered how to get more light from gas. He found that salts of thorium and cerium gave out an intense light when deposited on asbestos fibers and heated. By the 1890s, gas lamps were wearing little knitted covers known as mantles over their flames. When a lamp was lit, the metals in its mantle gave out enough light to rival an electric bulb.

Car

1885

Karl Benz, Gottlieb Daimler, Émile Levassor

The first car, the Motorwagen, was built in 1885 by German engineer Karl Benz. It was a three-wheeler with a single-cylinder engine. Soon Benz and others were making four-wheeled cars. In 1889, Gottlieb Daimler produced one with four gears. But it was French engineer Émile Levassor who produced the first car with its engine at the front, driving the rear wheels through a clutch and gearbox. His 1891 model was the forerunner of the cars we drive today.

Monotype typesetting system

1885

Tolbert Lanston

One of the slowest operations in traditional printing was setting up type. By the 1880s, several inventors were trying to mechanize the process. First to succeed was US inventor Tolbert Lanston. His Monotype system of 1885 had a keyboard and a machine for casting type from molten metal. The caster followed instructions created by the keyboard, delivering type almost ready to print. Monotype dominated book printing for more than 70 years.

Gasoline engine

1885

Gottlieb Daimler, Wilhelm Maybach

The gasoline engine evolved from engines that ran on natural gas. These could not run on liquid fuel, so the carburetor, which turns gasoline into a mist and mixes it with air, was an essential component of a gasoline engine. By 1885, German engineers Gottlieb Daimler and Wilhelm Maybach had designed an effective carburetor. They used it in a new high-speed engine, which was the first true gasoline engine and the forerunner of those that power most cars today.

Rabies vaccine

1885

Louis Pasteur

Rabies is an infection of the nervous system, which people can catch from animal bites, and usually kills if not caught in time. The French biologist Louis Pasteur developed the first vaccine against rabies by heating tissue from infected animals to create a weakened virus. On July 6, 1885, he gave a dramatic demonstration of its power by vaccinating a boy who had been bitten by a dog with rabies. The boy lived.

Car *This Benz car, made in 1888, was sold by Emile Roger, Benz's agent in Paris. It had a tubular metal frame, like a bicycle, and bodywork based on horse-drawn vehicles. The engine was at the rear, below the driver's seat.*

1884 The London Society for the Prevention of Cruelty to Children is founded following the passing of a cruelty law. Later, it will link with other societies to form the National Society for the Prevention of Cruelty to Children (NSPCC).

1884 The world system of standard time zones is established. Delegates from 27 nations meet in Washington, DC, to consider proposals about time zones made in the 1870s by Canadian railroad planner and engineer Sir Sandford Fleming.

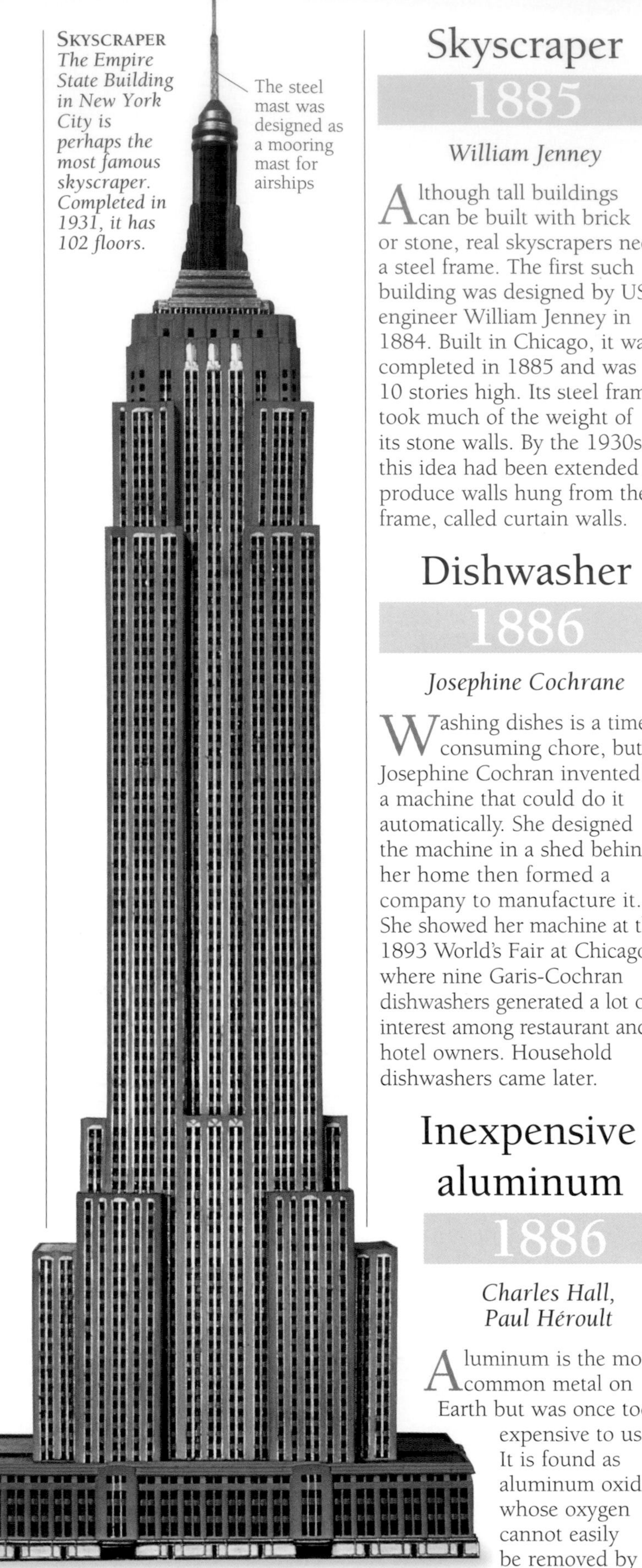

SKYSCRAPER *The Empire State Building in New York City is perhaps the most famous skyscraper. Completed in 1931, it has 102 floors.*

Skyscraper

1885

William Jenney

Although tall buildings can be built with brick or stone, real skyscrapers need a steel frame. The first such building was designed by US engineer William Jenney in 1884. Built in Chicago, it was completed in 1885 and was 10 stories high. Its steel frame took much of the weight of its stone walls. By the 1930s, this idea had been extended to produce walls hung from the frame, called curtain walls.

Dishwasher

1886

Josephine Cochrane

Washing dishes is a time-consuming chore, but Josephine Cochran invented a machine that could do it automatically. She designed the machine in a shed behind her home then formed a company to manufacture it. She showed her machine at the 1893 World's Fair at Chicago, where nine Garis-Cochran dishwashers generated a lot of interest among restaurant and hotel owners. Household dishwashers came later.

Inexpensive aluminum

1886

Charles Hall, Paul Héroult

Aluminum is the most common metal on Earth but was once too expensive to use. It is found as aluminum oxide, whose oxygen cannot easily be removed by chemical means. In 1886, both Charles Hall in the US and Paul Héroult in France dissolved aluminum oxide in molten cryolite (sodium aluminum fluoride) and used electricity to drag the aluminum and oxygen apart. The Hall-Héroult process has transformed aluminum from an exotic curiosity to the stuff of jumbo jets and soda cans.

Recording on wax

1886

Chichester Bell, Charles Tainter

The first sound recordings were made on foil wrapped around a grooved cylinder. A needle, moving up and down, created "hills and dales" in the shape of the sound waves. These recordings were fragile and inaccurate. In 1886, US inventors Chichester Bell and Charles Tainter patented the Graphophone, which recorded on waxed cardboard cylinders. The wax, along with a recording stylus that made a v-shaped groove, gave a better sound.

Function of the ear's semicircular canals

1886

Marie Flourens, Yves Delage

The semicircular canals of the inner ear are three fluid-filled tubes joined together at right angles. In 1824, French biologist Marie Flourens noticed that pigeons moved strangely after a tube was cut. In 1886, another French biologist, Yves Delage, realized what was happening. Moving the head moves the tubes, but the liquid inside lags behind. Hairs in the tubes detect the relative movement and tell the brain which way the head is moving.

Linotype typesetting machine

1886

Ottmar Mergenthaler

Until the 1970s, most newspapers were set in type using a machine invented by German-US engineer Ottmar Mergenthaler in 1886. The Linotype machine used molten metal, but instead of making individual letters like the Monotype machine (✱ *see* **page 157**), it produced whole lines of type—hence the name. Newspaper printers liked it because it was quick to use and needed only one operator.

Steam sterilization of surgical instruments

1886

Ernst von Bergmann

Once surgeons realized that infections were caused by germs (✱ *see* **page 146**), they had to decide what to do about them. Should they kill them with antiseptics or try to keep them out of the operating room from the start? Today, the second approach is normal practice. It was pioneered by German surgeon Ernst von Bergmann in 1886. He was the first person to sterilize instruments and dressings with steam. He later made everything else used in operations as germ-free as possible.

1886 French sculptor Auguste Rodin creates the first version of what will be one of his best-known works, *The Kiss*. Originally placed in a set of doors called *The Gates of Hell*, it is based on a scene from Dante's *Divine Comedy*.

1886 US president Grover Cleveland accepts one of the world's most famous symbols, the Statue of Liberty, as a gift from the people of France. Marking the centenary of US independence, it stands 306 ft 8 in (93.5 m) high.

Comptometer

1887

Dorr E. Felt

The Comptometer was one of two calculating machines used in accounting offices from the late 19th to the mid-20th century. While its rival, the Burroughs machine (✱ *see* **page 156**), could produce a printed record, the Comptometer was faster. Invented by US engineer Dorr E. Felt, it was first used in 1887. As with the Burroughs machine, numbers were entered using columns of keys—one for units, one for tens, and so on. The result was displayed in a set of windows for clerks to copy out by hand.

Esperanto

1887

Ludwik Zamenhof

International cooperation is hampered by the fact that people in different countries speak different languages. Many people have tried to solve this problem by inventing a universal language. The only one that has had any success is Esperanto, invented in 1887 by Polish oculist Ludwik Zamenhof. Based on European languages, it has simple, regular rules. Some of these seem strange to English speakers: plural nouns demand plural adjectives, for instance. Despite this, more than 100,000 people can speak it.

Fractal curve

1887

Giuseppe Peano

A fractal curve is a wiggly line that looks the same however much it is magnified. An example is the coast of a country, which looks just as wiggly on a small-scale map as on the actual shore where sand meets sea. The first fractal curves were described by Italian mathematician Giuseppe Peano, in 1887. They were viewed as a mere curiosity until the 1970s, when Polish mathematician Benoit Mandelbrot investigated them in more detail. He used them to create some stunning computer graphics.

Gramophone

1887

Emile Berliner

The first recording machines made cylindrical records. In 1887, German engineer Emile Berliner, working in the US, came up with a better idea—discs. He coated metal with wax, recorded sound by cutting through the wax, then etched the metal to make a permanent record. The cutter moved from side to side, not up and down as in earlier machines. On playback, the needle followed this "lateral-cut" groove more faithfully, giving better reproduction. More importantly, discs could be stamped out by the thousand, making Berliner's gramophone the best choice for music lovers.

Horn channeled the sounds from the disc

Handle was used to keep the turntable moving around

Drive belt

Disc was played on a turntable

Steel needle was lowered onto the disc

GRAMOPHONE *Early Berliner gramophones had no motor, so listeners had to turn a handle. The discs were the same size as a CD but played for only about a minute.*

1886 Scottish writer Robert Louis Stevenson publishes *The Strange Case of Dr Jekyll and Mr Hyde*, about a doctor who can turn into a fiend. A "Jekyll and Hyde" will come to mean anyone with two sides to their character.

1887 Two more classic fictional characters are born when Scottish writer Sir Arthur Conan Doyle writes *A Study in Scarlet* featuring ace detective Sherlock Holmes and his friend Dr. Watson. The story will be followed by many others.

MAIL ORDER *The Sears, Roebuck catalog became a part of the American way of life, allowing people in rural areas to enjoy the fruits of the nation's prosperity.*

Mail order

1887

Richard Sears, Alvah Roebuck

Richard Sears thought up mail order while working for a US railroad company. Acquiring some unwanted watches, he sold them by mail to other railroad workers. He used the profits to set up a company, which by 1887 had produced the first mail-order catalog. He later formed a new company with repairman Alvah Roebuck. By 1894, the Sears, Roebuck catalog was 507 pages thick.

High-voltage power transmission

1887

Sebastian de Ferranti

In the 1880s, there were many rival electricity systems. But British engineer Sebastian de Ferranti could see the future. Electricity would be generated in big power stations outside cities, not little ones inside them, and transmitted at high voltage. In 1887, he designed a giant power station at Deptford, just outside London, and cables that could take 10,000 volts. The station's directors pushed him out in 1891, and it was not completed to his plan. But Ferranti was right: high-voltage transmission is universal today.

Steam tricycle

1887

Leon Serpollet

At one time it looked as though steam, not gasoline, might be best for motor vehicles. Several inventors designed steam tricycles in the 1880s. In 1887, French engineer Leon Serpollet overcame their chief problem with a boiler that produced instant steam. He built this into a tricycle, then showed it off by driving it 282 miles (451 km) from Paris to Lyon. Later, he built steam cars. In 1903, one reached 80 mph (130 km/h).

Pneumatic tire

1888

Robert Thomson, John Dunlop

British inventor Robert Thomson patented air-filled leather tires in 1845, but these were never as popular as solid rubber ones. The first successful pneumatic tire was patented in 1888 by Scottish vet John Dunlop, after he experimented with rubber tubing on the wheels of his son's tricycle. The finished product was protected by a canvas cover. Dunlop's tire was ideal for bicycles and later became essential for cars.

Kodak camera

1888

George Eastman

Until 1888, photography was difficult. Cameras were complicated, and users had to process their own pictures. US businessman George Eastman changed that with his Kodak camera. It was simple to use and came already loaded with film. After use, the camera went back to Eastman, who returned it, reloaded, along with the pictures. With his slogan, "You press the button, we do the rest," Eastman became a rich man.

Radio waves

1888

James Clerk Maxwell, Heinrich Hertz

In 1864, Scottish physicist James Clerk Maxwell predicted the existence of electromagnetic waves moving at the speed of light. German physicist Heinrich Hertz wanted to generate such waves and see if they behaved like

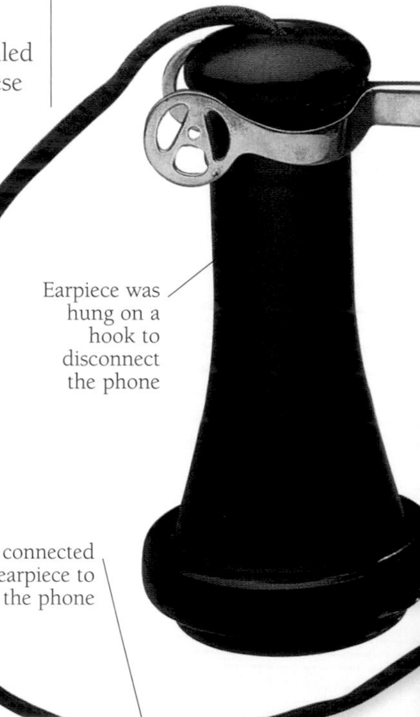

AUTOMATIC TELEPHONE EXCHANGE *This 1905 phone was designed for use with a Strowger exchange. Automatic dialing was available for local calls only.*

1888 Dutch painter Vincent van Gogh cracks under the strain of living with French painter Paul Gauguin in the south of France. He cuts off part of his left ear and later paints a portrait of himself with his head bandaged.

1889 A baby is born in the town of Branau, 30 miles (50 km) north of Salzburg, Austria. His father's surname, earlier changed from Schicklgruber, is Hitler. The baby is named Adolf. Fifty years on, he will plunge the world into war.

light, to find out if light itself was electromagnetic. He found that electrical sparks produced waves that could be received on a distant loop of wire, producing more sparks. He had discovered radio waves. Further experiments showed that they did behave much like light. Satisfied with these discoveries, complete by 1888, Hertz made no further use of them.

Automatic telephone exchange

1889

Almon B. Strowger

Telephone exchanges are needed to connect phones to each other. At first, connections were made by operators pushing plugs into sockets. Then, in 1889, Kansas City funeral director Almon B. Strowger, fed up with his operator diverting calls to a rival, devised the first successful automatic telephone switch. Callers could control it from their own phone by sending groups of electrical pulses down the line. The first automatic exchange opened at La Porte, Indiana, in 1892. At first, callers generated the control pulses by repeatedly pushing a button. Later, the more convenient rotary dial mechanism made this process automatic, too. (*See also* **Getting Connected**.)

Tabulating machine

1889

Herman Hollerith

As the population of the US grew, classifying the people took longer. Engineer Herman Hollerith decided to mechanize the 1890 census. Citizens were recorded as holes punched in a card. Hollerith's "tabulating" machines then sorted and counted the cards at high speed.

GETTING CONNECTED

TELEPHONES WOULD NOT WORK without exchanges. Your phone would have to be permanently connected to every other phone in the world, just in case you wanted to call it. In reality, connections are set up only when they are needed, by routing a call through a number of switches that connect you first to the exchange that handles the phone you want then to that particular phone.

An operator on a telephone exchange board connects callers to the number they ask for.

CALLING THE OPERATOR
Before automatic exchanges, all calls were connected by operators. To make a call, you would lift the receiver and, on some systems, alert the operator by turning a handle. You would then ask for the number you wanted and the operator would make the connection by plugging your line into a switchboard.

STROWGER'S SYSTEM
Strowger's basic idea was a remote-controlled switch that could connect one phone to any of several others. It was operated by electric pulses from the user's telephone line. Electromagnets and ratchets moved a connector to one of 10 rows of contacts, then along the selected row to reach the exact phone required.

1889 French engineer Gustave Eiffel builds a spectacular iron tower for the Paris World's Fair. It beats 100 other entries in a competition, pushing technology to its limits. Not everyone likes it, but it will become the emblem of Paris.

1889 In November, US investigative journalist Nellie Bly sets out to beat Jules Verne's fictional hero Phileas Fogg and travel around the world in less than 80 days. She does it in 72 days, 6 hours, 11 minutes, and 14 seconds.

Halftone screen

1890

Max Levy, Louis Levy

Black-and-white photos, with all their tones of gray, are printed by the halftone process. This turns them into dots—large ones in dark areas, small ones in paler areas. In the original process, the dots were made by copying the photo with a camera that had a screen carrying crisscross lines just in front of the film. The first successful halftone screen was made in 1890 by US inventors Max and Louis Levy. They cemented together two sheets of glass, each ruled with straight lines. Screens like this were in use until the 1970s.

Tetanus immunization

1890

Emil Behring, Kitasato Shibasaburo

Tetanus, or lockjaw, is an infection caused by germs in soil. These can breed inside a cut, producing poisons that make muscles contract and may cause death. In 1890, German and Japanese bacteriologists Emil Behring and Kitasato Shibasaburo found they could protect animals from tetanus by injecting serum from another infected animal. Today, most people in the West receive routine immunization with tetanus vaccine. If they suffer a deep, dirty cut, they will need only a booster dose to ensure continued protection.

TETANUS IMMUNIZATION *Tetanus vaccine, or toxoid, contains the poison produced by tetanus germs, made safe by heat or chemicals.*

Steam-powered airplane

1890

Clèment Ader

French engineer Clèment Ader was very nearly the first person to fly a plane. His steam-powered aircraft, the *Eole*, managed a longer flight than the more famous Wright brothers (✱ *see* **page 175**), but it didn't quite count. On October 9, 1890, Ader managed a 160 ft (50 m) "flight" near Paris, but the machine wasn't really flying because it wasn't under control. The experiment proved that a steam engine was just too heavy for flight.

Surgical gloves

1890

William Halsted

By the 1880s, many surgeons were convinced that germs were a threat to their patients. Sterilization and antiseptics could help, but what about the surgeon's hands? They were a source of infection, even when scrubbed, but could not be replaced by instruments. US surgeon William Halsted found the answer in 1890—he invented the thin rubber gloves that all surgeons wear today.

Gaslight photographic paper

1891

Leo Baekeland

In the 1880s, photographers made prints by daylight. This restricted their hours of work. The first photographic paper that worked in artificial light—usually gaslight—was invented by Belgian-US chemist Leo Baekeland in 1891. He sold his Velox paper to George Eastman in 1898, helping make photography affordable for all.

Long-distance telephone cable

1892

Oliver Heaviside, Michael Pupin

Early long-distance telephone calls suffered from blurring and distortion, an effect already noticed on telegraph cables. It could make it impossible to understand what someone was saying. Scientists were baffled until British telegraph engineer Oliver Heaviside invented a new mathematical method that showed where the problem lay. He published his results in 1892, and in 1900 US physicist Michael Pupin used them to improve long-distance lines by adding special coils at regular intervals.

Vacuum bottle

1892

James Dewar

Scottish physicist James (later Sir James) Dewar was one of the first to make oxygen so cold that it turned into a liquid. But he had storage problems, because at –183°C oxygen turns back to gas. So he invented a special bottle, the Dewar flask. It was made of two layers of glass, silvered like a mirror and with a vacuum between them. Infrared radiation, or radiant heat, was reflected from the silvering, while the vacuum stopped heat from being carried in through air currents.

Double walls greatly reduce heat transfer by air currents

VACUUM BOTTLE *Dewar flasks can be made of metal as well as glass. This model of a metal flask has been cut open to reveal its double wall. Metal flasks are not easy to make but have the advantage of being stronger and safer than glass flasks.*

1890 Norwegian dramatist Henrik Ibsen challenges accepted attitudes to women with his realistic play *Hedda Gabler*. Ignoring the conventions of 19th-century drama, Ibsen creates a powerful new form of theater.

1891 New York City opens a new concert hall, financed by industrialist Andrew Carnegie. Russian composer Tchaikovsky is guest conductor during its first week. Most important American and visiting musicians will perform here.

VISCOSE RAYON *This material has a glamorous, glossy finish. By 1903, when these samples were made, it was beginning to rival natural silk.*

MOVING PICTURE *Using a Kinetoscope was nothing like going to the movies. Peering through the eyepiece, the viewer saw a moving image that lasted about as long as a modern TV commercial.*

Viscose rayon

1892

Charles Cross, Edward Bevan, Clayton Beadle

The first artificial silk was expensive because it was made by a slow, dangerous method (✱ *see* **page 156**). In 1892, three British chemists, Charles Cross, Edward Bevan, and Clayton Beadle, invented the viscose process. Cellulose is converted into nonflammable cellulose xanthate and dissolved in caustic soda to form a yellow, sticky liquid. This is squirted through nozzles and reacts with further chemicals to make a silky artificial fiber called viscose rayon.

Viruses

1892

Dmitry Ivanovsky, Martinus Beijerinck

A virus is an infectious particle that can multiply only inside a living cell. It is basically just a set of genes wrapped in a protective coating. It takes over a plant or animal cell, forcing it to make copies of the invader. The first scientist to realize that bacteria were not the only infective agents was Russian micro-biologist Dmitry Ivanovsky. He published a paper on a virus infection of tobacco plants in 1892. Dutch botanist Martinus Beijerinck did similar work in 1898. Both discovered that viruses were far smaller than bacteria and invisible under an ordinary microscope.

Moving picture

1893

William Dickson, Thomas Edison

It is not clear who invented movies. A young US engineer, William Dickson, who worked for Thomas Edison, has a good claim. Edison thought that phonograph listeners might like something to watch and asked Dickson to provide it. Dickson devised a machine, the Kinetograph, which took 40 pictures each second on a long strip of film. The film was then viewed, by one person at a time, in another machine, the Kinetoscope. It held only 50 ft (15 m) of film, so a movie lasted only 20 seconds.

Film passed through in a continuous loop

1892 In the US, a five-month struggle between a big trade union and bosses of the steel industry starts in Homestead, Pennsylvania, after workers' wages are cut. The strike ends violently with several deaths.

1893 Norwegian painter Edvard Munch produces *The Scream*, a painting that conveys intense feelings of anxiety and emotional torment. It will become one of the most famous examples of the style known as expressionism.

Zipper

1893

Whitcomb Judson, Gideon Sundback

Chicago engineer Whitcomb Judson got tired of lacing his boots and invented a fastener that hooked them up with one pull. He patented it in 1893, but it tended to come unhooked. Swedish engineer Gideon Sundback realized that the hooks were the problem. By 1914 he had developed the modern fastener, with cups, not hooks, locking together. It was used in 1923 for a boot called the Zipper, and the name stuck.

Bubonic plague agent

1894

Kitasato Shibasaburo, Alexandre Yersin

Bubonic plague is a deadly disease carried by rat fleas. It has killed millions in repeated epidemics. Thanks to the discoveries of Japanese and Swiss bacteriologists Kitasato Shibasaburo and Alexandre Yersin in 1894, we now know that it is caused by a type of germ known as a bacillus. It is usually called *Yersinia pestis* in honor of Yersin's contribution.

Phototypesetting

1894

Eugene Porzolt

Photography offers an alternative to metal type. Letters can be projected on to film. The first phototypesetting machine, designed in 1894 by Hungarian engineer Eugene Porzolt, was a failure. But from the 1960s, with computers controlling the process, phototypesetting became the way most words got printed. Computers now store letter shapes in digital form. So, like metal type, phototypesetting itself is now a thing of the past.

Radio communication

1894

Guglielmo Marconi

Italian inventor Guglielmo Marconi started experimenting with radio waves in 1894, when he was only 19. Others, such as the British and Russian physicists Oliver Lodge and Alexander Popov, did the same. But it was Marconi who really got radio going. Within a year, he was sending signals 1.25 miles (2 km). By 1896, he was in Britain and had the world's first radio patent. After much further development, it was Marconi's "wireless telegraph" that sent the distress signals from the sinking ship *Titanic* in 1912.

Argon

1894

Lord Rayleigh, William Ramsay

Argon is known as an inert gas because it does not react chemically. It is used in light bulbs because it makes the filament last longer. It was discovered by British physicist Lord Rayleigh, who noticed that nitrogen from air was denser than nitrogen from chemicals. Both he and British chemist William (later Sir William) Ramsay thought that atmospheric nitrogen might be contaminated with an unknown, heavier gas. They both found it in 1894. Its name "argon" is Greek for "inactive."

Movies

1895

Auguste Lumière, Louis Lumière

Movies did not become a truly theatrical experience until French brothers Auguste and Louis Lumière invented the Cinématographe, the first system that could show an audience a moving picture that ran for several minutes. Their machine acted as both camera and projector. It gave its first public performance on December 28, 1895, in Paris. The program of 12 short films, including one showing Lumière factory workers, caused a sensation.

Helium on Earth

1895

William Ramsay

Helium, the gas that is used to fill party balloons, was first found on Earth by William Ramsay in 1895. He heated a mineral called cleveite, which contains uranium, and discovered that it gave off a gas. The gas's spectrum contained a yellow line matching that of helium in the sun, which proved its identity. Swedish chemists Nils Langlet and Per Cleve also found the gas at about the same time. Later, Ramsay and British chemist Frederick Soddy discovered that helium is produced whenever radioactive elements decay.

1893 On December 23, Richard Strauss conducts the first performance of German composer Engelbert Humperdinck's tuneful opera *Hansel and Gretel*. The story, by Humperdinck's sister Adelheid, is based on a well-known folk tale.

1894 London's Tower Bridge, started in 1886, finally opens. Built by Sir Horace Jones and Sir John Wolfe Barry, and powered by steam, it is London's only moving bridge. Its twin towers will become a well-known symbol of the city.

Liquid air

1895

Carl von Linde

If air is made cold enough, it turns into a liquid. The drop in temperature is produced by compressing air, letting it cool, then letting it expand so that it cools still further. The first to do this on a large scale was German engineer Carl von Linde. His system, invented in 1895, produced a continuous stream of liquid air. He later distilled air to produce liquid nitrogen, used as a coolant, and liquid oxygen, used in steel making.

X-rays

1895

Wilhelm Röntgen

German physicist Wilhelm Röntgen discovered X-rays in 1895 while he was investigating cathode rays (electrical discharges inside a tube containing very little air). He noticed that when the tube was working, some crystals lying nearby glowed, even though the tube was shielded so that no light could escape from it. He figured out that the cathode rays, hitting the glass of the tube, were producing other rays that made the crystals glow. He did some further experiments, which showed that the rays could pass through solid objects and affect photographic plates. This led him to make the first ever X-ray picture. At first, Röntgen was not sure that he should announce his discovery. He was worried that other scientists might not believe him. But soon everyone was talking about the new rays that made hidden things visible.

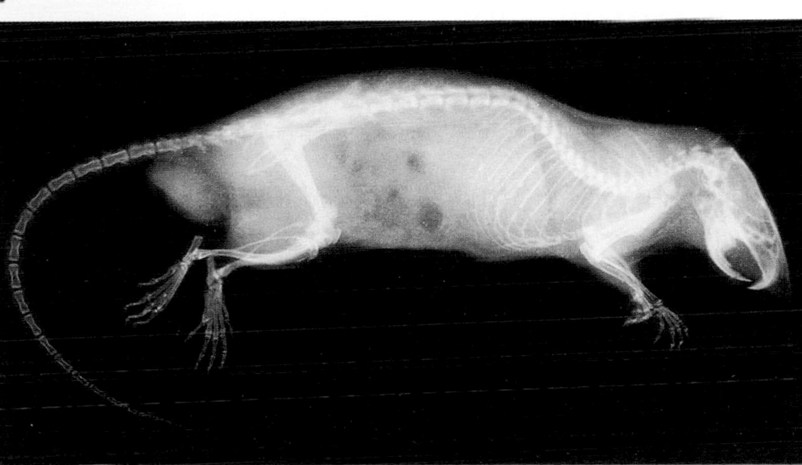

X-RAYS *Small animals like this rat made good subjects for early experimenters with X-rays. For the first time, their skeletons could be seen without dissection.*

Wheel guided the film into the mechanism

Rotating shutter has red, green, and blue apertures to give the film color

Lenses for red, green, and blue images

Handle was turned to show the film

Film wound onto a spool

MOVIES *The early movie camera (left) was hand-cranked. The projector (right) could show films in color.*

Radiation from uranium

1896

Henri Becquerel

French physicist Henri Becquerel wanted to see if crystals that glowed after exposure to sunlight gave out X-rays. In 1896, he found that certain uranium salts affected a wrapped-up photographic plate when placed on it in sunlight. Becquerel thought that sunlight may have made the crystals produce X-rays, which went through the wrapping. Then he discovered that the experiment worked in the dark. The crystals gave out penetrating radiation all by themselves.

1895 In April, the song *Waltzing Matilda*, by "Banjo" Paterson, is performed in Winton, Queensland, Australia, for the first time. Its title means "carrying a bag of belongings, or swag," and it tells the story of a wandering laborer, or swagman.

1896 The ancient Greek Olympic Games are revived in Athens by Pierre Fredi, Baron de Coubertin. Fourteen nations take part in the all-male competition. It includes a new event, the marathon, which is won by a Greek shepherd.

Surgical mask

1896

Johannes von Mikulicz-Radecki

With sterilization of instruments and surgical gloves in frequent use, one of the last sources of infection in the operating room was the surgeon's own breath. In 1896, a gifted Polish surgeon working in Germany, Johannes von Mikulicz-Radecki, blocked up this loophole by placing gauze over his mouth to form the first surgical mask.

Toothpaste in a tube

1896

William Colgate

Toothpaste existed in the 19th century but was packaged in jars. The first person to put it in a tube was US dentist Washington Sheffield. His Creme Dentifrice of 1892 was not very popular, and it was eclipsed four years later with the marketing of Colgate Ribbon Dental Cream by New York soap and candlemaker William Colgate. He changed the shape of the tube nozzle, and described the result with the successful slogan "Comes out a ribbon, lies flat on the brush."

Sphygmomanometer

1896

Scipione Riva-Rocci

The usual instrument for measuring blood pressure, the sphygmomanometer, was invented in 1896 by Scipione Riva-Rocci, an Italian children's doctor. A cuff around the arm is inflated until the blood stops flowing. The air pressure is then reduced until the flow just starts again, indicating the maximum blood pressure. Doctors now listen to the flow with a stethoscope, a refinement added in 1905 by Russian surgeon N. S. Korotkoff. This allows them to measure the minimum pressure as well.

SPHYGMOMANOMETER *This 1905 instrument is similar to those used today. The rubber bulb pumps air into the arm cuff.*

Blood pressure reading taken from here

TOOTHPASTE IN A TUBE *People who were accustomed to toothpaste from a jar seem to have had trouble with it when it came out of a tube, but Colgate's toothpaste behaved itself.*

Cathode ray oscilloscope

1897

Ferdinand Braun

Electric waves are invisible, so the cathode ray oscilloscope, which displays electrical signals on a screen, is a valuable tool. It was invented in 1897 by German physicist Ferdinand Braun. He took the still-experimental cathode ray tube (a glass tube containing very little air, in which a negative electrode, or cathode, gives off electric particles) and added magnetic coils to move the particles horizontally and vertically in response to signals. In this way, Braun managed to draw patterns on a screen inside the tube.

Exhaust casing received the spent steam

Diesel engine

1897

Rudolf Diesel

In 1892, German engineer Rudolf Diesel patented an engine that gave more power for less fuel. It compressed its fuel and air to a much higher pressure than a gasoline engine, making it so hot that it burned without the aid of a spark. In 1897, he built a fully developed engine, which

1896 Popular British newspaper the *Daily Mail* is founded by media tycoon Alfred Harmsworth. It includes features such as a women's column, competitions, and stories and will soon change the nature of newspaper publishing.

1897 Vampires get a boost from British writer Bram Stoker's horror novel *Dracula*. He bases it on the ancient Slavic religious belief that a buried body that does not decompose will leave its grave at night to drink human blood.

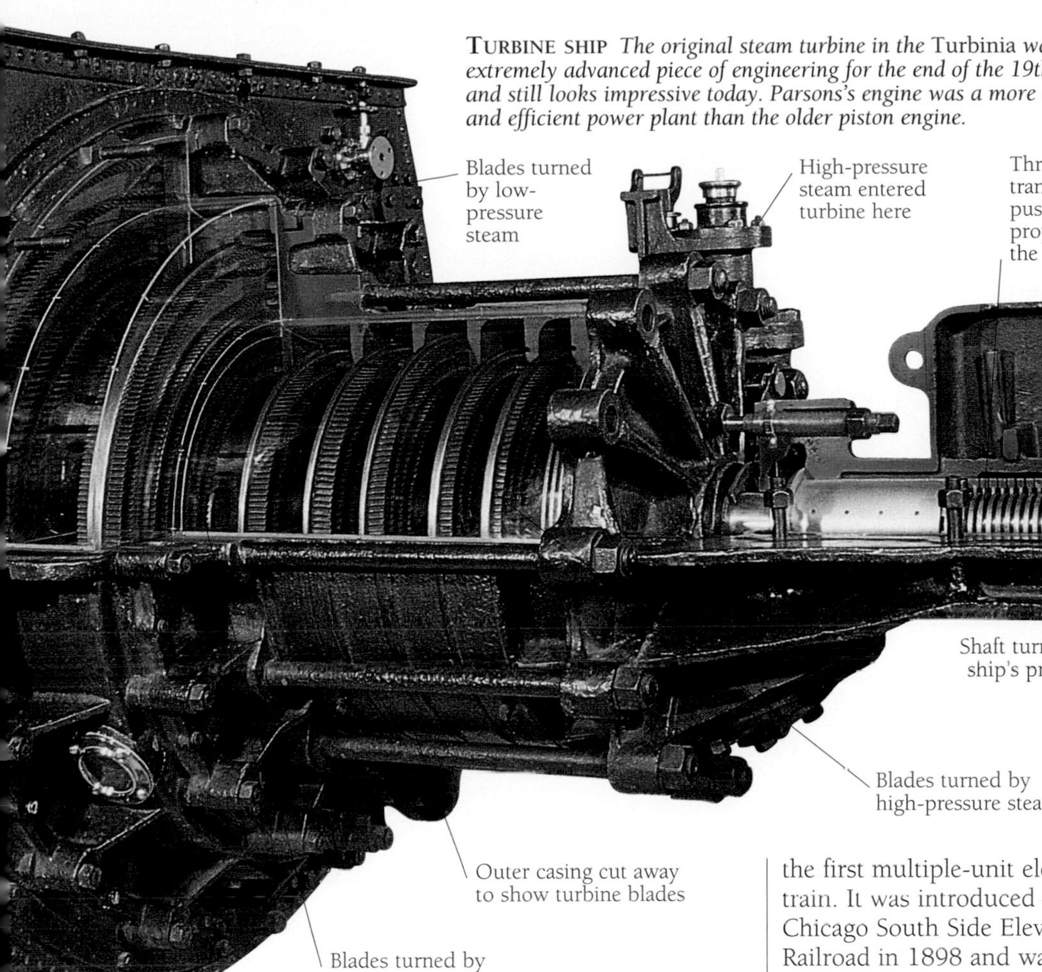

TURBINE SHIP *The original steam turbine in the* Turbinia *was an extremely advanced piece of engineering for the end of the 19th century and still looks impressive today. Parsons's engine was a more compact and efficient power plant than the older piston engine.*

delivered 25 horsepower from a single cylinder. Diesel engines can be expensive, heavy, and noisy but are unbeatable where fuel consumption really counts.

Electron

1897

J. J. Thomson

British physicist J. J. (later Sir J. J.) Thomson was the first person to show that atoms contain smaller particles. He studied cathode rays, and, by subjecting the rays to electric and magnetic fields, he showed in 1897 that they consisted of negatively charged particles. Thomson discovered that it made no difference what materials he used, and he concluded that the particles existed in everything. He believed that they were lighter and could move faster than any atom and realized that he had found something new. We now call the particles electrons.

Multiple-unit electric train

1897

Frank Sprague

Instead of one powerful locomotive at the front, many electric trains have smaller driving motors at several points along their length. This gives better acceleration and more passenger space, but the motors have to work together so that all the coaches speed up and slow down at the same rate. In 1897, US engineer Frank Sprague managed to control separate motors in this way and used them in the first multiple-unit electric train. It was introduced on the Chicago South Side Elevated Railroad in 1898 and was later used on New York's Manhattan Elevated Railway.

Transmission of malaria by mosquito

1897

Ronald Ross

Malaria is a disease caused by tiny parasites living in the blood. Patients suffer recurrent chills and sweats. Nobody knew how the parasites got there until British bacteriologist Ronald (later Sir Ronald) Ross studied infected birds in India. He proved in 1897 that the parasites are carried by mosquitoes and injected when they bite. A year later, three Italian scientists showed that only one mosquito, the *Anopheles*, gives malaria to humans.

Turbine ship

1897

Charles Parsons

Steamships changed forever when British engineer Charles (later Sir Charles) Parsons launched *Turbinia*, the first ship powered by his steam turbine. In 1897, he demonstrated it to the Royal Navy near Portsmouth, England. Navy ships were powered by piston engines, and *Turbinia* made them look ridiculous as it darted among them at the record speed of 34 knots (43 mph or 69 km/h). Tests in other ships confirmed the turbine's superiority.

Conditioned reflex

1898

Ivan Pavlov

A reflex is an automatic response, such as pulling a hand away from a hot object. In 1898, Russian scientist Ivan Pavlov started experiments that led him to discover a more complicated kind of reflex. When investigating digestion in dogs, he found that the sound of food being prepared made their mouths water. He later found he could train them to salivate whenever a bell was sounded. Pavlov called this kind of reflex conditional, because it happened only after learning, but it is now usually called a conditioned reflex.

1897 The world's first mass marathon is run in the US from Hopkinton, Massachusetts, to Boston—just over 26 miles (42 km). It will be repeated every April, but women will not be allowed to compete for another 75 years.

1898 Canadian adventurer Joshua Slocum reaches Newport on the US' northeast coast to become the first person to sail around the world single-handedly. He set out from Boston in a 95-year-old boat more than three years earlier.

Magnetic recording

1898

Valdemar Poulsen

Danish telephone engineer Valdemar Poulsen was worried by one obvious defect of the telephone. Unlike the telegraph, it didn't work without someone there to answer it. So in 1898, he invented the first telephone answering machine, the Telegraphone. To do so, he had to invent a totally new technology—magnetic recording. His machine recorded telephone messages on a reel of thin steel wire and could also be used for dictation. (* *See also* **Recording with Magnetism**.)

Polonium

1898

Marie Curie, Pierre Curie

Polonium is a very rare element. Highly radioactive, it can be used to discharge unwanted static electricity. The best source is pitchblende, but 1,100 tons (1,000 tonnes) of this yield only 40 mg of polonium. Polonium was the first element to be revealed by its radioactivity, and it was discovered by radioactivity pioneers Marie and Pierre Curie in 1898. They called it polonium after Marie's native country, Poland.

ASPIRIN *Soluble aspirin from Bayer is seen here in its original packaging.*

Radium

1898

Marie Curie, Pierre Curie

See **pages 170–171** for the story of how Marie and Pierre Curie discovered radium and made radiotherapy possible.

Aspirin

1899

Felix Hoffman

Other drugs have partly replaced aspirin as a painkiller, but it is still used for treating strokes and heart attacks. Chemically related to a plant extract, salicylic acid, it was first made by German chemist Felix Hoffman, whose father may have taken the acid for rheumatism. The compound was first marketed by Bayer, a German company, in 1899.

Street sweeper

1900

Florence Parpart

Florence Parpart had several patents to her name, including an improved icebox (an early form of refrigerator) that was easier to clean and a machine for sweeping the city streets. It was not the first street sweeper, but it became one of the most widely used.

RIGID AIRSHIP *Airships like this were used by the Royal Naval Air Service in World War I.*

Rudder steered the airship left or right

Cabin for the crew was called a gondola

Escalator

1900

George Wheeler, Charles Seeberger

The first escalator, invented by US engineer Jesse Reno, was just a sloping, moving walkway with a grooved tread to stop passengers from slipping. It wasn't even called an escalator. This name was used by US engineer Charles Seeberger to describe a design with folding steps originally invented by George Wheeler. Seeberger joined the Otis Elevator Company, which exhibited the escalator at the 1900 Paris Exposition. Later, the company added the grooved tread from Reno's design to complete the escalator we know today.

Fingerprinting

1900

Francis Galton, Edward Henry

Fingerprints are a good way of tracking down criminals, but they work only because there is a way of classifying them. Without this, a new print could not be compared with those on record. British scientist Francis (later Sir Francis) Galton, having confirmed that every fingerprint is different, devised a basic classification system. Police officer Edward (later Sir Edward) Henry developed this into the system widely used today. It was published in 1900. Two years later, fingerprints made their first appearance in court.

1899 What will become one of the most played piano pieces of all time, *Maple Leaf Rag*, is published in Missouri by US composer and pianist Scott Joplin. A later attempt by Joplin to break into opera will prove unsuccessful.

1899 Three years of war begin in South Africa when the Boers (descendants of the original Dutch settlers), led by Paul Kruger, start fighting with the British. Resentment had built up over the huge influx of Britons seeking gold there.

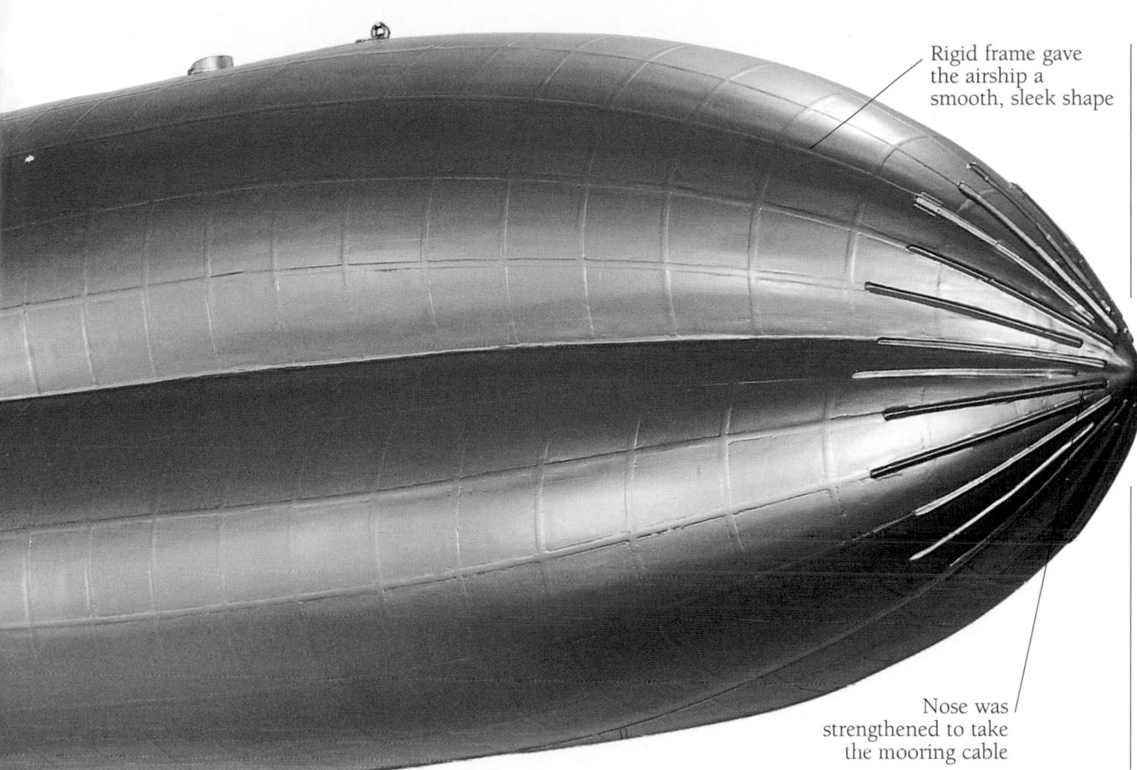

Rigid airship

1900

Ferdinand von Zeppelin

The first airships were just elongated balloons with an engine and passenger compartment. In 1900, German general Count Ferdinand von Zeppelin built the first airship with a rigid frame. Its lifting gas was held in separate gas bags inside the frame, allowing a more aerodynamic shape. Zeppelins, as they became known, were used as bombers in World War I. After this they carried passengers, until public confidence was destroyed in 1937 when the *Hindenburg* caught fire in a dramatic accident, killing 35 passengers.

Quantum theory

1900

Max Planck

In 1900, physicists had some problems. One was that the light from red-hot objects was not of the expected color. German physicist Max Planck found he could predict the color correctly by assuming that energy was radiated only in multiples of a fixed amount, or quantum. This also explained why the energy of electrons ejected from metals by light depended on the color, not the brightness, of the light. Over the next 30 years, quantum theory allowed Niels Bohr, Erwin Schrödinger, Werner Heisenberg, and others to develop a new view of the world in which matter and energy could be both waves and particles (✳ *see* **page 190**). This has transformed physics.

RECORDING WITH MAGNETISM

RECORDINGS ON WAX WERE FRAGILE and quickly wore out. The alternative, magnetic recording, also had problems, including noise and distortion. Both were eventually conquered. Magnetic recording proved ideal for recording computer data and television pictures. Its use with computers has more recently developed into digital magnetic recording, which produces the near-perfect tapes used to make CDs.

Valdemar Poulsen, inventor of magnetic recording

FROM METAL TO PLASTIC
Early magnetic recordings were made on steel wire or tape. During World War II, the first modern recorder, the Magnetophon, was developed by AEG and BASF in Germany. Like all later machines, it used coated plastic tape.

VIDEO RECORDING
Video signals contain very high frequencies. An ordinary recorder would need to run very fast to record these. Video recorders, invented in 1956, have a recording head that scans the tape at a high enough speed to record these frequencies.

Ampex VR1000 video recorder from about 1956

DIGITAL RECORDING
Since about 1950, computers have used magnetic recording for storing data. Unlike sound, data can be recorded without errors. Sound converted into digital form before recording gives a perfection unknown to the pioneers.

1900 Between 6,000 and 12,000 people die as a result of the Galveston hurricane, which devastates the port city of Galveston, Texas, in early September. The category 4 hurricane is the deadliest natural disaster in US history.

1900 US tennis player Dwight F. Davis donates a cup to be awarded at an annual international lawn-tennis tournament for men. It will become known as the Davis Cup. Intended for amateurs, it will later become professional.

PARTNERS IN DISCOVERY

Marie and Pierre Curie discover radium and make radiotherapy possible

HAPPY FAMILY
Marie and Pierre Curie were devoted to each other and their children as well as to science. They are seen here in 1904, two years before Pierre's tragic death, with their daughter Irene, who was then aged seven.

In 1891, Marie Sklodowska arrived in Paris, aged 23. She had done well in school in Poland, and now, after eight years as a governess, she had saved enough money for college. She registered at the Sorbonne, the university in Paris, and became a student, studying physical science and mathematics.

By 1894, Marie had her degree. Something else important happened that year, too. She met Professor Pierre Curie, and in 1895 they got married, forming one of science's most fruitful partnerships.

Marie decided to research the uranium radiation recently discovered by Henri Becquerel. She studied pitchblende, a mineral containing uranium, and found that it produced more radiation than the uranium alone could account for. It clearly contained something more "radioactive," as she called it, than uranium. With Pierre, she dissolved pitchblende in chemicals to produce compounds they could separate out. Work stopped briefly in 1897 for the birth of Marie's first daughter.

In the summer of 1898, the Curies found a new radioactive element, polonium, but there was more radiation still unaccounted for. Its source must be very radioactive indeed. Although they hadn't isolated it yet, they dubbed it radium, announcing their discovery in December.

After another four years' work, Marie had produced just one-tenth of a gram of pure radium chloride. She became a Doctor of Science—the first woman in Europe to do so—and in 1903 shared the Nobel Prize for physics with Pierre and Becquerel. As the first woman to win a Nobel Prize, Marie became famous. She and Pierre both got great jobs.

In 1904, the Curies had another daughter. Then, in

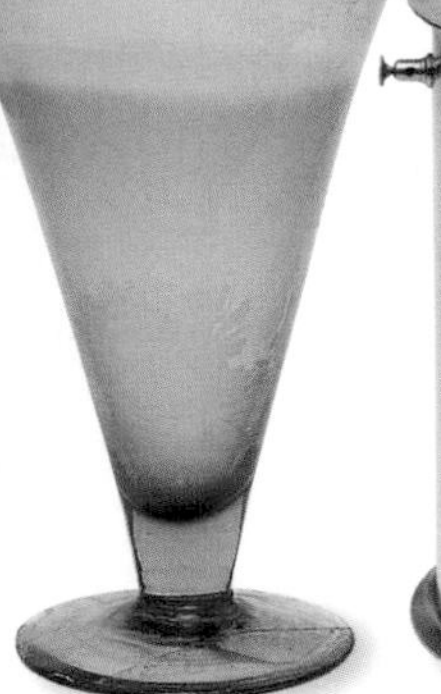

Quadrant electrometer built by Pierre Curie

Ionization chamber

Glass flask used by Marie Curie

Ionization chamber made by Pierre Curie

MEASURING RADIATION
The Curies had to build most of their research equipment for themselves. Radiation can make air conduct electricity, and Pierre developed several highly sensitive measuring instruments that made use of this effect.

1906, tragedy struck. Pierre was hit by a speeding cart and was killed. Marie had to take over Pierre's professorship at the Sorbonne—another first for a woman—and continue the research by herself. With the help of a colleague, she finally produced pure radium in 1910. The following year she received a second Nobel Prize. This time, there was nobody for her to share it with.

During World War I, Marie's research took a back seat. After the war, she toured the world, using her fame to drum up support for a new use of her great discovery. Doctors had found that radium, the most powerful source of radiation then known, could treat cancer. Marie Curie had made radiotherapy possible. Although radium is now little used for this purpose, it remains to remind us of a remarkable woman.

LASTING FAME
By 1927, when this photograph was taken, Marie Curie had earned her place at the Solvay Congress, a meeting of top physicists held in Brussels, Belgium. She is sitting in the front row, third from the left. Other famous names in the group include Bohr, Bragg, Einstein, Heisenberg, Lorentz, Pauli, Planck, and Schrödinger.

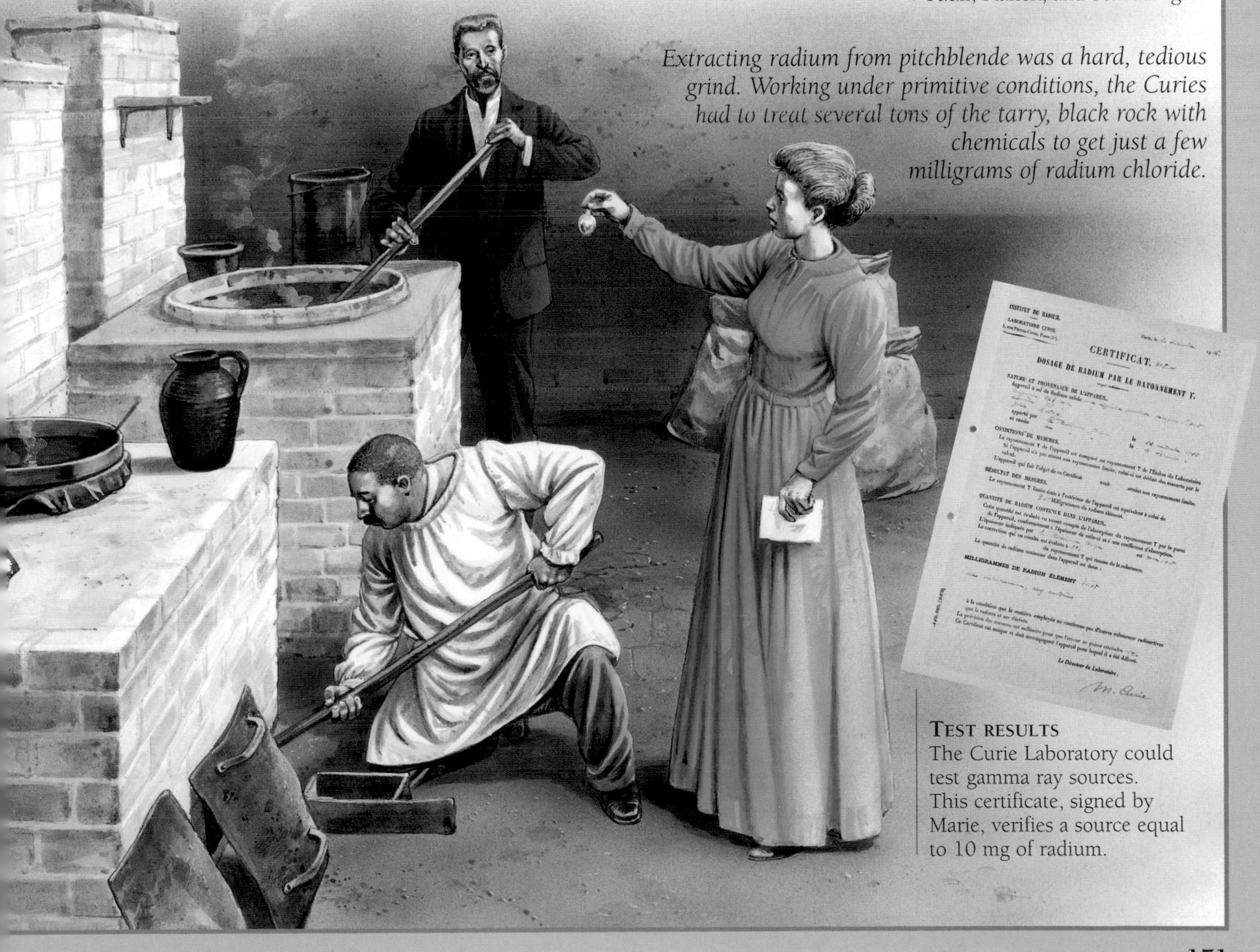

Extracting radium from pitchblende was a hard, tedious grind. Working under primitive conditions, the Curies had to treat several tons of the tarry, black rock with chemicals to get just a few milligrams of radium chloride.

TEST RESULTS
The Curie Laboratory could test gamma ray sources. This certificate, signed by Marie, verifies a source equal to 10 mg of radium.

INVENTIONS FOR EVERYONE

In the first 50 years of the 20th century, new inventions and discoveries transformed both everyday life and the world of science. Ordinary people got radio, lifesaving drugs, and cars. Scientists created a new physics that revealed the awesome energy hidden in matter. The modern world was nearly here.

Blood groups

1901

Karl Landsteiner

Early attempts at blood transfusion often killed the patient. In 1901, Karl Landsteiner, an Austrian pathologist (someone who studies the effects of disease on body tissues), showed why. Unless carefully matched, the red cells in one person's blood can destroy those of another. He discovered three groups of human blood, which he called A, B, and O. Only bloods of the same group could be safely mixed. He later found a fourth group, AB, and other groups have been discovered since. As well as ensuring safe transfusions, blood grouping can help eliminate suspects in murder cases.

Monorail

1901

Eugen Langen

Monorails are railroads with a single rail. The earliest was built in 1880 and had its rail underneath the cars. The more interesting suspended type, sometimes seen in amusement parks, has also been used for serious transportation. The earliest successful example, which still survives, is the monorail that runs along the Wupper River at Wuppertal in northwest Germany. It was designed in 1901 by Eugen Langen, a German engineer better known for his work on the internal combustion engine.

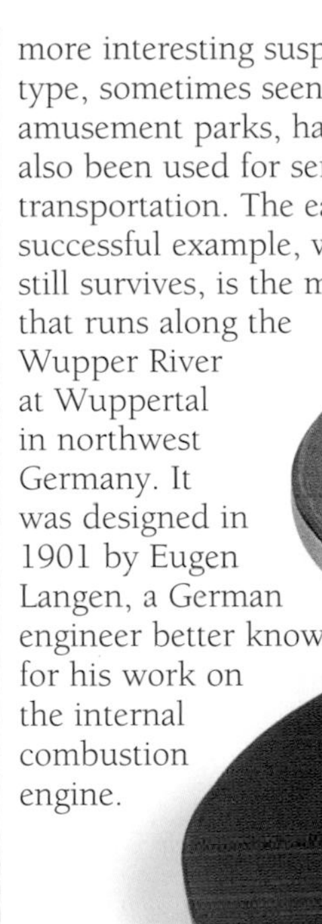

Disc brake *This Lockheed disc brake was made in about 1970.*

Safety razor

1901

King C. Gillette

King C. Gillette changed the life of men the world over when he followed the advice of a colleague and invented "something that would be used and thrown away." It was the disposable razor blade, which fitted into a new safety razor. Men may not have liked having to buy new blades all the time (by 1904, Gillette had sold more than 12 million), but they did appreciate a razor that was safer and quicker to use than the old, open-bladed straight razor.

Safety razor *An otherwise well-shaved King C. Gillette sports a moustache on this 1930s packaging.*

Disc brake

1902

Frederick Lanchester

Most modern cars have disc brakes. A steel disc is gripped between a pair of pads when braking is needed. The system was patented in 1902 by British car pioneer Frederick Lanchester, who, in 1896, also built the first all-British four-wheeled car. Lanchester's brake must have been rather noisy, because the pads were lined with copper. Another British engineer, Herbert Frood, substituted quieter, asbestos-lined pads in 1907.

Air-conditioning

1902

Willis Carrier

A combination of high temperature and high humidity is uncomfortable. When air is saturated with water vapor, sweat cannot evaporate. US engineer Willis Carrier realized in 1902 that refrigeration could deal with both heat and humidity. He designed an "apparatus for treating air," in which air was cooled to the temperature at which moisture condenses out of it. The water was then drained away, producing pleasantly cool, dry air.

1901 On New Year's Day, the six separate colonies of Australia become states in a new federation, the Commonwealth of Australia. It has an independent government, but it is still ruled by Britain's Queen Victoria.

1902 Britain's most exclusive club is formed as Edward VII founds the Order of Merit, an honor given for services to science or art. Only 24 people can hold it at any one time. The first female OM will be Florence Nightingale.

Hormones

1902

William Bayliss, Ernest Starling

Hormones are chemicals that control the body, such as adrenaline, which makes the heart pound in times of stress. The first hormone was discovered in 1902 by British physiologists (people who study how living things work) William (later Sir William) Bayliss and Ernest Starling. They found that the digestive system puts a chemical into the bloodstream when food reaches it, making the pancreas secrete digestive juice. They called the chemical secretin. Starling later coined the word "hormone" from the Greek for "setting in motion."

Tea-making alarm clock

1902

Frank Clarke

Although the British love their early morning tea, few can have risked Frank Clarke's 1902 automatic tea maker to get it. It was perhaps a little ahead of the technology. While you dozed, clockwork struck a match that lit a flame under a kettle. When the water boiled, the steam operated a mechanism that tipped the kettle to pour water into the pot and sounded an alarm—as if you'd need one!

Spark plug

1902

Robert Bosch, Gottlob Honold

A common problem with early internal combustion engines was how to ignite the fuel. One way was with sparks made by passing electricity through moving contacts inside the cylinder. In 1902, a German engineer, Gottlob Honold, who worked for electrical engineer Robert Bosch, invented a better method. He applied a much higher voltage to contacts with a fixed gap between them—a spark plug. Ignition was now controlled electrically.

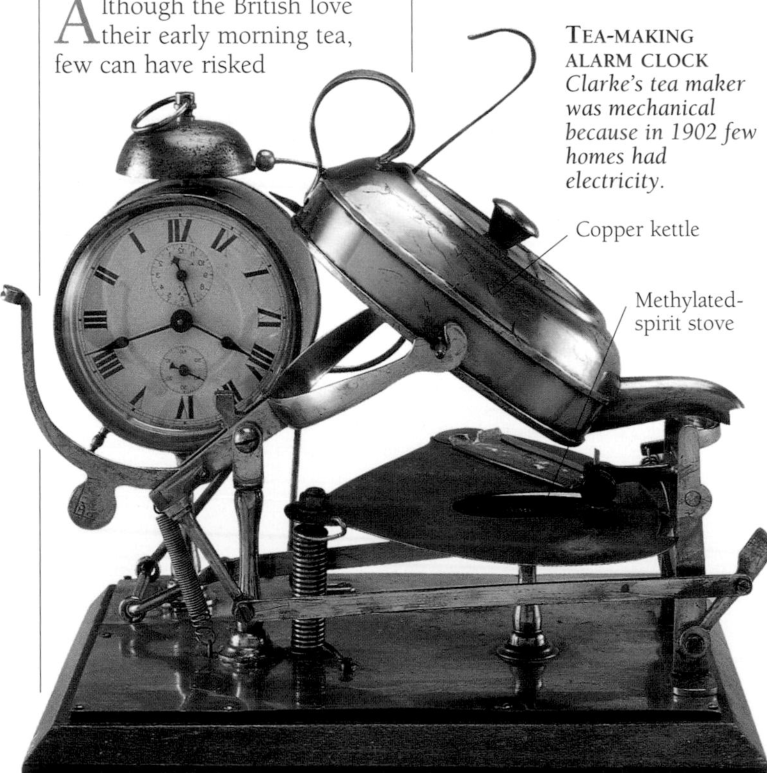

Tea-making alarm clock *Clarke's tea maker was mechanical because in 1902 few homes had electricity.*

Teddy bear

1902

Morris Michtom, Margarete Steiff

Popular US president Theodore "Teddy" Roosevelt became even more popular in 1902, when he went on a hunting expedition but refused to shoot a defenseless bear cub. Cashing in on this, New York retailer Morris Michtom began selling plush-covered bears with shoe-button eyes and jointed limbs, calling them "Teddy's Bears." They were a huge success, and their name soon became "teddy bears." At about the same time, German designer Margarete Steiff started making similar bears, which became bestsellers.

Cotton fabric stretched tightly over the framework of the wing

Propellers to push the plane through the air

Two wings linked by struts braced to combine their strength

Vacuum cleaner

1902

Hubert Booth

Early gadgets for removing dust just tried to blow it away. When British engineer Hubert Booth placed a handkerchief over his mouth and sucked the upholstery of a chair, the filth he collected convinced him that vacuum cleaning would be much better. His company, started in 1902, made cleaners, but they were so big they had to be parked outside the houses they cleaned.

Electrocardiogram

1903

Willem Einthoven

Doctors routinely check a patient's heart by making a record of its electrical activity, in what is called an electrocardiogram, or ECG. The first person to measure

1902 In April, French composer Claude Debussy's only opera, *Pelléas et Mélisande*, receives its first performance. Scottish soprano Mary Garden becomes famous for her interpretation of the female lead, Mélisande.

1902 British empire builder Cecil Rhodes dies. His will creates a new scholarship to Oxford University (for men only) meant to promote unity among English-speaking nations. Rhodes Scholarships will later be open to women.

the heart's electrical signals was Dutch physiologist Willem Einthoven. Using a sensitive instrument that he built in 1903, he set about finding out how a normal heart behaved.

Airplane *Striking features of the 1903 Wright* Flyer *included pusher propellers at the back, and no cockpit. The plane was controlled by wires that warped the wings.*

Multistage rocket

1903

Konstantin Tsiolkovsky

Russian scientist Konstantin Tsiolkovsky was thinking about interplanetary flight as long ago as 1895. In 1903, he suggested a way of getting large objects into space, using rockets with several stages that would be jettisoned as their fuel was used up. All major rockets are now built this way.

Windshield wiper

1903

Mary Anderson

Before windshield wipers, drivers had to get out of the car whenever they needed to clear rain or snow from the windshield. American entrepreneur Mary Anderson came up with a better idea: a swinging arm holding a wiper blade, operated by a handle inside the car. There was no electric motor as in today's cars. Another feature that seems strange now was that the wiper could be removed to give clearer vision in fine weather.

Airplane

1903

Orville Wright, Wilbur Wright

Although people had been going up in balloons since 1783, they were not satisfied. They wanted to fly like birds, not just drift with the wind. The first real flight was made in North Carolina on December 17, 1903. Watched by his brother Wilbur, US bicycle mechanic Orville Wright kept their fragile plane airborne for 12 seconds. The Wright brothers had at last solved the two great problems of flight: getting a machine to take off and controlling it in the air. (✱ *See also* **Up and away**.)

UP AND AWAY

IT TOOK A CENTURY of thought and experiment to conquer the air. The two big problems were lift and control, and the obvious masters of both were birds. One breakthrough came with the observation that a bird's tail is as important as its wings. The early pioneers also realized that flapping wings were not essential, which led to a practical airplane driven by a propeller.

GEORGE CAYLEY
A wealthy aristocrat, Cayley had established the basic shape of the airplane by 1799. It had a fuselage carrying fixed wings and a tail. After much research, he launched the first human-carrying glider in 1853.

OTTO LILIENTHAL
Lilienthal, a German engineer, studied the flight of birds before going on to develop effective fixed-wing gliders. In 1896, after thousands of experimental flights, he died in a crash.

OCTAVE CHANUTE
French-US engineer Chanute was in his 60s before he got interested in flying. During the 1890s, he made thousands of successful glider flights, accumulating data that he passed on to the Wright brothers.

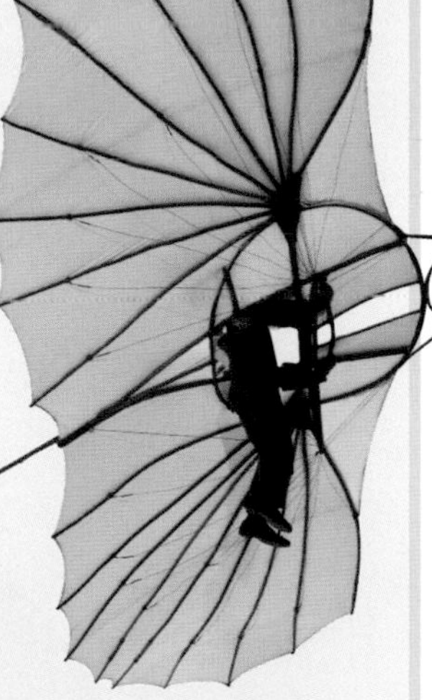

Lilienthal glider built in about 1891, seen here from underneath

1903 Emmeline Pankhurst founds the Women's Social and Political Union to campaign for votes for British women. Ignored at first, the "suffragettes," as they are called, are driven to violent methods, such as burning empty buildings.

1903 The Tour de France bike race is started by French journalist Henri Desgrange to provide a source of exciting stories for his paper. Out of 60 riders, only 21 finish. Maurice Garin wins after nearly 95 hours in the saddle.

The Landlord's Game

1904

Lizzie Magie

Ancestor of the popular Monopoly (✱ *see* **page 198**), The Landlord's Game was patented in 1904 by Lizzie Magie. It aimed to show that renting made landlords rich but tenants poor. Magie believed that wealth from the land should belong to all. Later, businessman Charles Darrow acquired the game and sold it to Parker Brothers, who removed the anti-capitalist message, changed the name, and made Darrow rich.

Lie detector

1904

Max Wertheimer, John Larson

Czech psychologist Max Wertheimer developed the first so-called lie detector in 1904, while he was still a student. In California, another medical student, John Larson, worked with police to build a better one in 1921. Known as a polygraph, it monitored blood pressure, pulse, and breathing, because these can change when people lie. They sometimes change when people are telling the truth, too, so not all courts accept lie detector tests.

Thermos flask

1904

Rheinhold Burger

James Dewar's vacuum bottle (✱ *see* **page 162**) was far too delicate. One of Dewar's students, Rheinhold Burger, saw how to make it more useful. He enclosed the glass bottle in a metal case with protective rubber mountings and a screw cap. Burger sold the idea to a German company and, after a competition to find a name, it was launched in 1904 as the Thermos flask.

Theory of relativity

1905

Albert Einstein

See **pages 178–179** for the story of how Einstein's theories of relativity shed light on Newton's universe.

Function of chromosomes

1905

Nettie Stevens, Edmund Wilson

US biologist Nettie Stevens was the first to link cell structures with genetics. In 1905, while experimenting with beetles, she discovered that two structures, the X and Y chromosomes, determine whether an animal is male or female. Another American, Edmund Wilson, discovered the same thing independently but later acknowledged the work of Stevens.

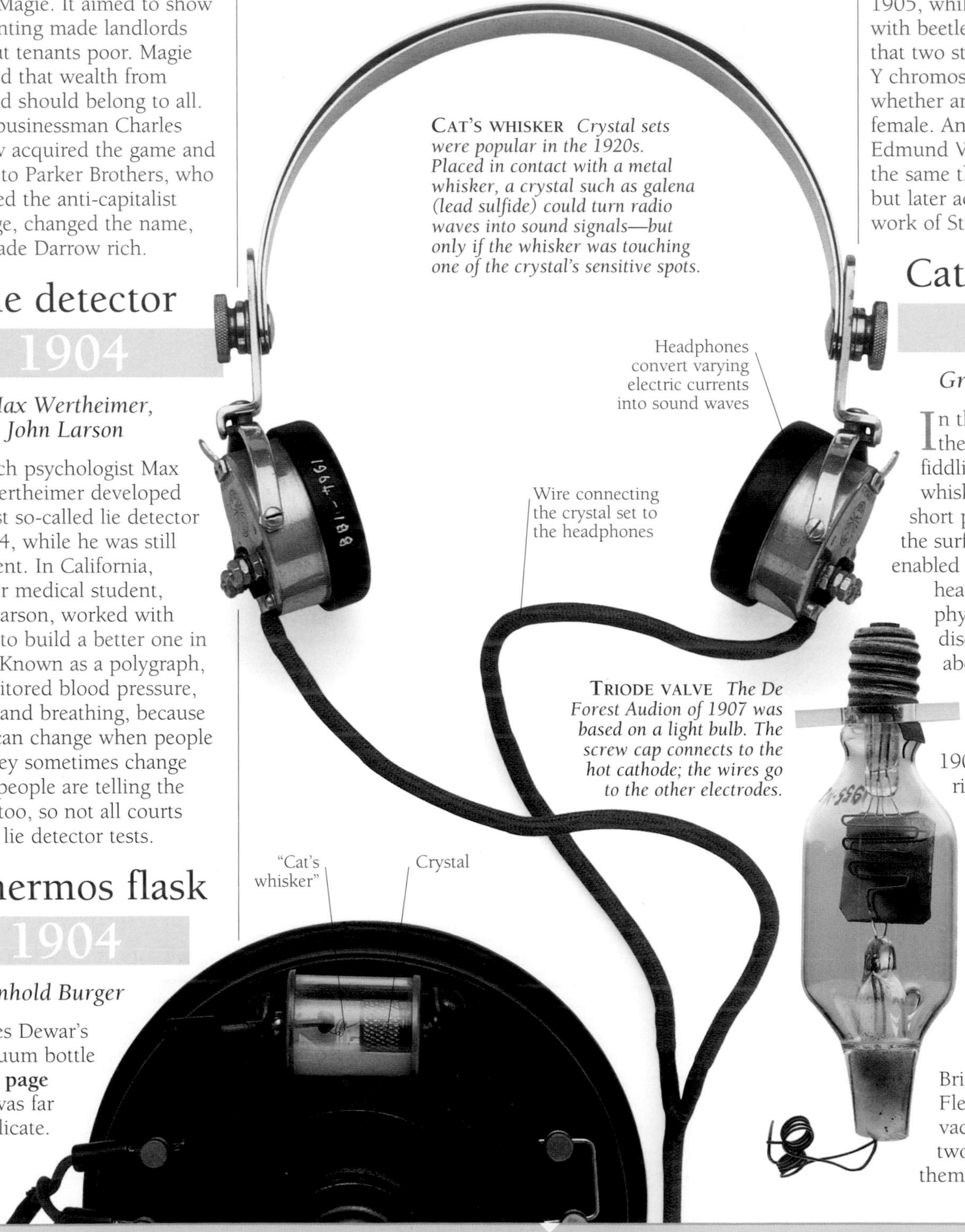

CAT'S WHISKER *Crystal sets were popular in the 1920s. Placed in contact with a metal whisker, a crystal such as galena (lead sulfide) could turn radio waves into sound signals—but only if the whisker was touching one of the crystal's sensitive spots.*

TRIODE VALVE *The De Forest Audion of 1907 was based on a light bulb. The screw cap connects to the hot cathode; the wires go to the other electrodes.*

Cat's whisker

1906

Greenleaf Pickard

In the 1920s, listening to the radio often meant fiddling with a "cat's whisker." The whisker—a short piece of wire—tickled the surface of a crystal and enabled radio waves to work headphones. German physicist Karl Braun had discovered this effect in about 1900, but US engineer Greenleaf Pickard patented the arrangement in 1906. His device gave rise to the transistor.

Triode valve

1906

Lee De Forest

Electronics started in 1904, when British scientist John Fleming found that a vacuum tube containing two electrodes, one of them heated, passed

1904 The US celebrates the 100th anniversary of the Louisiana Purchase by holding in St. Louis, Missouri, the World's Fair, where air-conditioning debuts, and the 1904 Summer Olympic Games, where the US wins 21 events.

1905 Chicago lawyer Paul P. Harris founds Rotary International, a worldwide group of business and professional people dedicated to higher ethical standards in their work. Meetings "rotate" from office to office, hence the name.

current in one direction only. In 1906, US inventor Lee De Forest added a third electrode. By varying its voltage, he could control the current between the other two. De Forest called his device the Audion. We would now call it a triode. He used it first to detect radio waves but was soon using it to amplify and generate them as well.

Sound radio

1906

Reginald Fessenden

Marconi got the first radio patent in 1896 (✳ *see* **page 164**), but it took 10 years for radio to get a voice. Early stations could send out radio waves only in short bursts, but to transmit sound, continuous waves are needed. In 1906, Canadian-US engineer Reginald Fessenden invented an electric generator that worked at 1,000 times the frequency of an ordinary power outlet, creating continuous radio waves that could carry sound. His first broadcast, on Christmas Eve, 1906, was a program of speech and music.

Color photography

1907

Auguste Lumière, Louis Lumière

Before French inventors Auguste and Louis Lumière introduced their Autochrome process in 1907, photographers had to take three photographs to get one color picture. The Lumière brothers coated glass with red, green, and blue starch grains, filled the gaps between them with black, then added a coating that was sensitive to all colors. The starch acted as filters, giving three images in one shot. These combined to form a pleasing color picture.

Color photography
Autochromes needed long exposures so most were of tranquil scenes.

Vitamins

1907

Frederick Hopkins, Casimir Funk

We all need carbohydrates, proteins, minerals, and fats, but these alone are not enough. British biochemist Frederick (later Sir Frederick) Hopkins found that rats died when fed on artificial milk with only these ingredients but thrived if real milk was added. He concluded in 1907 that the rats needed "accessory factors" in their diet. In 1912, Polish biochemist Casimir Funk identified one of these in rice. Finding that it was a chemical called an amine, he proposed the name "vitamine." Not all vitamins are amines, but the name, minus its "e," has stuck.

1907 Irish people wanting independence for their country are outraged by the portrayal of Irish peasants in the first performance of J. M. Synge's *Playboy of the Western World* at the Abbey Theatre, Dublin. They will later admire the play.

1907 Italian educator Maria Montessori begins teaching children in Rome with the system that will become known by her name. The Montessori method is based on children's ability to learn by themselves, with guidance.

RIDDLES OF SPACE AND TIME

Albert Einstein publishes his Theories of Relativity *and sheds light on Newton's universe*

When Albert Einstein was a small boy in Germany, he saw his first pocket compass. It made a great impression on him. Whichever way he turned it, its needle always pointed the same way. Some outside force was controlling it. The incident helped set him searching for the truth about the universe.

For a while, Einstein couldn't get a job because he had upset some important people. When he did get work in 1902, in Bern, Switzerland, it was only as a clerk in the Patent Office. But in his spare time, he began to develop a revolutionary theory.

Train is traveling at nearly the speed of light

The time it takes a beam of light to travel up to a mirror and down represents one tick of a clock

Man on the train sees a short "tick"

Train in starting position

Woman on the platform sees a long "tick"

Train has moved forward by the time the light beam hits the mirror

Train has moved further by the time the light beam reaches the detector

RUNNING LATE
Because relative motion cannot alter the speed of light, it must make moving clocks slow down.

In 1887, US scientists Albert Michelson and Edward Morley thought they would use light to measure the speed of Earth in its orbit through the ether, a theoretical medium thought to pervade all space. According to theory, light traveling in the same direction as Earth would slow down, just as a car looks slower when seen from the car behind. But the speed of light didn't change. Something was wrong with a basic theory of physics.

Einstein's *Special Theory of Relativity*, published in 1905, rescued physics from this embarrassment. With the help of ideas from Dutch physicist Hendrik Lorentz, Einstein modified the laws of physics to predict a constant speed of light. The modifications left almost all the old laws of physics unchanged at ordinary speeds but showed how, at speeds approaching the speed of light, strange things happen to moving objects. As seen by someone moving at a different speed, their length in the direction of motion decreases, their mass increases, and any processes within them slow down.

German-US physicist Albert Michelson

US physicist Edward Morley

FAILED EXPERIMENT
Michelson and Morley used a turntable with two light beams crossing it. Mirrors combined the beams into a pattern that would show up any difference in the speed of light in the two directions. But, whichever way they turned their table, they found no change.

ORIGINAL GENIUS
Albert Einstein was a highly original thinker who gave us a new view of the world. As well as creating the *Special* and *General Theories of Relativity*, he contributed greatly to the quantum theory of matter.

At its simplest, the Special Theory says that the mass of an object depends on its speed. If a force acts on an object, it accelerates, but as it speeds up, more energy goes into increasing its mass and less into increasing its speed. This prevents it from reaching the speed of light. One consequence is the equation $E = mc^2$, which says that mass and energy are interchangeable.

But the Special Theory was incomplete. It did not deal with gravity. Einstein put this right in 1915 with his *General Theory of Relativity*. Replacing space and time with space-time, it said that gravity was a property of space, not a force. At first this seemed to go against the law of conservation of energy, but German mathematician Emmy Noether proved that the law still held, thus saving the theory that also predicted black holes and gravity's ability to bend light.

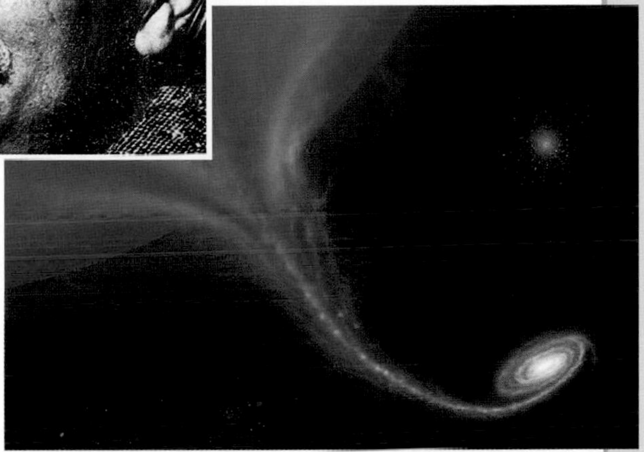

BLACK HOLE
Gravity, a warping of space and time, affects everything—even light. Black holes create gravity so intense that light is trapped, but they can be detected by their effects. In this picture, matter is being pulled away from a giant star.

Young Albert was ill in bed when his father gave him a compass to keep him amused. Einstein later recalled his vivid realization that "something deeply hidden had to be behind things."

Handle to engage the mangle drive

Mangle for squeezing water out of the washing

1919 advertisement for an early washing machine

Lifting the lid automatically disconnected the motor

Long drive belt

Wooden tub

ELECTRIC WASHING MACHINE *Early washing machines were often just hand-operated models with an electric motor bolted on. Even in 1920, Beatty Brothers of Canada, a pioneer of washing machines, was still making this wooden-tub machine with its alarmingly exposed motor.*

Faucet for letting out the water

Electric motor mounted under the tub

Wheels allowed the machine to be moved around easily

Tub was supported on a four-legged "dolly"

Electric washing machine

1907

Alva Fisher

Inventors tried for years to find a way of reducing the hours spent over a steaming washtub, but only electric power could offer real labor savings. The first electric washing machine, the Thor, was designed in 1907 by US engineer Alva Fisher. It had a drum that turned back and forth to tumble clothes clean. Its motor was simply bolted on to the outside, so it wasn't all that safe with water splashing around.

Umami

1908

Kikunae Ikeda

It used to be thought that your tongue could detect only four types of taste: sweet, sour, salty, and bitter. But in 1908, Japanese chemist Kikunae Ikeda realized that there was a fifth taste, which he named umami. Your tongue detects it as the meaty taste of foods rich in protein. He established that the umami taste comes from compounds called glutamates. Ikeda designed a process to mass-produce monosodium glutamate (MSG) as a flavor enhancer. This compound is still widely used today.

Tea bag

c.1908

Thomas Sullivan

Tea bags seem to have been invented by accident. A likely date is 1908. The story is that New York tea merchant Thomas Sullivan started

1909 Leaders meet in New York City to form the National Association for the Advancement of Colored People (NAACP) to fight for desegregation and equal rights for blacks in America. It will still be a powerful organization in the 21st century.

1910 Movie newsreels begin as French movie magnate Charles Pathé's company, Pathé Frères, releases the first of a weekly news compilation called Pathé Journal. The crowing rooster of Pathé News will be known worldwide.

sending out tea samples stitched into cloth bags. Rather than open these, people just poured boiling water over them, and Sullivan was soon getting orders for more. By 1920, proper tea bags were being used in the US, mainly large ones for the catering trade. Tea bags were introduced to Britain by Joseph Tetley & Company in 1953.

Neon sign

1910

Georges Claude

Several 19th-century inventors experimented with tubes containing gas at low pressure and found that electricity could make the gas light up. In 1910, French physicist Georges Claude tried the gas neon and found that it produced an intense orange-red glow. This was of little use for lighting, but after the new tubes had been used at the Paris Motor Show, an advertising agency suggested that they could be made into signs. By 1912, the first neon sign was in place over a Montmartre barber's shop.

Neon sign *New techniques had to be invented before neon signs could be widely used for advertising.*

Electric starter

1912

Charles Kettering

In early cars, the driver had to turn a handle at the front to start the engine. The handle could kick dangerously. Henry Leland, head of Cadillac Motors, found this unacceptable and asked US engineer Charles Kettering to create a self-starter. Kettering succeeded where earlier inventors had failed, and the 1912 Cadillac was the first car that could be started from the driver's seat.

Stainless steel

1913

Harry Brearley

British metallurgist Harry Brearley hit on stainless steel by accident while trying to make a steel that would resist the heat inside a gun. He was in charge of the Firth Brown Laboratories in Sheffield, England, an important steel-making center. In 1913, after a series of experiments, he made some steel containing about 13 percent chromium. He found that it was of little use for guns but realized that it was resistant to corrosion. Unlike other scientists, who had made similar steels, Brearley saw its potential for cutlery. It was a local Sheffield cutler who suggested the name that we now use for it.

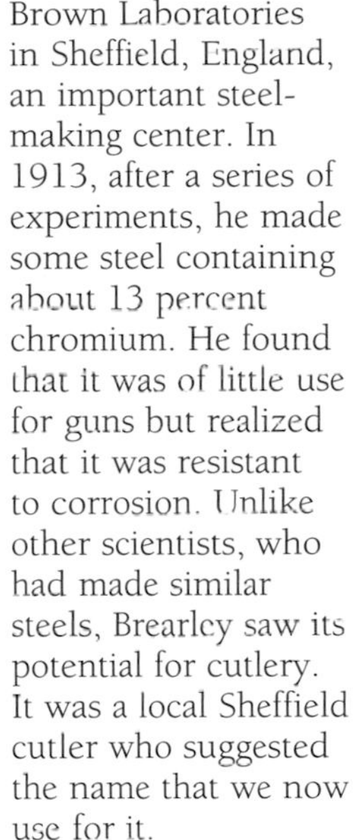

Stainless steel *This tea knife of 1915 was one of the first that did not need cleaning with an abrasive after a meal.*

Fertilizer from the air

1909

Fritz Haber, Carl Bosch

Plants need nitrogen. Although air is four-fifths nitrogen, plants cannot absorb it directly. Nitrogen rich fertilizers are one answer, but by 1900, natural supplies, such as bird droppings, were beginning to run out. In 1909, German chemist Fritz Haber succeeded in capturing nitrogen from the air. He used heat and high pressure to make it react with hydrogen, forming ammonia, which could be made into fertilizers and other products. By 1914, another German chemist, Carl Bosch, had found a way to increase the yield of ammonia, and developed Haber's method for large-scale use. The Haber-Bosch process is now essential to agriculture and much else.

Continental drift

1912

Alfred Wegener

If you look at an atlas of the world, you will see that South America and Africa would fit together like jigsaw-puzzle pieces. In 1912, German meteorologist Alfred Wegener said that this was not a coincidence. He said that all the continents had once been joined together as a continent he called Pangaea, which began to drift apart millions of years ago. His ideas were forgotten, but in the 1960s, scientists realized that he had been right.

Cosmic rays

1913

Victor Hess

The pioneers of radioactivity found their instruments responding to radiation from outside their labs. Its origin was a mystery until US physicist Victor Hess sent balloons carrying measuring instruments high into the atmosphere. By 1913, he had found that the radiation became stronger as the balloons went higher, suggesting that the "rays" came from beyond Earth. US physicist Robert Millikan confirmed this and in 1925 coined the term "cosmic rays" for this radiation from the depths of the universe.

Assembly line

1913

Henry Ford

See **pages 182–183** for the story of how Henry Ford adopted the assembly line to mass-produce the world's most successful car.

1911 On December 14, Norwegian explorer Roald Amundsen and his team become the first people to reach the South Pole. Powered only by dogs, they beat the motorized expedition led by Robert Scott, which sadly never returns.

1912 On the night of Sunday, April 14, the supposedly unsinkable *Titanic* hits an iceberg on its maiden voyage. By the next morning, it is on the bottom of the Atlantic Ocean. More than 1,500 people die, but about 700 are saved.

A MOTOR FOR THE MULTITUDE

Henry Ford adopts the assembly line to mass-produce the world's most successful car

MAN OF VISION
Henry Ford looked to a future in which efficient production methods would make everyone rich. His factory eventually had raw materials going in at one end and finished cars coming out at the other.

In 1891, when the first modern car was built, Henry Ford was a young engineer working in Detroit, Michigan, not far from the farm where he had been born. Most people still worked on the land. Ford would be one of the people who helped change this, transforming the US into an industrial nation.

By 1896, Ford had built his first car. In 1903, he set up the Ford Motor Company. At that time, cars were individually built and very expensive, so they were strictly for the rich. Ford realized he could keep costs down by producing just one type of car, and in 1908, he launched "a motor car for the great multitude"—the Model T.

TIN LIZZIE
Between 1908 and 1927, one of every two cars built in the world was a Model T. With its rugged construction and low price, it was ideal for the still rural US.

Model T Tourer (1916)

Demand for the "Tin Lizzie," as it was nicknamed, was soon running ahead of supply, and Ford moved to a new factory at Highland Park, just outside Detroit. Even here, people still had to walk from car to car to work on each one—and when they were walking, they were not working.

Ford wanted to find a faster, less expensive production method. In the US meat industry, workers stood still while carcasses were moved slowly past them. In 1913, Ford experimented with this "assembly line" idea for making part of the Model T. Output of the part went up by 300 percent, so he decided to make the whole car on an assembly line.

MORE CARS
The Ford story does not, of course, end with the Model T. Later designs included the sleek Edsel, the sporty Mustang, and the GT40, designed in Britain and built for serious racing.

Ford Edsel (1958)

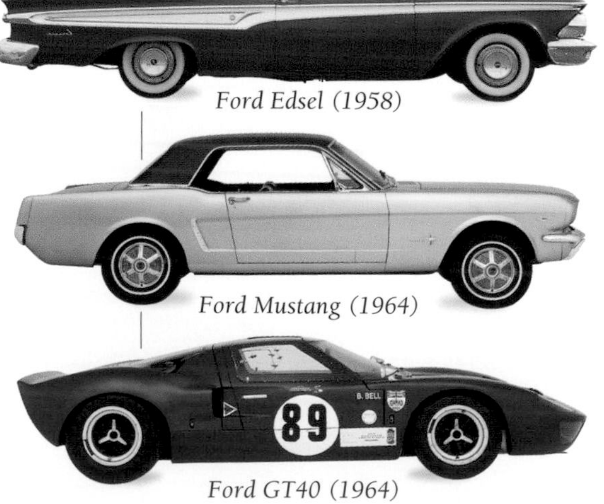

Ford Mustang (1964)

Ford GT40 (1964)

Ford succeeded in his mission to bring mobility to the masses, and in doing so changed the American way of life. As well as providing pleasure on picnics, low-cost vehicles made every industry more efficient.

Now, instead of wandering around the factory, workers spent all their time adding parts to cars as they passed by. Each worker did only one operation, and their pace was set by the moving line. By April 1914, Ford had cut the time it took to make a car from 12 man-hours to one and a half. Soon the factory was turning out a car every 24 seconds. The Model T became the world's most successful car, with total sales reaching more than 15 million.

The assembly line did have its disadvantages. Working in this way was stressful, so workers often left. Ford solved this problem by doubling his workers' pay and reducing the hours they had to work. It seemed crazy, but it was just good business. Ford realized that his employees had a private life and didn't just make cars. Thanks to his new methods, they would soon be buying them, too.

Modern manufacture
The first cars had their bodies bolted onto a separate chassis, but today's car body is a single, self-supporting steel shell. For many years, the shell was hand-welded together by skilled workers, but such heavy, repetitive tasks are now done by robots, like these at Ford's plant in Ontario, Canada.

Structure of the atom

1913

Niels Bohr

British physicist Ernest Rutherford pictured the hydrogen atom as a heavy nucleus with an electron orbiting around it. But classical physics said this could not be right because the electron would radiate energy and stop orbiting. Danish physicist Niels Bohr saved the situation in 1913 by showing that electrons could radiate energy only when jumping from a higher to a lower orbit. The radiation would appear as light whose frequency depended on the size of the jump.

Bra

1914

Mary Jacob

Although a "breast supporter" was patented in 1893, the idea didn't catch on. US innovator Mary Jacob was unsatisfied with the whalebone corsets popular with women at the time. She sewed together a couple of handkerchiefs and some ribbon and in doing so invented a precursor to the modern bra. In 1914, she changed her name to Caresse Crosby, patented the brassière, and started selling it. Although she was not very successful in this, she did manage to sell the idea to a big corset company, and by the 1920s women everywhere were wearing bras.

Lipstick

1915

Maurice Levy

Lipstick has been with us for centuries, but without a convenient package, women couldn't carry it around. In 1915, US inventor Maurice Levy attached a solid lipstick to a sliding carrier inside a metal tube with a lid. The lipstick could be slid out for use then put back safely inside its container to protect handbags and pockets. Lipstick soon became more widely used.

Lipstick *As this early print shows, lip color became popular when presented in convenient, solid form.*

Leprosy treatment

1915

Alice Ball

Leprosy is an infection that can cause the gradual loss of fingers and toes. Dr. Alice Ball developed the first effective treatment for it. She was the University of Hawaii's first female chemistry professor, having been the first woman and first African American to receive its master's degree. Her treatment was an injectable extract of the active part of a traditional herbal medicine. Ball developed this ingenious treatment at the young age of 23 but sadly died a year later, never getting to see its successful, widespread use.

Black hole

1916

Karl Schwarzschild

Using Einstein's General Theory of Relativity (✳ *see* **pages 178–179**), German astronomer Karl Schwarzschild figured out what happens near a massive star that has collapsed to a single point. He reasoned that gravity becomes so intense that within a certain distance from the point (now called the Schwarzschild radius) even light cannot escape its monumental pull. Black holes, as they are now known, emit no light but can be detected by the effect their gravity has on nearby stars.

Domestic food mixer

1919

Herbert Johnson

Bakers had been mixing dough by electricity for years before an effective mixer reached the

Domestic food mixer *By the 1930s, when many homes had electricity, appliances like food mixers were beginning to be more widely used.*

1914 Archduke Ferdinand, heir to the Austrian and Hungarian thrones, is assassinated on June 28. The resulting conflict escalates to involve 32 countries. It will end in 1918, after 47 million people have been killed.

1916 A work that will become a favorite of concertgoers and science-fiction producers alike, *The Planets*, is published by British composer Gustav Holst. His orchestral suite portrays the planets' astrological characters.

kitchen. Early domestic mixers were little more than motorized egg whisks, but the Troy Metal Products H-5, introduced in 1919 and later called the Kitchen Aid, was based on a professional mixer designed by US engineer Herbert Johnson. Its built-in bowl revolved in the opposite direction to the beaters, and this "planetary" action is now used in most mixers.

Central heating

1919

Alice Parker

The use of hot air for central heating goes back to the Romans, but African American inventor Alice Parker reinvented it for modern America. In the early 1900s, most buildings were heated by coal or wood, often in open fires. Parker's furnace ran on natural gas, a safer and more convenient alternative to solid fuel. A key feature of her invention was that it allowed different amounts of hot air to be sent to different parts of a building. Her exact design was never used, but it provided a crucial model for future central heating systems.

Public broadcasting service

1920

David Sarnoff, Guglielmo Marconi

Although US engineer Reginald Fessenden broadcast speech and music in 1906, and US radio executive David Sarnoff proposed a "radio music box" in 1915, real public broadcasting began only in the 1920s. By this time, electronics had developed greatly, allowing big transmitters to be built. The first regular service was started in Britain by Guglielmo Marconi in February 1920. In November 1920, US station KDKA began broadcasting from Philadelphia. Governments in both countries later stepped in to regulate the new medium. (✱ *See also* **Birth of Broadcasting**.)

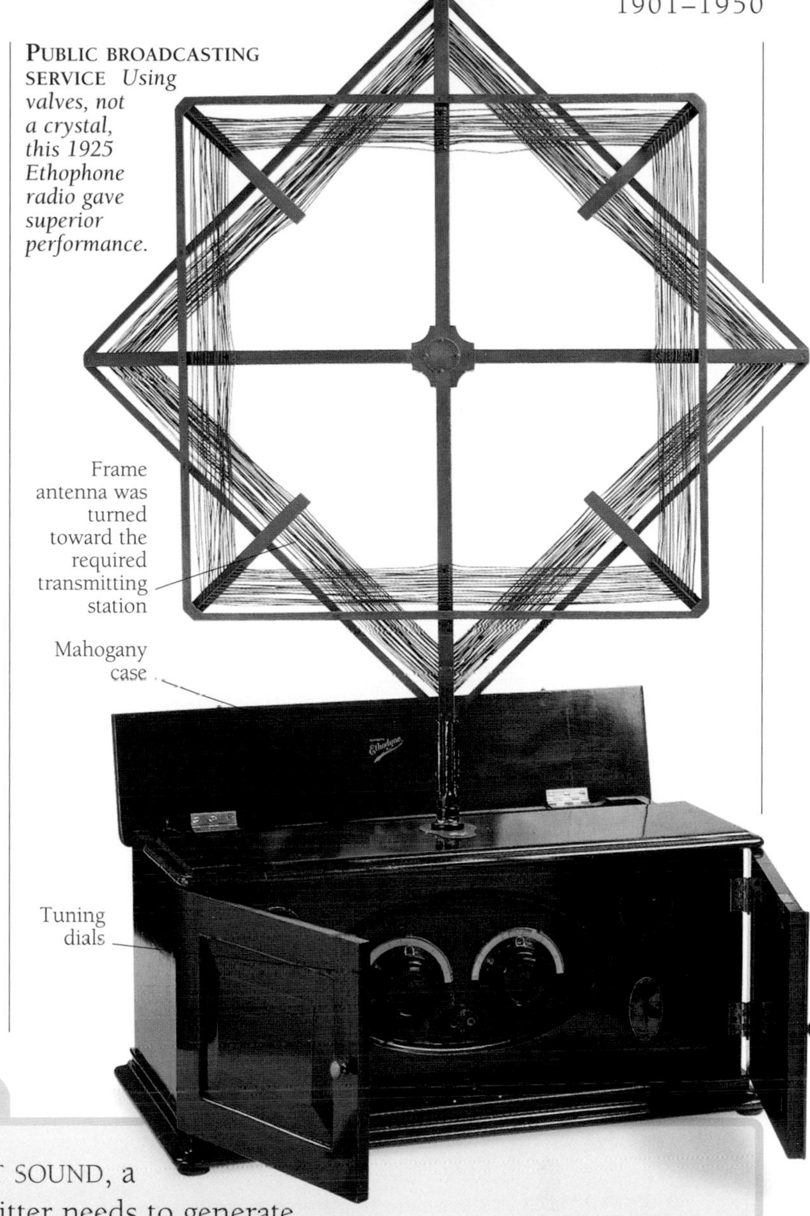

PUBLIC BROADCASTING SERVICE *Using valves, not a crystal, this 1925 Ethophone radio gave superior performance.*

BIRTH OF BROADCASTING

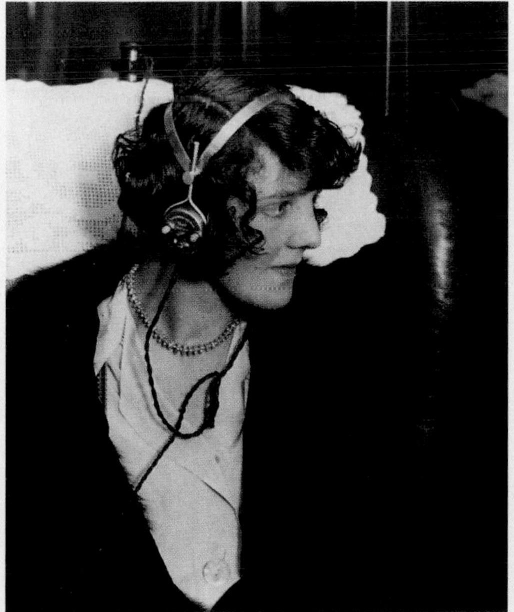

Listening to radio on a train in 1930

TO TRANSMIT SOUND, a radio transmitter needs to generate powerful, continuous, high-frequency waves. Reginald Fessenden pioneered these with high-speed electric generators, but it was the development of large electronic valves during World War I that really made broadcasting possible. The first listeners had to build their own receivers because the lack of regular broadcasts meant there was no market for ready-made radios.

BROADCASTING IN BRITAIN
Marconi's early radio broadcasts were banned, but after public pressure, his company was allowed to broadcast for 15 minutes a week from a hut near Chelmsford, starting in February 1922. In May, the station moved to London, and October saw the birth of the British Broadcasting Company. In 1927, this became a public corporation, the BBC.

BROADCASTING IN THE US
Unhampered by red tape, and led by visionaries such as David Sarnoff of the Radio Corporation of America, US broadcasting grew rapidly. By 1922, the US had 600 stations, mainly financed by advertising, while Britain still had only one. But competition threatened chaos, so in 1927 the industry finally came under government regulation.

1917 The Union of Soviet Socialist Republics, the USSR, is formed following the Russian revolution. The Congress of Soviets, controlled by the Bolsheviks under their leader Vladimir Lenin, takes over the former Russian Empire.

1920 American women are finally given the right to vote when the 19th Amendment to the US Constitution is ratified. With votes hanging in the balance, Tennessee finally votes to ratify the amendment, bringing the vote count to 36 states in favor.

Self-adhesive bandage

1920

Earle Dickson

Before ready-made dressings, cuts were covered with gauze stuck down with tape. Earle Dickson, of US surgical dressing manufacturer Johnson & Johnson, changed this in 1920. Working in his kitchen, he took a strip of adhesive tape, laid down squares of gauze on it, covered it with fabric and rolled it up for future use. His invention was soon on sale as Band-Aid. In 1928, T. J. Smith & Nephew introduced the similar Elastoplast to Britain.

Insulin

1921

Frederick Banting, Charles Best

Insulin is a hormone that tells the liver to remove glucose from the blood. People whose bodies cannot make enough insulin suffer from diabetes, in which blood glucose may reach dangerous levels. It was known that insulin came from a gland called the pancreas, but efforts to extract it from the pancreas of certain animals failed. The organ's digestive juices were also released and digested the insulin before it could be extracted. Then, in 1921, Canadian doctor Frederick (later Sir Frederick) Banting, assisted by a student, Charles Best, figured out a way to stop the pancreas's juices from destroying the hormone. Thanks to their work, insulin is now available for controlling diabetes.

Leaded gasoline

1921

Thomas Midgley Jr.

In a properly adjusted car engine, the fuel and air burn smoothly rather than exploding. When engineers made car engines more powerful by increasing the pressure inside them, they found that destructive explosions, or "knocking," became a problem. In 1921, US engineer Thomas Midgley Jr. discovered that adding lead compounds to the fuel could restore smooth running. Most cars used leaded gasoline until the 1980s, when concerns about pollution caused a switch to fuels that didn't need lead to stop the knock.

Ice pop

1923

Frank Epperson

Refreshing, flavored ice on a stick was patented by US salesman Frank Epperson in 1924, but its US brand name, Popsicle, was registered a year earlier. The legend is that Epperson invented the ice lolly by accident in 1905, when he was a boy, by leaving a drink with a stirrer in it out on a cold night. His patent describes cylindrical ice pops made in ordinary test tubes.

Traffic signal

1923

Garrett Morgan

A traffic signal was installed in London in 1868, but a more widely used signal was patented by US inventor

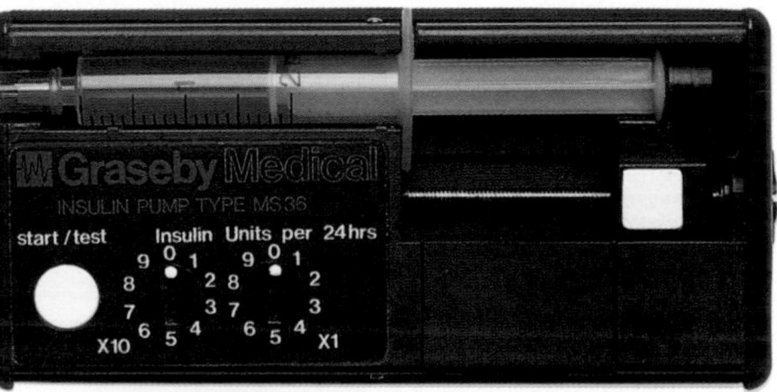

Insulin *This modern electric pump gives someone with diabetes a convenient way to inject themselves with insulin, slowly and continuously.*

Theremin

1920

Leon Theremin

The theremin was the first successful electronic musical instrument. Still played today, it produces those spooky wailing sounds popular in science-fiction films. It was invented in 1920 by Russian scientist Leon Theremin, who originally called it the etherophone. It is one of the few instruments played by waving the hands near it rather than touching it. The distance of the hands affects its tuning, giving total control over its unearthly notes.

Viewfinder

35mm camera *The Leica was not a single-lens reflex, as most 35mm cameras are today, but gave good results.*

1921 Nine years after the death of Emperor Meiji, who helped Japan become a modern industrial nation, a shrine to his memory is built in Tokyo. Its traditional wooden buildings will be destroyed in an air raid 24 years later.

1922 British archaeologist Howard Carter discovers the treasure-filled tomb of the Egyptian pharaoh Tutankhamen in the Valley of the Kings. Unlike most tombs, this one has not been looted, making it important to Egyptology.

Garrett Morgan in 1923. It had three movable arms with STOP and GO written on them, mounted on a pole. Signals were given by raising, lowering, and swiveling the arms to show or hide these words. The signal also had a position that stopped all traffic, to allow an orderly switch from one direction to another.

Frozen food

1924

Clarence Birdseye

US naturalist Clarence Birdseye got the idea for frozen foods on a trip to Newfoundland, Canada, in 1912. It's very cold there, and Birdseye saw people leaving freshly caught fish outside to freeze. He invented a machine that froze fish between refrigerated metal plates, and in 1924 helped found the General Seafoods Corporation. He was soon selling quick-frozen fruit and vegetables as well as fish. His name lives on as the familiar brand name Birds Eye.

35mm camera

1924

Oskar Barnack

The first precision miniature camera was the Leica, designed by German mechanic Oskar Barnack. It went into production in 1924. Barnack had started working on it much earlier but was delayed by World War I. To make the Leica, he adapted an instrument for testing 35mm movie film, made by the company he worked for, Ernst Leitz. He created the now standard frame size, 24 × 36 mm, simply by doubling the size of a movie frame.

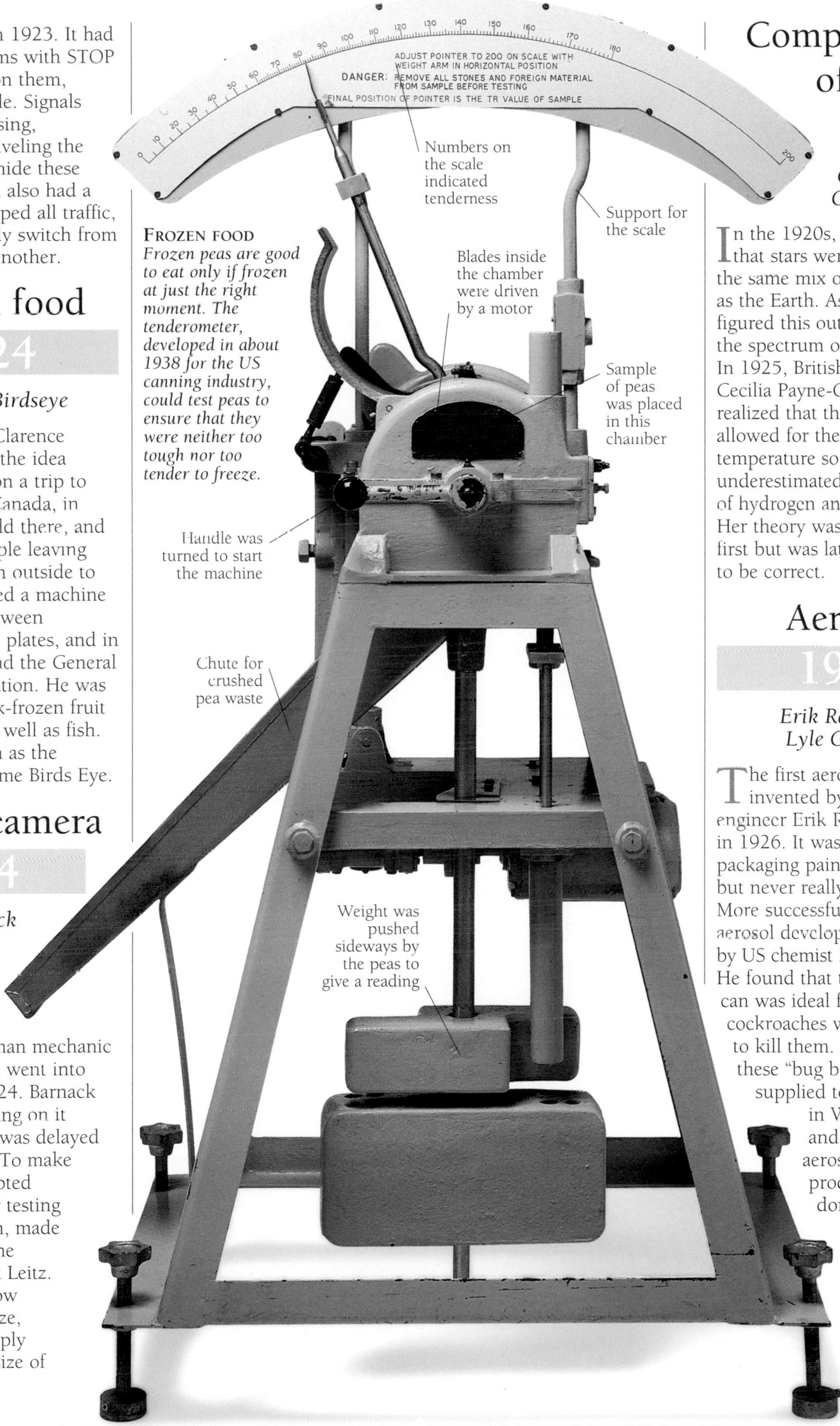

FROZEN FOOD *Frozen peas are good to eat only if frozen at just the right moment. The tenderometer, developed in about 1938 for the US canning industry, could test peas to ensure that they were neither too tough nor too tender to freeze.*

Composition of stars

1925

Cecilia Payne-Gaposchkin

In the 1920s, it was thought that stars were made of the same mix of elements as the Earth. Astronomers had figured this out by studying the spectrum of starlight. In 1925, British astronomer Cecilia Payne-Gaposchkin realized that they had not allowed for the effect of temperature so had greatly underestimated the amounts of hydrogen and helium. Her theory was rejected at first but was later proved to be correct.

Aerosol

1926

Erik Rothheim, Lyle Goodhue

The first aerosol can was invented by Norwegian engineer Erik Rothheim in 1926. It was used for packaging paint and polish but never really caught on. More successful was an aerosol developed in 1941 by US chemist Lyle Goodhue. He found that the new can was ideal for spraying cockroaches with insecticide to kill them. Millions of these "bug bombs" were supplied to US troops in World War II, and by 1946, aerosols were in production for domestic use. Fifty years later, world production was numbered in billions.

1925 One of the first films to use the technique of "montage"—telling a story by rapid cutting between shots—is made in Russia by Sergey Eisenstein. His *Battleship Potemkin* will become a model for many other filmmakers.

1926 The first woman to swim the English Channel unaided, US Olympic swimmer Gertrude Ederle, knocks two hours off the record as she makes it from Cap Gris-Nez in northern France to Kingsdown, Kent, in 14 hours, 31 minutes.

Film soundtrack

1926

Lee De Forest

Sound for the first films was supplied by live musicians. The only recordings available were gramophone discs, and it was difficult to keep these in step with the film. The obvious place for the recording was on the film itself. The first person to succeed in putting it there was US inventor Lee De Forest. His Phonofilm system of 1926 produced the first soundtrack—a narrow stripe down the side of the film, recording sound waves as a varying shade of gray. It was the forerunner of the later, more successful Movietone system.

Liquid-fueled rocket

1926

Robert Goddard

The first rockets used solid fuel. They were really just big fireworks. Modern rockets use liquid fuel, which allows much more controllable motors to be built. The first liquid-fueled rocket was launched by US physicist Robert Goddard. Burning gasoline and liquid oxygen, it lifted off briefly from his Aunt Effie's farm in Auburn, Massachusetts, on March 16, 1926. It was another 15 years before the same idea was used in Adolf Hitler's deadly flying bombs during World War II.

LIQUID-FUELED ROCKET *A Titan II rocket lifts off in January 1965 carrying an unmanned Gemini spacecraft. The 100 ft (30 m) long rocket was powered by the liquid fuel hydrazine.*

Plant growth hormones

1926

Friedrich Went

The life of plants is controlled by a number of different hormones. The first to be discovered was a group known as auxins. Dutch botanist Friedrich Went, a professor at the University of Utrecht, found them in 1926 while studying how plants grow. He discovered that auxins were not only responsible for stimulating plant growth but were also involved in the one-sided growth that makes plants bend toward the light.

Pop-up toaster

1926

Charles Strite

Burnt toast was normal with early electric toasters. They just kept toasting until someone turned them off. The first that turned off and popped the toast out automatically was patented in 1919 by US inventor Charles Strite. It was designed for caterers. The toaster as we know it, based on Strite's design, did not reach the breakfast table until 1926, when the Waters Genter Company, later known as McGraw Electric, marketed the first Toastmaster.

Expanding universe

1927

Edwin Hubble

Until US astronomer Edwin Hubble started studying the sky in the 1920s, nobody suspected that there were countless galaxies beyond our own Milky Way. Having proved the existence of such galaxies, Hubble discovered in 1927 that

1926 The Showa (bright peace) period begins in Japan with the enthronement of Emperor Hirohito. He is content to leave government to others until August 1945, when he ends World War II by insisting that Japan surrenders.

1927 Indian lawyer Bhimrao Ranji Ambedkar begins a campaign of direct action aimed at improving the social status of the Dalits, or "Untouchables." He will urge the Dalits, traditionally given the worst jobs, to take up Buddhism.

Pop-up toaster *By the 1960s, toasters were looking more stylish, but their principle—releasing the toast after a set time—was the same.*

they were rushing away from us, with speeds that increased the farther away they were. The universe, far from being changeless, was expanding. Cosmologists now accept this as evidence for the Big Bang that started it all.

Internal clock

1927

Curt Richter

Anyone who has had jet lag knows that we have a built-in clock that tells us when to be active and when to sleep. The first scientist to study this was US biologist Curt Richter, head of the psychiatric clinic at the Johns Hopkins University in Baltimore. In 1927, he published the results of research into the biorhythms, or internal cycles, that govern animal behavior. We now know they apply to humans, too.

Chain saw

1927

Emil Lerp, Andreas Stihl

The world's first gas-engined chain saw let rip on Mount Dolmar, Germany, in 1927. German engineer Emil Lerp's new, "portable" sawing machine had a moving chain like a modern saw but was too heavy for one person to pick up. A chain saw light enough for one person to wield didn't appear until 1950, made by a company founded by Lerp's rival, Andreas Stihl.

Big Bang theory

1927

Georges Lemaître, George Gamow

In 1927, Edwin Hubble discovered that the universe is expanding. In the same year, Belgian astronomer Georges Lemaître proposed a simple but radical explanation: everything had originally been squeezed into an incredibly dense "primeval atom" that had exploded to create the universe we know. In 1948, Russian physicist George Gamow revived Lemaître's idea in an attempt to explain how the chemical elements were formed. British astronomer Fred Hoyle scornfully dubbed this the Big Bang theory, and the name stuck. (✱ *See also* **Starting with a Bang**.)

Big Bang theory *It is impossible to know what the Big Bang was like, but this is an artist's impression.*

STARTING WITH A BANG

When Albert Einstein heard Georges Lemaître's Big Bang theory, he exclaimed, "This is the most beautiful and satisfactory explanation of creation to which I have ever listened." Although it doesn't explain where the "primeval atom" came from, an explosion about 15 billion years ago does account for the universe we see today. Backed up by recent evidence, the Big Bang is now the preferred picture of the beginning of time.

George Gamow (right) with Swiss US physicist Wolfgang Pauli

Evidence for the Big Bang
The strongest evidence for the Big Bang is the expansion discovered by Hubble. The theory also predicts that the universe should be filled with low-level microwave radiation, and this was found in 1965. Finally, about a quarter of the universe (by mass) is made of helium. Stars alone could not have produced this amount, but the first fireball could.

Steady State theory
In the same year that George Gamow revived the Big Bang theory, British astronomers Hermann Bondi, Thomas Gold, and Fred Hoyle proposed that the universe had always existed in a "steady state." They suggested that as the universe expanded, new matter filled the gaps to keep everything looking the same. Recent discoveries have made this theory seem unlikely.

1927 Australia's parliament moves from Melbourne to Canberra, a new city designed by US architect Walter Griffin. Building work had started in 1913. The name derives from an Aboriginal word meaning "meeting place."

1927 Intrepid US aviator Charles Lindbergh lands safely at Le Bourget airport, near Paris, after crossing the Atlantic single-handedly in his plane *The Spirit of St. Louis*. The flight from Roosevelt Field, Long Island, makes him a star.

Bubble gum *This Dubble Bubble advertisement from the 1940s is obviously aimed at children. Unlike chewing gum, bubble gum has always been seen as mainly a product for children and teenagers.*

Bubble gum

1928

Walter Diemer

Walter Diemer, a young accountant working for the Fleer Chewing Gum Company in Philadelphia, Pennsylvania, thought he could improve on the company's product. In 1928, he produced a gum that was so stretchy he could blow bubbles with it. He had created bubble gum. His company started selling it as Dubble Bubble. Diemer taught the sales force how to blow the perfect bubble, and the gum became a favorite worldwide.

Uncertainty principle

1927

Werner Heisenberg

Elementary particles, such as electrons, are described by the branch of physics called quantum mechanics (✱ *see* **page 169**). This says that a particle is not only a particle but also a wave. One consequence of this is that nobody can know both the momentum (mass × velocity) and position of a particle at the same time. Momentum comes from a spread-out wave, while position comes from a concentrated wave, and you can't have both at once. German physicist Werner Heisenberg announced this "uncertainty principle" in 1927.

Chlorofluorocarbons

1928

Thomas Midgley Jr., Albert Henne

Early refrigerators used chemicals like ammonia, which is extremely smelly and poisonous. In 1928, it took US scientists Thomas Midgley Jr. and Albert Henne just two days to find something better: chlorofluorocarbons, or CFCs. These compounds of chlorine, fluorine, and carbon had already been produced by Belgian chemist Frederic Swarts in the 1890s, but Midgley and Henne found a better way of making them. Unfortunately, they have a devastating effect on Earth's protective ozone layer, so they have not been made since the late 1990s.

Penicillin

1928

Alexander Fleming, Ernst Chain, Howard Florey

See **pages 192–193** for the story of how Ernst Chain and Howard Florey built on Alexander Fleming's lucky find.

Electric razor

1928

Jacob Schick

Attempts to do away with wet shaving go back to 1908 or earlier, but the first

Electric razor *Razors like this 1934 Schick allowed men to shave anywhere there was an electrical outlet.*

1927 Thin meets fat as two stars, Stan Laurel from Britain and Oliver Hardy from the US, team up at Hal Roach's Hollywood Studio for their first film, *Putting Pants on Philip*. The comic duo will make many more films together.

1928 British women finally get the same voting rights as men, after 10 years in which they could vote only if they owned a house, were married to a man who owned a house, or had a university degree and were over 30.

inventor to tackle the problem successfully was Lieutenant-Colonel Jacob Schick of the US Army. In 1928, he used the profits from an earlier invention, a razor that stored blades in its handle, to finance his new electric razor. Despite the Great Depression that hit the US in the following year, Schick's dry shaver was soon selling well.

Cinemascope

1928

Henri Chrétien, Claude Autant-Lara

Cinemascope squeezes a wide image onto normal movie film by distorting it with a special lens. A similar lens on the projector distorts the image back again to produce a wide-screen picture. French physicist Henri Chrétien invented the lens in the late 1920s, and experimental films were made in 1928 by French film director Claude Autant-Lara. But Cinemascope really hit the screens in the 1950s, as movies struggled to tempt audiences away from television.

Sliced bread

1928

Otto Rohwedder

Devising a machine that sliced bread can't have been that difficult, but US inventor Otto Rohwedder took 16 years to do it. One reason was that in 1917, after five years' work, he lost everything in a fire. More important was the fact that sliced bread quickly went stale. By 1928, Rohwedder had perfected a machine that not only sliced but also wrapped the bread into a handy, long-lasting package. Within five years, most bread in the US came sliced.

Prestressed concrete

1928

Eugène Freyssinet

Ordinary concrete tends to crack under loads that stretch it. One elegant solution was invented in 1928 by French civil engineer Eugène Freyssinet. He put stretched steel wires into concrete while it was wet. When it had set, he released the wires so that they squeezed the concrete together, canceling out the forces that would otherwise make it crack. Prestressed concrete is now used to produce light, strong structures of all kinds.

Electro-encephalograph

1929

Hans Berger

Electrodes placed on someone's head can reveal the electrical activity of their brain. This helps doctors diagnose disorders such as epilepsy. An electroencephalograph, or EEG, machine, records the activity as a set of squiggly lines. The first machine was built by German physiologist Hans Berger in 1929, after five years' work with dogs and humans. No one showed much interest in Berger's work at first, but a local optical company, Carl Zeiss, was impressed by his device and helped him build a better one.

Electrodes on scalp

Rubber cap holds electrodes in place

Wires connect electrodes to a recording instrument

Multipin connector plugs into the recorder

Electro-encephalograph
This modern EEG cap was made by Neuramedical Supplies.

Polaroid

1929

Edwin Land

Polaroid polarizes light. That is, it blocks all light waves except those whose vibrations are lined up in one particular direction. Polaroid sunglasses, which admit only vertically polarized light, can reduce troublesome reflections from smooth horizontal surfaces like water and roads. US physicist Edwin Land perfected this material, which has many other uses, in 1929. The thin plastic sheet, treated with optically active crystals, quickly replaced the bulkier polarizers that had been used earlier.

1928 A groundbreaking new dictionary of the English language, *A New English Dictionary on Historical Principles*, is published after years of work by James Murray and others. It will be better known as the *Oxford English Dictionary*.

1929 In October, prices on the New York stock exchange collapse, ruining thousands of people who had poured money into the market. The crash triggers a depression that lasts for years and makes millions of people jobless.

THE ANTIBIOTIC MIRACLE

Howard Florey and Ernst Chain build on Alexander Fleming's find to develop a lifesaver

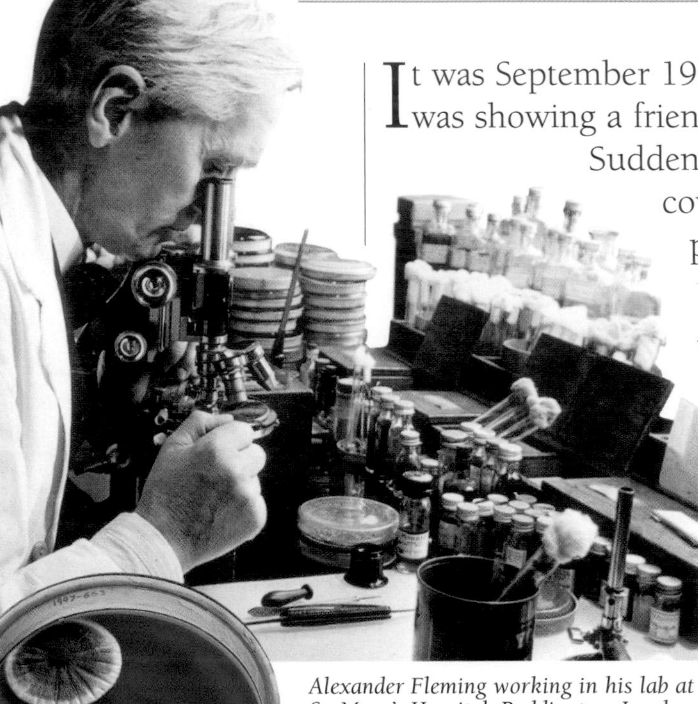

Alexander Fleming working in his lab at St. Mary's Hospital, Paddington, London

Culture dish showing the effect of penicillin on bacteria

HAPPY ACCIDENT
Bacteria can be grown in dishes filled with nutrient gelatin. Fleming had piles of these lying around, which led to his lucky find.

ANIMAL MAGIC
Fleming thought that penicillin would be good for getting rid of unwanted bacteria in the laboratory. But Florey and Chain saw its potential for curing disease and were the first to try it on mice.

It was September 1928. Scottish bacteriologist Alexander Fleming was showing a friend some plates he used for growing bacteria. Suddenly, he stopped. The plate in his hand was covered with bacteria, but there was also a patch of mold, and around the mold there were no bacteria. Fleming worked at Sir Almroth Wright's vaccine laboratories in St. Mary's Hospital, London. There, he grew more mold and made an extract he called penicillin. He tested it, used it to cure an eye infection, and wrote about it but pursued it no further. He was more interested in vaccines. Penicillin, he thought, would be best used in laboratories.

Ten years later, German biochemist Ernst Chain, working at the Sir William Dunn School of Pathology in Oxford, England, suggested to his boss, Australian pathologist Howard Florey, that they should investigate penicillin. Florey decided to see whether it would affect bacteria inside animals—something Fleming hadn't tried. Chain's job would be to isolate the active agent from the mold.

In May 1940, Florey injected eight mice with lethal bacteria. Then he injected four of them with penicillin. The next day, the untreated mice were dead, but the rest were fine. Florey phoned a colleague. "It's a miracle," he told her.

Florey wanted to test penicillin on human patients, but to produce enough he had to turn his lab into a factory. Soon it was filled with piping and chemical fumes. By February 1941, he had enough penicillin for the first human trial. Policeman Albert Alexander was gravely ill with a serious infection. On February 12, 1941, he started receiving penicillin. The effect was spectacular. He almost recovered, but Florey didn't have enough penicillin to keep the treatment going, and Alexander died. Later, five

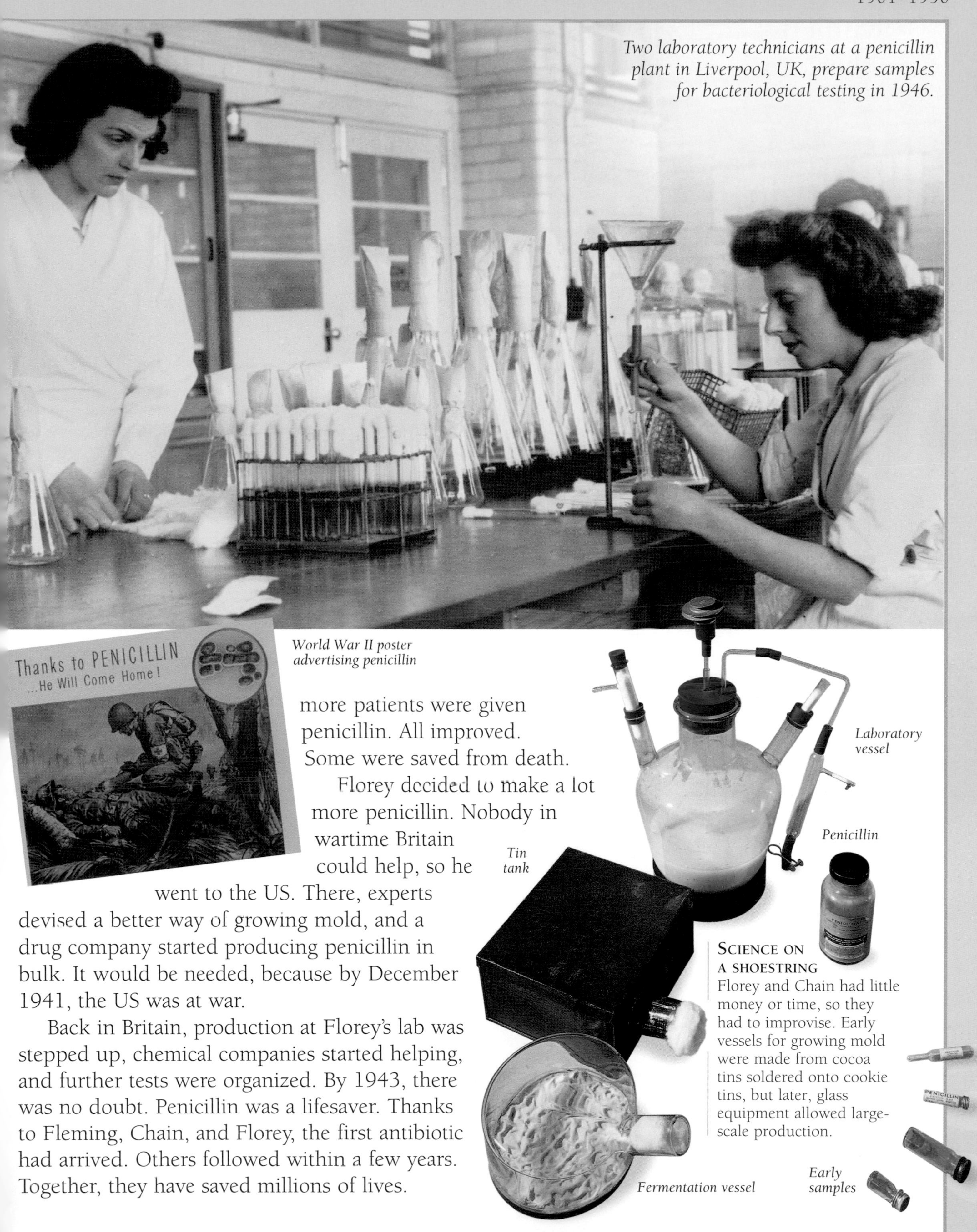

Two laboratory technicians at a penicillin plant in Liverpool, UK, prepare samples for bacteriological testing in 1946.

World War II poster advertising penicillin

more patients were given penicillin. All improved. Some were saved from death.

Florey decided to make a lot more penicillin. Nobody in wartime Britain could help, so he went to the US. There, experts devised a better way of growing mold, and a drug company started producing penicillin in bulk. It would be needed, because by December 1941, the US was at war.

Back in Britain, production at Florey's lab was stepped up, chemical companies started helping, and further tests were organized. By 1943, there was no doubt. Penicillin was a lifesaver. Thanks to Fleming, Chain, and Florey, the first antibiotic had arrived. Others followed within a few years. Together, they have saved millions of lives.

Science on a shoestring
Florey and Chain had little money or time, so they had to improvise. Early vessels for growing mold were made from cocoa tins soldered onto cookie tins, but later, glass equipment allowed large-scale production.

Synthetic rubber tires

1929

Walter Bock, Eduard Tschunkur

By the 1880s, scientists had some idea of the chemical composition of rubber, but their attempts to copy it failed. They had more success when they tried imitating its properties rather than its chemistry. In 1929, German chemists Walter Bock and Eduard Tschunkur made a synthetic rubber good enough for tires. This was important in World War II, when Germany's natural rubber supplies were cut off.

Supermarket

1930

Michael Cullen

The first essential of a supermarket is self-service. This was invented in 1916 by US grocer Clarence Saunders. His Piggly Wiggly store in Memphis, Tennessee, cut costs by letting customers take their purchases right off the shelves, something unheard of at the time. The other vital ingredients, bulk buying and quick turnover, were added in 1930 when another US grocer, Michael Cullen, opened his King Kullen store in an old garage in Long Island, New York. Customers flocked to this, the first true supermarket.

Jet engine

1930

Frank Whittle, Hans von Ohain

The jet engine was patented in 1930 by a young British Royal Air Force pilot, Frank (later Sir Frank) Whittle. He had great difficulty convincing anyone that it would be useful. Things were different in Germany. When Hans von Ohain thought up a similar engine, it was immediately taken up by a major plane company. The first jet plane, a Heinkel HE-178, flew from a German airfield in 1939, two years before the first British jet flight.

Clear adhesive tape

1930

Richard Drew

Cellophane appeared in the late 1920s. One of its main uses was for wrapping items like flowers and fruit to make them look attractive, so it demanded a clear sealing tape to go with it. First to solve the problem was US engineer Richard Drew of the Minnesota Mining and Manufacturing Company, now known as 3M. Having invented masking tape—an adhesive tape made from paper—in 1925, he coated Cellophane with a similar adhesive to produce Scotch Tape in 1930. Seven years later, Colin Kininmonth and George Gray produced Sellotape, a British competitor.

Radio astronomy

1931

Karl Jansky, Grote Reber

Radio astronomy started at Bell Telephone Labs in the US, where engineer Karl Jansky was tracking down radio interference. One source of interference eluded him until, in 1931, after months of frustration, he pointed his antenna upward. The mysterious interference was coming from the stars. Another US radio engineer Grote Reber built the first radio telescope, a 31 ft (9.5 m) dish, in 1937. By 1942, he had made the first radio map of the sky.

Electronic flash

1931

Harold Edgerton

The flash in most of today's cameras took 50 years to perfect. It started as a bulky device used when taking research photographs

JET ENGINE *The Gloster E28/39 was the first plane to be equipped with the jet engine designed by Frank Whittle. It took to the skies in April 1941, four years after Whittle's first engine was started up, and two years after the first successful German jet flight.*

1930 After 19 days' solo flying in a converted De Havilland Moth, British aviator Amy Johnson reaches Darwin, Australia, from England. The feat, achieved after only 50 hours' flying experience, wins Johnson a £10,000 ($48,500) prize.

1930 After the formation of the soccer organization FIFA in 1904, the World Cup finally kicks off in Montevideo, Uruguay. Only 13 teams compete, which do not include any from Britain. Uruguay takes the cup.

of high-speed objects, such as bullets. US engineer Harold Edgerton realized as early as 1926 that a high voltage applied to a tube containing xenon gas could produce very brief but intense pulses of light. By 1931, he had devised a practical flash.

Scrabble

1931

Alfred Butts

The world's best-known word game was invented in 1931 by an unemployed New York architect, Alfred Butts. He called it Criss-Cross. Nobody wanted to make the game, so Butts went into partnership with a retired government official, James Brunot, who started making it in his garage. Renamed Lexico, the game went on sale in 1946. Within two years, games makers Selchow & Righter had snapped it up and were selling it under yet another name—Scrabble. The letter values were fixed by counting the number of times each letter appeared on a page of the *New York Times*.

SCRABBLE *The Scrabble board contains 225 squares, of which 81 are "premium" squares that increase a player's score.*

Ailerons control banking and turning

High-speed jet of hot gases from the engine pushes the plane along

Heavy water

1932

Harold Urey, Edward Washburn

Heavy water has the same chemical properties as ordinary water but is nearly 11 percent heavier. This is because it contains a heavier form of hydrogen, called deuterium. US chemist Harold Urey discovered deuterium in 1931. He then realized that electrolysis of water releases more hydrogen than deuterium, leaving behind water enriched with deuterium. Using this process, he and fellow chemist Edward Washburn created the first heavy water. They published their discovery in 1932.

Button-up shirt

1932

Cecil Gee

British tailor Cecil Gee opened his first shop in 1929 in London. His customers didn't want fussy shirts that had to be pulled on over their head. Nor did they like separate collars attached with fiddly studs. So in 1932, Gee designed a shirt with buttons all the way down, which could be slipped on like a jacket, and also had its collar sewn in place. After years of resistance by traditionalists, Gee's design became the standard men's shirt.

Full-color movie

1932

Herbert Kalmus

Several color movie processes were invented in the early 20th century, but most used only two colors, giving unrealistic results. One of these two-color processes was Technicolor, invented by US engineer Herbert Kalmus. In 1932, it was redesigned to work with three colors. The first full-color movies had arrived. Although hampered by a huge camera taking three reels of film at once, Technicolor was used for many classics, including *The Wizard of Oz*.

FULL-COLOR MOVIE *The Technicolor camera was really three cameras in one. After processing, its three films were printed on to a single film for projection.*

1931 The Empire State Building, the world's tallest skyscraper, is completed in New York. It will eventually be outdone by taller buildings, but with 102 stories, and a starring role in the movie *King Kong*, it will remain a tourist attraction.

1932 On May 20–21, American aviator Amelia Earhart becomes the first woman to fly nonstop solo across the Atlantic Ocean, sealing her reputation as a great pilot. She sets a record time of 14 hours, 56 minutes in a Lockheed Vega 5B.

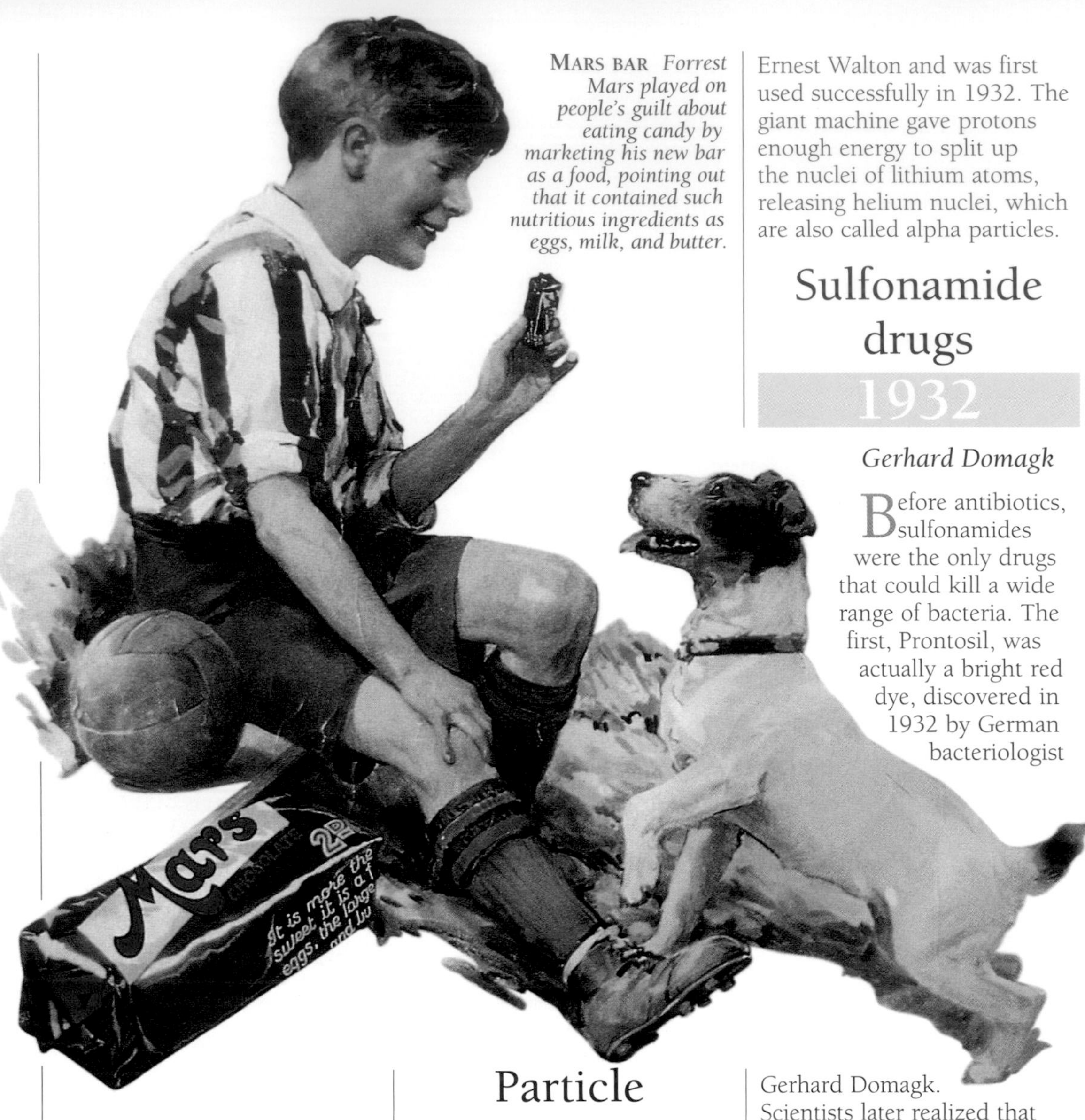

MARS BAR *Forrest Mars played on people's guilt about eating candy by marketing his new bar as a food, pointing out that it contained such nutritious ingredients as eggs, milk, and butter.*

Mars bar

1932

Forrest Mars

The Mars bar started with the idea of turning malted milk into confectionery. In 1922, Forrest Mars suggested this to his father, US candy maker Frank Mars, who created a chocolate-covered nougat and caramel bar called Milky Way. After an argument with his father, Forrest left for England in 1932. He set up his own company in Slough, near London, where he perfected the Mars bar, a version of his father's product cleverly adapted to British tastes.

Particle accelerator

1932

John Cockcroft, Ernest Walton

Nuclear physicists can study the structure of matter by firing subatomic particles such as protons and alpha particles (helium nuclei) at other atoms to smash them up and see what comes out. At first, the physicists had to use particles emitted naturally by radioactive materials like radium. Today, they nearly always use particle accelerators, which produce energetic particles artificially. The first was built by British physicists John Cockcroft and Ernest Walton and was first used successfully in 1932. The giant machine gave protons enough energy to split up the nuclei of lithium atoms, releasing helium nuclei, which are also called alpha particles.

Sulfonamide drugs

1932

Gerhard Domagk

Before antibiotics, sulfonamides were the only drugs that could kill a wide range of bacteria. The first, Prontosil, was actually a bright red dye, discovered in 1932 by German bacteriologist Gerhard Domagk. Scientists later realized that this broke down in the body to give a more potent drug, sulfanilamide. From 1936 onward, after clinical trials by British doctor Leonard Colebrook, this and other related "sulfa" drugs began to save thousands of lives. They are still used today when antibiotics fail.

Electron microscope

1933

Ernst Ruska

An image cannot contain detail smaller than the waves used to form it. Because of this, ordinary light microscopes cannot reveal really tiny objects. In 1933, German engineer Ernst Ruska invented a microscope that worked with much smaller waves. The waves were electrons. Although these were once regarded as particles, quantum physics (✳ *see* **page 169**) shows that they are also waves. Using them, electron microscopes can now reveal objects as small as molecules.

Stereophonic sound

1933

Alan Blumlein, Harvey Fletcher

Stereophonic sound was developed independently on both sides of the Atlantic. In Britain, engineer Alan Blumlein, seeking realistic sound for large-screen films, obtained a patent covering the fundamental principles of stereophony in 1933. He also developed a microphone technique for stereo recording and developed the basic system that is used to make stereophonic discs. In the US, physicist Harvey Fletcher of Bell Telephone Laboratories gave his first public demonstration in 1934, in New York City.

FM radio

1934

Edwin Armstrong

The letters FM on a radio station stand for "frequency modulation." This means that the transmitted frequency goes up and down slightly with the ups and downs of the sound wave it is carrying. It's more complicated than the earlier "amplitude modulation" (AM) system but resists interference better. FM was perfected

1933 US President Franklin D. Roosevelt begins speaking directly to the American public by means of regular radio addresses. These "fireside chats" boost the public's confidence in their country's leader.

1933 Adolf Hitler is appointed Chancellor in Germany. He uses his position to establish the absolute rule of the National Socialist (Nazi) Party. Violently suppressing all opposition, he establishes himself as a dictator.

in 1934 by US engineer Edwin Armstrong, who first demonstrated it using a transmitter on top of the Empire State Building.

Front-wheel drive car

1934

Andrè Citröen, André Lefèbvre

Many modern cars have their engine connected to the front wheels, avoiding lengthy transmission systems and giving them better grip. A lot of inventors tried this in the early 20th century, but the first to succeed in a big way was French carmaker Andrè Citröen, whose chief engineer was André Lefèbvre. Their "*traction avant*" system appeared in 1934, and car manufacturers Citröen have been making front-wheel drive cars ever since.

Hammond organ

1934

Laurens Hammond

The sound of the Hammond organ comes from lots of spinning magnetic wheels, one for each note. Teeth on the wheels create pulsating currents in magnetic coils, and these are mixed and amplified to produce the final sound. US engineer Laurens Hammond built his first organ in 1934, using a constant-speed motor he had invented earlier. Each wheel could have only a whole number of teeth, so the scales he got were slightly out of tune. His solution was to add a wobble to every note, covering up the errors while creating the unique Hammond sound.

Cat's eyes

1935

Percy Shaw

Cat's eyes are the little reflectors set in the road that make driving at night safer. Possibly inspired by real cats' eyes, British engineer Percy Shaw invented them in 1934, but they were not used until the following year. Their secret was in the rubber that housed the reflectors. Whenever a car ran over a cat's eye, a flexible "eyelid" wiped the reflectors clean, ready for the next driver. Shaw became a millionaire but never left his hometown in Yorkshire.

Polyethylene

1935

Eric Fawcett, Reginald Gibson

Chemists Eric Fawcett and Reginald Gibson were part of a team at British chemical company ICI. They were investigating the reactions of the gas ethylene at high pressure. In 1935, they found a white, waxy solid in one of their reaction vessels. It was a new plastic, polyethylene. It was an excellent insulator and easy to mold. ICI marketed the new material in 1939 as Alkathene.

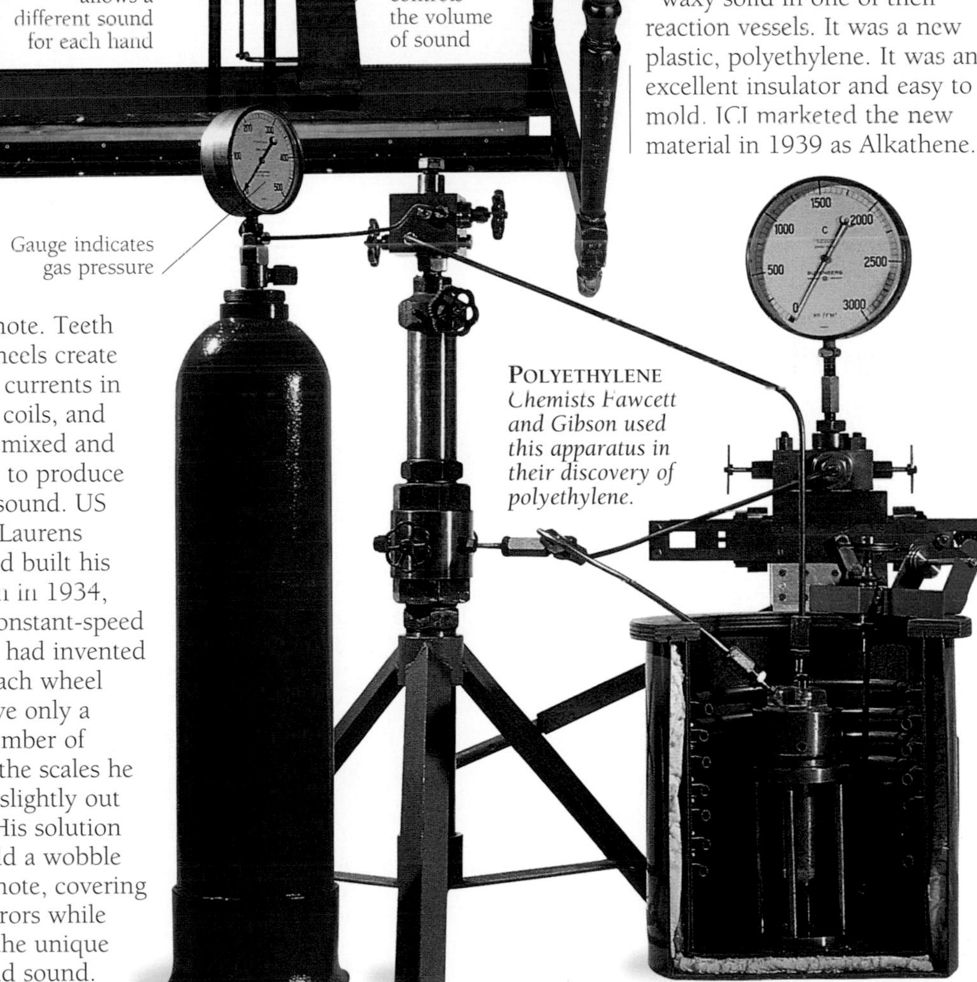

HAMMOND ORGAN *One of the Hammond's great advantages was that it was much smaller than a traditional pipe organ. It could compete with the piano as an instrument for the home.*

POLYETHYLENE *Chemists Fawcett and Gibson used this apparatus in their discovery of polyethylene.*

Perspex

1934

Rowland Hill, John Crawford

The first thick, clear plastic available in large sheets was Plexiglas. Developed by German chemist Otto Röhm, it was introduced by the Röhm & Haas companies in Germany and the US in 1931. The following year, two British chemists, Rowland Hill and John Crawford, discovered how to make sheets of a related but more glasslike material, polymethyl methacrylate. Produced by chemical company ICI, it went on sale in 1934 under the more user-friendly name of Perspex.

1934 "Bollywood," the Indian version of Hollywood, gets started with the opening of a major movie studio, Bombay Talkies, in Mumbai. It is the brainchild of Indian producer Himansu Rai and a London-based Indian playwright, Niranjan Pal.

1934 Following the death of President Paul von Hindenburg, German chancellor Adolf Hitler becomes Führer ("leader"). This gives him the powers of chancellor, president, and leader of the army, cementing his dictatorship.

MONOPOLY *The British version of Monopoly, with London street names, appeared in 1936. Its advertising traded on its success in the US.*

Monopoly

1935

Charles Darrow

This popular board game was invented by US heating engineer Charles Darrow. He based it on a less successful game invented in 1924 by Lizzie Magie (✳ *see* **page 176**). His first board featured streets in Atlantic City, a favorite vacation spot. The tokens—dog, hat, and so on—were copies of charms on his wife's bracelet. Manufacturers rejected the game at first, but it finally appeared in time for Christmas 1935.

Radar

1935

Robert Watson-Watt

In 1935, the British government, fearing war, asked Scottish engineer Robert Watson-Watt whether he could produce a radio "death ray." Watson-Watt knew that radio could not destroy enemy aircraft but thought it might be able to detect them. On February 26, using signals from a BBC transmitter, he detected a distant bomber. After this, he supervised the construction of radar stations along the English coast. These started working just as the war with Germany began in 1939. They helped the Royal Air Force win the Battle of Britain. (✳ *See also* **Seeing by Radio**.)

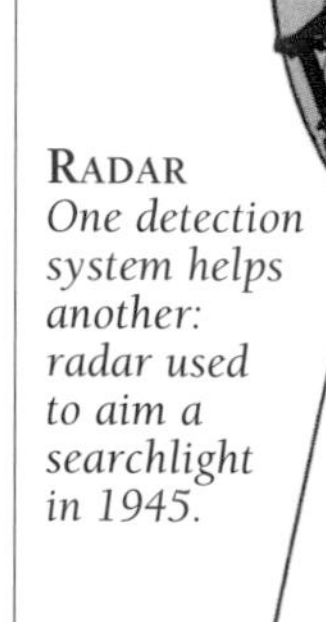

RADAR *One detection system helps another: radar used to aim a searchlight in 1945.*

Color film

1935

Leopold Mannes, Leopold Godowsky

Color film was invented by two US classical musicians, Leopold Mannes and Leopold Godowsky. Their film had three separate light-sensitive layers. Each layer formed an image in one of the three primary colors. Although its processing was complicated, the pictures it produced were so good that, in 1930, Kodak invited Mannes and Godowsky to work in its research laboratories. The result, Kodachrome, was launched on April 15, 1935.

1935 US composer George Gershwin writes his folk opera *Porgy and Bess*, a unique blend of jazz, pop, and opera that will come to be thought of as his greatest work. Its lyrics are written by his elder brother, Ira.

1936 On December 11, Britain's King Edward VIII tells the nation that he must leave his throne for love of the woman he has been forbidden to marry, Mrs. Wallis Simpson. He settles in France and marries her the next year.

SEEING BY RADIO

"RADAR" GETS ITS NAME from "radio detection and ranging." It detects objects and measures their distance, or range, by sending out short pulses of radio waves and showing if anything reflects them back. The time between sending a pulse and getting it back shows the distance of the reflecting object. Its direction is found by using a steerable antenna.

EARLY RADAR
The discoverer of radio waves, Heinrich Hertz, showed that they were reflected from metallic surfaces, and several early radio experimenters thought that they might be used to detect objects. German engineer Christian Hülsmeyer patented a detection system in 1904, and a crude form of ranging with radio pulses was achieved in 1925.

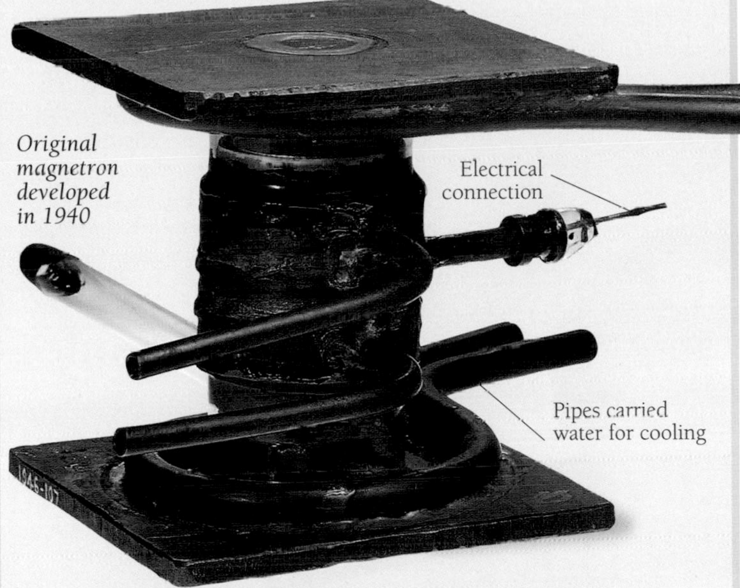

Original magnetron developed in 1940

LATER DEVELOPMENTS
The first radar stations worked with quite large wavelengths. This made their measurements rather imprecise and also meant that the stations had to be big. In 1940, the invention of the magnetron, which could produce much shorter waves called microwaves, allowed compact, precise radars to be installed in aircraft. Radar is now essential to aviation.

Parking meter

1935

Carlton Magee

The hated parking meter first appeared in 1935, on the streets of Oklahoma City. It was invented by Oklahoma businessman Carlton Magee, who wanted to stop all-day parkers from clogging the streets. He also thought it might make a little money for his city. The Park-O-Meter, as Magee called it, was remarkably similar in appearance to the meters used today. Much to the annoyance of inconsiderate parkers, Magee's idea has proved a hit with city authorities everywhere.

Richter scale

1935

Charles Richter, Beno Gutenberg

News reports usually rate earthquakes on the Richter scale. Devised in 1935 by US seismologists Charles Richter and Beno Gutenberg, the scale relates to the energy released by an earthquake at its center, with each step representing 10 times the energy of the previous one. So an earthquake measuring 8 on the Richter scale, which would usually be catastrophic, releases a million times as much energy as one rated at 2, which wouldn't be noticed.

Structure of Earth's core

1936

Inge Lehmann

Deep below the Earth's crust, right at the center of our planet, is the core. Scientists can study this entirely hidden layer by measuring and interpreting seismic waves generated by earthquakes. In 1936, Danish seismologist Inge Lehmann realized that her measurements of these waves did not fit with the widely accepted theory that Earth had an entirely molten core. She instead argued that the way the waves travel through the core shows that it must have a solid center.

HELICOPTER *The Fw 61 looked more like a wingless plane than a helicopter. Its rotors spun in opposite directions to make it fly straight.*

Helicopter

1936

Heinrich Focke

It took a long time to develop a really usable rotating-wing aircraft. Early helicopters had little lift, and because the way the rotor worked was not fully understood, they tended to flip over sideways. The French Breguet-Dorand gyroplane of 1935 solved most of these problems, but the first helicopter to develop into a practical production machine was the Focke-Wulf Fw 61. Designed by German engineer Heinrich Focke, the machine had two rotors and took to the air in 1936.

Suntan lotion

1936

Eugène Schueller

The first mass-market suntan lotion was produced in 1936, after Paris designer Coco Chanel acquired a house in the south of France and made tanning fashionable. The perfumed, golden oil that helped prevent the skin from burning was created by a small company founded by French chemist Eugène Schueller. Today, his company, L'Oréal, is much larger, and the name of his oil, Ambre Solaire, is known worldwide.

1936 Adolf Hitler fails to demonstrate white racial superiority at the carefully stage-managed Olympic Games in Berlin, when black US athlete Jesse Owens wins four gold medals. Hitler simply refuses to acknowledge the fact.

1936 After years of strife between Nationalists and Republicans, the Spanish Civil War starts on July 17. People from many nations join in. After three years and 100,000 deaths, Nationalist General Franco will control Spain.

Television

1936

Vladimir Zworykin, Isaac Shoenberg

See **pages 202–203** for the story of how Vladimir Zworykin and Isaac Schoenberg perfected all-electronic television.

Pulse code modulation

1937

Alec Reeves

In 1937, British engineer Alec Reeves came up with a new way to reduce interference on telephone calls: convert them into code, like telegraph messages. The code would resist interference during transmission and could be converted back into speech once received. Reeves called his idea pulse code modulation. With the electronics of his day, it was too expensive to use widely, but it is central to the digital communications revolution of today.

Trampoline

1937

George Nissen

As a child, US businessman George Nissen loved to watch trapeze artists bouncing on their safety nets. So he later designed his own, more effective bouncing rig. In 1937, he learned that the Spanish for springboard was "*trampolín.*" This, in English form, would become the trademark of his new product. Children loved the Trampoline, and when war came Nissen sold lots to the US air force to help pilots with fitness training. The first world trampolining championship was held in 1964.

Epoxy resin

1937

Henry Moss

Epoxy resins are found in glues that come in two tubes. One tube contains resin, the other a hardener. When the two are mixed, they set hard because the hardener contains chemical groups that link the resin molecules together. British chemist Henry Moss made the first epoxy resins in 1937, and a two-part glue was marketed in 1946. Its Swiss makers, Ciba (now Ciba-Geigy) named their new product Araldite.

Superfluidity

1937

Peter Kapitsa, John Allen

It normally takes an effort to make a fluid flow. But at really low temperatures, things can be very different. In 1937, Russian physicist Peter Kapitsa discovered that below about –456°F (–271°C), liquid helium loses its resistance to flow and also develops strange habits, such as climbing up the walls of its container as a thin film. Kapitsa published his findings in 1938, as did Canadian physicist John Allen, who discovered it independently.

Grocery cart

1937

Sylvan Goldman

US retailer Sylvan Goldman noticed that people in his Humpty Dumpty supermarkets never bought more than they could carry. He reasoned that if they could carry more, they would buy more. So, in 1937, he got a local odd-job man to weld wheels and baskets to metal folding chairs. Customers resisted the strange-looking contraptions at first, so Goldman hired people to push his first crude grocery carts around the store until everyone got the idea and started to use them.

ESPRESSO COFFEE *Small espresso machines, like this one from about 1950, use steam pressure to force water through the coffee.*

Pressurized aircraft cabin

1937

Lockheed Corporation

Aircraft fly more smoothly and use less fuel at high altitudes. But the low pressure at these heights does not agree with people, so passenger cabins have to be pressurized. The first fully pressurized aircraft was the experimental US Lockheed XC-35, which was based on an existing Lockheed plane, the Electra. Built in 1937, the modified plane's reinforced fuselage had few windows, causing pilots to dub it the "Can't see-35."

Espresso coffee

1938

Achille Gaggia

When Italian engineer Achille Gaggia wanted coffee, he wanted it fast. So he invented a pump that forced nearly boiling water through finely ground coffee. Because the water moved so quickly, there wasn't time for bitter flavors to develop. A cup of espresso took only the pull of a lever, so it soon became popular with café owners. Gaggia patented his invention in 1938, and his name is now likely to be seen wherever coffee lovers gather.

1937 San Francisco's elegant Golden Gate Bridge opens to traffic, after heroic struggles with rock and water by engineer Joseph Strauss. For another 27 years, its 4,200 ft (1,280 m) main span will be the longest in the world.

1937 American aviator Amelia Earhart sets out from Oakland, California, on a planned flight around the world. She and her navigator, Fred Noonan, lose radio contact a month into the flight and disappear, never to be found.

Nylon

1938

Wallace Carothers

Nylon was launched by US chemical company DuPont in 1938. Its inventor, US chemist Wallace Carothers, specialized in polymers—molecules made by joining lots of identical molecules together. He was trying to imitate silk, which is a protein, so he tried joining molecules with a linkage found in proteins, called the amide bond. In 1934, he succeeded so well that he could pull a continuous strand of "polyamide," or nylon, straight out of a laboratory beaker. The first nylon stockings went on display, to wild acclaim, in 1939.

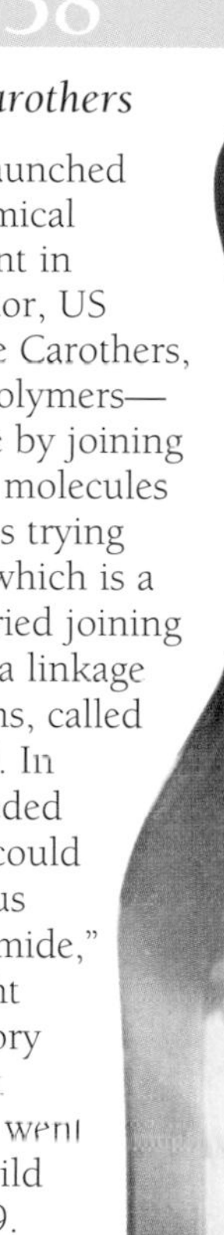

NYLON *After being knitted, stockings are shaped to ensure a wrinkle-free fit by pulling them over dummy legs, a process known as boarding. It is seen here in a factory of 1946.*

Ballpoint pen

1938

Ladislao Biró, Georg Biró

Hungarian artist Ladislao Biró and his brother Georg, a chemist, thought they were making a totally new writing instrument. In fact, US inventor John Loud had invented something similar in 1888. New or not, Ladislao's ball-tip rolled on, lubricated by Georg's greasy, smudge-proof ink. The Biro pen was patented in 1938. Later, the brothers met British entrepreneur Henry Martin. He noticed that ballpoints didn't leak at high altitude and sold them to the Royal Air Force. Ballpoints reached British shops in 1945—in time for Christmas.

BALLPOINT PEN *The original ballpoint pen of the 1940s, made by the Miles Martin Pen Company, was a luxury product, which cost more than an ordinary fountain pen.*

Teflon

1938

Roy Plunkett

The slippery, heat-resistant plastic used for coating pans was discovered by accident. On April 6, 1938, Roy Plunkett, a research chemist for US chemical company DuPont, was testing the refrigeration gas tetrafluoroethylene. He had some in a cylinder, but it wouldn't come out. When he investigated, he found that it had turned into a white powder. The gas molecules had joined together to form polytetrafluoroethylene. Its more familiar trademark, Teflon, was registered in 1945. In the 1960s, researchers found a way to make the nonstick plastic stick to metal.

1938 The world's first large oceanarium, Marineland, in Florida, opens to the public. Visitors are thrilled by fish such as sharks and rays, normally seen only in the open sea. Later, they will get soaked as dolphins do tricks.

1938 On March 13, the Nazi chancellor of Austria, brutally installed by Hitler, asks in German troops to suppress disorder. Next day, Hitler and troops are in Vienna, declaring *Anschluss* (union) between the two countries.

MAKING THE DREAM COME TRUE

Vladimir Zworykin and Isaac Shoenberg work to perfect all-electronic television.

Saturday, January 30, 1937, was a sad day for Scottish television pioneer John Logie Baird. That was when the British Broadcasting Corporation (BBC) finally abandoned his mechanical television system, with its whirring wheels and messy chemicals. He had come a long way since his first experiments with television in 1923, but it wasn't far enough. His dream was over. The future was electronic.

Three months earlier, on November 2, 1936, the BBC had started the world's first regular, high-definition, public television broadcasting service. In alternate weeks, it used two different sets of equipment. The idea was to test two rival systems. One was Baird's; the other had been created by a team at Electrical and Musical Industries (EMI) led by Russian-born engineer Isaac Shoenberg. The all-electronic EMI system won easily. Its pictures were sharper, its cameras were more mobile, it was more reliable, and it cost less. In all but detail, it was the system we use today.

Shoenberg's team had been formed five years earlier. They had worked with remarkable speed, but they weren't the first to research all-electronic television. On the other side of the Atlantic, a lone pioneer, Philo T. Farnsworth, had started work on his electronic "image dissector" in 1926. He gave the first demonstration of all-electronic television in 1934. Unfortunately, his cameras needed too much light, and his work came to a dead end.

John Logie Baird

ELECTRONIC EYE
The strange shape of the Emitron camera reflected the shape of the image tube inside it. The drooping nose held the tube's electron gun. Above this were two lenses, one of which was a viewfinder.

PICTURES FROM A SPINNING DISC
Baird did much to create interest in television. He used a rotating disc to sweep a spotlight over the subject to be televised, with a matching disc in the receiver. This mechanical system could not make pictures good enough to compete with electronics.

Baird Televisor, 1926

Isaac Shoenberg

Vladimir Zworykin

TV PIONEERS
The two main pioneers of all-electronic television were both born in Russia. Shoenberg was born in 1880 and Zworykin in 1889. Shoenberg emigrated to Britain in 1914, and Zworykin to the US in 1919. It was Zworykin who developed the first successful camera tube. It scanned the image with a beam of electrons. Tubes of this type were highly sensitive and could show fine detail.

Modern television owes far more to another US engineer, Russian-born Vladimir Zworykin. He was the first to take up the suggestion, made in 1908 by Scottish engineer Alan Campbell Swinton, that a cathode ray tube could create as well as display pictures. In 1929, Zworykin took charge of television development at the Radio Corporation of America. By 1931, he and his team had created the first successful electronic camera tube, the Iconoscope. Shoenberg's team later used Zworykin's basic idea to develop their own Emitron tube, which formed the heart of the cameras they designed for the BBC.

On September 1, 1939, as war gripped Europe, the BBC television service was closed down. Just four months earlier, the US' first regular television service had started, when the National Broadcasting Company (NBC) broadcast the opening of the New York World's Fair. Zworykin, Shoenberg, and a host of other engineers and enthusiasts had finally made the dream of television come true.

Britain's first television receivers were very expensive, worked only in London, and offered only a single channel. But they were the start of something big.

TELEVISION IN THE US
Regular television broadcasts began later in the US than in Britain, but the US system expanded more quickly. This National Broadcasting Company studio, equipped by the Radio Corporation of America, is seen in 1939, broadcasting where war had forced the BBC to stop.

Xerography *Chester Carlson did much of the basic research into dry photocopying in his kitchen.*

Xerography

1938

Chester Carlson

US physicist Chester Carlson wanted to make office work easier. He studied various methods of copying documents, then, in 1938, produced his first xerographic copy, using a zinc plate coated with sulfur. The original was on a microscope slide, and the copy was formed from moss spores stuck to wax paper. (✳ *See also* **Making Copies**.)

DDT

1939

Paul Müller

The chlorine-based chemical DDT had been known for years before Swiss chemist Paul Müller discovered, in 1939, that it made a good insecticide. It kills insects but has little effect on warm-blooded animals. In World War II, DDT was used to protect troops from insect-borne diseases. Later, it was used to kill insects that attack crops. Because DDT tends to persist in the environment and can find its way into food, it is now little used.

MAKING COPIES

Xerography gets its name from the Greek "*xeros*" meaning "dry." A lens projects an image on to a drum, the surface of which conducts electricity when exposed to light. Where the image is bright, the drum becomes more conductive and the electricity leaks away. Powdered resin dusted on the drum is attracted to the parts that are still electrified. The resin is transferred to paper and heated until it melts to form a permanent copy.

Early xerographic copiers were big and slow. This is part of one from 1960.

Life without xerography
Copying documents used to be difficult. They could be photographed with a special camera, but this was expensive and too big for an office. Or they could be made by the diffusion-transfer process, invented in 1939. This made copies in the office, but used wet chemicals and was very slow.

Xerography at work
Carlson's process has transformed office work. Machines that make 60 copies a minute are now commonplace. Xerography is also used in laser printers, which produce documents directly from digital data, rather than from other documents. Color copiers, basically three machines in one box, now offer excellent quality.

Nuclear fission

1939

Lise Meitner, Otto Frisch

When uranium is bombarded with neutrons, the nuclei of its atoms can split, releasing energy. This was discovered by German chemists Otto Hahn and Fritz Strassmann in 1938, but it was Austrian physicists Lise Meitner and Otto Frisch, her nephew, who explained the details and coined the term "nuclear fission." Realizing that it could be used to make a bomb, they quickly alerted other physicists and, through them, the US president.

Single-rotor helicopter

1940

Igor Sikorsky

The first successful helicopter, made in 1936, had two rotors that went

1939 On September 1, German troops invade Poland. Two days later, Britain and France declare war on Germany. The French rely on their heavily fortified "Maginot Line" along the German border. Britain prepares for all-out war.

1940 US writer Ernest Hemingway writes his novel *For Whom the Bell Tolls*, based on his experiences in the Spanish Civil War. Its main idea is that everyone, wherever they live, should be concerned by oppression occurring anywhere.

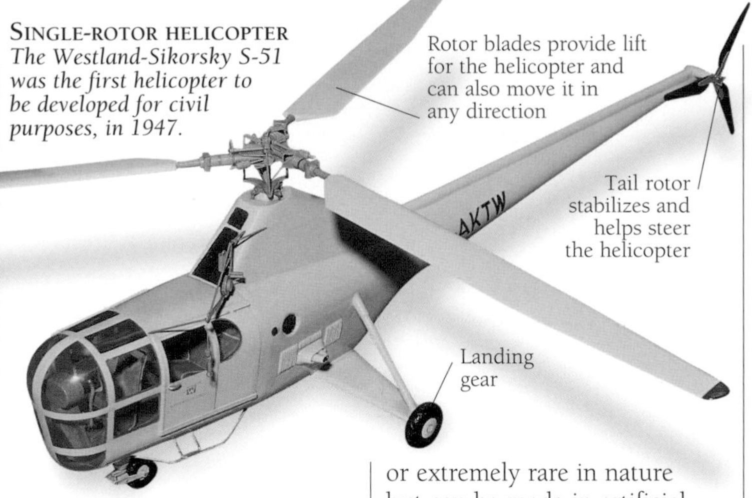

SINGLE-ROTOR HELICOPTER *The Westland-Sikorsky S-51 was the first helicopter to be developed for civil purposes, in 1947.*

around in opposite directions. This stopped the machine from spinning around. By 1940, the Russian-born US engineer Igor Sikorsky had flown a single-rotor helicopter. He stopped the spin with a small tail rotor that pushed sideways. It could also be used to help the helicopter turn left or right.

Digital logic design

1940

Claude Shannon

Digital logic circuits operate machines from computers to dishwashers. They would be almost impossible to design without US engineer Claude Shannon's thesis of 1940. He said that the work of British mathematician George Boole (✳ *see* **page 140**) could be used to simplify the design of electrical circuits that worked out what a machine should do next. To prove it, he built a robot mouse that could find its way around a maze.

Plutonium

1940

Glenn Seaborg

Plutonium is one of several elements, all heavier than uranium, that are nonexistent or extremely rare in nature but can be made in artificial nuclear reactions. US chemist Glenn Seaborg and his colleagues discovered 10 of these between 1940 and 1955. Plutonium is the most important because of the special properties of one form called plutonium-239. This highly toxic material, which is produced in some types of nuclear reactors, can be used to make atomic weapons.

Binary electronic computing

1940

John Atanasoff, Clifford Berry

Early computing machines used the decimal system to represent numbers. This is not a good way of using electronic circuits. US mathematician John Atanasoff and his student Clifford Berry realized this as early as 1940. Their unsuccessful attempt at a computer, the ABC, used the binary system, which works with the base 2 instead of 10. It was more efficient because logic circuits work best when switching between just two voltages. Although the ABC was little known at the time, it may have influenced EDVAC, the first modern computer design (✳ *see* **page 208**).

Anti-g flying suit

1941

Frederick Banting, Wilbur Franks

A fighter plane making a tight turn acts like a spin dryer. The so-called "g" force drains blood out of the pilot's brain, possibly causing a blackout. When a team under Sir Frederick Banting, better known for his work on insulin (✳ *see* **page 186**), discovered this, US scientist Wilbur Franks started work on an anti-g suit. The design his team produced was made from two layers of rubber with water in between them. When the suit was laced tightly around the pilot, it kept the blood in place, allowing tighter turns. The Franks Flying Suit Mk II was ready by 1941. Sadly, on his way to Britain to demonstrate it, Banting died in an airplane crash.

ANTI-G FLYING SUIT *By the 1950s, suits like this one by Dunlop were filled with air, not water.*

1941 On December 7, the US wakes up to the reality of world war as Japanese submarines and carrier-based planes attack the US Pacific fleet based at Pearl Harbor. Eight battleships and 10 other vessels are sunk or damaged.

1941 US sculptor Gutzon Borglum completes his giant heads of presidents George Washington, Thomas Jefferson, Abraham Lincoln, and Theodore Roosevelt carved into the granite of Mount Rushmore, South Dakota.

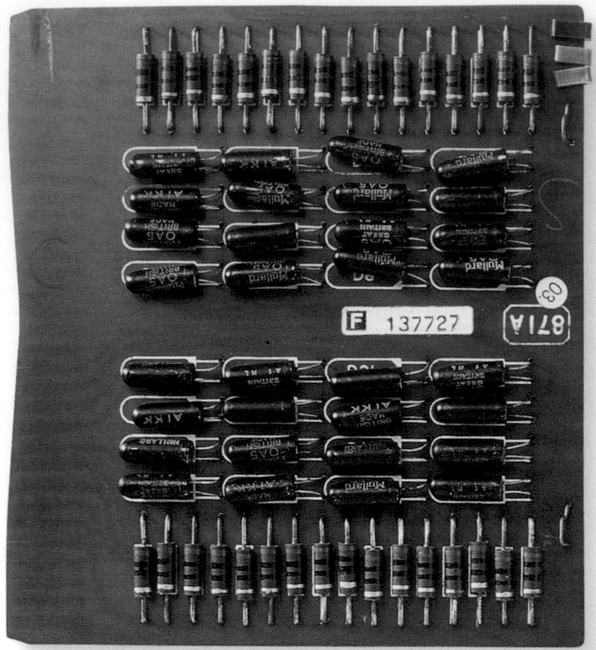

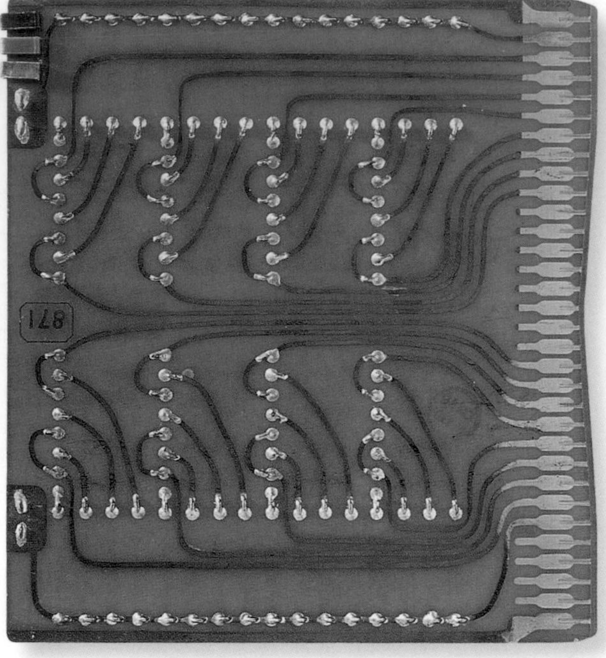

Printed circuit board *The front and back of a board from a 1959 Ferranti Orion computer reveal its simple, hand-drawn design.*

Electro-mechanical computer

1941

Konrad Zuse

The first true computer was built in 1941 by German engineer Konrad Zuse. It was controlled by a program and represented numbers in binary form, but it was not electronic. It used relays—switches operated by electromagnets. As these have actual moving contacts, they are extremely slow compared with electronic switches. So Zuse's Z3 computer was really the last of the mechanical computers, not the first of those we use today.

Printed circuit board

1941

Paul Eisler

Until Austrian engineer Paul Eisler invented the printed circuit board, or PCB, all electronic equipment was laboriously wired by hand. In 1941, Eisler printed wiring patterns on to copper foil stuck to plastic sheet, then placed this in an etching bath to remove the copper not protected by printing. After cleaning, and drilling holes for wires, the board was ready to receive components. The first PCBs were fitted inside anti-aircraft shells.

Polyethylene terephthalate

1941

Rex Whinfield, James Dickson

Clothes, duvet filling, bottles, and photographic film can all be made from polyethylene terephthalate, better known as PET. It was invented in 1941 by British chemists Rex Whinfield and James Dickson. Because Britain was at war, it was not until 1954 that the new material went into production there, as Terylene. By then, the US DuPont company had already developed and launched their own version of the material, which they called Dacron.

Silicon solar cell

1941

Russell Ohl

Solar cells convert sunlight into electricity. Modern cells can convert about one-third of the sunlight that falls on them, but the very first devices, made from about 1890, converted less than 1 percent. The breakthrough came with a cell invented in 1941 by US scientist Russell Ohl. He used two types of impure silicon, rather than pure silicon and a metal. When brought together and exposed to light, current flowed from one to the other.

Ballistic missile

1942

Wernher von Braun

A ballistic missile is a rocket with a warhead that flies high into the sky and then falls on to its target. The development of such weapons has now led to the design of large rockets for peaceful purposes. The first effective ballistic missile was the V-2, designed for Hitler by German engineer Wernher von Braun and first launched in October 1942. It carried 1,600 lb (725 kg) of explosive 50 miles (80 km) above Earth to drop on London as the most feared weapon of World War II.

Scanning electron microscope

1942

Vladimir Zworykin, Dennis McMullan

Scanning electron microscopes, or SEMs, combine high magnification with great depth of focus to produce vivid pictures of tiny three-dimensional objects. They work by scanning objects with a beam of electrons. The first SEM was built by Russian-born US physicist Vladimir Zworykin and others in 1942. It didn't seem as good as existing electron microscopes (✱ *see* **page 196**), so it was

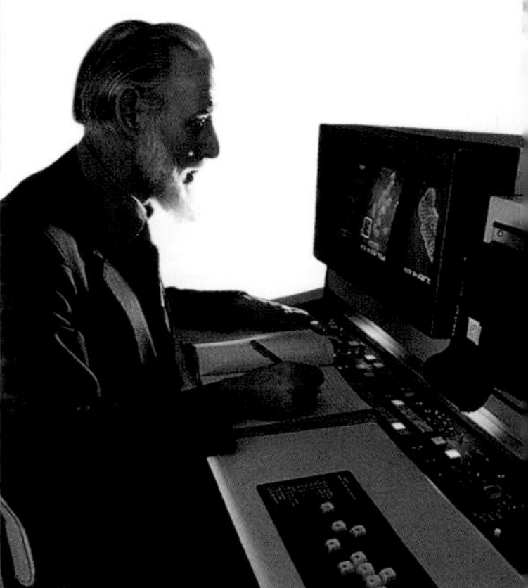

Scanning electron microscope *The picture from a SEM is viewed on a screen, not through an eyepiece.*

1942 The elegant French luxury liner *Normandie*, holder of the Blue Riband for the fastest Atlantic crossing—which it won with a time of 3 days, 22 hours, and 7 minutes—catches fire in New York harbor and is destroyed.

1942 In Oxford, England, an organization called Oxfam is created to raise money for hungry children in Greece, which is ravaged by war. It will continue after the war to provide aid for refugees and for poorer parts of the world.

dropped. Later, British engineer Charles Oatley got his student Dennis McMullan to try again, and by 1951 he had built a working instrument. The first commercial SEM, producing the striking images familiar today, was launched in 1965.

Nuclear reactor

1942

Enrico Fermi

When a uranium-235 nucleus splits under bombardment by neutrons, it gives out further neutrons. These can split other nuclei, which release yet more neutrons. This process was first kept going in a controlled "chain reaction" by a team led by Italian-born US physicist Enrico Fermi. Their nuclear reactor, built in a squash court at Chicago University, was used for research that helped build the first atomic bomb.

Frequency-hopping radio

1943

Hedy Lamarr, George Antheil

Eavesdropping enemies or radio interference can be overcome by making the radio frequency jump about. Hedy Lamarr, who is also known for her work as an actress, patented a system for military use based on this idea. A punched paper roll, similar to those in automatic pianos, made the transmitter switch between many different frequencies, while an identical roll kept the receiver in step. The same basic idea is used in Bluetooth technology today.

Aqua-Lung

1943

Jacques Cousteau, Émile Gagnan

Before French explorer Jacques Cousteau and engineer Émile Gagnan thought up the Aqua-Lung in 1943, divers got air through pipes or by using a snorkel. They could not swim freely far below the surface. The Aqua-Lung had compressed air cylinders worn on the body and connected to the diver's mouthpiece through an automatic pressure regulator. It changed our view of the oceans and created the popular sport of scuba diving.

Function of DNA

1944

Oswald Avery

The first step toward unlocking the mechanism of genetic inheritance was taken in 1944 by Canadian-born US bacteriologist Oswald Avery, who explained an observation made by British researcher Fred Griffith in 1928. Griffith found that pneumonia bacteria were either rough or smooth and that an extract of the smooth bacteria could make the rough ones smooth. More important, all their descendants inherited this characteristic. In a long series of experiments, Avery showed that the substance responsible was not a protein, as expected, but a nucleic acid, DNA (✱ *see* **page 149**).

AQUA-LUNG *Scuba divers, like this one exploring Red Sea corals, take their own air with them, which gives them greater freedom.*

1943 The Rodgers and Hammerstein musical *Oklahoma!* opens on Broadway, New York, to wild acclaim. Including songs such as *Surrey with the Fringe on Top*, it will win a Pulitzer Prize and continue for 2,248 performances.

1944 Kiri Te Kanawa is born in Gisborne, New Zealand, to an Irish mother and an aristocratic Maori father. After success as a soprano in her own country, she will study singing in London and eventually become an international star.

ARTIFICIAL KIDNEY *Home dialysis machines appeared in the 1960s. This machine, discreetly disguised as furniture, was used by one of the first home patients.*

Myers-Briggs Type Indicator®

1944

Katharine Cook Briggs, Isabel Briggs Myers

In the 1940s, Katharine Cook Briggs and her daughter Isabel Briggs Myers developed the Myers-Briggs Type Indicator®. It is a questionnaire that aims to reveal people's different ways of seeing the world, dividing them into 16 types, based on how much they lean toward one end or the other of four scales: Extrovert–Introvert; Sensing–Intuition; Thinking–Feeling; and Judging–Perceiving. This test is still used by employers to determine the right people for the right roles.

Electronic computer

1944

Tommy Flowers, John Mauchly, John Presper Eckert

Mechanical computers were in use by the 1930s, but electronics, using tubes, promised greater speed. The first all-electronic computer, known as Colossus, was developed by UK engineer Tommy Flowers and used at Bletchley Park, UK. Programmed by switches and plugs, not a stored program, it was the first working machine to use electronics for logic and counting. It was part of the top-secret work that cracked the German army's Enigma code during World War II. US engineers Mauchly and Eckert developed a similar machine a year later.

Modern computer architecture

1945

John von Neumann

Most modern computers keep their programs, and the data on which they work, in one and the same memory. This makes them more flexible. It is not clear who invented the idea, but the best candidate is Hungarian-born US mathematician John von Neumann, who was heavily involved in designing the "stored program" computer EDVAC. This design appeared in 1945, but the concept was first proved by an experimental computer in Manchester, England, in 1948. (✱ *See also* **Computer Pioneers.**)

Atomic bomb

1945

Robert Oppenheimer

Most people would prefer that the atomic bomb had not been invented. But in 1940, with Germany at war with the world and possibly working on a bomb of its own, the development of an atomic weapon seemed essential. US physicist Robert Oppenheimer took charge of the Manhattan project, which developed the technology needed to purify the right kind of uranium or plutonium and make it explode. After a test in July 1945, the first atomic bomb used in war was dropped on August 6, destroying the Japanese city of Hiroshima and most of its inhabitants.

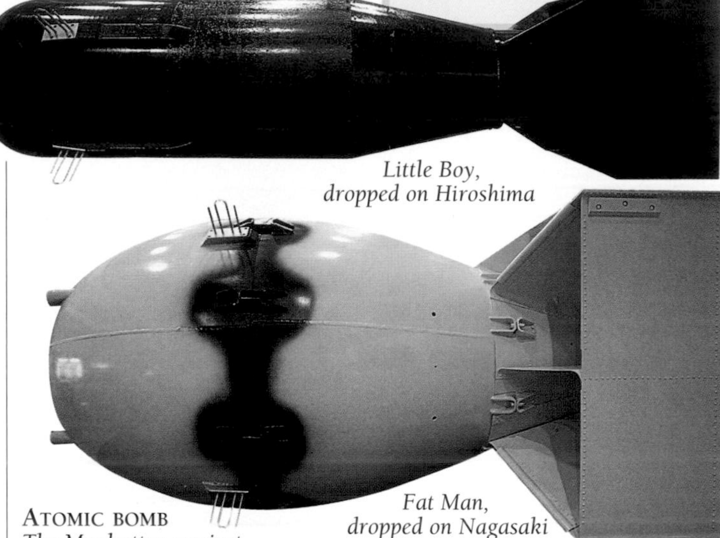

Little Boy, dropped on Hiroshima

Fat Man, dropped on Nagasaki

ATOMIC BOMB *The Manhattan project produced two types of bombs. Little Boy was a plutonium bomb and Fat Man was a uranium bomb.*

Only part of Charles Babbage's Analytical Engine was completed before Babbage's death in 1871. This is part of the "mill" or processor of the machine, with its printing mechanism.

Bikini

1946

Jacques Heim, Louis Réard

Skimpy two-piece swimsuits get their name from Bikini Atoll in the South Pacific. French fashion designer Louis Réard chose the name to upstage rival designer Jacques Heim who, in 1946, had started selling a two-piece called the Atome. On July 5, four days after the US tested an atomic bomb over Bikini, Réard launched his explosively small creation under the suddenly well-known name.

1944 US composer Aaron Copland writes *Appalachian Spring* for US ballet dancer Martha Graham. The music from the ballet perfectly expresses the open-air, pioneering spirit of the US and will become a concert classic.

1945 On May 8, the end of war in Europe is formally declared. as the Germans surrender in France. On August 14, the Japanese surrender to the US and Allies. World War II is finally over.

COMPUTER PIONEERS

THE COMPUTER ARCHITECTURE pioneered by John von Neumann is basically simple. A single memory stores data coming from outside and from the arithmetic unit that does the computing. Instructions and data are retrieved from the same memory by the control unit—which sequences and decodes instructions—and by output devices such as displays. Earlier computers used several different architectures and often worked with inefficient decimal arithmetic.

BEFORE ELECTRONICS
The idea of a programmable computer goes back to British mathematician Charles Babbage's Analytical Engine, conceived in 1834 but never built. The first working, nonelectronic computer was built in 1941 by German engineer Konrad Zuse.

EARLY ELECTRONIC COMPUTERS
The first all-electronic computer, Colossus, was big and slow. Better architecture and use of the binary system gradually improved things. The first practical stored program machine, EDSAC, was built by British computer scientist Maurice Wilkes in the 1940s.

MODERN COMPUTERS
The arrival of integrated circuits (ICs) transformed computers from the early 1960s onward. Computers had already been shrunk by transistors, but ICs made them even smaller and could also form compact, high-speed memories.

Motor scooter

1946

Corradino d'Ascanio

The shape of the modern motor scooter was determined in 1946 by Italian engineer Corradino d'Ascanio. His boss, Enrico Piaggio, wanted something to get him around the aircraft engine factory he owned. D'Ascanio soon came up with the basic design: U-shaped body, two-stroke engine under the seat, and small, easy-to-change wheels. Cheap to make and fun to ride, the Vespa (Italian for wasp) was named after the sound its engine made, and it became an engineering classic.

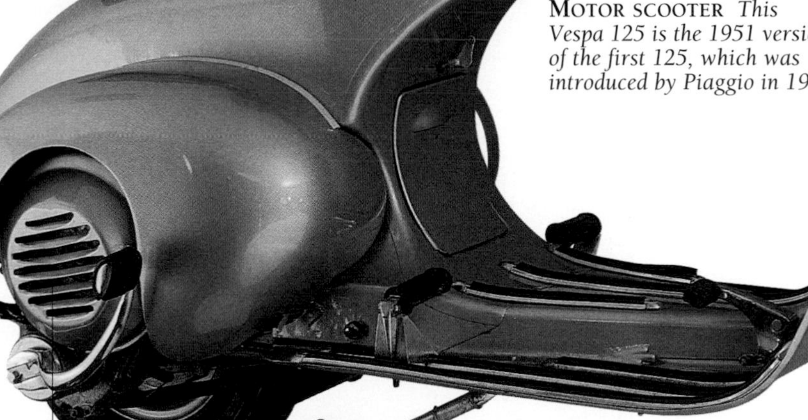

Grip was twisted to control the throttle

Engine and gearbox directly connected to the rear wheel

Easily changed wheels

MOTOR SCOOTER *This Vespa 125 is the 1951 version of the first 125, which was introduced by Piaggio in 1948.*

Microwave oven

1946

Percy Spencer

When US engineer Percy Spencer was working on radar for the Raytheon Company in 1945, he noticed that the powerful microwaves had melted some candies in his pocket. After experimenting with popcorn and eggs, Spencer built the first, crude microwave oven. In 1946, Raytheon took out a patent, and in 1947 the Radar Range went on sale at $5,000.

Tupperware

c.1946

Earl Tupper

Plastic refrigerator boxes were invented by US plastics manufacturer Earl Tupper, in about 1946. He found the right plastic and designed an airtight seal, but people did not seem to want the boxes. In 1948, after meeting ace saleswoman Brownie Wise, Tupper hit on a new sales technique. Hostesses invited their friends over, then demonstrated and sold the boxes to them.

1946 Former British prime minister Winston Churchill popularizes the term "iron curtain" in a speech warning of the dangers of communist expansion and Soviet isolationism. The Cold War begins.

1946 Perhaps the most widely read book about babies, *Common Sense Book of Baby and Child Care*, written by US pediatrician Benjamin Spock, is published. It will be blamed for many things, including the youth culture of the 1960s.

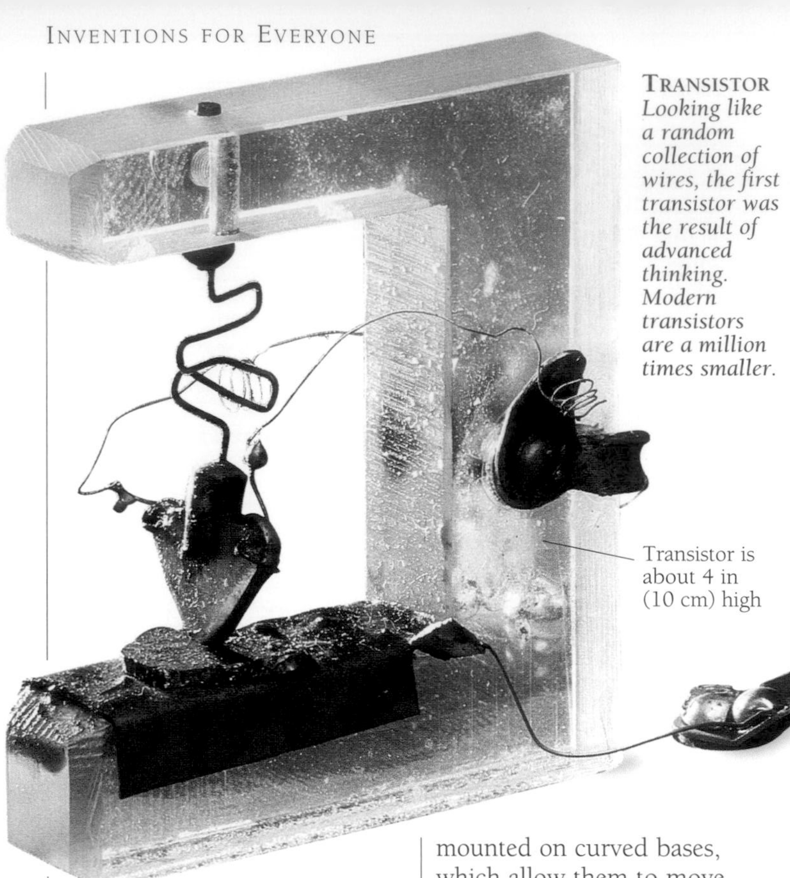

TRANSISTOR *Looking like a random collection of wires, the first transistor was the result of advanced thinking. Modern transistors are a million times smaller.*

Carbon dating

1947

Willard Libby

Carbon dating enables archaeologists to estimate the age of organic materials. It was developed by US chemist Willard Libby in 1947. He showed that Earth's atmosphere contains a tiny proportion of a radioactive form of carbon, carbon-14, and that living organisms take up both this and ordinary carbon. After the death of an organism, its carbon-14 starts to decay, so the smaller the proportion of carbon-14, the older the sample must be.

Subbuteo

1947

Peter Adolph

Subbuteo is a popular tabletop soccer game played with model soccer players mounted on curved bases, which allow them to move without falling over. Players flick their chosen players at an oversized ball. The game was invented in 1947 by British birdwatcher Peter Adolph. He named it using the Latin name of a bird called the hobby, *Falco subbuteo*. When its current maker, Hasbro, said in 2000 that production would have to stop, there was an international outcry. They relented and the game lives on.

False eyelashes

1947

David Aylott, Eric Aylott

The first convincing false eyelashes were made for the movie industry. In 1947, British studio makeup artists David and Eric Aylott created strips of false eyelashes that were easy to apply and could stand the scrutiny of a close-up. The Aylotts later developed lashes for everyday use under the name Eyelure. By the 1960s, Eyelure was selling eight million pairs a year.

Transistor

1947

John Bardeen, Walter Brattain, William Shockley

A transistor is a tiny piece of silicon within which the flow of electricity is controlled, making the whole of modern electronics possible. There are many different types of transistors. The first one, invented in 1947 by US physicists John Bardeen, Walter Brattain, and William Shockley, was made of germanium, not silicon, and worked on a different principle from those in modern computer chips. But it started a revolution. Within 25 years, electronics based on vacuum tubes (✳ *see* **page 176**) was virtually dead.

Holography

1948

Dennis Gabor

Unlike an ordinary photograph, a hologram captures every detail of the light waves reflected by an object. This makes objects appear with startling realism; in a hologram viewed at an angle, objects look just as they would from that angle. The technique was invented in 1948 by Hungarian-born British engineer Dennis Gabor. It works by recording the interference pattern created when light reflected from an object mixes with unreflected light. The best light source is a laser. As this was not invented in 1948, Gabor had to make do with ordinary light shining through a small hole.

Long-playing record

1948

Peter Goldmark

Before 1948, a 12 in (30 cm) record played for only four minutes each side, produced poor sound, and broke easily. So a disc that

LONG-PLAYING RECORD *By 1967, when The Beatles released the record* Sgt. Pepper's Lonely Hearts Club Band, *LP cover design had become high art.*

1947 Jack R. (Jackie) Robinson becomes the first African American major league baseball player of the 20th century. As a player for the Brooklyn Dodgers, he wins rookie of the year for leading the league in stolen bases.

1948 The General Assembly of the United Nations adopts the Universal Declaration of Human Rights at a session in Paris on December 10. The vote is carried unopposed, but eight members, including the USSR, abstain.

offered 25 minutes of pure sound per side, and was made of flexible vinyl, created a sensation. It was developed by Hungarian-born US engineer Peter Goldmark for Columbia Records. Rival company RCA-Victor soon brought out a record that played for the same time as the old "12-incher"—ideal for a single song—but was only 7 in (18 cm) across. Both were highly successful.

Polaroid camera

1948

Edwin Land

US inventor Edwin Land had a successful company making Polaroid material. When his daughter asked to see a picture he had just taken of her, he asked himself, "Why not?" In 1948, after a few years' work, he launched the Polaroid Land camera. The secret was in the film, which contained its own developing system and could produce a brown-and-white print 60 seconds after the picture was taken.

Tennis shoes

1949

Adolf Dassler

Tennis shoes can be traced back to a design that German sports shoe manufacturer Adolf "Adi" Dasler registered in 1949—a year after he split with his brother Rudolf to found the company Adidas. Dasler's shoes were worn by some notable athletes, including the American Jesse Owens, who won four gold medals in the 1936 Olympics. The new shoes had three stripes down each side, which gave extra support. The stripes were probably the start of the elaborate decoration seen on tennis shoes today.

Plastic wrap

1949

Dow Chemical Company

Traditional plastic wrap is a plastic called PVDC. It is related to PVC, a material used for window frames and electrical insulation. Plastic wrap was supposedly discovered in 1933 by accident, as an indestructible sticky residue on laboratory glassware. It was first marketed in the US by the Dow Chemical Company in 1949. The first users were professional caterers, but a domestic version, Saran Wrap, appeared in 1953.

Error-correcting code

1950

Richard Hamming

Today, much information comes in the form of digital codes. Cell phones and CDs, for example, use digital codes. Unfortunately, the media that transmit or store these codes are not perfect, and errors occur. If these were not corrected, many systems would not work. US mathematician Richard Hamming solved this problem as early as 1950. He devised codes that showed when an error had been made and also how to correct it.

POLAROID CAMERA *The first Polaroid Land camera looked much like the roll-film cameras many photographers were using at the time.*

1949 On October 1, China becomes a socialist country as Mao Zedong, having defeated Nationalist opposition, proclaims that the government of the People's Republic of China is now established in Beijing.

1950 US scientist and science-fiction writer Isaac Asimov publishes a collection of short stories entitled *I, Robot*. It includes his three laws of robotics, a moral system that should be built into all robots to stop them from hurting humans.

INFORMATION & UNCERTAINTY

IMPROVEMENTS IN information technology, and a new understanding of the machinery of life, dominated the years after 1950. These developments were related—scientists needed computers to help them map human genes. They used them for many other discoveries, too. Suddenly, we knew almost too much. How should we use this knowledge?

Airbag

1952

John Hetrick

The first airbag was patented in 1952 by US inventor John Hetrick. But it was not until 1973, when the rising death toll on US roads began to cause concern, that General Motors developed a practical airbag and offered it as an option. In spite of consumer resistance, and worries about deaths caused by early airbags, by 1988, most US cars were equipped with airbags. European car makers followed suit later.

High-level computer language

1952

Grace Hopper

In the early days of computing, programs were written in code that suited a computer but was difficult for people to read. Mathematician (and US Navy Rear Admiral) Grace Hopper made computers more user-friendly. She wrote a program that could translate a language quite like English into a list of instructions a computer could follow. This led to one of the earliest high-level languages, COBOL, still in use today.

Polio vaccine

1952

Jonas Salk, Albert Sabin

Poliomyelitis, or polio, is a viral infection that can cause paralysis. It posed a serious threat until US physician Jonas Salk developed a vaccine that could create resistance to the virus. It contained an inactive (dead) virus and was first used in a successful trial in 1952. After further trials, the Salk vaccine was approved in 1955. Later, Polish–US physician Albert Sabin developed the vaccine more widely used today, which contains weakened polio virus.

Color television

1953

National Television Systems Committee

It was hard to make televisions show color without making existing black-and-white receivers useless. The US National Television Systems Committee (NTSC) provided the solution in 1953. Their system splits pictures into brightness variations, which can be displayed on a normal black-and-white set, and color information, which color receivers use to add color to the picture. Later variants of NTSC that transmit colors more accurately are now in use.

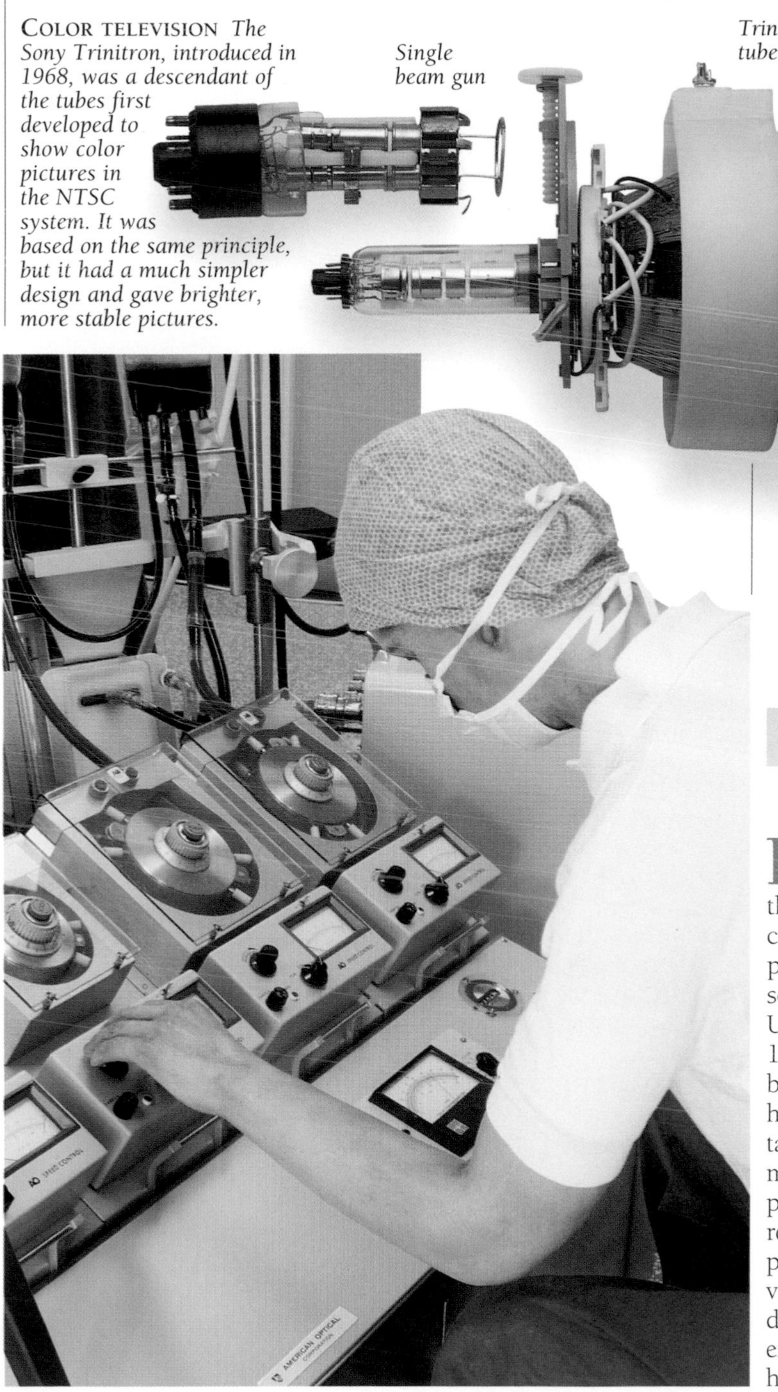

Single beam gun

Trinitron tube

Color television *The Sony Trinitron, introduced in 1968, was a descendant of the tubes first developed to show color pictures in the NTSC system. It was based on the same principle, but it had a much simpler design and gave brighter, more stable pictures.*

Use of heart–lung machine *This reconstruction of a 1980 operating room shows a heart–lung machine in use. The circular devices in the center pump blood.*

Use of heart–lung machine

1953

John Gibbon Jr.

Heart surgery was once almost impossible because the heart is full of blood and constantly moving. The first person to drain a human heart so that he could work on it was US surgeon John Gibbon Jr. in 1953. He was able to do this because the job of the patient's heart had been temporarily taken over by a heart–lung machine. This continually pumped blood out of the body, recharged it with oxygen, and pumped it back. Modern versions are the result of decades of development by experimenters. Their use in heart surgery is now routine.

1952 In Kenya, the British declare a state of emergency and arrest Jomo Kenyatta, leader of the Kenya African Union, in an effort to crush the Mau Mau—armed members of the Kikuyu tribe rebelling against British rule.

1953 Nepalese Sherpa Tenzing Norgay and New Zealand mountaineer Edmund Hillary reach the top of Mount Everest, on May 29. They are the first people who can prove they have climbed to the summit. Hillary is later knighted.

Structure of DNA

1953

Francis Crick, James Watson, Rosalind Franklin

See **pages 216–217** for the story of the race to find the structure of DNA.

Breathalyzer

1954

Robert Borkenstein

The difficulty in proving that a driver had been drinking led US policeman Robert Borkenstein to invent the Breathalyzer in 1954. Alcohol in the bloodstream passes into the breath, so the more alcohol there is in a driver's blood, the more there will be in their breath. The Breathalyzer has a glass tube containing chemicals that change from orange to green as they react with alcohol. Drivers blow into a bag to give a measured quantity of breath. If the green goes too far along the tube, they are over the limit.

BREATHALYZER *A police officer would fit a fresh sample tube into this 1979 Breathalyzer before asking a driver to blow into the bag.*

Bag inflated to measure breath

Turboprop airliner

1953

Vickers Armstrong Aircraft

The turboprop led the way toward today's mass air travel. Basically, a jet engine driving a propeller, it gave higher speeds and a smoother flight than a piston engine. The first turboprop airliner was the British Vickers Viscount. It carried its first paying passengers in 1953. The makers liked to boast that it was so smooth you could balance a coin on the arm of your seat—on its edge.

Pleasure center in the brain

1954

James Olds, Peter Milner

Laboratory rats can be trained to work a lever in return for food. But in 1954, US psychologist James Olds and physiologist Peter Milner found a part of the rat's brain that they could stimulate electrically to give a reward greater than any food. By wiring this "pleasure center" to a lever, they could get the rat to push it thousands of times an hour. The center is now thought to be involved in human behaviors such as drug addiction.

Kidney transplant

1954

Joseph Murray

All early attempts to transplant organs failed. Scientists eventually realized that rejection was caused by the body's immune system. US surgeon Joseph Murray confirmed this when he tried to graft skin on to wounded soldiers. He noticed that the only successful grafts came from an identical twin. In 1954, he and several colleagues tried transplanting a kidney from one twin to another. The twin given the new kidney survived for years. In the 1960s, after drugs to suppress the immune system were developed, Murray made successful kidney transplants from unrelated donors.

Nuclear power station

1954

Institute of Physics and Power Engineering

The first operational nuclear power station was built at Obninsk, near Moscow. It started working in June 1954. The station was designed by the USSR's Institute of Physics and Power Engineering, which started work on it in 1951. It was small and simple and had a power output of only 5 megawatts (MW), as compared with 1000 MW for a modern reactor, but it was still a triumph for the USSR.

Polypropylene

1954

Karl Ziegler, Giulio Natta

In 1953, Italian chemist Karl Ziegler discovered a catalyst (a substance that speeds up a chemical reaction) that allowed polythene to be made from the gas ethylene more easily. In 1954, Italian chemist Giulio Natta discovered that Ziegler's catalyst also worked with the related gas propylene. The result was polypropylene, the tough, flexible plastic now used for everything from garbage cans to carpets. Commercial production began in 1957.

Atomic clock

1955

Louis Essen, Jack Parry

In 1955, working at the National Physical Laboratory with his colleague Jack Parry, British physicist Louis Essen made a clock that would gain or lose less than one second in 300 years. It worked by electrically sensing a natural vibration of cesium atoms.

1954 British medical student Roger (later Sir Roger) Bannister runs a mile in less than four minutes, breaking both a record and a psychological barrier. Bannister's time will be beaten seven weeks later by Australian John Landy.

1954 Japanese director Akira Kurosawa blends Japanese tradition with western technique in *The Seven Samurai*, perhaps the best-ever film about the Samurai, a powerful warrior caste. It wins silver at the Venice Film Festival.

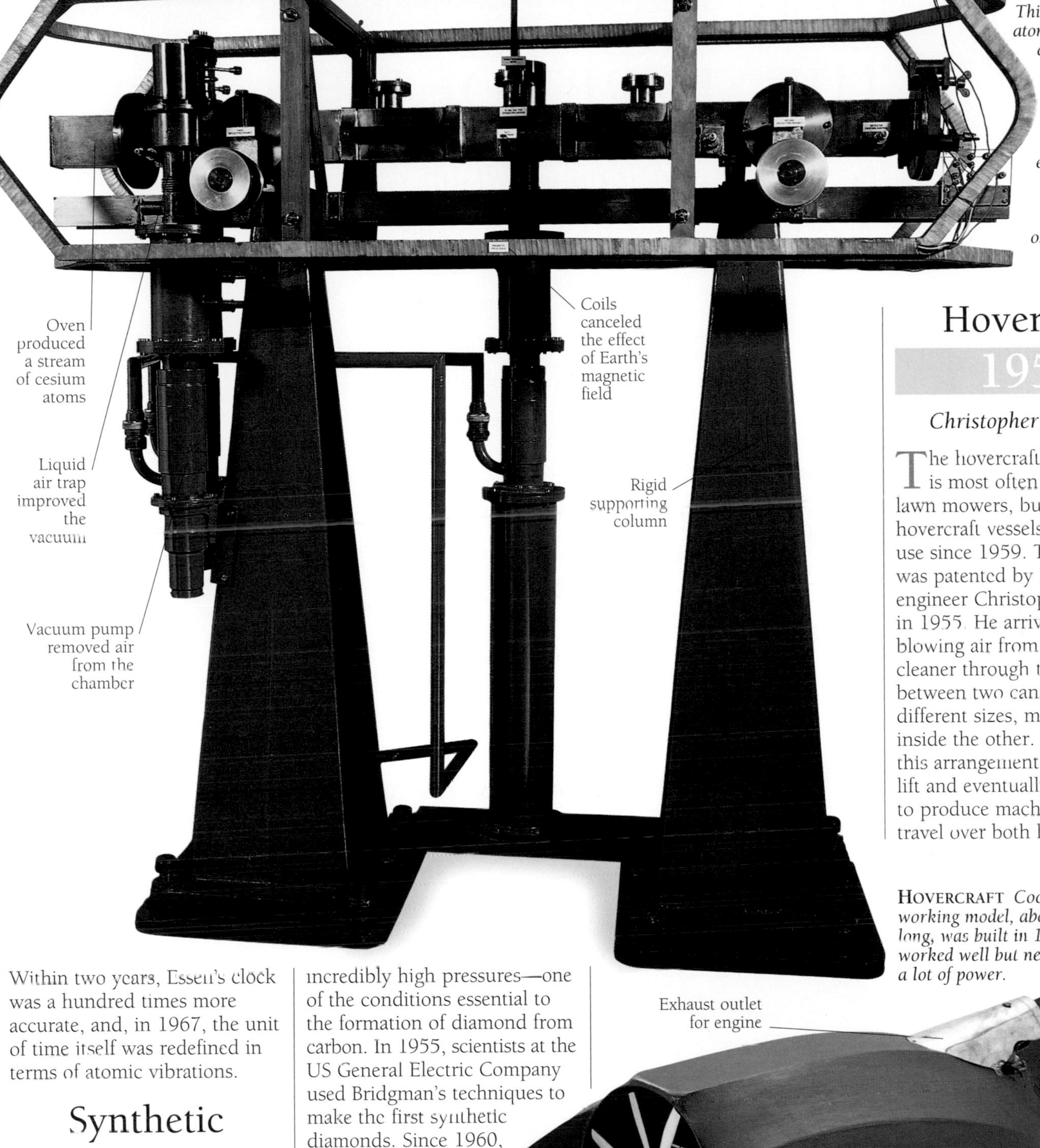

ATOMIC CLOCK *This part of the first atomic clock created a beam of cesium atoms that could absorb radio waves of only one precise frequency. This effect was used to monitor the frequency of a separate quartz oscillator, keeping it very accurate.*

Within two years, Essen's clock was a hundred times more accurate, and, in 1967, the unit of time itself was redefined in terms of atomic vibrations.

Synthetic diamonds

1955

Percy Bridgman, General Electric Company

US physicist Percy Bridgman never made diamonds himself, but he did develop ways of subjecting materials to incredibly high pressures—one of the conditions essential to the formation of diamond from carbon. In 1955, scientists at the US General Electric Company used Bridgman's techniques to make the first synthetic diamonds. Since 1960, industrial diamonds have been made in quantity by this process. These diamonds, which are a bit like grains of sand, are used to add bite to cutting tools like saw blades and drill bits.

Hovercraft

1955

Christopher Cockerell

The hovercraft principle is most often seen in lawn mowers, but seagoing hovercraft vessels have been in use since 1959. The principle was patented by British engineer Christopher Cockerell in 1955. He arrived at it by blowing air from a vacuum cleaner through the space between two cans of slightly different sizes, mounted one inside the other. He found that this arrangement gave increased lift and eventually scaled it up to produce machines that could travel over both land and water.

HOVERCRAFT *Cockerell's first working model, about 3 ft (1 m) long, was built in 1955. It worked well but needed a lot of power.*

Exhaust outlet for engine

Smooth skin reduced drag

1954 British writer William (later Sir William) Golding publishes his first and best-known novel, *Lord of the Flies*. Schoolboys stranded on an island descend into savagery as they struggle to survive. It will be filmed in 1963 and 1990.

1955 Rock 'n' roll gets its first wide airing as US band Bill Haley and the Comets shoot to the top of the charts with *Rock Around the Clock*. Its blues-based harmony and strong backbeat enrage the old and enchant the young.

THE SECRET OF LIFE

Francis Crick and James Watson race to find the chemical structure of DNA

CRICK AND WATSON World War II interrupted Francis Crick's studies, so he was still working on an advanced degree when biologist James Watson arrived at the Cavendish. Crick's official work was soon put aside as he took up the challenge of DNA.

Francis Crick

James Watson

In February 1953, two men rushed into the Eagle, a pub in Cambridge, England. The English one, Francis Crick, said that they had found the secret of life. The American, James Watson, wondered if they really had.

The race to find the structure of DNA began in 1944, when US immunologist Oswald Avery showed that bacteria inherited their characteristics through DNA. This has four key components—A, T, G, and C for short. In 1949, Austrian biochemist Erwin Chargaff noticed that the amount of A is always the same as the amount of T, and likewise for G and C.

This was all that was known about DNA when biologist James Watson arrived at Cambridge's Cavendish Laboratory in 1951. The Cavendish specialized in X-ray analysis of molecular structures, and physicist Francis Crick was an expert there. Watson was convinced that unraveling DNA

Original laboratory model of DNA

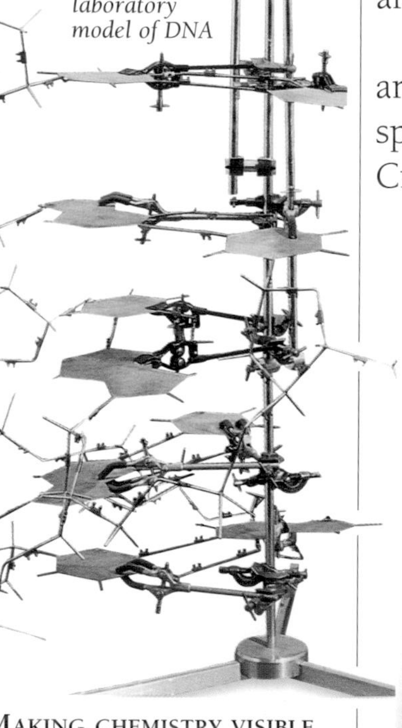

MAKING CHEMISTRY VISIBLE The ways that atoms fit with each other follow known rules. Before computers, it was hard to see the effect of these rules without building a physical model. This double helix was assembled by James Watson using metal plates shaped to represent the chemical groups he knew were present in DNA.

Structure of DNA

1953

Francis Crick, James Watson, Rosalind Franklin

See **pages 216–217** for the story of the race to find the structure of DNA.

Turboprop airliner

1953

Vickers Armstrong Aircraft

The turboprop led the way toward today's mass air travel. Basically, a jet engine driving a propeller, it gave higher speeds and a smoother flight than a piston engine. The first turboprop airliner was the British Vickers Viscount. It carried its first paying passengers in 1953. The makers liked to boast that it was so smooth you could balance a coin on the arm of your seat—on its edge.

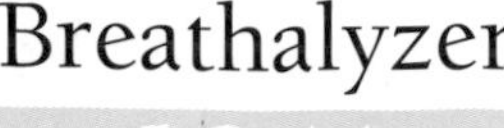

Breathalyzer

1954

Robert Borkenstein

The difficulty in proving that a driver had been drinking led US policeman Robert Borkenstein to invent the Breathalyzer in 1954. Alcohol in the bloodstream passes into the breath, so the more alcohol there is in a driver's blood, the more there will be in their breath. The Breathalyzer has a glass tube containing chemicals that change from orange to green as they react with alcohol. Drivers blow into a bag to give a measured quantity of breath. If the green goes too far along the tube, they are over the limit.

BREATHALYZER *A police officer would fit a fresh sample tube into this 1979 Breathalyzer before asking a driver to blow into the bag.*

Bag inflated to measure breath

Pleasure center in the brain

1954

James Olds, Peter Milner

Laboratory rats can be trained to work a lever in return for food. But in 1954, US psychologist James Olds and physiologist Peter Milner found a part of the rat's brain that they could stimulate electrically to give a reward greater than any food. By wiring this "pleasure center" to a lever, they could get the rat to push it thousands of times an hour. The center is now thought to be involved in human behaviors such as drug addiction.

Kidney transplant

1954

Joseph Murray

All early attempts to transplant organs failed. Scientists eventually realized that rejection was caused by the body's immune system. US surgeon Joseph Murray confirmed this when he tried to graft skin on to wounded soldiers. He noticed that the only successful grafts came from an identical twin. In 1954, he and several colleagues tried transplanting a kidney from one twin to another. The twin given the new kidney survived for years. In the 1960s, after drugs to suppress the immune system were developed, Murray made successful kidney transplants from unrelated donors.

Nuclear power station

1954

Institute of Physics and Power Engineering

The first operational nuclear power station was built at Obninsk, near Moscow. It started working in June 1954. The station was designed by the USSR's Institute of Physics and Power Engineering, which started work on it in 1951. It was small and simple and had a power output of only 5 megawatts (MW), as compared with 1000 MW for a modern reactor, but it was still a triumph for the USSR.

Polypropylene

1954

Karl Ziegler, Giulio Natta

In 1953, Italian chemist Karl Ziegler discovered a catalyst (a substance that speeds up a chemical reaction) that allowed polythene to be made from the gas ethylene more easily. In 1954, Italian chemist Giulio Natta discovered that Ziegler's catalyst also worked with the related gas propylene. The result was polypropylene, the tough, flexible plastic now used for everything from garbage cans to carpets. Commercial production began in 1957.

Atomic clock

1955

Louis Essen, Jack Parry

In 1955, working at the National Physical Laboratory with his colleague Jack Parry, British physicist Louis Essen made a clock that would gain or lose less than one second in 300 years. It worked by electrically sensing a natural vibration of cesium atoms.

1954 British medical student Roger (later Sir Roger) Bannister runs a mile in less than four minutes, breaking both a record and a psychological barrier. Bannister's time will be beaten seven weeks later by Australian John Landy.

1954 Japanese director Akira Kurosawa blends Japanese tradition with western technique in *The Seven Samurai*, perhaps the best-ever film about the Samurai, a powerful warrior caste. It wins silver at the Venice Film Festival.

Airbag

1952

John Hetrick

The first airbag was patented in 1952 by US inventor John Hetrick. But it was not until 1973, when the rising death toll on US roads began to cause concern, that General Motors developed a practical airbag and offered it as an option. In spite of consumer resistance, and worries about deaths caused by early airbags, by 1988, most US cars were equipped with airbags. European car makers followed suit later.

High-level computer language

1952

Grace Hopper

In the early days of computing, programs were written in code that suited a computer but was difficult for people to read. Mathematician (and US Navy Rear Admiral) Grace Hopper made computers more user-friendly. She wrote a program that could translate a language quite like English into a list of instructions a computer could follow. This led to one of the earliest high-level languages, COBOL, still in use today.

Polio vaccine

1952

Jonas Salk, Albert Sabin

Poliomyelitis, or polio, is a viral infection that can cause paralysis. It posed a serious threat until US physician Jonas Salk developed a vaccine that could create resistance to the virus. It contained an inactive (dead) virus and was first used in a successful trial in 1952. After further trials, the Salk vaccine was approved in 1955. Later, Polish–US physician Albert Sabin developed the vaccine more widely used today, which contains weakened polio virus.

Color television

1953

National Television Systems Committee

It was hard to make televisions show color without making existing black-and-white receivers useless. The US National Television Systems Committee (NTSC) provided the solution in 1953. Their system splits pictures into brightness variations, which can be displayed on a normal black-and-white set, and color information, which color receivers use to add color to the picture. Later variants of NTSC that transmit colors more accurately are now in use.

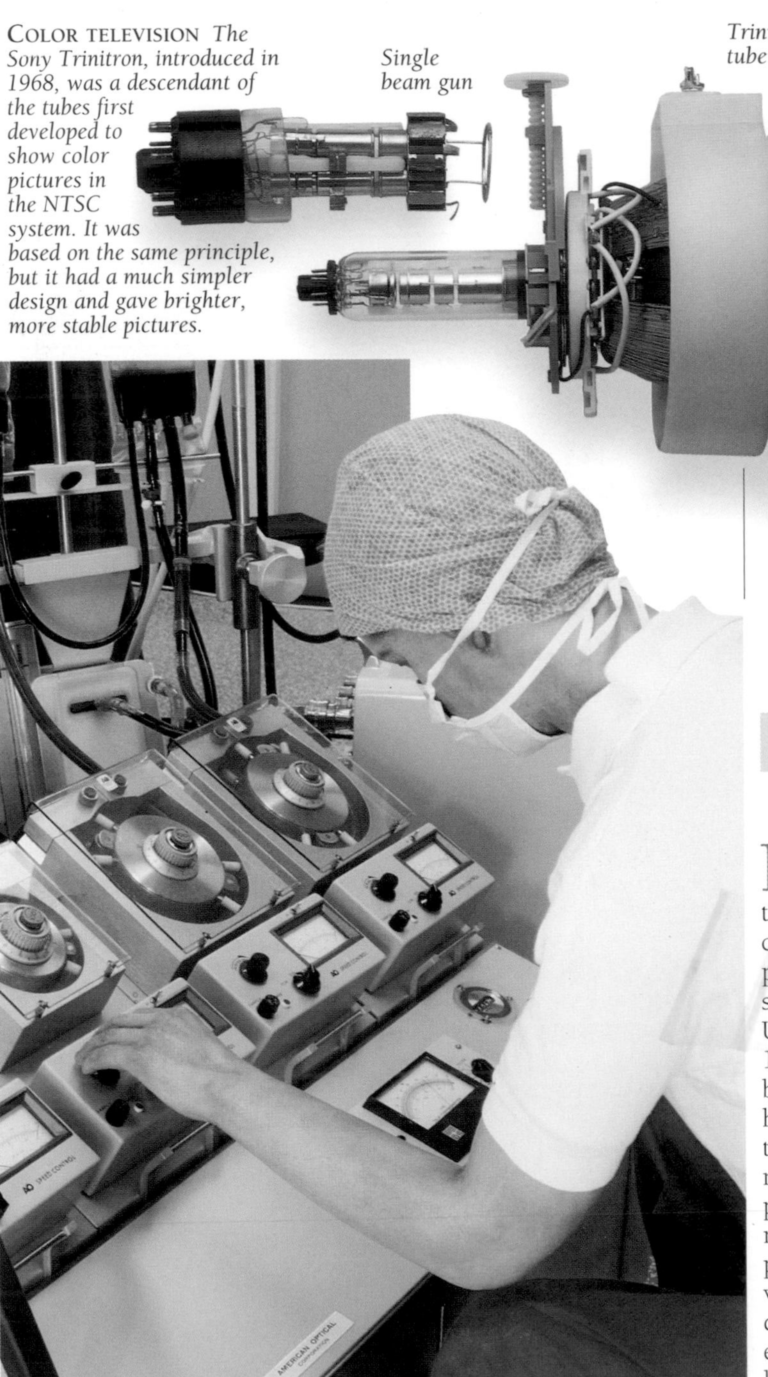

COLOR TELEVISION *The Sony Trinitron, introduced in 1968, was a descendant of the tubes first developed to show color pictures in the NTSC system. It was based on the same principle, but it had a much simpler design and gave brighter, more stable pictures.*

USE OF HEART–LUNG MACHINE *This reconstruction of a 1980 operating room shows a heart–lung machine in use. The circular devices in the center pump blood.*

Use of heart–lung machine

1953

John Gibbon Jr.

Heart surgery was once almost impossible because the heart is full of blood and constantly moving. The first person to drain a human heart so that he could work on it was US surgeon John Gibbon Jr. in 1953. He was able to do this because the job of the patient's heart had been temporarily taken over by a heart–lung machine. This continually pumped blood out of the body, recharged it with oxygen, and pumped it back. Modern versions are the result of decades of development by experimenters. Their use in heart surgery is now routine.

1952 In Kenya, the British declare a state of emergency and arrest Jomo Kenyatta, leader of the Kenya African Union, in an effort to crush the Mau Mau—armed members of the Kikuyu tribe rebelling against British rule.

1953 Nepalese Sherpa Tenzing Norgay and New Zealand mountaineer Edmund Hillary reach the top of Mount Everest, on May 29. They are the first people who can prove they have climbed to the summit. Hillary is later knighted.

ATOMIC CLOCK *This part of the first atomic clock created a beam of cesium atoms that could absorb radio waves of only one precise frequency. This effect was used to monitor the frequency of a separate quartz oscillator, keeping it very accurate.*

Within two years, Essen's clock was a hundred times more accurate, and, in 1967, the unit of time itself was redefined in terms of atomic vibrations.

Synthetic diamonds

1955

Percy Bridgman, General Electric Company

US physicist Percy Bridgman never made diamonds himself, but he did develop ways of subjecting materials to incredibly high pressures—one of the conditions essential to the formation of diamond from carbon. In 1955, scientists at the US General Electric Company used Bridgman's techniques to make the first synthetic diamonds. Since 1960, industrial diamonds have been made in quantity by this process. These diamonds, which are a bit like grains of sand, are used to add bite to cutting tools like saw blades and drill bits.

Hovercraft

1955

Christopher Cockerell

The hovercraft principle is most often seen in lawn mowers, but seagoing hovercraft vessels have been in use since 1959. The principle was patented by British engineer Christopher Cockerell in 1955. He arrived at it by blowing air from a vacuum cleaner through the space between two cans of slightly different sizes, mounted one inside the other. He found that this arrangement gave increased lift and eventually scaled it up to produce machines that could travel over both land and water.

HOVERCRAFT *Cockerell's first working model, about 3 ft (1 m) long, was built in 1955. It worked well but needed a lot of power.*

Exhaust outlet for engine

Smooth skin reduced drag

1954 British writer William (later Sir William) Golding publishes his first and best-known novel, *Lord of the Flies*. Schoolboys stranded on an island descend into savagery as they struggle to survive. It will be filmed in 1963 and 1990.

1955 Rock 'n' roll gets its first wide airing as US band Bill Haley and the Comets shoot to the top of the charts with *Rock Around the Clock*. Its blues-based harmony and strong backbeat enrage the old and enchant the young.

THE SECRET OF LIFE

Francis Crick and James Watson race to find the chemical structure of DNA

CRICK AND WATSON World War II interrupted Francis Crick's studies, so he was still working on an advanced degree when biologist James Watson arrived at the Cavendish. Crick's official work was soon put aside as he took up the challenge of DNA.

Francis Crick

James Watson

In February 1953, two men rushed into the Eagle, a pub in Cambridge, England. The English one, Francis Crick, said that they had found the secret of life. The American, James Watson, wondered if they really had.

The race to find the structure of DNA began in 1944, when US immunologist Oswald Avery showed that bacteria inherited their characteristics through DNA. This has four key components—A, T, G, and C for short. In 1949, Austrian biochemist Erwin Chargaff noticed that the amount of A is always the same as the amount of T, and likewise for G and C.

This was all that was known about DNA when biologist James Watson arrived at Cambridge's Cavendish Laboratory in 1951. The Cavendish specialized in X-ray analysis of molecular structures, and physicist Francis Crick was an expert there. Watson was convinced that unraveling DNA

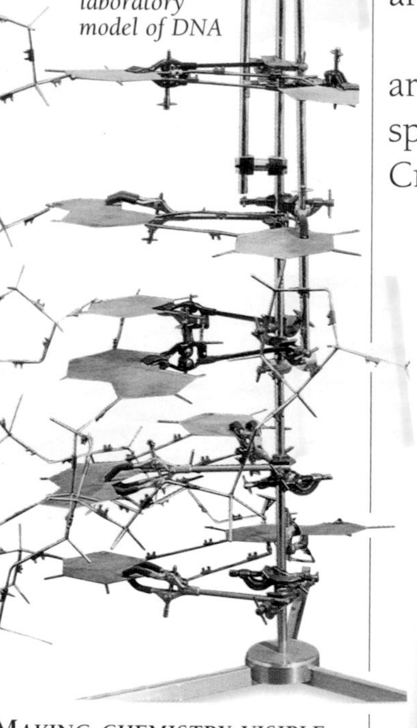

Original laboratory model of DNA

MAKING CHEMISTRY VISIBLE The ways that atoms fit with each other follow known rules. Before computers, it was hard to see the effect of these rules without building a physical model. This double helix was assembled by James Watson using metal plates shaped to represent the chemical groups he knew were present in DNA.

ROSALIND FRANKLIN
Using X-rays alone, Rosalind Franklin nearly found the structure of DNA. Her work was vital to Crick and Watson. She died in 1958, four years before they and Wilkins got their Nobel Prize.

would be the breakthrough of the century. He needed Crick's help because in the US, the great chemist Linus Pauling was already hot on the trail.

At King's College London, UK, physicist Maurice Wilkins was working on DNA, and his assistant Rosalind Franklin had managed the difficult task of producing clear X-ray images suggesting its structure. Crick and Watson got hold of Franklin's images and used them to help build models. Their first attempt was obviously wrong and Franklin told them to think again. All the time, Pauling was breathing down their necks. Crick and Watson eventually saw a draft diagram of his proposed structure, but they knew that it too was wrong.

Watson studied Franklin's latest X-ray picture and became convinced that a DNA molecule was spiral, or helical, in shape. He wondered whether it could be a double helix, rather than the triple helix they had considered, because important biological objects come in pairs. Then Franklin suggested that DNA's "backbone" was on the outside. Suddenly, Watson saw that T fit with A, and C with G, like rungs between the uprights of a twisted ladder. It explained Chargaff's observation and, more importantly, how DNA was copied. He told Crick, and that was when they rushed to the Eagle.

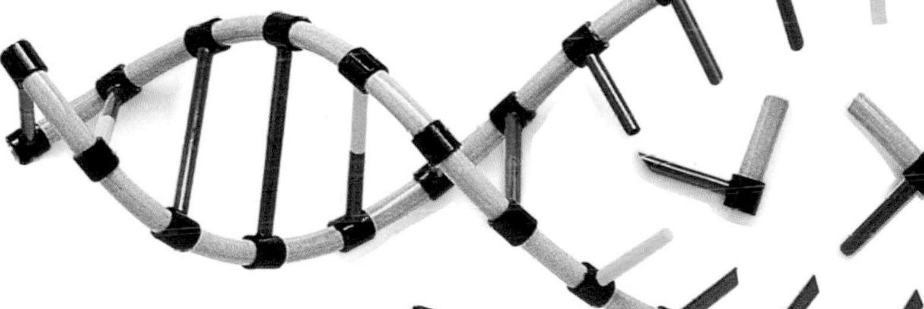

COPYING MACHINE
Life continues through the ages because DNA, with the help of several enzymes, can reproduce itself. As the molecule untwists and splits down the middle, a new T bonds to each A, and a new C to each G, forming two identical copies.

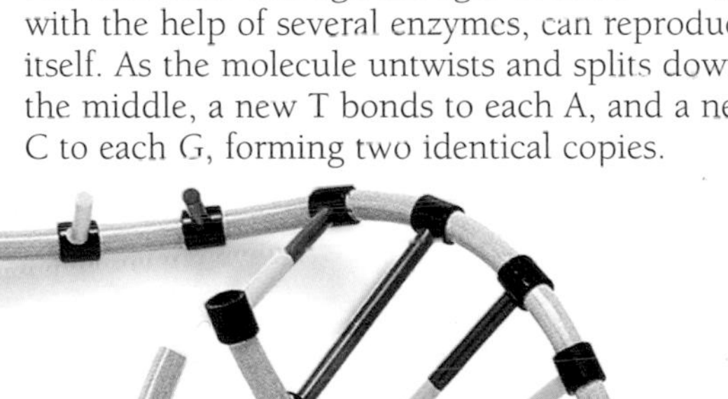

PAIRING OFF
In DNA, atoms forming a type of sugar are linked by groups containing phosphorus. Between these, hydrogen atoms link thymine (T) to adenine (A), and cytosine (C) to guanine (G). This model is diagrammatic only.

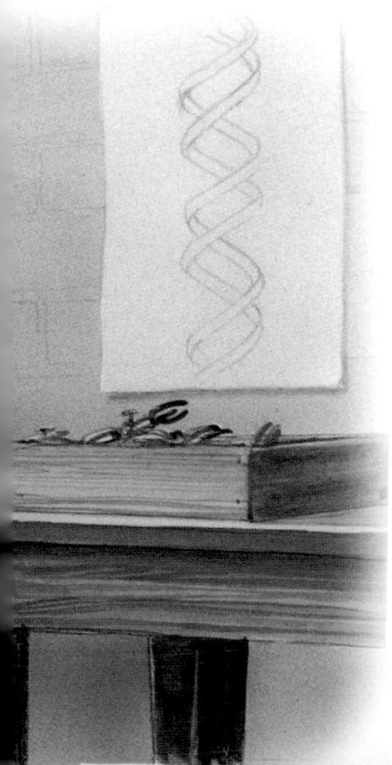

Watson and Crick were worried in case they were mistaken, so they raced to build an accurate model. There was nothing wrong with it. It was definitely the structure of DNA. Later, even Pauling was delighted to agree that Crick and Watson had indeed found the secret of life.

VIDEO RECORDER *Video cameras of the early 1970s needed a heavy box like this to make the actual recording on a reel of wide tape.*

Parity violation

1956

Chien-Shiung Wu

In physics, parity is the concept that an object and its mirror image act exactly the same, but with left and right reversed. By 1956, it had been shown that this theory held true for the electromagnetic and strong nuclear forces, but to the astonishment of physicists, Wu established that it was not true of the weak nuclear force. This parity violation, as it is known, means that the mirror world is somehow different. Her male collaborators in the experiment received the 1957 Nobel Prize in Physics, but Wu received only a separate mention.

Video recorder

1956

Charles Ginsburg, Ray Dolby

Television signals contain much higher frequencies than those recorded on audio tape (✳ *see* **page 169**). Capturing them by running the tape faster is not practical. The problem was solved by US engineers Charles Ginsburg and Ray Dolby in 1956. They used a wide tape running horizontally at low speed while a rotating head scanned it vertically at high speed, effectively folding up a long, fast tape into a short, slow one. Domestic video recorders, such as VHS, use a related principle.

Velcro

1956

George de Mestral

The name Velcro comes from the French for velvet (*velours*) and hook (*crochet*). It is actually two materials: one covered in tiny hooks, the other in tiny loops. Placed in contact, the hooks catch in the loops and the surfaces cling together to fasten clothes and much else. Swiss inventor George de Mestral got the idea in 1941 by noticing plant burrs clinging to his dog. It took 15 years of research to copy the burrs' hooked surface in a fabric.

Artificial satellite

1957

Valentin Glushko, Sergey Korolyov

The first artificial Earth satellite was Sputnik I, launched on October 4, 1957. It weighed only 184 lb (84 kg) and went only 584 miles (942 km) into space but proved that the USSR was well ahead in space technology. The engineers responsible, Valentin Glushko and Sergey Korolyov, received many honors. The US responded by creating the National Aeronautics and Space Administration (NASA) in July 1958. The space race was on.

Chemical mechanism of nerves

1957

John Eccles, Alan Hodgkin, Andrew Huxley

Nineteenth-century scientists knew that nerves worked electrically. By 1957, the exact mechanism had been unraveled by Australian physiologist John Eccles and British physiologists Alan Hodgkin and Andrew Huxley (all later knighted). They found that an excited nerve releases a substance that opens pores in the outer membrane of the next nerve cell. Sodium ions then flow in, making the cell electrically positive and also making more pores open. The process continues, causing an electrical wave to travel down the nerve.

Rotary internal combustion engine

1957

Felix Wankel

Car engines go around and around, but their pistons go up and down. German engineer Felix Wankel thought this was bad. By 1957, he had built and tested an engine without pistons. The Wankel engine has a rotor that spins inside a fixed chamber to carry out the various stages of combustion. Although it has

Engine is mounted in the rear compartment

Car body is basically the Bertone-styled Sportprinz

ROTARY INTERNAL COMBUSTION ENGINE *The first production car with a Wankel engine was the German NSU Spider, a sports car launched in 1963. It won the German GT Rally Championship in 1966 and all classes of the German Hill Climb Championship in 1967.*

1956 Soviet writer Boris Pasternak's only novel, *Dr Zhivago*, is published in the West. Because it describes an individual's struggle for identity within the USSR, it is considered subversive and not published there until 1987.

1956 Egyptian president Gamal Abdel-Nasser nationalizes the Suez Canal. France and Britain, fearing he will close it to vital oil shipments, launch an invasion of the area, with Israel as an ally, but pull out under international pressure.

been used in cars, it has proved difficult to maintain a gas-tight seal between rotor and chamber. So the piston engine, in spite of needing more parts than the Wankel, still rules the road.

FORTRAN

1957

John Backus

Early computer programmers had to write thousands of virtually unreadable coded instructions to make their machines work. US researcher John Backus changed this with the first successful high-level programming language, which could translate English-like statements into machine code. FORTRAN, released by IBM in 1957, produced results nearly as good as those achieved by hand coding, but in a fraction of the time.

Penrose triangle

1958

Lionel Penrose, Roger Penrose

Many drawings by the Dutch artist M. C. Escher show "impossible worlds" that include baffling tricks of perspective. Inspired by these, British geneticist Lionel Penrose and his physicist son Roger invented the Penrose triangle in 1958. It looks like a triangle until you realize that it contains three right-angle joints so could not be made. Escher was in turn inspired by the Penroses' work to draw some more impossible worlds.

The impossible looks possible from this angle

In reality, the sides of the triangle do not meet

PENROSE TRIANGLE *A real Penrose triangle is impossible, but this object looks like one when viewed from the correct angle.*

Liquid Paper®

1958

Bette Nesmith Graham

Before PCs and laptops, people used electric typewriters. They worked well, apart from the fact that any mistakes were hard to erase. Bette Nesmith Graham, an American typist and bank secretary, hit on the idea of covering up errors with quick-drying white paint. She invented this "correction fluid" and, after making some improvements, put it on the market as Mistake Out, later changing its name to Liquid Paper®. She eventually sold her company for more than $45 million.

Superglue

1958

Harry Coover, Fred Joyner

Superglue bonds surfaces carrying any trace of water. The water triggers a reaction that turns the liquid glue into strong plastic. The chemical involved—cyanoacrylate—was discovered in 1942, but it was 1951 before US researchers Harry Coover and Fred Joyner realized its potential. Superglue became a product in 1958, and Coover demonstrated it on television by using just one drop to lift the show's host right off the floor. Many careless people have since confirmed how well it sticks to skin.

Flap conceals the gas cap

Radiator and fan at the front

1957 The Treaty of Rome creates the European Economic Community, joining the economies of six European countries. The EEC establishes a common trade policy and makes it cheaper and easier for member nations to trade with each other.

1958 The US establishes the independent government agency responsible for the exploration of space, the National Aeronautics and Space Administration (NASA). The first seven astronauts will be chosen the next year.

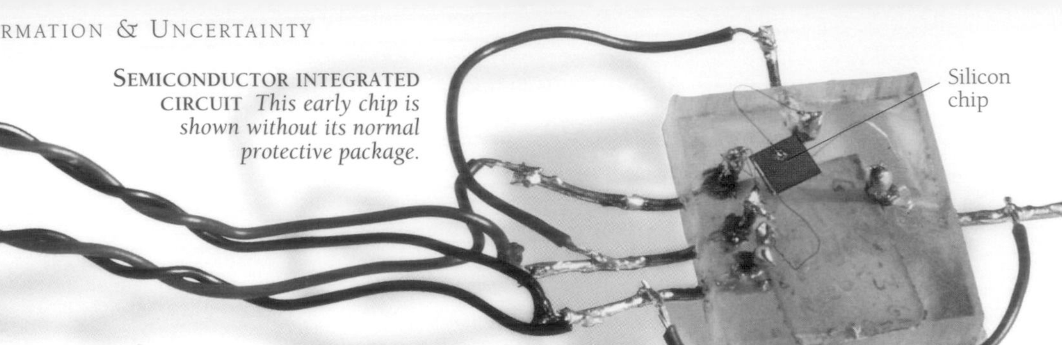

SEMICONDUCTOR INTEGRATED CIRCUIT *This early chip is shown without its normal protective package.*

Laser concept

1958

Charles Townes, Arthur Schawlow

The laser started out in 1953 as a type of amplifier for microwaves called a maser (from Microwave Amplification by Stimulated Emission of Radiation). One of its inventors, US physicist Charles Townes, and another US physicist, Arthur Schawlow, later showed that the same principle could apply to light. Changing the initial M to L for light gave the name laser. Most lasers are, however, used not as light amplifiers but as light sources with very special properties. (✱ *See also* **Masers and Lasers**.)

Lego

1958

Godtfred Christiansen

Lego bricks existed in 1949 but were reinvented in their modern form in 1958 by Godtfred Christiansen. He was the son of a Danish carpenter, Ole Christiansen, who, in 1932, founded a company making wooden products, including toys. By 1934, the toys were taking over, and the company was renamed Lego, from the Danish *"led godt"* meaning "play well." Godtfred, who joined the company when only 12, was also the force behind the creation of Legoland.

Semiconductor integrated circuit

1958

Jack Kilby, Robert Noyce

Modern electronic devices, such as laptop computers, pack a lot into a small space. They do this with integrated circuits—silicon chips containing thousands or millions of transistors and other components connected to form a complex circuit. The first of these, made in 1958 by US engineer Jack Kilby, contained only a few components but demonstrated the principle. The following year, another US engineer, Robert Noyce, invented a better way of making integrated circuits. He used a film of metal to connect up transistors buried beneath the surface of a silicon chip. With many improvements, this process is still used today.

Van Allen radiation belts

1958

James Van Allen

Earth is surrounded by electrically charged particles that come from the sun and are captured by Earth's magnetic field. They gather in two doughnut-shaped belts around the equator. The inside of the inner belt is about 600 miles (1,000 km) above Earth's equator, while the outside of the outer belt is about 15,000 miles (25,000 km) up. These dangerous regions are called the Van Allen belts, after US physicist James Van Allen, who discovered them in 1958 by studying cosmic-ray data gathered by equipment on board the Explorer 1 satellite.

LEGO *Massive, accurate molds like these are needed to make bricks that will always snap together.*

1959 Twelve nations sign the Antarctic Treaty. Its goal is to keep the world's last wilderness free of military operations, including nuclear weapons, and make it somewhere science can flourish in a spirit of international cooperation.

1959 Through two separate acts, Alaska and Hawaii become the 49th and 50th states of the USA. President Eisenhower declares Alaska a state in January, and dissolves the territory of Hawaii in August to create the newest state.

MASERS AND LASERS

WHEN ATOMS OR MOLECULES absorb energy, they become "excited." If they are then struck by radiation of a suitable frequency, they release their energy as a wave exactly in step with that radiation. This "stimulated emission" was predicted by Albert Einstein in 1917. In a laser, the new radiation strikes other excited atoms, which then emit further light. This chain reaction produces high-intensity radiation with all the waves in step with each other.

LASER LIGHT

Laser light is pure—that is, it consists of waves of a single frequency, all in step. This makes it useful where a light bulb's uneven waves of many frequencies would not do. It can be very intense, allowing industrial lasers to cut through metal, and can also be formed into a much narrower beam than ordinary light.

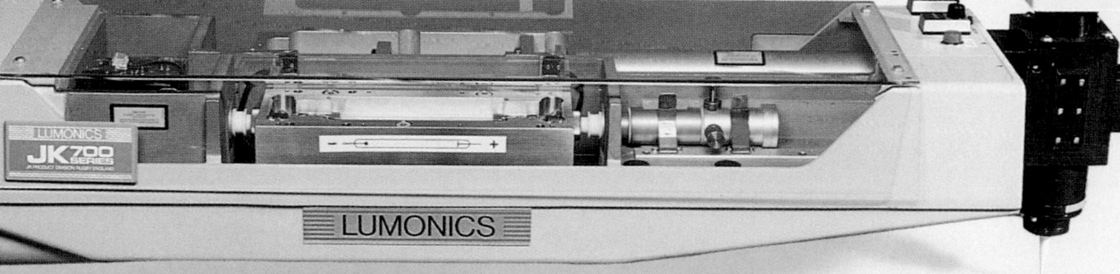

Lasers in machines like this cut metal without distorting it.

This enlarged view of the music layer of an audio CD shows fine depressions that a laser can read.

LASERS IN ACTION

Lasers are ideal for measurement. Their narrow beam is used in surveying to bounce off distant reflectors and give pinpoint positioning. Tiny, low-powered infrared lasers detect the microscopic messages written on CDs. Lasers are essential for making holograms (✳ *see* **page 210**) as well as great for putting on light shows.

Float glass

1959

Alastair Pilkington

Nearly all window glass is made by the float glass process. A ribbon of molten glass is poured on to the mirrorlike surface of a pool of molten tin. The tin smooths the underside of the glass while flames play on the top to smooth this. Alastair Pilkington of British glass company Pilkington thought up the idea in 1952. After seven years' development, it was ready to use.

Seat belt

1959

Nils Bohlin

When a car stops suddenly, as in a crash, Newton's first law (✳ *see* **page 96**) says that its occupants will carry on at their original speed. This means that they will hit the inside of the now stationary car and be injured. The way to prevent this is to anchor them to the car so that they stop when it stops. Various seat belts were tried before Swedish engineer Nils Bohlin came up with today's lap-and-diagonal design. His belts were first used in a 1959 Volvo.

Cause of Down syndrome

1959

Jérôme Lejeune

Human cells usually have 46 chromosomes containing their genes. But in 1959, French geneticist Jérôme Lejeune showed that the cells of people with Down syndrome, a condition that can cause learning difficulties and medical problems, have an extra copy of one particular chromosome, known as chromosome 21, making 47 in all. As a result of later work, babies can now be checked for this and other gene problems before they are born.

Bubblewrap

1960

Alfred Fielding, Marc Chavannes

Bubblewrap consists of two layers of soft plastic with rows of air bubbles trapped between them. Used to pack delicate articles, it is cleaner and more effective than materials like shredded paper. It appeared in its earliest form, AirCap cellular cushioning, in 1960. Its US inventors, Alfred Fielding and Marc Chavannes, were originally trying to make textured wall coverings but soon realized that packaging offered a bigger market.

1960 In Sharpeville, South Africa, a crowd gathers in protest against laws that restrict the movement of black Africans. Police open fire; 67 people are killed. A state of emergency is declared, and black political groups are outlawed.

1960 One of the U-2 spy planes regularly flown over Soviet territory by the US is shot down. Pilot Gary Powers parachutes to safety but is put in prison for 10 years. The incident wrecks an East–West summit meeting in Paris.

Communications satellite

1960

John Pierce

Communications satellites are radio relay stations in space. They enable signals to reach places far away from the transmitter. In 1960, to convince people that this would work, US engineer John Pierce made use of the experimental satellite Echo 1. This giant aluminum-coated balloon made a good radio reflector, and Pierce showed that signals could be bounced off it over long distances. His work led to the launch of *Telstar*, the first satellite to relay television, in 1962.

Artificial neural network

1960

Frank Rosenblatt

An artificial neural network (ANN) is a lot of electronic "nerve cells" joined together. It processes information in a similar way to the brain. Electronic models of natural nerve cells were developed in the 1940s by US researchers Warren McCulloch and Walter Pitts to help them understand how the brain worked. Another US scientist, Frank Rosenblatt, put these cells together to form the first ANN, a pattern-recognizing network called the Perceptron, He demonstrated it in 1960. ANNs are used in deep learning—training computers on real-world data, for use in tasks such as speech recognition.

SI units

1960

11th General Conference on Weights and Measures

Science and technology need consistent units of measurement for things like length, mass, force, and electric current. The Système International d'Unités, or SI, provides such units. Adopted in 1960, SI cleaned up an older system called MKS (meter–kilogram–second) by defining six basic units (plus a seventh added in 1971) and deriving all the others from them. It also standardized the prefixes, such as kilo (a thousand) that are used to express measurements.

Synthetic ruby rod

Lamp lies next to the ruby rod when the unit is closed

Synthetic ruby rod

Mirrorlike surface ensures that the ruby is bombarded with as much light as possible

Closed laser unit

RUBY LASER *Flash tubes pumped energy into the pale pink ruby rod of this 1960 laser. The inside of the casing was silvered to prevent energy from being wasted. The ends of the rod had to be precisely parallel to get laser action.*

Quasar

1960

Allan Sandage, Maarten Schmidt

Quasars are starlike objects. They are found in some parts of the sky that also give out strong radio waves. US astronomer Allan Sandage found the first in 1960. Its spectrum was puzzling. In 1963, Dutch-born US astronomer Maarten Schmidt suggested that it was a normal spectrum shifted sideways by a huge amount. According to astronomical theory, this showed that the quasar was billions of light-years away and therefore must be fantastically bright. Further observations indicated that quasars are also quite small, suggesting that they are active black holes (✳ *see* **page 184**).

Ruby laser

1960

Theodore Maiman

A year after it was shown that lasers were possible (✳ *see* **page 220**), US physicist Theodore Maiman made one. He used a rod of synthetic ruby with silver-coated ends, surrounded by flash tubes. Light from the tubes excited atoms in the rod, making them give out light. Trapped between the reflecting ends, this stimulated further atoms, creating the first pulses of laser light.

Disposable diaper

1961

Vic Mills

From the mid-1940s onward, many attempts were made to invent a disposable diaper.

1960 In an unsuccessful effort to prevent communist North Vietnam from invading and taking over the weaker, pro-Western government of South Vietnam, the US sends military advisors and weapons and the Vietnam War begins.

1961 The Communist East Germany stems the flow of illegal emigrants by building a wall across Berlin to prevent them from getting into West Germany. Temporary at first, it soon becomes 29 miles (47 km) of solid concrete.

None were really successful until US engineer Vic Mills, fed up with the cloth diapers worn by his granddaughter, put the US company Procter & Gamble to work on the problem. After several years of tests, Pampers were launched in 1961.

Shape memory alloys

1961

William Buehler, David Muzzey

When strongly heated and then cooled, shape memory alloys (SMAs) "remember" the shape they had when hot. However much they are bent while cold, heating them restores their original shape. They are useful for making, among other things, sleeves to join metal tubes and valves to control the rate of fluid flow. The first SMA was made from nickel and titanium by US researcher William Buehler. Another US scientist David Muzzey discovered its properties in 1961, supposedly by heating a bent metal strip with his lighter.

Industrial robot

1961

George Devol, Joseph Engelburger

Industrial robots are jointed arms controlled by computer. They can do complex jobs, such as welding and painting cars. They are also good at tedious jobs like unloading finished parts from a machine. The first working robot did this. It was developed by US engineer George Devol and installed in 1961. With businessman Joseph Engelburger, Devol went on to found the first industrial robotics company. (✳ *See also* **Willing Servants.**)

WILLING SERVANTS

THE WORD "ROBOT" comes from the Czech word for forced labor. It first appeared in 1920, in the play *R.U.R.* by Karel Čapek, but people have been making machines that imitate life for centuries. By the 18th century, clockwork dolls were serving tea in Japan, while French inventor Jacques de Vaucanson had made a realistic mechanical duck. But a self-sufficient, intelligent robot remains the stuff of science fiction.

A robot arm spot-welding the suspension unit of a car. Robots are ideal for dangerous, repetitive jobs like this.

Following the rules
Most modern robots have little intelligence or awareness of their surroundings. They have to be programmed in great detail to tell them what to do. Some robot arms can learn what movements to make by recording the actions of a human operator. They then simply repeat them.

Breaking free
More advanced robots have less need of humans. With sensors to detect obstacles, they can move around freely, while a computer gives them enough intelligence to do complex tasks like cleaning, cooperating with other robots, or even exploring Mars.

1961 US writer J. Heller invents a new phrase in *Catch-22*. To be grounded, airman Yossarian has to be crazy, and he must be crazy to be flying, but if he asks to be grounded, he can't be crazy any more, so he has to keep flying. Catch 22!

1961 On May 5, Alan Shepard becomes the first American in space. The Mercury 3 mission is the first mission to study the physiological changes of the pilot in space flight. Shepard flies in suborbital space for a little over 15 minutes.

advanced aircraft and for high-performance sports equipment. Carbon fiber technology was pioneered in 1963 by British engineer Leslie Phillips at the Royal Aircraft Establishment. It is now used throughout the aircraft industry.

Space flight

1961

Yuri Gagarin

The first person to fly through space was Yuri Gagarin, a major in the USSR's air force. He went into orbit around Earth in the spacecraft Vostok 1 on April 12, 1961. Gagarin's flight lasted for 1 hour, 48 minutes. He reached a speed of 17,000 mph (27,400 km/h) and a height of 203 miles (327 km). Gagarin was an international hero on his return. Sadly, he was killed seven years later, while he was testing a new plane.

SPACE FLIGHT *This poster was produced in 1973 to commemorate Russian cosmonaut Yuri Gagarin's space flight. It reads, "Cosmonaut Day USSR 12 IV 1961."*

Hip replacement

1962

John Charnley

As people grow older, their hips can wear out. The first successful hip replacements were largely the work of British surgeon John (later Sir John) Charnley in 1962. He inserted a metal ball into the top of a patient's thigh bone with a new kind of cement and matched this with a cup made of tough polythene attached to the pelvis. With improvements, this became the method now used for millions of people every year.

HIP REPLACEMENT *Many designs of artificial hip have been tried since Charnley's work in the 1960s. This "Exeter" joint, made in 1985, uses stainless steel for its metal part.*

Resealable plastic bag

1962

Steven Ausnit, Kakuji Naito

Plastic bags with little toothless zippers built in were conceived by Danish inventor Borgda Madsen in the 1940s. Romanian engineer Steven Ausnit, working in the US, produced the first practical versions of these about 10 years later. His zippers were formed separately and then welded onto the bags. In 1962, Japanese inventor Kakuji Naito created even better bags by forming bag and zipper from the same piece of plastic.

Carbon fiber

1963

Leslie Phillips

Fibers of carbon, made by stretching synthetic fiber then toasting it to blackness, are twice as stiff as the same weight of steel. Plastics reinforced with them are both stiff and light, making them ideal for critical structures in

Push-button phone

1963

AT&T

Phones with buttons began to replace phones with dials in 1963, when US phone company AT&T introduced its Touch-Tone system. Dial phones work by disconnecting the phone line once for 1, twice for 2, and so on. Push-button phones send musical tones down the line. There are four tones for the four rows of buttons, and three for the three columns. Pressing a button sends out the pair of tones corresponding to its row and column.

Polaroid color photograph

1963

Edwin Land

Polacolor film, launched in 1963, has three layers, each sensitive to light of one color—red, green, or blue. Each layer contains a dye that absorbs just the light to which the layer is sensitive. The blue-sensitive layer, for example, contains yellow dye, which absorbs only blue light. Pulling the film out of the camera activates it and squeezes it into contact with a white print sheet. As the layers

1962 War threatens as presidents Kennedy of the US and Khrushchev of the USSR stage a standoff over the installation of Soviet nuclear missiles in Cuba. After a tense few days, Khrushchev backs down and the missiles go home.

1962 After thousands of babies are born with abnormally short arms and legs, the sedative drug thalidomide, introduced in 1958, is finally withdrawn. Doctors had traced the malformations to mothers taking the drug while pregnant.

develop, their dyes are trapped in proportion to the exposure received, and the remaining dye moves into the print. Where the subject absorbs blue, for example, the blue layer receives less exposure, so more of its yellow dye reaches the final print, making it, too, absorb blue. The process takes just 60 seconds.

POLAROID COLOR PHOTOGRAPH *In 1975, Polaroid launched a new camera, the Color Swinger. It was designed to encourage use of a new and improved Polacolor film introduced the same year.*

MINISKIRT *Ultra-short skirts and dresses were a symbol of the social upheaval of the 1960s. In Britain, they even created problems for the tax man, because their length allowed them to be classified as children's clothes, which were tax-free.*

Electronic music synthesizer

1964

Robert Moog

Several people had already attempted to produce electronic music before US inventor Robert Moog invented the Moog synthesizer in 1964. Unlike most of its earlier, less successful rivals, it could be played from a normal keyboard. It produced each of its different sounds by starting with a note that was rich in harmonics—multiples of the note's basic frequency—and passing it through filters that reduced the loudness of each harmonic by a different amount. This is known as subtractive synthesis. The Moog could also vary the way in which sounds started, continued, and stopped, giving effects that varied from plucked strings to organ notes.

Miniskirt

1964

André Courrèges

Miniskirts, shorter than any that women had worn before, first appeared in the collection of French fashion designer André Courrèges, who showed them in Paris in 1964. His models wore them with boots. By December 1965, the fashion had reached Britain, where London designer Mary Quant offered skirts that stopped more than 6 in (15 cm) short of the knee.

Quarks

1964

Murray Gell-Mann

In the early 1960s, nuclear physicists observed more and more new subatomic particles. It seemed that even protons and neutrons were made up of particles, which could combine in previously unseen ways. In 1964, US physicist Murray Gell-Mann, building on earlier work with Israeli physicist Yuval Ne'eman, proposed a set of truly basic particles that explained the new observations. He called them quarks. He and other scientists then developed an elaborate, and now accepted, theory of how they work.

Electronic telephone exchange

1965

AT&T

Old-fashioned automatic telephone exchanges (✷ *see* page **161**) were built from unreliable electro-mechanical switches in which electromagnets moved mechanical contacts. They were replaced in the 1960s by so-called "electronic" exchanges. Calls were actually switched by a new type of electromechanical switch, because purely electronic switching proved difficult to combine with the existing network. The first such exchange was the ESS No. 1. Developed by the US company AT&T, it went into service in 1965.

1963 On November 22, US president John F. Kennedy is assassinated as he travels in an open car through Dallas, Texas. The alleged killer, Lee Harvey Oswald, is himself killed by a nightclub owner before he can be tried.

1963 Comic art meets the serious kind when US artist Roy Lichtenstein paints *Whaam!* a 13 ft (4 m) wide blowup of a comic strip frame. His careful rendering of the comic's crude printing helps start the Pop Art movement.

Computer mouse

1965

Doug Engelbart

US engineer Doug Engelbart was leader of the Human Factors Research Center of the Stanford Research Institute in California. The computer mouse was one of several similar devices his team tried out in the 1960s. It was the clear winner. Despite its ease of use and friendly nickname, it was nearly 20 years before the mouse was introduced to the public with the launch of the Macintosh computer in 1984.

Cable attaches to the computer

Transparent plastic matches modern Macs

Shape suits left- or right-handed users

COMPUTER MOUSE *The Apple Pro Mouse, introduced in 2001, uses optical tracking rather than the rolling ball of the conventional mouse. It also does away with a separate mouse button: users click by pushing its whole body.*

Minicomputer

1965

Kenneth Olsen

In the 1960s, computers were huge—and cost at least $1,000,000 apiece. US engineer Kenneth Olsen thought that smaller might be better. In 1965, he produced the PDP-8, one of the first computers to use integrated circuits (✱ *see* **page 220**). It was small (about the size of a two-drawer filing cabinet), powerful, and cost an affordable $18,000.

Designed mainly for laboratory use, it was an instant success with scientists and engineers around the world.

MÁRIA TELKES *The inventor of the portable solar still, shown here in her lab at MIT, Massachusetts, spent much of her career working on solar energy.*

Solar still

1966

Mária Telkes

For someone adrift in a lifeboat, a big worry is getting enough water to drink. Mária Telkes solved this problem in 1968 with a lightweight device that uses sunshine to convert seawater into drinking water. The seawater goes into a shallow black bag with porous walls. Sunlight heats the bag, making pure water evaporate and collect in a separate chamber. This idea has saved many lives.

Pull tab can

1966

Ermal Fraze

The first canned drinks had to be opened with a separate opener. If this got left behind on a picnic, everyone went thirsty. So, in 1965, US engineer Ermal Fraze patented a new kind of can with a pull tab on the top. Pulling the ring peeled off a metal tab to open the can. Sharp-edged can tabs became a menace on streets and beaches, but in 1976, US engineer Daniel Cudzik saved the pull tab by inventing the stay-on type used today.

Dolby noise reduction system

1966

Ray Dolby

Tape recordings were plagued by background hiss until US engineer Ray Dolby invented his noise reduction system. It works by boosting quiet, high-frequency sounds during recording. On playback, these sounds are reduced to their original volume. Since the hiss is a high-frequency sound, it gets reduced, too. Dolby delivered his first batch of noise reduction units to the Decca Record Company in 1966.

Jump jet

1966

Hawker Siddeley Aviation

Most aircraft get lift from wings or rotors, but jump jets get off the ground by directing the thrust of their jet

Cockpit holds single pilot

Air for engine is sucked in here

JUMP JET *The Harrier GR1 showed its capabilities at Britain's Farnborough air display in 1968, and in a transatlantic air race. Powered by a Bristol (later Rolls-Royce) Pegasus Mk 101 engine, it entered service with the Royal Air Force in 1969.*

1965 US artist Andy Warhol achieves fame with his painting of a can of Campbell's tomato soup. By choosing such an everyday object, he states that painters have no exclusive claim to call their work art.

1966 On St. Valentine's Day, Australian currency goes decimal. The nation rejects the British Pound and its proposed replacement, the Royal, and opts for the Dollar. The switch goes smoothly and is completed in 1967.

engines downward, giving them the versatility of a helicopter with the speed of a jet. Once the plane is airborne, the thrust is directed backward for forward flight. The first operational "vectored thrust" aircraft was the Harrier, made in Britain by Hawker Siddeley Aviation. Based on the earlier, experimental Kestrel fighter, it jetted off the ground in August 1966. Needing no runway, it could be used to fly in and out of combat areas to support troops. The Harrier is now used by several air forces.

Heart transplant

1967

Christiaan Barnard

The world's first heart transplant was carried out by South African surgeon Christiaan Barnard in 1967. The patient survived for only 18 days, but he would have died anyway if he hadn't had the operation. During the following year, more than 100 heart transplants were attempted by Barnard and other surgeons around the world. Results continued to be poor at first, but new techniques and better drugs to prevent rejection have made transplants more successful.

Pulsar

1967

Jocelyn Bell, Antony Hewish

In 1967, in Cambridge, England, a young astronomer, Jocelyn Bell, found a new kind of radio source that emitted short, closely spaced pulses. She and fellow astronomer Antony Hewish later realized that it was the spinning remnant of a supernova (✳ *see* **page 82**) sending out a rotating beam of radiation, like the lamp on a police car. Whenever the beam hit Earth, it created a pulse. Since then, more than 300 pulsars have been discovered.

Dark matter

1968

Vera Rubin

American astronomer Vera Rubin found that some galaxies rotate so quickly that the gravity of their stars is not enough to hold them together. Because they do not fly apart, there must be some extra mass that we cannot see keeping them intact. This necessary but invisible mass, greeted at first with skepticism, is now known as dark matter. It has changed our view of the universe.

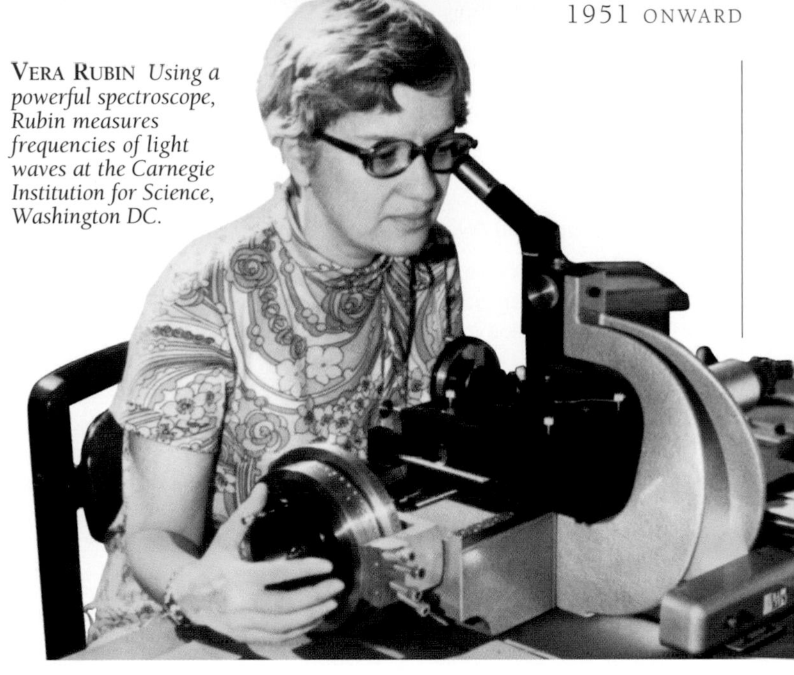

VERA RUBIN *Using a powerful spectroscope, Rubin measures frequencies of light waves at the Carnegie Institution for Science, Washington DC.*

Graphical user interface

1968

Doug Englebart, Alan Kay

Computer screens with a graphical user interface—windows, icons, and menus—seem normal now. But when US engineer Doug Engelbart and his team showed the beginnings of such a system, the "electronic office," at the National Computer Conference in San Francisco in 1968, the audience were stunned. Among them was graduate student Alan Kay, who later developed the idea of the computer screen as a virtual desktop, complete with icons.

Movable nozzles direct thrust downward for takeoff

Main undercarriage with wheels for landing

Pylons for attachment of weapons

Outrigger wheels stabilize aircraft on the ground

1968 Black US civil rights leader Martin Luther King Jr. visits Memphis, Tennessee, in support of a strike by sanitation workers. While standing on his motel balcony, he is killed by a sniper. The gunman, James Earl Ray, gets 99 years in prison.

1968 In May, increasingly rebellious French students bring turmoil to the streets of Paris with political protests and riots. The same year sees demonstrations worldwide against US involvement in the Vietnam Wsar.

Sailboard

1968

Newman Darby, Jim Drake, Hoyle Schweitzer

Windsurfers get closer to the waves than do most other sailors. The idea started with US enthusiast Newman Darby, but the first people to get a patent were two Californian surfers, Jim Drake and Hoyle Schweitzer. Their 1968 Windsurfer was 12 ft (3.5 m) long and weighed 60 lb (27 kg). Modern boards are shorter and lighter, typically weighing only 26 lb (12 kg).

Video home security system

1969

Marie Van Brittan Brown, Albert Brown

African American nurse Marie Van Brittan Brown and her electrician husband, Albert, invented the first home security system that used television. A camera at the front door of the house enabled the occupant to see visitors before opening it with a remotely operated lock. The system also allowed audio communication.

Structure of insulin

1969

Fred Sanger, Dorothy Hodgkin

Insulin (✱ *see* **page 186**) is a hormone that is essential to health. The sequence of its 51 amino acids was determined by British biochemist Fred Sanger in 1955, but the way its atoms are arranged in space—useful information for people trying to make a synthetic version—was finally figured out in 1969 by British crystallographer Dorothy Hodgkin. She analyzed the structure of insulin crystals with X-rays, a technique pioneered by physicist Lawrence (later Sir Lawrence) Bragg in the early 20th century.

Floppy disk

1970

IBM

Floppy disks were originally 8 in (20 cm) across and held only 100 kilobytes of data. IBM engineers used them from about 1970 onward to update programs on mainframe computers. By 1973, IBM had a disk drive that could accept input from users, but the disks were just as big. Small, 3.5 in (9 cm) floppy disks were introduced by the Sony Corporation in 1980. Today, disks are largely obsolete as new media, such as online sharing and storage, have taken over.

Microprocessor

1971

Ted Hoff

The microprocessor, which made personal computers possible, was invented by accident. In 1969, Japanese calculator makers Busicom asked US microchip company Intel to develop a new scientific calculator chip. Engineer Ted Hoff at Intel thought it would be much easier to design a programmable chip than to build in all the required functions. When Busicom went bust in 1970, Intel bought back the rights to the chip and, in 1971, launched it as "a micro-programmable computer on a chip," the Intel 4004. Although very slow by modern standards, it was the first in a series of devices that led to today's powerful microprocessors.

MICROPROCESSOR *Two Intel 8008 processors, successors to the original 4004, are seen with their top covers removed to reveal the chip inside.*

MILITARY USES *Strong and light, Kevlar® is used to make military-grade protective gear.*

Kevlar®

1971

Stephanie Kwolek, Herbert Blades, Paul Morgan

Kevlar® is a plastic that, weight for weight, is five times as strong as steel. It was developed in the US by chemists Stephanie Kwolek, Herbert Blades, and Paul Morgan. Chemically, it is related to nylon, but the addition of an extra chemical group adds strength and stiffness. This makes it suitable for demanding applications such as radial tires and bullet-proof vests. Kevlar® is also used in fiber-reinforced panels for aircraft and boats and in golf clubs and flameproof clothing. It can even stand the heat in brakes, replacing asbestos.

1969 In September, Arab nationalist Captain Muammar al-Qaddafi seizes control of the government of Libya in a military coup that deposes King Idris. Al-Qaddafi later allegedly supports international terrorist groups.

1972 China and the US creep toward a better relationship when Chinese premier Zhou Enlai and US president Richard Nixon sign the Shanghai Communiqué in March. Formal diplomatic relations will start in 1979.

Image converter for space

1972

George R. Carruthers

Image converters can make ultraviolet images visible. They usually have a tube containing electrodes in a vacuum, with a glass window to let light in. African American engineer George R. Carruthers realized that in space you don't need the window—the tube can be open, as space provides the vacuum. This admits more light, increasing efficiency.

Video game

1972

Nolan Bushnell

The first successful video game, Pong, was designed by US computer enthusiast Nolan Bushnell in 1972. Although extremely simple—just two on-screen paddles that flipped a ball back and forth—it fascinated customers in bars and pubs, who had never seen anything like it before. The prototype, installed in Andy Capp's Tavern in Sunnyvale, California, quickly broke down as its makeshift coinbox filled up and jammed. Later adapted into a phone app, Pong can still be played today.

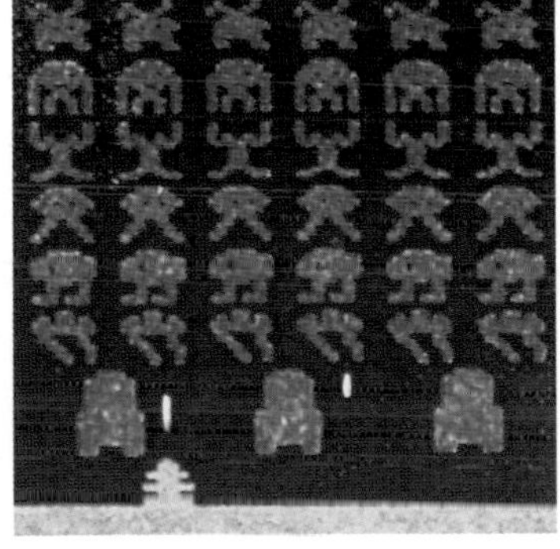

VIDEO GAME *Toshihiro Nishikado's classic game* Space Invaders *was written in 1978 and is still played.*

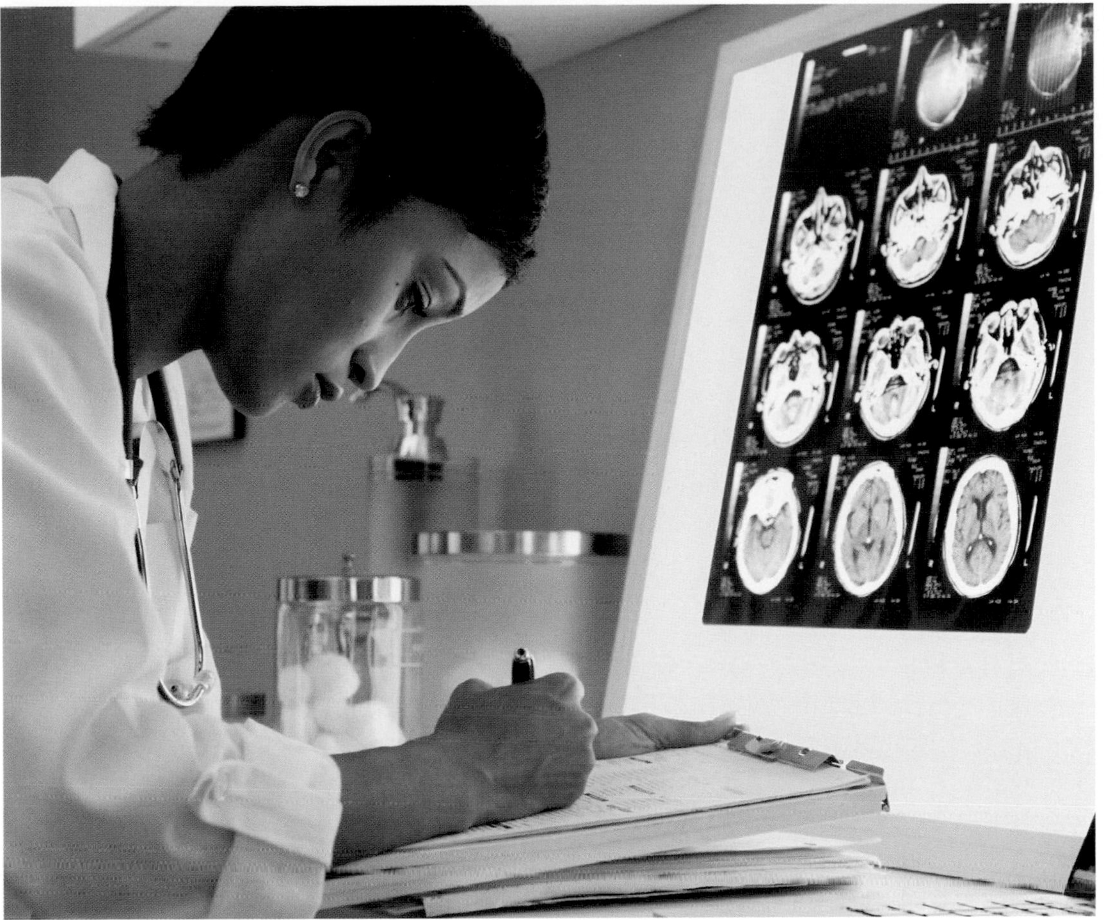

CAT SCAN *A doctor consults X-ray images of a brain, taken using a CAT scanner, to inform her diagnosis.*

CAT scanner

1972

Godfrey Hounsfield, Allan Cormack

Normal X-ray pictures are taken from just one angle. By taking them from several angles, and doing some calculations, much more can be revealed. British engineer Godfrey (later Sir Godfrey) Hounsfield and US physicist Allan Cormack worked independently on this idea. Cormack developed much of the math, while Hounsfield built the first practical machine. His computerized axial tomography (CAT) scanner used X-rays and a computer to produce images of successive slices across the long axis of the body. ("Tomography" comes from the Greek "*tomos*" a "slice".) When the scanner was tested in 1972, it gave doctors their first three-dimensional glimpse inside a living human body.

Pocket calculator

1972

Jack Kilby, Jerry Merryman, James van Tassel, Clive Sinclair

The earliest "pocket" calculator, the Canon Pocketronic, weighed 880 g (31 oz). Released in 1970, it was based on work by US engineers Jack Kilby, Jerry Merryman, and James Van Tassel at Texas Instruments. British inventor Clive (later Sir Clive) Sinclair developed his pocket calculator later, and benefited from advances in technology. His Executive calculator, launched in 1972, was only 0.4 in (1 cm) thick.

Genetic engineering

1972

Stanley Cohen, Herbert Boyer

An organism's genes are carried in its DNA. In 1969, US biochemists discovered how to snip DNA into smaller pieces. Then, in 1972, US biochemists Stanley Cohen and Herbert Boyer began work on altering organisms by cutting up the DNA of one organism and inserting genes from another. This is called genetic engineering. It has produced useful new bacteria and plants, but some people worry about its long-term effects.

1972 At the Munich Olympics in Germany, 22-year-old US swimmer Mark Spitz wins a record seven gold medals. He also sets a new world record in each of the seven events that bring him gold.

1972 The nuclear arms race slows down as the first series of Strategic Arms Limitation Talks (SALT 1) between the US and the USSR finally bears fruit. The most important outcome is a treaty to limit deployment of missiles.

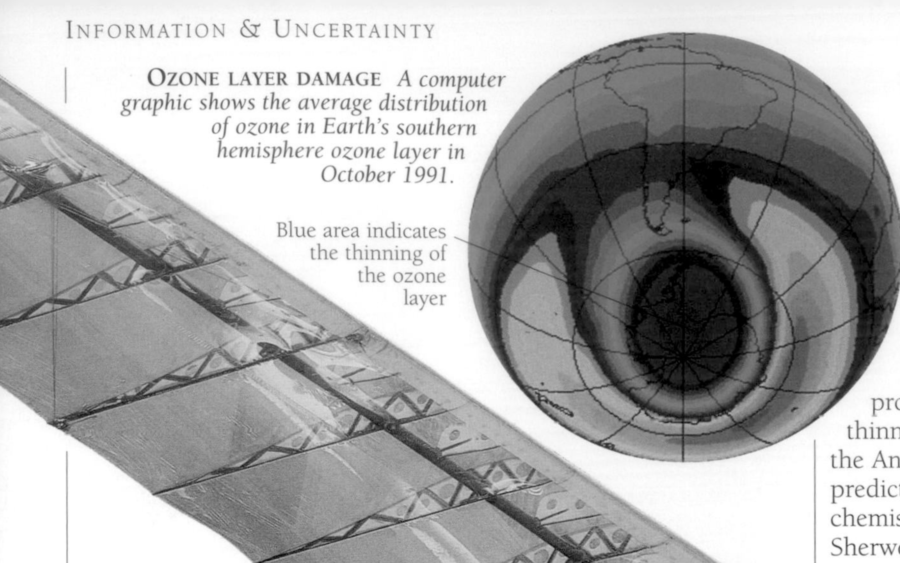

OZONE LAYER DAMAGE *A computer graphic shows the average distribution of ozone in Earth's southern hemisphere ozone layer in October 1991.*

Blue area indicates the thinning of the ozone layer

Plastic soft drink bottle

1973

Nathaniel Wyeth

Most plastics can't stand up to the pressure exerted by carbonated drinks, so for a long time bottle manufacturers stuck to glass. Then US engineer Nathaniel Wyeth figured out a way of using the plastic PET (✳ *see* **page 206**) to make a stronger bottle. Knowing that synthetic fibers were strengthened by being stretched during manufacturing, he designed a tool that stretched PET in two dimensions as it was molded. The result, patented in 1973, was the first carbonation-proof bottle.

Space station

1973

NASA

A space station is a base in space with accommodation and laboratories for several people. The earliest attempt was Salyut 1, launched by the USSR in 1971, but this crashed back to Earth within six months. The first successful space station was the 83 ton Skylab, launched by NASA in May 1973 and occupied until February 1974. It was used to observe the sun and a comet and to experiment with manufacturing in space. It survived until 1979.

Binary pulsar

1974

Joseph Taylor Jr., Russell Hulse

In 1974, US astronomer Joseph Taylor Jr. and his student Russell Hulse discovered an unusual pulsar (✳ *see* **page 227**). The time between its pulses varied over an eight-hour period. Taylor and Hulse deduced that the pulsar was orbiting another, unseen star. The Doppler effect (✳ *see* **page 134**) squeezed the pulses together when the pulsar was approaching Earth and stretched them apart when it was receding. The orbit seems to be shrinking gradually, suggesting that the system is radiating gravitational waves, as predicted by Einstein (✳ *see* **pages 178–179**).

Ozone layer damage

1974

Mario Molina, Sherwood Rowland

In the 1980s, scientists noticed that Earth's protective ozone layer had thinned dramatically over the Antarctic. This had been predicted. In 1974, US chemists Mario Molina and Sherwood Rowland had figured out that the gases used in aerosols would decompose in intense sunlight, releasing chlorine that destroyed ozone. Dutch chemist Paul Crutzen had earlier predicted a similar effect for nitrogen oxides from cars. Many governments had taken action to reduce these pollutants, but too late.

PET scanner

1974

Michael Phelps, Edward Hoffman

A PET (positron emission tomography) scanner can produce images that show events inside a living body, particularly the brain. It works by responding to the gamma rays produced when positrons meet electrons. A substance modified to make it emit positrons is tracked inside the body by combining information from several gamma ray detectors. The first PET scanner for human studies was built in 1974 by US chemist Michael Phelps, assisted by his student Edward Hoffman.

Supercomputer

1976

Seymour Cray

Even with the enormous power of today's computer chips, scientists with really serious calculations to do have to use supercomputers. These big machines crunch numbers at high speed by using several processors at once. The first was the Cray-1, produced by US engineer Seymour Cray in 1976. It could perform 240 million calculations a second, operating not just on pairs of numbers, like a normal computer but on lists of pairs. By 1985, the Cray-2 was churning out more than a billion results per second.

Long, thin wings like a glider

Modified bicycle in the cockpit powered the propeller

1973 In Australia, Sydney's world-famous opera house is completed. Its beautiful shape, like the sails of a boat, is the result of a long political struggle, which included the resignation of Joern Utzon, its Danish architect, in 1966.

1974 Richard Nixon is the first US president to resign. He steps down rather than be charged with misconduct over the Watergate scandal. People connected with him had burgled the offices of his election rivals, the Democratic party.

Conductive plastics

1977

Alan Heeger, Alan MacDiarmid, Hideki Shirakawa

Metals conduct electricity. Plastics don't. Unless they're conductive plastics, created in 1977 by US chemist Alan Heeger, New Zealand chemist Alan MacDiarmid, and Japanese chemist Hideki Shirakawa. They used iodine to free up the electrons in polyacetylene, creating a plastic a billion times less resistant to electricity. It can even, in some cases, emit light. The possibilities seem endless.

Magnetic resonance imaging

1977

Paul Lauterbur, Raymond Damadian

Placed in a magnetic field, some atomic nuclei absorb energy. If someone is probed with radio waves while inside a huge magnet, a picture of the inside of their body can be created. When the nuclei release this energy, using Magnetic resonance imaging (MRI). MRI reveals chemical differences, so it can detect abnormal cells. US chemist Paul Lauterbur and US physician Raymond Damadian both contributed to its invention. Damadian produced the first human body image in 1977.

MAGNETIC RESONANCE IMAGING *This experimental MRI headset fed radio waves into people's heads.*

Public-key cryptography

1977

Whitfield Diffie, Martin Hellman, Ron Rivest, Adi Shamir, Leonard Adleman

Public-key cryptography, conceived in 1975 by US cryptographers Whitfield Diffie and Martin Hellman, allows people to send electronic messages securely. The system was given practical form by US researchers Ron Rivest, Adi Shamir, and Leonard Adleman in 1977. People give out a public key that specifies how messages sent to them should be scrambled. Once in this form, messages can be read only by someone with the matching private key. A public key is a huge number containing hundreds of digits. It could take a powerful computer years to find the matching private key.

Human-powered aircraft

1977

Paul MacCready, Bryan Allen

Dreams of human flight faded in the 17th century, when scientists realized the size of the wings and muscles required. Then, with the invention of modern plastics, long, light wings became possible. Using these, human leg muscles are just big enough for flight. US engineer Paul MacCready provided 96 ft (29 m) long wings with *Gossamer Condor*. Cyclist Bryan Allen provided muscles to drive a propeller. They achieved human-powered flight on August 23, 1977. Two years later, Allen pedaled *Gossamer Albatross* across the English Channel.

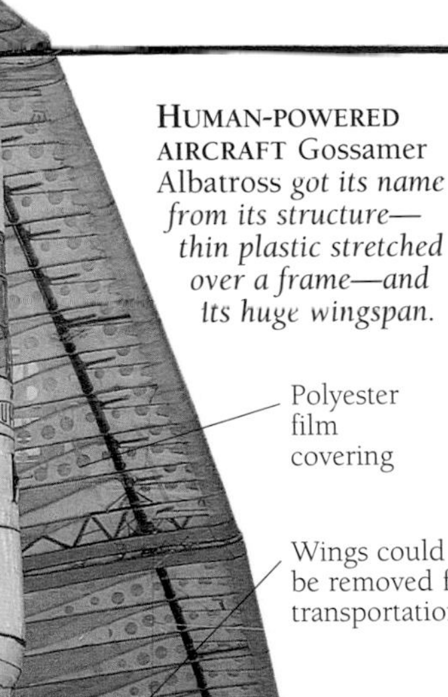

HUMAN-POWERED AIRCRAFT Gossamer Albatross *got its name from its structure—thin plastic stretched over a frame—and its huge wingspan.*

Gene exons and introns

1977

Phillip Sharp, Richard Roberts

When scientists discovered that DNA carries genes, they thought that these would be strung along the molecule one after the other. Then, in 1977, US biologist Phillip Sharp and British biologist Richard Roberts both discovered that genes are often separated or split by stretches of DNA that don't do anything. They called the active parts exons and the inactive parts introns. Before genes get to work, the cell makes a copy with the introns chopped out.

1975 Former Portuguese colony East Timor is taken over by Indonesia, despite protests from Portugal, who had granted it independence, and the UN. It will become an Indonesian province in 1976 and will suffer continuing unrest.

1976 Popular interest in black history is increased by the publication of US writer Alex Haley's book *Roots*. Built around the life story of an African slave, Kunta Kinte, it explores black identity while promoting racial understanding.

Personal computer

1977

Steve Jobs, Stephen Wozniak

The first three computers for personal use appeared in 1977. The Commodore PET and Tandy TRS-80 are now almost forgotten, but the third was the Apple II, a machine with its own monitor and plug-in expansion cards. The other machines were good, but the dedication of the Apple's promoter and designer, US computer enthusiasts Steve Jobs and Stephen Wozniak made all the difference. (✱ *See also* **Computers for All.**)

Global positioning system

1978

US Air Force

If you had a global positioning system (GPS) receiver, you would never get lost. The present GPS began in 1978 with the launch by the US Air Force of the first two NavStar satellites. Receivers now tune in to four out of 24 satellites, each of which carries a highly accurate atomic clock. By comparing the received times with the actual time and the known positions of the satellites at that time, the receiver can determine where it must be.

CELL PHONE *The first cell phones were called "car phones" because they were too big to carry around.*

Test-tube baby

1978

Patrick Steptoe, Robert Edwards

Louise Brown, the world's first "test-tube" baby, was born in England on July 25, 1978. British gynecologist Patrick Steptoe took an egg from her mother. His colleague Robert Edwards added sperm from her father. The doctors placed the fertilized egg in her mother's womb, where it grew into a healthy baby. Twenty-one years later, Louise had a job in a nursery.

COMPUTERS FOR ALL

IN 1975, ENCOURAGED by his friend Steve Jobs, US computer hobbyist Stephen Wozniak built and marketed the Apple I computer—a bare circuit board aimed at electronics hobbyists. Jobs saw that computers had a wider market and got Wozniak to design a more complete, stylish-looking machine that simply plugged in and worked. Apple II transformed the computer industry, making even giants like IBM take notice.

Apple I computer

RISE OF THE HOBBYIST
The personal computer came out of the work of countless electronics hobbyists—some of them now big names—who, in the early 1970s, built and programmed their own crude machines in their bedrooms and garages.

THE ALTAIR 8800
The first kit computer appeared in 1975. The Altair 8800 had no screen, no keyboard, and hardly any memory, but its very simplicity made it ideal for computer pioneers to cut their teeth on.

Cell phone

1979

Bell Labs

Cell phones were pioneered in the US by Bell Telephone Laboratories. After a trial in Chicago in 1979, the first public service opened in 1983. Meanwhile, Scandinavia had launched its own system in 1981. All cell phones use the same idea. There are relatively few radio frequencies, but millions of users, so the base stations that relay calls to the fixed phone network are given a limited range. Outside that range, frequencies can be reused. As callers move, computers automatically retune their phones to a frequency in the new area. It nearly always works.

Word processing software

1979

Seymour Rubinstein

By the late 1970s, personal computers could display a page of text. With cheaper printers available, they looked set to replace typewriters. US software developer Seymour Rubinstein, seeing his chance, started writing word processing software. Unsuccessful at first, he launched a second attempt, WordStar, in 1979. This used short, easy-to-remember, non-printing codes typed into a document to specify its fonts and formatting. Although it cost $450 (about $1,150 today), the program quickly took a two-thirds market share, selling nearly a million copies in five years. People were still using it in the late 1980s.

1979 Margaret Thatcher becomes Britain's first female prime minister after a decisive election victory for her Conservative party. Her time in office will bring more freedom for private companies and less for trade unions.

1979 The nuclear power industry reels when the "impossible" happens at the Three Mile Island nuclear power station in Pennsylvania, An accidental meltdown damages the plant and dents public confidence in nuclear safety.

Apple II computer

COMPUTER LIBERATION In the early 1970s, some people, including Ted Nelson, son of a Hollywood actress, began to demand computing power for all. Personal computers and the internet have given this to many in the West, but most of the world's population still has no access to computers.

Transparent area allows tape to be seen

Adjustable headset

Cord plugs into the cassette player

Headphones allow the user to listen to music without disturbing other people nearby

WALKMAN *Sold in Britain as the Stereo Stowaway, this early Walkman had some facilities absent from later models, including provision for two sets of headphones.*

Spreadsheet software

1979

Daniel Bricklin, Bob Frankson

A spreadsheet program displays a constantly updated table of related numbers. This simple idea has probably sold more personal computers than any other piece of software. When US student Daniel Bricklin and programmer Bob Frankson launched the first spreadsheet program, VisiCalc, in 1979, it was a revelation. People were amazed by the way they could make changes to one number and instantly see the effect on all the others. They had a new management tool.

Walkman

1979

Akio Morita

Akio Morita, cofounder of the Japanese firm Sony, invented a cassette player small enough for people to carry around. His name for it was Walkman. This was considered bad English, so at its launch in 1979, it was the Soundabout in the US and Stowaway in Britain. Morita got his way in the end—it is now the Walkman everywhere.

Cellular address code

1980

Günter Blobel

Healthy people have all their different proteins in the right places, wherever they are needed. By 1980, German doctor Günter Blobel had discovered how this happens. He found that every protein carries a molecular code, a sequence of amino acids, which controls its movement through the body. Responding to the code, a cell membrane either blocks the protein or lets it through—unless it is needed by the membrane itself, in which case it hangs on to it.

1979 Soviet Union troops cross the border into Afghanistan to prop up the country's communist regime, which has been weakened by years of infighting between its leaders. Within days, the USSR has installed a new leader.

1980 Strikes over food prices in Gdansk, Poland, lead to workers getting the right to form free trade unions. Under their leader, Lech Walesa, they form the union Solidarity, which will later defeat the communist government.

Genetic control of embryonic development

1980

Edward Lewis, Christiane Nüsslein-Volhard, Eric Weischaus

The fruit fly breeds quickly and has large chromosomes (✻ *see* **page 176**) so is ideal for genetics research. In 1978, US geneticist Edward Lewis found that its genes are arranged along its chromosomes in the same order as the body parts they control. By 1980, German geneticist Christiane Nüsslein-Volhard and US geneticist Eric Weischaus had found that only 140 of the genes are essential during development. Some control the body plan, others create segments of the body, and others determine features within segments. Work like this helps scientists to understand development in humans.

G proteins

1980

Martin Rodbell, Alfred Gilman

Bodies wouldn't work if cells didn't respond to things. Heart cells respond to adrenaline (✻ *see* **page 174**) by pumping harder. Eye cells respond to light with nerve impulses. US pharmacologist Alfred Gilman used the work of US biochemist Martin Rodbell to help find the link between stimulus and response. By 1980, he had found G proteins. Activated by a stimulus, these make cells containing them respond. Gilman's finding has helped to explain some diseases, including cholera.

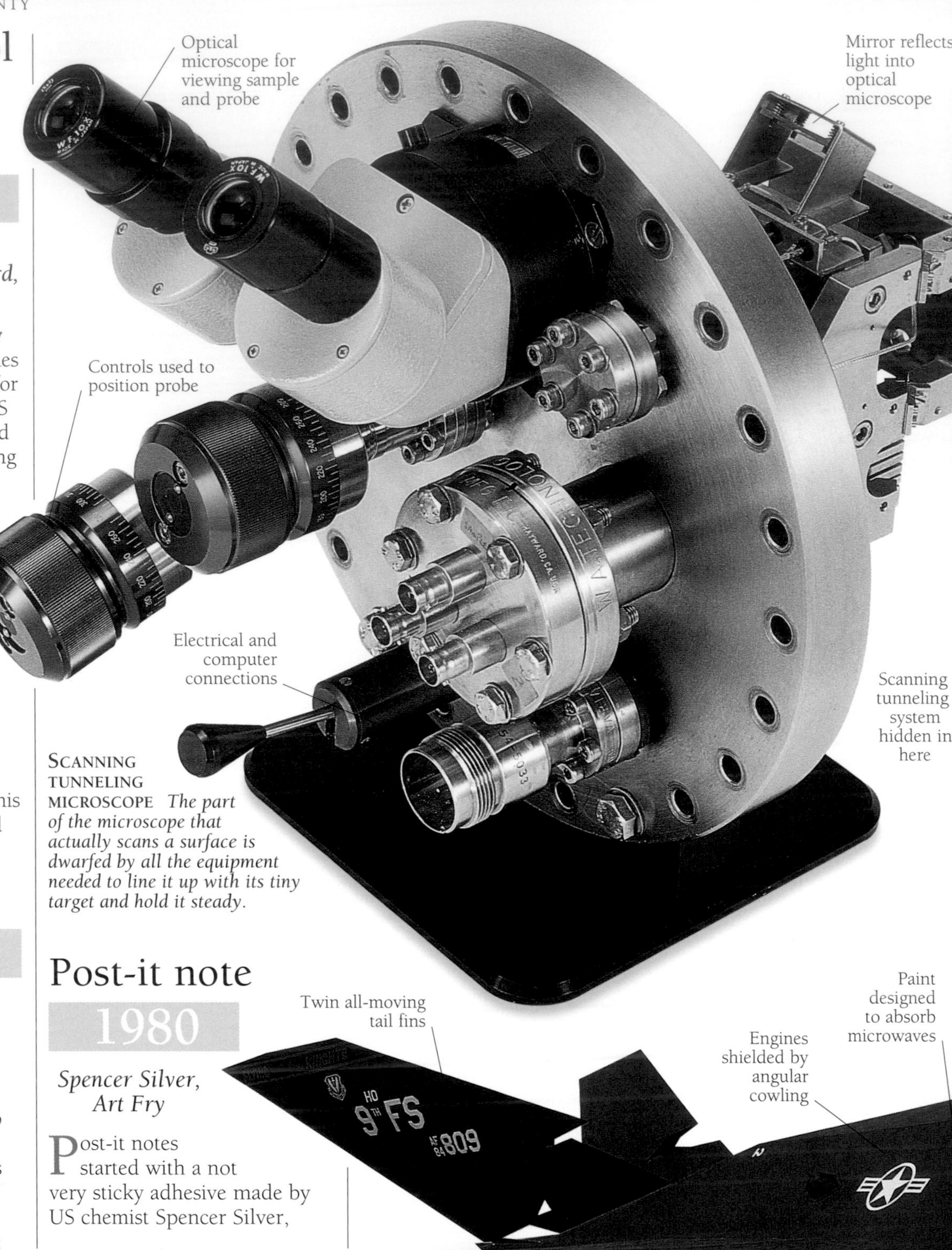

SCANNING TUNNELING MICROSCOPE *The part of the microscope that actually scans a surface is dwarfed by all the equipment needed to line it up with its tiny target and hold it steady.*

Post-it note

1980

Spencer Silver, Art Fry

Post-it notes started with a not very sticky adhesive made by US chemist Spencer Silver, who worked for US manufacturing company 3M. He had a feeling that the adhesive might be useful but couldn't think of a use for it. Eventually, his colleague Art Fry found one. Art sang in a choir and needed bookmarks that wouldn't fall out of his music. A strip of Silver's adhesive was the answer. After much development, and the realization that the peelable, sticky sheets had many other uses, 3M's Post-it notes were launched in 1980.

1982 In April, Canada gets total independence from the British parliament when Queen Elizabeth II signs the Constitution Act. Canada's new status is largely the result of a long campaign by its prime minister, Pierre Trudeau.

1982 Argentine troops invade the British-run Falkland Islands, off South America. Britain's prime minister, Margaret Thatcher, sends troops to defend the islands. Altogether, about 900 British and Argentine troops die. Argentina is defeated.

Scanning tunneling microscope

1981

Gerd Binnig, Heinrich Rohrer

The scanning tunneling microscope, invented by Swiss physicists Gerd Binnig and Heinrich Rohrer in 1981, reveals the three-dimensional reality of individual atoms. It scans a metal surface with a sharp probe that doesn't quite touch it. A small voltage makes electrons "tunnel" out of the metal, creating a current, and a control signal raises or lowers the probe to keep this current constant as the surface is scanned. Fluctuations in the control signal can then be converted into an amazingly detailed picture of the surface.

IBM PC

1981

William Lowe, Don Estridge

In 1980, US computer giant IBM saw the desktop computer as both a threat and an opportunity. One of its managers, William Lowe, suggested that the company should develop a personal computer. A small company called Microsoft provided the operating system. By fall, the design was ready, and another manager, Don Estridge, took over production. The IBM PC was launched in New York on August 12, 1981. Within days, output had to be quadrupled as demand outstripped supply.

Space shuttle

1981

NASA

A space shuttle blasts into space, then glides home like a plane. Unlike a plane, it starts each journey attached to a huge fuel tank and booster, rockets, the whole thing weighing 2,000 tons. The tank is discarded, but the boosters are reused. After trials in which shuttles were launched from jumbo jets, the shuttle *Columbia* lifted off from Cape Canaveral in Florida on April 12, 1981. Its 54-hour mission, ending at Edwards Air Force Base in California, was the first of many.

Compact disc

1982

Philips Electronics, Sony Corporation

Competing companies Philips and Sony did not want a repeat of earlier mistakes, in which their rival video systems had both been beaten by the VHS recorder (✳ *see* **page 218**), so they worked together to invent the CD. When commercial CD players appeared in 1982, the Philips player included a key component made by Sony.

Cause of AIDS

1983

Flossie Wong-Staal

The cause of acquired immunodeficiency syndrome, or AIDS, was unknown until Chinese–American virologist Flossie Wong-Staal and her team at the US National Cancer Institute identified the human immunodeficiency virus, or HIV. The same discovery was also made by Luc Montagnier and Françoise Barré-Sinoussi in France. Wong-Staal went on to clone the virus and establish its genome, which led to the design of blood tests for HIV. Today, antiretroviral therapies prevent people with HIV from developing AIDS by reducing the amount of the virus in the blood to very low levels.

Stealth aircraft

1983

Lockheed Martin Corporation

Stealth technology tries to make planes invisible to radar (✳ *see* **page 198**). The idea is not new: in World War II, German submarine snorkels were coated with radar-absorbing material to reduce the risk of detection. Another technique is to shape objects so that they do not reflect radar waves back to where they came from. Both ideas were used in the first stealth aircraft, the US Lockheed F-117 fighter, which became operational in 1983. Despite its weird shape and special paint, one was shot down over Yugoslavia in 1999.

Cyclonic vacuum cleaner

1983

James Dyson

See **pages 238–239** for the story of how James Dyson took on the world with the first cyclonic vacuum cleaner.

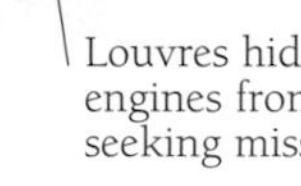

STEALTH AIRCRAFT *The angular shape of the F-117A deflects radar pulses, while its special black paint absorbs them and also makes it less visible at night.*

1983 On Wednesday February 16, which will be known as "Ash Wednesday," Australia's worst ever bush fires kill 72 people, including 12 firefighters, and cause $400m of damage. Some fires are the work of arsonists.

1983 At Black Rock, Nevada, British businessman Richard Noble makes land speed history in his jet car *Thrust 2*. His speed of 633.468 mph (1,019.467 km/h), is 11.061 mph (17.797 km/h) faster than the world record.

Internet

1983

J. C. R. Licklider, Larry Roberts

US psychologist J. C. R. Licklider, head of Information Processing at the US military's Advanced Research Projects Agency (ARPA) started his Intergalactic Computer Network—officially known as Arpanet—in 1963. Its goal was to link research computers together. Network specialist Larry Roberts took over in 1966. By 1970, Arpanet was using packet switching, the transmission technique that makes the internet possible. Procedures for transferring data were fixed by 1978, and became compulsory in 1983, effectively creating the modern internet. (✱ *See also* **Network of Networks**.)

Dust-free builder's chute

1984

G. H. Vlutters, A. J. Vlutters

Dutch building equipment suppliers G. H. and A. J. Vlutters invented their garbage chute in 1984. Before then, builders made their own chutes from planks. Dust went everywhere, and large objects sometimes bounced out and fell. The Vlutters were inspired by a stack of disposable cups. If the cups had no bottoms, they would form a flexible tube. They made the cups bigger, added chains and a winch, and persuaded builders to buy them.

Top "cup" is attached to the building

Sections link together to form the chute

DUST-FREE BUILDER'S CHUTE *A chute like this, erected in minutes, is safer than earlier chutes, which took hours to build.*

3-D graphics computer

1984

James Clark

Computer-generated images for films and advertising are made with specialized graphics computers. The first person to see the need for such computers was US engineer James Clark. He intended them for scientific and military work, but when his company, Silicon Graphics, gave one of its first workstations to *Star Wars* director George Lucas, in 1984, it opened up a new market. Today, digital actors can replace extras in a movie, and entire films are created without a single actor.

DNA fingerprinting

1984

Alec Jeffreys

Every person's DNA is unique. DNA fingerprinting compares DNA found after a crime with DNA from a suspect. It was invented in 1984 by British geneticist Alec (later Sir Alec) Jeffreys. The DNA is first split into fragments with an enzyme. Everyone's DNA will split differently. When drawn through gelatin by electricity, some fragments move faster than others. The resulting pattern of spots is revealed by making radioactive DNA stick to the original DNA. It can be used as evidence in a trial. In 2013, advanced DNA sequencing techniques were developed that can distinguish between identical twins.

Figures' movements based on those of real actors

3-D GRAPHICS COMPUTER *Graphic computers generated hundreds of "actors" for the movie Titanic.*

1983 Germany's *Stern* magazine excites world interest with excerpts from what it says are Hitler's diaries. Despite the approval of British historian Hugh Trevor-Roper, they turn out to be the work of a forger called Konrad Kujau.

1984 In Bhopal, central India, a leak at an insecticide plant releases 50 tons of deadly gas into a populated area. About 2,500 people are killed, 50,000 are temporarily disabled, and many more will claim lasting effects.

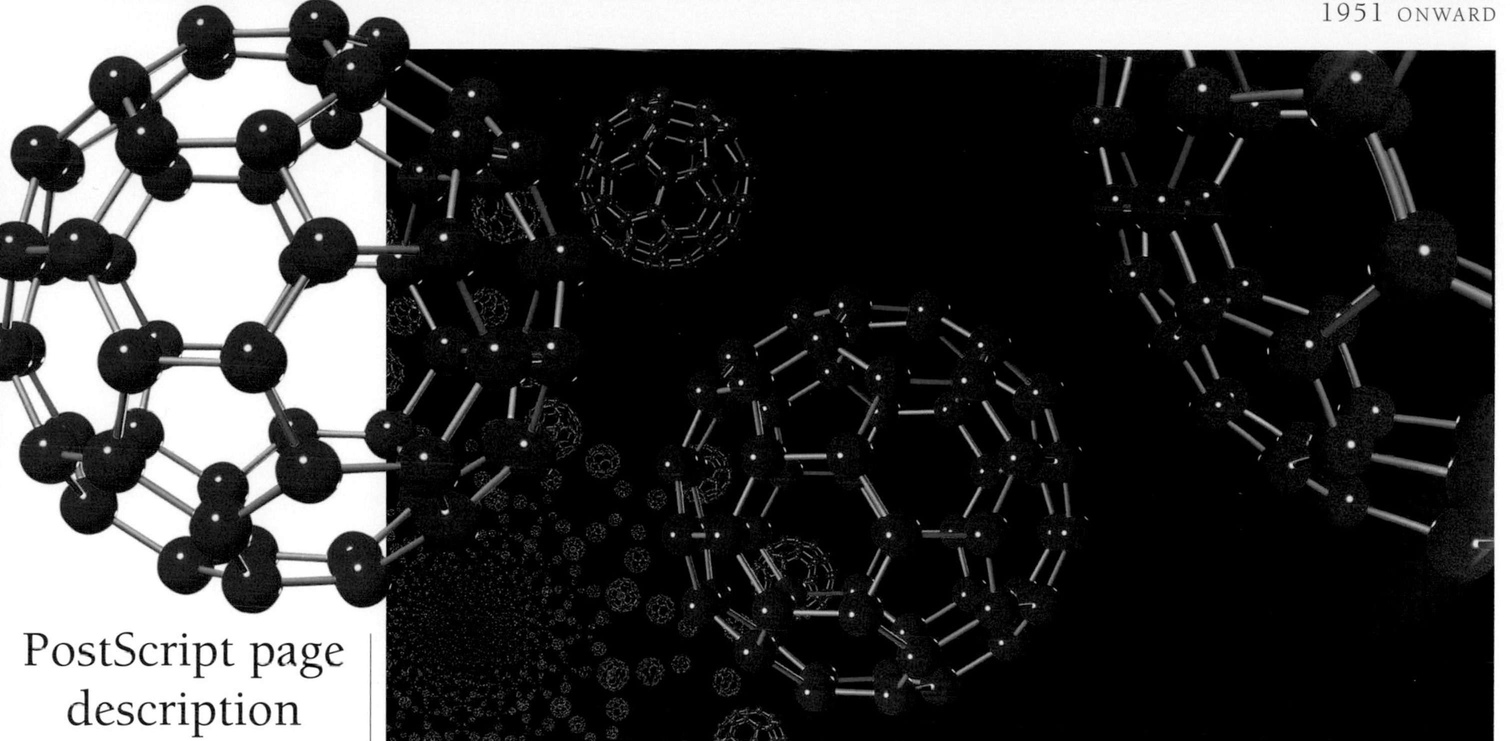

FULLERENES *A buckminsterfullerene molecule is a semiregular polyhedron. Buckminster Fuller based designs for huge domes on polyhedra of this kind.*

PostScript page description language

1984

John Warnock, Charles Geschke

PostScript is a language that describes printed pages. Any printer that understands PostScript can print a PostScript file. Because the language describes shapes, instead of issuing instructions, the result is limited only by the quality of the printer. PostScript was devised by US computer scientists John Warnock and Charles Geschke and released by their company, Adobe, in 1984. When Apple used it in their LaserWriter printer, and a third company, Aldus, added a layout program, PageMaker, desktop publishing was born.

Fullerenes

1985

Harry Kroto, Richard Smalley, Robert Curl

Scientists once knew only three forms of carbon—diamond, graphite, and amorphous. Then, in 1985, British chemist Harold (later Sir Harold) Kroto and US chemists Richard Smalley and Robert Curl vaporized graphite with a laser beam. This formed molecules containing 60 carbon atoms arranged as a hollow ball. They named the new form of carbon buckminsterfullerene, after a US architect famous for his domes. Other fullerenes have since been found.

Windows operating system

1985

Microsoft Corporation

The Apple Macintosh set a new standard. Its point-and-click interface made the IBM PC's text-based operating system, Microsoft's MS-DOS, look old-fashioned. In 1985, Microsoft hit back with Windows, but because PC users wanted to keep their old programs, Windows operated through MS-DOS, making it slow. An improved version, so Maclike that it provoked a lawsuit, appeared in 1987. Finally, Windows 3, launched in 1990, helped the PC dominate the computer it had once imitated.

NETWORK OF NETWORKS

THERE ARE MANY INTERNETS but only one "internet." An internet is any network that interconnects several smaller networks. The internet connects thousands of internets to form a vast global network. It consists of "backbones," such as NSFNET in the US and EBONE in Europe, into which are plugged smaller regional and local networks. These connect to individual computers.

GETTING THE MESSAGE

A home computer connects to the internet through a computer belonging to an Internet Service Provider (ISP). This computer is connected through the ISP's network to the internet and has a unique address. Data travels as independent "packets," which find their way with the help of special computers called routers.

EXCHANGING DATA

Computers using the internet have to talk TCP/IP, its official "language." This is actually a pair of protocols, or standards. TCP is Transmission Control Protocol, responsible for the exchange of data between programs running on different computers. IP is Internet Protocol, which ensures that data can find its way around the net.

1984 India's prime minister, Indira Gandhi, is killed by her Sikh bodyguards. It is the end of a conflict in which Sikh extremists in the Punjab violently sought independence and resented the use of troops to clear the Sikh temple at Amritsar.

1985 Irish musician Bob Geldof organizes Live Aid, a 16-hour charity concert at London's Wembley Stadium, with further time at Philadelphia's JFK Stadium. World-class performers take part, and money rolls in for the world's poor.

TAMING THE WHIRLWIND

James Dyson takes on the world with the first vacuum cleaner that doesn't need a bag

EARLY VACUUM CLEANER
From their invention in about 1902 until Dyson applied the cyclonic principle, all vacuum cleaners sucked air through a bag. Some early models were powered by hand. Electricity made cleaning easier and a little more efficient.

Dyson got the idea for his cleaner from the industrial cyclone, which is used to collect unwanted particles, such as the sawdust from a sawmill. His challenge was to get the principle to work on a much smaller scale inside a domestic machine.

It was late at night. An intruder was creeping around a factory yard. For a long time, he stared at and examined a giant metal cone sticking out of the factory roof. He made several sketches of the cone, then he was off into the darkness. James Dyson had just had his first encounter with an industrial cyclone, a device that removes dust from the air coming out of a factory. It was to change his life.

The next morning, Dyson built a copy of the cyclone in his own small factory, where he was making wheelbarrows. He wanted it to trap the paint powder that filled the air when his wheelbarrows were sprayed. There was already a fan in the factory that sucked air through a cloth filter, but the cloth needed cleaning hourly. In the cyclone system, the air whirled around inside a cone. The powder was flung out like water out of clothes in a spin dryer and deposited at the bottom of the cone.

Then Dyson thought of something else. At home, near Bath, England, he used a powerful vacuum cleaner. The design of vacuum cleaners hadn't changed much since they were invented. They worked well only with a new bag, because the dust they sucked up from the carpet quickly clogged the pores in the bag, reducing suction. The bag was like the cloth filter in Dyson's factory, which he had replaced with a cyclone, and he wondered if he could replace the bag with a cyclone system, too.

Dyson rushed home and made a cardboard model of the industrial cyclone. He ripped the bag off an old vacuum cleaner and replaced it with his cardboard cone. To his delight, he found that the bagless vacuum cleaner worked well. He had made an important invention.

That was in 1978. It would be another 15 years before Dyson's Dual Cyclone cleaner was launched, although his first cyclonic cleaner, the G-Force, featured on the cover of *Design* magazine in 1983 and reached Japan in 1986. Those years were filled with intensive engineering, which he loved, and dealing with businessmen and lawyers, which he hated. In the end, he had to manufacture his invention himself. He didn't want his idea stolen or suppressed by jealous rivals.

When the Dual Cyclone was finally launched in 1993, the first reaction from customers was shock—it looked so different. Then sales grew. After two years, Dyson's invention was the number one vacuum cleaner in Britain and was generating worldwide sales of well over $1 million a day. The whirlwind was tamed.

Dyson G-Force cyclonic vacuum cleaner, sold in Japan from 1986

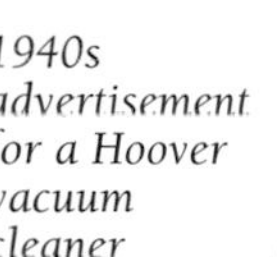

1940s advertisement for a Hoover vacuum cleaner

FORCE FOR CHANGE
Japanese customers loved the unusual pink of the G-Force, the first cyclonic cleaner to go into production. The color was suggested by the early morning light in the fields of Provence in the South of France.

JAMES DYSON
The multi-cyclone cleaner seen here is just one of many ideas Dyson has produced. Training at the Royal College of Art, London, helped him develop his creativity. Before the cyclonic cleaner, he had invented a new kind of boat and a wheelbarrow with a ball-shaped wheel. Just as important as his creativity, though, was his determination to see things through.

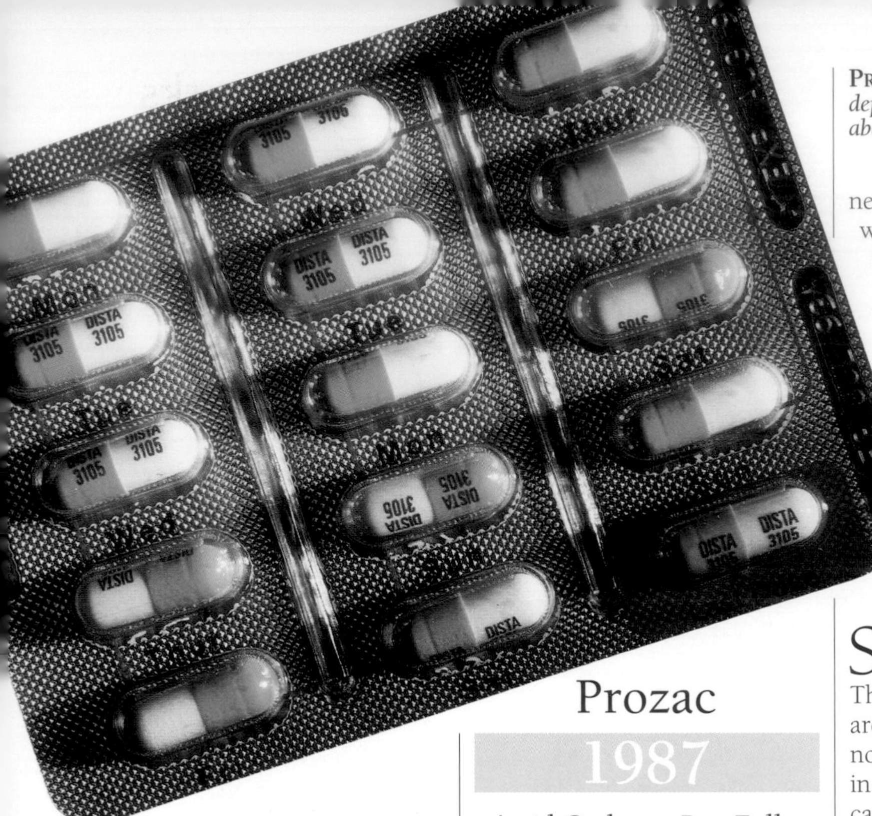

PROZAC *A drug prescribed for depression, Prozac is taken by about 40 million people worldwide.*

High-temperature superconductors

1986

Georg Bednorz, Alex Müller

Superconductors, used in powerful electromagnets, show no resistance to electric current. But they work only at very low temperatures. In 1986, German physicist Georg Bednorz and Swiss physicist Alex Müller found a superconductor that worked at a higher temperature. Their new barium-lanthanum copper oxide sparked off a search for others. By 1988, researchers had found a similar oxide that was superconductive at –234°F (–148°C), which could be made to work by being cooled with cheap liquid nitrogen.

HIGH-TEMPERATURE SUPERCONDUCTORS *Electromagnets like this use superconductors to carry their huge currents. The magnet is enclosed in a cooling chamber.*

Prozac

1987

Arvid Carlsson, Ray Fuller

In 1972, a team led by US biochemist Ray Fuller synthesized the compound fluoxetine. Fifteen years later, it became the antidepressant Prozac. Fluoxetine reduces the rate at which serotonin, a nerve chemical, is reabsorbed. This makes more serotonin available, which eases depression. Fuller's work used some research by Swedish neurologist Arvid Carlsson, who developed another anti-depressant, later withdrawn because of side effects.

Supermassive black hole

1987

John Kormendy, Alan Dressler, Douglas Richstone

Supermassive black holes have the mass of millions of suns. They can destroy everything around them, but astronomers now believe they are involved in the creation of galaxies. They can be detected by the way nearby stars and matter orbit them at colossal speeds. In 1987, a 30-million-sun black hole was found independently by Canadian astronomer John Kormendy and US astronomers Alan Dressler and Douglas Richstone. Many more have been found since then.

Gene that causes cystic fibrosis

1989

Lap-Chee Tsui, Francis Collins

In cystic fibrosis (CF), thick, sticky mucus clogs the lungs and intestines. A child can inherit the condition if both parents are carriers. The faulty gene that causes it was found in 1989 by Canadian geneticist Lap-Chee Tsui at the Hospital for Sick Children in Toronto, Canada, and US geneticist Francis Collins at the University of Michigan. Their discovery makes it possible to detect CF carriers and may one day make the condition curable.

World Wide Web

1990

Tim Berners-Lee

The World Wide Web grew from the work of British physicist Tim Berners-Lee at the European Centre for Nuclear Research (CERN) in Switzerland. CERN's scientists needed to get at information scattered among computers worldwide. Berners-Lee's answer was the web. In 1990, when he had written the software and defined the standards that would make it work, the web became available to CERN scientists. The public saw it a year later.

Gene therapy

1990

French Anderson

Gene therapists attempt to restore health to people with genetic disorders by replacing faulty genes. The first person to receive officially approved gene therapy was a four-year-old girl who had inherited a defective immune system. In 1990, US geneticist French Anderson removed some white cells from her blood, inserted normal copies of a faulty gene, then replaced the cells. With regular follow-up treatments to maintain enough gene-corrected white cells, the girl became able to lead a normal life.

Digital cell phone

1991

Groupe Spécial Mobile

The first cell phones used a simple but insecure analogue radio system, in

1986 Chernobyl power station in the USSR explodes, showering much of northern Europe with long-lasting radioactive fallout. Coming after several other nuclear disasters, this one finally shatters dented confidence in the industry.

1989 TV screens worldwide fill with scenes of jubilation as the Berlin Wall is torn down after 28 years. Berliners of all ages join in cracking up the concrete barrier between East and West. Bemused East German soldiers just watch.

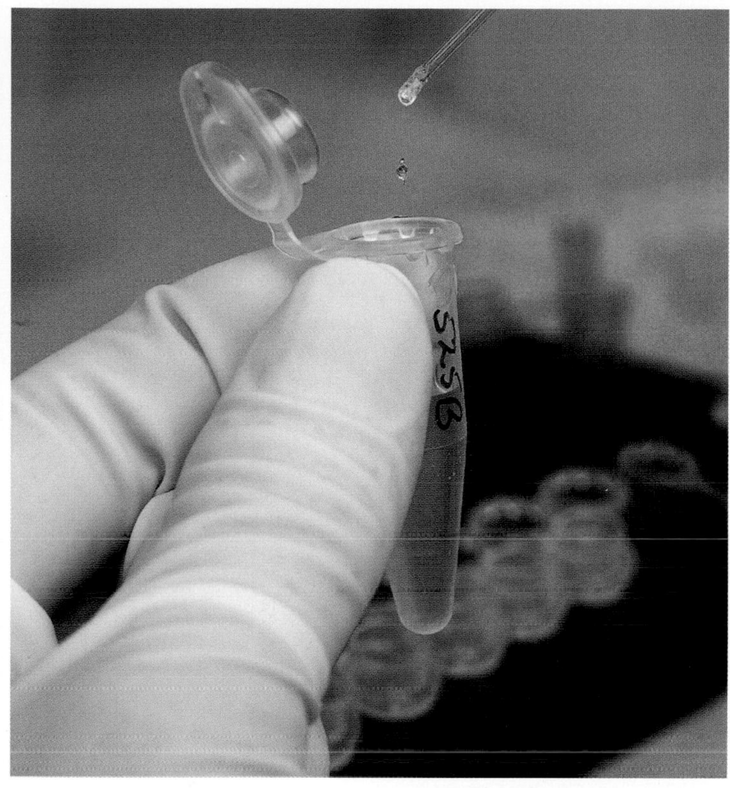

GENE THERAPY *A scientist pulls a thread of pure DNA out of solution to isolate it from an organism.*

which speech was converted more or less directly into radio waves. In 1982, the Groupe Spécial Mobile was formed to develop a digital system for Europe and beyond. Digital phones convert sound waves into numerical codes describing their shape, then send these codes by radio. By 1991, trial versions of the GSM system were ready, and the following year all major European operators began to use it. GSM now powers cell phones in 85 percent of the world market.

Separation of stem cells

1991

Ann Tsukamoto

Your body is made up of trillions of tiny cells, which carry out a huge range of functions. They produce antibodies, regulate the immune system, detect foreign substances, protect against rogue cells, help with clotting, and carry oxygen around your body. Despite this incredibly wide range of functions, all of these cells spring from one basic type—stem cells. In 1991, Tsukamoto and her team devised an ingenious way of separating stem cells from other types of cells and keeping them alive for further research. Stem cells can be used to treat a large number of conditions, including heart disease and diabetes.

Disposable TV camera

1992

Smith & Nephew Dyonics

In surgery, the smaller the incision, the better. So one essential tool of modern surgery is the endoscope, a fiber-optic device that lets surgeons peer through a "keyhole" incision. In 1992, US company Smith & Nephew Dyonics patented a more flexible alternative: a tiny camera that could be passed into the body. As it is difficult to sterilize, the camera is designed to be used only once, then thrown away.

Graphical web browser

1993

Marc Andreessen

The first World Wide Web sites (✱ **see page 240**) were entirely text-based. The web could deliver pictures but not with text. This changed in 1993, when the US National Center for Supercomputing Applications released Mosaic, the first graphical web browser. Developed by 21-year-old US student Marc Andreessen, it changed the way we use the web. The richness and convenience of Mosaic's direct descendants, Netscape (by Andreessen) and Internet Explorer, are now taken for granted by web users.

GRAPHICAL WEB BROWSER *Mozilla Firefox, released in 2002, is available in 75 languages and is used by more than 500 million people around the world.*

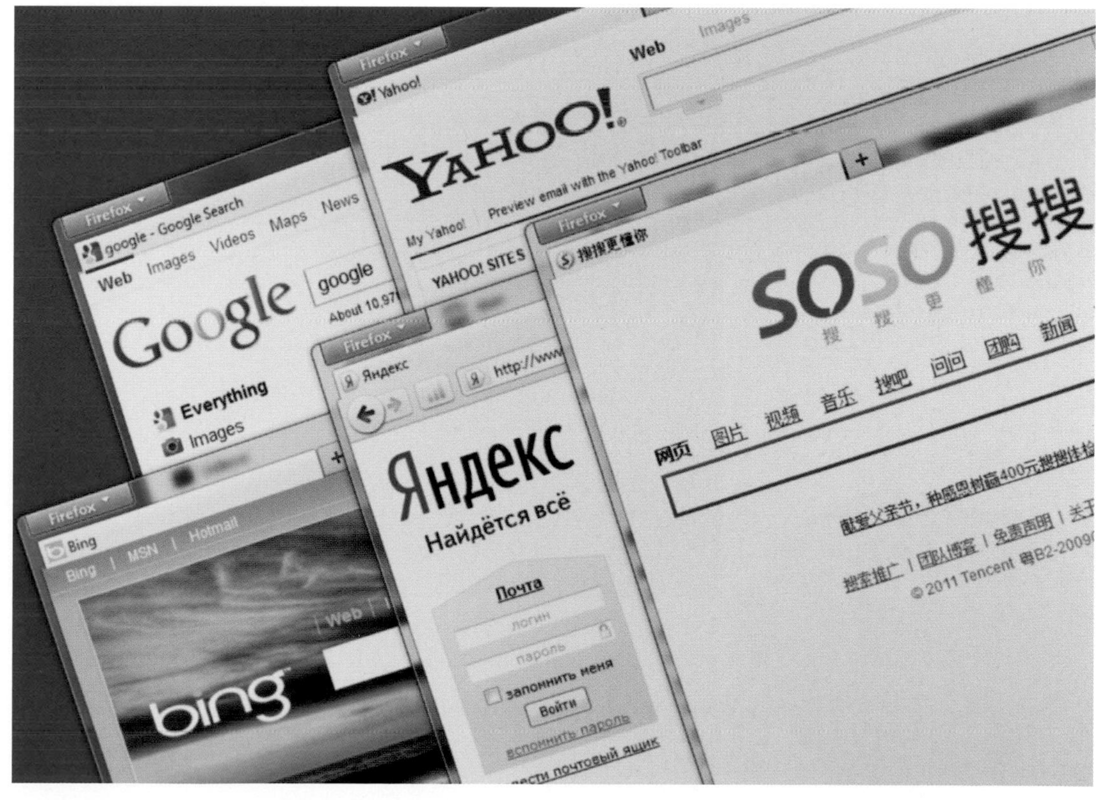

1990 After 27 years in prison, South African antiapartheid activist Nelson Mandela is released by President F. W. de Klerk. Mandela and de Klerk work to create a nonracial democracy. Mandela will win the first election open to all races.

1993 Steven Spielberg wins a best picture Oscar for *Schindler's List*, his World War II drama about German concentration camps. The same year, his dinosaur movie, *Jurassic Park*, grosses a record $725 million in four months.

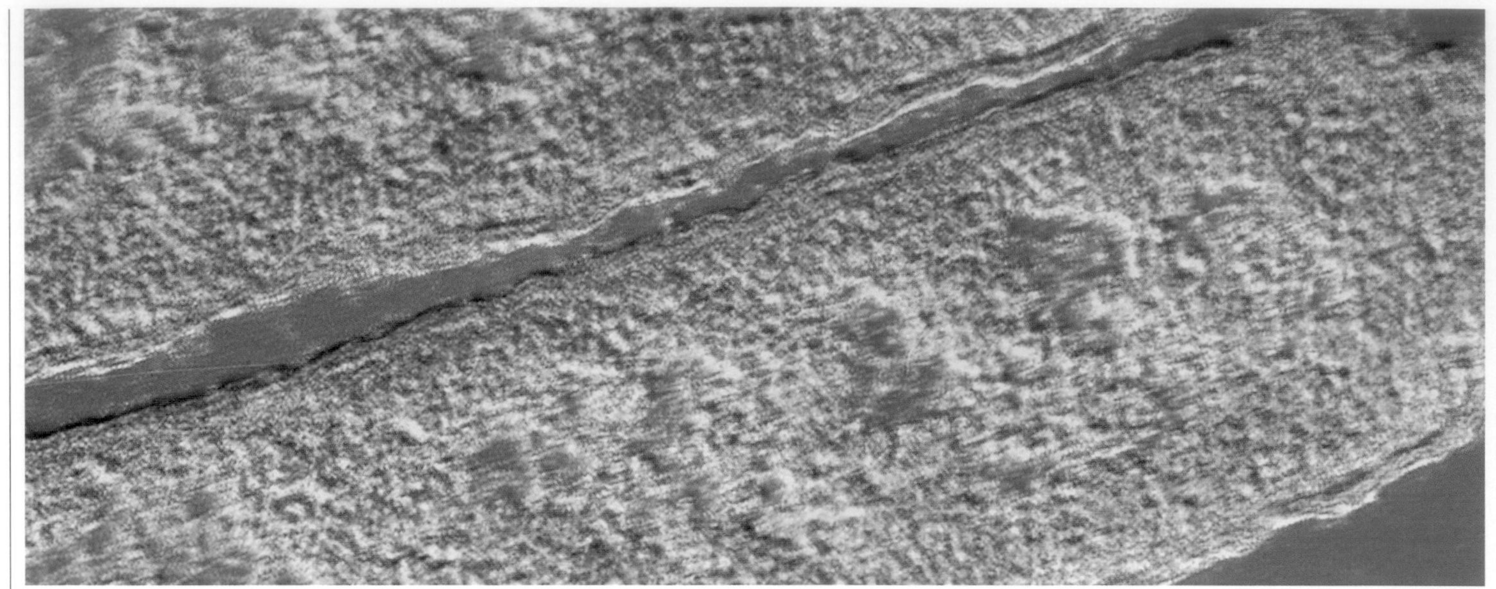

Comet Hale-Bopp *When Hale-Bopp was at its closest to the sun, in April 1997, its dust tail was longer than the distance from the sun to Earth.*

Genetically modified food

1994

Calgene Inc.

Farmers and growers have been changing the genetic makeup of our food for centuries. The first genetically modified (GM) food produced by genetic engineering (✻ **see page 229**) and approved for sale was the Flavr Savr tomato, produced by US company Calgene. A modified gene made it firmer, allowing it to be picked later without its being too soft to transport. This meant it had more flavor. Other GM foods, such as soybeans, followed.

Comet Hale-Bopp

1995

Alan Hale, Thomas Bopp

In 1995, two US amateur astronomers, Alan Hale and Thomas Bopp, independently discovered a new comet. At seven times further away from Earth than the sun, it was the most distant ever spotted by amateurs. The professionals found that it was a thousand times as bright as Halley's comet, with a nucleus about 30 miles (50 km) across. By 1997, it was much closer to the sun and was clearly visible to the naked eye. It has now retreated into space and will not be seen from Earth for another 2,400 years.

Complete bacterial DNA sequence Haemophilus influenzae *(above) was the first of several organisms to have its entire DNA sequenced by The Institute for Genomic Research in the mid-1990s.*

Complete bacterial DNA sequence

1995

Robert Fleischmann

An organism's complete set of genes—its genome—is hidden among the millions of chemical units making up its DNA (✻ **see pages 216–217**). To study a genome, scientists first have to list these units in the right sequence. The first free-living organism to have its entire DNA sequence revealed was a bacterium that can cause meningitis—***Haemophilus influenzae***. A team led by US geneticist Robert Fleischmann at The Institute for Genomic Research (TIGR) used the "shotgun" method. The team first broke the bacterium's DNA into thousands of random fragments, then used a computer to put these into a complete sequence. The result was presented, to great acclaim, in May 1995.

1994 The dream of decades is realized when the Channel Tunnel, which runs under the English Channel to link Britain and France by rail, is opened. Construction of the tunnel has taken more than six years and cost £10.5bn ($15bn).

1994 South Africa rejoins the Commonwealth after holding its first election open to people of all races. The clear winner is the African National Congress, led by Nelson Mandela, who becomes the country's first black president.

Internet retailing

1995

Jeff Bezos

While hundreds of internet retailers crashed in 2001, the oldest of them all remained healthy. Amazon.com, the internet bookstore (which now sells other things as well) was founded by US computer scientist Jeff Bezos in 1994. It sold its first book in July 1995. Following a great US tradition, business whizz Bezos started the website in his garage. He also wrote his own software for the site, which he named after the world's longest river.

Full-length computer-generated movie

1995

The Walt Disney Company

Making a full-length animated film is laborious and expensive. In the early 1990s, specialized graphics computers (✳ **see page 236**) became capable of doing most of the work. The first movie that was made in this way was Disney's *Toy Story*, a tale of rivalry between a handcrafted cowboy and a mass-produced space ranger. It was released in 1995. Its success led to the making of other computer-generated films, including *A Bug's Life* and *Monsters, Inc.*

Proof of Fermat's last theorem

1995

Andrew Wiles, Richard Taylor

The last unproved theorem of 17th-century French mathematician Pierre de Fermat stated that, for n greater than 2, there were no positive whole numbers x, y, and z such that $x^n + y^n = z^n$. Fermat said he had a proof but never wrote it down. In 1993, British mathematician Andrew Wiles produced his own 200-page proof. Other mathematicians spotted some gaps, but by 1995, with the help of Richard Taylor, one of Wiles' former students, these were plugged and Fermat's last theorem was proved.

Life on Mars?

1996

David McKay

In August 1996, US geologist David McKay made an announcement about a meteorite. It contained evidence, he said, that there may once have been life on Mars. The 4.5 billion-year-old meteorite was found in Antarctica in 1984, but its Martian origin was not confirmed until 1994. Two years' work revealed organic chemicals within it that suggested the presence of living bacteria at some time in the past. The surface of the meteorite carried no such chemicals, ruling out Earth contamination. There were also inorganic compounds that are secreted by bacteria. Scientists regard the evidence as inconclusive.

INTERNET RETAILING
Amazon.com is the world's biggest internet business. It has more than 80 giant warehouses worldwide.

Dolly the sheep

1997

Ian Wilmut, Keith Campbell

See **pages 244–245** for the story of how Ian Wilmut and Keith Campbell created Dolly the sheep.

Growth of new brain cells

1998

Fred Gage, Peter Eriksson

People used to think that once all our brain cells are in place, no more can grow. In 1998, neurologists Fred Gage in the US and Peter Eriksson in Sweden showed this is not so. They labeled brain cells in terminally ill patients with a chemical that revealed cell division. On examining the brains after death, they found that they had been producing up to 1,000 new cells every day.

MicroStar air reconnaissance vehicle

1998

Lockheed Martin Corporation

Small aircraft are harder to detect than large ones. In 1989, the US Lockheed Martin Corporation took this to an extreme with their military reconnaissance plane MicroStar. Its wingspan was 5 in (12 cm), and it weighed 3 oz (85 g). It carried a tiny television camera and transmitter. Designed to fly at a height of 200 ft (60 m), it could send vital spy pictures to people below.

1996 Afghan Islamic fundamentalists, the Taliban, capture the capital, Kabul, in the civil war that broke out in Afghanistan when Soviet troops left in 1989. They seize power and impose a strict rule based on Islamic law.

1997 J.K. Rowling's *Harry Potter and the Philosopher's Stone* is published in the UK. The popular franchise captures the world's attention, and will go on to include seven novels, eight movies, a play, and a vast merchandising empire.

CLONING AN ADULT MAMMAL

Ian Wilmut and Keith Campbell create Dolly, a perfect copy of a grown-up sheep

IAN WILMUT
Born in 1944, Ian Wilmut joined the Animal Breeding Research Station (now the Roslin Institute) near Edinburgh, Scotland, in 1974. There, with Keith Campbell, he developed a way of cloning animals from partly developed embryos. The results, two sheep called Megan and Morag, were born in 1995. They were forerunners of the first clone from an adult.

Harry Griffin picked up the phone. It was the evening of Saturday February 22, 1997, and he was enjoying a break from the busy Roslin Institute, Scotland, where one of his jobs was to deal with journalists. The call shattered his weekend. Tomorrow, a Sunday newspaper was going to publish a story that was supposed to be kept secret until the following week. Scientists at the Institute, collaborating with the biotechnology company PPL Therapeutics, had created a sheep that was an exact copy—a clon—of an adult sheep.

Lamb 6LL3—Dolly—had been born in July 1996. Journalists tried to figure out what she meant for humanity. Could humans now be cloned? Should they be? British genetic engineer Ian Wilmut, who led the Dolly team, didn't think so. He wanted to produce sheep that delivered medicines in their milk. If he could make one sheep do this, cloning might turn it into a flock.

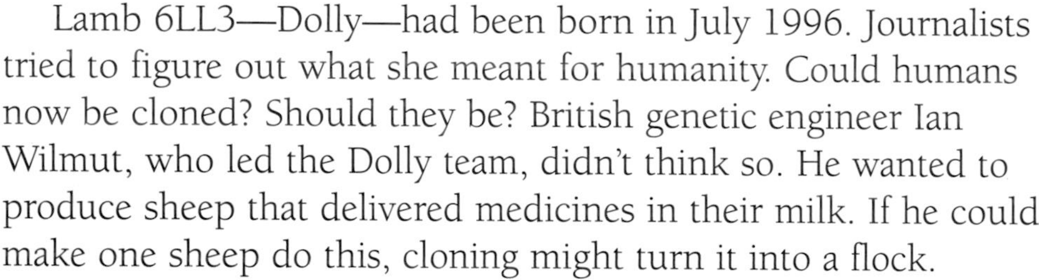

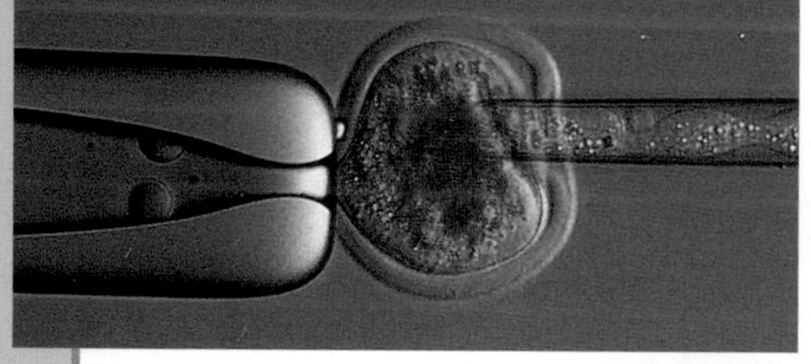

An egg cell has its nucleus removed.

HOW ANIMALS ARE CLONED
To create a copy of an animal, one of its cells is grown in a laboratory under special conditions then injected into a cell from which the nucleus has been removed. The fused cells are usually given a brief electric shock to activate them. Although the basic technique for moving genetic material from cell to cell dates from 1952, success rates for cloning are still low.

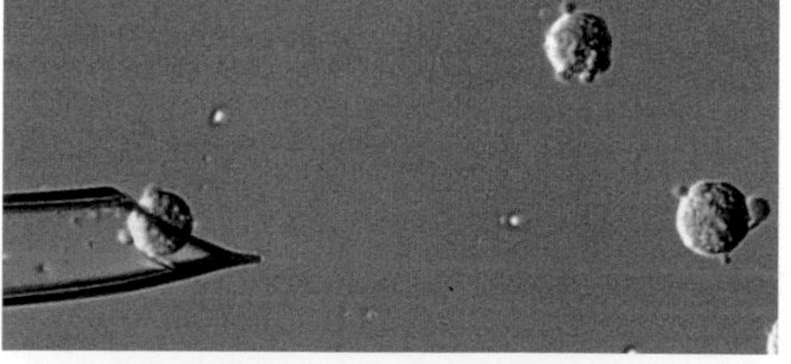

A laboratory-grown adult cell is collected.

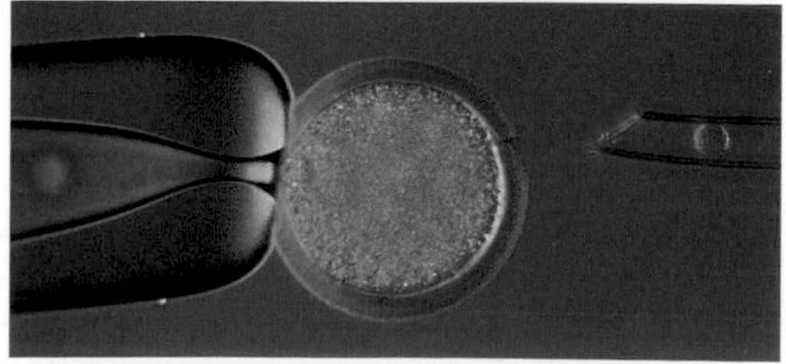

A pipette, on the left, holds the nucleus-free egg cell in place while the complete adult cell is pushed into it by the tube seen on the right.

Animals had been cloned before, but all from cells at an early stage of development. As an embryo grows, its cells become specialized. Some of them form nerves, some form muscles, and so on. The genes not needed in any particular type of cell are "turned off." It is this that allows many different types of cells to be created from just one set of genes. So although every adult cell contains every gene, none has all its genes available in working form.

In 1995, another scientist at the Roslin Institute, Keith Campbell, had found a way to turn back the clock and make an adult cell behave like an early embryonic cell.

The world's press converged on Dolly after Britain's Observer *newspaper printed her story on Sunday February 23, 1997.*

He kept adult cells alive in culture dishes using a medium that contained very little "growth factor"—in effect putting them on a starvation diet. This starvation turned the genes that had been turned off during development back on again. A cell treated in this way, because it had a full set of genes available for work, could, when fused with an egg that had had its nucleus removed, form the starting point for a new animal.

Wilmut and his colleagues took an egg from a sheep and sucked out its genetic material with a tiny tube. Then they inserted a "starved" cell from the udder of a different sheep. A tiny electric shock started the egg dividing to produce an embryo. They implanted this in the womb of another sheep. They had to do this 277 times to get just one Dolly—the others all died at some stage.

When Dolly was born, she didn't look like the sheep that had carried her, or even like the sheep that had provided the egg. She looked exactly like the sheep that had provided the udder cell. Shaped by the genes from that cell, Dolly was that sheep's clone—a world first. A little ahead of schedule, Dolly was front-page news.

DOLLY BECOMES A MOM
On April 13, 1998, Dolly proved that she was a fully functional sheep by giving birth to a healthy lamb named Bonnie. The following March, Dolly produced triplets, seen here with their mother. The lambs are completely normal, but Dolly seems to be older than her chronological age.

MP3 compression standard

1998

Fraunhofer Institut, Moving Picture Experts Group

Downloading music from the internet would take forever without compression to remove unnecessary information. This could reduce quality, but MP3 (or MPEG Layer-3) ensures that the effects of compression are masked by louder sounds. It was developed by the Fraunhofer Institut in Germany and released by the Moving Picture Experts Group (MPEG) in 1998. Although its use on the internet created some copyright problems, a little MP3 player is a really neat way to carry music around.

SATELLITE CELL PHONE *Ordinary satellite phones use satellites in high orbits. They are not truly mobile because they have to be carefully aimed at the chosen satellite before use.*

Satellite cell phone

1998

Iridium Satellite LLC

Cell phones will not work in remote areas where there are no base stations. Phones working through satellites in high Earth orbits have been available since 1982, but the mobile network Iridium, which went live in 1998, uses 66 satellites in much lower orbits. At first, demand fell short of expectations, and Iridium had to close down, but it is now back in business.

Carbon nanotube "muscle"

1999

Ray Baughman

Better robots came closer in 1999 with the demonstration of "muscles" made from fullerenes (✷ see page 237). Robots are normally operated by electric or pneumatic actuators. These are slow and heavy, but an actuator made from "buckypaper"—a sheet containing billions of tubular carbon molecules—promises superior performance. Developed by an international team led by US scientist Ray Baughman, the muscle flexes when a low voltage is applied. The movement is small, but the force is greater than with human muscle. With the right leverage, it could work a robot.

Biological molecular motor

1999

Carlo Montemagno

Molecular motors are so small that they contain only a few molecules. In 1999, researchers led by US engineer Carlo Montemagno demonstrated a motor whose shaft, 12-millionths of a millimeter in diameter and made from a protein molecule, rotated at 200 revolutions per minute. The movement was created by a reaction between the protein and the enzyme ATPase. It occurred when the motor was immersed in a solution of the energy-rich molecule ATP. Such motors may one day power invisible pumps inside human bodies.

Homegrown replacement organ

1999

Anthony Atala

Rejection problems and lack of donors make replacing human organs difficult. In 1999, US doctor Anthony Atala showed that an entire new organ could be made from just a few cells of the old one. He took muscle and lining cells from the bladders of dogs and grew them around plastic balls to form new bladders. When he replaced the dogs' bladders with the artificial ones, they worked perfectly.

1999 South African novelist J. M. Coetzee becomes the first author to win the prestigious Booker Prize twice. Having won it in 1983, with his novel *The Life and Times of Michael K*, he completes the double with *Disgrace*.

2000 The century's most feared "insect," the millennium bug, bites only mildly, as computer clocks flip from 1999 to 2000. Although some older chips think it is now 1900, the worldwide chaos predicted by doomsters fails to materialize.

Leech neuron computer

1999

Bill Ditto

In 1999, US physicist Bill Ditto demonstrated the first computer made by connecting living nerve cells together. His "leech-ulator" could do only simple operations and needed an ordinary computer to help it display the results, but it worked. Ditto's goal was to develop a computer that could "think" without detailed programming.

Gene targeted sheep

2000

Kenneth McCreath

Gene targeting is inserting a new gene at a specific point in an organism's genome (✱ *see* **page 242**), rather than adding it at random. It allows the gene to work properly and be inherited by offspring. The first person to target genes in a large animal was Scottish geneticist Kenneth McCreath. He put the gene for an enzyme into the DNA of sheep cells, moved the nuclei to egg cells, and grew these into sheep. The enzyme appeared in their milk.

Growing bone outside the body

2000

Julia Polak

In 2000, Julia Polak and her team at the Chelsea and Westminster Hospital in Britain discovered that human bone cells could be made to grow outside the body. The cells were helped to bond together using Bioglass, a ceramic material containing silicon, calcium, and phosphorus. This had been developed in the 1960s by British researcher Larry Hench. It is now hoped that it will be possible to inject liquid Bioglass enriched with bone cells into patients to aid the healing of broken bones or to treat brittle bones in older people.

Human genome

2000

Francis Collins, Craig Venter

The human genome—a human being's complete set of genes—is contained within a long sequence of chemical units (A, T, G, or C) that is unique to human DNA (✱ *see* **pages 216–217**). A draft of the sequence was announced on June 26, 2000, by two rivals, the public Human Genome Project (HGP), led by Francis Collins, and the private Celera Genomics, led by Craig Venter. Neither genome was actually complete. Celera had done more but charged people to see theirs, while HGP's less-complete genome was free. Both organizations published more complete information in February 2001. (✱ *See also* **Start of Something Big**.)

Cloned endangered animal

2001

Philip Damiani

The gaur, an ox found in Asia, is on the list of endangered species. In January 2001, a baby gaur named Noah was born to a domestic cow in Iowa. Researcher Philip Damiani cloned it (✱ *see* **pages 244–245**) from skin cells from a dead gaur, frozen eight years earlier. He fused these with cow eggs whose genes had been removed, producing embryos that he implanted into cows. Noah was the only calf to come through alive, but he later died from an infection.

START OF SOMETHING BIG

THE HUMAN GENOME is only the start of a project that could last another century. Scientists will use it, among other things, to find connections between genes and diseases. There will be several areas of study. Important among these will be functional genomics, which is about what genes do, and structural genomics, which deals with the shape of the proteins that enable them to do it.

Dr. Craig Venter, former president of Celera Genomics

HUMAN GENOME PROJECT
This international project was started in 1990, with the goal of completing it by 2005. This was later brought forward to 2003. There are four major participants in the US and one in Britain, with research centers in at least 18 other countries making contributions. Its results are freely published.

CELERA GENOMICS
Celera was founded in 1998 by the PE Corporation, a US biological laboratory equipment company, and Craig Venter. It operates the world's largest genomic production plant and makes extensive use of supercomputers. Academic and commercial organizations pay a subscription to make use of the company's genomic information.

CLONED ENDANGERED ANIMAL
The gaur is found in forests in Asia. It eats grass and bamboo shoots.

2000 It's "happy birthday" to Queen Elizabeth the Queen Mother, affectionately known as the Queen Mum, as she reaches 100 on Friday, August 4. Crowds see her on the balcony of Buckingham Palace with three generations of royal children.

2001 On September 11, the US is attacked by terrorists flying four hijacked planes—two destroy the World Trade Towers in New York. The US and other countries unite together to fight terrorist organizations around the world.

Self-cleaning glass

2001

Kevin Sanderson

Window cleaning may soon be a thing of the past. In 2001, Britain's Pilkington glass company announced the invention of self-cleaning glass, developed by a team under chemist Kevin Sanderson. Its secret lies in a special coating, which makes rain run off the glass, taking dirt with it. The coating, which is extremely thin, also acts as a catalyst, allowing ultraviolet light and oxygen to unstick any dirt that might be left behind .

iPod

2001

Steve Jobs, Lee Black

Apple launched its now-famous music player, the first pocket device able to hold 1,000 songs, in 2001. Early models used the MP3 music compression system (✳ *see* **page 246**), but later iPods can also use an even more efficient file format unique to Apple. By 2005, more than 1.5 million songs, and even the album art that goes with them, were available for downloading through Apple's iTunes website. Despite the sleek white box and ultra-cool user interface, the iPod did not contain any new technology, just a hard disk drive and a little computer to control it and decode the music. With its distinctive look and ability to find any tune in seconds, it quickly displaced the portable CD player and the Walkman. (✳ *see* **page 233**)

IPOD *Since 2001, the basic iPod has acquired enough capacity for 10,000 tunes and a color screen that can show photos and album art.*

More moons for Jupiter

2002

Scott S. Sheppard, David Jewitt

In 2002, astronomers from the University of Hawaii revealed that the planet Jupiter has even more moons than we thought. Using a 140 in (3.6 m) telescope atop a Hawaiian volcano, they discovered 11 new satellites. This took the total number of Jupiter's known satellites up to 39—far more than any other planet in the solar system. It is perhaps a bit of an exaggeration to call these moons—they are not large, round bodies, but relatively small, irregularly shaped lumps of rock that were captured by the giant planet's huge gravitational field. By 2013, 67 moons had been found orbiting Jupiter.

Single-atom transistor

2002

Paul McEuen, Dan Ralph

The first transistor built around a single atom was created by scientists at Cornell University in 2002. Buried inside a specially designed molecule was a lone atom of cobalt. When the molecule was hooked up to an electronic circuit, the cobalt atom responded to a control voltage by changing the current through the device. This is only what an ordinary transistor would do, but the invention could be a step toward something new—molecular electronics. This technology would involve the building of circuits by chemical synthesis, replacing the current technique of etching shapes onto silicon.

Synthetic virus

2002

Jeronimo Cello, Aniko V. Paul, Eckard Wimmer

Any virus can easily mass-produce itself by using the genetic machinery in the cells of a suitable victim. In 2002, however, a team from the State University of New York was the first to synthesize a virus from scratch. Using the genome (genetic makeup) of the polio virus, as downloaded from the internet, they made a copy using ordinary chemicals.

Outer coat made of four different proteins (false color)

SYNTHETIC VIRUS *The polio virus has 20 five-sided faces around its genetic core.*

Super-tough fiber

2003

Ray Baughman

The plastic fibers in bulletproof vests are tough, but in 2003, scientists at the University of Texas and Trinity College, Dublin, spun a fiber 17 times tougher. It was made from carbon nanotubes—tubular molecules consisting entirely of carbon—dispersed in a soft plastic. Possible uses include better seat belts and explosion-proof blankets.

2002 The traditional currencies of many European countries cease to be accepted for payment as 12 eurozone nations switch their coins and banknotes to the euro. Money in other forms has been euro-based since 1999.

2003 The US, Britain, and other nations invade Iraq. Within three weeks, Saddam Hussein and his Ba'ath party are toppled, leaving the country free of its cruel dictator but devastated and under the control of foreign troops.

Water on Mars

2004

NASA

In 2003, NASA landed two robot rovers, Spirit and Opportunity, on Mars. Their job was to explore the planet, looking in particular for signs of past life. Opportunity was the first to find geological evidence of water that had flowed long ago. In 2004, Spirit found even clearer signs of water, backing up the evidence of its twin. Although the rovers didn't actually find liquid water, the presence of sedimentary rocks and water-cut shapes show that water must once have been present. In 2013, Curiosity—a rover launched in 2011—heated soil from the planet's surface and detected water vapor. The dust on Mars contains 2 percent water, which is bound to chemicals in the soil.

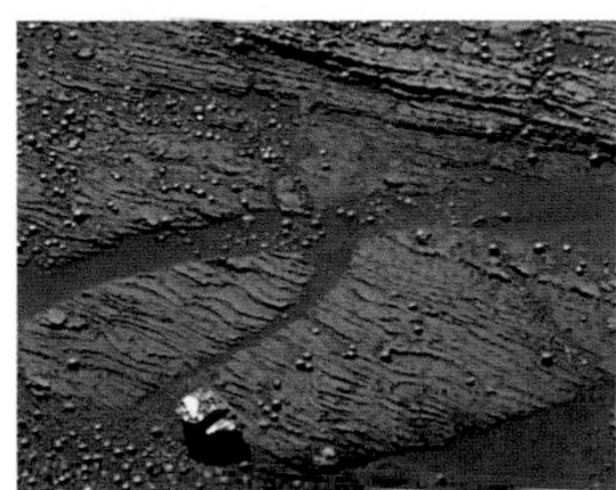

WATER ON MARS *Opportunity (left) sent back images (above) showing layers of sediment and the effects of rippling water on rock.*

OLDEST PLANET *Floating 380 miles (611 km) above the Earth, the Hubble Space Telescope can detect remote objects like Methuselah normally hidden by our atmosphere.*

Oldest planet

2003

Donald Backer, Stephen Thorsett, Steinn Sigurdsson

Although the universe is about 13.7 billion years old, the planets in our solar system were formed a mere 4.5 billion years ago. In 2003, the existence of a planet formed 12.7 billion years ago—a billion years after the universe—was confirmed by the Hubble Space Telescope. Planet PSR B1620-26C, or Methuselah, belongs to a star system 5,600 light-years from Earth. The planet showed up as a "wobble" in some star data for many years before it was caught on camera.

2004 An earthquake in the Indian Ocean creates a huge, fast-moving wave called a tsunami, causing terrible destruction in the coastal areas of surrounding countries. Nearly a quarter of a million people lose their lives.

2005 Sir Bob Geldof organizes Live8—11 concerts designed to put pressure on world leaders to help Africa by canceling debt, increasing aid, and trading more fairly. More than 1,000 musicians are seen by billions on 182 TV networks.

Low-cost mine clearance

2005

Paul Richards

The world is littered with land mines, which kill or maim more than 15,000 people every year. Getting rid of them was costly until 2005, when British engineer Paul Richards, based in South Africa, invented MineBurner. Instead of explosives, it uses bottled gas and oxygen to cut into land mines and destroy them, making disposal much cheaper.

Smartphone

2007

Steve Jobs, Jonathan Ive

In 2007, Apple launched the iPhone, which had an operating system, iOS, making it into a handheld computer on which the internet could be accessed and phone calls could be made. The phones can also run apps whose functions include organization, news, social networking, and games. With an iconic design similar to the hugely popular iPod and a touch screen, iPhones were in great demand. Soon, other cell phone companies created smartphones with similar designs.

SMARTPHONE *The first iPhone was made mostly of aluminum and had a simple design, which quickly became iconic.*

First lab-grown, synthetic organ transplant

2011

Alexander Seifalian, Harvard Bioscience, Dr. Paolo Macchiarni

The world's first successful transplant of a synthetic organ grown in a laboratory was performed in July 2011. A plastic, Y-shaped model of the patient's trachea, or windpipe, was created and then lined with the patient's stem cells. This meant his body would accept the synthetic organ. This operation paved the way for organ transplants that don't need a donor. Previous synthetic transplants were created from a patient's body tissue or a segment from a donor organ.

Higgs boson particle

2012

François Englert, Peter Higgs

On July 4, 2012, scientists at the CERN laboratory in Switzerland found a particle that could be the Higgs boson, a subatomic particle theorized to be responsible for the fact that objects have mass. In the 1970s, its existence was proposed by Peter Higgs and François Englert. Although the found particle is yet to be confirmed as the Higgs boson, Higgs and Englert were awarded the Nobel Prize in Physics in 2013 for its likely discovery.

HIGGS BOSON PARTICLE *The Large Hadron Collider is a huge machine in which particles were smashed together to find the Higgs boson.*

Fuel from plastic

2012

Azza Abdel Hamid Faiad

Unwanted plastics can be difficult to get rid of. They can be buried or partially recycled, but they often end up in the sea, which leads to catastrophic consequences for wildlife and the environment. In 2011, a 16-year-old Egyptian student won a prize at the EU Contest for Young Scientists for her way of turning plastics into fuel. Using an aluminosilicate catalyst, she transformed trash into methane, propane, and ethane. She estimated that the fuel generated from Egypt's plastic waste could be worth up to $78 million a year.

Life in the deep

2013

Mark Lever

Life, it seems, can exist almost anywhere there is water. A team of scientists led by Mark Lever studied rock samples from the crust under 1.6 miles (2.6 km) of ocean and 1,150–1,900 ft (350–580 m) below the seabed. Even with no light, oxygen, or nutrients, there were living microbes present, seeming to live off energy from chemical reactions between rock and water. Similar life-forms may live on other planets.

Earth-like planets

2013

Erik A. Petigura, Andrew W. Howard, Geoffrey W. Marcy

In 2013, astronomers studying data from NASA's Kepler space telescope discovered more than 3,000 possible

2008 The bankruptcy of the huge Lehman Brothers bank is the start of a worldwide financial crisis.

2009 Barack Obama becomes the first African American to be elected president of the US.

2010 Starting in Tunisia, demonstrations and protests, the "Arab Spring," challenge the governments of the Arab world.

2011 The population of Earth exceeds 7 billion. It is predicted to reach 8 billion by 2024.

planets outside our solar system. Many of these were found to orbit at the right distance from their stars to support Earth-like temperatures that could make them habitable for life.

Reusable rocket

2015

Elon Musk

Traveling into space is expensive. Much of the cost goes toward the enormous rocket needed to escape Earth's gravity, and once this has done its job, it becomes space junk. In 2011, the entrepreneur Elon Musk set up SpaceX to develop a rocket that could return to Earth and be used again. He reached his first milestone in December 2015, when the exhausted first stage of a Falcon 9 rocket flipped itself around to land vertically near the launch site.

Smart speaker

2015

Amazon.com

Ever since the talking computer HAL in the 1968 film *2001: A Space Odyssey*, people have dreamed of a machine they could speak to and get a response from. The first machine to get close was Apple's iPhone, with its Siri assistant, in 2011. Amazon's Echo brought the idea into the home. Responding to the wake word "Alexa," it can control almost anything around the house, including heating and lighting.

AlphaGo

2016

Demis Hassabis

In 1997, a computer called Deep Blue played against the world chess champion, Garry Kasparov, and won. This was impressive, but 20 years later, an artificial intelligence system called AlphaGo beat Lee Sedol, the world's best player of a far more difficult game called Go. The system amazed onlookers by making moves never seen before in the game's 2,500-year history.

Human-carrying drone

2016

EHang

Highly efficient batteries and electric motors make it possible to build machines that fly in a new way, using four or more small, high-speed rotors instead of fixed wings or one large, slower rotor. These machines—known as drones—come in all sizes but do not usually carry people. At the 2016 CES® in Las Vegas, the Chinese drone-maker EHang showed EHang 184, the first commercial machine designed to carry a passenger.

James Webb Space Telescope

2018

American, European, and Canadian space agencies

The biggest space telescope ever built, the James Webb, dates back to 1996 but is not yet in space. The project got its final green light in 2018. Its mirror—18 hexagonal segments that unfold to 21 ft (6.5 m) wide after launch—dwarfs those of previous space telescopes. Its four instrument systems, using mainly infrared light, will soon enable us to see stars and planets currently beyond our reach.

JAMES WEBB SPACE TELESCOPE *Engineers check the telescope after testing the primary mirror.*

Black hole image

2019

Astronomers worldwide

A black hole is a region in space with gravity so strong even light can't escape. In 2019, astronomers put together a global network of radio telescopes. They then used an algorithm developed by computer scientist Katie Bouman to produce a picture of the superheated gas at the edge of a supermassive black hole. It was hard evidence that black holes, predicted by Albert Einstein in 1915, actually exist.

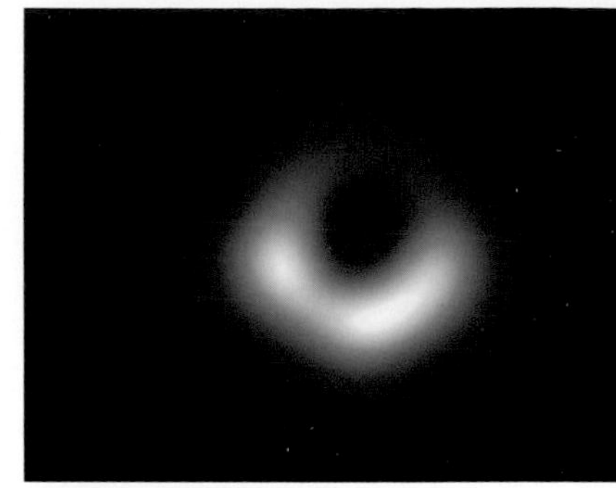

BLACK HOLE *This image is a composite, made up of many different images all put together.*

Ultra-high-speed video

2019

Feng Chen, Lidai Wang

Most high-speed video cameras capture separate frames. But by allowing frames to overlap and tagging them so they could be separated later, Feng Chen and Lidai Wang managed to get their camera up to nearly four trillion frames per second. At this speed, the motion of individual light pulses can be seen in detail.

Mars probes

2020

UAESA, NASA, CNSA

Hope, the Arab world's first mission to Mars, will launch from Japan in 2020 to track the escape of hydrogen and oxygen from the planet's atmosphere. In the same year, NASA will launch a Mars probe to search for signs of past life, while China plans to send an orbiting spacecraft plus a rover.

2014 Malala Yousafzai shares the Nobel Peace Prize, becoming the youngest-ever winner at the age of 17.

2018 Technology company Apple becomes the first company to be valued at $1 trillion.

2020 Following a referendum held in 2016, the UK leaves the European Union on January 31.

INTO THE FUTURE The best part of this book remains unwritten—because it hasn't happened yet.

Index of inventions & discoveries

AB

aberration of light 101
achromatic lens 101
acupuncture 26
adder-lister 156
adding machine 122
aerosol 187
agriculture 10, 12–13
air brake 147
air-conditioning 173
airbag 213
airplane 175
airship 139
albumen print 137
alchemy textbook 70
algebra 58
algebraic notation, modern 84
alphabet 35
AlphaGo 251
aluminum 124, 158
amalgam filling 124
Amazon Echo 251
amber, attraction of objects to 37
ambulance 113
anesthetic 136
Andromeda galaxy 64
anemometer 74
aniline dye 141
anti-g flying suit 205
antiseptics 145
Aqua-Lung 207
arc light 118
arch 27
Archimedean screw 36
Archimedes's principle 47, 48–49
argon 164
armor 33
artificial: neural network 222; satellite 218; silk 156
aspirin 168
assembly line 181, 182–183
asteroid 116
astrolabe 60
astronomical observatory 52
athletic shoes 211
atom, structure of 184
atomic: bomb 208; clock 214 theory 45; weights 118
automatic keyboard instrument 78
automatic telephone exchange 161
automaton 44
ax 15
Babbitt metal 133
Babylonian calendar, improved 43
bacteria 95
ballistic missile 206
ballpoint pen 201
barbed wire 149
barometer 91
barrel vault 29
basket weaving 16
bathroom 29
battery 116
BC and AD dates 60
bell chime 29
Bernoulli effect 103
beryllium 114
bicycle 156; hub gear 156
bifocal eyeglasses 110
Big Bang theory 189
bikini 208
binary electronic computing 205
binary system 95
biological clock 189
biological molecular motor 246
black hole 184; image of 251
blast furnace, improved 105
block printed book 60
blood groups 173
blood pressure, measurement 102
bloomers 140
boat 15; built from planks 21
Bode's Law 108
book carousel 83
book with pages 59
Boolean algebra 140
boomerang 9
botanical garden 80
bottle cork 82
bow and arrow 8
Boyle's law 93
bra 184
Braille 127
brass 32
Breathalyzer 214
brick 17
bridge for boarding ships 47
bronze 20
bubble gum 190
bubblewrap 221
bubonic plague agent 164
button-up shirt 195
buttonhole 69

C

cable car 149
calculus 96
calendar 21
camel 34
camera obscura 81
can opener 140
canal lock 71
candle 20; flame, structure of 88
canning 118
cannon 70
capillaries 92
car 157
carbon dating 210
carbon dioxide 105
carbon fiber 224
carbon nanotube "muscle" 246
carbonated drinks 108
carillon 78
carpenter's brace 71
carpet 27
cash register 154
CAT scanner 229
cat's whisker 176
cat's eyes 197
catapult 43
cataract operation 58
cathode ray oscilloscope 166
cause of AIDS 235
cave painting 8
celestial spheres 44
cell: as the basic unit of living things 132; nucleus 127
cellular address code 233
cell phone 232, 250
celluloid 148
Celsius scale of temperature 103
central heating 41, 185
centrifugal governor 111
chain mail 51
chain store 51
chain saw 189
chair 26
champagne 94
chariot 29
chemical nerve mechanism 218
chemistry, modern 112
chewing gum 147
chisel 11
chlorofluorocarbons 190
Christmas card 135
chromatic harp 116
chromatic keyboard 70
chromium 114
chromosomes, function of 176
cinema 164
Cinemascope 191
circulation of the blood 89
city 18
clarinet 97
clavichord 71
clay tablet book 25
clear adhesive tape 194
clepsydra 33
clinical thermometer 145
cloned endangered animal 247
clouds, names for 117
coal 45
cobalt 101
cobalt blue 36
code breaking 73
coded correspondence 43
color: film 198; photography 177; television 213
comet Hale-Bopp 242
communications satellite 222
compact disc 235
complex numbers 80
compound microscope 85
compound pulley 47
compound steam engine 118
compressed air 46
comptometer 158
computer architecture 208
computer mouse 226
computer program 135
condensed milk 141
conditioned reflex 167
condom 82
conductive plastics 231
conservation of energy 135
continental drift 181
convection heating 89
cookbook 45
copper 14
corset 32
cosmetics 21
cosmic rays 181
cotton 21
cotton gin 114
crank 58
cream separator 151
crossbow 43
cryptographic frequency table 78
cutting holes in the skull 10
cyclonic vacuum cleaner 235, 238–239
cylinder printing press 119
Cyrillic alphabet 63

D

dam 25
dance notation 75
dark matter 227
DDT 204
decimals 83
deep-sea life 250
dice 30
dictionary 89
diesel engine 166
differential gear 126
diffraction of light 94
digital logic design 205
digital cell phone 240
dinosaurs 134
disc brake 173
dishwasher 158
disposable diaper 222
disposable TV camera 241
dividing engine 107
diving: bell 101; suit 122
division of labor 109
DNA 149; bacterial sequence 242; fingerprinting 236; function of 207; structure of 214, 216–217 dog 10
Dolby noise reduction system 226
Dolly the sheep 243, 244–245
dome 56
domestic food mixer 184
Doppler effect 134
Down syndrome, cause of 221
drill 7
drum 15
dry cleaning 123
dry photographic plate 149
dust-free builder's chute 236
dynamite 147
dynamo 148

EFG

ear: semicircular canals 158
earth, air, fire, and water 41
Earth, size of 47; structure of core 199
earthquake detector 57
electric: motor 128; razor 190; starter 181; train 154; tram 154; washing machine 180
electromechanical computer 206
electrocardiogram 175
electroencephalograph 191
electrolysis of water 116
electromagnetic induction 127
electromagnetism 123
electron 167; microscope 196
electronic: computer 208; flash 194; music synthesizer 225; telephone exchange 225
electroplating 133
engraving tool 8
epicyclic universe 58
epoxy resin 200
error-correcting code 211
escalator 168
Esperanto 159
espresso coffee 200
Euclidean geometry 45
evolution by natural selection 142
expanding universe 188
factory 108
false eyelashes 210
fertilizer from the air 181
fiber, super-tough 248
film soundtrack 188
fingerprinting 168
fire: making 11; use of 7
firearms 71
fireplace 65
fireworks 64
fishhook 8
flag 32
flamethrower 62
flax 11
flint mining 10
flintlock musket 87
floppy disk 228
flour from potatoes 103
fluorspar 80
flush toilet 84
flute 51
flying actor 42
flying shuttle 102
flywheel 74
FM radio 196
folding fan 61
formal logic 45
formula for area of triangle 57
FORTRAN 219
Foucault's pendulum 139
four-stroke engine 150
fractal curve 159
Franklin stove 103
frequency-hopping radio 207
freezer pop 186
front-wheel drive car 196
frozen dessert 45
frozen food 187
fuel cell 133
fuel from plastic 250
full-color movie 195
full-length computer-generated movie 243
fullerenes 237
G proteins 234
gas: engine 142; lighting 113; mantle 156
gases, as distinct from air 91
gaslight photographic paper 162
gasoline engine 157
gene: exons and introns 231; targeted sheep 247; that causes cystic fibrosis 240; therapy 240
genetic control of embryonic development 234
genetic engineering 229
genetically modified food 242
germs 146
glass 27; float 221; laminated 176
glassblowing 55
glasses (eyeglasses) 69
glider 140
global positioning system 232
gloves 32
Gothic arch 65
gramophone 159
graphical user interface 227
graphical web browser 241
gravity 97, 98–99
greenhouse effect 126
Gregorian calendar 82
grid-plan city 42
grindstone 16
groin vault 53
growing bone outside body 247
growth of new brain cells 243
gunpowder 63
gyroscope 140

H

halftone: screen 162; woodblock print 79
Halley's comet 96
Hammond organ 197
hand ax 7
handles for tools 8
harp 24
harpsichord 74
heart: transplant 227; valves 47
heart–lung machine, use of 213
heat engine efficiency 124
heavy water 195
helicopter 199
helium: Earth 164; sun 147
Higgs boson particle 250
high-level computer language 213
high-temperature superconductors 240
high-voltage power transmission 160
hip replacement 224
holography 210
home security system, video 228
homegrown replacement organ 246
hormones 174
horse 28; collar 60
horse-drawn tram service 129
horseshoes 53
hot-air balloon 109
house 9
hovercraft 215
human anatomy: based on dissection 47; practical manual of 70; scientific study of 80
human-carrying drone 251
human genome 247
human-powered aircraft 231
hydrogen 107; balloon 110
hypodermic syringe 140

IJK

IBM PC 235
ice pop 186
ice skates 34
iced dessert 45
image converter for space 229
index to a book 88
inductance 128

induction motor 155
industrial robot 223
infinity of the universe 83
ink 27
inner ear, mechanism of 139
insulin 186; structure of 228
interchangeable parts 125
internet 236; retailing 243
iPod 248
iron 30; in building 41
iron bridge 109
iron plowshare 53
iron-framed printing press 116
iron-hulled ship 112
iron-tipped plowshare 35
irrigation 16
Jacquard loom 116
James Webb Space Telescope 251
jeans 149
jet engine 194
jointed fishing rod 59
Julian calendar 55
jump jet 226
kaleidoscope 119
Kevlar® 228
kidney transplant 214
kiln-fired pottery 19
kimono 62
knitted socks 42
knitting 34; machine 84
Kodak camera 160

LM

lace-making machine 118
Landlord's Game, The 176
laser concept 220
latent heat 106
lathe 24
laudanum 80
laughing gas 115
law of refraction 88
lawn mower 127
laws of: chance 100; heredity 145; motion 96; planetary motion 88; thermodynamics 137
lead 14; pipe 45
lead acid battery 142
leaded gasoline 186
leather 16
leavened bread 26
Leclanché cell 146
leech neuron computer 247
Lego 220
lemonade 95
leprosy treatment 184
letterpress printing 75, 76–77
level 93
lever 24
Leyden jar 103
lie detector 176
life raft, practical 154
life table 93
light bulb 151
light, speed of 94
lighthouse 46; indestructible 105
lightning, electrical nature of 105
linoleum 143
linotype typesetting machine 158
lipstick 184
liquid air 164
Liquid Paper™ 219
liquid-fueled rocket 188
lithography 114
lock 30
lock-stitch sewing machine 136
logarithms 88
long-distance telephone cable 162
long-playing record 210
longitude at sea, finding 106
loom 16
lost-wax casting 26
lubricants 21
lyre 24
macadamized road 126
magnet 34
magnetic: compass 37; poles 69; recording 168; resonance imaging 231
magnetism of Earth 85
magneto 128
mail order 160
malaria, and mosquito 167
male and female plants 31
mammals from eggs 125
margarine 147
Mars: life on 243; polar caps 94; probes 251; rotation of 92; water on 249
Mars bar 196
mass production 117
match 126
mathematics of the rainbow 69
math for fun 87
mechanical clock 65
mechanical equivalent of heat 137
mental hospital 64
Mercator map projection 82
mercury 45; thermometer 101; vacuum pump 145
metabolism, study of 88
metal: casting 18; coins 37; movable type 73; printing plate 75
mezzotint engraving 91
microphone 151
microprocessor 228
microscope condenser 149
MicroStar air reconnaissance vehicle 243
microwave oven 209
milking machine 143
mine clearance, low-cost 250
miners' safety lamp 119, 120–121
minicomputer 226
MiniDisc 241
mining 7
miniskirt 225
mirror 27
Monopoly 198
monorail 173
monotype typesetting system 157
moon craters 87
moons of Jupiter 87, 248
Morse code 129, 130–131
mortise and tenon joint 14
mosaic 46
motorcycle 156
motor scooter 209
movable type 64
moving picture 163
MP3 compression standard 246
Möbius strip 147
mule 42
mule spinning machine 109
multiple fire tube boiler 126
multiple-unit electric train 167
multistage rocket 175
multistage steam turbine 156
music type 80
musical notation 64
musical ratios 37, 38–39
Myers-Briggs Type Indicator® 208

NO

navigation chart 69
neon sign 181
Neptune 136
nerve impulses: electrical nature of 137; speed of 137
New World, the 78
news bulletin 55
newspaper 87
nitroglycerine 137
non-Euclidean geometry 123
nuclear: fission 204; power station 214; reactor 207
numbers in tens, writing 20
numerals, modern 68
nylon 201
oars 34
occupational disease 81
Ohm's law 126
oil lamp 35
oil painting 74
oil well 142
olive 18
open-hearth steel making 143
opium 18
Orion nebula 87
oven 10
oxygen 108
ozone 134; layer damage 230

P

pack mule 18
package vacation 134
paddle wheel 62
paintbrush 9
painting with wax 24
paper 55; boat 147; money 64
papyrus 24
parabolic path of a projectile 90
parachute 110
parchment 28
parity violation 218
Parkesine 144
parking meter 199
particle accelerator 196
pasteurization 145
paved road 30
peep show 74
pen nib 44
pencil 82
pendulum: clock 92, constant swing of 82
penicillin 190, 192–193
penny-farthing bicycle 148
Penrose triangle 219
periodic table 148
personal computer 232
perspective 73
Perspex 197
PET scanner 230
phlogiston theory of combustion 97
phosphorus 94
photographic motion capture 151
photography 132
photosynthesis 109
phototypesetting 164
piano 100
pickproof lock 110
pineapple 79
pipe organ 50
piston 52
planets, Earthlike 250; oldest 249
plant groups, two separate 100
plant growth hormones 188
plastic drink bottle 230
plastic wrap 211
platinum 112
pleasure center in the brain 214
plow 16; with wheels 60
plutonium 205
pneumatic tire 160
pocket calculator 229
Polaroid 191; camera 211; color photograph 224
polio vaccine 213
polonium 168
polyethylene 197
polyethylene terephthalate 206
polypropylene 214
polystyrene 133
pop-up toaster 188
porcelain 62
Portland cement 124
Post-it note 234
postage stamp 134
PostScript page description language 237
potato 28
potter's wheel 19
pottery 9; painted 14
power loom 111
prestressed concrete 191
precession of the equinoxes 53
precision boring machine 109
prefabricated building 139
pressure cooker 96
pressurized aircraft cabin 200
printed circuit board 206
printer's type case 69
printing ink roller 113
printing telegraph 140
proof of Fermat's last theorem 243
propaganda dropped from air 68
protozoa 94
Prozac 240
public: broadcasting service 185; electricity supply 154; hospital 60; steam railroad 124
public-key cryptography 231
puddling process for wrought iron 111
Pullman sleeping car 145
pulsar 227; binary 230
pulse code modulation 200
punctuation 51
push-button phone 224
Pythagoras's theorem 37

QR

quantum theory 169
quarks 225
quasar 222
quill pen 60
quinine 123
rabies vaccine 157
radar 198
radiation from uranium 165
radio astronomy 194
radio communication 164
radio waves 160
radium 168, 170–171
railroad locomotive 117
railroads in mines 81
ramp 24
resealable plastic bag 224
reaping machine 125
recording on wax 158
red blood cells 92
reflecting telescope 93
reflex 129
refrigerator 139
repeating watch 96
reusable rocket 251
revolving stage 91
Richter scale 199
rigid airship 169
ring-pull can 226
river tunnel 135
road 19
rocket 69
roller skates 144
roman type 75
rope 9
rotary internal combustion engine 218
rotary quern 36
rubber 102
ruby laser 222
rudder 68
running water 32

S

saccharin 154
saddle 46
safety: fuse 128; lift 140; pin 50; razor 173
sail 19
sailboard 228
sari 52
satellite cell phone 246
saw 30
scales 17
scanning microscope: electron 206; tunneling 235
scientific botany 46
scientific names for plants 105
scissors 57
Scrabble 195
screw 56
screw press 54
screw-cutting lathe 114
scurvy, prevention of 105
seal 16
seat belt 221
secret writing 32
seed drill 97
self-adhesive dressing 186
self-cleaning glass 248
self-trimming candle wick 124
semaphore telegraph 114
semiconductor integrated circuit 220
sensory and motor nerve fibers 119
sexagesimal number system 31
sextant 102
shadow clock 36
shape memory alloys 223
sheep 11
ship 31; propeller 132
shoes 33; sizes 69
shop 37; scales 94
shorthand 51
SI units 222
sickle 14
signs of the zodiac 42
silicon solar cell 206
silk 27
silver 17
silver-plated tableware 103
single-rotor helicopter 204
skis 28
skyscraper 158
sliced bread 191
slide rule 90
sling 31
slip casting 103
smallpox vaccine 115
smallpox, diagnosing 63
smelting iron with coke 89
smartphone 250
soap 58
soccer 51
socks 35
sodium and potassium 118
solar eclipses, cause of 41
solar hydrogen 144
solar still 226
solar system 80; stability of 111
sound radio 177
sound recording 150
southern star constellations 84
space: flight 224; shuttle 235; station 230
spark plug 174
spear thrower 8
spectroscope 142
speech center in the brain 143
speech synthesizer 113
sphere, surface area/volume 50
sphygmomanometer 166
spinning jenny 106
spoked wheel 31
spreadsheet software 233
stage lighting 81
stained-glass window 62
stainless steel 181
standardized Chinese writing 50
stars: composition 187; magnitudes 53; naming of 86
stealth aircraft 235
steam: aeolipyle 57; bus 128; engine 100; engine, high-pressure 117; engine, improved 107; hammer 134; ship 112; sterilization of surgical instruments 158; tractor 107; tricycle 160
steam-powered airplane 162
steel 52
stem cells, separation of 241
stereophonic sound 196
stereoscope 129
stereotype 101
stethoscope 122
Stirling engine 122
stirrups 53
stone: buildings 24; tools 7
stove 78
stratigraphy 115

street lamp 56
street sweeper 168
striking clock 70
Subbuteo 210
submarine 88
sulfonamide drugs 196
sunspot cycle 135
suntan lotion 199
supercomputer 230
superfluidity 200
Superglue 219
supermarket 194; cart 200
supermassive black hole 240
supernova 82
superphosphate fertilizer 122
surgical: gloves 162;
mask 166
swing, child's 32
sympathetic nervous system 58
synthetic: alizarin 148; diamonds 215; organ transplant 250; rubber tires 194; virus 249

TU

tabulating machine 161
tapestry 61
tea 26; tea bag 180
tea-making alarm clock 174
teddy bear 174
Teflon 201
telegraph 129
telephone 150, 152–153
telescope 87
television 200, 202–203
tennis 71
test-tube baby 232
tetanus immunization 162
theater scenery 41
theory of relativity 176, 178–179
theory of shadows 86
theory of vision 64, 66–67
theremin 186
thermos flask 176
thermoscope 84
thermostat 86
35mm camera 187
3-D graphics computer 236
three-field system 65
three-phase electricity supply 155
threshing machine 112
thyroid gland, function of 154
tin can 54
titanium 113
tongs 31
toothpaste in a tube 166
topiary 56
tower windmill 73
trading 15
traffic signal 186
tram 50
trampoline 200
transatlantic telegraph 141
transistor 210;
single atom 248
transit of Venus 91
triangle of forces 83
trigonometry 53
triode valve 176
trombone 74
trumpet 33
truss bridge 57
tungsten 110
tunneling shield 122
tunneling with explosives 96
Tupperware 209
turbine ship 167
turboprop airliner 214
two-stroke engine 151
type-rotating printing press 136
typewriter 150
ultraviolet light 116
umami 180
umbrella 90
uncertainty principle 190
underground railroad 144
university 43
uranium 112
Uranus 109

VW

vacuum bottle 162
vacuum cleaner 174
vacuum, strength of 92
valves in the veins 86
Van Allen radiation belts 220
Velcro 218
vending machine 56
Venn diagram 154
Venus 25
Vernier scale 90
video: game 229; recorder 218
viruses 163
viscose rayon 162
vitamins 177
vulcanized rubber 132
Walkman 233
watch 79
water: frame 107; turbine 126
water-powered iron works 73
waterproof cloth 123
waterwheel 54
wave theory of light 97
welding 28
wet-plate photography 139
wheat and barley 11
wheel 19
wheelbarrow 56
wheeled vehicle 19
whistle 10
white light, composition of 100
wind-driven sawmill 84
windmill 61
Windows operating system 237
windshield wiper 175
woodcut 71
woodworking plane 54
word processor software 232
World Wide Web 240
writing 20, 21–22; brush 37

XYZ

X-rays 165
X–Y coordinates 90
xerography 204
Yale lock 144
zero to represent nothing 61
zero, systematic use of 62
zipper 164

Index of inventors & discoverers

A

ab Aquapendente,
Hieronymus Fabricius 86
Abbe, Ernst 149
Adams, Thomas 147
Ader, Clèment 162
Adleman, Leonard 231
Adolph, Peter 210
Aeschylus 41
Al-Kalka-shandi 73
al-Khwarizmi, Muhammad 58, 62
Alberti, Leon 73, 74, 78
Alfred Gilman 234
Alhazen 64, 66–67
Allbutt, Thomas 145
Allen, Bryan 231
Allen, John 200
Amazon.com 251
Anaxagoras 41
Anderson, French 240
Anderson, Mary 175
Andreessen, Marc 241
Ångström, Anders 144
Antheil, George 207
Appert, Nicolas 118
Archer, Frederick 139
Archestratus 45
Archimedes 47, 48–49, 50
Archytas of Tarentum 44
Aristophanes of Byzantium 51
Aristotle 45
Arkwright, Richard 107, 108
Armstrong, Edwin 196
As-Sufi 64
Aspdin, Joseph 124
AT&T 224, 225
Atala, Anthony 246
Atanasoff, John 205
Attaignant, Pierre 80
Ausnit, Steven 224
Autant-Lara, Claude 191
Avery, Oswald 207
Aylott, David 210
Aylott, Eric 210

B

Babbitt, Isaac 133
Backer, Donald 249
Backus, John 219
Bacon, Francis 88
Baekeland, Leo 162
Bakken, Earl 219
Ball, Alice 184
Banting, Frederick 186, 205
Bardeen, John 210
Barlow, Peter 122
Barnack, Oskar 187
Barnard, Christiaan 227
Bauer, Andreas 119
Bauer, Georgius 80, 81
Baughman, Ray 246, 248
Bayer, Johann 86
Bayliss, William 174
Beadle, Clayton 163
Beasley, Maria 154
Becquerel, Henri 165
Bednorz, Georg 240
Behring, Emil 162
Beijerinck, Martinus 163
Bell Labs 232
Bell, Alexander Graham 150, 152–153
Bell, Charles 119
Bell, Chichester 158
Bell, Jocelyn 227
Bell, Patrick 125
Bell, Thomas 124
Bénédictus, Édouard 176
Benz, Karl 157
Berger, Hans 191
Berliner, Emile 159
Berners-Lee, Tim 240
Bernoulli, Daniel 103
Bernoulli, Jakob 100
Berry, Clifford 205
Best, Charles 186
Bevan, Edward 163
Bezos, Jeff 243
Bi Sheng 64
Bickford, William 128
Binnig, Gerd 235
Birdseye, Clarence 187
Biró, Georg 201
Biró, Ladislao 201
Bissell, George 142
Black, Joseph 105, 106
Black, Lee 248
Blades, Herbert 228
Blanquart-Évrard, Louis 137
Blobel, Günter 233
Bloomer, Amelia 140
Blumlein, Alan 196
Bock, Walter 194
Bode, Johann 108
Bohlin, Nils 221
Bohr, Niels 184
Bolyai, János 123
Boole, George 140
Booth, Hubert 174
Bopp, Thomas 242
Borden, Gail 141
Borkenstein, Robert 214
Bosch, Carl 181
Bosch, Robert 174
Boulsover, Thomas 103
Boyer, Herbert 229
Boyle, Robert 93, 94
Bradley, James 101
Brahe, Tycho 82
Brahmagupta 61
Braille, Louis 127
Bramah, Joseph 110
Brand, Hennig 94
Brandt, Georg 101
Brattain, Walter 210
Braun, Ferdinand 166
Brearley, Harry 181
Brewster, David 119
Bricklin, Daniel 233
Bridgman, Percy 215
Briggs Myers, Isabel 208
Bright, Charles 141
Broca, Paul 143
Brown, Albert 228
Brown, Mike 250
Brown, Robert 127
Brunel, Isambard 135
Brunel, Marc 117, 122, 135
Brunelleschi, Filippo 73
Bruno, Giordano 83
Budding, Edwin 127
Buehler, William 223
Bunsen, Robert 142
Burdin, Claude 126
Burger, Rheinhold 176
Bürgi, Joost 88
Burgkmair, Hans 79
Burroughs, William 156
Bushnell, Nolan 229
Butler, Edward 156
Butts, Alfred 195

C

Calgene Inc. 242
Calley, John 100
Callinicus of Heliopolis 62
Cambacères, J. J. 124
Campbell, Keith 243, 244–245
Campin, Robert 74
Canadian Space Agency 251
Cardano, Gerolamo 80
Carlisle, Anthony 116
Carlson, Chester 204
Carlsson, Arvid 240
Carnot, Sadi 124
Caro, Heinrich 148
Carolus, Johann 87
Carothers, Wallace 201
Carré, Ferdinand 139
Carrier, Willis 173
Carruthers, George R. 229
Cartwright, Edmund 111
Cassini, Gian 94
Cavendish, Henry 107
Caventou, Joseph 123
Cayley, George 140
Cello, Jeronimo 248
Celsius, Anders 103
Chabaneau, P. F. 112
Chain, Ernst 190, 192–193
Chang Heng 57
Chappe, Claude 114
Chardonnet, Hilaire 156
Charles, Jacques 110
Charnley, John 224
Chavannes, Marc 221
Chrétien, Henri 191
Christiansen, Godtfred 220
Citröen, Andrè 197
Clark, James 236
Clarke, Frank 174
Claude, Georges 181
Clausius, Rudolf 137
Clerk, Dugald 151
CNSA 251
Cochrane, Josephine 158
Cockcroft, John 196
Cockeram, Henry 89
Cockerell, Christopher 215
Cohen, Stanley 229
Colgate, William 166
Collins, Francis 240, 247
Columbus, Christopher 78
Colvin, L. O. 143
Cook, Thomas 134
Cook Briggs, Katharine 208
Cooke, William 129
Coover, Harry 219
Copernicus, Nicolaus 80
Cormack, Allan 229
Cornelisz, Cornelis 84
Cort, Henry 111
Corti, Alfonso 139
Courrèges, André 225
Cousteau, Jacques 207
Cranach, Lucas 79
Crawford, John 197
Cray, Seymour 230
Crick, Francis 214, 216–217
Cristofori, Bartolomeo 100
Crompton, Samuel 109
Cross, Charles 163
Ctesibius of Alexandria 46, 50
Cugnot, Nicolas 107
Cullen, Michael 194
Curie, Marie 168, 170–171
Curie, Pierre 168, 170–171
Curl, Robert 237

D

d'Ascanio, Corradino 209
D'Elhuyar, Fausto 110
D'Elhuyar, Juan 110
Daguerre, Louis 132
Daimler, Gottlieb 156, 157
Dalton, John 112, 118
Damadian, Raymond 231
Damiani, Philip 247
Daniel, Ralph 103
Darby, Abraham 109
Darby, Newman 228
Darrow, Charles 198
Darwin, Charles 142
Dassler, Adolf 211
Davenport, Thomas 128
Davis, Jacob 149
Davy, Humphry 115, 118, 119, 120–121
de Colmar, Thomas 122
de Ferranti, Sebastian 160
De Forest, Lee 176, 188
de la Condamine, Charles-Marie 102
de La Rive, Auguste 133
de Laval, Gustav 151
de Maricourt, Petrus Peregrinus 69
de Mestral, George 218
de Méziriac, Claude-Gaspar 87
de Moivre, Abraham 100
de Peiresc, Nicolas 87
de Roberval, Gilles 94
de Rochas, Alphonse Beau 150
de Vaucanson, Jacques 116
De Vick, Henry 65
de' Luzzi, Mondino 70
Delage, Yves 158
della Porta, Giambattista 81
Democritus 45

Denner, Johann 97
Descartes, René 90
Devol, George 223
Dewar, James 162
Dickson, Earle 186
Dickson, James 206
Dickson, William 163
Diemer, Walter 190
Diesel, Rudolf 166
Diffie, Whitfield 231
Dionysius Exiguus 60
Diophantus of Alexandria 58
Ditto, Bill 247
Dolby, Ray 218, 226
Domagk, Gerhard 196
Doppler, Christian 134
Dow Chemical Company 211
Drake, Edwin 142
Drake, Jim 228
Drebbel, Cornelis 86, 88
Dressler, Alan 240
Drew, Richard 194
Du Bois-Reymond, Emil 137
Dudley, Dud 89
Dunlop, John 160
Durand, Peter 118
Dyson, James 235, 238–239

EF

Eastman, George 160
Eccles, John 218
Eckert, John Presper 208
Edgerton, Harold 194
Edison, Thomas 150, 151, 154, 163
Edwards, Robert 232
EHang 251
Einstein, Albert 176, 178–179
Einthoven, Willem 175
Eisler, Paul 206
11th General Conference on Weights and Measures 222
Ekeblad, Eva 103
Elkington, George 133
Empedocles 41
Engelbart, Doug 226, 227
Engelburger, Joseph 223
Englert, François 250
Epperson, Frank 186
Érard, Sébastien 116
Erasistratus of Ceos 47
Eratosthenes of Cyrene 47
Ericsson, John 132
Eriksson, Peter 216
Essen, Louis 214
Estridge, Don 235
Euclid of Alexandria 45
Eudoxus of Cnidus 44
European Space Agency 251
Evans, Oliver 117
Fahlberg, Constantin 154
Fahrenheit, Daniel 101
Faiad, Azza Abdel Hamid 250
Fallopius, Gabriel 82
Faraday, Michael 127
Farisi, Kamal 69
Fawcett, Eric 197
Felt, Dorr E. 159
Fermi, Enrico 207
Fessenden, Reginald 177
Field, Ben 145
Field, Cyrus 141
Fielding, Alfred 221
Fisher, Alva 180
Fitch, John 112
Fleischmann, Robert 242
Fleming, Alexander 190,192–193
Fletcher, Harvey 196
Florey, Howard 190, 192–193
Flourens, Marie 158
Flowers, Tommy 208
Focke, Heinrich 199
Ford, Henry 181, 182–183
Foucault, Jean 139, 140
Fourier, Joseph 123, 126
Fourneyron, Benoît 126
Fowler, John 144
Fox Talbot, William 132
Franklin, Benjamin 103, 105, 110
Franklin, Rosalind 214, 216–217
Franks, Wilbur 205
Frankson, Bob 233
Fraunhofer Institut 246
Fraze, Ermal 226
Freyssinet, Eugène 191
Frisch, Otto 204
Fry, Art 234
Fuller, Ray 240
Fulton, Robert 112
Funk, Casimir 177

G

Gabor, Dennis 210
Gagarin, Yuri 224
Gage, Fred 243
Gaggia, Achille 200
Gagnan, Émile 207
Gaius Duilius 47
Galen 58
Galilei, Galileo 82, 84, 87, 90
Galle, Johann 136
Galton, Francis 168
Gamow, George 189
Geber 70
Ged, William 101
Gee, Cecil 195
Gell-Mann, Murray 225
General Electric Company 215
Geschke, Charles 237
Gesner, Conrad 82
Gibbon, John Jr. 213
Gibson, Reginald 197
Giffard, Henri 139
Gilbert, William 85
Gillette, King C. 173
Ginsburg, Charles 218
Glidden, Carlos 150
Glidden, Joseph 149
Glushko, Valentin 218
Goddard, Robert 188
Godfrey, Thomas 102
Godowsky, Leopold 198
Goldman, Sylvan 200
Goldmark, Peter 210
Goodhue, Lyle 187
Goodyear, Charles 132
Gorrie, John 139
Gramme, Zénobe 148
Graunt, John 93
Greathead, James 122
Gregor, William 113
Gregory, James 93
Groupe Spécial Mobile 240
Grove, William 133
Guido of Arezzo 64
Gurney, Goldsworthy 128
Gutenberg, Beno 199
Gutenberg, Johann 75, 76–77

H

Haber, Fritz 181
Hadley, John 102
Hale, Alan 242
Hales, Stephen 102
Hall, Charles 158
Hall, Chester 101
Hall, John 125
Hall, Marshall 129
Halley, Edmond 96, 101
Hallidie, Andrew 149
Halsted, William 162
Hamming, Richard 211
Hammond, Laurens 197
Hancock, Walter 128
Hargreaves, James 106
Harington, John 84
Harrison, John 106
Harvard Bioscience 250
Harvey, William 89
Hassabis, Demis 251
Hawker Siddeley Aviation 226
Heathcoat, John 118
Heaviside, Oliver 162
Heeger, Alan 231
Heim, Jacques 208
Heisenberg, Werner 190
Hellman, Martin 231
Henlein, Peter 79
Henne, Albert 190
Henry, Edward 168
Henry, Joseph 127, 128
Hero of Alexandria 56, 57
Herophilus of Chalcedon 47
Héroult, Paul 158
Herschel, William 109
Hertz, Heinrich 160
Hess, Victor 181
Hetrick, John 213
Hewish, Antony 227
Higgs, Peter 250
Hill, Rowland 134
Hill, Rowland 197
Hillman, William 148
Hipparchus 52, 53
Hippodamus of Miletus 42
Hodgkin, Alan 218
Hodgkin, Dorothy 228
Hoe, Richard 136
Hoff, Ted 228
Hoffman, Edward 230
Hoffman, Felix 168
Hollerith, Herman 161
Honold, G. 174
Hooke, Robert 94
Hopkins, Frederick 177
Hopper, Grace 213
Horrocks, Jeremiah 91
Horsley, John 135
Horsley, Victor 154
Hounsfield, Godfrey 229
Howard, Andrew W. 250
Howard, Luke 117
Howe, Elias 136
Htai Tjong 73
Hubble, Edwin 188
Hughes, David 140, 151
Hulse, Russell 230
Hunt, Walter 136
Huxley, Andrew 218
Huygens, Christiaan 92, 97
Hyatt, John 148

IJ

IBM 228
Ingenhousz, Jan 109
Institute of Physics and Power Engineering 214
Iridium Satellite LLC 246
Ivanovsky, Dmitry 163
Ive, Jonathan 250
Jacob, Mary 184
Jacquard, Joseph-Marie 116
Jansky, Karl 194
Janssen, Hans 85
Janssen, Pierre 147
Jeffreys, Alec 236
Jenner, Edward 115
Jenney, William 158
Jewitt, David 248
Jobs, Steve 232, 248, 250
Johnson, Herbert 184
Joule, James 137
Joyner, Fred 219
Judson, Whitcomb 164
Julius Caesar 55

K

Kalmus, Herbert 195
Kapitsa, Peter 200
Kay, Alan 227
Kay, John 102
Kepler, Johannes 86, 88
Kettering, Charles 181
Keyser, Pieter 84
Kilby, Jack 220, 229
Kirchhoff, Gustav 142
Klaproth, Martin 112, 113
Kormendy, John 240
Korolyov, Sergey 218
König, Friedrich 119
Kroto, Harry 237
Kwolek, Stephanie 228

LM

Laënnec, René 122
Lamarr, Hedy 207
Lanchester, Frederick 173
Land, Edwin 191, 211, 224
Landsteiner, Karl 173
Langen, Eugen 173
Lanier, Jaron 240
Lanston, Tolbert 157
Lap-Chee Tsui 240
Laplace, Pierre-Simon 111
Larrey, Dominique 113
Larson, John 176
Lauterbur, Paul 231
Lavoisier, Antoine 112
Le Verrier, Urbain 136
Leclanché, Georges 146
Lee, William 84
Lefèbvre, André 197
Lehmann, Inge 199
Leibniz, Gottfried 95, 96
Lejeune, Jérôme 221
Lemaître, Georges 189
Lenoir, Étienne 142
Lenormand, Louis 110
Lerp, Emil 189
Levassor, Émile 157
Lever, Mark 250
Levy, Louis 162
Levy, Maurice 184
Levy, Max 162
Lewis, Edward 234
Libby, Willard 210
Licklider, J. C. R. 236
Lillienthal, Otto 140
Lind, James 105
Linnaeus, Carolus 105
Lippershey, Hans 87
Lister, Joseph 145
Lobachevsky, Nikolay 123
Lockheed Corporation 200
Lockheed Martin Corporation 235, 243
Lockyer, Norman 147
Lovelace, Ada 135
Lowe, William 235
Ludwik of Zamenh 159
Lumière, Auguste 164, 177
Lumière, Louis 164, 177
Macchiarni, Dr. Paolo 250
MacCready, Paul 231
MacDiarmid, Alan 231
Macintosh, Charles 123
Maddox, Richard 149
Magee, Carlton 199
Magie, Lizzie 176
Maiman, Theodore 222
Malpighi, Marcello 92
Mannes, Leopold 198
Marconi, Guglielmo 164, 185
Marcy, Geoffrey W. 250
Mariotte, Edmé 93
Marius, Simon 87
Mars, Forrest 196
Martin, Pierre 143
Mauchly, John 208
Maudslay, Henry 114, 117
Maxwell, James Clerk 160
Maybach, Wilhelm 157
McAdam, John 126
McCormick, Cyrus 125
McCreath, Kenneth 247
McEuen, David 248
McKay, David 243
McMullan, Dennis 206
Mège-Mouriès, Hippolyte 147
Meikle, Andrew 112
Meitner, Lise 204
Mendel, Gregor 145
Mendeleyev, Dmitry 148
Mercator, Gerhard 82
Mergenthaler, Ottmar 158
Merlin, Joseph 144
Merryman, Jerry 229
Microsoft Corporation 237
Midgley, Thomas Jr. 186, 190
Miescher, Johann 149
Mills, Vic 222
Milner, Peter 214
Michtom, Morris 174
Molina, Mario 230
Montagu, Lady Mary Wortley 115
Montemagno, Carlo 246
Montgolfier, Étienne 109
Montgolfier, Joseph 109
Moog, Robert 225
Morgan, Garrett 186
Morgan, Paul 228
Morita, Akio 233
Morse, Samuel 129, 130–131
Morton, William 136
Moss, Henry 200
Moving Picture Experts Group 246
Mobius, August 147
Müller, Alex 240
Müller, Paul 204
Murdock, William 113
Murray, James 122
Murray, Joseph 214
Musk, Elon 251
Muybridge, Eadweard 151
Muzzey, David 223

N

Naito, Kakuji 224
Napier, John 88
NASA 230, 235, 249, 251
Nasmyth, James 134
National Television Systems Committee 213
Natta, Giulio 214
Nesmith Graham, Bette 219
Newcomen, Thomas 100
Newton, Isaac 96, 97, 98–99, 100
Nicholson, William 113, 116
Nissen, George 200
Nobel, Alfred 147
Noyce, Robert 220
Nüsslein-Volhard, Christiane 234

O

Ohl, Russell 206
Ohm, Georg 126
Olds, James 214
Olsen, Kenneth 226
Oppenheimer, Robert 208
Ørsted, Hans Christian 123, 124
Otis, Elisha 140
Otto, Nikolaus 150
Oughtred, William 90
Owen, Richard 134

PQ

Papin, Denis 96
Paracelcus 80
Parker, Alice 185
Parkes, Alexander 144
Parpart, Florence 168
Parry, Jack 214
Parsons, Charles 156, 167
Pasteur, Louis 145, 146, 157
Patterson, John 154
Paul, Aniko V. 248
Pavlov, Ivan 167
Paxton, Joseph 139
Payne-Gaposchkin, Cecilia 187
Peano, Giuseppe 159
Pecqueur, Onésiphore 126
Pelletier, Pierre 123
Penrose, Lionel 219
Penrose, Roger 219
Pérignon, Dom 94
Perkin, William 141, 148
Petigura, Erik A. 250
Phelps, Michael 230
Philips Electronics 235
Phillips, Leslie 224
Piazzi, Giuseppe 116
Pickard, Greenleaf 176
Pierce, John 222
Pilkington, Alastair 221
Pisano, Leonardo 68
Pixii, Hippolyte 128

Planck, Max 169
Planté, Gaston 142
Plimpton, James 144
Plunkett, Roy 201
Polak, Julia 247
Pope Gregory XIII 82
Porzolt, Eugene 164
Poulsen, Valdemar 168
Pravaz, Charles 140
Priestley, Joseph 108
Pritchard, Thomas 109
Ptolemy 58
Pullman, George 145
Pupin, Michael 162
Pythagoras 37, 38–39
Quare, Daniel 96
Qutb ash-Shirazi 69

RS

Rabinowitz, David 250
Ralph, Dan 249
Ramelli, Agostino 83
Ramsay, William 164
Ramsden, Jesse 107
Ray, John 100
Rayleigh, Lord 164
Réard, Louis 208
Reber, Grote 194
Reeves, Alec 200
Remsen, Ira 154
Richards, Paul 250
Richstone, Douglas 240
Richter, Charles 199
Richter, Curt 189
Riquet, Pierre 96
Ritter, Johann 116
Ritty, James 154
Riva-Rocci, Scipione 166
Rivest, Ron 231
Roberts, Larry 236
Roberts, Richard 231
Rodbell, Martin 234
Roebuck, Alvah 160
Rohrer, Heinrich 235
Rohwedder, Otto 191
Rømer, Ole 94
Rosenblatt, Frank 222
Ross, Ronald 167
Rothheim, Erik 187
Rowland, Sherwood 230
Röntgen, Wilhelm 165
Rubin, Vera 227
Rubinstein, Seymour 232
Rusch, Adolf 75
Ruska, Ernst 196
Sabin, Albert 213
Salk, Jonas 213
Sandage, Allan 222
Sanderson, Kevin 248
Sanger, Fred 228
Santorio, Santorio 88
Sarnoff, David 185
Savot, Louis 89
Schawlow, Arthur 220
Scheele, Carl 108
Schick, Jacob 190
Schleiden, Matthias 132
Schmidt, Maarten 222
Schönbein, Christian 134
Schueller, Eugène 199
Schwabe, Samuel 135
Schwann, Theodor 132
Schwarzschild, Karl 184
Schweitzer, Hoyle 228
Seaborg, Glenn 205
Sears, Richard 160
Seeberger, Charles 168
Séguin, Marc 126
Seifalian, Alexander 250
Semmelweis, Ignaz 145
Senefelder, Aloys 114
Serlio, Sebastiano 81
Serpollet, Leon 160
Shamir, Adi 231
Shannon, Claude 205
Shao Yung 95
Sharp, Phillip 231
Shaw, Percy 197
Shaw, W. T. 156
Shen Nong 26
Sheppard, Scott S. 248
Shi Huangdi 50
Shibasaburo, Kitasato 162, 164
Shirakawa, Hideki 231
Shockley, William 210
Shoenberg, Isaac 200, 202–203
Sholes, Christopher 150
Siebe, Augustus 122
Siemens, William 143
Sigurdsson, Steinn 249
Sikorsky, Igor 204
Silver, Spencer 234
Simon, Eduard 133
Sinclair, Clive 229
Singer, Isaac 136
Skirlaw, Walter 73
Smalley, Richard 237
Smeaton, John 105
Smith & Nephew Dyonics 241
Smith, Adam 109
Smith, Francis 132
Smith, William 115
Snell, Willebrord 88
Sobrero, Ascanio 137
Sony Corporation 235, 241
Sophocles 42
Sostratus of Cnidus 46
Soulé, Samuel 150
Spencer, Percy 209
Sprague, Frank 167
Sprengel, Hermann 145
St. Fabiola 60
Stahl, Georg 97
Stanhope, Charles 116
Starley, James 148
Starley, John 156
Starling, Ernest 174
Steiff, Margarete 174
Stephenson, George 119, 120–121, 124, 126
Stephenson, John 129
Steptoe, Patrick 232
Stevens, Nettie 176
Stevin, Simon 83
Stihl, Andreas 189
Stirling, Robert 122
Strauss, Levi 149
Strite, Charles 188
Strowger, Almon B. 161
Sturgeon, William 128
Su Sung 65
Sullivan, Thomas 180
Sundback, Gideon 164
Swammerdam, Jan 92
Swan, Joseph 151, 156
Symington, William 112

TUV

Tainter, Charles 158
Taveau, August 124
Taylor, Joseph Jr. 230
Taylor, Richard 243
Telkes, Mária 226
Tesla, Nikola 155
Thales of Miletus 37
The Walt Disney Company 243
Theophrastus 46
Theremin, Leon 186
Thomson, J. J. 167
Thomson, Robert 160
Thomson, William 137, 141
Thorsett, Stephen 249
Tiro, Marcus 54
Titius, Johann 108
Torelli, Giacomo 91
Torricelli, Evangelista 91
Townes, Charles 220
Train, G. F. 129
Trevithick, Richard 117
Trujillo, Chad 250
Tschunkur, Eduard 194
Tsiolkovsky, Konstantin 175
Tsukamoto, Ann 241
Tull, Jethro 97
Tupper, Earl 209
UAESA 251
Urey, Harold 195
US Air Force 232
Vail, Alfred 129, 130–131
Van Allen, James 220
Van Brittan Brown, Marie 228
van Eyck, Jan 74
van Helmont, Jan Baptista 91
van Leeuwenhoek, Antoni 94, 95
van Musschenbroek, Pieter 103
van Tassel, James 229
Vauquelin, Nicolas 114
Venn, John 154
Venter, Craig 247
Vernier, Pierre 90
Vesalius, Andreas 80
Vesconte, Petrus 69
Vickers Armstrong Aircraft 214
Viète, François 84
Vlutters, A. J. 236
Vlutters, G. H. 236
Volk, Magnus 154
Volta, Alessandro 116
von Baer, Karl 125
von Bergmann, Ernst 158
von Braun, Wernher 206
von Guericke, Otto 92
von Helmholtz, Hermann 137
von Kempelen, Wolfgang 113
von Kleist, Ewald 103
von Linde, Carl 165
von Mayer, Julius 135
von Mikulicz-Radecki, Johannes 166
von Neumann, John 208
von Ohain, Hans 194
von Siegen, Ludwig 91
von Welsbach, Carl Auer 157
von Zeppelin, Ferdinand 169

W

Walker, John 126
Walton, Ernest 196
Walton, Frederick 143
Wang Chen 69
Wankel, Felix 218
Warnock, John 237
Washburn, Edward 195
Waters, Elisha 147
Waters, George 147
Watson, James 214, 216–217
Watson-Watt, Robert 198
Watt, James 107, 111
Wegener, Alfred 181
Weischaus, Eric 234
Went, Friedrich 188
Wertheimer, Max 176
Westinghouse, George 147, 155
Wheatstone, Charles 129
Wheeler, George 168
Whinfield, Rex 206
Whitney, Eli 114
Whittle, Frank 194
Wiles, Andrew 243
Wilkinson, David 114
Wilkinson, John 109, 112
Wilmut, Ian 243, 244–245
Wilson, Edmund 176
Wimmer, Eckard 249
Wong-Staal, Flossie 235
Wood, Alexander 140
Woolf, Arthur 118
Wozniak, Stephen 232
Wright, Orville 175
Wright, Wilbur 175
Wu, Chien-Shiung 218
Wyeth, Nathaniel 230

XYZ

Yale, Linus 144
Yeates, Robert 140
Yersin, Alexandre 164
Zara, Antonio 88
Ziegler, Karl 214
Zimmerman, Tom 240
Zuse, Konrad 206
Zworykin, Vladimir 200, 202–203, 206

Picture credits & acknowledgments

The author would like to thank the staff at the Smithsonian: Kealy Gordon, Product Development Manager; Jill Corcoran, Director, Licensed Publishing; Brigid Ferraro, Vice President, Consumer and Education Products; Carol LeBlanc, President; National Museum of American History, Kenneth E. Behring Center; National Air and Space Museum. **Also:** Louise Pritchard and everyone at Bookwork, who made this book happen; plus Caryn Jenner for proofreading.

The publisher would like to thank the following people for their help with making the book: Nimesh Agrawal for picture research and Jessica Cawthra for proofreading.

The publisher would like to thank the following for their kind permission to reproduce their photographs (Key: c=center; b=bottom; l=left; r=right; t=top)
Courtesy of Apple: 249bl. **Advertising Archives:** 166bl, 180tc, 184br, 190tl, 193cl, 229cl. **AKG London:** 38cl, 56–57t, 71, 74t, 79tr, 83br; Erich Lessing 15tr, 18tr; Gilles Mermet 43tr; Instrumentmuseum, Berlin 116; Paris Bibliotheque Nationale 64tl; Postmuseum, Berlin 129cr. **Alamy Images:** ZUMA Press, Inc. 250bl. **Alamy Stock Photo:** EHT / Xinhua / Alamy Live News 251tr; Granger Historical Picture Archive 106br; Imaginechina Limited 55cra; Rocketclips, Inc. 229tr; Science History Images 37tr. **Ancient Art & Architecture Collection:** 39cr, 39br, 11tr, 24bl, 26br, 29cr, 32–33t. **Antiquarian Images:** 38tl. **The Art Archive:** 58; Biblioteca Nazionale Marciana Venice/Dagli Orti 52bl. **Ashmolean Museum:** 35c. **Bradbury Science Museum:** Los Alamos 208cra, 208cr. **Bridgeman Images, London / New York:** 86–87b, 105tl; Bible Society, London 59tr; Bibliotheque Nationale, Paris 69tr; Christie's Images, London 66tl; Down House, Kent 143cr; Giraudon 62tr; Natural History Museum, London 79tc. **British Library:** 22bl, 23br, 76bc. **British Museum:** 7r, 8l, 12tc, 16–17, 19, 22b, 22tl, 22tc, 22cl, 23tr, 24–25t, 26tl, 27, 30cl, 44t, 46br, 48tl, 49tr, 60bl. **Corbis:** 41bc, 59b, 70, 95br, 96cr, 98tl, 105b, 112–3, 140bl, 147tr, 183cr, 247b, 63cr, Martial Trezzini/EPA 250tc; Minnesota Historical Society 118cl. **The Culture Archive:** 134tr, 149cr. **Danish National Museum:** 53. **Dreamstime.com:** Pressureua 241b. **Mary Evans Picture Library:** 2–3t, 12cl, 31tr, 63bl, 66bl, 66bc, 80–81, 104, 131tr, 132bl, 135, 184c; Engraving by Emile Baynard 2tl, 6, 18br; Illustrated London News 2tc, 40. **Football Museum:** 51t. **Linton Gardiner:** 182bl3. **Getty Images:** Alfred Eisenstaedt / The LIFE Picture Collection 226clb; Daily Herald Archive / SSPL 193t; De Agostini / A. Dagli Orti 60–61t; Frans Lemmens 14–15b; Simon Dawson/Bloomberg 243; Thomas Koehler / Photothek 228cb. **Glasgow Museum:** 202bc. **Ronald Grant Archive:** 20th Century Fox 236br. **Robert Harding Picture Library:** 92bl; Dr. Denis Kunkel/Phototake NYC 95tr; Ellen Rooney 41t. **Hulton Archive:** 3tl, 3tc, 118–9, 138, 172. **iStockphoto.com:** Bbuong 102ca. **Museum of London:** 12tl. **NASA:** 249tl; JPL/Cornell 249l, 249br; Kepler Mission/Wendy Stenzel 250br; NASA/Chris Gunn 251bcr. **Natural History Museum:** 14bl. **Peter Newark's Pictures:** 76cla. **Robert Opie Collection:** 160tl, 195cl, 196, 198tl. **Christine Osborne:** 13r. **Quadrant Picture Library:** The Flight Collection 226–7. **Royal Horticultural Society, Wisley:** Lindley Library 21. **Saint Bride Printing Library:** 76clb. **Saxon Village:** Crafts 69ca. **Science & Society Picture Library:** 2tr, 4–5, 7c, 7l, 8–9b, 10–11c, 10b, 16cl, 17tr, 20r, 24bl, 30–31, 33br, 34tl, 34–35, 37c, 42cl, 44bl, 45, 47, 52tr, 54b, 60r, 62cl, 65c, 67tc, 68c, 73r, 73tl, 74–75, 75br, 78, 80cl, 80t, 82c, 82b, 84–85, 84tl, 85c, 86tl, 86–87cb, 88, 89tl, 89br, 90, 91tc, 91r, 92, 92–93, 93tr, 93c, 96tl, 97b, 99cr, 100bl, 101, 102–103b, 103cr, 106tl, 107br, 108–9, 109tr, 110–1, 111tr, 112tl, 114–5t, 115tr, 115c, 115b, 117, 119, 120cl, 120bl, 120bc, 121tr, 121br, 122–3, 124, 125cl, 125t, 126bl, 126–7, 128, 130cl, 131cr, 131bc, 132tl, 133cl, 133t, 134bl, 137c, 137t, 139tr, 139tc, 140c, 141, 144tl, 144–5, 145, 146b, 148–9, 149tc, 150tl, 150–1b, 152bl, 152tl, 152c, 153br, 154cl, 153cr, 154–5, 155tr, 156tr, 156cr, 156bl, 157, 159, 160–1, 161r, 162bl, 162br, 163tl, 163r, 164-5, 165cr, 166ca, 166–7, 168bl, 168–9, 169c, 169br, 170tl, 170bc, 170cl1, 170cl2, 171tr, 171br, 173tr, 173bl, 174bl, 175br, 176bl, 176br, 177, 178clb, 179tr, 180c, 181l, 181r, 182tl, 185tr, 185bl, 186b, 187, 188–9, 189br, 190–1, 191tr, 192cla, 192cl, 193br, 194–5, 195tr, 197br, 198br, 199cl, 200cb, 200–1b, 201, 202cl, 203tc, 203br, 205tl, 205br, 206tl, 208tl, 208tr, 209b, 210tl, 210br, 211, 213bc, 213cr, 214l, 215br, 215t, 218tl, 218–9, 219ca, 219cra, 220tl, 220–1b, 221tr, 222cl, 222bc, 224tc, 225l, 226tl, 228cr, 230tc, 230–1, 231tr, 232bl, 232–3t, 233tr, 233br, 234tr, 240tl, 240bc, 241tl, 242tl; Graseby Medical 186c; NASA 94, 188bl, 174–5. **Science Photo Library:** endpapers, 3tr, 48cl, 66tl, 178bc, 179cra, 189cr, 202cb, 203tr, 204tl, 207br, 212f, 216tl, 216tc, 217tr, 221ca, 223, 236t, 244cla, 244cl, 244cb, 244bc, 246, 247tr, 248bl; CNRI 242cb; Emilio Segre Visual Archives / American Institute of Physics 227tr; James M. Hogle, Harvard Medical School 248br. **Statens Historika Museum:** Stockholm 50–51. **Superstock Ltd.:** 46tl, 77tr. **Topham Picturepoint:** 245cr. **TRH Pictures:** 199tr. **Art Directors & TRIP:** 39tr, 85br, 236l, 33c. **University Museum of Archaeology and Anthropology, Cambridge:** 50br. **University of Archaeology and Anthropology:** 20c. **Matthew Ward:** 182bl1, 182bl2. **Barrie Watts:** 192bl1, 192bl2, 192bl3.

All other images © Dorling Kindersley. For further information see: **www.dkimages.com**
Illustrations by Peter Dennis.